HENRY
AND
CLARE

ALSO BY RALPH G. MARTIN

Charles and Diana

A Hero for Our Time: An Intimate Story of the Kennedy Years

Golda: The Romantic Years

Jennie: The Life of Lady Randolph Churchill—The Romantic Years: 1854–1895

Jennie: The Life of Lady Randolph Churchill—The Dramatic Years: 1895–1921

Cissy

The Woman He Loved: The Story of the Duke and Duchess of Windsor

Skin Deep (Novel)

Boy from Nebraska

The Best Is None Too Good

The Bosses

Ballots and Bandwagons

World War II: A Photographic Record of the War in the Pacific from Pearl Harbor to V-J Day

The Wizard of Wall Street

The G.I. War

A Man for All People

Lincoln Center for the Performing Arts

President from Missouri (Juvenile)

Front Runner, Dark Horse (with Ed Plaut)

Money, Money, Money (with Morton D. Stone)

Eleanor Roosevelt: Her Life in Pictures (with Richard Harrity)

The Human Side of FDR (with Richard Harrity)

Man of the Century: Winston Churchill (with Richard Harrity)

Man of Destiny: Charles DeGaulle (with Richard Harrity)

The Three Lives of Helen Keller (with Richard Harrity)

World War II: A Photographic Record of the War in Europe from D-Day to V-E Day (with Richard Harrity)

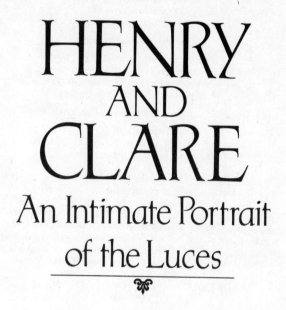

HENRY
AND
CLARE

An Intimate Portrait
of the Luces

Ralph G. Martin

A PERIGEE BOOK

Perigee Books
are published by
The Putnam Publishing Group
200 Madison Avenue
New York, NY 10016

First Perigee Edition 1992

Library of Congress Cataloging-in-Publication Data

Martin, Ralph G.
Henry and Clare: an intimate portrait of the Luces/
Ralph G. Martin.—1st Perigee ed.
p. cm.
Originally published: New York: G. P. Putnam's Sons, © 1991.
Includes bibliographical references and index.
ISBN 0-399-51781-2
1. Luce, Henry Robinson, 1898–1967—Marriage. 2. Publishers and
publishing—United States—Biography. 3. Journalists—United
States—Biography. 4. Luce, Clare Boothe, 1903–1987—Marriage.
5. Dramatists, American—20th century—Biography. 6. Ambassadors—
United States—Biography. 7. Legislators—United States—
Biography. I. Title.
Z473.L89M37   1992   92-9864 CIP
070.5′092—dc20
[B]

Designed by Rhea Braunstein

First photo insert: Page 1, photo #1: Library of Congress, #2: UPI/Bettmann, #3: AP/World Wide Photos   Page 2, photo #1: State Historical Society of Wisconsin, The Nettie McCormick Collection, #2: Courtesy of Elisabeth Moore   Page 3, photo #1: Culver Pictures, #2: Library of Congress   Page 4: Yale University Archives   Pages 5, 6, 7: UPI/Bettmann   Page 8: The South Carolina Library, University of South Carolina   Page 9, photo #1: Photoworld/FPG International, #2: UPI/Bettmann   Page 10, photo #1: AP/Wide World Photos, #2: UPI/Bettmann   Page 11: Columbia University   Page 12: Alfred Eisenstaedt, *Life* magazine, © Time Warner, Inc.   Page 13, photo #1, #2: AP/Wide World Photos   Page 14, photo #1: UPI/Bettmann, #2: George Karger, *Life* magazine, © Time Warner, Inc.   Page 15, photo #1: UPI/Bettmann, #2: New York Public Library Picture Collection   Page 16: Elton Lord, *Life* magazine, © Time Warner, Inc.

Second photo insert: Page 1: George Carver, *Life* magazine, © Time Warner, Inc.   Page 2: Library of Congress   Page 3, photo #1: UPI/Bettmann, #2: AP/Wide World Photos   Page 4, photo #1, #2: AP/Wide World Photos   Page 5, photo #1: UPI/Bettmann, #2: Photoworld/FPG International   Page 6: AP/Wide World Photos   Page 7: UPI/Bettmann   Page 8, 9: AP/Wide World Photos   Page 10, photo #1: Pictorial Parade, #2: Courtesy of Lady Jean Campbell   Page 11, photo #1: UPI/Bettmann, #2: Yale Joel, *Life* magazine, © Time Warner, Inc.   Page 12: AP/Wide World Photos   Page 13: NARA—Lyndon B. Johnson Library   Page 14: Debs Metzong   Page 15, photo #1, #2: UPI/Bettmann   Page 16: UPI/Bettmann

Cover design by One Plus One Studio
Cover photo by Alfred Eisenstaedt, *Life* magazine, © Time Warner, Inc.

Printed in the United States of America
1   2   3   4   5   6   7   8   9   10

This book is printed on acid-free paper.

∞

ACKNOWLEDGMENTS

Tina Martin was absolutely indispensable. In the early months, we worked together at the Library of Congress and in Boston archives. When I began my interviews, she did her own archival research around the country, finding assistants, directing their efforts, supervising their incoming material, then coding and editing it for the computer. She also did most of the initial picture research and the selection of photographs for the book. But, most of all, she not only organized my work, but made probing editorial suggestions about my various drafts and rechecked everything for accuracy. She is an excellent editor.

My wife, Marjorie Jean, as always, was the first to read my manuscript, and, as always, made highly perceptive comments, which greatly enriched my book. Her editing has always been superb.

Phyllis Grann, my publisher, dear friend and neighbor—who has been my editor on previous books—shared the inception of the idea for this biography on a Sunday morning walk. Her support since then has been strong and unstinting and she has always been full of sage advice.

My editor, Andrea Chambers, is surely one of the best editors in the business—highly intelligent, intensely conscientious, with the rare ability to make cuts so seamlessly that while they hurt the author, they definitely help the book.

Many thanks to my agent, Sterling Lord, for his friendship and constant encouragement.

The heart of this biography is the interviews. I was fortunate that so many family members, friends, and associates of the principals are still alive. I am particularly grateful to the first Mrs. Luce, Mrs. Lila Tyng, and to Mrs. Elisabeth Moore, Henry Luce's favorite sister and best friend, who were so generous with their time and their remarkable memories. I am also grateful to Mrs. Moore for giving me access to the family album of photographs. Mrs. Sheldon Luce, Henry Luce's sister-in-law, was also most helpful.

The two women who changed Luce's life most dramatically—Jean Dalrymple and Lady Jean Campbell—the two women he truly loved and wanted to marry—were marvelously cooperative and forthcoming. They both told me previously untold stories that gave an extra human dimension to Henry Luce.

Of the many interviews, too numerous to mention, with Time Inc. associates scattered around the world, the most important were with Allen Grover, the so-called "Vice President in Charge of Luce," and his wife, Bea, who was such a close friend of Clare Luce. Richard and Shirley Clurman were also invaluable—Richard was one of the few Time Inc. people invited to the family funerals, and Shirley was one of the few outsiders mentioned in Clare's will. I was fortunate to have had long conversations in England with T. S. Matthews before he died, and he made available to me his private papers and correspondence. Robert and Patricia Coughlan both gave me key background information.

My interviews with Andrew Heiskell were both important and fruitful, and so were my interviews with Ed Thompson, John Hersey, Hugh Sidey, John Steele, Frank White, Tom Griffith, George Harris, Robert Manning, Oliver Jensen, Robert Sherrod, William Buckley, Jr., Dave Richardson, Curt Prendergast, A. B. C. Whipple, Kelly Brook, Otto Fuerbringer, Joseph Kastner, Dimitri Kessel, Milt and Nan Orshefsky, Ted Sorensen, Bernard Yudain, Mrs. Pierrepont Isham Prentice, Dorothy Ferenbaugh, Marian MacPhail McDermott, Osborn Elliott, H. D. Quigg, and Jerry Goodman.

I am particularly grateful to Dr. David Read, Henry Luce's pastor, for giving me his memories and his insight and to Mrs. Ralph Ingersoll, who not only told me much I needed to know, but made available to us her husband's important letters and papers. I am similarly grateful to Wilfrid Sheed for his perceptive memories and to my dear friend Helen Swinton for sharing her memories with me. My old friend from third grade, Dr. Murray Krim, who has been head of the William Alanson White Institute, gave me the benefit of his psychological wisdom in probing the actions of my principals.

Dorothy Sterling was most kind in making available to me her unpublished manuscript, "The Luce Empire"; her private papers and interviews were most revealing. I am grateful also to David Halberstam for making available his papers at the Special Collections Library at Boston University. Particularly important were his excellent interviews with those who are no longer alive.

Clare Boothe Luce's papers at the Library of Congress Manuscript Division proved to be a rich resource of letters, papers, diaries, clippings, speeches, and articles. The staff there was most helpful, especially Mary Wolfskill and John Haynes. Equally important were the papers of John Shaw Billings at the South Caroliniana Library at the University of South Carolina. The Billings diaries were a gold mine of revealing material. Allen Stokes, director of the archive, and Charles Gay were helpful there; the researcher who earned our greatest gratitude is Miles Richards, who worked so tirelessly and intelligently in combing out what we needed.

A valuable source of key interviews came from the Oral History Division of Columbia University, and we thank its director, Ronald J. Grele, for all his help. At Columbia, too, there were Bernard Crystal and Patrick Lawlor at the Rare Books and Manuscript Division of Butler Library. The most important papers here were those of W. A. Swanberg, Laura Z. Hobson, and Daniel Longwell. The Swanberg papers were the most valuable.

Most cordial and helpful were Elaine Felsher, director, and Bill Hooper, who is in charge of photographs, at the Time Inc. archives. They cooperated in a variety of ways. Special thanks to John Manners, also at Time-Warner, for providing additional information. Harold L. Miller and Andrew Kraushaar facilitated access to the most important Nettie F. McCormick Papers at the State Historical Society of Wisconsin. Linda McCurdy and Patricia Webb aided us with the Matilda Young papers at Duke University. Carmen Hurff and researcher Scott Howard were most helpful at the University of Florida, where the invaluable Alden Hatch papers are located. The Hatch interviews were most important, particularly with people who have since died. I am thankful to the family of my old friend Theodore White for permission to research his private papers at Harvard University. I also thank Eva Moseley at the Schlesinger Library at Radcliffe for helping me with access to the Mary Bancroft papers.

John Hersey very kindly made his private papers at Yale University available to me. Other important papers there included those of Thornton Wilder and Dwight Macdonald. The staffs at Yale's Sterling Memorial Library and the Beinecke Rare Book and Manuscript Library were most helpful. Gail A. Ferris, director, and Ruth Penkala at the Alumni Records Office also provided important research material. Emmet D. Chisum, research historian at the American Heritage Center at the University of Wyoming, provided assistance with John K. Jessup's papers. The able staff at the John F. Kennedy Library was most helpful, as was Mildred Mather at the Herbert Hoover Presidential Library. At the Franklin D. Roosevelt Library in Hyde Park, New York, we thank Elizabeth Denier and Mark Renovitch, as well as Benedict K. Zobrist, director, and Liz Safey at the Harry S Truman Library in Independence, Missouri. We especially thank Tom Kirker for his important research at the Dwight D. Eisenhower Library at Abilene, Kansas.

My special thanks to Richard Kroll for all his help in research and in so many other ways.

Our local reference librarians at the Westport, Connecticut Library were a constant support group, and they include Kathy Breidenbach, head of Information Services, and her staff: Marta Campbell, Barbara Murphy, Sylvia Schulman, and Joyce Frymann.

We also want to thank Sandy Rosoff at Nyack Library and Ed DiRoma at the New City Library, who helped with key information. Althea Anderson at Clearwater Public Library in Florida was most helpful, as was Ruth Nerendorffer at the Historical Society of the Tarrytowns. I would also like to thank Professor John Robertson at Paducah Community College in Kentucky.

Mari Walker, my dear friend, who has typed so many of my manuscripts, and has the difficult job of transcribing all of my interviews, again deserves my heartfelt thanks. Janice Murray did the complicated job of converting the coded research material onto the computer and typing the final manuscript. Her humor and skill are much appreciated. Radha Ramanathan also helped with the typing. Special thanks to my computer guru Ted Shapiro. My close friends John Weaver, Ed Plaut, and Paul S. Green, as always, supplied me with a stream of clippings, anecdotes, and excellent background. Paul Green was also invaluable as a proofreader.

At Putnam, among those who were so helpful were Dolores McMullan, particularly with the final compilation of photographs, Lucia Tarbox for her copyediting expertise, and Karen Mayer for her legal advice. We also thank Aaron Shmulewitz of Parker, Duryee, Rosoff and Haft for his legal counsel.

I cannot list the names of all people who deserve mention, but some I must: Arthur Greenbaum, Herb Klynn, Peter Porcino, Sidney Shore, Ed Wergeles, Bob Pastel, Chet Hansen, Shirley Green (for her advice on photographic sources), Daniel Greenbaum, and Elizabeth Martin.

My special thanks to my good friends Max Wilk (my ultimate theatrical reference), Enrico Caruso (who so expertly copied old photographs for the book), and Vincent Aitoro, Stan Adelman, and Julius Gold who gave such strong moral support.

*To my Marge, who has enriched my books
as much as she has enriched my life*

1

OFTEN, it is the simplest detail that helps explain the enigma of a man's life. For Henry Robinson Luce, that clue lay inside his passport. Most husbands would want their wives or families notified in case of death; Luce, however, listed his next of kin as Time, Inc.

Luce's first wife, Lila Ross Hotz, would often say that *Time* was the love of her husband's life. It was his passion and his creation. To call it a next of kin was almost an understatement, for *Time* was part of Luce's very soul. Readers quickly discerned a very powerful presence behind the magazine, and the presence was Luce.

Once, speaking to an assembly of students in Boston, Luce was asked how he could call *Time* a news magazine when it was so filled with opinion. He paused, then said, "I invented the idea, so I guess I can call it anything I like." He also believed that he could *do* anything he liked with his magazine. When he felt strongly about an issue or a personality, he had no qualms about twisting the facts to present his version of the truth.

Luce often repeated his contention that the most astonishing thing about a human being was his range of vision, his willingness to suffer grief and frustration for a dream. Luce himself began dreaming about *Time* as a prep school student, and later refined his ideas at Yale. With a scant $86,000 in seed money, Luce and his school friend Briton Hadden were able to expand their dream into an influential journal of news and opinion. When Hadden suddenly died at age thirty-one, Luce carried on alone, turning a piecemeal news operation into the most powerful publishing empire in the world. *Time* became a part of the lives of millions of Americans and prodded people to think about not only the news, but religion, medicine, science, and culture in a way they never had before. Many critics felt that much of *Time* was predigested pap and very superficial, and some of it was. But the magazine stirred the mind and made a profound impact on how daily papers reported the news.

With the creation of *Life* and *Fortune,* Luce grew so influential that he became the most important advocate—even more than President Roosevelt—in leading a reluctant United States into World War II. Luce deeply believed that the war was the only way to stop fascism. He was so powerful that he could pluck out a politically naive general named Eisenhower and help make him president. "Harry," as those close to him always called Luce, once told his friend William F. Buckley, Jr., that though he was proud of being an editor, he was really a promoter. And so he was. Luce promoted not only patriotism, but God. More than anything, he yearned to be a great American and a true Christian. It was a small secret that he prayed every morning in the elevator he rode up to his office. Moreover, when he viewed a person or a cause as godless, he was a forceful opponent. The major reason for Luce's lifelong hatred of communism was that it was godless.

Luce could be wrong and vengeful in his actions, but few questioned his integrity or his personal honesty. Many hated some of the causes he stood for, but few hated him. He was the cool handle on a hot teapot, an ideological curmudgeon who could roil the waters, upset political apple carts, and prick the comfortable conscience of a nation. Yet this was a conservative-minded man, an avowed Republican. He told his staff that it was the business of *Time* to make enemies and *Life* to make friends.

Luce was a lonely man, and part of his loneliness came from his power. He was a man on top of a mountain with few true peers and fewer friends. "We looked at him as a god," said a *Time* researcher, "but he was never godlike."

He was a man of contradictions, seemingly cold and controlled with a highly disciplined mind, yet capable of an almost boyish enthusiasm. He had an unceasing, omnivorous curiosity for trivialities, yet believed in the epic sweep of events. He was a man of conscience in terms of the larger mission in life, but he could resort to petty and shortsighted methods.

Basically a shy man, he had married a well-bred, wealthy young woman from Chicago who wanted nothing more than to be his helpmate. Lila adored and admired her husband, and earlier she had satisfied his romantic yearnings, but now he wanted something more. Luce fantasized himself as a swashbuckling lover, a man capable of sweeping any woman off her feet. His Presbyterian conscience had managed to hold him in check, but his days as a faithful husband were nearing an end. Luce was a man aching for a great love in his life, aching for an affair.

When he received an invitation to a cocktail party one night, he did not know that the evening would change his life. He hated small talk, but he accepted the invitation from his friends the Hobsons because Thayer Hobson was an old Yale classmate and his wife, Laura, had an intriguingly sharp mind.

It was the fall of 1934, and the president of the United States was Franklin Delano Roosevelt, a man so beloved that prominent politicians publicly proposed that the Constitution be changed so that F.D.R. could be made an hereditary monarch. Americans had just celebrated their first year without Prohibition, and newspapers reported that 560 had been jailed in a recent drive on drugs. In Germany, the people had elected Adolf Hitler as their Fuehrer. And in Hollywood, *It Happened One Night,* starring Clark Gable and Claudette Colbert, won the Academy Award.

If the Depression was still dark and deep in many parts of the country, in the upper echelons of New York, the parties continued almost as if nothing were wrong. The gaiety was brittle, the women slinky, and the view from the terrace of the seventeenth floor of the Hobsons' Manhattan apartment absolutely spectacular.

It was one of those small moments of magic. A beautiful woman makes a grand entrance at a cocktail party, the noisy chatter stops dead and the crowd stares.

She wore a striking black dress and exquisite diamond jewelry and tilted her blonde head ever so slightly to one side. She simply stood under the hallway arch, clutching a nosegay of white flowers in her hands. Her extraordinary blue eyes looked demure and slightly expectant as she waited for the hostess to scoop her up and introduce her.

Most women hated Clare Boothe Brokaw because she was so young and beautiful and had such a tart tongue; most men loved her for the same reasons. She had been the celebrated editor of *Vanity Fair* and the author of a deliciously satirical novel that tore apart the High Society in which she had lived. Since her divorce from a multimillionaire drunk who was old enough to be her father, a line of admirers had waited impatiently for her attention.

A long time before, Clare's heart had been broken by her first lover, and the pain never went away. She promised herself that she would never be hurt again, and she held that promise. "She was no vamp, but all she had to do was just smile at a man and the guy would fall down dead," noted a Time executive. She was a worldly, sophisticated woman capable of real conversation. When she talked to a man, it often seemed as if she knew the answers before she asked the questions. Her life was full of outstanding men, because it took such men to please her. She would seek them out—and excite them. But the passion was theirs, rarely returned.

Clare's careful game plan at a party was to survey the scene as soon as she arrived, target someone worth talking to, and then zoom in. The man she wanted to meet that night was tall and intense-looking with brooding blue eyes and a strong jaw. Harry Luce wore a preoccupied frown and seemed so aloof as to appear inattentive. Some years before, Clare had tried to interview him, but he had been too busy to see her.

Luce seldom had problems with people because he found the easiest way to reach out to someone was to ask a question. Any person who answered his question intelligently caught his interest. His intense focus was flattering to most women because it was something they did not often get from men. Women felt Luce was strongly sensual yet tremendously masculine. They also felt attracted to his vulnerability, his unwillingness to hurt anybody. "He could have had loads of affairs, no question, if he made the effort," said Lael Wertenbaker, a *Time* correspondent.

Yet Luce didn't reach out for other women, because he was naive about the opposite sex. He talked to women as he talked to men. He could understand their minds, but he knew nothing about their hearts.

The night Harry met Clare, all that changed. Hostess Laura Hobson watched their first encounter with special interest: "They stood a little apart from everybody, talking by themselves, she leaning back into the curve of the piano, facing the room, and Harry ignoring the room, holding forth intensely, and then listening intensely. Clare was too clever to be impressed with him; she would say something light, and laugh, then change moods and seem totally impressed by what he was saying. She had an odd little trick of clipping off certain words and phrases. It gave her speech a staccato brightness."

Clare focused on subjects she knew interested him and piqued his curiosity. Part of her charm was that when she talked to a man, it was as if there was nobody else in the room. She also looked him straight in the eye, which pleased him. To talk to Luce, even Clare had to shift her mind into high gear, because his was never in neutral. A friend depicted Harry as "so fierce, so obsessed, so narrow, a man who could operate at a frightening velocity without coming apart."

Confronted with the force of Luce's personality, Clare was careful not to make a point too forcefully, lest she seem strident. She began with a short, fervent summary of conditions in Europe, then a pointed critique of his magazines. She was careful never to be too caustic. She then baited him about his beloved *Fortune,* tossing out little mots about how easily it could be made better. Finally, she added, "I hear that you're getting out a picture magazine . . ."

"No, I don't think it would work."

"But why not?"

She then proceeded to detail her own idea for a picture magazine, which she had once proposed to her former boss, Condé Nast. Intrigued, Luce asked many questions.

He was so sure of himself and what he wanted, so little bothered by doubt, and so impressively energetic. The initial attraction for Clare was that this man was even more forceful and domineering than she. This was a man of such terrific power and sheer strength that friends said he might well have been a gangster, had he not been so stirred by God.

Clare also found Harry physically appealing. She liked his tall, lanky frame and large head, which she called the Gary Cooper look. She was drawn to his dark, bushy eyebrows. Everything about Luce was compelling.

Suddenly, in the middle of their conversation, he pulled out his pocket watch and abruptly announced, "Well, got to go!"

Men didn't do that to Clare. Luce was unforgivably rude, but she was intrigued.

Harry was more than intrigued; he was caught. He appreciated intelligent women who could express themselves, but this one also had a scintillating kind of beauty, as well as the aura of being a celebrity.

Clare and Lila were poles apart, yet both represented a part of him. He had married Lila when he was a young man, not long out of college. Harry now wanted a woman who better meshed with his own exalted status. The more he brooded, the more he wanted. And the more he thought of Clare, the more he wanted her.

The life they later built together was once described as a mating of eagles. Clare was never an eagle, and her power was largely a reflection of his. But she would break her own ground, build her own pedestal. She became a celebrated congresswoman, the first female ambassador to a major country, an internationally known playwright, and the most influential woman in the Republican Party. He would grow into an elder statesman and advisor to presidents, a man both feared and admired. Secretly, he yearned to hold office, but contented himself with behind-the-scenes politics.

To the outside world, Harry and Clare were two powerful people living in an idyllically privileged world. They enjoyed many homes and all the money they needed, but happiness eluded them. Their marriage was tarnished by constant competition, sharp cuts, and deep hurt. Most of the cuts came from Clare and most of the hurt was his. Still, they sparked each other's minds and, in their own way, enriched each other's lives. But in the end, they remained lonely people searching for love and excitement. She found it with other men and other adventures; he found it with other women and with the expansion of his empire.

Theirs is the story of a royal American marriage, fabulous but bitter, and ever fascinating to watch.

2

GOD and country and China: this was the passionate core of the Luce heritage.

God shaped the life of Henry Winters Luce as he sat in his small study in the old North Hall at Yale University on Easter Sunday, 1892. It was there that Luce, a tall, freckled-faced young man with red hair and blue eyes, claimed he had heard the clear call of evangelism. He felt, he said, "intoxicated with God and inebriated with the Holy Ghost." He decided to become a missionary and chose China as the country where he would put God's will to work.

Had he needed any further inspiration, Luce could have taken some from his very name. "Luce" comes from the Latin meaning "light." The Welsh origin of the word describes a man in charge of a lighthouse. The Luce family crest is actually an eagle holding a sword—all of which fit the senior Luce and, later, his son.

Henry liked to tell people that all Luces were related and came from a place in Scotland called Luce. According to one genealogy, the Luces can be traced back to a Norman family which reached British soil about 1066 with William the Conqueror. The first Luce to come to America in 1643 was another Henry: Martha's Vineyard records described him as a surveyor, a selectman, a property owner, and the father of ten sons. He was also known as a member of the "Dutch Rebellion." Another ancestor, Rear Admiral Stephen Bleecker Luce, married a grandniece of Martha Washington, helped General Sherman capture Charleston in the Civil War, and later founded the Naval War College.

The father of Henry Winters Luce was a pious, unpretentious grocer in Scranton, Pennsylvania, despite his fancy name of Van Rensselaer W. Luce. He soon dropped the "Van." His wife Adelia Tedrick, tiny and gentle, was firm enough to be a member of the board of managers of the Friendship House.

Their fiery son Harry, as everybody called him, was a man of seemingly endless energy who liked to lead. His mother often told him, "Harry, you can't be captain all the time."

At Yale they called Luce "Lucifer," because of his red hair and hot temper. Not only did he edit the Yale newspaper, but he also ran the school's twice-weekly prayer meetings and discussions. He was intent on studying law until his friend "Pit" (Horace Tracy Pitkin) proselytized him, urging him to become one of "Jesus' Little Lambs." Pit warned him, however, that eleven missionaries had been killed in China in the previous two years and that the Chinese regarded red hair as a badge of the devil. Luce was undaunted.

Before going to China, Luce got his Doctor of Divinity at Princeton, and chose a bride in his hometown of Scranton. Elizabeth Middleton Bloodgood Root, born in Utica, New York, was a social worker with the Young Woman's Christian Association in the drab factory section of Scranton. Like the Luces, the Roots came from English stock (they had settled in Connecticut in 1639). Elihu Root became President McKinley's secretary of war and President Theodore Roosevelt's secretary of state and won the Nobel Peace Prize in 1912. Other Roots, like other Luces, had been prominent public servants in law, medicine, education, and the military. Elizabeth's father was a lawyer and many of her ancestors served in public life. Though she had not gone to college, Elizabeth had a fine mind and was well read. When Harry Luce proposed marriage, Elizabeth had been contemplating a mission in India. Childhood typhoid fever had impaired her hearing but not her judgment, and the dark-haired Elizabeth decided to go to China with Harry rather than go alone to India.

They married in the Second Presbyterian Church on June 1, 1897. Pastor Charles E. Robinson urged them, "Strive to learn the Chinese way of looking at things." He impressed them both so much that they gave their first son the middle name "Robinson."

China was a country of challenge and danger for the 1300 Protestant missionaries (half of them women). Most of the 400 million souls in China did not want to be "saved" by Americans or anyone else. Their cultural heritage dated back long before the Christian era. Many felt that the missionaries were insolent to their god Buddha. The Chinese who converted (some 55,500 converted to Protestantism and 500,000 to Catholicism) were regarded by other Chinese as "rice Christians," who mainly wanted to get their bowls filled. Wild rumors circulated about missionaries kidnapping Chinese children, killing them, and making them into medicine.

The Luce mission was in the northern province of Shantung, 150 miles from

Shanghai. Larger than England, Shantung was considered the Chinese Holy Province because Confucius had been born and buried there twenty-four centuries ago. Once known for its poets and persimmons, Shantung had become a hotbed for robbers so vicious that women reportedly hanged themselves when such thieves invaded their village.

When the Luces arrived, two coolies waded out to their sampan and carried them on their backs to shore. A muleteer who knew no English then took them on their two-day trek to their Presbyterian mission at Tengchow. The Luces traveled in a shend-zi, an elaborate network of ropes fastened on two long poles to the wooden saddle frames of two mules. Since the mules seldom kept in step, the resulting trip shook bones and demoralized nerves. Their son, already in his mother's womb, would one day write a sentimental poem about the shend-zi.

Tengchow was the "city of heights," an ancient walled city, steep and rocky with narrow dirt streets filled with beggars and swarms of surly dogs, pigs, chickens, and stray cats. Local peasants circulated rumors that missionaries put "a peculiar powder" in the wells which caused all who drank the water to come under their spell. There were peasants who hissed openly at missionaries and spat on the ground when they walked by. In towers nearby, missionaries had been burned and crucified.

The Presbyterian mission compound in Tengchow was built like a fort surrounded by a high brick wall. It was when the Luces were unceremoniously dumped in front of the enormous gate of this compound that Elizabeth, filled with homesickness, thought, "All abandon hope, ye who enter here." But Harry was exultant, still filled with his mother's words, "Remember, I have given you to God!"

Years later, his daughter Elisabeth (who was called "Beth") would describe her father's pure pleasure in China: "You could see the faith just shining in his face and the determination to share that faith with the Chinese. A beautiful thing."

Beth continued, "Father was soon steeped in Chinese culture and language and he respected Chinese heritage as a very great heritage. He found in the writings of Confucius, references to a 'superior man,' which, again, suited him as it did his son: 'The Superior Man wishes to be slow in his words and earnest in his conduct.' "

Life for the Luces was Spartan. Their house had no gas, no electricity, no steam heat or plumbing. Light came from kerosene lamps. Reverend Luce set a strict schedule: up at six, cold bath, Bible study before breakfast, three hours of Chinese lessons before lunch, a nap, three more hours of Chinese lessons, supper at six, a long walk, general reading with more Chinese study.

Most missionaries had a short-range goal of individual conversion, but Luce concentrated on the long-range vision of educating Chinese for Christian leadership. He also wanted to unify the varied missionary denominations into a single educational force. His fellow missionaries quickly assessed him as a man of strong will and vigorous intellect, "who was too eager to try new experiments and had too little regard for proven methods." The Chinese gave him the name Lu Ssu-i, "one who seeks righteousness."

His fellow missionaries also said of him that "he believed in Truth with a capital 'T,' no matter where it takes you, but he always found God at the end of the road."

The Luces' first child, Henry Robinson Luce (soon called "Harry" like his father), was born on April 3, 1898 and baptized by Reverend Calvin Meteer, who had pioneered the Mission. The Chinese soon gave its own name to the son: Lu-Shao-i, "Small Boy Luce."

"Small Boy Luce" was born the year President William McKinley voiced the view of many American missionaries that God had given the United States a manifest destiny to spread its goodness elsewhere in the world. To save their "little brown brothers" in the Philippines, the United States had fought and defeated Spain in 1898.

Two years later in China, Americans and other citizens of the Western world faced what Reverend Luce called "the days of blood and death." The Empress Dowager, Tzu Hsi, had helped revive a secret society, I Ho Chuan, "Fists of Righteous Harmony," known as "The Boxers." They claimed a supernatural power, an immunity from death, and they had a single mission: Kill the foreign devils. Before the rebellion was put down, the Boxers killed some two hundred missionaries plus many of their wives and children as well as some 30,000 Christian converts.

"It was terrifying," said Beth, who had heard the family story many times. "Harry was not yet three years old and my sister Emmavail was only a month old. So, imagine my mother holding her baby and my father holding Harry's hand and all of them running in the dark of night through the fields of sorghum. That sorghum saved their lives. It grew fifteen feet high and could hide them that night until they got to the shore."

The family escaped to Korea and spent the summer in a hot, single room in a temple. The heads of missionaries, including that of their friend Pitkin, were displayed in cages around the country. An international force of 18,000 Japanese, Russian, American, English, French, German, Italian, and Austrian troops finally defeated the Boxers. This international force indulged in their own orgy of looting and brutality and demanded harsh indemnities.

Within another year, Small Boy Luce was back in Tengchow, attending Sunday services with his parents. In the family archives, recorded by his mother, there is the text of a sermon that Harry wrote when he was six years old, based on II Timothy 1:7: "For God hath not given us the spirit of fear but of power . . ."

"His sermons weren't long but they had very good ideas and were very intense, and he would preach them!" said Beth. "He later made us line up and listen, and the little Chinese kids, the servants' children, would also have to line up and listen, and we didn't care for that at all!"

At six, he wrote a poem for his father, which described heaven as a place without fear of robbers or darkness.

For all his wisdom, Harry was still a small boy, tempted by the usual mischief. "He remembered crawling under the bed when his mother wanted to spank him. Eventually he grew so big that he couldn't get entirely under the bed, and she was able to grab him by the leg and pull him out," said a family friend. "Mother could never manage to spank me properly," said Luce later, "because we would both get to laughing before she got the old hairbrush really swinging."

Missionary pay was pitifully small but the Luces were partly subsidized by wealthy friends in Scranton, Pennsylvania. Peasant pay was minuscule. Servants could be hired for four dollars a month. The Luces had six: a cook (who was a steady opium smoker), gardener, table boy, laundry boy, and two female amahs (nannies) to care for the children. Harry learned most of his kitchen Chinese from his amah. His playmates were the children of the servants: they played such games as whip top, cat and bat, and blindman's buff.

The Luce family soon moved to another compound in Weihsien, a bigger city 125 miles to the southeast, inland near the center of the province. At Luce's insistence, the Christian college was being moved there and a bigger one built.

"Actually we lived a mile or two outside of the walled city, in the middle of a great plain where grain grew—winter wheat and millet and sorghum fifteen feet high," recalled Luce of his youth. Surrounding them too, in the fields, were Buddhist burial grounds, great places to play and hide. "I was at home in the countryside," Luce said. He had very vivid memories of his surroundings.

"The roads were just ruts in the plain, worn down through the centuries. Until now they were fifteen feet below the level of the fields. Big-wheeled cars were the only vehicles. You can't say it was primitive because it was part of such an ancient civilization. There, I saw the whole life of China. I saw the country people pouring in before dawn and wandering back at twilight, some of them staggering. I saw the flow of bridal processions. Once a week we went into the town, where I saw the crowded jostling alleys. I came to know the

Chinese with their strange tenderness, sentimentality, and paradoxical cruelty."

Sometimes, the family went to a Chinese show set up in the fields, or to a parade or festival. His mother was most concerned about disease—black smallpox had killed a missionary child, and the province was periodically ravaged by bubonic plague.

As Harry grew older, his father occasionally took him on expeditions to various little villages. "He had very vivid recollections," said his Presbyterian pastor, Dr. David Read. "I'll bet he was asking questions all the time."

Luce had a wistfulness about not having American roots: "How did I come to know about America?" he said. "My father and mother told me about it. They told concrete things—like about uncles and aunts and about the home church back in Scranton, Pennsylvania. My mother read to me a *Child's History of America*. And I cannot remember a time when I did not know about the Declaration of Independence and the American Constitution. I was brought up as an American. . . ." There is a note in the family archive quoting Harry at six saying that he was ready to teach the history of George Washington.

Harry's mother had a hard life, but she was totally committed to their existence in China. Partially deaf, she wore a primitive hearing aid and demanded her children speak loudly and clearly. Despite her hearing loss, she played the piano.

Most evenings, the family sang songs with the mother at the piano and the father playing the violin.

"Harry loved music," said his sister. "We had a big Victrola horn and he later collected lots of records, particularly opera. He loved opera. And he loved to sing. He had a lovely voice."

In the Luce household, there was an emphasis on strictness and rules. But the undercurrent was Harry's intense admiration for his father and love for his mother. "There was no warmth from his father," said a Luce intimate. "Everything came from the mother."

His father had merged his patriotism and his religion into a moral force, and so, too, would young Harry.

The Mission decided to send Reverend Luce back to the United States to raise money for their new college at Weihsein, the first united college of a dozen missionary groups. Since the tour would take more than a year, the Luce family of five went together.

It was in Chicago that they met the woman who would be their lifelong benefactor, Mrs. Cyrus Hall McCormick, who was matriarch of the International Harvester Company dynasty, and was a petite, kindly, graceful woman.

She lived in a private palace in Chicago on Rush Street with an hydraulic elevator.

"I shall never forget my first meeting with Mrs. McCormick," said Reverend Luce. "I had been in China eight years and came home in 1905. During the eight years we had never been able to buy a book or any apparatus except as we filched it from our all too meager salaries. Coming to Chicago, I of course wanted to see Mrs. McCormick. A mutual friend gave me a letter of introduction. Sitting opposite and close to each other (she on a window seat and I on a chair) she asked me very earnestly: 'Why do you want money for this college?' In two or three sentences, I told her about our needs as I have given it above. That was all that was ever said. Her reply was, 'Mr. Luce, you are tired. Come with me.' (In later years how often we heard that wonderfully gracious command, 'Come with me.') And then she led me to a room, pulled back the bed clothes, sent for pajamas, and urged me to rest awhile. She said she would be in the drawing room at about five-thirty. I shall never forget my feeling, for at one o'clock I had entered the house a perfect stranger and at three o'clock I was resting in the lovely bed. Never again did we talk of finance; but one day a check arrived for twenty thousand dollars, which laid the foundation for the endowment of Shantung Christian University."

Forever after, the Luce family would refer to her as "The Dear Lady." Mrs. McCormick was so struck with young Harry that she made the Luce family an offer they found generous and terrible. Harry himself remembers sitting on a couch and listening to Mrs. McCormick's plans. If his father would let her bring Harry up, she'd give so much to the missionaries. Harry felt that his father was selling him. He recalled that discussion as a time of terror, the most awful experience he could remember from his childhood.

After private prayer, the Luces gently refused to part with their son. Harry was deeply relieved.

Mrs. McCormick had seen something special in this boy. She became his patron, his sympathetic ear, his refuge. He would write her things that he would not tell his parents. Without her ready financial help, always available, his rough early school years would have been even more formidable, perhaps even impossible. As for the Luce family, Mrs. McCormick was more than "a dear lady"—she was a fairy godmother with a magic wand. For Dr. Luce, she was the entrée to the world of fund-raising. For Mrs. Luce, she became an extraordinary confidante. Mrs. Luce wrote to Mrs. McCormick how shy her son was in showing affection, and how much it meant when he signed a letter with "a million kisses."

The family spent Christmas together with their benefactors and friends, the Linens, where the children had their first Christmas tree in their homeland.

Mrs. Luce wrote Mrs. McCormick, saying how much Childe Henry appreciated her Christmas gift—*Whitman's Compilation of Childhood Verse*—and that he already had learned a great deal of its poetry by heart.

Soon after Christmas, Harry had to undergo a difficult tonsillectomy. Before the surgery ended, the anesthesia wore off, and Harry was in considerable pain. Forever afterward, his parents blamed that for the difficult stammer he developed. His stuttering made Harry a more private person, and more of a reader. Years later he would largely overcome this stuttering. Yet, in moments of stress, the m's and the s's would again stick in his throat. His words often came out in short, staccato bursts, with a slight catch in his speech. His sentences were often unfinished.

The Luces soon visited his mother's family in Utica, New York, and attended church there. As family members recalled the story, "Harry saw a stained glass window containing the quotation, "I am the Vine and ye are the Roots," meaning Jesus and his disciples. On returning home, Harry told his parents he hadn't known he was directly related to God.

They then settled on a beautiful country farm outside his father's hometown of Scranton. The farm belonged to the family of their sponsor, James Linen. In a sense, Dr. Luce now became a missionary in reverse, trying to explain China to Americans. What appalled him most was the minimal concern and knowledge Americans had about China. To them it was "more remote than the moon." Yale gave Reverend Luce an honorary degree, but his former Yale classmates were much more reluctant to give him money.

It took fifteen months before the Reverend Luce felt they could return to China.

"Not long before we returned to China, Mrs. McCormick asked me, 'Mr. Luce, in what house are you going to live when you return to China?' I replied that we did not know, and that it was dependent upon some missionary coming home on furlough, as the University was short a house. That was all that was said, but one day a check for the house was sent to the Presbyterian Board," recalled the senior Luce.

Despite the excitement of America, Harry loved China. Years later he would reminisce about the way the mountains swept down to the sea, the neatness of the tilled fields, the drama of the walled cities, the kindness of the people he knew best.

"I loved China, but I was immunized against illusions about her. What the great intellectuals never understood was that Chinese civilization had fallen in terrible decay. They saw only the outward forms of a graceful old culture but the dynamism was gone."

During those days, the Chinese greeted each other by asking, "Have you eaten rice yet?" Hunger was rampant. Disease was everywhere. Missionaries returning from visiting villages were quarantined in rough huts near the compound.

Harry always remembered some stone towers he saw on his hikes. Families would put their children there to die because they couldn't feed them. Not one woman in a thousand could read, and young girls were often sold to those who wanted them. Sun Yat Sen had announced the program for a Chinese Democratic Republic but would not be proclaimed provisional president for another five years.

For the Luces, to simply maintain a sense of normal family life in this stark, brutal land was a major achievement.

"Our home," recalled Beth, "was a very simple brick house. It had a moderate-size living room with an upright piano. Opposite that, was Father's study, which was bigger. With lots of books, books, books, and a fireplace. Father always had visitors to talk about his various projects, and many of these long-gowned scholars worked with him on translations. Father always wanted to be certain that what he wrote was in idiomatic Chinese.

"The living room was on the left, and Father's study on the right. And behind the living room, a very nice dining room, with old Victorian furniture that Mother had brought from her home in New York . . . always a white damask tablecloth. We had a full-time laundry boy who was just washing linen all the time. He was also washing Mother's beautiful white, lacy dresses and petticoats with ruffles. . . . Father wore white ducks, and jackets because they were supposed to be hygienic.

"We had an inside toilet," she continued. "Our bath was only Saturday night; and then it was in a tin tub, brought up into our room. Harry loved that tin tub. The table boy would bring the hot water up from downstairs in five gallon cans. There were also the oil lamps that had to go down to the pantry every day to have their wick trimmed and kerosene added. Each room had its own oil lamp. We also carried candles around a lot, too. Father had a huge lamp with a green glass globe and he'd grab it by the neck when he went downstairs in the middle of the night—he was a very bad sleeper.

"We had a wonderful garden," Beth recalled. "We had corn, sweet potatoes, and peas. And we had marvelous strawberries. Mother was fierce about every bit of food that came into the house. It not only had to be washed but some of it had to be dipped into a disinfectant. No foreign woman would shop in the market. Doc Fu ran the kitchen and much of the household, a big man and a wonderful cook. Mother taught him Victorian cooking—isn't that terrible! Instead of Chinese food, we had cream sauces."

Elizabeth Luce also insisted on reading the classics. "She would always read aloud to Harry. . . . I think this accounts for his beautiful use of the English language," noted Beth. "She would read sometimes for hours on end—Shakespeare, the Bible, Dickens, everything. And there was one book he loved her to read, *Water Babies.*"

"That was the origin of my love of reading aloud," Luce later said.

His mother also taught him writing, arithmetic, and discipline. Harry later confided to a friend that his mother was lovely and he loved her very dearly, and that she adored him "but that she was very self-controlled."

In this environment, Harry learned to be resilient and self-sufficient. He mapped military strategies of battles with his own collection of tin soldiers. As he grew older, he even reconstructed famous battles of the Civil War. "He would take over part of the nursery with his damn forts and soldiers," said Beth, "always marshalling armies. Sometimes a friend would come in and join him. My sister and I resented it because he sometimes would take over the whole floor and we wouldn't dare to touch his forts and we had to be very careful where we stepped. Everything he did was always very intense. There was nothing sort of casual."

Harry later remembered all kinds of things about his house: "It was a great, big, mysterious world filled with a thousand objects, pictures, keys, the frayed edges of the rug, the crack in the window pane, the photograph album exactly placed, the sound of the doorbell—just so, year after year—each of these objects was woven with long threads into the pattern of life."

Part of the annual pattern was the impatient wait for the arrival of their shipment from the Montgomery Ward Company in Chicago. The children helped unpack everything—everything they couldn't buy in China—and the school schedule was forgotten that day. One thing Harry later requested was a small chess set he could carry anywhere—his insurance that he would not waste time.

It was said of Dr. Luce that he never gave orders to his children. Instead, he tried to be a counsellor, drawing out their thoughts and opinions, stating his own views, but leaving the final decisions to them. What he *did* do was set an example of work and dedication. Specific discipline came from the mother. Even the family games often had a learning context. One such game was "Clumps," a variation of Twenty Questions, based on the Scripture. "Harry won most of those games," said Beth.

In 1909, a younger brother was born, Sheldon Root. Sheldon's later memory of his father and brother was that they were both serious, undemonstrative "and almost zero on small talk." Yet Harry and his father were always able and ready to talk to each other about substantive issues. "The great thing that I owe my father," said Luce later, "is that he would talk to me as one adult to another. We would go on walks, and he would tell me the problems of the college and about Teddy Roosevelt or about his own quest for the historical Jesus." In these talks, the big word was "balance." Put your life in balance, his father told him.

For young Harry, it was soon time to prepare for Yale, the Luce alma mater. The first step on the long journey to New Haven was a British boarding school at Chefoo.

3

CLARE'S grandfather, John William Thomas Boothe, was a man of divinity and a man of God. From 1890 to 1898 he served as pastor of the Second Baptist Church in Holyoke, Massachusetts. He preached a powerful sermon without notes and was known for his very fine mind. One of his parishioners was once quoted as saying that Dr. Boothe was "vigorous in style and a close reasoner. You will seldom find a man who will carry out a line of thought in the systematic style he is capable of." He believed that all sermons should be written on Friday so that Saturday could be a day of rest. Ministers could then go to the pulpit on Sunday in full spiritual vigor.

His granddaughter Clare discussed the possibility that the original family name was "Booth," but that her grandfather had added the "e" to distinguish them from John Wilkes Booth, who had murdered Lincoln. Yet, another relation called this "a preposterous lie." With her sardonic humor, Clare found this amusing. In her private papers, she kept a piece of fabric with a painted photo of Booth.

Genealogists trace the family back to 1634, when a Boothe ancestor arrived in Maryland on the *Ark & Dove* with Lord Baltimore. Another ancestor served in the Maryland militia during the War of Independence. Still another relation signed the Declaration of Independence.

The Reverend Boothe had been born in Maryland in 1838, the son of a sea captain. As a boy, he clerked on a steamer, learned the machinist's trade and fashioned some of the ornamental iron work on the U.S. Senate building. He married a woman named Sarah Rebecca Deaver, who bore him four sons and seven daughters. One of those daughters created a scandal when she married the manager of a theater company and shot herself in a New York hotel room. This news caused the Reverend's resignation.

Clare later commented: "All the people of my youth firmly believed in the Ten Commandments, even when they broke them."

Clare's father broke them often. William Franklin Boothe, one of John and Sarah's eleven children, was born in Poolesville, Maryland, in 1861, attended Purdue University for several years, then left to study violin at the Cincinnati Conservatory of Music. A handsome man, strongly built and athletic, he had thick eyebrows, dark hair, and a bushy mustache. He was a brilliant raconteur, "dreamily artistic . . . a man who loved music more than he loved anything or anybody," a newspaper reporter later wrote about Clare's father. His great lack was strength of character.

After working as a salesman in the piano business in Philadelphia, "Billy" Boothe went to Europe for more serious study of the violin. He settled in New York for a while, where he played and taught the violin. After traveling restlessly around the country, Billy then entered the family piano business. When that floundered, he became a salesman for George Washington Coffee, playing violin whenever he could. In his infrequent letters home, Billy informed his parents that he had worked in various orchestras, married, divorced, and planned to marry again.

The woman he loved was Anna Clara Snyder. She was "tiny but perfectly formed—a pocket Venus. She had wonderful eyes like wet violets," an observer would later write.

Her mother, Louisa, was the impoverished daughter of a German immigrant, but Anna Clara later insisted that her mother had been an aristocrat, and even produced a picture of a woman in court costume, covered with jewels.

Genealogists record Anna Clara's birth as 1862 (although her daughter said it was ten years later). Anna Clara's father, John Snyder, had left Germany to escape conscription into the army and settled in Weehawken Heights, New Jersey, less than a mile from Manhattan. The surrounding Hoboken area was described by a chronicler of New Jersey's Hudson County as a "little Eden . . . no lovelier spot dotting the bosom of the Hudson River . . . a haven for American writers like Washington Irving and Edgar Allen Poe. Here, also, had been the historical dueling ground where Aaron Burr killed Alexander Hamilton, the rising star of the American revolution."

John Snyder started a livery stable business in New Jersey. He and Louisa had two sons, both of whom died young. Anna Clara was the only child to survive. At eighteen, she changed her name to Ann Clare and traveled across the river to New York City to work as a salesgirl, then as a typist. But secretly, Ann Clare yearned to go into show business and finally landed a job as a chorus girl in a musical comedy. It happened that handsome Billy Boothe played in the orchestra. Six months later, in 1894, they eloped. Both families were shocked by the marriage because of differences in religion. The Snyders were devout Lutherans. To them, their daughter was now living in sin. The Reverend Boothe felt equally dismayed. Their son's divorce was contrary to his beliefs, and his marriage to a Lutheran contrary to his faith.

Abandoned by both families, the newlyweds managed well without them. Their first child, David Franklin, was born on April 10, 1902. Their second child, Ann Boothe, was born March 10, 1903, though for some unknown reason, thereafter she celebrated her birthday in April, rather than March.

Ann Boothe, called Clare, was born just as the world around her seemed to be taking on a new sense of urgency. The year 1903 marked the first coast-to-coast crossing of the American continent by an automobile—in sixty-five days. Great Britain set a new speed limit for motor cars—twenty miles an hour.

The Boothes were then living on West 124th Street in one of the poorer parts of New York City, the so-called "respectable slums." "The small foyer of the dismal apartment house perpetually smelled of stale cabbage. An iron elevator cage opened on to a narrow, dank hall, which led to their three-room apartment." Clare later vividly described the clutter of garbage cans in the hallway, and the night a mouse got into her bed and she ran screaming to her mother, who was solicitous. "I didn't want for love," Clare said of her mother.

Billy was a convivial man with many friends, a large number of them in music or the theater. His wife was of a similar spirit. They always seemed to be moving to different places in different jobs, never settling anywhere long enough to put the children in school. Billy Boothe, who reportedly got music hall engagements as "the Irish Fiddler" and was often between engagements, was then a patent medicine salesman.

"We traveled all over the place," said Clare. "Memphis, Racine, Des Moines." Home was a succession of cheap apartments and boarding houses "where the great problem was paying the grocer." But, wherever they were, both parents read aloud and often to their children, mostly from the ten-cent volumes of the Little Leather Library. Clare remembered her father reading until they fell asleep. It was Billy who taught them to read at an early age. Clare insisted that her father had introduced her to *The Decline and Fall of the Roman Empire* when she was only nine years old.

"I had no formal education," Clare said, "but books, books, books." History was a favorite subject, but randomly taught. "I knew little about Washington, but everything about Marie Antoinette," she recalled. Other children were given toys or dolls for Christmas or birthdays, she said, "but my parents were always giving us books." She devoured a series of books about a very good little girl named Elsie Dinsmore, and Clare later said, "I couldn't understand why I had to be like her when men could be like Frank Merriwell [a teenage hero of the times]."

Her father also taught her a little Latin, some French, and German. Since they moved so often, the children had no time to form close friendships, which brought the two of them even closer. With both parents working, or searching for work, the children dug deeper into books and games, and formed a tighter bond to each other. Clare later said, "Childhood is a blissful time of play and fantasizing." She loved to exaggerate.

Later in life, Clare tended to ignore the ugly and idealize the truth. Yet she would often remember bitterly the loneliness of her childhood. She changed her mother's birthday and invented a variety of dramatic anecdotes to brighten up her life story. "As far as I know," wrote Clare's friend Helen Brown, "she has never lied about her age." Helen, however, did suggest that if you believed everything Clare said or wrote, you would discover that she went to different schools in different parts of the country at the same time.

In 1911, the Boothe family fortunes changed dramatically. Billy got a job as a concert violinist with a traveling symphony orchestra and took his family with him. When the tour ran out of money in Nashville, Tennessee, the Boothes settled there for a while. "I have a faint memory of having spent a few days in a convent in Nashville," recalled Clare. "Mother had been taken ill . . . and father was on a concert tour. I remember the white faces of black-robed sisters leaning over me, and that they gave me little paper-frilled holy pictures which I liked. But the memory, no doubt because it was connected with a separation from my lovely mother, remains a melancholy one."

One of the searing nightmares of Clare's life took place in Nashville: She was in a small dark room which seemed to be under a staircase. The only light came through a red and purple stained glass window high up in the wall. The windows opened and a witch in a basket hovered in the opening. The witch reached for her to put her in the basket and take her up to the moon to cut her throat. She never dreamed this again, but never forgot it.

When Billy went to work in a soft-drink bottling business, his family was delighted. They lived regular lives with regular hours and saw each other every night at supper. The children attended the fashionable Ward Belmont School in Nashville, where Clare was in kindergarten. She later described her life during that period as "middle-class comfort."

In later years, when Clare was in a storytelling mood, she would say that her father became a part-owner of the bottling plant and sold it to buy a piano factory. She also reported that the bottling company had produced Coca-Cola, and, if they had not sold it, they would have been very, very rich. She told that story with many variations. The truth was that Billy received an offer to play the violin in the Chicago Grand Opera orchestra, and that's why he left the bottling plant.

Chicago was a happy time for the Boothes, but only at the beginning. They lived modestly but comfortably. The children went to school and made friends. Clare even enrolled at the Chicago Latin School.

Suddenly, one day in 1911 Billy was gone. Their mother simply told them their father was dead. There was no grief, no funeral, and their mother never again mentioned his name. Many years later, Clare and David learned that their father had gone away with another woman. "I was about seven when my father left us and my mother had to struggle for a bare existence," Clare said. Inevitably, Ann Clare grew bitter. Her mother's attitude toward men, Clare said in later years, was "You shouldn't let none of them out except on a leash."

In 1913, Ann Clare obtained a formal divorce on grounds of desertion. She was still beautiful, bitter, and unbowed.

"I live in my children," Mrs. Boothe told her daughter. As for young Clare, she was convinced of this. "She had persuaded me, early, that her whole existence would somehow be justified in me," Clare later recalled. "My mother felt she had given up a promising career in the theater to marry. When my father later ran off with another woman, my mother decided she had been a complete failure. She began pressuring me to excel. 'You,' she would say, 'are the real reason I was born'—because I would become all she had ever hoped to be. I believed my mother, and I tried hard to justify her reason."

Mrs. Boothe took her children home to Hoboken. With the advent of the motor car, her father's livery stable was a dying business. Her family could provide little help, so she worked as a waitress in a luncheonette. Her ambitions for her children were still fierce and she had no qualms about asking for help from friends. Her children remember going to spend summers in the country with their mother's friends.

After her father's death, Mrs. Boothe moved back to New York City, to a two-room flat on Columbus Avenue. Clare remembered bathing in the kitchen sink and later described it as "a poor and starving" existence. "Clare's youth had been so very hard," said her childhood friend Buffy Cobb. "Her mother was in the chips one moment and flat broke the next. Once Clare had to sleep on a cot in the kitchen while her mother entertained her friends." Clare also remembered there were many men. "I don't know about *her* morals," she said of her mother, "but I had to be pure."

"Clare's roots came out of hell," said her friend, writer Wilfrid Sheed. "And of course the worse it was, the more we admired her."

"My mind and heart grew so bewildered, I could no longer function intelligently, much less happily," Clare recalled. "I grew moody, distracted, restless, fickle, subject to fits of inexplicable depression. I was constantly being accused

of being selfish and thoughtless and stupid and ungrateful and changeable in
my views."

In the midst of this confused, unhappy youth, there were two summers when
Clare and David were sent to stay with their mother's friend on a lake in
Wisconsin. The children ran barefoot and wild ("like little Indians," as Clare
recalled). They climbed trees, canoed on the lake, played in the woods, fished,
and smelled the pines. They learned to roll logs with their bare feet at a nearby
logging camp and also how to shoot a gun.

When some boys dared Clare to slide down a log chute two-and-a-half-
stories high onto the frozen lake, Clare boldly obliged. She got so many ice
splinters in her small bottom that she spent the next ten days on her stomach.

Still, she thought of those days as the only happy ones she ever knew.

Financially, things were looking up for the family. Mrs. Boothe had received
a small inheritance from her father, and with advice from a friend, she had
multiplied it in the stock market. Billy Boothe also reportedly still sent irregular amounts at irregular intervals for the children's education. He had settled
in Los Angeles where two of his brothers lived. He worked for a time as a violin
teacher, then founded the Boothe Violin School with his brother John. Once
again, he was on his financial feet.

In 1913, Mrs. Boothe felt flush enough, with two thousand dollars to her
name, to send her son to military school for a year while she took her ten-year-
old daughter to Europe. David always resented being shunted aside, and Clare
felt guilty about being so preferred and so pampered.

She always remembered her growing pains and how her mother once soaked
her legs in very hot water and mustard to relieve the ache as tears poured down
Clare's face.

Basically, Mrs. Boothe was a romantic—but a pragmatic one. She believed
there was a symbolic pot of gold at the end of the rainbow, but it took a lot
of specific steps to find it. One of the steps was to expand her daughter's
horizon, give Clare a sophisticated exposure to the world, and hence prepare
her for the inevitable road to success. Mrs. Boothe constantly repeated the
slogan, "Up the ladder, up the ladder . . ."

"She wanted me to be beautiful, rich, charming, creative, to spend my time
with people worth knowing. The beautiful part seemed impossible. From my
earliest youth people said to me, 'You'll never be as pretty as your mother.'
I took it for granted that if I hoped to make my way in the world, I'd have
to study and be bright," said Clare.

Curiously, Clare never seemed to resent her mother's pushiness. She described her as the most perfect woman. Ann Clare's only fault was her naiveté—too many rosy expectations of things that could never happen. For

instance, Mrs. Boothe rationalized to her friends that Europe was then so cheap that she would actually save money by going.

Mother and daughter lived in Paris on the cheap, but they saw everything in style. The theater, the festivals, the museums, all the sights—everything but the concerts. Mrs. Boothe now had an unforgiving bias against all musicians. Clare, slightly plump and very pretty, absorbed it all and was ready and willing for more. She read about what she didn't see. She listened when she didn't know something. She dreamed about what she didn't have. While they lived in a small pension in Paris on the Rue Balzac, she studied French from a tutor.

By this time, an Austrian archduke had been assassinated and war had come to much of Europe. It was time for the mother and daughter to go home. The trip had consumed most of Mrs. Boothe's savings and they faced a most uncertain future.

On the trip home, Clare later remembered a man aboard the ship who was caught by her mother's beauty and she thought he proposed to her mother on the spot. Joseph Jacobs was a most untypical kind of prince to rescue a lost lady. Clare recalled him as "rough but kindly." In the months and years to come, he continued to court Mrs. Boothe and pressed his proposal. While her feeling for him was deep and abiding, she told her children that she could not marry him because, "I can't have a Jewish father for my children. They'll never get anywhere."

Joseph Jacobs, a retired tire merchant, still became Mrs. Boothe's greatest benefactor, friend, confidant, protector, and admirer. Whenever Mrs. Boothe was in any need, she could always turn to him for help. What was equally important to her was that her children liked him. They called him "Riggie," and Clare would later comment, "Riggie is so good to both of us. He's a dear, sweet man and I love him . . ."

Mrs. Boothe had her own pride of independence. She sold imitation pearls at Tecla's, a costume jewelry store, and later got a better job selling all kinds of costume jewelry. Her salary was enough to maintain her son at military school. When David came home on holidays, she found it hard to cope with him, as he had become a difficult child. When David was accused of stealing from a bakery truck, she berated him bitterly: "You're just like your father." Whatever love and affection he received came from his sister, not his mother.

Mrs. Boothe's ambitious hopes centered on Clare, not David. She decided that her pretty, curly-haired daughter might catch some producer's eye and become a child star. So she wangled a meeting with the great theatrical impresario David Belasco, who hired her to understudy Mary Pickford in *The Good Little Devil,* a play he was scheduled to produce. Clare never got a chance to get on stage—Mary Pickford played every night.

Mary Pickford, "America's Sweetheart," became Clare's ideal because she was "innocent, original, gay, pathetic, good, mischievous, tender, helpless." She later said she did not aspire to the Pickford ideals, "but was subconsciously influenced by them."

The persistent Mrs. Boothe found another part for her daughter, understudy for a child star in a play called *The Dummy*. This time, Clare appeared on stage for six performances. "My memory of my big (and only) scene is quite clear," she later said. "I played that scene gagged and bound by the kidnappers to a chair."

Fort Lee, New Jersey, was then a film production center, and Mrs. Boothe took Clare there for a screen test at the Biograph Studios. Clare listened to the director explaining the art of expressing the three necessary emotions: fear, abject fear, and stark horror. "Her test was terrible," wrote Frederick Van Ryn in a 1942 article entitled "Dream Jobs." She got a tiny part as "the girl over the fence" in a short film called *The Heart of a Waif.* She was also cast in some children's scenes in *Over the Hill to the Poor House.*

Since stardom seemed elusive, Mrs. Boothe swiftly made other plans for Clare. She still wanted Clare to fulfill her own frustrated dream of being a star in the theater. She was most persuasive and enrolled her daughter in the Major's School, a New York drama academy. Mrs. Major put a black wig on Clare, and told the apple-cheeked child to be a geisha girl. For the students' first public performance, Clare drew a slip from a bowl: "You are a cave man," it read, "and your whelps are starving. You go out and slaughter an animal for food, drag the carcass home, and you and your family have it." Baffled by the game, Clare squared her elbows, planted her feet wide apart, twisted her pretty face into a savage snarl, and rocking from side to side in a bloodthirsty manner, uttered a piercing growl. The audience collapsed into helpless laughter.

"This is ridiculous," Clare then announced. She quit the course, but the theater would always be part of her life.

The undaunted, irrepressible Mrs. Boothe then began finagling to get her twelve-year-old daughter a scholarship at the Cathedral School of St. Mary in Garden City, Long Island. Clare qualified for a scholarship in 1915 because her grandfather had been a clergyman.

"Because my mother was beautiful, she was determined I'd never find myself in her situation, depending on sheer physical beauty. She saw it was not enough to protect one against the misfortune of an unhappy marriage and no money. She was determined I was to have a good education," Clare explained.

St. Mary's was set in a long, rose-colored brick Tudor building covered with vines. The downstairs reception room was dark and gloomy with heavy Victorian furniture and glass-covered bookcases. The only way to get to Clare's room on the fourth floor was through the old chapel, which was called "Paradise" because it was painted with angels.

"There were two very crummy-looking stucco praying angels on the wall," Clare remembered. "I thought they were rather pretty and I used to say my prayers trying to look and feel as pious as those angels. One night, a girl from the room next door popped in and caught me imitating the angels' pose. She burst into laughter and called me 'Angel Face.' I was stuck with that nickname for years."

Clare was then still plump and unhappy. "I was so lonely I became a compulsive eater," she later said. She was soon twenty pounds overweight. Some classmates amended her nickname to "Angel Face Tubby." Among her private papers, there is an advertising booklet for "Lily of France Corsets" with different styles and models, telling what they do. Clare wrote on the cover, "I need 'em."

Prior to St. Mary's, Clare's formal education had been almost zero. She had never learned proper grammar rules, and her spelling was poor. But she had read books most of the girls had never heard of, and her English composition was excellent. Besides that, she could speak and write French. What she did practice, and practice hard, was her penmanship. She also wrote a proverb and kept it: "A note in the hand is worth two in the dictionary."

At first, Clare was deeply homesick. She had been away from her mother on an occasional summer, but never in the winter. Also, she felt so much older than most of the other girls who had never known her world of adults. When they talked about their clothes and their homes and their vacations, she felt awkward, a stranger among strangers. All this pushed her deeper into herself. She found solace in reading books, and selected a favorite secret place in an old apple tree. She would climb up there and read. The other girls noticed how withdrawn she was. They were also struck by Clare's poise and compulsive neatness.

When Clare came home that first Christmas, her mother was living in a cheap hotel on upper Broadway. Snow on the ledges stayed a long time because there was no sun to melt it, and the two windows were always covered with soot.

"Cooking was forbidden," Clare later wrote, "but a neighbor showed my mother dozens of ways to economize in a hotel like this . . . how to set up a little stove rigged with a rubber hose from the gas jet on the sill of the slightly opened bathroom window. The trick was to plug the bathroom door with towels so that no smells would leak into the hotel corridor. And she showed her what kinds of food to cook which gave forth the least odors and how to put the bottle of breakfast milk in a jar of cool water just inside the sill, so that by morning it would be cold, and not soured or frozen."

In later years, Clare tended to omit mention of her youth, rather than glamorize it. Friends felt that she was happy to forget the past and move on.

One of the few bright spots of Clare's childhood was meeting her St. Mary's classmate, Elizabeth Cobb, whom everybody called "Buffy." Buffy still vividly remembers the day she met Clare:

"I had been forced to play hockey about three days after I got there [to St. Mary's]," said Buffy. "I loathed the game. The ball ran up the stick and hit me in the eye. It was just too much. I ran off the field and climbed an apple tree, just to be alone. Pretty soon, there was a beautiful little girl standing under the tree. She was fat as butter but she had long golden curls and clear blue eyes and lovely pink and white skin. She looked up and asked, 'Is that your private apple tree or may I come up?' I said, 'Sure you can.' Up she came and we introduced ourselves."

Clare's version of that meeting was that, "I was lonely, and homesick. I wanted to shed a tear where none of the other girls could see me. What did I find up in that tree? Why another little girl just as lonely and home-sick. . . . I stopped crying because at once she made me laugh. And she stopped crying because I told her it made more sense to. We were both going to be writers when we grew up. We decided we were going to write mystery stories and create sleuths far more famous than Sherlock Holmes."

Soon, Clare confided to her diary her determination to make Buffy Cobb her "bestest" friend. She then added the sad note that she didn't have anyone she knew in the whole world who liked her better than someone else.

"Neither Clare nor I were used to other children," said Buffy, who was an only child. "Clare was loathed by many of the girls, but much of her early arrogance was a defense. We were inseparable, wrote stories and painted together. . . . We were both twelve years old. Clare was perfectly square, though beautiful. Both of us were square, but I was anything but beau-tiful . . .

"There have been so many Clares, but they always followed a pattern. There was always a terrific drive in her that almost amounted to psychosis, a drive to achieve, to have, to learn. Everything! There was no contentment in her."

Buffy's father was Irvin S. Cobb, a former Kentucky newspaper columnist who wrote for *The Saturday Evening Post,* which was then the most popular magazine in America. Cobb was a pot-bellied man, warm and joyful and at the peak of his fame. Invited to their home for Thanksgiving, Clare was quickly accepted as part of the family. She even called Cobb, "Daddy Cobb."

The Cobbs were so taken with Clare that when Mrs. Cobb drove out every

Friday to Garden City to bring Buffy home for the weekend, she took Clare, too. Finally Clare's mother came to call on the Cobbs. "Mrs. Boothe was very beautiful and funny with a delightful wit," said Buffy. "She described herself as a poor widow trying to bring up her children and see them through school. Naturally, my mother became friendly with her and even fascinated by her. She often drove Mrs. Boothe out to Garden City." Mr. Cobb, too, was impressed. "She was the loveliest little lady I ever saw, a pretty little partridge of a woman, all soft and sad and fluttering . . ."

The Cobb house was a hangout for literary and theatrical celebrities and Clare met everybody from the celebrated war correspondent Richard Harding Davis to the theatrical producer, Florenz Ziegfeld. Many were surprised that this little girl talked to them on an adult level and was unawed by them.

One day, Clare and Buffy had a bitter parting over a boy from a nearby military school who asked Buffy to go to his prom. She said she would let him know. In the interim, the boy asked Clare to go if Buffy couldn't. When Buffy delayed her answer too long, the boy took Clare. "You are a cold, scheming, and unscrupulous woman," Buffy wrote Clare.

In her diary, Clare confided her prayer that she and her dear friend would be reconciled. Eventually, of course, they were.

For Mrs. Boothe during this period, the picture suddenly brightened. She had acquired a serious suitor, a wealthy Philadelphia man with two children. When things didn't work out, Clare described him as "a nasty little toad, a selfish snob." Clare remembered her mother crying so hard it seemed as if her body would break. She felt her mother was simply tired of struggling with poverty. Clare wondered why money was so all-important in the world and vowed that she would never be in a position like her mother.

As a tenth grader, Clare was admitted to the Castle School overlooking the Hudson River in Tarrytown, New York. Castle had huge rooms with beamed ceilings, dark wood, and wonderful views of the Hudson. Clare's own room had white-painted iron beds placed close together. Clare's bed was the one near the tall, draped window. There were two desks, an ugly chandelier with two lights, a wash basin, and closet. She and her roommate placed pictures of their mothers over their beds.

Clare was delighted with the school. At St. Mary's, the headmistress was stern and dry; at Castle, headmistress and founder "Cassy" Mason was gentle and inspiring.

"She was the one who said to me, 'Clare, I think you will go far. You have talent. But always remember only two things you need: confidence in yourself and confidence in God and *She* will protect you," Clare recalled of this amazing woman who was years ahead of her time.

Clare's confidence in herself was indeed heightened when she lost weight. Her old friend Buffy visited and said, "Honey, you're really pretty!"

She now even had a boy friend, Lloyd Miller. Clare was certain she was in love with him and sadly waved him off to war when he enlisted in the Air Corps. Lying about his age, her sixteen-year-old brother, David, also enlisted, but in the Marines. Clare wrote daily letters to both of them and volunteered to roll bandages for the Red Cross. As a fund-raising effort for the Red Cross, Clare wrote and directed an all-women play called *Cinderella.* She even painted the scenery and sewed the costumes. The benefit netted $75.

As a student, Clare excelled so that Headmistress Mason offered her a chance to graduate a year early. She was particularly good in history, literature, and French. Clare was also business manager of the yearbook, *The Drawbridge,* and was widely known for her intensity. Dorothy Burns, Clare's close friend at Castle, recalled: "When the other girls were reading a racy, contraband account of their favorite movie star, Clare would have a volume of Racine or Molière. She wasn't stuffy about it. She just didn't have time for trash. She even read while she brushed her hair or when she bathed, propping a book on the faucet of the tub. She took longer baths than any girl I have ever known before or since." Burns also remembered how at a school party, Clare pretended she was French when a boy asked her to dance. "All evening, she pretended she could not understand a word he said, and answered him in French. He called up the next day and came for tea. She kept it up through tea. We were in stitches."

"Clare was always boss," said another of her schoolmates. "She always knew what she wanted."

Clare abruptly decided she wanted to be a writer. She wrote a one-act comedy called *The Lily Maid,* whose heroine had a "wealth of golden hair, eyes demurely lowered, cheeks that have carefully cultivated a convent blush." She also wrote articles for her school paper and drew cartoons.

One of her favorite writers was Somerset Maugham, and she sent him a letter telling him about her unhappy childhood and how unsympathetic her mother was about her writing ambition. Somerset Maugham replied with a six-page letter, advising her that an unhappy childhood could be a great blessing because it could spur her to seek happiness in life and communicate with others. He added that those with a happy childhood were seldom ambitious in later life because they already had the best.

During this period, Clare was deeply troubled by the war. Her brother and her romanticized young lover were both now fighting overseas and Clare was seriously concerned. She took copious notes when Rabbi Stephen S. Wise lectured at The Castle on "Why did Germany go into the war?"

When Lloyd Miller was reportedly shot down over France, Clare wept bitterly. But at the end of the war, Miller reappeared to tell Clare about another girl he wanted to marry. Clare noted in her diary how boring he now was, and how it all had really been puppy love.

The class prophecy for Clare was that she would marry a college professor and dedicate one of her books to The Castle. About this time, a palm reader advised her to take up public speaking, journalism, or art, but said she must first develop willpower. Clare listened. She quietly promised herself that she would also have a serious love affair.

Clare's mother and Joe Jacobs came for her graduation on May 27, 1919. Her mother attracted an unending stream of suitors who came and went, but Jacobs always remained part of her life. Clare had hoped "Riggie" would give her some stocks as a graduation present. Instead he presented her with a four-cylinder Essex automobile. Earlier, he had given her a white puppy, whom she called Lord Kitchener, and a leather-bound set of the works of Alexandre Dumas. He would then take mother and daughter out on a boat ride, then for a ride in his new car, and on to the theater in New York, and dinner at the Ritz Carlton. For Christmas, he gave Clare's mother a gold mesh bag, embellished with diamonds and sapphires, and Clare a diamond wristwatch. Like a father figure, he was openly concerned when Clare went on a midnight escapade to a nearby neighborhood that had a rowdy reputation.

Clare was indeed fond of Riggie, but felt he was too impatient and restless. But he was a part of their lives. Thanks to Riggie, Clare's mother made some stock investments that netted her a rich return. Clare hoped that the day would come when she would find her *own* Riggie.

At sixteen, Clare was summa cum laude, the youngest graduate in the school's history. There was a symbolic bonfire of parting with the past in which she burned a large package of letters. She wore a white georgette crepe dress, "straight lines flowing from shoulders, with the most exquisite silk underwear I always dreamed the princesses in fairy tales wore . . ." she wrote. The yearbook said of her, "Yes, yes, she is our prodigy and our genius, yet just the same she is as lovable as she is brilliant. You all know her wit. . . ."

In her diary, Clare wrote that what she wanted out of life was to write something memorable, marry a publisher, have three children, and be fluent in four languages. Her class voted her the prettiest, cleverest, and most artistic. But she ranked only second in the class for ambition, which she regarded as a major slight. "Oh God, help me to succeed. Success is not life, but life should be success," Clare said at the time. She described herself then as someone with "ten thousand dreams."

4

CHEFOO, the home of the China Inland Mission School, was a squalid, uninteresting town 450 miles north of Shantung on the Yellow Sea. The surrounding countryside undulated gently for a little distance from the town, before meeting the rising hills. Since the climate was so mild, foreigners quickly turned it into a resort.

Most of the 120 students at the Chefoo school were children of Christian missionaries and, like the staff, English or Scottish. The fourteen American boys had second-class status because the British were the foreigners who dominated China, especially in trade. Many of the students came from so far away that they did not see their parents for years. Most of the parents felt the school a boon, sparing them the need to send their children home for their education.

Basically it was a British boarding school "with none of the swank and all the severity," said Beth. "It could be brutal, really brutal."

"We were a strong, conspicuous minority," Luce said. "The British code—flogging and toadying—violated every American instinct. No wonder hardly an hour passed that an American did not have to run up the flag. A master insists that Ohio is pronounced O-hee-o. What are you going to do? Will you agree? The American can't agree; it would betray every other American. So, first your knuckles are rapped, then you get your face slapped by the Master, then you are publicly caned. By this time, you are crying but you still can't say O-hee-o."

Years later, Luce confided that he associated the smell of chalk dust with having his face rubbed on the floor for insisting that Ohio wasn't pronounced "O-hee-o."

One of Harry's classmates suffered one hundred strokes because he questioned the Master's dictum, "If I tell you the moon is made of green cheese," said the Master, "I expect you to agree . . ."

Luce's memories of the school were always vivid and intense: "I hated it and loved it." It was a rough, tough school, and he recalled bloody noses, skinned knees, swollen hands, and "a shameful, futile, endless two hours one Saturday afternoon when I rolled around the unspeakably dirty floor of the main school with a little British bastard who had insulted my country."

"There were millions of rules. We boys were always in trouble," said Harry. The most strictly enforced rule was that they could not communicate with the Chinese.

Harry saw local Chinese only when he and his classmates marched to church services on Sunday in their white pith helmets and white suits with knee-length pants. What shocked them most were the crippled and blind children, most of them starving skeletons.

Harry's close friend at Chefoo was Thornton Wilder, whose father had been a newspaper editor, then consul general in Hong Kong and Shanghai. Luce admired Wilder because he was a year older, born in the United States, had a hometown (Madison, Wisconsin), and was such a good talker. Luce still stammered, and was often mocked for it. Like Luce, Wilder was a reader, and even devoured French and English dictionaries. The two also shared a common resolve to go to Yale.

Determined to overcome his stuttering, Harry helped start a debating society. He would not sit there and suffer his embarrassment, but would cope with it and conquer it. He was like an actor with stage fright, pushing himself before an audience. When troubled by his stutter, he would cock his head to one side and wag his hand.

He wrote home that they planned to debate whether Mary Queen of Scots should have been beheaded. The remarkable thing was that he somehow managed, by sheer willpower and practice, to eliminate any stammering from his speech during any debate. Then, immediately afterward, his stutter returned.

Summer vacations with the family meant the most to him. They took their holiday at Tsingtao which Harry called one of the most beautiful of all places on this earth. Tsingtao was a magnificent port sprawled on a hundred little hills on one side of a long narrow channel which opens into a huge bay. Harry wrote of the joy of coming home for vacation. He had a mild complaint: his baby brother was a great pleasure to everybody but was monopolizing his mother.

As part of their redemption for losses in the Boxer Rebellion, the Germans has seized the bay of Tsingtao and the surrounding hundred miles and proceeded to build a German town out of a scatter of villages. They built a German church with a deep clanging bell, which Harry always remembered.

They built German homes with stucco walls and trim little gardens and paraded on the promenade along the beach to the music of a German band. The only Chinese visible were rickshaw coolies and servants.

Harry always had strong memories of the Germans. What also lingered in Harry's mind was the way they beat the rickshaw coolies, using sticks on their bare backs. The British never did this, Harry noted. What they did do was give the coolies a minimum fare and sneer slightly. The Americans didn't beat coolies either, but then they tipped heavily, especially if they lost their temper for any reason during the ride.

All this had an unforgettable impact on Luce. The extremes of beauty and brutality he observed did much to shape his concept of China, which influenced a large part of his thinking life.

His view of America at that point was admittedly more distorted. He had experienced no evil in the Americans he grew up with. His young vision of America was idealistic and romantic. Later, he came to feel his view was false.

The Chinese have an adage: A great man has the heart of a boy. "Harry was never a young boy," said Beth. "We children were always 'old' in those days. I mean, we were very grown-up much sooner."

Their father had set a pattern of discipline and determination. He had instilled in them an ambition to achieve, so overpowering that it swept away most childish concerns. But for Harry, part of this growing up was his closeness with God. He reported to his parents the best sermon he ever heard at school was "on the redemption of what the death of Christ means."

Harry had his own vision of God, that God would help him get into the fourth form, that God would help him get one hundred percent in algebra.

Chefoo closed down in the winter for six weeks because the school could not afford to heat the place. Harry returned home, where a typical day began at six-thirty A.M. "We all went downstairs to the sitting room for prayers. Mother played the hymns on the piano. Then we had a little Bible reading," said Beth. "Then we'd kneel down with our heads on the chairs—I liked the one with the cane bottom. I was always putting my little fingers in the holes. At breakfast, Harry always ate very fast—he was mostly talking with Father. They'd *both* eat fast; they were always so interested in what they were talking about that they didn't have much time to eat, or think about that.

"A meal was an occasion to talk. Everyone talked, which was a wonder because Father talked all the time! It was understood that if you were sitting at the table, you were supposed to contribute to the conversation. Father went around the table at some points to give everybody a chance. Then I think he was very relieved when he completed the rounds and could turn back to Harry, where it was much more fun. They would really talk about interesting things—

about America, China, about what was going on. Don't forget, we had no radio, no newspapers. And Father always had a new theory, a new project, a new concern. And of course, this was always very important to Harry. He never had any qualms about debating Father because Father always encouraged him to do so.

"We were always over-awed by all the long-gowned scholars in Father's study, but Harry, even as a young boy, was never over-awed by anybody. Harry would always be going in and out of Father's study to look at a dictionary or check for some reference. Father was very pleased for Harry to have the run of his study. Father was a tremendous influence on Harry."

Harry's mother, too, had a deep influence on his upbringing. She believed in decorum and good breeding and strived for a sense of propriety that seemed almost English. Her children promptly went to their rooms after breakfast, Harry to do his homework and the girls for their German lessons. Lunch was "dinner," the big meal, always with a white damask tablecloth. After lunch was the quiet time, the siesta. Afternoon was playtime for the children. Tea was served promptly at four "with beautiful white bread, very thin, carefully buttered . . . a proper English tea. All of Father's confrères on the faculty somehow knew that Mrs. Luce had the nicest tea in town, so for some reason many of them came to see Father about four in the afternoon 'on college business,' " said Beth. Years later, Luce also reminisced fondly about the "thin" corn bread in China.

Supper was light, and there were often visitors to spend the night. The children were not happy then because it meant that they had to be particularly quiet. But there was almost always the family musical concert before an early bedtime.

Back at Chefoo after the winter break, Harry wrote weekly letters home. They dealt with everything including the way he traded stamps for picture postcards of the country (he had a large collection), the pros and cons of having white mice as pets, the terrible school food, and the consequences of flood and famine in China. In discussing the attempted revolution of 1911 to replace the Manchu dynasty, Harry wrote that his sympathies were with the rebels as long as they had good and honest leaders. He then saw a revolution as the hope of the future.

For a boy not quite thirteen, this was quite a profound dictum. His sisters cherished another letter from that same period in which he said how horrified he was by any ignorant women and how proud he was of his intelligent, well-read sisters.

Another letter revealed that he still wanted to write a long epic on the rewards and sacrifices of a missionary. He was also busy doing an essay on capital punishment. The big news was that a weekly paper was being started and he would be editor in chief. The paper would include everything from classical poetry to burlesque.

His mother observed in a note to a friend that Harry "spends all his free time going over old Yale catalogs trying to figure out what the courses will be like five years from now. . . . Some specimen exams are given and yesterday I found him working over a French exam paper—isn't it funny?"

Few boys had greater intellectual curiosity about absolutely everything—and a phenomenal memory to retain it. He was always near the top of his class, but had a secret longing for something more spectacular.

There was little fault to find with Harry at fourteen. He was ready to face the world and conquer it. He was highly serious, highly moral, and highly determined. If he lacked anything then, it was a sense of humor. He had never learned to laugh enough. He almost never would. The largest laugh he had was a chuckle. He also lacked an ease with people.

Thornton Wilder's father had written his children that he hoped they would grow up to be "gracious, jolly, sympathetic commanding men and women who do not follow the fashion but make it." Harry fit the description well except for the word "jolly." Life was too earnest.

Harry's father wanted *other* things in his children. He wanted them to be liberal in their views of strangers, conservative with themselves; humble in victory, confident in defeat. To a child who temporarily failed in something, Dr. Luce wrote: "There is only one problem for you and that is how to apply your native Luce-power to your studies." His father's favorite maxim came from the Greeks: Character means destiny. These were two maxims Harry often repeated, never forgot.

Here, then, was the early mold of the man: the religious zeal and the moral force of a missionary father mixed with the intense patriotism of someone born abroad. Add to this equation the powers of utter determination and probing curiosity, the hallmark of Luce's life.

His father took care of his intellectual and academic needs, while remaining distant emotionally. Dr. Luce knew his son's strength of character and intense intellect. Yet, he quietly fretted over Harry's stuttering. When he heard about a man in England at a small school in St. Albans near London who was highly successful in curing stutterers, he arranged for Harry to go there. They had talked to him as an adult and now treated him as one. "Father and Mom figured that the best way to let a boy learn was to turn him loose," said Harry's brother Sheldon. They allowed this fourteen-year-old boy to go alone aboard a German ship to Southampton by way of the Indian Ocean and the Suez Canal.

"I didn't have much money," Harry recalled later, "so I'd attach myself to a group of Cook's tourists who were being led around, and they'd explain everything." Harry liked the botanical gardens in Singapore but decried the city where time "could be sold for a flower an hour." He admired the bazaars in Ceylon and described a funeral where a man preceded the coffin doing tricks with a firebrand lit at both ends. He marveled at the magnificence of the churches in Italy but wondered "with all its beauty . . . its ecclesiastical finery, there is a terrible poverty and hence a hotbed of socialism—no wonder!"

Harry arrived in St. Albans in October 1912. Stutters could be helped but not cured. Therapists tried to abort stuttering with a short, silent breath before each sentence. The breaths presumably relaxed the vocal cords enough to allow the person to speak fluently. Most therapists regarded the physical therapy as only part of the treatment. After five months, Harry felt helped, but not enough. His stammering hadn't stopped. His own intense willpower and practice helped him much more in later years, but for the rest of his life, he stuttered when he got overly excited.

In 1913, fifteen-year-old Henry Robinson Luce arrived at the Hotchkiss School in Lakeville, Connecticut, looking "sandy-shaggy" in his unstylish Chinese-made suit and his well-worn shoes, feeling himself a minority of one. And so he was. Of the 250 boys, he was the only one born abroad. The others promptly nicknamed him "Chink." In telling of this afterward, Luce sometimes softened it by saying his nickname was "China Boy." He always had the sense of being an outsider. It was not simply as if he had come to a country foreign to him—it was really another world.

Hotchkiss was one of the most prestigious prep schools in America. "The school boasted a pride of spirit and a social discipline comparable to the ancient schools of England," wrote a journalist in a piece about a Hotchkiss professor. "Hotchkiss was a *very* rich school, and pre-war United States was a much more elitist society than it is today." All Hotchkiss boys lived high on the hog. Maids made their beds and cleaned up after them. At a single dinner in 1915, 262 students consumed 350 pounds of steak.

The school consisted of an impressive row of brick buildings overlooking Connecticut's Lake Wonoscopomuc and the magnificent Berkshire wooded hills. The students at Hotchkiss were mostly white, Protestant, Republican, and rich, with the exception of a few "townies" given free tuition and six scholarship students.

As one of the scholarship boys, Luce swept, cleaned rooms, waited on tables, and was generally treated like a second-class citizen. "Harry did these chores very badly," said Beth, "because at home he had never cleaned anything—he had Chinese servants to do it. So, when he was supposed to clean the class-room, he didn't have the remotest idea how to do it."

"I detested [the cleaning], but I wasn't humiliated," Luce later insisted, saying he felt no injustice and was happy to be there on those terms. To novelist Pearl Buck, another mishkid (the name for a missionary child), Luce was more revealing, telling her how he hated being so poor at Hotchkiss, how painfully embarrassed he was by his poverty. Nor could he understand the students' frame of reference. Coming from China, he knew none of the current American slang and found himself listening to jokes he didn't find funny. All this pushed him further to one side and made him seem more aloof. His stammering didn't help.

The headmaster at Hotchkiss was the Reverend Dr. Huber Gray Beuhler, whom students called "the King," a pompous, cold, excessively shy man, never known to touch a boy. He once told an old friend that he would give anything if he could bring himself to put his arm around a student's shoulder. In his annual speech, he always said, "There is only one rule in this school, 'Be a gentleman.' "

Being a gentleman meant wearing three-button herringbone jackets, silk shirts, and proper plus-fours as knickerbockers. Being a gentleman also meant living with a strict unwritten code. Upperclassmen brought violators to trial and those found guilty ran naked past a gauntlet of other boys who whipped them with knotted towels.

The school talk was most of girls, sports, clothes, and Harry cared for none of these things. His fellow students saw their young lives in terms of fun and laughter, and Harry couldn't understand why their fun was fun and why they would waste their time like that. Life to him now was serious, serious, serious. He had come here with goals and purpose. His father had ingrained in him such a sense of mission that he didn't know how to really relax.

Since Luce could afford neither clothes nor a social life, he made some early choices: no girls, no smoking, no drinking. Instead, he would concentrate on classwork. Some said that he was prudish about sex then, but the greater likelihood is that he disdained girls simply because he didn't have the money for dates. He felt he could never have the ease of an insider. The hurt of the humiliated outsider always stayed with him.

His mother came to visit and reported to Mrs. McCormick that "I came away greatly troubled about some things—I am glad that I went and had the chance to quietly see for myself, because it is impossible to find out from Henry if things are not what they should be. He never complains about anything. He goes steadily on his way, doing his work, and meeting all difficulties in his brave, quiet manner. It seems that the scholarship boys are required to room in the village, at least during their first year. Harry had a little room a mile away, going down about nine o'clock in the evening and coming up at six-forty-five A.M., through heavy storms of snow and wind—and when I was there, a blizzard raged, and it was eighteen degrees below zero. He was sleeping in a three-quarter bed, with a husky farmer boy from Kansas! I had given Henry warm blankets and quilts, and there he was sharing with his roommate. When I mentioned to Henry that the blankets and quilts were meant for use on a single bed, he said, 'this boy hasn't any of his own and I am so glad to share them with one who needs them.' I also found out that Henry was spending many days during the week, helping this boy with his lessons."

Harry was soon known as the "the Brain." His classmate Culbreth Sudler recalled that "even when we took a walk, his eyes would still be remembering a passage from Milton we had to memorize for the next day's English class."

The purpose of a walk for Luce "was to sort out the contents of his mind on such questions: Was Alexander Hamilton or Thomas Jefferson ultimately right for the American people?"

Still, Harry never stopped trying to be good at everything at Hotchkiss. He tried out for the dramatic club, traveled with the football team as a photographer, and even played center on the team. He managed to stay on the eight-man tennis squad but was "in daily fear of being fired from the squad." But he did become captain of the soccer team, sang first bass in the glee club, and wrote the words for the school song.

But no matter how he tried, Harry simply was not a typical Hotchkiss boy. While he wore the standard stiff collar to chapel every day, his tie wasn't straight or maybe a button was missing. Few other students made special trips to New York on holidays to hear special sermons and almost nobody felt free to embarrass the headmaster on Bible class by asking, "Why should we have to ask an all-protecting God not to lead us into temptation?" As one of Luce's friends later noted, "In a kind of dour, Presbyterian way, Harry was thinking in ultimate terms, almost as if he were playing chess with God."

Nor was Harry overwhelmed by the headmaster's private lecture to him about his nonconformist attitude. Harry could not understand why they should "fuss so much about my attitude." He followed his father and Ralph Waldo Emerson on this: "A foolish consistency is the hobgoblin of little minds. With consistency, a great soul has nothing to do. Your conformity explains nothing. Greatness appeals to the future."

Harry and his father also exchanged letters on the foundation of American leadership in the world, a refrain that would echo in so many of Harry's later ideas.

"Harry wasn't very popular at Hotchkiss," said one of his few friends, John

Hincks, "but one thing we all envied was that he had come there all alone from China by way of India and the Suez Canal and Constantinople and Rome and taken a month to do it. We thought that was wonderful." Hincks and Harry decided they didn't want to go to the junior prom so they went to New York together, stayed with Harry's family who were there then on church business, and saw three operas, one on Friday and two on Saturday. "We'd save money by buying standing room tickets. After the first act was nearly over, if you gave the usher a half dollar, he'd lead you to an empty seat."

Of Harry's few friends, one of the most important was Briton Hadden, nicknamed "Cat" because of the way he grinned and wrinkled his nose. "Cat" was everything "Chink" was not—gregarious, full of fun, sports-loving. Son of a wealthy Brooklyn banker, Brit Hadden had come to Hotchkiss determined to outdo his older brother who had been captain of the baseball team. His one ambition was to become a big league baseball player, but the best he could do was successfully adopt the swagger and the scowl of his hero Ty Cobb. Despite Brit's rugged build, he was no athlete.

Harry had no such frustrations. His prime aim was literary. What tied these two young men together was not warm friendship, but a mutual admiration and a love of language. Their competition was keen. Both tried out for staff positions on the school weekly newspaper, *The Record,* and both were accepted. Harry's first journalistic assignment was to report on a soccer game. Brit eventually became editor and Harry his assistant but Hadden wrote his mother that he would rather have gotten his "H" in baseball "than be the editor of all the papers in the world."

With all Harry's frenetic activity, he still felt lonely, especially after his family returned to China. "I can see Henry now, waving his brave good-bye as the ship pulled out and slipped off on the long journey," wrote his mother. She referred to their separation as "the sword that must pierce our hearts."

At graduation time, neither Luce nor Hadden was voted "most likely to succeed." That honor went to the star athlete. Harry was named "Class Poet." He ranked third as the brightest, fourth as the most absent-minded, sixth as the most pious, and ninth as the worst woman hater. His scholastic record read, "Honor Roll, Leader of the Class." A class book comment about him read, "All wisdom's armory this man could wield." Brit won the Declamation Award for his rendition of "Casey at the Bat," wrote the lyrics for the class song, and delivered the class oration on the need "for bettering the political conditions of the land we live in."

After Hotchkiss, there never had been any doubt that Harry would go to Yale. He scored the highest mark in the college board Greek exams in the history of Yale. Hotchkiss's headmaster thought this event important enough to declare a school holiday.

Asked in a class poll about his future career, Luce had answered, "Undecided." But, to his family, Harry wrote of his interest in returning to China and getting involved in some big economic movement, such as railroads, farming, or newspaper syndicates. Harry told his father that he would depend on God to help him choose.

That summer, Harry got a job on the Springfield, Massachusetts, *Republican,* working at the front counter of the business office handling subscriptions, complaints, and local advertisements. For two thirds of a week's work, he received $5.34. He described himself as being at the foot of the newspaper ladder, and even wondered whether he would ever "get wise" to the awful detail of the clerk job, although he saw it as good training in precision and accuracy. But he wrote home with pride that he felt a closer kinship with democracy than he had before.

When his editor let him do some reporting, his excitement increased. Harry wrote home of his fascination with courtroom drama and seeing the inside of a prison cell for the first time. "I never before saw a brave tear-stained mother coming to bail out her son on the sure charge of forgery," he said.

Furthermore, Luce was now convinced that journalism came closest to the heart of the world. For Harry Luce, it was a prophetic comment that his family would soon comprehend.

5

SEVERAL days after graduation from Castle, Clare took the train to New York, settled down to read her book on Plato, and soon became aware that an older man sitting next to her was examining her very closely. She now knew how pretty she was and expected men to stare at her occasionally. But this man never stopped staring, and she gradually felt more and more uncomfortable. Finally, he spoke up and asked if she understood what she was reading. "Yes, I do. At least I think I do, and I enjoy it." They discussed Plato for a while "and he talked wisely and well," Clare recalled. Then, as the train approached Grand Central Station, the man asked, "Is your name, by any chance, Clare Boothe?" Astonished, she said yes. He then asked if her mother was as beautiful as ever and if she was well.

Clare looked more closely at the man. His hair was thick and gray, and he was good-looking, but slightly shabby. Mostly, he looked somewhat familiar. She told him about her mother and he then asked about her brother, David. She replied that David was still in the Marine Corps, en route from Nicaragua. Finally, Clare asked him how he knew their family.

"Why, child, I am your father," he told her. "We haven't seen each other for a long, long time, but your mother sent me a snapshot of you and David a few years ago."

Clare was too shocked to say anything or ask anything more. He said he had been visiting his brother who was a professor at Yale, and that he now lived in San Francisco. They parted at the exit.

Every time she told that story Clare seemed to change her age.

"People with disappearing fathers are prone to fantasies about them. In dreams, she may have met him in every age," said the author Wilfrid Sheed, who was Clare's friend and confidant in later years. Clare confided to her diary about the father she had fabricated for her friends, making him out to be some superb creature with every admirable attribute, and how wrong she was to do this.

Clare then confronted her mother. Why had she told them ten years ago that their father was dead? Tearfully, her mother insisted that she had done so to make it easier for them. The truth, she said, was that their father had run off with the famous opera singer, Mary Garden.

Several days later, Clare's father called and said he wanted to see her again. Over dinner with Riggie and the family, Billy Boothe told them he had married three more times after the divorce. He also made no pretense of apologizing for the way he had deserted them. Clare noted that Riggie felt only contempt for a man who contributed so little to his family, and she agreed. She wrote in her diary that she hated her father, but she later crossed that out and noted that she couldn't care less about him. But the following week he came to dinner again, and Clare felt forced to admit that he was indeed personable. She marveled at his nerve in coming to face them without any regret or shame after all the years, yet confided to her diary that she wanted to wipe him out of her mind.

During this final visit, Billy Boothe and his former wife quarreled because Clare and David had never learned to play the violin or the piano. In her diary, Clare admitted that her heart ached to master the violin or the piano but that she couldn't play a note because she was tone-deaf. If her daddy had been a good daddy, she wrote, and had taught her, maybe she would have learned to play anyway because she wanted to make music, and because she felt her father rising up within her.

Many years later, Clare received a letter from a male cousin in Massachusetts who claimed that Clare's father had visited him frequently before he went to California. "I liked him. He had a charm of his own," the cousin said. Clare replied that she was pleased her father visited her cousin but only wished he also could have visited her, too.

If having an absent father was the major regret of her life, Clare once said, another was that she never went to college. She attended Lee's Business Course in Stamford, Connecticut, to study shorthand and touch typing, but only, she said, to help her at Columbia University. Columbia didn't accept her, she complained, because she was too young. That seems unlikely, since she was sixteen. More likely, Clare needed a scholarship and didn't get it—*if* she applied at all.

Not long after that, Clare left home, rented a small room in New York, and got a job cutting paper flowers and painting paper nut cups for Christmas for Dennison's on lower Fifth Avenue for eighteen dollars a week. She adopted a new name, Jacqueline Tanner, because it made her break from her family complete. Possibly, she was getting back at her father for leaving her and her mother for concealing the truth. Yet, all Clare has said of this period was: "I had to get away." But three months later, Clare had an attack of appendicitis and was admitted to Greenwich Hospital. Soon after, she moved back with her mother.

In many ways, Clare and Ann Clare were of the same mold. She had long envied her mother's beauty, but, now, finally, she had her own. She had longed envied her mother's warmth and easy popularity, yet these were qualities that still eluded her. She envied her mother's ambition, and she knew that this was directed mainly at her. She and her mother were two fierce women fighting the world and they needed each other to continue the fight. Three months in a tiny room in Manhattan doing a dull job, and being lonely most of the time, had convinced her of this. She was happy to come home.

In her diary, Clare once wrote, "When I am with mother, I am always so happy."

Buffy Cobb had a different memory of Mrs. Boothe: "Clare had a dreadful mother, really appalling. Mrs. Boothe had groomed her to use her beauty, to be a predatory woman. She [Clare] had to be secretive, careful, protecting her mother and the dreadful things she knew." Among the secrets she kept, said Buffy, were "the awful men who had been keeping Mrs. Boothe." Buffy admitted, however, that Mrs. Boothe was "wonderful with kids," a quality she came to appreciate when she had stayed with them for part of a summer because of a polio epidemic near her own home.

One of the men Mrs. Boothe knew well was Yves de Villers, who lived in a terraced penthouse on Madison Avenue and gave lavish parties for celebrities. Once, he took Mrs. Boothe to a society ball in Greenwich. "She was still a truly beautiful woman with violet eyes, glossy brown hair, and a voluptuous figure," he remembered. They were giving a prize at the ball for the most beautiful woman there. "She knew no one there, of course, except me," said de Villers, "but she found out, God knows how, who the judges would be and she made a point of talking to each in turn, weaving her spell. The result was that she was awarded the prize to the indignation of all the other women present."

De Villers also recalled that Mrs. Boothe once called him in the middle of the night to tell him how worried she was about Clare, who was then sixteen. She had a request: Would Yves marry Clare? "Of course, I told her it was an insane suggestion."

Finally, at age thirty-eight, Clare's mother decided to concentrate on herself. When her appendix ruptured, she was rushed to the same hospital where Clare's appendix was removed two months earlier. Mrs. Boothe's surgeon was Dr. Albert Elmer Austin, whom she had met before socially. She told everybody that she had been dying and that this surgeon had saved her life. Clare thought early on that he was very much in love with her mother, "though he tried very, very, very hard to conceal it from both of us."

Austin, then forty-two, was a very proper and conservative man with graying hair. A former Latin teacher, he had served in the World War as a regimental surgeon, then became head of the Greenwich Hospital staff. He believed that too much sleep dulls the intellect. Austin was then in the midst of a difficult divorce. He could not propose to Ann Clare, but he could court her. Clare called her mother's suitor "the most adorable man on the planet. He came almost every night to take us to dinner and the movies or theater." He later taught Clare Latin "with the patience of love."

While her mother and Austin were courting, Clare, too, enjoyed herself. There were soon a variety of young men calling on her, most of them in the Army: a former lawyer with thin hair and a quick wit (her mother liked him, but Riggie thought him too talkative); a tall, dignified young man of twenty-four who acted ten years older; and a Captain Quigley who left a dance early because he decided not to compete with Clare's cutting comments. When she questioned his leaving, he said she had drawn enough blood for the evening. Some men made her blush and tremble, and one proposed regularly, but none of them were "Mr. Right."

What Clare most wanted, and what she repeated again and again in her diary was the love of a strong man. She didn't feel she was too young to want someone to love her because, after all, she was already sixteen and Juliet was only fourteen when she fell wildly in love. But unlike Juliet, Clare at sixteen was determined not to marry until she was a famous writer or artist.

The man she envisioned was tall, with a firm chin. He should be sensitive, brave, and a little reckless. She didn't care what religion he had believed in, but she wanted him to love her more than he loved God or honor or country. She wanted a masterful man, and she prayed that he would not be poor—she wanted someone who made at least $12,000 a year. She also wanted a man who cared for his hands and polished his boots. Somehow, she had a feeling that she would eventually marry an Englishman. Never would she fall in love with an ordinary man and have an ordinary courtship and an ordinary wedding.

Her brother, David, returned in his Marine uniform, and Clare was sad to see that he was the same selfish, complaining boy he had always been. She didn't like his companions, who were invariably tough. She no longer fought with him, although he did try to stir her up. Despite everything, she was happy he was home, happy to be with him.

Her mother now came up with a romantic, preposterous idea. The prince of Wales was staying at The Greenbrier hotel in White Sulphur Springs, West Virginia and Mrs. Boothe was absolutely certain that as soon as the prince met Clare, he would be dazzled by her and promptly propose. She knew The Greenbrier hotel manager, and he actually arranged a ball where the prince might meet Clare. Clare called her mother's dreams "bubbles," and this bubble burst because their luggage didn't arrive on time. Clare couldn't go to the ball because she had nothing to wear. Then, the prince unexpectedly departed early. Little did Clare realize that years later, she would befriend him and dine with him.

For Mrs. Boothe, the world brightened when Dr. Austin proposed marriage. He was a gentle, considerate man. Clare was delighted, even though she described him as "New England cold." She nicknamed him "Cicero," because he taught her Latin. Clare found it odd watching her mother being coquettish and teasing. Much as Clare liked Riggie, she preferred Austin because he was more intellectual. This marriage now gave her mother a sparkling new community status.

Clare wasn't concerned about status—she was sixteen and too busy having fun. A friendly pilot took her on her first plane ride, a wild one complete with looping-the-loop. She bought a book called *Eat and Grow Thin,* because she was desperate to attract her dream man, whoever he was.

Her stepfather provided a fresh adventure, another trip to Europe in 1920, only this time first class. Dr. Austin was awarded a grant to investigate plastic surgery techniques in Berlin and wanted his new family to accompany him. Joining them was her mother's old friend, Adele Schmeider, who came mainly as a companion for Clare. Clare later described Adele as lovable, unselfish, unsophisticated, and unspoiled. "And, wonder of wonders, she likes to hear me talk."

Germany was in a period of economic chaos, partly because of the heavy reparations it faced to pay for the war. Adolf Hitler announced his twenty-five-point program at the Hofbrauhaus in Munich. All over Europe, 1920 was a year of chaos. Mussolini had made his march on Rome and formed a Fascist government. The soviet states had combined into a single government, the Union of Soviet Socialist Republics.

En route to Germany, they stopped in England. Clare found Englishmen very charming and soon revealed that she had been infatuated twice and planned to marry a foreigner. Friends told her one young man was a rake, but she said she didn't care. She was a young woman living in a whirlwind of excitement. In her letters to friends, she poured out how she loved London with all her heart.

After a stay in Paris, the travelers' next stop was Berlin. Inflation was running so high in Germany that the Austins were able to stay at the luxurious Adlon Hotel: They had the royal suite with three bedrooms, two baths, and a reception room for twelve dollars a day.

Clare studied German and she and Mrs. Schmeider saw a lot of theater, including Max Reinhardt's *Schauspielhaus.* She also observed the chaos of German politics and blamed much of it on France for grinding Germany's face in the mud, demanding reparations that it could never pay. She now felt she was becoming somewhat pro-German. She later told author Luigi Barzini that she was so stirred by what she saw that she had decided to become a journalist so that she could "really do something about it." After observing some of these political profundities in her letters, Clare noted how handsome the German men looked in their dinner jackets with their military bearing straight out of a newspaper ad.

While Dr. Austin was happily at work, Clare and Adele went for a week to Vienna, where they learned the tricks of riding over five-foot hurdles in an English saddle. She then joined the Austins on a trip south to the Riviera, where she won a beauty contest. She was five foot six and willowy, "with the most beautiful legs of any woman I know," gushed a reporter. Clare saved newspaper clippings of the time, one of which headlined: VOTED MOST BEAU-TIFUL GIRL.

After a few months abroad, Clare decided that she would select as a husband "a full-blooded American" because she had discovered that she was too poor to attract a duke.

Nevertheless, her plan had always been to fall in love, and when it happened, nationality was no barrier. The object of her passion was a war hero, Major Julian Simpson, tall and handsome, and an Oxford graduate who planned to go into politics. They met at a party at the Guards' Club, and before the evening was over, Clare was completely entranced.

Here was her romantic fantasy come true. In their four days before her ship sailed, they were constantly together: breakfast, lunch, tea, dinner. They toured the city, saw the sights, went to the theater. Simpson knew exactly how to stir Clare. He drove her to Liverpool in a Rolls-Royce sedan to catch her ship. During the four-hour trip, he recited Francis Thompson's long poem, "The Hound of Heaven," to prove that he loved poetry as much as she did. They talked about their future and he promised to come to

Greenwich as soon as he could to continue the courtship. An eager seventeen, she gave him her heart.

Aboard ship, she wrote several long love poems, saying how perfect Julian was, how utterly she loved him with her body and soul and how she would not let him go.

Few young women believed it more; few young women could have been happier or more miserable. Sighing at the ship's rail, she said, "Everything is love. Love is the most important thing in the world."

6

WHEN eighteen-year-old Harry Luce entered Yale in 1916, the looming question was when the United States would join the war in Europe. Yale already had a volunteer field artillery battery ready to go. However, the mood was still basically boola-boola. Students were more concerned with secret societies than with the war. "A Yalie was known to be a clear-eyed, clean-cut, high-minded, upright, downright, forthright Christian young man who went to hops and tea dances and parted his hair in the middle," wrote author Gilbert Harrison in a biography of one of Luce's classmates, Thornton Wilder. Philosopher George Santayana, in his autobiography, described Yale as characterized by a muscular Christianity and an undirected moral enthusiasm. "You were trained merely to succeed. And in order to be sure to succeed, it was safer to let the drift of the times dictate your purpose. Make a strong pull and a long pull and a pull all together for the sake of togetherness. Then you will win the race. . . . 'Rah, rah, rah! Whooper-up! Onward, Christian Soldier!' " Long afterward, in a talk on education, Luce announced that when he went to Yale, "the last thing they told him was the truth."

In describing his years at Yale, Luce once said: "An undergraduate's day began with prayer in chapel, the proctors noting empty seats and the back rows half-filled with kneeling, muffled figures in white ties and tails who had been partying in New York and had just got off the milk train."

Harry, however, was not one of the party-goers. At Yale, he exhibited his usual discipline. He made time for singing bass in the glee club, rowing number two with the freshman crew six miles a day, and waiting on tables. He had arrived with five hundred dollars from his father—the rest was for him to earn. Harry wrote Mrs. McCormick that his father was financing his freshman year but he would have to work his way through after that. Tuition was $175, room $125, and board about $200. Mrs. McCormick continued to send him needed checks.

*   *   *

Harry's class (Yale 1920) included the son of a partner at Morgan Brothers, the prestigious banking house, a du Pont, an Adams, and an Auchincloss. Luce developed an awe of social aristocracy that never left him.

During his first year at Yale, Harry told a friend: "I couldn't decide whether to be an anarchist or a great publisher. It was only after much thought that I decided to be a publisher."

It is difficult even to imagine Luce ever considering anarchism with any seriousness. He may have well resented the constant rub of the rich, but he wanted to emulate them, equal them, better them—not destroy them.

With the notion of being a publisher in mind, Harry started "heeling" for the Yale *Daily News.* "Heeling" was a process of points. You earned them by the quantity and quality of the stories you suggested and wrote, the number of ads you sold, and the time you spent running errands for the staff. Harry called the competition "awful . . . a blind desperateness. . . . It not only uses up all your energy, it robs you of the mood or frame of mind to do anything like studying or reading or writing letters." He was worried that he had made a "very poor start." Hoping to get ahead, he asked if Mrs. McCormick, who was "so widely acquainted with men in this country who are doing things," would send him a letter of introduction to someone who might want to be interviewed for the paper. In particular, he mentioned a man whose photograph he had seen on her library table.

Obsessed with his task, Harry got up at five-forty-five each morning to give the newspapers the once over. "If there's no news, I go back to bed again, but if there is, I put on an overcoat and a pair of shoes over my pajamas and beat it across Elm Street to the *News* office . . . where I drop a card for a 'scoop' . . . and then go back to bed again," he wrote home.

His major scoop was an exclusive interview with the commander of a German submarine which had unexpectedly blundered into New London, Connecticut. At last, Harry was on his way and exuberant sent home a one-word cable: SUCCESSFUL.

The Luces knew exactly what that meant. Of the several dozen freshman candidates for the *News,* Harry was one of four chosen. So were Brit Hadden and Thayer Hobson, whose wife, Laura, would later stage the party where Harry met Clare. Hobson himself would become a successful publisher and have a special presence in Harry's personal life.

The four winners were at a party celebrating when somebody rushed in with a newspaper headlined, U.S. DECLARES WAR. Patriotism at Yale reached a new fervor. Luce believed in pursuing the war with fierce determination. He and Brit persuaded their class to buy a $1000 Liberty Bond.

Freshmen were urged to stay at school, while older students went to train as officers at Yale's field artillery unit in South Carolina. Still a freshman, Harry earned a term's tuition working for a tailor soliciting orders from students for ROTC uniforms. He resisted the temptation to sign up with Theodore Roosevelt's Flying Corps.

Students were even encouraged to work on farms during the summer to raise crops to feed the soldiers. Harry's family had returned to China, so he went to Pennsylvania to work on the farm of his family friends and financial supporters, the James Linens. What he liked least was cleaning out chicken coops. Yet, there was something about the Linens that Harry emulated and admired. James Linen III, a future Luce publisher, "somehow got the impression that Harry either wished that his father had been more like Jim's father, or regarded Jim's father as his own."

As close as he was to the Linens, Harry felt an even stronger bond to Mrs. McCormick. He regarded her as a surrogate mother and sent her a steady flow of letters, plus copies of all his speeches and articles.

The departure of senior students intensified competition for top editorial positions on the *News.* Hadden later beat out Harry for chairman of the board by a single vote. Luce wrote home about his deep disappointment in not being able to follow in his father's footsteps. In *his* letter home, Brit wrote, "Luce is the best competition I ever had. No matter how hard I run, Luce is always there. I have to get better acquainted with 'Chink' Luce, with whom I will have to work in the next few years," Hadden continued. Harry himself said he had the greatest admiration and affection for Brit, which he hoped was reciprocated.

As their friendship grew, Brit and "Chink" one day went crow-shooting, got gloriously lost, and wallowed home through soggy woods. Afterward, they went to a party where the music was superb. Although Harry was not at that point a good dancer, "I guess I got away with it," he said. That night, until three in the morning, they discussed the girls at the party.

At other more serious moments, Hadden and Luce concentrated enthusiastically on the war effort. If a course interfered with military training, the Yale *News* editorialized: drop the course. If there was a question about having a junior prom: make the price of admission a Liberty Bond. Harry proudly wrote home that the Yale *News* had played a great part in changing the spirit at Yale. "There is now no college in the country more thoroughly and intensely patriotic—and intelligently!" he told his family.

In the summer of 1918, Luce and Hadden and most of their class went to Camp Jackson, South Carolina. They were part of a cadre of student-officer instructors for the incoming flood of draftees. They traveled for two days and two nights in coaches, three men in two seats, and took an open bath in Washington. In camp, they were soon firing imaginary guns at imaginary enemies. They weren't in the army, but they almost thought they were. In a way, it was a reminder for Luce of life in a Chinese compound: selected people in a compressed area with a special mission.

Harry was delighted to report home that he got the coveted position of corporal. As corporal, he lectured to his platoon on how the German sinking of the *Lusitania* meant a terrible loss of American lives. He roused the men to such an emotional pitch that he regarded his speech as "one of the greatest successes of my life."

Since he wasn't yet a commissioned officer—you had to be twenty-one— Harry couldn't accompany his soldiers when he took them on the eight-mile march to the troop train. "The one thing we wanted to do," said Harry, "was to go to the front and fire at the enemy." Many of those he had helped train didn't fire at the enemy either—they were drowned when their transport ship, the *Ticonderoga*, was torpedoed in mid-Atlantic.

Harry and Brit were finally commissioned second lieutenants and celebrated by smoking big cigars. They were then shipped to Camp Zachary Taylor near Louisville about a month before the war ended. "What are we going to tell our grandsons that we did in the war," Harry asked. "Cleaned a horse's hoof at Camp Jackson!"

Twenty-five years later, Luce talked about it: "It was sickeningly hot that summer, but it cooled off a little at night. One night Brit and I were walking back to our barracks through the vast sprawling camp. At each step, our feet sank ankle-deep into the sand. But we ploughed on for hours, and talked and talked.

"For many months we hadn't talked about anything except artillery, mess, inspection." Brit and Harry discussed how the soldiers were enormously ignorant of the war and the world. Or, as Luce later put it, "Their knowledge didn't equal their interest." They felt the dire need to produce a news magazine so interesting that everybody would want to read it. "Here we were, talking about 'that paper,' about something we would do—cross our hearts—someday. I think it was in that walk that *Time* began."

With the end of the war in November 1918, Luce and Hadden returned to Yale and their college newspaper. If Yale now seemed tame, it was still a place of great meaning for Harry. At Hotchkiss, he had felt on the fringe, but here he blossomed. He would later say of Yale, "In this place it is impossible to be entirely selfish. In this place it is impossible to think wholly in terms of oneself, of one's own desires, pleasure, pursuits, ideas, and ideals."

But he *had* to think of himself and the future. His newspaper dream with Hadden was so nebulous. Now, he had to consider more pragmatic possibilities. "Family and friends could think of no way to get on in the world except to be a lawyer. Accordingly, I spent a summer at summer law school," he explained. Harry studied criminal law and read the famous murder cases in seventeenth-century England, but could never predict who was guilty or innocent. "I could follow the judge's logic but I could not foresee it. Clearly I had no aptitude for law."

By January 1919, Hadden was considered king of the campus. Even Harry admitted that if ever a class had one big man, it was Brit. On most issues, Brit was the conservative and Harry the rebel. They argued frequently about everything, and their different points of view made the paper more alive.

Everything about Harry seemed geared up for purpose. He was crossing the campus one day, his face screwed up with concentration. "I was there when he stumbled and almost fell," said Allen Grover, then a Yalie, two years behind Luce, "and I heard this voice yelling, 'Watch out, Harry, or you'll drop the college!' It might have been Brit, but I wouldn't swear to it.

"I felt sorry for Harry, really sorry," added Grover, who later became Luce's closest associate and confidant. "I felt sorry for him because he had so few friends. It was almost as if he were *afraid* of giving his friendship. He was rather remote, rather distant, a humorless man in the sense that he wasn't a jokester. But I never found him arrogant. He was never short with me, never bad-tempered. Another thing: he was not a chatterer, no small talk. His way of reaching out to people was to ask questions. His curiosity was infinite."

Some still called him "Chink" but others called him Harry or Hank. One classmate described him later as "intent and brilliant, never deviating and ever attaining . . . said by some to sweat ice water . . ."

"Tap Day" was a crucial turning point for Luce. He yearned to be "tapped" for Skull and Bones, the supreme secret society at Yale, the ultimate honor. For most Yalies, nothing was more prestigious. The philosophy of "Bones" was that there were only a limited number of outstanding positions in the world and Bones men were destined to fill them. The fifteen tapped for Bones each year were not simply the most successful in the school, but those with the greatest potential. Luce's father had not been tapped for Bones. This made Harry more ecstatic when he was selected. Harry also made Phi Beta Kappa—and Hadden did not.

At his Yale graduation in 1920, Harry was summa cum laude and was regarded, along with Stephen Vincent Benet and Thornton Wilder, as one of the three outstanding poets of his class. Harry later said, "I came to the conclusion that I was never going to be a really good poet, so the hell with it."

Brit Hadden, Harry's friend and nemesis, was voted "most likely to succeed" and "the man who had done most for Yale." The two were locked in a fierce competition that was only beginning.

The issue now for Harry was what to do next. Mrs. McCormick tried to pressure him to consider a future in the ministry, but he recapped for her his interest in the profession of newspaper work, which appealed to him not only because of the writing, but because of the political aspects and the chance to influence public policy.

"Harry, don't. Don't go into journalism. It will turn you into a cynic. It will corrupt and corrode you. It will turn your wine into vinegar. You will lose your soul," advised his friend's father, former newspaper editor Dr. Amos Wilder. He pleaded with Harry for "nearly an hour . . . with tears in his eyes." Dr. Wilder, to Harry, was "perhaps the most brilliant man on the New Haven campus, and certainly the most overpoweringly eloquent."

Mrs. McCormick was also highly persuasive. Harry had spent some of his vacations with her and they would discuss everything from the integrity of the mind to the question of the morality of exporting munitions. She gave him a thousand-dollar graduation gift and the promise that there was a job always waiting for him in her family business, International Harvester.

Harry was in no hurry. Besides the McCormick gift, he had earned $1500 from his share of the profits from Yale *News,* all of which he planned to use for travel in Europe plus a postgraduate year at Oxford. Prior to that, there was an invitation he could not refuse. Yalie Morehead Patterson, who would be his Oxford roommate, had invited him to share his father's private railroad car en route to the Republican National Convention in Chicago.

There, Luce was entranced with General Leonard Wood, who claimed the mantle of Theodore Roosevelt. But the man who won was strikingly handsome, silver-haired, United States Senator William Gamaliel Harding, "the only man in the United States who might have worn a toga and gotten away with it," as an observer wryly noted. The disappointed Harry wrote home that he hadn't yet decided what political party he preferred.

In July 1920, Harry sailed on the *Olympia* to England with two Yale friends. He hiked with them through Devon and Cornwall. The three young men carried walking canes and wore army fatigues with rolled leggings. They examined Roman ruins, ate Cornish pasties, paid a pilgrimage to the grave of Elihu Yale in Wales, socialized in London, then toured the Lake District and Edinburgh. Luce left the group to go to Paris. Originally, he had planned to spend the summer with a French family and learn the language; instead, he joined another Yale friend, Hugh Auchincloss (who would later become

Jacqueline Bouvier's stepfather) on a trip to Turkey on the Orient Express. What impressed Harry about Turkey were the thick woods, the magnificent air, and the great devotion he observed at a mosque.

Wherever he went, Harry always visited the American Embassy mainly for information and occasionally for lunch. He reflected that he felt as if he knew 500 percent more about Europe and its problems than he ever knew before. Harry and Hugh crossed the closed Rumanian border into Bulgaria, and toured Yugoslavia on a seventy-hour train trip. In Budapest, when they couldn't find a hotel room, their cabdriver suggested a bordello for the night. Instead, they slept in bathtubs at the Ritz.

Now he was ready for Oxford, and a year's study of history.

"What history?" asked his tutor.

"A little impatiently, I spelled it out," he recalled. "I intend to read eighteenth- and nineteenth-century European history."

"Luce," said his tutor, "I am bound to tell you that here in Oxford we believe that modern history ends with the Glorious Revolution of 1688. After that, all is mere hearsay and rumor."

Life was serene. "Harry considered Oxford a holiday," said Beth. "He had worked so hard all those school years, and now he needed a holiday, and deserved it." There was research reading, of course, but he always found reading fun. Afternoons meant bicycling and tennis, followed by tea. Evenings meant conversation, literature, and chess. Discussions with his tutor often focused on choice bits of historical scandal, such as whether James I could hold his liquor or whether Cromwell married for love or money.

Harry's Oxford life boarded on opulence. His roommate, "Pat," (Morehead Patterson) believed in spacious rooms with proper servants. Pat's own major interest in Oxford seemed to be fox hunting.

Journalism was no longer a primary goal, but merely a means to an end for Luce. What Harry now wanted, he said, was a financial independence so he could go into politics without being entirely dependent upon anyone "for bread and butter."

That Christmas of 1920, Harry journeyed to Rome with an Oxford friend and accidentally bumped into Thornton Wilder, his old classmate from Chefoo, Hotchkiss, and Yale. Listening to Harry's convictions and opinions, Wilder said, "I never knew when I liked him better, not even in China . . ."

On New Year's Eve, they all went to a party at the American Academy. Harry suddenly noticed a tall girl with curly brown hair. Lila Ross Hotz was a light-hearted, spirited young woman who spoke fluent French and Italian and loved music. A student at the fashionable Miss Risser's School in Rome, Lila came from a wealthy Presbyterian Chicago family. Her brother was a Yale man. Lila was just what Harry needed.

"He was the most intriguing person I had ever met," said Lila. "His conversation, his *extraordinary* knowledge of everything interesting. He wasn't shy, not a bit. He was sort of low-key. He didn't boast. He didn't talk loud. Harry and I then discovered our common love of poetry."

In the midst of their first conversation, Harry abruptly asked: "Are you popular?"

Indeed, Lila was, but she was so intrigued with this different young man who "talked a blue streak," that she let him monopolize her that evening. Harry was dazzled. As for Lila, she later said, "I think I knew the day I met Harry that I wanted to marry him."

The day after the party, Harry left for Florence. "I wasn't sure if I'd ever see him again," Lila recalled. Two days later, there was a letter from him and he asked me to write back. So, then we started a correspondence. And he said something quite wise. He said, 'We mustn't write long letters, the way we had long conversations, because it would just interrupt our work. So, let's be very wise and disciplined, and write short letters.' "

Yet, the disciplined Harry could barely contain his excitement. In Florence, he bumped into another Yalie, Pierrepont Isham Prentice, who would one day become a publisher of *Time*.

"I was standing outside the Pitti Palace when all of a sudden I got socked in the back and there was Harry Luce," said Prentice. "He told me he had met the most wonderful girl in the world and he was going to marry her."

On his return to Oxford, Harry continued their correspondence, which became regular and heavy. "He wrote the most heavenly letters. I kept one big brown envelope and on the outside it said, 'Letters from HRL' (Harry Luce) 'to LRH' (Lila Ross Hotz). We loved that our initials were turned around."

During spring vacation, Lila stayed with her aunt in Paris. Harry had also come to Paris for a little sight-seeing, and he and Lila arranged a meeting. The once awkward young man in ill-kept suits had been influenced by Oxford. He now owned a Savile Row suit and sported a mustache and a cane.

Not long after the rendezvous in Paris, Harry invited Lila to be his guest at Oxford for three days at the Common Balls, "where everyone danced till dawn . . . great fun," she reported. Harry and Lila also attended an American-British polo match at Hurlingham and went on picnics and punting excursions.

Their relationship at this point was totally chaste. If Harry had any yearnings, he suppressed them. As Lila recalled, "I was brought up like all the girls of families who want their kids to behave well. There was no holding of hands, absolutely no kissing, until a *long time* after."

In London, Harry decided to explain to both Lila and her mother. "I have no money at all. I have a job that's been promised in Chicago by the McCormicks," he said. "So I'm going out there. I want to marry Lila; but I can't ask her to wait for me."

Harry then told Lila privately, "Now, I have no idea when I'll *ever* be able to support myself and you. Marriage is out of the question now, for me. And you are absolutely free to get interested in anybody else."

But Lila would not listen. "I am not going to be interested in anybody else. I will wait for you!" she told Harry. Furthermore, she considered herself engaged.

By the spring of 1921, Lila had completed her studies at her Rome finishing school and headed home to Chicago. In midsummer, the Oxford year over and his funds almost depleted, Harry decided it was time to enter the real world, which seemed to be in Chicago. Lila was there and so was International Harvester, where a job was supposedly waiting.

"My rather simple-minded notion at the time was that you didn't get anywhere in the newspaper business by starting as a cub reporter and climbing to be editor," Luce said. "So I thought, 'Well, I'll go out and make some money.' "

He promptly went to see Mrs. McCormick's son, the president of International Harvester who introduced Harry to the vice president, saying, "Well, you know, Momma has always hoped Henry would come into the company." And the vice president replied, "Well, of course, if Mrs. McCormick wants us to do it, we'll do it." He then turned to Harry, and said: "But now, Luce, do you want us to do it? If we take you on, you know, we'll have to fire someone else."

Poor Harry was taken aback. "What could I say?" he asked. "Of *course* I don't want you to fire anyone."

While he pondered what to do next, Harry lived part of the time in Mrs. McCormick's house on Rush Street. He also stayed on occasion with his former roommate, Culbreth Sudler. Four or five nights a week, Harry would go over to Lila's house for dinner. One day, they took the train to Lake Forest, just to have a picnic lunch on the beach.

"And there he said, 'Well, now, I really think it's time that you and I tried this,' " remembered Lila. "And he kissed me."

Lila's mother was fond of Luce, but her stepfather, a senior vice president of the biggest bank in the Middle West, thought little of the man or his prospects. One night over dinner, he sputtered: "That man Luce will never get anywhere in life because he doesn't hang up his pajamas!"

Lila never did learn how her stepfather knew that.

While he was courting Lila, Harry was conscientiously trying to find a job. He applied to the Chicago *Daily News.*

"When I asked for a job, Mr. [Henry Justin] Smith said no. Keeping in mind what I read in schoolboy stories, I decided that the thing to do was to go back again and again and say that I would sweep the floor," Luce remembered. "The third time I tried, Smith said, 'Well, it just happens that Ben Hecht says he's behind in his work and needs an assistant.' "

Ben Hecht never let facts interfere with his fiction. His daily column, "One Thousand and One Afternoons," featured stories about the city's odd characters. The staff called Hecht "a hack of a genius." In asking Smith for an assistant, he had asked him not to send him a reporter because "a reporter doesn't react to anything but the mangled body of a society leader." What he wanted, he said, was "a very naive fellow who will notice everything going on and bring me tidbits that I can work into columns." When Hecht saw what he described as this "eager-eyed young man about my own age, just out of college, I hired him on sight."

From the outset, Harry did not fit in. With his Yale and Oxford background and society fiancée, he never felt at home in the city room. His worst moment by far came one Saturday when he had a date to take Lila for a drive. "We met at the corner. I was dressed to kill in my one Savile Row suit, and I think I still had a mustache and I was carrying a cane," Harry recalled. "Suddenly, I realized that I had forgotten a book at the office. I had to pick it up, but did I dare to show myself there in that get-up? I asked Lila to wait. Since it was Saturday, I thought I could get in and out without anyone seeing me. In the old, ratty elevator in the *Daily News* building, there was room for only two or three people coming down. Our editor, old Henry Justin Smith, stepped in. For me it was an interminable ride. As he stepped out, H. J. Smith looked me over from top to bottom and said, with withering scorn, 'Ah, Luce, a journalist, I see . . .' I shall never forget it."

Lila called Harry's stint at the *Daily News* "an annoying, stupid little job, not really a writing job. Harry would go out and notice things that happened and Hecht would write up those things. Very boring. Harry was bored stiff."

His job at the *News* lasted five weeks. Hecht told Smith that Luce was "much *too* naive; nothing he writes makes any sense. Reams of copy come in about lemonade stands and traffic jams and people who lost suitcases in railroad stations. I haven't been able to get a paragraph out of it."

Soon afterward, in September 1921, Harry wrote home that his department had been instructed to eliminate five men and since he was the last one hired, he was the first one fired. Henry Justin Smith told an associate that he considered Luce an unsolvable puzzle and "could never figure out what he was doing." Smith's final advice to Harry, reportedly, was: "Get out of newspapers."

*   *   *

"If we're ever going to start that paper, this looks like our chance." This message came in a letter from Brit Hadden about their fantasy and their future. Their Yale friend Walter Millis was doing so well at the Baltimore *News* that his editor had asked him, "Do you know any more Yale boys who write as well as you?"

Luce couldn't resist rubbing it in and wrote to his former boss, Henry Justin Smith, saying that he had considered taking Smith's advice to "get out of newspapers" when he got this offer for $40 a week. He hoped Smith could restrain any Rabelaisian laughter. Harry then mentioned his "signs of pernicious insanity," as evidenced by his and Brit's plans to undertake a new publishing venture in a few months. As a postscript, Harry invited Smith to dine with him at the Manhattan Club anytime they both happened to be in New York.

Luce and Hadden were then not quite twenty-four years old. Just as Luce's professional reporting career on the Chicago *Daily News* had been unremarkable, Hadden's writing experience on the New York *World* was largely confined to animal stories.

Harry and Brit moved to Baltimore and snapped up an apartment on West Biddle Street for $37.50 per person a month. They found Baltimore a pleasant, old-fashioned city where people were even-tempered and tactful. Harry had been deeply reluctant to leave Lila and found that he missed her terribly.

"We were more emotional about each other after he left Chicago for Baltimore," Lila Hotz later reflected. "We wrote to each other probably twice or three times a week. Of course, we never knew what his future was going to be."

But they knew *their* future. Harry confided to Mrs. McCormick a secret he called "the most secret in human history"—that Lila had promised to marry him someday. They had not yet told his parents, or hers. After Oxford, he had decided they should be "just friends" until his financial future seemed clearer. But they had found this situation impossible, just as they found it impossible to be apart. She seemed to have even more faith in him than he had in himself. He knew all this was utterly impractical and illogical, but he also knew it was inevitable, and that there was now no limit to his happiness. He remembered in the old Elizabethan drama that love was called a disease. If so, it was incurable. For Luce, love also had a will of its own.

Yet, even Lila was pushed into the back of Luce's mind as he and Brit began work on their dream: starting a news magazine.

The *News* job was perfect for their project. Their newspaper work ended by mid-afternoon, which gave them the rest of the day and night to work on their magazine.

They kept busy cutting stories from *The New York Times,* classifying them by subject, and condensing seven days of news on any subject into a single, concise story. They made it feisty and provocative, then pasted the finished stories into a dummy layout. They had no qualms about rewriting printed news stories because a noted editor had told them that news was public property at least within twenty-four hours of its publication.

The concept of a news magazine was not new. *The Literary Digest* had made an enormous success of it for thirty-two years, and eventually boasted more than a million in circulation. *The Literary Digest* was also assembled with scissors; the editors were conscientious about crediting sources, carefully giving both sides of every subject without offering any editorial comment of its own. Luce and Hadden, on the other hand, not only wanted their stories bright and tight, but opinionated.

Within three months, they had assembled a sample issue and a prospectus, which said: "There will be no editorial page, but the editors recognize that complete neutrality on public questions and important news is probably as undesirable as it is impossible. . . ."

The two brash young men also persuaded their editor to give them seven weeks' leave of absence without pay, plus a promise to take them back.

Next stop for Harry and Brit was New York. They wanted to show their magazine dummy layout to some thirty or forty editors, publishers, and businessmen to get their advice and counsel. Then, if advisable, they would start raising money, and New York seemed the center for that. They were not certain yet where they wanted to publish, but were leaning toward Washington, D.C. If they could not finance it themselves, they were considering selling their idea to a large publishing house. So, they took off for New York with their dummy and their dream.

7

THE grande dame and an undisputed queen of New York society was Mrs. Oliver Hazard Perry Belmont. The granddaughter of a southern general, the former Alva Elizabeth Smith came from Mobile, Alabama, and had married William K. Vanderbilt, whose wealth could not compensate for his philandering. His wife shocked society by suing for a divorce on grounds of adultery.

"For a woman of my social standing to apply for a divorce from one of the richest men in the United States on such grounds, or for any cause, was an unheard of and glaring defiance of custom. . . . All around me, were women leading these half-lives, practically deserted by their husbands, who not only neglected them but insulted them by their open and flagrant and vulgar infidelities," she said at the time.

Once the divorce and all the unpleasantness were behind her, Alva selected another well-needed spouse, O. H. P. Belmont, who ordered his horses covered at night with pure linen sheets. Mrs. Belmont soon managed to outdo her eccentric husband: When she had her Chinese Ball at Newport, she converted her home into a "reasonable replica of the Imperial Palace at Peking, and added pelicans for extra authenticity." By marrying off her daughter Consuelo to the Duke of Marlborough, she achieved prominence abroad, too. And then, after Belmont died and left her his many millions, Mrs. Belmont became a woman of many causes. Her interests included music and French literature. She also spearheaded a campaign to eliminate the brownstones she felt disfigured New York's best residential section. At other moments, Mrs. Belmont was busy promoting a secret formula for Victory Laxative Tablets that she had received from a German doctor. She insisted that her staff take them once a day to maintain a bloom of health.

Mrs. Belmont also had a deep interest in women's suffrage. This was neither a whim nor a fad, and it later became one of the major concerns of her life.

* * *

By some twist of fortune, Mrs. Belmont was traveling on the same ship as Ann Clare and Clare Boothe. It was, perhaps, more Ann Clare's manipulation than fate that found Clare and Mrs. Belmont in adjoining deck chairs.

The two women quickly charmed each other. Clare was nineteen, vividly pretty and bright, and filled with news of her adventures abroad. The seventy-year-old Mrs. Belmont was captivated. She saw in Clare much of her younger self—the wit, the enthusiasm, the drive. "You stick with me," she told her.

Mrs. Belmont enthusiastically promoted her feminist political cause to Clare. She visualized Clare as a brilliant ornament of her new Women's National Party.

In her memoirs, Elsa Maxwell confided that she had seldom seen Mrs. Belmont "so animated" when she later told her, "I met a girl on the boat who has all the earmarks of talent and success. . . . She's poor, but she has the beauty and brains to go as far as ambition will take her. Remember her name: Clare Boothe. If she gets half the advantages she deserves, you'll be proud to know her twenty-five years from now. I'm going to give her a push in the right direction. . . . The world is going to notice that girl."

Maxwell promptly offered to invite her to a party. "Whatever happens then, she'll get a rich husband."

Another passenger who also saw a future for Clare was Max Reinhardt. En route from Berlin, the famous impresario was heading for New York to produce a morality play entitled *The Miracle.* Part of his mission was to search for a blond virgin for the leading role of the nun. As soon as he met Clare, he felt that his search was over. "You *must* be in the theater," he told her. When she protested her lack of experience, he insisted that was no problem. In this play, the nun had no lines—all she had to do was look beautiful.

For Clare, such attention was heady stuff. This was what happened in so many of the books she had read, but not in real life. Still, her heart and thoughts were back in London with Major Julian Simpson, the handsome young Englishman with whom she was so in love. The young man would surely soon come to America, sweep her off her feet and marry her.

Photographers were waiting for Clare at the New York dock. News of her first prize in a beauty contest had already reached them, and now they wanted the usual cheesecake picture.

From the moment she docked, Clare impatiently awaited the arrival of her lover. He had written letters from the Guards' Club in London, telling her about a trip to Poland and about another projected trip to France, explaining that he was soon headed for France—all part of his work for the special branch of the foreign office. This made him seem worldly and important. Soon a letter arrived at the Austins, properly asking their permission for him to come and court. Clare was ecstatic. Her brother, David, was skeptical enough to hire Joseph Madigan, a former detective inspector, New Scotland Yard, to investigate Mr. Simpson.

When Julian finally came, a bewildered Clare found a different young man, his ardor cooled, his manner almost distant. Soon after his arrival, he announced suddenly that something unexpected required him to leave. Clare quickly discovered what the "unexpected" was. Their mutual friend, Vernon Blunt, admitted that Julian's sole objective in America was to find an heiress. Blunt had told Julian, "as a joke," that the Austins were very wealthy. When Julian saw the modest Austin home in Connecticut, the romance was over.

About that time, David received his report that Julian Hamilton Cassian Simpson had no known record of foreign service.

Clare refused to give up. She wrote Julian how much she loved him, that love would find a way. They were letters reflecting a young woman's dream and a young woman's heartbreak. She was not brittle then. She was soft and yielding and wanting. She was offering him more of herself than she would ever offer to any man. He was her first real love. He was her fantasy come true. She did not want to lose him. If she did, she would never be the same—and she never was.

Simpson's reply was unsentimental. He was unemployed, deeply in debt, and could not afford love without money.

The lesson was sharp and deep. It would be a long time before Clare again let her heart rule her mind.

She then went to work for Mrs. Belmont in the women's movement. She put on airplane goggles, got into an open-cockpit World War Jenny, and scattered handbills announcing the 75th anniversary of the Women's Rights Conference. She also helped stage a pageant for the convention, and an article headlined that she and Mrs. Belmont would "STUMP THE COUNTRY" on behalf of the National Women's Party.

Clare also found time for two other shipboard friends, Mr. and Mrs. James Stewart Cushman, who were very social, rich, philanthropic, and religious. The Cushmans had no children and perhaps this made Clare particularly appealing to them—especially since she recited poetry. When Clare came to visit them in New York one Sunday, they took her to hear the celebrated Dr. Harry Emerson Fosdick at the morning service at the Fifth Avenue Presbyterian Church.

Sitting in the same pew was "a rather distinguished older man," as Clare remembered him. Whenever she sneaked a sidelong glance, she noticed how he keenly observed her. The Cushmans later introduced them. He was George Tuttle Brokaw, forty-three, a multi-millionaire and one of the most eligible bachelors in New York, described as the "object of assault by more than one generation of debutantes."

George Brokaw had graduated from Princeton in 1902, traveled extensively, worked in the family's clothing business, became a lawyer, and formed his own firm in the Guaranty Trust Building. George was a member of the Huguenot Society, St. Nicholas Society, Society of Colonial Wars, Sons of the Revolution, New York Historical Society, and the New York Genealogical and Biographical Society. He was also President of the Industrial Christian Alliance and a member of the following clubs: University, Union League, Racquet and Tennis, Princeton, Piping Rock, Garden City Gold, Riding, Rumson County, Uptown, Ardsley, Ivy, and the Oakland Golf Club. He was head of the Young Men's Temperance League at his church, despite the fact that he had a serious drinking problem. George was also a playboy and was well known about New York for his love of parties, women, and scotch.

The Cushmans, playing matchmaker, invited Clare and George to lunch at their Fifth Avenue home. Clare thought he was nice enough, good-looking, with a courtly charm. It is doubtful that Clare then had any thoughts of marriage with this man twenty-four years her senior. But George was smitten enough to phone Clare's mother the next day to ask if he could call on them. Mrs. Austin, who read all the society and gossip columns, knew all about the wealthy George Brokaw and was absolutely delighted. Her husband was not. He knew George's reputation and didn't want his stepdaughter added to a long list of George's cast-off women.

George drove up to the Austin cottage in Greenwich in his impressive yellow Locomobile and took the whole family to dinner at the Greenwich Pickwick Arms Hotel; he played the perfect, considerate gentleman, and even Dr. Austin was impressed. The man was plainly in love. As the courtship continued, Clare's mother pressed her daughter to give George serious consideration.

She pointed out that this was a once-in-a-lifetime chance to marry wealth. "She went to the drawer where she kept her 'pretty things,' and pulled out a little package wrapped in tissue," said Clare. "I opened it and found a silk chemise embroidered with my name and one little cupid. Mother said, 'That's for your trousseau, dearie.' Then she put her hands on my shoulders [and said] 'I hope when you are married you will be as happy as I've been.'"

Clare dreaded the necessary visit to George's mother. The Brokaw family mansion at One East 79th Street was gloomy, and the Brokaw matriarch a slightly forbidding woman in her eighties. Rumor had it that she was loath for her George or "Dawdie" (a baby pronunciation of his name) to get married. The old mansion, fronting Central Park on the north corner of Fifth Avenue, was built by their ancestor Isaac Vail Brokaw in 1877 and had jagged gables, protruding turrets, and an impressive marble staircase. A plaque that once hung on the house recorded that it was conscientiously modeled after "the French chateau of Chenonceaux on the River Cher in France."

The furniture was upholstered in red velvet and trimmed with gilt and the woodwork ornately carved. Most of the furniture was covered, the drapes were removed, and the shades down. Mrs. Brokaw was preparing to go to her summer home in New Jersey.

Clare later remembered that it was "like going to a house where nobody lived." The walls were so thick that they made any sound seem unreal. Mrs. Brokaw had greeted Clare graciously. The tea was uneventful until Mrs. Brokaw suddenly asked Clare to stand near the window where the light was better. Clare later recalled standing there an interminable time, feeling like a pinned butterfly under a microscope while the old woman stared at her intently, then loudly announced, "She's a good girl and a healthy girl. Dawdie, you marry her."

George hugged his mother, kissed Clare for the first time, and rushed her to Cartier in their chauffeured car to pick out a seventeen-carat blue-white diamond solitaire engagement ring. Clare later insisted that the marriage had been maneuvered by her mother behind her back, like a baseball trade. The scene that stuck in her mind was her mother, stepfather, and George discussing her future and the wedding, while she felt like a fly on the wall, invisible and ignored. George wanted to marry quickly, mainly because his mother was ill, and he wanted to give her grandchildren quickly. Brokaw also knew his brothers and sister opposed his marriage. If anything happened to him while he was a bachelor they would inherit his share of the family millions. "I was about as popular as the smallpox," Clare said afterward.

For once in her life, Clare was curiously complacent. She could have said no at any time, but her mother said, "Get married." "So I did what my mother said," explained Clare, who soon busied herself spending the greater part of her time in town, keeping appointments with dressmakers and milliners.

In the engagement announcement, a newspaper headline read, "BEAUTY PREFERS REAL AMERICAN TO TITLE" and the subhead added "Pretty Clare Boothe, back from Europe, declares stalwart 'Yank' her ideal."

The stalwart Yank, according to Clare's confidante Buffy Cobb, "was a very old forty-three. He seemed terribly ancient, stuffy and pompous . . . a mass of complexes." Another family friend described Brokaw as "inherently sweet, thoughtful, kind . . . and dull."

The engagement announcement came as a shock to George Brokaw's friends, who had regarded him as the perennial Fifth Avenue bachelor.

Through all the excitement and drama of the engagement, there had been no real courtship, no love, at least on Clare's part. She had her share of qualms, all of which she confided to her friend Buffy. The night before the wedding, her mother tried to console her weeping daughter. Ann Clare brought in all the jewelry George had given, and said, "You can't throw all this away." That night, Clare's brother David climbed up the drainpipe to her window. "You don't have to marry him. I've saved up some money," David told her. "We'll run away together."

Clare never, never ever forgot that. It seemed to explain why the bond between them always remained tight no matter what trials and trouble he would bring to her in later life.

The wedding took place at Christ Episcopal Church in Greenwich, Connecticut, on August 10, 1923. Though the nation was mourning the death of President Warren G. Harding, the wedding was still hailed as "the most important social event of the season." Yet, there was an omen of problems ahead when George's brother Howard, who had been originally scheduled to be his best man, used the presidential mourning period as his excuse for not coming. Clare's brother replaced him. The mourning also excused the absence of George's other brother and sister and their families. The Brokaw siblings, from the first, regarded Clare as a fortune-hunter. (The greater truth was that her mother was the hunter; Clare was simply the bait.)

Even in her fantasy, Clare had never imagined such a wedding. There were more than a thousand guests. "Not only were the motorcars lined up for several blocks but there were photographers and motion picture men grouped near the entrance to the church. Isn't it funny?" Clare wrote afterward. "There must have been a thousand people at the reception and I can't remember anyone who came. I can only remember the ones who *didn't* come."

As a society columnist duly noted, "The bride wore a very old and rare rose-point lace. An old fan of exquisite rose-point was worked into a cascading fichu at the waist. She carried a shower bouquet of white bridal roses and lily of the valley. . . . The bridesmaids were attired in gowns of pastel shades. They wore picture hats of chiffon and tulle. All the frocks were noticeably simple and girlish. The wedding gown worn by the bride, with its long train and cloudy tulle veil being particularly graceful in its simplicity."

Clare was twenty years old. The thoughts she had that day were surely mixed: The money must have seemed like a fairy tale, but the prince was old enough to be her father. Reflecting on this later, she said that she married the first man who was kind to her.

The Austins gave a wedding reception for 150 friends at the Pickwick Arms Hotel ballroom in Greenwich. Because of the mourning for the president, there was no dancing. There was also a smaller party at the Austin family home at Sound Beach. That night, the newlyweds stayed at The Plaza in New York and sailed the next morning aboard the *Majestic* for a four-month honeymoon in Europe.

Clare's wedding night is probably best described in a story she wrote some years later. She named the husband Peter Towerly and wrote of "the bride guiding her drunken husband into their room and laying a white satin negligee across the foot of the bed." In Clare's story, the bride began with slow shaking fingers to unpack Peter's effects. "She came to a beautiful pair of pink and white peppermint-stick silk pajamas, and she laid these on the chair which partly hid his red, swollen face from her view. He was still unconscious, with his mouth drooping open. She looked at him for a moment, closed her eyes to wink back a sudden rush of tears, laughed uncertainly, and then walked to the desk to light a comforting cigarette. . . ."

Materially, at least, the honeymoon was everything she might have wanted. George was a lavish spender, buying her clothes, and jewels, anything that caught her fancy—and many things did. He was also surprisingly tender, and much more knowledgeable than she had supposed, particularly about art. George filled in many of her gaps. Writing of the honeymoon later, Clare noted that it was not a great success. "A honeymoon never is. It is a period of readjustment."

On the trip home, their ship hit a storm near Nantucket. Fourteen passengers were injured, including Clare, who suffered cracked ribs. The storm was simply a small sign of things to come.

Though her mother had assured her that love would come, it never really did, not with George. Clare herself wrote later: "That the very nature of love was that it could only be felt between equals . . ." Whether George considered her inferior because she was so much younger, so much less sophisticated, she did not then know. But she felt it, and sensed it.

Soon enough Clare learned that George was one of the better known drunks in New York. Worse, because he didn't need to work, he stayed home most of the time, except when he was busy touring the country's top golf courses, winning more golf trophies in which he hid his gin. Clare often said afterward, "He was always drunk, drunk, drunk."

Nevertheless, Clare tried to turn her back at first. Of course she had married this man for his money, but she was determined to make him a proper wife. She had an intuitive sense of what made society move, a great grasp of the pattern of the social and class structure, and she was determined to shine in it and make him proud of her. His family, however, wanted no part of her and actually tried to boycott Clare socially.

Still, Clare was cheerful. At this point in her life, she was still rooted in traditional middle-class values, as the following verse she wrote for her brother reveals:

> *A wife should be pretty*
> *But never perverse*
> *A wife should be easy*
> *On heart, mind and purse . . .*

Clare found it harder and harder to live up to her verse, particularly in this "very quarrelsome family." "From the moment I stepped into the house until the moment I stepped out, the family never stopped quarreling," she recalled. "A good deal of every day's conversation was taken up with fighting about one thing or another. . . ." She once overheard George quarreling with his brothers and one of them saying, "If you do this . . . I will never allow you and Clare to enter Palm Beach or Newport."

When Clare started giving some small dinner parties of her own, she carefully combed George's guest list and eliminated anyone too friendly to his brothers or sister. Their only friend in the Brokaw family was George's mother; the newlyweds stayed with her and her seventeen servants for almost a year. The situation became intolerable, however, when Clare discovered that her mother-in-law always carried the keys to all the doors in the house (even closets) in her petticoat pocket.

Ready for her own home, Clare picked a palatial colonial house, set on six acres fronting Long Island Sound in socially correct Sands Point. The prince of Wales had once slept at the Brokaw's new house, and so had the English polo team. When George bought the estate, he also bought the yacht *Black Watch* on which the prince had sailed. Clare liked that, plus the fact that her good friend Mrs. Belmont was now a neighbor. For the moment, all was relatively serene. George behaved himself and bought Clare plenty of beautiful frocks, splendid jewels, and a luxurious motor car.

That December, Clare gave George the news he most wanted—she was pregnant. The idea of a possible son and heir made George ecstatic. He even hired the Russian artist Savely Sorine to paint Clare's portrait, which the New York *World* reprinted in rotogravure.

Several months later, in February 1924, Captain Julian Simpson returned to the United States. This time he was in pursuit of an heiress in Chicago and found himself short of funds. He felt little hesitation in seeking help wherever he could find it, for there is a record in Clare's personal papers of $500 in money transfers sent to Simpson from her brother, David. No matter what

Julian had done and how he had hurt her, he had still been her first love. In fact, Julian also wrote to Clare asking her to correspond with him again and wondering when she might be coming over to England, so that they might meet. There is no record that they did. Or that they didn't. Someone who saw Simpson years later said he still carried a picture of Clare in his wallet.

Clare celebrated her pregnancy with a baby party and invited all the guests to come dressed as kiddies. Upon arrival, they received a teddy bear, a doll, and a horn. Those who didn't come in costume were given hair ribbons and bibs. George obligingly wore a white blouse and bloomers. Clare was dressed as a French doll. Golden curls hung down her back and she wore a big pink bow.

Despite all this gaiety, Clare was often alone. George was frequenting golf tournaments, or getting drunk. "George wrote me to come and spend the summer with them because Clare was lonely," said Clare's friend from Castle School, Dorothy Burns Hallorand. Clare would later ask: "If there is any process more active, more positive, more strenuous, more exhausting, more 'creative' than that of bearing a child in the womb, do tell me what it is."

The baby was a girl, born August 25, 1924, at the Greenwich Hospital. She was christened Ann Clare Brokaw, just like her mother. Clare named Mrs. James Stewart Cushman as one of the godmothers. As a peace offering, she asked George's brother Irving to be the godfather. Only his mother's urging made Irving accept. The whole family convened for the christening. The only other time the whole family again convened would be at the funeral of the elder Mrs. Brokaw ten months later.

As much as she had wanted a child, Clare quickly learned that she was not a natural or giving mother. In one of the short stories she would write years later, one of the characters asked another: "Do you like children?"

"Other people's," was the telling reply.

Like most women of her social class, Clare delegated most of Ann's care to nannies. "Rich women are not too put upon by their children," she later said. "You don't have to do all those things for a child that those women who had to stay at home did. My Ann had a French governess who took care of her until she was twelve years old and went off to boarding school."

Her pushy mother basked in Clare's social sunshine. She went to most of Clare's parties and Clare came to hers, including an Austin luncheon at the Japanese Garden at the Ritz Carlton. Clare not only improved her mother's social standing, but she also tried to help her brother, David. "David Boothe was a complete no-good, coarse and vulgar," said Buffy Cobb. "David pulled something crooked and Clare sold her jewels to bail him out. Then David went back into the Marines."

Clare's image changed dramatically when her mother-in-law died in June 1925. The Manhattan mansion passed on to George to live in for his lifetime, but was held in trust for all the children. "It was a frightfully difficult house," Clare said of her new home. "It took at least fourteen servants to run it, and they all lived in tiny, tiny rooms at the top of the house with one bathroom between them. Most of the ceiling was covered with gold leaf which crumbled away all day. There was a huge stairway with the most horrible yellow marble I had ever seen. It was not well proportioned, definitely not a thing of beauty. For example, it was full of cupolas. Now, what are you going to put in cupolas? I finally filled them with aspidistras."

She also complained about the imitation tapestries, the clutter of soiled Japanese screens, the bad plumbing, and the "execrable carvings . . . nothing there at all that had the smallest sense of taste or charm. After a year, I tried to re-decorate the thing, but it was impossible. Really, the ugliness of the house was just appalling."

Clare went to work. Why not tear the house down, she proposed, and build an apartment house with a penthouse? They could live on the top two floors. After getting over his initial shock, George explained that his two brothers were co-owners in trust, and he would need their permission. The brothers, who lived in houses nearby, hated the idea. Such a thirteen-story building would cut the light from their windows and lower the value of their own homes. When Clare persisted, George brought the case to court. The brothers won their case, and George and Clare had to content themselves with a complete renovation of the interior. In the interim, they lived at the elegant Sherry Netherlands Hotel.

The Brokaw family usually spent summers on the shore in Brookville, Long Island, but that summer of 1925, Clare easily persuaded her husband to head for Newport, Rhode Island, where she hoped to truly enter society. Clare and George rented the so-called "cottage" occupied the previous season by Mrs. William K. Vanderbilt II and her daughters. Barely old enough to vote, Clare faced Newport society wives many years her senior. Some of them were envious of her and many were openly resentful. Clare was much too pretty and much too young. How dare she? Newport thought even less of Clare than Clare thought of Newport. It was a case of hatred at first sight.

But something inside Clare told her not to give up. She sat there bravely at tea parties and other gatherings, being snubbed by the world's finest. Clare persisted, perfecting her poise. She invited the celebrated violinist Albert K. Spaulding to her home for the weekend and more than 150 guests came to listen. Clare also played Beauty in *An Enchanted Forest,* a benefit pantomime for the Newport County League for Animals. She was assured of the part because George Brokaw was the president and financial backer of the dramatic group.

Gradually, Clare won over the brittle cadre of Newport society matrons. She became the first Mrs. Brokaw to do so. "It is dollars to doughnuts that certain other Mrs. Brokaws are *vert* with envy, and are indulging in the well-known gnashing-of-teeth pastime," wrote a local columnist. "That loveliest of matrons, Mrs. George Tuttle Brokaw, can now sit back and fold her hands, happy in the knowledge that her first season at Newport was a howling success."

Yet, Clare was still naive and idealistic. Despite her minimal schooling, she had always filled her brain with batteries of ideas and found that she had little use for the intellect in Newport. She had simply assumed that these very rich people, all properly educated at the best Ivy League schools, would easily discuss the issues of their time. She found them much more concerned with handsome motor cars, splendid yachts, and beautiful clothes. In the long run, she determined that the reality of society was "more apt to be rather dull, dispirited, unenlightened, indifferent, and usually a little discontented."

One society woman who did seem to have an interest in the world outside was Clare's neighbor and friend, Mrs. Belmont. Clare joined her in Washington, D.C., at the crypt of Susan B. Anthony to pay homage to the Women's Rights pioneer. Feminists from forty-eight states placed wreaths and listened to the women's Magna Carta read by poet Edna St. Vincent Millay. Clare loved being part of the excitement. Mrs. Belmont was also directing her energies toward abolition of child labor and improvement of overall working conditions for women.

Clare enjoyed being center stage virtually anywhere. She happily played leading lady in several amateur theater productions and also kept busy arranging a series of benefit mah-jongg and bridge tournaments at New York's Biltmore Hotel.

She and George vacationed on the Riviera and even consulted real estate agents about leasing a villa at Cannes. They spent a month at Hot Springs in Virginia and photographer Alfred Cheney Johnston named Mrs. Brokaw as "the most beautiful society woman in New York." Told of this, Clare said she was surprised and somewhat flattered. "It seems to me that beauty is something quite apart from externals. To be beautiful, a woman must first of all be gracious; the quality must come from within. That is how it seems to me. All the beautiful women I know are gracious. But if you ask me about creams and beauty parlors, I couldn't say anything. I have never thought much about that sort of thing." She told an interviewer, "There's no harm in looking pretty. My own theory of dress: Buy as few things as possible but as good as you can afford. Look pretty, bright and clean in becoming things. And then forget it all."

Nevertheless, she marched into Saks Fifth Avenue one day and bought a silver-fox scarf, a broadtail coat, two silver-fox skins, an ermine coat, a natural eastern mink coat, and several other items. Clare was, after all, only twenty-three, a moneyed princess. Everything was available to her.

Somehow, Clare managed to keep her perspective. She had intuitive good sense. Society was simply a game, and she learned how to play it. She had earlier training from her mother, who knew how to take advantage of any situation. But if Clare absorbed society, society never absorbed her. She made long mental lists of everything silly, phony, and preposterous. One day soon she would put it into a book.

Meanwhile she was generous with her family. Not only did she continue to promote her mother's entry into society, she persuaded her husband to find David a job as a stockbroker after he got out of the Marines. David had an easy way about him. With his good looks and charm, he did well.

Clare also helped her father, who had read of his socialite daughter and knew where to reach her and asked her for money. Billy Boothe needed it. He was then sixty-eight and seriously ill and had lost his music school. Clare sent money to him regularly without telling her mother. There is some record that he had come east once to see Ann when she was a baby. There is also a letter in Clare's papers from cousin Edward Boothe, discussing her father's illness: "During the last phase, he lived on the fringe of lunacy."

Clare's mother moved in with her. They badly needed each other. Ann Clare had separated from her husband because the doctor had taken up with a nurse. And Clare needed to talk about her disintegrating relationship with George.

Shortly before the elder Mrs. Brokaw's death, the matriarch had had a long talk with Clare about George's drinking. She had pleaded with Clare not to leave George "until I've gone," adding, "I can't live that long."

After his mother's death, he stopped trying to keep his drinking secret. The gin came out of the golf trophies onto the table and George was a mean drunk. Sober, he was generally kind and thoughtful, pleasant and charming. He even faithfully attended church on Sundays. Drunk, he was jealous, even vicious. He beat Clare—sometimes badly. During this period Clare had at least three miscarriages. She told a friend that "she once tried halfheartedly to abort herself with hot baths, etc., because she thought a baby would upset Brokaw just then." After her last miscarriage, doctors told Clare she could no longer have children.

"I know all about violence and physical abuse," Clare later confided to the author Dominick Dunne. "Once I can remember coming home from a party and walking up our vast marble staircase at the Fifth Avenue house while he was striking me. I thought, if I gave him one shove down the staircase I would be rid of him forever."

In his drunken delirium, George even talked about once wanting to be a Presbyterian missionary. When he was only partly drunk in the morning, he might serenade the sleeping Clare by playing glee club songs on his banjo.

When he was sober, George was guilt-ridden, disconsolate, despondent, making the usual alcoholic promises never to do it again; he even gave Clare the keys to the liquor cabinet. She, in turn, threatened to fire any servant who provided George with liquor.

For Clare, the situation grew intolerable. All the money, all the mansions, all the jewels, all the clothes were not worth the terror of a beating by a vicious drunk—a drunk who even raped her on the night she returned from the hospital after a miscarriage. When George drank too much, he was simply out of control. Clare confided this to several of her friends.

Clare's mother, always the pragmatic, urged Clare to play for time: George could not live too long this way. When he died, Clare would still be a very young, very, very rich widow with her whole life ahead of her. Wait, counseled the mother, wait! Besides, she noted, there was no evidence of any adultery, and therefore no grounds for divorce in New York. And George, when sober, was a kind, generous man. And, then, added Mrs. Boothe, there was their daughter to consider.

Clare considered. She could not and would not wait until her husband drank himself to death. Nor did she want her daughter to grow up in that atmosphere. She refused to allow her life to grow bitter and fearful. She would no longer be what she later contemptuously called "a sperm-pot." She would leave him. "I was a rich man's darling for six incredibly boring years. I couldn't take it, so I walked out."

Her mother returned to Greenwich, and Clare moved into the Stanhope Hotel. She hired a top lawyer, Arthur Garfield Hays, and then left for Reno, Nevada, taking her four-year-old daughter with her. Clare described the scene at the station: Her pale, crestfallen husband was "armed with a bunch of orchids." As the train began to pull out of the station, he leaped upon the platform, and, seizing her in his arms, kissed her hungrily. She felt tears upon her cheek, but as his figure receded in the gloom of the station, and the train gathered momentum, she realized they were her own.

Clare had chosen Reno because she did not want to recount the story of the drunken beatings. In Reno, she would not have to; "mental cruelty" was sufficient grounds for divorce for some 2,000 women there every year.

She described Reno in 1929 in a story she wrote for *Vanity Fair* under the pseudonym Julian Jerome. It is revealing that Clare chose as her first pseudonym the name of her first love. Reno was "a typical western desert town," she wrote, "small but prosperous, gray and dun-colored main street, with a single stop-and-go sign, a courthouse, a three-story brick hotel, innumerable cheap cars, moving picture palaces, filling stations, corner drug stores, hair-dressing parlors, a five and ten . . . hybrid churches, a dry goods emporium, Chinese and Italian restaurants, quick lunches, a post office, railway station and speakeasies." The town of 18,000, noted author Jerome, was called "The Divorce Capital of the World," "The City of Broken Vows," "The Mecca of Lost Ladies," and "Purgatory."

Clare and Ann stayed at the Riverside Hotel, "along with smart Eastern women in well-cut Long Island riding togs or rich furs, tripping along in high French heels," she noted. Clare called the hotel "the psychological heart of Reno . . . a prosaic, dull-looking temple of disbelief." It was midway on the north bank of the Truckee River, into which the divorcées traditionally tossed their wedding rings as soon as they received their official decrees tied in a pink or blue ribbon.

For the women awaiting their decrees, Reno was a frustrating, deadly place. To get the necessary residence requirement for divorce, it was necessary to stay six weeks. What made it worse was that there were two women for every man in town. Any man became an object of prey. Some women even drove to the airport to meet the mail plane and invite the pilot back to town for a drink.

When it came time for Clare to meet with the judge, she asked why people get divorces; he named the seven statutory reasons but noted that the prime one was incompatibility, "which always means they are tired of sleeping together," he said. Clare asked the judge if he believed in divorce and he answered, "I believe in anything that takes courage. And it takes courage to come to this dull place. . . . [Women] are in search of some mythical freedom, some spiritual salvation and all they get is the relief of the courts. Often they come back."

For Clare, the stay in Reno gave her time alone with Ann. To her surprise, she found she enjoyed this time of togetherness. They rode horseback together and visited old gold mines, ghost towns, and lovely blue lakes. They drove fifty miles over the mountains to Virginia City, the site of the famous Comstock Lode where some $900 million in gold had been found. "I spent an hour looking over the register in the only place in Virginia City—the Crystal Bar. A great shiny bar, backed by a long, fly-specked mirror," Clare later wrote, again under her pseudonym Julian Jerome. She noted the historical names she saw: Mark Twain, Thomas Alva Edison, Henry Ford, Charles Lindbergh. "It must have been crowded, reckless, and gay in the old gold rush, faro bank, gun-toting days. Now they sell milk chocolate and postal cards."

When it came time for the final divorce arrangements, Clare tried to be fair. Though she could easily have bled George for a considerable slice of his fortune, she didn't. "I may have married for money," Clare said, "but I certainly didn't divorce for it."

The elder Brokaw had left an estimated $12 million to his children. Clare quickly settled for a lifetime yearly income of $26,000 plus a trust fund of $425,000 to revert to Ann after her death. Her lawyer later said, "I got most of what Clare wanted out of George." George agreed to pay for Ann's education, which was to begin at Miss Beard's School in Orange, New Jersey. Ann would spend the first half of each vacation with her father, the second half with her mother. Otherwise, Clare would have custody from January 1 to June 30, and George would have Ann for the rest of the year.

In one of her autobiographical stories, Clare wrote of being "assailed by a doubt or two about the well-being of her child under this arrangement." Yet, she agreed to it and set forth as a well-situated divorcée.

That same year twenty-six-year-old Clare not only lost a husband, she lost a father. Billy Boothe died at the age of seventy. Clare was not named in his obituary, and she was not present at his funeral.

8

HARRY Luce called 1922 "the hardest year of my life." It was also his best.

Young men of Henry Luce's class at Yale were calling themselves members of F. Scott Fitzgerald's "Lost Generation." Confused and emotionally adrift, many identified with T. S. Eliot's "The Wasteland." But Luce and Hadden were different. They knew exactly what they wanted and where they were going. Their news magazine was no longer an adolescent dream, but a real business venture.

Harry's father, who was in New York fund-raising, helped them find their new office space. "It was a hell-hole, just a junk place in a funny area," said Harry's sister Beth, who occasionally volunteered to help. "I remember working in the basement, with windows on the sidewalk. There was just Harry and Brit and me and some shadowy characters like an office boy doing I-don't-know-what. And there was no joking around. You were there and you worked. You just sat down at your desk and pounded out whatever it was. I remember there was this big brass container, perhaps eighteen inches in diameter. In China we called it 'a gong.' Harry and Brit smoked end on end and never put down their cigarettes. They used this brass bowl just for butts. When they moved offices, Father later rescued that bowl and gave it back to Harry."

The dilapidated brownstone office on 9 East 17th Street rented for $55 a month and wasn't worth more. They furnished it with a filing cabinet and four secondhand desks stacked against the wall. Nobody thought of washing the windows. Two young ladies sat in the back room clipping newspaper articles for possible rewrite. They were New York debutantes hired "in a spirit of good-humored sorority fun." They would later be replaced by researchers who would check the correctness of every statement that appeared in the magazine. This sexual division of labor later became so crystallized that a male researcher "would feel like a choir boy in the chorus of Minsky's burlesque," Luce would later say. "We invented most of the women who are here, because we invented a thing called the researcher."

He also admitted that he had created a "sex war" between male writers and editors and female researchers. For now, however, the system worked. Around the office, the atmosphere was that of a college newspaper. Harry and Brit managed to feed off each other's strengths and weaknesses. "I think Harry cared more about the substance of stories than Hadden," said Beth. "Hadden was more the decorator; he liked the language.

"Harry and Brit were such a strange combination, but they knew how each other worked and they respected each other," she continued. "Brit was very strange. He came from a good family in Brooklyn but he affected this Brooklynese accent and was very proud of it because he was very good at it. He liked shocking people with it—especially young ladies. Those were the speakeasy days of Prohibition. Brit knew every speakeasy west of Third Avenue and I later went to quite a few of them with him. You had to ring a bell and they'd look through a peephole at you. Of course, they all recognized Brit and we never had any trouble getting in. Then we'd go upstairs to some horrible dingy quarters and Brit would talk his tough Brooklynese to the bartender, usually about baseball. Harry wouldn't waste his time doing anything like that. He just felt he didn't have time for sitting around, chewing the rag. A lot of people thought that was a weakness in him."

Harry worried about everything and a major concern was raising money. "Part of the advantage of going to Yale was to get to know rich people. We thought the fund-raising would be just easy arithmetic—but it turned out differently," he told the Yale *Daily News.* "Our classmates weren't rich, their fathers were, and they wouldn't put up money for such crazy schemes."

Moreover, Harry was a poor fund-raiser "because he was shy, soft-spoken, and sincere," a journalist would write of him in the *Saturday Review.* Hadden failed for the opposite reason: His badgering and blustering scared prospective investors away in droves.

Potential investors thought Luce and Hadden were mad trying to compete with *The Literary Digest.* Charles Seymour, later president of Yale, told noted archivist Dr. Howard Gotlieb, "If I had listened to that boy and invested some money, I would be rich, rich, rich!"

Somehow, Harry and Brit managed to get to see the famed magazine editor and critic H. L. Mencken, who listened to them quietly, then said: "It will never work. Nobody will read it." The pair even offered newspaper mogul William Randolph Hearst a percentage of their profits if he financed them. He looked over their dummy and said in effect, "I don't feel I can participate in this in good conscience because I've never been interested in a rewrite."

Their former professor, William Lyon Phelps, told them they had a wonderful idea "but that it would be impossible to make it financially successful." The
consensus of most people they talked to in eight months was a firm "Don't do
it!"

Harry was then living with his mother and sister Beth on the fourth floor
of an old building near Columbia University. "Harry would usually come
home very late dead tired, but Mother always had a nice warm dinner waiting
for him," said Beth. "Then he'd go to his room and play some music on his
funny old-fashioned Victrola."

In writing to his traveling father, Harry expressed his wish that he had not
spent his money on Oxford and travel so that he could have had it for the
magazine. His father, who had been battered so often in his own fund-raising
attempts, tried to raise his son's spirits. To a waiting and worried Lila Hotz,
a discouraged Harry questioned if they could really raise enough money to
float their project or whether the thing was "too big for us."

One of the magazine dummies featured Bernard Baruch on the cover; it was
filled with "Imaginary Interviews," called itself "The Weekly News-Paper,"
and listed Hadden as president and Luce as secretary-treasurer. Harry's
younger brother Sheldon, then fourteen, recalled that sometimes they would
continue working on a dummy at home and that he was their office boy,
running out to get cigarettes. He would later proudly remember, "I sharpened
all those pencils."

Luce showed one of their dummies to Henry Seidel Canby, their former
creative writing teacher at Yale, who was most encouraging. He suggested they
search out a provocative style, condensed, but not telegraphic, with a point of
view so that people don't have to think too hard as they read.

The style Luce and Hadden eventually developed discarded the news lead.
Each article began like a short story, setting the stage. Since the news was four
to ten days old, the editors tried to enliven it. They used the most vivid
adjectives and verbs possible and relied on bold, teasing headlines. They aimed
for a facetious tone mixed with an underlying seriousness: thought and meaning with a light touch. They also felt that since the average American had no
time to form his own opinions, the magazine must do it for him.

Over the next year, consorting with golfing friends and their fathers, they
raised some $86,000 from seventy-two investors. (Adlai Stevenson, later to
become a presidential candidate, told how they had approached him to invest
and how he had refused, putting his money instead in an Illinois dairy "that
went bust.") Their biggest contributor was a Yalie's mother, Mrs. William L.
Harkness of Cleveland, whose hearing was so poor that she could not under-

stand the fervent pitch delivered by Luce and Hadden. Still she said, "That will do, boys. You may put me down for $20,000."

"I didn't hear a word," she later admitted, "but I sat there looking at these two sweet youngsters and couldn't resist their expression of enthusiasm and utter dedication to what they were doing." When she later lost her money in the Wall Street crash, her investment in *Time* helped support her old age.

Luce and Hadden now had enough to set up shop near their printer in the Printing Crafts Building on Eighth Avenue. "People were so squeezed that if Luce wanted to get to his desk, his secretary had to stand up to let him go by," said Joseph Kastner, then an office boy, who would later write for *Life*.

The search was on for a name. They had considered "Facts," but discarded it. "Time" finally came to Luce while coming home from work.

"Going home one night on the subway, my half-glazed stare fell on an advertisement with the headline, TIME TO RETIRE, or TIME FOR A CHANGE. I remember the name *"Time"* occurring to me. It stayed with me overnight and when I went in the next morning, I suggested it to Hadden and he accepted it immediately," said Luce.

Culbreth Sudler, Harry's old Yale friend, came from Chicago with $548.88 to invest and became advertising manager. Manfred Gottfried, another Yale man with money to invest, started working without pay as their first writer. He later became the first salaried employee.

The most important of the new staff was Roy Edward Larsen, who would play a pivotal role in Time Inc.'s development. They called him "Dapper Dan" because he always looked well dressed, even in his shirt sleeves. He arrived with the reputation of having made an unprecedented profit while business manager of the Harvard *Advocate*. Medium height, clean-cut, he was considered the hardest working man on the staff, "a grim but smiling terrier." Luce would later say of him, "If I drop dead or get bumped off, Roy Larsen will be boss."

Harry was taking home a salary of thirty-five dollars a week and trying to bank his money for his future marriage. To save money, Luce later shared an apartment with "Gott."

Through all these frenzied months, Lila did not let Harry forget her. About once a week, she would come by train from Chicago. "I would spend three or four days in New York at a little hotel on 39th Street and Park Avenue . . . sometimes he could get away for an hour a day to come and see me. He'd arrive in the evening, and we'd read some books aloud together. And mind you, nobody would believe this, but no embraces! It's incredible because we were terribly in love . . ." said Lila.

Lila's visits were a great comfort to Luce, but his mind and energy was focused on *Time*. On February 27, 1923, the entire staff piled in three taxis that would take them from their new office on East 40th Street and Eleventh Avenue, to the printing plant on Vesey Street in lower Manhattan. They all watched as the first issue of *Time* magazine went to press.

Luce later reminisced about working around the "stone" (tables) of the composing room until dawn, rewriting to cut and fit, "and everyone tried his hand at captions."

"It was daylight when I got home and went to sleep," Luce added. "That afternoon, I found an uncut copy of the little magazine in my room. I picked it up and began to turn through its meager thirty-two pages (including cover). Half an hour later, I woke up to a surprise: what I had been reading wasn't bad at all. In fact, it was quite good. Somehow, it all held together, it made sense, it was interesting."

Now came the matter of circulating the issue. An initial mailing brought in some 6,000 trial subscriptions, and the newsstands took 5,000 copies—of those, 2,500 went unsold. Roy Larsen, then circulation manager, sat on the floor of the office surrounded by all the magazine wrappers for the mailing, hopelessly mixed up. Larsen was trying to sort them by states. They were still mailing out the first issue when the third went to press.

Volume I, Number I of *Time,* The Weekly Newsmagazine was dated March 3, 1923. Sales price: fifteen cents. Reading time: one hour. It compartmentalized the weekly news into twenty-two departments, with only four meager pages of advertising. It sold about 8,500 copies and received praises from a variety of people. Franklin D. Roosevelt, then an unsuccessful vice presidential candidate, was one of those who thought that the articles were "just about right in length and they are as unbiased as far as it is possible for red-blooded Americans to make them so." Their former teacher, William Lyon Phelps, read it and said, "Bully."

On the cover of the first issue was eighty-six-year-old Speaker of the House James G. ("Uncle Joe") Cannon, who was retiring after twenty-three years. Humorist Robert Benchley remarked that the pictures "looked as if they had been engraved on slices of bread." But no matter, the news seemed fresh and the national affairs section dealt with the controversy over U.S. membership in the World Court. In the foreign affairs section, the main article discussed the big sale of Soviet wheat to western Europe. The aeronautics section described a possible dirigible service between Chicago and New York. Education debated the question of whether or not Yale should retain Latin and Greek for a bachelor of arts degree. The editors believed that they would make news out of subjects most people didn't consider news, such as education and religion. Medicine eventually became the most popular of these "back-of-the-book" sections.

The style for everything was saucy with an air of omnipotence. "Let all stories make sharp sense. Omit flowers. Remember you can't be too obvious. People talk too much about things they don't know," Luce said at the time. The basic belief was that busy, influential people preferred a digested substitute to the long original stories. "The job of journalism," Luce continued, "was to foment and formulate. Facts should be married to imagination and passion." If Luce had an adage, it was, "People aren't interesting in the mass; it's only individuals who are exciting."

Every story has its slant. Luce no longer believed in all the facts, nothing but the facts. "When you put facts together to make stories of them, you endow them with values they did not have before. And that can raise hell with the truth. But since you also make them much more readable . . . you are successful in your field, which is communicating beyond your wildest dreams."

Asked once why *Time* did not present two sides of a story, Luce answered: "Are there not more likely to be three sides or thirty sides?" And he added later, "Show me a man who claims he's completely objective, and I'll show you a man with illusions." His idea was that the American press had a mission which could influence the fate of American civilization: "Give the public the truth we think it must have."

Get all the facts, surely. First-rate writing meant a base of facts. But then predigest them and arrange them—or misarrange them—according to the "truth" you want to tell. "We went in every week to remake the world," said one writer. This was the thread that tied *Time* together.

Time, each week, was a world of good guys and bad guys, absolute and dogmatic. The editors got the facts, then re-arranged them according to the truth they wanted to tell.

Sales zigzagged up and down that first year, then up again because the audience was there, and it kept growing. People seemed to like their news tasty, snappy, short, and in gulps. Within four months, things were going well enough for *Time* to take half a floor in an old brewery building on East 39th Street between Second and Third avenues. Their offices were directly over a gun shop which tested rifles on Sundays, *Time*'s busiest day. By this time, even Lila's stepfather, who had once described Luce as "a person of no position . . . worthless," now felt forced to agree that this young man was bright with promise, and gave permission for the marriage.

For Lila and Henry, this was an enormous relief. Lila had loyally supported his efforts and had toured the Chicago newsstands demanding they stock *Time.*

She contented herself with a flow of letter writing. He called her "Darlingest," "Carissima," and "Angel" and wrote that, "what Harry needs is you." She called him "Belovedissimo" and urged him not to work too hard. "Dearest, do you HAVE to stay in your office till two AM and then get there at the crack of dawn the following morning? That sort of thing worries me a lot."

Finally, on December 22, 1923, the long wait was over.

"They had this enormous wedding in the big Presbyterian Church in Chicago," said Beth. "I was one of the bridesmaids and we had silver-brocaded dresses with ermine hats. Wow!" Lila also described the wedding as "the most gorgeous . . . unbelievably highbrow. We had forty-two people for dinner . . . a *very* distinguished evening."

"Father Luce came to our wedding reception. Mother Luce was in China; she couldn't come," said Lila. Harry's father was a great, wonderful, devoted Christian, who could sell anybody into Christianity because he was so sold on it himself. My stepfather, who was completely without any religion—a hardheaded banker. . . . He used to call Father Luce something like 'Sky Man,' meaning 'always in the religion.' When he came to the wedding reception, he had never tasted anything with liquor in it. There was a little bit of rum in the punch—maybe a *lot* of rum! And he drank that, and said, 'Oooh, this is good!' "

The discreet announcement in *Time*'s Milestone simply said: "Married, Miss Lila Ross Hotz, 23, of Chicago, to Harry Robinson Luce, editor of *Time*, The Weekly Newsmagazine."

After a honeymoon in Homestead, Virginia, Harry and Lila found a four-room flat on Fifth Avenue and 97th Street overlooking the park but "very much at the edge of nothing," as Lila noted. Rent was cheap and they filled the apartment with some of Lila's mother's expensive antiques. Her mother also quietly supplemented their income so that Lila could afford regular help.

"Harry and I entertained not at all, when we got married. He was working. My very best friend, Helen Stanton, used to be very discouraged because she and I had made our debuts (she in New York, and me Chicago) in 1919. For two years, we were very gay. We went to all the dances, visited our school friends all over the country. We traveled together in Europe—and had a wonderful life. Then, when I was married, she couldn't get us to come to dinner! Harry was working. Except on Wednesday nights."

Harry and Brit's original agreement was that they would alternate as editor and business manager. "Brit won the toss of the coin and got to edit first," said Beth. "Harry was so upset about that because the one thing he prized above all was the title of just plain editor. Anyway, Harry concentrated on the advertising and the money. He was thrilled the next year when they switched jobs, but, after a short time, they could see that Brit was floundering on the financial end. And so Harry reluctantly had to take over the business end again to make it work." *Time*'s annual report in 1924 showed a net profit of $674.15.

Brit later referred to Harry as "a financial genius." Hadden, meanwhile, put his firm imprint on *Time* style. For a guide, he relied on the Greek *Iliad*, where adjectives were often used as verbs, and words were hyphenated. Brit's copy of the *Iliad* had hundreds of words written on the back cover "which seemed to him fresh and forceful." When he saw something like "pig-faced" or "bald-domed," he would say, "Great word!" Luce also admired the *Iliad* language, especially the inverted sentences. In a letter home, Luce often wrote in the same style. "Puppets of Time and Fortune are we all" was a classic Luce line.

But it was Hadden who was the true wordsmith. He liked to make everything flip and feisty, so tightly edited that everything seemed compressed, even encapsulated. He invented words like "tycoon" and also used foreign words like "pundit"—from the Hindu meaning a learned man. "Kudos" was another Hadden word that received wide acceptability.

He also liked alliteration and typically referred to George Bernard Shaw as "mocking, mordant, misanthropic." Hadden urged the use of words that packaged two meanings into one, such as "uprighteous," which combined "upright" and "righteous," or "sarcastigator" (sarcastic and instigator). The most successful "blended" word was "socialite" (a combination of social and light). And then there was "smog," a blend of smoke and fog. *Time* talk was not totally new. Lewis Carroll had telescoped "lithe" and "slimy" into "slithy." Columnist Westbrook Pegler mocked all this as "a nervous disease on the typewriter."

Though Harry and Brit basically agreed about style, they differed about many other matters. The careful, businesslike Luce and the flippant, disorganized Hadden were an odd, mismatched team.

"I know that Harry and Brit had hot arguments but never in front of us," said Joseph Kastner. "They'd go off to the Yale Club or somewhere to settle it."

"Hadden is hard to convince," Luce once told his wife. "If I can convince Hadden, then I know my idea is good." One of their important discussions concerned salary. Should they give themselves a ten-dollar raise? Brit the bachelor said no, but Harry the married man, needed it. They were still then on a salary of only forty dollars a week.

Harry and Lila were not happy in New York City. Lila was pregnant and preferred the quiet of a home in the suburbs. Harry and Brit had talked about moving *Time* to the Midwest to assure earlier delivery to the West Coast but Brit was against leaving New York. When Hadden took his first holiday, a six-week trip to Europe, he made Manfred Gottfried managing editor and warned him, "Make sure that Harry doesn't meddle." By the time Brit returned, plans were set to move the magazine to Cleveland, adjoining a printing plant. Roy Larsen reportedly suggested Cleveland because he was courting a girl there. Only after a furious, private argument and only after Luce showed how much money they would save, did Brit reluctantly agree.

Lila and Harry liked Cleveland. They found it not too big, and not too pressured. They liked the friendly neighbors and quiet streets for their brand-new son, Henry III (who would become known as "Hank"). The Luces fell happily and neatly into the social pattern, joined the local country club, and bought season tickets to the symphony orchestra. Harry even talked to the Chamber of Commerce. "We had a lot of friends there," said Lila, "and they were lovely to us. It was really a much different kind of life. . . . One did nothing but just count on playing bridge, after a dinner conversation—no intellectual interest. But I must say, we thought we were going to be there the rest of our lives. So we accepted it, and we were happy."

Because Harry was a terrible driver, bordering on the dangerous, Lila habitually drove the family Chrysler to pick Harry up at about two in the morning after he had helped put the magazine to bed.

In contrast Hadden hated Cleveland. "He was a Brooklyn boy, an almost violent Dodger fan, and New York was his playground," said Lila. "Brit did crazy things. He'd get a friend to sit in the car with him, and they'd go through the streets of Cleveland . . . it was just after Sinclair Lewis had written his book, *Main Street.* I suppose they thought of Cleveland as *Main Street.* And Brit would shout out the window of his car at almost anybody who went by in a car or was walking along the street, *Babbit!* It got something off his chest."

The breach between Harry and Brit kept widening. In almost every way, they were opposites. One staff member put the contrast the following way. Luce/Hadden: moral/amoral, pious/worldly, respectable/raffish, bourgeois/bohemian, introvert/extrovert, sober/convivial, reliable/unpredictable, slow/quick, dog/cat, tame/wild, efficient/brilliant, decent/charming, puritanical/hedonistic, naive/cynical, Victorian/eighteenth century.

The contrast was not quite that simple. Each man had parts of the other and envied the rest. This was part of their bond. And the birth of *Time* needed them both. John Martin, Hadden's cousin who became a *Time* staffer, once observed, "Without a fellow competitor, Brit might have lost, as Dempsey without a sparring partner. In Harry Luce, I always felt, he had the ideal combination of partner and critic. Equally energetic, equally hardheaded, equally brilliant each in his way, they complemented each other to an extraordinary and fortunate degree, their very differences spurring them both on to results better than they might have accomplished singly."

The breech widened when Yale made Luce the youngest man to ever receive an honorary degree from the school. He was praised as the man who had done the most for Yale because of his accomplishments in journalism. No mention was made of Hadden. Nor did Harry tell Brit about the degree. But when Brit found out about it, his resentment deepened. Why did they pick Luce, not Hadden? Perhaps because Luce conformed more to the desired Yale pattern of respectability.

Harry made a new and very good friend when his sister Beth married a lawyer named Maurice Thompson ("Tex") Moore in the fall of 1926. "Harry had absolute trust, absolute confidence in Tex," said Beth. "The wonderful thing was that Harry knew that he could tell Tex anything, anything at all, and it wouldn't go any further—even to me. Harry really needed somebody like that. Tex became Time Inc.'s general counsel and, later, chairman of the board.

"Both were very stubborn, strong-minded men," said Beth Moore, "and they would have some very hard discussions and really yell at each other. They'd roar at each other so loudly that you would think they were fighting bloody murder in the battle of the century. But, then, suddenly, it was over as quick as it had started, and it was all calm again. Their arguments centered mostly on corporate business when Tex told Harry that he couldn't legally do what Harry *wanted* to do."

Beth herself contributed to *Time* by writing book reviews. "Nobody told me what to do," she remembered. "The books just poured in and all I knew was that I had two pages to fill." Harry was a big help to her. "He had a knack of focusing your attention on the essentials . . . 'I think the point is this,' he would tell you, 'but I don't want more than a hundred words.' "

In June 1927, Harry and Lila took a month's vacation in Europe, leaving Hank with Lila's parents. They started off in Paris, where they looked up two part-time *Time* correspondents, Stephen Vincent Benet and Archibald MacLeish, who were being paid $10 a week.

The Luces then went to Rome, where they had first met and fallen in love. Luce unsuccessfully tried to arrange an interview with Benito Mussolini, the new fascist dictator of Italy, a man who much intrigued him. "My greatest thrill of the entire trip was the day we arrived at a tiny hotel with only four bedrooms on the top of the highest mountain in Corsica," Lila said, "and found a two-year-old copy of *Time* in the hotel's little vestibule."

On their return, Luce discovered Hadden had turned the tables. He had successfully persuaded the board of directors to move *Time* back to New York, using the argument that the magazine had outgrown the Cleveland presses.

Hadden, though, had resisted the urging of friends who had tried to convince him to buy out Luce. By the time Luce returned, he found that "there was no use arguing with Hadden about the move back to New York." In an earlier letter to his wife, Harry had complained about his relationship with Hadden, citing the differences between them—but he saw no way out. Harry's brother Sheldon felt, too, that Hadden had become a problem because he drank so much.

Luce would always have his reservations about being in New York, but he reluctantly agreed it was "the great workshop," the center of power and competitive ideas. Lila recalled that they were really happy to be back in New York.

"We had a red-brick house at 225 East 49th Street, and we furnished it with mother's glorious period furniture," she said. "It was owned by Efrem Zimbalist, the violinist, and Alma Gluck, the opera singer, who lived next-door. We had a backyard. And we used to go to the Zimbalists' parties, if Harry could get away from work. . . . Later on, when *Time* was older, we could go to more of their parties and meet all their musician friends."

Friends recalled that Lila was a good wife and a fine mother. She knew the niceties of being the perfect hostess, no matter what guests Harry invited. "They were almost entirely *Time* people. . . . I didn't even try to invite my own friends," she said. "I sacrificed my own social relationships, and had no thought of doing anything else."

Most of all, she was protective of Harry. "Harry is working on a speech . . . I can't disturb him," she would tell those who tried to see him.

That summer, Lila stayed with her son at a house they had rented in Roxbury, Connecticut, while Harry remained in town. Harry came home on Tuesday and Wednesday, after the magazine had gone to press. During their absences, they exchanged frequent short notes. Hers would be wifely, advising him to get his pants pressed, giving him the latest news about their son, telling him not to work so hard, suggesting they go to The Grand Street Follies. She threatened to kidnap him and take him to "some leafy solitude . . . to laugh or lie and listen to the sweet silences." She signed one note: "Always your lover." In another, she wrote, "Adored! My love may be imperfect but it is very great."

In 1928, Harry Luce was thirty years old. He had told his wife then that he expected to be a millionaire before the year was out, and indeed he was. What made 1928 *more* important for him was that Hadden had promised to stay on the business management side all that year and let Harry be the editor. All the better, this was a presidential election year, Democrat Alfred E. Smith vs. Republican Herbert Hoover. Smith had been a four-time governor of New York, wore a brown derby, smoked cigars, and was a Roman Catholic. Hoover was a tall, round-faced engineer from Iowa who wore high, stiff collars. Each man rated a *Time* cover story. When a reader accused *Time* of being Republican, the reply was that one editor (Hadden) had voted for Hoover and the other (Luce) for Smith.

Luce took his role as editor very seriously. Instead of too frequent use of the heavy black pencil, editor Luce concentrated on steering the story line straight, keeping the main idea clear and concise. "He'd galvanize a page by putting two pencil marks on it," recalled Eliot Janeway, a later consultant to Luce.

Luce was a man of ideas and there were those who felt he cared more for ideas than for people. With people, he never seemed completely comfortable. Partly, it came from shyness. He was not a cold man and was never deliberately impolite, but he simply was not the kind who could stretch out a hand and touch somebody. People sensed an awkwardness and unease in him. His demeanor was grave, never gregarious. He couldn't seem to navigate through human relationships. An observer once said that if he could get a book to tell him how to be a father and friend, he probably would've been able to do it. But he had no natural intuition about those rules.

Some found it funny that one of Harry's favorite desserts was a kind of eclair called, "Frozen Smile." When he did smile, however rarely, it was a marvelous smile that would transform his face. His blue eyes would twinkle and his whole face would soften. This was a side of him few saw and few knew. He was a controlled man who was proud of his control. He saw it as a protection of his privacy.

Though Luce had a basic kindness in him, many felt he was very rude. An associate once explained that he never meant to hurt or snub people, it was just that he was impatient. He couldn't stand things getting in the way and got testy if he was kept waiting, or if he felt people were wasting his time. Then he could be brusque "and chew the hell out of people," said Tom Griffith. On the other hand, if you caught his interest in something, he would want to know all about it.

Here was a man who was never afraid of seeming stupid. His curiosity was insatiable and he wanted to know everything. "After you had been with Luce for a day, you felt as if a suction pump had been applied to your brains and pulled every bit of information out . . . I always felt exhausted and sometimes exasperated, but always excited," said one of his secretaries.

He was basically a loner, the little boy in China who went off by himself into the fields on his donkey. Almost nobody ever came into Luce's office uninvited. Later, even his sons had to make appointments to see him.

If Luce was truly passionate about anything, it was *Time*. He believed anything important could be made understandable and popular, that there was no such thing as a dull important subject. "And he could be interested in the damndest things . . . and so he was never ever bored," said *Time* writer James Bell. It would be difficult to find things in which he was *not* interested. He was not a man who could be put in a mold. "He could be utterly boring or dazzling, and you never knew which it would be." Yet he seldom talked in simple slogans. There was a kind of intellectuality about most of his discussions.

For a multi-faceted man, he was not devious. He didn't say one thing to one person and something else to another person. There was no slickness in him, and sometimes he had to grope toward his subject, taking a long time to make a point.

He was a very thoughtful man, often benevolent, and found it terribly difficult to fire anybody. Despite his rough edge, there was no cruelty in him. He was a man of complexity. He enjoyed living comfortably, but seemed to have no concern about food or clothes. He was not chatty and hated small talk, but he loved gossip. He even occasionally made the rounds with a Broadway columnist. And yet his idea of a perfect evening was to go to bed with a book of theology.

Luce was not a man of self-doubt. He believed in himself implicitly. He saw life in simple, heroic terms. His faith was a shining thing. The passion in him was compartmentalized. He had a passion for being an American with an almost boyish enthusiasm. His great strength was recognizing brilliant ideas and brilliant people. When he found them, he backed them. He had a passion for words, the right ones, and he instinctively seemed to know what they were. When he found the writer who used them well, he forgave almost everything else—drinks, politics, eccentricity.

Luce enriched the magazine with his wide range of interests and cultural values. A *Time* researcher once depicted Luce as "the best of all editors because of his temperamental ability to be constantly surprised and delighted by what he didn't know before." As author Robert Elson observed in his authorized history of *Time*: If Hadden's contribution was his sense of word and style, Luce's was his curiosity "which contributed as much to the liveliness of the early *Time*."

"He really loved Time Inc. He really just loved the company and the people," said his secretary Gloria Mariano. "I always wished more people had the chance to know him better. He didn't care if people had odd hours, as long as they worked hard, did their work, and cared about Time Inc. In those days, you'd have gone to work without being paid. I mean, that was really the feeling. It was just a joy; it was fun."

It was also a place without pretense. Luce made no effort to exalt *Time* beyond what it was. Asked by *Editor & Publisher* where *Time*'s news items came from, Luce promptly replied: "We pick them up out of newspapers." *Editor & Publisher* then raised the question whether any magazine has a moral right to scissor news and present it in print as if it were an original creation.

"If anybody who objects doesn't know this by now," sputtered Luce in reply, "why the hell are they still spending thirty-five cents for the magazine?"

But Luce clearly wanted *Time* to be *more* than a rewrite of newspapers, and so it was. The careful use of the right, bright anecdote, the snappy word, the pointed opinion gave a more human dimension to the news. But the real success of the magazine was the Back of the Book, which popularized culture in grass roots America. "Luce did more of that than anybody in history, I think," said Dave Richardson, a *Time* correspondent. "Luce had a profound effect on Americans by telling them that a symphony orchestra in your town is a good thing for business. And so is an art museum. The Back of the Book made that magazine." In fact, a surprising number of readers started with the back of the book and still do today.

In the winter months of 1928, Brit had seemed listless and called in frequently to say, "I'm not well. I don't know what's wrong with me."

At his mother's insistence, he moved back home to Brooklyn where she could care for him.

He soon got worse. Hadden came down with influenza and an infection in his blood stream that affected his heart. Some said the infection came from the scratch of a tough butcher's cat Brit had brought home to his apartment. Whatever the source, it was virulent. Hadden was swiftly hospitalized and in need of blood. Harry, the first to donate blood, was a daily visitor. But Hadden quickly deteriorated. He died on February 27, 1929, at the age of thirty-one.

The New York Times saluted him for his "touch of genius." The *Time* obituary read in part, "to Briton Hadden, success came steadily, satisfaction never." The epitaph on his tomb read, "his genius created a new form of journalism."

In Hadden's personal notebook on a page headed "Expansion" were: "Business Mag, Fiction Mag, Spt. Mag, Secy Mag, Letter Mag, Time monthly, School Time, Women Mag, Daily Newspaper, US history ok."

They had had bitter differences in the past, but those who knew Harry and Brit well felt they had resolved them on Brit's deathbed. Harry would never afterward speak disparagingly of Hadden. He missed his friend, and his death presented him with a deep sense of loss. "I don't know what I'll do without Hadden," Luce said.

He soon found out.

9

CLARE had expected to feel happy and free after her divorce from Brokaw, but instead she drifted through her days in a miserable, lonely daze. She had neither direction nor goal. The money was there, the posh apartment and the maids, but what was she going to do with her life? She felt, she said, "like a useless member of the world."

Friends failed to understand Clare. Here she was living in surroundings almost anyone would envy. Her penthouse on East 52nd Street was decorated in modern Chinese red, black, and white; the view of New York and the East River below were spectacular. An impressionable young visitor, Leo Lerman, who later became an editor of *Vogue* and *Vanity Fair,* was one of those struck by the rarefied environment enjoyed by pretty Ms. Brokaw.

"I can remember driving up on 52nd Street in my father's truck seeing this exquisite blonde standing on the corner with her dog," said Lerman, whose father had been hired to paint Clare's apartment. "I think she was wearing the first Chanel suit I ever saw. It was black with a saw-toothed hem, and with it she had on the most beautiful blouse. When I was introduced to her, however, she was surprisingly cold, almost charmless. I can remember thinking she had no interest in children at all. There was no sign of her daughter in the apartment," observed Lerman, who was then fifteen. He recalled that her dining room was covered with silver tea paper decorated with a panorama of the New York City skyline in Matisse colors. "The table, which seated twenty, was made of smoked glass, reflecting the skyline on the paper. She had a wood-burning fireplace, walls lined with books, rooms filled with fresh flowers, and weeping willow trees on the terrace."

Even Clare gradually came to appreciate the seductive charms of her home and social position.

"I breathed in deeply of the air of irreligion and materialism. For a long time, I liked it," Clare confessed. "It had a tang to it, bitter and sharp and a little heady. It made the senses reel pleasantly. The New York of my youth was a fat, rich, glittering, exciting, glamorous place. The goal of Everybody one knew was to be either flush or famous, preferably both. And practically Everybody was within shooting distance of his objective. Fame and fortune were measured then, as now, by newspaper lineage. The least of my friends made the society columns. Many made national headlines."

She analyzed that success was like anesthesia. "You increase the dosage and you increase it and finally it doesn't work. Most of the successful people I know are unhappy. I think now this is because we did not know that no man possesses anything he owns or holds or even what he takes into his mouth, his arms, his heart, his mind, but only that which he holds in his very soul."

She tried to understand her own angst, despite all her material pleasures, and was puzzled: "After an amicable divorce from a man with whom I had been violently unhappy, I still found myself violently unhappy. This struck me at the time as utterly unreasonable, which it was. For I did not lack for money or health, or the affection of friends or attention from the opposite sex. But some vast uneasiness, restlessness, spoiled every pleasure and heightened every pain, and poisoned every relationship. I concluded with considerable shame that I must be neurotic, which I wasn't. I was just not at peace with God. Now, in those days, the most fashionable 'ism' for expecting a cure of [such a condition] was Freudianism. Indeed Freud was the patron saint of the liberal elite. I was psychoanalyzed in the middle thirties."

She later described the thirties as the Age of Psychoanalysis. You went to one, she said, even if you didn't need one, "in keeping with the fashion." The psychiatrist she selected was considered one of the best in America, a pupil of Freud's. He estimated that she would probably need daily sessions for a minimum of two years. He also promised to "shake off her psychic angularity" and make her "a happy woman." At the very least, she was ready to be told why she was the way she was.

Clare described herself to friends as a plum cake of complexes. Her analyst told her she had both a father complex and a mother complex. He seemed to believe strongly that her lingering desire to be loved by God reflected her childhood desire to be loved more by her earthly father. Her current wish to become a writer seemed to signify that she wanted to spite her father by becoming more masculine. In thinking about it, she sensed that while it was true that her father had deserted the family when she was a child, still, all her earlier memories of him had been loving. Her father never had punished her for anything, always had called her "my darling girl."

Typically, Clare started "sopping up Freud's own books." She decided that she was being adjusted to a world "so shorn of beauty and goodness that a sane person might be better to leave it than try to live in it." She decided that her analyst was trying to show her that all art, architecture, music, painting, all the great works of the human spirit were merely sublimated sexual atavism. She felt he was trying to transfer all her love, faith, and confidence to him "as a child helpless before the father." She disliked his willingness to relieve her of all guilt and transfer it to her father, mother, and society. She could accept him as a father confessor, because she needed one, but she could not accept him as a father.

Clare finally decided that she had become his psychological guinea pig. Whether this was because he was reaching too close to a raw nerve of truth, or because she was "running out of real dreams" and kept busy inventing them, she quit her analysis. Her analyst warned her that if she left her treatment unfinished, "you will have psychic scars all your life."

Indeed, she admitted, "I was still to struggle, to strive, to suffer, to sin, to betray, and to be betrayed. And to be unhappy. The 'Big Question,' the meaning of life and death, the real goal of human life, did not yield to psychoanalysis." But then she added, "Of all the things I have ever done in my life, my abrupt retreat from that office has given me the most pleasure and the least regrets. I demonstrated that I possessed a free will: I could choose my own path to doom! Nevertheless, I am deeply grateful for this experience."

After discarding analysis, her impulse was to meet men—interesting men, important men. Gossip columnists soon associated her with some of the most celebrated men in the city. She became a season party guest, a highly decorative adjunct for any hostess. At many of the parties she attended, Condé Nast was also a guest.

Nast, whose mother was French, was a born New Yorker. He held a law degree from St. Louis University and had worked for *Collier's* magazine at the turn of the century, where he became the highest paid general manager in American magazine publishing.

Nast bought *Vogue* magazine in 1909 when it was a sick society paper. He brought in noted artists such as Salvador Dali as fashion illustrators, and made *Vogue* one of the first modern illustrated magazines. His *Vogue* patterns became famous and made him a fortune. Four years later, he transformed a magazine called *Dress and Vanity Fair* into *Vanity Fair*. He was a patriarch in his fifties who believed that if you make a gesture, make a *grand* gesture. When he gave one of his editors a box of ties, there was a thousand dollar bill stuffed in the back of each tie.

At his twenty-room Park Avenue penthouse, Nast was a lavish host. He was often selected as one of the ten best-dressed men in America. Despite losing some two million dollars in the stock market crash, he continued to live with

Edwardian elegance. His ballroom was covered with eighteenth-century Chien-Lung wallpaper and opened onto a covered terrace to seat a hundred. One guest recalled that there was "such an array of flat silver that I was thankful my mother had taught me to start from the outside and simply work my way in without having to watch and see which fork the hostess picked up." Nast's guests might include everybody from the young pilot Charles Lindbergh, to George Gershwin playing the music of a future show. A Nast party often caused a squabble among invited magazine staff members: "I'm going to wear my red Chanel—you'll have to wear your white." The host believed in making each party a statement of fashion.

Nast was a man who always seemed to be between marriages, always en route to Europe, always in the company of the world's most beautiful women—even though he was not brilliant, witty, or erudite, or even physically attractive. Yet, he fascinated women.

At one of those midnight parties, Clare cornered him. Knowing she needed the discipline of a job, she asked for a position on one of his magazines. "He gave me a long sales talk about all the women who wanted jobs on *Vogue*," said Clare. He said he knew her type—rich, restless, gay divorcée wanting a temporary job until the man came along, or the next vacation. "I was persistent," said Clare. Reminiscing about it later, Nast recalled, "I didn't think she was serious . . . [I] thought it was just one of those sudden notions she'd soon forget. I told her 'I'm off to Europe tomorrow. You see Edna Chase.' I was counting on Edna to get me off the hook."

Edna Woolman Chase seemed to have a sixth sense about coming fashions. She liked to say that *Vogue* was a democracy and anyone could come into her office and pose a problem. She said everyone had a voice in her magazine, but her voice was the strongest, and it was her magazine.

"Edna gave me the same runaround," said Clare, "the same talk. She too was off to Europe and when she got back, well, maybe, perhaps."

"Mrs. Brokaw was an ambitious young woman intensely interested in magazines," said Mrs. Chase, "but as her alimony settlement from Mr. Brokaw had been widely publicized, she had considerable difficulty persuading possible bosses she was in earnest."

Yet she was. Clare returned to the *Vogue* office sometime later, but Mrs. Chase was still not back. "By this time I knew the set-up. I walked along the corridor peering into offices until I came to one in which there was a dear old lady writing a social letter. It was the office of the caption writers. There was one empty desk. I kind of oozed in."

"Whose desk is that?" Clare asked.

"No one's at present."

"Then it's mine," said Clare.

"What are you doing?"

"Writing captions."

"Well, here are some to write."

She promptly began writing captions for pictures on what the well-dressed woman will wear. "I worked there every day," said Clare. "I was scared to death somebody would find out I hadn't really been hired, but nobody noticed me until the girl came around with the pay envelopes. Nobody knew anything about me, not even the accountant. It was three weeks before I got a pay envelope." (Her salary was $21 a month.)

The halls of Condé Nast publishing company were set up in such a way that anyone bound for the *Vogue* offices had to pass by the door of *Vanity Fair.* Most of the ladies on *Vogue* were married, and so many of them were pregnant so much of the time that certain assistant editors of *Vanity Fair* took to leaving the office doors open and making bets on the condition of the next *Vogue* editor to pass by. Accustomed to a long procession of maternity dresses, the *Vanity Fair* speculators got a jolt the first morning Mrs. Brokaw arrived to report for work at *Vogue.* She was slim and pretty in a simple gray frock with touches of white at the throat and wrists, and the light from a window at the end of the hall celestially illumined her face and hair. "Geez, what was that?" a *Vanity Fair* editor murmured as she passed.

Still, no one quite knew how she got there. "Condé and I were on one of our transatlantic shuffle routines," said Mrs. Chase, "and each assumed that somewhere—Paris, London, New York, or the high seas—the other had engaged her. Her status was vague, but after a bit she began to prove herself." Clare was simply following an aphorism by La Rochefoucauld: "To establish oneself in the world, one does all one can to seem established there already."

Condé Nast had his own aphorism about promising young people: "You never know how far they can go until you try them out." He liked to roam the office corridors, sociable, convivial, and searching. He was not the kind of editor who opposed any fraternizing with pretty employees. He fraternized. A staff member described the scene at *Vanity Fair* as having an "air of sexual democracy." You could never be sure that the receptionist wouldn't be the next Mrs. Condé Nast.

Surprised to find Clare working on his magazine, Nast promptly invited her to dinner. "Those were still the days when at the end of a dinner, the ladies left the room while the men remained for brandy and cigars," he said. "At this dinner, however, Clare blandly stayed on with the men, while the other women, banished into the drawing room, fumed helplessly."

"When Clare came into the office, all the editors' backs would stiffen like cats watching a confident dog stroll by," Edna Chase said. An art director recalled his first impression of her: nice shoes and a mink coat. Then he added, "Clare wasn't a clothes horse, a clothes worshiper like the others on *Vogue*. From a *Vogue* viewpoint, she was an unbeliever. To meet important people, she used to think she had to dress like a Southern belle—beige, rose, organdy— things that really weren't in character for her." She would sometimes wear Mainbocher clothes, too, not that she cared about it, but because she thought it was part of the "thing" to be well-dressed. Some *Vogue* observers insisted Clare was seen by a hairdresser and manicurist—before coming to work.

She also had two tailored suits, one gray and one tan, both very mannish and businesslike, "but very female on you," a staff woman later told her. The staff vividly recalled the day she arrived with *all* her jewels, just prior to placing them in a safety-deposit box. It was also noted that she couldn't spell, though no one seemed to care.

She seemed to fluster everyone around her. "Clare had a hypnotic effect on me when she came to my studio," said a woman photographer who was taking pictures of Clare. (As an acknowledged beauty of the era, she was often asked to pose.) "I could hear myself saying idiotic things that I wasn't conscious of thinking and, if I tried to say what I meant, I would get deeper in the sticky mess—as if my words were taffy candy that wasn't cooked enough to pull. I suspected that it amused her to see me flounder. I didn't blame her for this; she didn't like women very much, nor did I at that time. I would have liked to have had the same wit and power as she had, and I would have had no desire to use it in a more gentle way."

When Clare came into Cecil Beaton's studio, it was often filled with tulle and flowers and stuffed white doves. The phrases he used most often were "darling," "divine," and "too, too lovely." Beaton, reportedly, was the one who called Clare "drenchingly beautiful." He later told a mutual friend, "I never said it about her. I said it about someone else and Clare pinched it." But the phrase still fit. The essential quality of her beauty was the luminosity of her flawless skin, which had a curious kind of pearl-like translucence. Her eyes were not large, but there was, said Beaton "a magical loveliness in her gaze, which was level, disquieting, spellbinding. She could enter a room where there were other women more beautiful, better dressed, with better figures, and they faded into the background."

Clare's ambition was to move to Nast's other publication, *Vanity Fair*, which was centered in three semi-partitioned rooms between *Vogue* and the elevators. She described her work at *Vogue* as "monkey jobs" while *Vanity Fair* was a showcase for some of the best, wittiest writing in the country. Contributors included Dorothy Parker, Robert Benchley, P. G. Wodehouse,

Edna St. Vincent Millay, Colette, Aldous Huxley, Edmund Wilson, Robert Sherwood, Gertrude Stein, with art by Picasso and Matisse.

"*Everybody* wrote for it," said another contributor, Jay Carter. Nast called *Vanity Fair* an intellectual exercise for nice people. Its credo was to chronicle the progress of American life cheerfully, truthfully, and entertainingly. As an organ of the elite, it tried to define much of the taste of the time. It assumed that a magazine should be "talked about, laughed at, and enjoyed."

The celebrated editor in chief of *Vanity Fair* was Frank Crowninshield, a New York legend. "Crownie," as he was called, was dapper with curly hair and a curly mustache, a constant twinkle and a complex, remarkable mind. Born in Paris of a distinguished New England family, educated in Rome, Crownie was both a gentle man and a gentleman. The love of his life was his collection of French modern art. Nast regarded him as the custodian of his taste. He was courtly, kind, and urbane. He also had a sense of fun. "Married men," he once said, "make very poor husbands."

His office luncheons were memorable. Recalling a typical repast, Edna Chase described the guests: "a prominent Hollywood director, a diabetic who sat weighing his food on little scales, the magician who was making coins disappear, a girl wandered through with some lingerie she wanted photographed and bumped into serious pundit Walter Lippmann, murmuring his apologies for being late. . . ."

Crownie was adored by his staff, even though he, like Nast, had a deserved reputation for pawing and pinching. One of his secretaries, looking exhausted, commented, "Mr. Crowninshield's been dictating to me all morning, and I'm black and blue from shoulder to ankle." Yet, when a secretary was ill— especially if she was not pretty—he personally brought flowers to her bedside. And, in hiring a new secretary, he often took out a painting of a nude and said, smiling, "This was my old secretary. She was awfully good at dictation. I hope you'll be able to do as well."

Crownie wrote charming rejection slips. In one, he said: "My dear boy, this is superb! A little masterpiece! What color! What life! A veritable gem! Why don't you take it to *Harper's Bazaar?*" And when a bride introduced her new husband at a party, "This is my new husband, everybody: he makes love to me like Casanova and titillates me like the Marquis de Sade," Crownie instantly replied, "Oh, dear, poor darling—I'm afraid that means he does neither."

When Clare came for her interview, Crownie was sixty years old. He told her to come back in a week with a hundred suggestions suitable for publication. When she delivered them, he read them, patted her arm, then said, with a twinkle, "Well, well, you've done a lot of work . . . you and I understand each other. Now confess, who was the bright young man under your bed who thought up all these ideas for you?"

Clare was so angry she almost cried. Crownie quieted her, then warned her never to take him, or life, too seriously and then hired her. He also told her that some of her story ideas were terrible but at least two were excellent and that was more than one could expect from a starting assistant. Crowninshield later described Clare in a *Vogue* article as "a creature combining the various capacities of a superfortress, a battleship, and a tank."

Frank Crowninshield was the editor and unique spirit of the magazine, but twenty-nine-year-old Donald Freeman, who had been managing editor since 1924, was its working genius. Short, balding, and slightly fat, Freeman was one of the best editorial minds in the country. A New Yorker by birth, his background included journalism in Paris and Vienna. He was a chevalier of the Legion of Honor, descended from old American families, a member of the Society of Colonial Wars, the Huguenot Society, and Sons of the Revolution.

Clare still used "Julian Jerome," as a byline on her first article, "Talking Up and Thinking Down," poking fun at café society, and enclosed it with a group of other manuscripts she passed on to Managing Editor Freeman.

"These first three pieces are useless," he told her, "but find this fellow Jerome. I'd like to print more of his stuff." When she confessed she was the author, Freeman said, "You're really a first-class writer. Stick with it. Write what you know best and you will go a long way."

As soon as he met Clare, Freeman was hooked. He was delighted to discuss her ideas and problems, and she was even more delighted to have gained his interest. He wangled invitations to parties for her, introduced her to important literary people, loaned her his car, and praised her to Crowninshield. It was Freeman, according to Condé Nast, who persuaded Clare to drop the "Ann" in front of her name.

But Freeman's major contribution to Clare's welfare was keeping her mind in focus, her work disciplined.

Before meeting Donald, she admitted, she had not been very ambitious. "The minute I was good at something, I tended to quit it and go on to something else. It wasn't that I was bored, it was just that I was insatiably curious." She was, she insisted, lazy and procrastinating. Her greatest strength, she admitted, was her nervous energy.

She was soon doing everything at *Vanity Fair*. Clare read unsolicited manuscripts, helped photographers make appointments with celebrities, and listened hard to everything Freeman said. He put her in charge of some free-lance writers, including Henry Morton Robinson, later a noted novelist. Robinson remembered his first meeting with Clare. She sat at a temporary-looking desk near an arch with nothing on her desk but a pencil. She appraised him with an impersonal glance, quizzed him coolly, quickly sorted out his ideas, and within five minutes gave him an assignment. "Whether she intended it or not," Robinson said, "Clare gave the impression of being La Belle Dame sans Merci, but très, *très* intelligent . . ."

When the magazine needed someone to translate some stories by French writer André Maurois, Clare quickly volunteered. Her knowledge of French was more schoolbook than fluent but she worked long hours at home every night with the help of a French-English dictionary. The result was so good that she was asked to translate other French writers.

Behind the scenes, Freeman was always there to help Clare. He fell hopelessly in love with her and was willing to do anything for that love. He had no illusions about what he had to offer, or what she wanted. He was too bright and too sensitive not to know. And, yet, he was willing to give what he had and get what he could. Clare needed everything he had: his experience, his wisdom, his advice, his watchful eye, and all the supporting love he could give her.

"He encouraged me at a critical time in my life to believe in myself and my talents," she later said. "I loved him for that, but not in the same way he loved me."

He wrote her passionate letters such as this:

I love you so deeply dearest that the thought of being separated from you for even two days makes me despair. You are so lovely, so sweetly pure, so infinitely sweet of all women that my love for you seems always to grow and become strengthened. . . . I am fully aware of my unreasonableness and still more fully aware of your gentle forbearance. . . . I am such a dunce and such a nut. You know how sincerely I love you and how much I am yours.

With men she needed, Clare maintained a tight hold. She had said, "The only way to dominate a man or command a man is through affection." With Freeman, it was more than that, much more. They had formed a Pygmalion relationship and he was shaping her style, her habits, her personality, her life—and she loved it. She insisted to him, again and again, that she loved him. He was a possessively jealous man, as he explained, because most of the other men she knew were so much more handsome, richer, and more sophisticated than he was. As she once reminded him, "You know how much of my heart and time belong to you already. I've spent the past four weekends with you, seen you all of every day and every night (the best part of it too)."

With Freeman, Clare exhibited a coquettishness she had suppressed since her ill-fated relationship with Simpson. In one of her frequent letters to him, she wrote that he was the only one who really cared whether or not she succeeded, and she loved him for that. She told him he had expanded her talent and gave her such faith in herself that she knew no one could beat her down anymore.

She knew what he wanted to hear, and she told it to him. He was not only the love of her life but she wanted to marry him and live in the French countryside for eight months a year, where he would help write her book. She needed his wisdom on all things, she said. She wrote him from her daughter's camp in Loon Lake, in New York. She told him all her worries because Ann was so timid and so sullen and seemed to be turning into a brat. She needed his wisdom. What should she do? She wrote her "darling Donald" two long letters within twelve hours.

Donald replied that Ann had all the symptoms of a child of divorce living out her mother's fears, but this would disappear if she could live with Clare all the time. He also told her to drop the Brokaw out of her byline and stop smoking. She replied that the reason he nagged her so much about smoking was because he was jealous of anything that gave her pleasure; and it only raised the imp in her to disobey him.

Within months after her return to work, Clare was made associate editor. She knew she could write, edit, think, and organize. She could produce ideas filled with imagination. Finally, she had a function and an excitement in her life.

In her new position, Clare busily set about creating new features. One of the most popular was called, "Ike and Mike—They Look Alike." Clare would sit in her office searching hundreds of photographs, pairing pictures of mismatched people who looked like each other. Another department she created was called "We Nominate for Oblivion," to counterpoint the magazine's well-known "Hall of Fame." And she dreamed up an idea of putting Roosevelt's New Deal cabinet on playing cards. When an idea was presented to her which was not for *Vanity Fair,* but good, she was highly encouraging: "You can't kill it. It's such a good idea, any editor will rewrite it for you if he has to. You keep at it." She could be equally discouraging. When Condé Nast suggested a satirical cover on the Forgotten Man during the Depression, Clare gave him a cold look. "I don't see anything even remotely funny about people being hungry."

Such directness was Clare's style. If she wanted a secretary who was working for somebody else, she simply offered the young woman a huge raise and paid for it out of her own pocket. If she saw some theater tickets on the drama editor's desk to a play she wanted to see, she simply took them.

Clare also had a miniature gray town car with a chauffeur named Tansy that always aroused attention wherever she went. Clare adored cats so much that she had kittens embroidered on all her lingerie.

Not everyone admired her at *Vanity Fair.*

In a letter to a Vassar friend, Helen Brown wrote:

> *Mrs. Brokaw is twenty-eight. She comes sweeping into the office around ten or eleven in the morning, looking blond, beautiful, expensive, her perfume leaving people on her route practically in an olfactory swoon . . . she lives in a Beekman Place penthouse with four servants, including a personal lady's maid to draw her bath and help her dress, just like a movie star.*

Yet, gradually Clare won her over. "Clare always gave me credit for ideas I suggested, even when it wasn't necessary to do so, instead of passing them off as her own, a habit many female executives have been known to practice with subordinates," she recalled. She described Clare as encouraging and scrupulously fair, and added, "She's clever and quick-witted. If we need a title, a caption, a word, an idea, she can think of one right off the bat. She's not a profound thinker, but she's one of the fastest, trigger-quick." Summing Clare up, she called her "so ambitious that it hurt."

Another friend, the actress Arlene Francis, put Clare's aspiration more pointedly. "She wanted to be queen, and why the hell not?"

"When she left the house," Francis noted, "one maid would help her into her magnificent fur coat and another would spray her with perfume from a big atomizer. Very different from the life of the dear queen."

The queen kept enlarging her court. She organized parties by calling a famous actress she didn't know, introducing herself, mentioning *Vanity Fair,* then saying, "I'm giving a little party for Maurice Chevalier and he suggested I ask you." Then she would call Chevalier—whom she didn't know—and go through the same routine. It usually worked. Or she would call some important man to whom she was barely introduced at some party and tell him that somebody had sent *Vanity Fair* two complimentary tickets to a hit play and would he accompany her? He usually would. She then called her ticket broker and ordered two tickets. Her contacts expanded with her horizons.

"I remember being at a great big cocktail party once," said Henry Luce's sister, Beth. "I don't believe I'd even met her. But somebody said, 'Oh, you know, that's Clare Boothe.' And she was sitting on a huge kind of couch . . . red-velvet . . . it was more like a huge bed, almost—sort of an Arabic kind of thing. And she was in the middle, this queen, in a black dress with a full skirt, and lots of pearls. And there must've been four or five men all around her, just hanging on every word that she had to say. She was so beautiful and had this classic facial structure. Men were crazy about her . . . this was a year before I knew that she was going to have a very significant part in our lives."

As Clare's power and prestige grew, her relationship with Freeman changed. "The two of them squabble a lot," Helen reported to a friend. "Sometimes he gets so furious he rushes out to the elevator and calls her on the telephone there so his secretary won't hear him, but I can hear Mrs. B. yelling back at him. She treats him like a faithful old dog that gets on her nerves. He has a pudgy face, a snobbish voice, and a bald head on which he is trying desperately to raise a crop of fuzz. I have a feeling Mrs. B. has other fish to fry."

As was her habit, Clare dealt with Freeman—and many others who followed—in her writings.

In one of her later plays, her heroine talks of her series of affairs, and how bored she got with men who fell in love with her.

But Freeman was dogged. He knew he still held great sway as her mentor and intellectual guide. He sent a manuscript of Clare's collection of stories, entitled *Stuffed Shirts,* to noted critic H. L. Mencken for possible review. Mencken replied that he had taken a solemn oath not to review any more fiction "but maybe I can be induced to break it . . . it looks immensely interesting." When *Stuffed Shirts* was published, it became a social sensation. "I predict the fashionable game for the fall this year will be guessing the identity in Clare Boothe Brokaw's stories," observed a New York *Telegraph* columnist.

"Gracious, I didn't know there were so many piano-playing cads in New York," a society matron exclaimed. Clare had mentioned a piano player who "kissed and told," and five piano players had called to protest.

Clare's dreams of being celebrated as a successful author were smashed when she got her first accounting from her publisher. *Stuffed Shirts* sold only 2,600 copies, netting Clare $600. Clare ruefully announced that she would concentrate on writing plays "for cash and kudos."

Meanwhile, she put aside any pretense of fidelity to Freeman. Her name was romantically connected with a great many men from millionaire Jock Whitney to noted author John O'Hara. She claimed that David Rockefeller, Averell Harriman, and a long list of others wanted to marry her. In her private papers, Clare gleefully claimed that Strom Thurmond had goosed her.

One of Clare's favorite stories was the one about the time a concierge in Europe returned her passport, except that it was the passport of another hotel guest, a man Clare described as "incredibly handsome." She studied his passport thoroughly before returning it to the concierge. On the train the next day, Clare saw the man and managed to seat herself in the same compartment with him. In the course of the conversation, she volunteered to read his palm, then proceeded to tell him when he was born and where he had traveled. She never confessed how she knew and the man was fascinated and amazed. "This led to the most wonderful affair," Clare later confided to a friend.

Whatever sympathy, guilt, or contriteness Clare felt about Freeman, she successfully submerged it. He had been a vital stepping stone in her life. She had loved him in her fashion, and for a period of time, but now she had moved on. There were worlds to conquer beyond Donald Freeman. Conquering them called for a hard heart, sharp mind, and cool head. She had them all.

Now that she had put Freeman behind her, Clare was seen more often with Condé Nast. One newspaper even reported their romance as "one of the more interesting . . . of our town" and predicted that they would soon "march up the aisle." Clare called the story malicious and unfounded and worried that it put her in a false light with her colleagues, raising the charge of favoritism. Though Nast was in the process of getting another divorce, Clare had no interest in marrying Nast.

Her letters to him, though, were intimate and affectionate. When he went to France, she wrote that if he decided to pawn his cuff links and spend the rest of his life sipping liqueurs in some charming French bistro, that he should let her know and she would be on the next boat.

"Clare was Nast's showpiece," said his art director, M. F. Agha. "He liked to have her around when he was entertaining important people. She was the only one with the brains enough to talk with them. But she wouldn't play the social game. She was too satirical, too outspoken."

Clare was also seeking someone very special in her life, a sentiment she voiced in an interview, saying that it wasn't necessary to have a series of affairs to broaden one's experience—one affair would do.

Soon she would find a man she subconsciously had been waiting for.

10

WITH Hadden's death, Luce became "the spark plug as well as the transmission of the machine," and started remaking *Time* in his own image. Hadden's will had decreed that his stock be held by his heirs for forty-nine years, which would have prevented any Luce control. But Harry persuaded the Hadden family to sell him their stock. In subsequent years, Brit Hadden's distinct style disappeared, though his name remained on the masthead.

As *Time* blossomed, so did Harry and Lila.

Lila then was "very likable, very gay, very talkative." She presided over a posh new apartment in the Turtle Bay section of New York near the *Time* offices.

Lila maintained a full household staff, including uniformed footmen to serve meals. All this mattered much to Lila, but very little to Harry.

What *did* matter to Harry at this point in his life was his concept for a new magazine, a business monthly that would simplify, and illuminate finance the way *Time* had done for news. Before Hadden took ill, a friend had confronted him about Harry's idea for a business magazine. Brit had pounded the table and said, "If we do, it'll be over my dead body."

Luce didn't really understand business, but he knew it was important, and he agreed with former President Coolidge that, "The business of America is business." He felt that most people were more ignorant about business than he was, and felt that the great businessmen were the new supermen of civilization. He believed their lives represented a romantic adventure, a story of high drama and excitement. He wanted a magazine that made all this come alive. He saw it as a challenge, an untold story.

Luce selected Parker Lloyd-Smith, a calm, almost languid, young man with a Mona Lisa smile, to explore his notion of a business magazine. If Luce suggested an idea he didn't like, Lloyd-Smith might simply say, "Harry, it stinks." Luce could accept this from Parker without anger.

The tentative title of the new magazine was "Power," but Harry wasn't happy and asked Lila to jot down some other names. "I put four down; at the top was 'Fortune,'" she recalled. "And he read that, and said, 'That's it!'"

Privately, Harry expected only a limited audience, and repeated, "All businessmen are divided into two kinds: those who can read and do; those who cannot read and don't." Yet this did not dampen his enthusiasm. Harry hired Margaret Bourke-White as his first photographer, because he agreed with her that photographs could catch the power of the story as well as words could. Asked to describe the new magazine, Bourke-White said, "Oh, a sort of industrial *National Geographic.*"

Bourke-White had a distinct impression of Luce, "He was strikingly powerful in build with a large head over large shoulders. His words tumbled out with such haste and emphasis that I had the feeling he was thinking ten words for every one that managed to emerge. He began questioning me at once. Who was I and what was I? Why was I taking these industrial pictures? Was it just for fun? Or was it my profession? He went on talking in that abrupt and choppy manner, racing from one thought to the next, breaking off into short silences, then leaping again from point to point in a kind of verbal shorthand. He left such gaps that at first I had difficulty in following him. Then suddenly I became accustomed to his manner and it all came into focus. . . . [They] were planning to launch a new magazine of business and industry. Did I think this was a good idea, he asked, pausing for breath."

Luce showed the same eagerness when he accompanied Bourke-White on one of her stories. "On arriving at each new plant, he would hurry through, his leonine head thrown forward between his huge shoulders, his questions tumbling over one another. It seemed to me he was curiosity personified and magnified into a giant, as though he were being curious in advance for all his readers."

Bourke-White was particularly awed by Luce during a visit to a foundry. She had started to photograph a ladle conveying molten metal into a row of sand molds, when the mechanism holding the ladle slipped. The red-hot metal started splashing out all over the floor. "With gallantry I have never forgotten," she said, "Harry Luce dashed forward, grabbed my bulk camera and light stands out of the path of molten metal and swept all the equipment back to safety."

Fortune seemed a very poor idea all of a sudden when the stock market crashed in 1929. As some of his wealthy cronies plunged from windows, Luce grew nervous and tight with his money.

He wrote a memo to his staff cautioning them against extravagance, including extravagant ideas. He asked them not to make a long distance call if a telegram would work, not to leave the lights on when they were going home, not to send personal mail with company postage, not to scribble office notes on *Time* letterhead paper, and above all, "Don't waste time!"

But nothing, not even economic collapse of the world around him, would stop him from publishing *Fortune.* Volume I, Number 1, was born on February 1930. It weighed two pounds six ounces, and was described as being "fat as a flounder." Priced at a dollar, handsome with handsewn binding, *Fortune,* said Luce, was "designed to be the most beautiful magazine in America. It deals with the factors which control the fortunes of every man."

"Fortune," added a *Time* executive, "is half the size of the New York telephone book and almost twice as interesting."

That first issue featured pages of magnificent color photographs by Bourke-White, who found poetry in big hulking machines and the people who worked them. Luce had invented the "corporate profile," which wove excitement and drama into the story of a company. The first issue featured a profile of the Radio Corporation of America. There was also a family album on the Rothschilds, which Harry's sister Beth had researched while she was in Paris. She recalled that she had returned with a massive amount of material, "confused and bogged down." Then Harry asked questions "and the story suddenly took shape." Other articles dealt with how to live on $25,000 a year and a personality profile of Mr. Gamble of Procter and Gamble. Harry knew the Gamble son at Hotchkiss, and had stayed at their California home.

Most corporations came out looking good in a *Fortune* story, but there were enough exceptions to make many companies nervous. The first public relations man hired by General Motors was hired shortly after the launching of *Fortune.* Asked what his primary assignment was, he replied, "To keep *Fortune* away from GM."

To create stories with sufficient punch and depth, Luce argued that writers, not editors, should be the heart of the magazine.

"We don't give a damn how he gets the story done—whether it's written out of his head or after months of scholarship," said Luce about a talented *Fortune* writer. "It could be written sixteen different ways. All that we care is that it should be a knockout *Fortune* story."

"He didn't mind if *Fortune*'s stories were *endless,"* said Allen Grover, a Yalie, who became a *Fortune* editor. "When Harry realized I knew the difference between a stock and a bond, he shifted me to *Fortune,* and I was soon assistant managing editor. I think I was the only one there who knew anything about finance."

The hope was that *Fortune* would attract staff writers from *Time* and create a family atmosphere. Instead, the staffs were generally hostile. *Time* reporters regarded *Fortune* writers as pretentious interlopers, and *Fortune* writers regarded *Time* people as hacks who had sold out to the conservatives. "We read their weekly sheet sometimes with admiration, sometimes with fury and contempt."

What was remarkable about the early staff of *Fortune* was that the strongly Republican Luce had hired mostly ardent liberals, much to the left of him politically. He once told a friend that the reason most of his writers were not Republicans was because "I guess Republicans don't write so good."

Luce supplemented his liberals with a collection of poets in the belief that they would help give *Fortune* the prestige he so badly wanted. The best of the poets Harry hired was Archibald MacLeish, who had been ahead of him at Hotchkiss and Yale. MacLeish had done some part-time writing for *Time* in Paris. Luce now offered him a full-time job as a *Fortune* editor. When MacLeish replied that he knew nothing about business, Luce thundered: "That is exactly why I want you! There are men who can write poetry and there are men who can read balance sheets. The men who read balance sheets cannot write. It is easier to turn poets into business journalists than to turn bookkeepers into writers." His goal, Luce later explained, was to find "writers who could see beyond the balance sheets and describe the lights and shadows of factories and the men who ruled them."

Luce told MacLeish that he thought poetry involved perceptiveness of beauty and that MacLeish would soon see the beauty of business and industry. When MacLeish protested that he'd need time for his poetry, Harry had a ready solution. "I'll tell you what I'll do," he said. "You work for *Fortune* as long in any year as you need to pay your bills, and when you get your bills paid, you can go off and no questions will be asked and you won't be bothered."

Delighted with the arrangement, MacLeish was determined to disprove the cliched description of the poet. He worked hard, didn't drink too much, dressed neatly, shaved, and was friendly. He arrived at nine, produced clean copy with tinges of poetry, and went home every day at five.

Luce's editors admitted that he was a critical gadfly who kept them on their toes. He kept the staff "from getting soft and flabby . . . and his running comments kept us jacked up and taut . . ."

Another keen observer was Hubert Kay, an editor at *Time* and later at *Life*. "It was not so much that we were afraid of Harry (although we were a little) as that we busted our guts trying to keep pace with him and please him," he said. "We didn't love him in those days—he wouldn't permit it. He was too preoccupied, intense, supercharged, explosive, too driving and hard-driven. He was a generous, just, inspiring boss, but also a demanding one, a rigorous perfectionist with a prodigious mind, inexhaustible energy, and a total devotion to Time Inc. We viewed him with a mixture of awe, alarm, and hero-worship, almost an idolatry, and one of his rare words of praise was worth all the suffering."

Harry Luce was emerging with his own tart style. If an interviewer began pleasantly by saying, "I hope I'm not disturbing you," Luce might say, "Well, you are!"

He almost never complimented a hostess on a good dinner, a pretty dress, or a pleasant evening. He knew no amusing anecdotes. And, yet, when he entered a room, his presence was compelling. It was not the kind of aura that seemed to announce, "I am the king!" It was not in the least self-inflating. And, yet, it was there, tangible. It came from the absolute confidence of position. "Luce doesn't have to say anything . . . his power is felt and smelled," said *Life* staffer Dorothy Sterling.

"When Harry really disagreed with somebody, and didn't like the person, he was, oh, very polite. Harry never really got angry about anything," said his sister, Beth. "But to hear him *talk,* you'd think he was angry, because he was so violent about his ideas. You should hear him and my husband yell at each other," she continued. "You'd think that *they* were having a fight, but he never got *mad* at anybody. It was the *idea* he pursued. He had a passion for the truth. He was passionate about his patriotism, about his religion, and about China."

The television host and columnist William F. Buckley, who was thirty years behind Luce at Yale, said that the genius of Luce was that he was always three weeks ahead of people. "If he had been five weeks ahead, he'd have been avant-garde and that wouldn't work."

Understandably, guests seldom relaxed with Luce. His tendency was to dominate a conversation, control the subject. He usually approached social gatherings with a tight, coiled intensity. If a guest made a simple statement, Luce might snap, "Who told you that? What makes you so sure it's true?" At a formal dinner for twelve, Luce ignored the casual conversation, raised his gruff voice loudly enough to drown all the table talk, and, with his typical intensity, made a rapid-fire demand: "How many marriages and divorces at this table?" He ignored a woman's giggle and continued, "We've been reading about the divorce statistics in the U.S. and here we are, a pretty good sample of the U.S. best. So how many?" When somebody reluctantly volunteered that she had been divorced once and married twice, Luce said, "Good. Let's go around the table."

"The table sprung alive," recalled hostess Laura Hobson. "It was Harry Luce, the serious guest who had done it."

* * *

While *Fortune* was busy winning an audience, the Luce empire now had begun growing in different directions. *Time* was branching into radio with *The March of Time,* a program in which a small cast of actors reenacted and dramatized the news of the week.

National reaction to the first network radio show in February 1931 was mixed. Some felt it was too sensational, too much editorializing of the news. "Certain public characters are sneered at, and others made ridiculous. The nifty purpose of giving us world news has deteriorated into an apparently young editor's opinion of that news. The public may be dumb, but it is not half so dumb as a lot of publishers think it is," Rob Wagner commented on the radio.

But Luce was confident that *The March of Time* would eventually find a large audience, and once again he was right. He left the details of the show to others and focused on creating the right leadership at his magazines. He was shocked and saddened during the summer of 1931 when Parker Lloyd-Smith, then twenty-nine, climbed to the top of his fifteen-floor apartment building and plunged off the roof in a perfect swan dive.

Luce swiftly replaced him with Ralph McAllister Ingersoll, who had been several classes behind Harry at Hotchkiss and Yale. Ingersoll came from a socially prominent family, who had originally organized Manhattan's so-called Four Hundred.

Ingersoll was a biting, witty man, who had worked as a mining engineer in Mexico and wrote a book about it before editing *The New Yorker.* He was tall, almost lordly, except that he stooped slightly. He had "as much hair under his nose as on his head, sad eyes, full lips," Wolcott Gibbs would later write about Ingersoll in *The New Yorker.* Staff people regarded him as a hypochondriac, "twelve yards of quivering mucous membrane." His desk was littered with pills and Kleenex and included a glass ant colony, which he often studied. Ingersoll loved big game fishing and fast driving and seldom missed a Yale football game. Few considered him endearing, but they respected his editorial talent, judgment, and ideas. He radiated vitality and nervous energy, describing himself as "a cocky bastard." Many women found him fascinating. Most of all, he and Luce liked each other.

At *Time,* Luce's general was managing editor John Martin, Brit Hadden's cousin. Martin had lost an arm when his brother accidentally shot him. Whether this contributed to his explosive temper, no one quite knew. Staffers knew to keep a distance from Martin when he was in a dark mood. It was said that he could edit the magazine lying down, and often did. A strong, able editor, Martin was determined to maintain Hadden's legacy. He believed in what had become known as *Time* style, a supercilious, convoluted way of saying things. Martin continued that style to the point that the magazine sometimes seemed a burlesque of itself. Even Luce was troubled. "We went too far," he later said. "The original reason for jolting the story off the page was to put it into the reader's head. But you can destroy the importance of a story by overemphasizing physical traits. It may be more important to show what's inside a man's head than the size of his nose."

To Luce, Martin remained the last vestige of Hadden on *Time.* In November 1933, he dispatched Martin to become editor of a new Time Inc. venture, *Architectural Forum.* Luce had bought the magazine because he believed that "to influence architecture is to influence life." (Luce would eventually suspend publication years later; he learned that he did better creating magazines than buying them.)

As a replacement for Martin, Luce selected a southerner, John Shaw Billings, a Harvard man of encyclopedic knowledge who looked to Luce "as a critical gadfly to keep me and the staff from getting soft and flabby." As a young man, Billings had wandered around New England, slept in barns and talked to farmers with a copy of Vachel Lindsay's poems in his pocket. In World War I he had been an ambulance driver in France, and an aviation cadet. Billings was also socially registered, solemn, and snobbish, and harbored racial and religious prejudices. He had a bitter wife and no children. He would love Luce and hate him, and, most of all, envy him.

Once he had placed an editor in a position of authority, Luce did little to coddle him. He had no time for social niceties and liked to gather his editors for small working lunches. Or, if he summoned them to his office, they could tell by his curtness that the session was to be intense and earnest. Luce simply assumed that those who worked for him would do a good job, and he parceled out scant praise.

In May 1932, Luce felt that his magazines were running smoothly and were thriving. He felt comfortable enough to leave on a planned three-month trip around the world. His companion was his sister Emmavail's husband, Leslie Severinghaus, then head of the English department at the Haverford School in Pennsylvania.

Severinghaus was a big, friendly fellow who was highly cultured and fairly fluent in Chinese. He was the perfect companion for Luce.

Lila arranged to meet Harry at the end of his journey in Paris. It was strange that he would make such a long trip without her, Hank, and a new baby, Peter Paul, but it was too long and hectic a trip for the whole family. Besides, perhaps Harry felt an urge for some freedom. The pace of his life had been so intense that he surely felt a need to stretch out on his own. His wife, who had been so close and so loving and so loyal, deserved the trip, and he may have felt some guilt about that. But he was moving forward too fast to be too introspective—or guilty.

Stopping in Seattle, en route to Vancouver, Luce bought a new hat on the condition that they mail the old one back to New York. Luce fired off a sharp note to the *Time* offices, saying that every time he traveled out of New York, he always ran into a great story that should have been in *Time*. He complained that *Time* didn't seem to care about news west of the Hudson.

They sailed for Japan on the *Empress of Canada*. In his detailed diary, Severinghaus reported how Luce insisted upon extensive sightseeing wherever they went. In Japan, they visited everything from the Gold Pavilion to the red-light district in Yoshiwara. "We entered several houses and looked at the pictures of the various prostitutes, many of them really good-looking. The women themselves poked their hands through the curtains, called to us, laughed and jabbered," he wrote. Later, they went to a dance hall and a beer parlor where, said Severinghaus, there was "some scratchy dance music and a great deal of lap-sitting and cuddling quite openly." And, finally the two men visited a geisha house.

Luce's initial reaction to China was intense. China had changed, and so had he. But, once inside the old compound at Weihsien, recalled Severinghaus, "Harry could not talk fast enough . . . Harry was like a ten-year-old, scrambling over the walls and into the cemetery where he had played so many games with his friends." The old college buildings were still there, and so was his Latin teacher and some of his parents' friends, like white-haired Mrs. Mateer. They spent five days in the mission compound. Harry showed his brother-in-law through their old home, even pointing out the donkey stall and the chicken coop. Severinghaus spent much of the night listening to the rush of Luce's memories.

"It was moving to watch Harry walking along the shaded paths. I could only imagine the feelings coursing through his mind and heart," said Severinghaus. At Chefoo, he added, "Harry's pleasure was boundless." The students asked endless questions and Luce proudly pointed out his name on the honor roll of 1910.

Luce and Severinghaus spent five weeks in China, dined with bankers, argued with Communists, philosophized with philosophers, "always the center of active conversation," noted Severinghaus. "I am continually astounded at this grasp of facts in so many fields." He was also amazed that, when they climbed to the summit of 3,500-foot Lao Ting, Harry "hopped from boulders like a mountain goat."

In Shanghai, his crowded itinerary included a visit to La Dow's, a famous cabaret where lovely Russian girls were willing to dance with anyone for a fee.

Harry danced several times with a stunning Russian girl in a black evening gown. Severinghaus went back to the hotel at two AM. "Harry was still talking to the young lady when I left," he noted. Years later, lunching with an interviewer, Luce waxed nostalgic and said, "Screwing in Shanghai is the best in the world." Few ever heard Harry use language like that.

Luce sent streams of notes back to *Time,* including the thought that they might give Chiang Kai-shek the nickname of "iguana" because of the Chinese belief that Chiang was the reincarnation of a great sea beast. *Time* had featured Chiang on several covers ever since he had broken with the Russians, fought the Communists, and turned Methodist. Luce now saw Chiang as the new Christian warrior who would return China to the world he knew.

Soviet Russia was next on their itinerary. The trip started badly and grew worse. Luce and Severinghaus took the Trans-Siberian Railway, a six-day trip on a wood-burning train that traveled twenty-five miles an hour and took on assorted passengers who were often barefoot and unwashed. Harry described an unexpected Russian roommate as smelling like "the odor of rotten eggs in a damp cellar." Harry was not altogether unhappy when he got a bad cold. In Moscow, the pair found that the hotel service was slow, the plumbing unpredictable, and the people sloppy and boorish. Luce's dislike of Soviet Russia was immediate and violent. He felt that the recent *Fortune* story on the Soviets omitted the stink and sourness of the country. He found it a disgusting place.

This only reinforced Luce's feelings about the Soviet Union. He could not forgive the Bolshevik long-standing campaign of bitterness against God. He saw the state's inequities as infamous. His magazine frequently highlighted Russian atrocities. Luce considered the attempts of American capitalists to seek Soviet trade so traitorous that he listed the names of specific American companies on the cover of a *Time* issue—even though many of the companies were advertisers. Luce was in the forefront of those who wanted an international capitalist economic boycott of Soviet Russia. His Russian trip only intensified his contempt.

The trip ended with a family reunion in Paris. Lila even brought over a maid, chauffeur, and the family Chrysler. She wrote home that Harry wasn't wasting any time in Paris, that he was already playing in a tennis tournament. In these years, Lila seemed to get less and less of his time.

While Luce was away on tour, the Democrats had nominated Franklin D. Roosevelt as their presidential candidate. Luce, though he voted for Hoover, was not unhappy at Roosevelt's victory and put F.D.R on *Time*'s cover as Man of the Year. Harry's friend Archibald MacLeish arranged for Harry to meet the new president at the White House.

The two shared a room at the Carleton, waiting for word from F.D.R.'s secretary Missy Le Hand as to when the president would see them. "I thought Harry would go crazy, pacing the floor," said MacLeish. Then, when the president greeted them, F.D.R. turned on the charm, "so powerfully that he seemed to use up all the oxygen in the room . . ."

"My God!" Luce said afterward. "What a man! What a man!" He amplified that, saying that the press hadn't praised F.D.R. enough for his dynamic personality and his charm.

A few months later, *Time* celebrated its tenth anniversary; the magazine now boasted one million readers. Luce was feeling both proud and magnanimous. He decided the time had come to give not only to his magazines, but to his family. He knew that Lila loved the world of the seventeenth century and that what she wanted most was a Norman castle. One day, a real estate agent told him that an estate on fifty acres had come up for sale in New Jersey.

"So Harry rushed out," remembered Lila, "and he came back and said, 'It looks all right to me.' So we bought it."

This would be their home until they built their stone castle. There was also a working farm on the property, with several barns and eighty cows. While Harry never liked working on a farm, he enjoyed the feeling of a farm—the space and smell of a fresh-cut crop. He wanted his two sons to share it.

For Lila, this was a wonderful time. She had spent many of the previous years confined by a succession of pregnancies. Between Henry and Peter Paul, another son, Christopher, had died at birth. Then, after the birth of Peter, Lila suffered six miscarriages in the seventh month. "Harry and I were Rh-negative," she explained.

Building her dream house was a much needed diversion for Lila. As the house took shape, Lila and Harry decided it was time to find the right furniture to fit into the enormous rooms. So, in 1934, Harry took Lila and their son Henry to England to buy antiques. When they returned, Manfred Gottfried, a *Time* editor who would soon become managing editor, was a weekend guest at their New Jersey home. He noticed some friction between the Luces. When some prominent person called from a country club where the Luces had been expected to attend a lunch, noted Gottfried, Lila returned to the table and reported this to Harry with some embarrassment. She had forgotten all about the lunch. This was the third time she had done something like this with this same friend and his wife. "Harry was furious," Gottfried recalled.

Another time, Lila greeted some arriving guests at the door in her nightgown because she had forgotten they were coming. Once, Lila also gave some friends their opera tickets when the Luces couldn't go—only the tickets turned out to be singles for two different nights. "It broke your heart to laugh at her," said Ralph Ingersoll, "because she was so lovable and pretty and sweet."

Harry had some of these same problems of forgetfulness himself, but he found it hard to tolerate them in others—especially in his wife. Yet, it was Lila who drove her convertible to New York to pick up Harry in the early morning hours after the magazine went to press—just as she had done in Cleveland. No wife could have been more concerned or protective or more loving of her husband. Still, there were those friends who felt a growing distance between Harry and Lila. Harry was so absorbed with his work that it dominated everything they did. If Harry was expanding his horizons, some felt Lila was not. If there was a change in his feelings for Lila, a change in their relationship, she did not sense it then. Perhaps, Harry didn't either.

11

IN the course of his lifetime, Bernard Mannes Baruch would become an advisor to seven presidents and a global statesman. A national monument, he even looked like one. Baruch was six-foot-four and built like a heavyweight. In Hebrew, Baruch means "blessed," which had indeed been his path upward from a New York tenement.

"I grew up a poor boy," Baruch told the writer John Hersey. "When we first moved to New York, we lived in the attic of a boarding house . . . I went to City College." He then told the story of how, as a boy, his mother took him to an aged phrenologist who felt his head. "He wants to be a doctor," said Mrs. Baruch. "He'll be a pretty good doctor," said the phrenologist, "but he'd be a better lawyer." He felt Baruch's head again. "Get him into finance and business if you can." Baruch's mother never rested until she did so.

Young Bernie discovered Wall Street when he delivered some papers to financier J. P. Morgan. He was so impressed with the scene that he promptly quit his three-dollars-a-week job with a glassware company and never looked back. "Some men can make funny faces," he said, "others can make fools of themselves, others can make money. How do you define a talent?"

Before he was thirty, Baruch was one of the richest men in the country, and one of the most powerful.

Asked once how many millions he had, Baruch replied, "Right up to the day they put the coffin lid over me, I'll always have a dollar more than I need."

Early on, Baruch's wealth exposed him to government investigations. "The first time I was ever investigated in January 1917, these Congressmen asked me my occupation, and I guess they expected me to say I was a banker, or something dignified like that. I sat up straight and said I was a speculator. I went on to tell them I made my money in perfectly legal ways, just by being faster than the next fellow." The word "speculator," he noted, came from the Latin "speculari," "to observe."

Baruch was one of those surprising men who quit fortune-making to dedicate the rest of his life to public service. During World War I, President Woodrow Wilson put him in charge of the vital War Industries Board, and called him "Dr. Facts." He soon acquired a reputation as a sage and an oracle, and held court sitting on a park bench in the center of Lafayette Park under a chestnut tree, facing the White House. Photographs soon appeared of Baruch on his bench meeting politicians who came seeking his advice. Dorothy Parker once said that the two things she never understood were the theory of the zipper and the precise function of Bernard Baruch.

Baruch himself could not always explain his public appeal other than the fact that, "people believe in me. They think I'm honest and they think I'm always right. That's the greatest satisfaction I've had in life—being right. Nothing makes me madder than something that isn't fair. You've got to have a sense of justice and fair play if you want to succeed. You've got to be ready for anything and fearful of nothing. I believe I can say I'm afraid of nothing. I used to be a fighter in the ring, and I wasn't afraid of taking a beating."

At a dinner party at the Colony Restaurant in New York, in the early nineteen thirties, Bernard Baruch met Clare Boothe. Immediately, they were engrossed in conversation. Clare was entranced and later described Baruch as "a king, or some gangster chieftain, always surrounded by an impressive entourage whose duty it was to protect and promote the Baruch cause of the moment."

Clare fell for Baruch hard. "They soon became lovers," said the highly respected *Life* writer Robert Coughlan, who wrote extensively about Baruch.

A mutual friend of both Clare and Bernie told how Baruch had taken her on a tour of his Long Island home and pointed to a room, saying, "And this is Clare's bedroom." That same woman discovered that there was a sales person at Tiffany specifically assigned to serve Baruch whenever he ordered jewelry for his various women. This salesperson confided that Baruch sent a lot of jewelry to Clare, who once returned a watch to Tiffany "by special messenger," because she was wearing it when she took a bath and wanted it checked: It was going perfectly, but she wanted to make certain that science had conquered nature.

"Women should get the idea out of their heads very quickly, and very early, that the real love of a fine man is anything they are entitled to as a birthright," Clare had said. "They are not entitled to it at all. If it happens, it is a miracle." Yet, for Clare, Baruch was a miracle, one of the great influences on her life.

Her longtime friend, Wilfrid Sheed, confirmed this. "Clare was passionate about Baruch. You could tell by the intensity with which she talked about him."

Baruch was similarly entranced. "I remember little wispy curls on her forehead. But under that was a matter-of-fact, thoughtful person," he said. "Character, work, courage. When courage was given out, she was sitting in the front bench. Clare has the spirit that only generals have, and it shines in her eyes. She reacts automatically against injustice, against anything that is wrong; and she is very soignée, wearing the latest things. Yet there is nothing feminine about her looks. Men become afraid of her because of her mind, but she has a very tender heart and deep sentiment. She has never forgotten her struggles, or the people who were with her then."

For Clare, the attraction was not only his reputation, but his personality. He was charming, courtly, and impressive.

The fact that Baruch was sixty-one when they met and more than twice her age, mattered little to Clare. She had already married a man old enough to be her father. But unlike Brokaw, Baruch was vital and vibrant and Clare, after all, had always preferred the mature man and the mature mind—not to mention power.

A mutual friend quickly observed that Baruch wanted to marry Clare. The major difficulty was that his wife was mentally ill and Baruch would not leave her. If his wife died, Clare "would have married him without hesitating a second," commented her *Vanity Fair* friend Helen Brown.

But the pair seemed content being lovers. Baruch often swept the willing Clare away to his great estate, Hobcaw, near Georgetown, South Carolina. On that huge plantation, it was a life of walking, sitting around the fire, riding, and shooting. "I taught her to shoot," Baruch said later. "She went about it with concentration and determination, as she does everything else, thoroughly. She became a first-class shot."

Clare later remarked that Baruch, with a gun at his shoulder, or wearing that Inverness cape of his, had all the dignity and nobility of a Scottish chieftain and that she "was surely in love with him."

Her friend always felt that Baruch touched something extraordinary in Clare. "She once pulled out some pictures of him," reminisced Shirley Clurman, an intimate of Clare's later years. "I hadn't realized he was as gorgeous as all that. But you could see that she was madly in love with him. He really was the great love of her life."

In an article Clare wrote on "The Great Garbo" for *Vanity Fair* in 1932, she seemed almost to be writing about her own relationship with Baruch:

"History has never reserved a place for a beautiful woman who did not love, or who was not loved by at least one interesting, powerful, or brilliant man. Love, magnificently, a little recklessly, and certainly publicly—loves of the great can no more be hidden than the burning of the topless towers of Ilium."

For his part, Baruch seemed to put Clare first among his women. Constantly traveling, he always brought back gifts for his women friends, and Clare always had first pick. "Poor little rich kid," Baruch commented. "It's hard to refuse her anything." His favorite gifts were antique gold snuff boxes, "and Clare practically cornered the market," Helen Brown reported. "She had about two dozen." Helen, who had had her own affair with Baruch years earlier, possessed her own collection of snuff boxes.

Baruch began introducing Clare to the leading lights in the Democratic Party. She attended the 1932 Democratic National Convention in Chicago, where Franklin D. Roosevelt, the Governor of New York, crippled by polio since childhood, received the nomination. Clare described the convention as "a great eye-opener—a significant event in my life."

By this point in her career, Clare had recognized the power of politics. Even before Baruch steered her through Democratic pathways, she had been indoctrinated by Arthur Krock, the nationally known columnist for *The New York Times*. As with most men in Clare's life, Krock could not keep his interest strictly friendly or educational. The tough newspaper man found himself tenderly comparing Clare's curly, golden hair to a baby's and even described her gown with its floating ruffles of chiffon. He gushed about her slender figure and her intelligence.

Clare did nothing to discourage Krock's infatuation, for he was an excellent political guide. Through Krock, and then through Baruch, she defined her political sensibilities to the point that she even envisioned founding a new party. The "New National Party" endorsed a program similar to Roosevelt's, but called for a stronger President. "WANTED, A DICTATOR!" Clare wrote in *Vanity Fair,* and she was serious.

However, with Roosevelt's nomination, there were no funds available for Clare's party, and she wisely abandoned it. From that point on, she declared herself a liberal, politically and philosophically.

To those who observed Clare during this period, her liberalism extended to many facets of her life. Her ideas about men and relationships indeed seemed far more liberal than the times. She loved Baruch deeply, but was pragmatic enough to know that he had other women and that he could never commit himself to her. She then proceeded to fill her life with an admiring coterie of other men, most of whom were useful to her in one way or another.

Men gravitated to Clare almost automatically. Up to the age of forty, she thought something was wrong if a man didn't make a pass at her. She had watched her mother use men for what she could get out of them, maneuver them skillfully without conflict, and somehow keep them all—except her husband. Clare did the same. Baruch held a special part of her heart, as did Freeman. Freeman had helped her develop her talent, served as a literary springboard and even as a father-mother figure. The other men, until then, were all short-term affairs, most of them serving a specific purpose or need.

She managed to make each man feel wanted without really giving of herself. She could never really give to anyone but Baruch—and her first lover, Major Simpson. But Clare seemed to sense what each man most wanted and transformed herself briefly to fulfill each man's desire. She had become a shrewd judge of men—and a good actress. Each of her lovers thought he knew a different Clare. And, of course, they were jealous of each other. Yet, she was generally able to juggle many men in her life, largely because these lovers were also terribly busy and mostly married. They were the college education she never had, and they enriched her beyond her imagination. They enlarged her personality, increased her sophistication, heightened her self-confidence. They gave her everything but roots.

This manipulation of men was exciting, even though it didn't really satisfy her or make her happy. In her own way, perhaps, Clare was getting back at Julian Simpson, who had jilted her. Now *she* would do the jilting. Another compensation was that she was seldom lonely. One of the snide circulating remarks about Clare was, "I didn't sleep with her. Not everyone can say that."

Clare rarely discarded her men. They all seemed willing to wait in the wings, willing to return at the crook of her finger.

One man who seemed to enjoy most favored status was Mark Sullivan. Sullivan was one of those forceful men who automatically appealed to Clare. He described himself to her as a cheerful Irishman and not the grim, grouchy presence that emerged in his nationally known, highly respected conservative political column.

Clare knew about Sullivan's easy access to the White House and all government circles. She soon discovered that he was a physically passionate man and a romantic. Among Clare's personal papers are love letters from Sullivan that are intense and remarkable.

Sullivan was a good friend of Baruch and, like Baruch, much older than Clare. But he had none of Baruch's power or money or physical presence. Sullivan frankly told Clare that when he first met her, he thought her forlorn, frustrated, and slightly pathetic; and he wanted to be kind to her. He was also a married man and introduced Clare to his wife and children.

The relationship progressed, ironically, at Hobcaw, Baruch's plantation where Clare could come whenever she wanted. She took Sullivan walking along the river bank at sunset, to a small church, and riding through the woods.

That summer, of 1932, Clare leased small, deserted Crotch Island, six miles off the coast of Maine, available only by launch or seaplane, with no telephones. She planned to write another book there and invited Sullivan to join her for as long as he wanted. He later told her of a friend of his, who happened to be on a seaplane and saw him getting off on what looked like a deserted island to be welcomed by a wild beautiful woman, in tight shorts, who pulled him into the woods. When Sullivan left her six days later, Clare wrote him that she was instantly lonely and wanted him back, that he had inspired her enough for a lifetime, that his charm, dignity, and sweetness were unparalleled. She later described their time together there as savage and free, and she declared that nothing would ever be as perfect as that.

Sullivan told Clare more about politics than she could ever imagine, brought her books to read, introduced her to the most important people, and sent her research for various articles. He also volunteered to write captions for political pictures and proofread political articles for *Vanity Fair.* Sullivan was happy to do all those things. He also worried when he saw her having two cups of coffee before dinner, another cup after, and two brandies. He told her she was much too fragile for that, and that there must be something wrong if she needed so many stimulants.

While Clare was on her island, Donald Freeman went to Europe to sort out his feelings for Clare. Earlier, he had written that he couldn't understand why she thought he wanted to eat her alive, that he knew his defects, knew that she had always put him in competition with richer, more successful, handsomer men, and that Clare never had accepted him in her heart. He described himself as being in a state of nervous agitation so that he often seemed almost hysterical. He felt she wore an iron mask, and he could not reach her. But, finally he did say that her love had enriched him. "You have done far more for me than I could ever do for you."

Clare sent him a long letter saying she wanted their relationship to evolve from love to friendship. Their three years together had been memorable and tender, but that was over now. She had moved into a political world in which he had no interest. What she did not say was that she had learned much of what he had to teach her, and there were now other men, many others, who had much more to teach her.

Back in New York on the night of October 2, 1932, Donald Freeman crashed his roadster into a dividing post on the Bronx River Parkway and died without regaining consciousness. "I knew him very well," said Jean Dalrymple, a theatrical producer who would years later become intimate with Harry Luce. "He was madly in love with her. She led him on and used him. He taught her everything. He made her career at Condé Nast. Then she just dismissed him. He couldn't take it. He drove head first into that dividing post."

Indeed, the consensus among Freeman's friends was that it was suicide. He had been supporting a mother and two orphan children in Vienna, and he had a surviving sister. Yet he still named Clare in his will.

Clare was shocked but not shattered. There had been a transition period of many months in which their relation had eased and cooled. Their three years together had been a time of true affection and tenderness. Yet the quality of her love was always in considerable question.

Soon after Freeman's death, she inherited his job, his office, and his secretary. She would always talk warmly about Freeman as her great good friend and "severest critic," and she never minimized his importance in her life. But she never described the depth of their relationship.

As *Vanity Fair*'s managing editor, Clare ruled over a celebrated intellectual circle. She described her job as one of stage manager and scene shifter and claimed to be the anonymous power behind the throne, though anonymity was never Clare's forte in life. Condé Nast brought her a corsage of roses which he said should be pinned on *him* for having the good fortune to have a managing editor with such charm, beauty, and intelligence.

It was all very heady. Clare had moved into a new orbit and it was exactly what she had wanted. *Vanity Fair* was a literary stage of quality and distinction, and she was now in charge of that stage. The New York literary world not only accepted her, but catered to her. She was welcomed everywhere, wanted everywhere.

She had met celebrities all her life and was never awed by them. Yet, she had envied so many of them, especially the talented ones, who won all the literary prizes. Now they were all knocking at her door, inviting her to lunch, dinner, drinks, waiting for her to say yes or no. One moment, the Eugene O'Neills were inviting Clare to dinner and the next she herself was giving a little soirée for her literary hero, Somerset Maugham—remembering well the long handwritten letters of literary advice he had sent her when she was a teenager.

Clare met many of the literary figures she had long admired. Walter Lippmann was a contributor to *Vanity Fair,* as was Ernest Hemingway; Nobel Prize winner Sinclair Lewis and a parade of others presented manuscripts to Clare. When she turned down an article by Lewis, he wrote to her that female editors were simply horn-rimmed battle axes.

Clare had no problem calling on friends for help. She asked George Gershwin to find a critic who wrote on modern music with authority and a bit of humor. She asked Mark Sullivan to send her some research for an article on women in politics. Clare's feeling was that a woman was Republican or Democrat first and a woman second, that she voted just as intelligently as men—

which she said wasn't saying much—that in fifty years there would be as many outstanding women in politics as men.

Since she had no peer models, Clare really seemed to be reinventing herself. Politics had always been an excitement for her, perhaps because it required her to use her intellectual capabilities while appealing to her theatrical sense. Through politics, she met fascinating people, some of whom served causes, as well as themselves. Clare made politics a part of her magazine.

One of those Clare brought into her magazine and into her life, was Buckminster Fuller. "Bucky," as he was known to Clare, was an intellectual, adventurer, and the inventor of the geodesic dome. A small, wiry, balding man, he was also on the list of Clare's warmest admirers. She had written about him in *Vanity Fair* and would later say of him, "I helped him get started on his career. He invented the Dymaxion dome in my living room." He once escorted Clare to a Picasso show in his newly invented Dymaxion car—black and shiny and shaped like a gigantic teardrop.

Clare's efforts to bring new voices into *Vanity Fair* angered Condé Nast. Nast felt that Clare wanted complete editorial command and the authority to make final decisions—and he refused to surrender this responsibility. He felt that when he made any decision Clare didn't like, she responded with overbearing stubbornness. He was willing to discuss his decisions, but not abrogate them. And when he made final decisions, he expected them to be cheerfully accepted. Once he wired her in Chicago, THIS IS NOT A REQUEST. THIS IS A COMMAND.

Clare quickly apologized. She insisted she had never consciously contradicted his final authority and blamed her reaction on her misplaced zeal. She was soon back in groove. The magazine's editorial focus again became a "what the well-dressed man should think." Yet, Clare managed to create a "Who's Zoo" feature, showing prominent people and the animals they resembled, accompanied by a suitable limerick. She complained that there were too many sacred cows and struggled to expose them. Clare was one of the first editors to spoof *Time* style. She printed a fabricated, protesting letter to *Time* from a woman noting that the magazine had called her cross-eyed and pigeon-toed but had neglected to add that one of her legs was shorter than the other.

For all her fresh self-assurance as an editor, she was still sorting herself out as a person. She found it difficult to cope with the members of the Algonquin Round Table which at that time included Dorothy Parker, Robert Benchley, Harpo Marx, and Alexander Woollcott. Clare found the lunches there "too competitive. You couldn't say, 'Pass the salt,' without somebody trying to turn it into a pun or trying to top it," she complained.

In 1931, Nast asked Clare to suggest a new magazine idea. Clare and her art staff proposed a prospectus for a large-format magazine with a heavy emphasis on photographs. "I wrote a long memo called 'On Turning *Vanity Fair* into a Picture Magazine Called LIFE,' " recalled Clare. Strong on celebrity, with minimal satire and streamlined, the magazine would be "a sort of *Vanity Fair* for the masses."

In her papers there is even a letter indicating she contracted for some articles for the magazine. She suggested Nast buy the title "Life" from a defunct magazine. Nast instead decided to merge *Vanity Fair* with *Vogue* and make it a weekly as Clare kept fighting to revive and refinance the magazine. Baruch had already invested heavily in it. She joined Bernie in London, and he introduced her to Winston Churchill who he felt might be a possible literary contributor. Churchill was charmed enough to ask Baruch to join him for the weekend "and invite that pretty Mrs. Brokaw."

Although the weekend did not convince Churchill to join Clare's list of contributing writers, he did make a romantic contribution to her life. Churchill tried to serve as a matchmaker between Clare and his son Randolph. Randolph was going through a tough time with drinking and divorce. Moreover, he was struggling to create a separate identity. "It is very difficult," Randolph said, "for a sapling to grow up in the shadow of a giant oak."

Churchill, whose own mother, Jennie Jerome, had been an American from Brooklyn, felt that an American woman might revitalize his son.

For an intense romantic time, Clare and Randolph conducted a passionate affair, but Clare would not regard this as a serious match. She had paid her dues with one alcoholic, and didn't want another. Besides, she didn't want to marry the *son* of a great man—she wanted to marry a great man. On the day Randolph died nearly four decades later, there was a photograph in his bedroom of Clare, signed, "To the boy wonder from the girl vamp."

"I've never known a man who could resist her spell, once she set her mind to it and had him face-to-face," said Helen Brown. "One after another, she knocked them off like sitting ducks. Even those who, before meeting her, were critical and scornful—John O'Hara, John Mason Brown, to name two I knew personally—succumbed." Helen told of going with Clare on a double date with two young men. Clare told her, "Don't bother to dress." Then she showed up "in a long, white satin evening dress, cut low in front and blazing with diamonds—bracelets galore, necklace, earrings, brooch, rings—an altogether breathtaking vision." Over dinner in a speakeasy called Moriarty's, Helen's date was soon smitten. "Clare was covering the young man steadily with her beautiful deep eyes," said Helen. "I might just as well have been one of the waiters. It was over coffee that she gave him the coup de grace. 'Let me read your palm,' she said, taking his hand, gently running her fingers over it, murmuring softly, and finally when he was in a state fast approaching levitation, pressing his palm for a brief moment against the bare, pearly skin above where her dress began. He was a gone goose. In our taxi afterward, he was still mesmerized. 'She's so feminine, I never dreamed she'd be so feminine.' "

"Feminine as a meat-ax," novelist Irwin Shaw later commented. But Shaw, too, was captivated. He arrived at the Norse Grill at the Waldorf to meet Clare and found her reading a copy of his play *Bury the Dead* and dressed simply in a tailored dark dress without jewelry. She asked him to autograph her book and her manner was so friendly and respectful that twenty-four-year-old Shaw had to admit, "She's quite a girl." Later the two became lovers.

There seemed to be no end to the stream of men in Clare's life. Partly, she simply didn't like being alone at night. She wanted company, the company of men. Clare wanted to be adored and complimented and stimulated. Some men discovered, unhappily, that Clare often preferred conversation to caresses. The lieutenant governor of New York, Charles Poletti, discovered this but persisted. When he tried to call her at a hotel one night, he was told by the operator that the only calls she answered automatically were transatlantic or from wrestler Strangler Lewis. At the time, Clare seemed enamored of wrestlers and also romanced World Champion Jim Londos.

Still, she seemed more interested in the conquest than the affair. "I've known men who have slept with Clare, and who said she was just like a dead fish. She just laid there and didn't seem to enjoy it at all," said a woman who later competed for her husband. Raymond Bret-Koch, a French artist who dated Clare several times, told her friend Helen, "It's a beautiful facade, well-constructed, but without central heating . . . she's not *real.*"

To the contrary, when Clare wanted something, she was very real and often quite calculating. She knew exactly how to court her ex-husband's lawyer when there were legal problems about her daughter. She sat humbly at his feet listening to his various opinions and asked him to join her for a swim at the beach and some dinner. And when she decided that Donald Freeman had been right on her need to write another book, she zeroed in on the probable publisher, Thayer Hobson, husband of her dear friend Laura. In a short time, Thayer was "mad about her," and their affair began. She invited him to share a weekend with her at her Crotch Island hideaway. Thayer said such a visit was impractical because it meant two days and two nights driving and all they would have would be a few hours. Besides, he told her, it would be difficult explaining this to a wife who was intuitive about such things. No, they would find ways and means and time to meet often in New York because he adored her, wanted her badly, and besides they could talk about her book which he would publish. It bothered him that she was alone on that island, but then he added that she probably wouldn't be by herself for long. Clare did go off to the island, but found time for Hobson in New York, seemingly oblivious to the fact that she was betraying one of her closest friends.

Indeed, Clare always put her own interests first. Jeanne Winham, Clare's co-worker at *Vanity Fair,* described her as "a female who had male ideas." When Clare and Dorothy Parker were at a formal affair, both were escorted to the front door to enter the dining room first. Clare stepped aside, graciously commenting, "age before beauty, dear Dolly." At which dear Dolly swept by with "and pearls before swine, dear Clare." Parker also said, "Clare would be nice to her inferiors—if she could find any."

Clare's hectic social life, the many pressures of her job, and the energy required to juggle so many men left little time for anything or anyone else. Clare's only child got minimal attention. In fact, Clare rarely mentioned Ann and kept her far from the public. Some said this was because the presence of a young daughter interfered with Clare's sophisticated image. Others insisted that Clare wanted her daughter to have a more normal life, outside intrusive publicity that surrounded Clare.

Entitled to possession of daughter Ann for six months a year, she sent her away for some of that time to a camp near Lake Placid, New York. Clare was pleased because Ann seemed to be completely happy with children her age, without too many rules. Clare soon had some of her own rules, warning her daughter to take care of her cold, not to fall off her horse, and not to wear her elaborate fairy dress costume because the other children might think she was putting on airs. Instead, Clare sent her masquerade costumes of a pirate and a little Dutch maid. She also notified her that she had arranged for two piano lessons a week when she returned and that both cats were in the veterinary hospital with the flu. Superficially, at least, she tried to be motherly. Yet Clare once told a friend that Ann complained that when they were in the same room together, she felt that her mother was hardly aware of her presence. Clare admitted this and said it was the result of trying to live three lives at the same time. There was little question that their time together was minimal enough for Clare to feel guilt, and later remorse, and for Ann to be lonely.

Two years after the divorce, Ann's father married someone even younger than Clare, Frances Seymour, who would later wed actor Henry Fonda. Clare and George continued to have legal fights, particularly over Ann. When there was an attack of mumps near the Atlantic Beach Club, where father and daughter were spending the summer, Ann was returned to her mother. There was a dispute at the time as to when Brokaw was to regain temporary custody.

He went to court. "The child became hysterical when her father demanded her return," Clare testified. " 'Daddy' to Ann Brokaw is not a great big kindly person, but someone who scares her. . . . And for the sake of her health, I did not force her to go to Mr. Brokaw's home. I have no desire, except for Ann's health, to interfere."

Clare even sued her former husband for $500 as back salary for their daughter's governess. She talked then of getting her revenge one day by writing a book about "the horrors of that unbelievable family."

Clare's brother was an equally persistent problem. He was always reappearing. David had been an unsuccessful stock broker, rejoined the Marines after Clare's divorce, and had gone to Nicaragua. He returned in 1931 with an honorable discharge, became a broker again, and opened an office. Clare paid the rent. She let him manage much of her money, and he lost much of it. In reminding him that he owed her $49,719.84, she added that she didn't see how he could possibly repay her and so she might as well write it off as a tax loss.

"They were the most ill-matched siblings I've ever seen," said Helen Brown. "It seemed incredible that they could have had the same parents. There wasn't the slightest trace of resemblance between them. He looked like a black Irishman: swarthy skin, rugged features, black hair, dark eyes, husky build, handsome in a tough, virile way with a hard-boiled manner that matched his appearance . . ." He was also a heavy drinker.

By this time, Clare's mother and stepfather had separated, but Ann Clare still lived alone at the home in Greenwich. She was in her nightgown, ready for bed when two men entered her bedroom one night and tied her up with sheets. The local papers reported that the intruders had tied Mrs. Boothe's hands behind her back, and pulled another sheet up between her legs, and wrapped it about her body. They also tied her legs and placed a gag in her mouth. They then took all her jewelry, including a $4,000 diamond brooch.

Typical of her character, she had struggled and was covered with bruises. She was at the edge of a nervous collapse, and Dr. Austin was called to attend her. She went to a country sanitarium in Massachusetts, where Clare joined her that Easter. Clare and her mother were in contact, but the contact was no longer close. And when her stepfather wrote her a note correcting her grammar, Clare countered by saying that instead of spending so much time at the Masons, he should have devoted a little more time to her English lessons when she was young.

Clare was restless. She was always thinking of her next trip, her next man, her next leap of ambition. Baruch reportedly offered to buy *Vanity Fair* for her, but she saw the lack of advertising intensifying and the financial problems worsening. Her more flip excuse was that she didn't like to work in an office anymore. Her real reason was she had decided she wanted to write plays. So in February of 1934, she handed Frank Crowninshield her resignation. "You have been a source of continual wonder to me," Crownie told her. He also put her in the magazine's Hall of Fame and sent her a clipping from a Broadway column listing Clare's current suitors as a noted publisher, a "title," and a rich widower.

Being playwright not only seemed a romantic thing to do but it would enrich her claims as "the glamour girl of letters," and put her on a new creative level.

While Clare had a large ego, she still lacked the self-confidence needed to write plays. Ardent admirer Paul Gallico was waiting and willing to collaborate. A famed sportswriter on the New York *Daily News,* Gallico wrote briskly and well. Their combined effort was *The Sacred Cow.* They needed a producer, and Baruch introduced her to John Golden. In sending him the manuscript, Clare coyly admitted that it lacked mystery and charm, and contained no message. She even apologized for all the profanities which she blamed on Gallico. Was it worth bothering about, she wondered? Golden replied that the play needed a lot of work, but it was fresh and lively. He did not, however, volunteer to produce it.

In a restless, sentimental mood, Clare revisited her literary scene of glory at *Vanity Fair* and looked up her old friend Helen Brown. Clare began talking about her uncertain future and Helen kidded, "Maybe you'll wind up in the White House."

Clare replied unsmilingly, "Stranger things could happen."

Politics no longer seemed as much fun as it used to be, and she now seemed disappointed in some of Roosevelt's policies. But she was still pleased to accept an appointment Baruch had managed to get for her as a nonvoting member of the Code Authority for the Motion Picture Industry under the National Recovery Act. She was one of three appointed representatives from the public sector. It was as bureaucratic as it sounded and she resigned several months later, saying, "In a free country, this program can't work. It can only be done with bayonets."

She was soon negotiating to do a radio series on society and social snobbery for a face cream advertiser. She wrote purple, gushing descriptions of a Park Avenue dinner party, describing somebody as being so chic that she made a visitor's stockings wrinkle.

None of these endeavors worked, and Clare was disconsolate. She retreated to a small island called St. Simons off the Georgia coast. Broadway gossip intimated that Clare was simply having another affair. This time it wasn't true;

this time she was really alone. She was not only alone, but she insisted to friends that she was very happy being alone. She liked the island, she said, because it was near the home of Blackbeard, her favorite pirate, fierce and lusty, who used to pillage and rape in the days of the Spanish Main.

She had found a hotel on a semi-circular beach with dunes and palm trees and a background of live oaks covered with Spanish moss. Her neighbors, the Eugene O'Neills, had a large beach house filled with books and African masks and framed pictures of the important people they knew. The O'Neills had been married only two years and Clare described their contentment with a kind of envy. Wondering aloud, she confided that if she had married a playwright and lived out here, she would be happy for a year and then want to hurry back to New York and the meat ax boys.

Clare used her time there to begin another play, which she wrote in long-hand. When she returned to New York, she gave it to one of her three secretaries to type. She dictated her speeches as well as letters and magazine articles and used a dictaphone to record other thoughts when she was in a car en route to an appointment. She hated wasting time. She tried writing a syndicated newspaper column, but she was soon fired because "nobody wants to read any woman's views of politics."

For Clare, this was a thoughtful time. She had done so much and was left with so little. She couldn't marry Bernard Baruch, the man she loved, and the other men didn't matter much. Her magazine episode was fun and brilliant, but it was over. She had not yet managed to reach her daughter. Her friends were few, very few. She had a posh apartment but it was empty of real sentimental value. What was left was a play she harbored in her mind, a play still being shaped, still to come alive.

Whenever she wanted peace or a place to work, she went to Hobcaw. John Golden had requested to see a new script she had worked on in Georgia with the intention of bringing the play to Broadway that fall if certain suggested revisions were made.

"I was working for John Golden," said Jean Dalrymple, a vivacious theatri-cal agent, who would become increasingly important in Clare's life. "She called me up and wanted to have lunch with me; and I was thrilled because she was a leading person around town, very beautiful and very hot. She wanted me to read her play *Abide With Me*. It was about her husband, about Brokaw. He was a terrible drunk. She gave me the script; and I took it home and read it that night. I was horrified that any woman would tell about this awful life and this terrible man that she had been married to. She called me up the next day, to see if I'd read it. I said, 'You must never have this produced. It is an awful thing for people to know, even to know that you'd write about this!' She didn't like that a bit! I said, 'Please don't let this go around. It's very private, personal information you're giving here.' It didn't bother her at all."

Abide With Me opened that summer at the Beechwood Theater in Scarborough in Westchester, New York. The stars were Rosamond Pinchot and Dorothy Hale. "All three young ladies [including Clare] are very close friends and what a lot of fun they are having," wrote the New York *Evening Journal.* Years later, both Pinchot and Hale committed suicide, which left Clare devastated.

Abide With Me was a shocker. A sadist threatens to kill his child, and his wife kills him. But there is a happy ending because her mother-in-law persuades the world that it was a suicide, and the wife marries her psychiatrist and lives happily ever after.

The play died quietly. John Golden wrote Clare that the play had fine writing in it, and that even though it was not his kind of play, he might still produce it on Broadway. But he did want her to change it to make it right.

Clare was exultant. She now saw everything in a brighter light, and she viewed this as a time of tremendous growth.

The young rich society matron now seemed to belong to a distant, faded past. She had found much and wanted more. She was being shaped by her driving ambition, the knowledge that she could get what she wanted. Yes, she was happy, but she wanted to be much happier. This was her mood when she accepted a dinner party invitation from Laura Hobson, who did not yet know of Clare's special relationship with her husband. The two women had always liked each other, and besides, Laura always had the most interesting guests.

It would turn out to be a monumental evening.

12

HENRY Luce never had met a woman like Clare, and he wanted to see her again. He was delighted, two months after their first brief encounter at Laura Hobson's, when they finally met at a dinner at the apartment of Countess Rose Waldeck.

Harry again found himself struggling with his Presbyterian conscience. As a supposedly happily married man, he now fought his growing desire.

During dinner, Clare sat at Luce's right but he largely ignored her. She was not used to being ignored. She was now more than affronted; she was aroused. After dinner, he wandered over to her and suddenly said, "I want to talk to you more about this magazine—the idea you have for a picture magazine."

Luce then posed a hypothetical question, the death of Japan's emperor: "All right, you have a picture magazine published here in New York. The Emperor Hirohito dies. You're thousands of miles away. What are you going to do about it? How would you cover it?"

"Well, you know, Mr. Luce, I should think anyone like yourself would have complete access to the best photographers in Japan. Make a contract with them to buy the first magazine rights. You could also have a corps of your own photographers."

"That solves the problem if you can get it from Japan in time."

"I don't know why that worries you, because if you can't get it from Japan, I don't think anyone can. Besides you could also build up a library of such pictures."

He probed with more questions and she supplied pointed replies. Then, once again, out came the pocket watch and he mumbled, "Time to go. Good night."

"And here I was, giving my all," Clare remembered.

She had never encountered this kind of man before. She was both angered and attracted. Clare knew that it wouldn't be long before she and Luce met again, and so they did on December 9, 1934, at a dinner party given by Condé

Nast. Among the guests were Mr. and Mrs. Henry Luce. The party was a prelude to a birthday ball at the Waldorf Astoria in honor of Cole Porter, whose latest musical comedy, *Anything Goes,* had just premiered on Broadway. Nast had persuaded Harry to come with them afterward "just for an hour" especially since Porter was a fellow Yalie.

By the time they all arrived at the Starlight Roof of the Waldorf, it was close to midnight. The hostess was Elsa Maxwell, a short, plump balloon of a woman. This party was a Turkish Ball attended by four hundred celebrity guests including Hearsts, Harrimans, Rockefellers, Kennedys, Whitneys, Astors, and Ethel Merman.

Clare Boothe was dancing when she saw Henry Luce striding across the floor with a glass of champagne in each hand. She remembered thinking, "Here comes that rude man!" But as he approached her, she excused herself from her dancing partner, hurriedly approached Luce, and said, "Oh, Mr. Luce, is that champagne for me?"

Almost at that moment, the lights went out and they sat down in a far corner of the hall and talked.

Hostess Maxwell unveiled a tiny birthday cake for Cole Porter, and he recoiled from it in mock disgust. Maxwell then sounded a trumpet and curtains parted to reveal another cake, fifteen feet high, which served as the backdrop for the evening's entertainment. Maxwell, who was no singer, proved it by tearing apart a tune Porter had written in his student days, "I Have a Shooting Box in Scotland." Mrs. Cornelius Vanderbilt Whitney, another non-singer, also made her unfortunate debut as a prostitute singing "Love for Sale." Ethel Merman then put the evening's entertainment into professional gear by belting, "I Get a Kick Out of You."

Clare Boothe and Harry Luce heard none of this. Long after the entertainment was over and the lights came on, Clare and Harry still seemed oblivious to everyone and everything, both still talking intensely.

As he sat with her, talking with her, absorbing her, admiring her, fantasizing a life with her, suddenly it was as if something within him had exploded. His conscience was gone, his family was gone, and he wanted this woman more than he had ever wanted anything.

"I could see them at a distance," Lila recalled. "They were just talking. They disagreed and sort of quarreled, and then a few minutes later went right on talking. This was the second time I had ever seen Clare. The first time I met her, she came late to a cocktail party that was given by a German journalist in a hotel suite. I was talking to a tall man and Clare came in and put herself right between us, pushing me back. What could I do but go away? I couldn't fight her. I couldn't try and talk to him, hoping he'd protect me, because he wanted to talk to her. So I backed out quickly. I don't know if she knew who I was or not. But she just jumped in—she was going to get rid of me!

"Now, Harry came over to me, and he said, 'Would you mind going home? I've been asked to stay here.' That was a bit of a surprise! And of course, I said, 'Fine.' He said, 'Could you get somebody to take you home?' I said, 'Oh yes, oh yes.' 'Course, I didn't ask anybody. I got in a taxi and went home!"

"At four in the morning, Harry and Clare were still at the same table deeply absorbed in each other," Elsa Maxwell recalled. "When I told them the party was breaking up, they looked around in bewilderment, as though they were coming out of a trance. Still, I didn't think anything of it. Luce was married and had two sons."

Clare later remembered that Harry asked her then, "Would you come downstairs in the lobby with me? I have something important I must tell you. I can't say it here and I must tell you now."

The only thought that crossed her mind, she later confessed, was that he might be offering her a job on *Time*.

They went down to the main floor and stood at the ticket booth and he said, "I've heard about this happening, but it has just been happening to me. It isn't easy to say it. I've just made the most important discovery. I want to ask you a question, possibly the most important question I shall ever ask and you will ever answer. How does it feel to be told that you are the one woman, the only woman, in a man's life?"

"Whose life?"

"Mine."

She stood there speechless—a rare condition for her—and then she started to say, "Mr. Luce . . ." As if reaching for some support to steady herself, she gasped and said, "Perhaps we've had too much champagne?" Then she saw her friend Helen Brown racing through the lobby and yelled, pleading, "Come and talk to us. Stay with us."

Helen shook her head and rushed out to find a taxi. The next day, Helen reported to her boss Condé Nast about seeing Clare and Harry in the lobby the night before.

"I know," Nast said. "I got stuck for hours with Mrs. Luce."

Harry again left Clare hurriedly, but not before he asked where she lived and made an appointment for the following afternoon.

If Clare felt bewildered, she also felt bewitched. She was clearly stunned, and so was Harry.

"Infatuation, that's what it was," insisted Allen Grover, Luce's friend and confidant, later known as the vice president in charge of Luce. "Harry was infatuated, completely, and utterly. Look up the word 'infatuation.' Part of the definition indicates a sort of loss of judgment. And that's what happened to Harry with Clare. Absolutely. Here was Harry, this very simple, hard-working, God-fearing American son of a Chinese missionary, and he was completely infatuated. No doubt about it. And the word infatuation is stronger than the word love. Absolutely. It was overpowering. There was no doubt that he wanted to marry her, no matter what."

The next morning, after Elsa Maxwell's ball, Harry called his old Yale friend Archibald MacLeish. Could MacLeish meet him at the Commodore Hotel ballroom? MacLeish later described Harry standing in the semi-darkness of the stale-smelling ballroom, "shaken, overwhelmed, infatuated. He was in love with another woman, Harry said, a case of *coup de foudre,* love at first flash. He wanted to marry her and wondered whether he had the *right,* the sheer Christian right to leave his wife for another woman." He regarded Clare as somebody socially glamorous, almost beyond his reach, and himself as a crude country bumpkin, and he was afraid he had made a fool of himself in asking her to marry him. He said she had laughed when he had said that.

MacLeish listened sympathetically. His own reaction to Clare then was that she was a brassy blonde, cold and power-hungry. But he could understand that Luce felt he and his wife no longer had the same interests.

"And he gave me my answer," Harry said afterward to Ralph Ingersoll, the managing editor of *Fortune.* "Love is all there is. I haven't any choice. I have to leave Lila because I love Clare."

The next night, at another Waldorf party, Harry saw Ingersoll, pulled him into the men's room of the hotel, and carefully looked under the stall doors to make certain they were alone. Ingersoll described him as "eyes shining, whole body quivering." He then blurted, "I'm in love, Mac, with Clare Brokaw—*the* Clare Brokaw. I'm going to marry her. I've told Archie, but no one else, Mac. You can't believe how wonderful she is. Oh God, how wonderful she is! It's absolutely unbelievable."

Ingersoll was stunned. "I was not an intimate of his—or didn't consider myself one. So his choosing to share his big secret with me came as a numbing shock." He knew Clare and ticketed her as "a flashy bit, too flashily pretty for her own or anyone else's good." He disparaged her as a notorious woman who had shown terrible judgment by marrying George Brokaw, a "lightweight and near lush." He noted that his own sister had rejected Brokaw's advances. Ingersoll went on to call Clare "a rather wild young lady not to be taken seriously as a writer or an editor or a social figure." To this he added that Clare used to be known as "a party girl from Greenwich, Connecticut, of whom other men talked, a very pretty girl who 'got about'—blond, good figure, could dance, would neck, but look out!" In his view, Clare was targeted for nowhere.

This view, some later said, was distorted by the fact that he himself had been one of her rejected suitors.

Harry now needed some help. "How do I break the news, Mac, to Lila?" Then he paused. "To everybody."

"For chrissakes, Harry, get the hell out of here and go tell Lila right away—before someone else gets to her with the news and *really* breaks her heart!"

When it came to women, Harry was still a naif. He knew almost zero. He was a romantic who wrote passionate love letters, but this was a man who never even kissed his wife until *after* they were engaged. He was not a physically demonstrative man. Courting to him meant holding hands and reading poetry. In Asia and in his Presbyterian missionary home, he had been brought up to conceal his emotions. His ideas of love were formed by the Waverly novels, not by Hollywood.

Harry arrived at Clare's penthouse apartment at the Sherry Netherlands Hotel on Fifth Avenue. He wasted no time in coming quickly to the point. This was a woman he had never held in his arms. And yet he could say to her, "What has happened to me is very important, and I know it's going to be the most important thing in my life—unless you kick me out of it. I think I want to marry you . . ."

This sophisticated woman looked at this highly intense young man, laughed a little nervously, and didn't really know what to say. There was no doubting his seriousness. But it seemed so bizarre, so unreal. She hedged her answer, and he left.

What interested her most in a man, Clare later revealed, was his mind and soul. She regarded sex as the least attractive thing about men. Still, she admitted, the only way to secure a man was to get a physical hold over him. Her first husband, she had said, made her feel that she was really missing something.

In one of her autobiographical short stories, one of the women said she wanted a husband to be neat, kind, slightly boring, dull and stupid, but also faithful and acquiescent.

Harry was sometimes naive, but never stupid. He was certainly kind. He *was* opinionated. Until then, he had been as faithful as most husbands. A little boring and dull? Sometimes, but usually he brought electricity with him into a room.

If Harry knew nothing about flirting or courting or love, Clare saw him as brilliant, rather rough-hewn, and unusually vulnerable. But she was still not certain.

Harry was. To him it was an overwhelming thing, the challenging faith of his life. "I *will* not fail it!" he told Ingersoll. "I have faith in love now and I will not lose it! I do not know how I am going to fulfill it, but only that I have to and that if it takes the rest of my life, I will, and to hell with Time Incorporated!"

For Luce to have said that about *Time* seems inconceivable. *Time* was the heart of his life. Clare would say years later, and bitterly, "The only thing he ever loved was *Time.*"

Yet, the distraught Harry Luce had temporarily divorced himself from *Time.* Nobody there saw him. Nothing seemed to be functioning smoothly anymore without him. Senior editors began feuding and snapping. His absence seemed an invitation to chaos.

As Luce pressed his suit, Clare was drawn in by the urgent, burning need of this man. He was visibly and pathetically in love with her. If he could not fully sweep her senses, never be a great lover, he could make her mind jump and reel. He was still not the giant that Baruch was, but he was so much younger and the potential was there. He would never be the romantic, as a dozen others were, but she might shape him and smooth him into more of the man she wanted. He surely was the antithesis of George Brokaw. It was time, too, that her daughter Ann, now ten years old, had a proper father and a proper home. He was also rich, and he did have that craggy look that so much stirred her. And, of course, there was his power, BIG power, strong and almost magnetic. Still, she insisted to herself that it wasn't just "power calling to power," because, in his way, he was the fulfillment of her mother's ideal man—a decent man who knew his way in the jungle.

She still wanted time to think. She fled to Florida to stay with her mother, and he followed her. She moved on to Cuba to be with friends, and he chased her there too.

"It was like breaking open an eggshell," Clare later confided to a friend. In this time together, the awkward missionary boy disappeared. He finally convinced Clare of the absolute certainty of his intention, revealed himself as never before. He didn't want an affair. He wanted marriage.

What he did not know about the techniques of courtship sex, Clare was now happy to teach him. He never had a sexual experience of that kind and it was a chemistry that worked. In analyzing their married life, Clare told a friend that, sexually, this was their best time together.

Back in Washington, attending a Gridiron dinner, an associate observed that Harry left his table four times during the evening to telephone Clare.

The March of Time was in its earliest stage of film production and Harry took Clare for an inspection tour. Editor John Dullaghan opened the door of the projection booth to find Harry and Clare in a tight embrace. When they saw him looking stunned, both of them laughed.

"She and Harry had a *very* romantic courtship," said his sister Beth. "She was very much like Harry. She never talked small talk; she always asked some very searching questions, and so she'd have all the men vie with each other, to make a smart answer. Clare and Harry had a lot in common—the whole *world!* It's not hard to see why he was captivated."

As Harry continued the calls and correspondence, Clare made up her mind. She finally said yes, she would marry him. Friends insisted that her decision was more "a surrender to sentiment than a victory of tactics." Back in New York, she had a small dinner party for old friends. As dinner ended, Clare tapped her fork against the glass to get everybody's attention, then dramatically announced, "I have a big secret but I am only going to tell you part of it. I am going to be married."

She enjoyed the quick commotion, then added, "I told you this has to stay a secret for a while, but I'll give you a clue. He's connected with the movies."

Her friends excitedly began a guessing game, naming leading movie stars, but Clare only looked happily enigmatic and simply added that they would know about it in due time.

Later, Laura Hobson insisted on knowing who he was.

"You ought to know who it is—you know him," Clare said.

"I know him? I don't know a soul in the movies."

"You know him quite well."

Laura looked blank.

"I'll give you one more clue: he's powerful and he's young and he's rich."

Laura still looked blank.

Clare faked a lisp, "Laura, it's Hawwy, Hawwy Luce!"

"Harry Luce? But you said the movies."

"*The March of Time* is connected with the movies, isn't it?"

Clare seemed relieved and delighted. "I just had to tell somebody who knows Harry or I'll go mad not being able to talk about him for the next few months."

Hobson later contemplated the adjectives Clare had used to describe Luce. The first obviously meant the most to her: powerful.

Laura and Thayer Hobson afterward spent an evening with Harry and Lila Luce, who lived just a block away. Laura told Thayer, "You've been driving yourself too hard, Thayer. You sound tired out. Why don't you take off for a while." That night, Lila said the same thing to Harry Luce. "The next night," said Laura afterward, "I got the news from Thayer [that he wanted a divorce in order to marry another woman] and Lila got her [divorce] news from Harry."

Shortly after, a friend saw Lila Luce sitting at a table at Schrafft's. Lila was crying.

"I was absolutely destroyed," said Lila, "because I really cared. He was my religion; he was my life, my intellectual everything. You see, I never suspected he wasn't happily married. If only he had told me!"

The irony was that the great communicator could not communicate. Harry's guilt over the divorce was almost as great as his passion for Clare. But not quite.

"Harry obviously fell madly for her," Lila reminisced. "She was incredibly pretty. . . . She had the reputation of having the face of an angel, and the morals of a prostitute. Because she really did have love affairs all the time. Undoubtedly, she lived with him; and they went to Europe together, briefly, for perhaps a week or so. He asked for a divorce before he went to Europe."

Later, Lila asked Laura about Clare. When Laura said that Clare was unusual and brilliant, Lila answered simply that this is what she had heard. Mrs. Luce soon went to visit her widowed mother in Chicago, then to Bermuda with her two sons. Harry wrote to her there, called her "Darlingest," which he said would always be his private word for her. He went on to say that one day he would try to tell her of his love and his deep appreciation for all her troubled times caused by his unkindnesses which he himself could not defend. He still hoped he could be a good father to their sons.

In a strange, brighter mood, Luce sent Lila a telegram on her birthday, that he would give her the moon for a thimble ring, if he were king.

All this revealed a man helplessly caught in the wave of his infatuation, a man who saw clearly what he was losing, but could not stop himself. As a young man, Harry had told a Hotchkiss classmate that if he ever married, it would be forever. Now, he was not living up to his principles.

In another letter Harry wrote to Lila on June 8, 1935, he again repeated that part of his deep hurt at their separation was that he knew she still loved him just as he would always love her in a way he would love no one else. Why then was he divorcing her? Harry abjectly confessed that he didn't understand it.

In Bermuda, Lila pondered her future—and Harry's. She had heard that Clare was very beautiful and brilliant but also ruthless, tough, vulgar, selfish, and immoral. Would she make Harry happy? Lila finally decided that no matter what Clare was like inside, Harry was evidently very much in love with her and therefore she had no right to hold him back. Her friends disagreed and tried to persuade Lila not to grant a divorce because Harry was mainly infatuated. It would not last, they told her.

"But, I thought, 'If he doesn't want me for a wife, I have no moral right to prevent his getting a divorce.' I never allowed myself to say anything against Clare, because I knew that would just start a lot of gossipy talk. And I would get the reputation of being a jealous, discarded wife."

Lila was clearly hoping that Harry would change his mind. Friends said that she continued to love him the rest of her life. Lila decided to fight by insisting on stiff financial terms. She hoped this would discourage the divorce.

Throughout this time, Harry wrote to Lila about his shame, his silent loneliness, and his growing agitation. But he did not change his mind about Clare.

Harry had isolated himself from his family, shocked his parents, bewildered his sons—then eight and twelve years old. To his older boy Hank, he wrote how sad he was that he couldn't get to Bermuda, but he was busy reorganizing the distribution of *The March of Time*. His other son Peter Paul had lunched with him earlier and had reported that his father didn't have much time for him because at the lunch there was also a prince, two governors, and an opera singer (Lily Pons).

Harry had moved to the Pierre Hotel. At lunch there, he confided to John Shaw Billings that Lila had been "swell," and that his family thought he was a dirty dog to ditch her. He had been going through hell for weeks, he reported, and couldn't work.

"I was shocked and surprised," Billings recorded in his diary. "I thought Harry had settled, was not really interested in women physically—all he wants is a new fact. But at least he seems to handle himself like a gentleman."

Allen Grover's wife, Bea, who knew both Lila and Clare, reflected, "Lila Luce was sweet but tried too hard. She was so nervous that she was not a good hostess, fluttering around looking too assiduously after her guests and making them nervous. There was no great community of spirit between Lila and Harry. Their marriage just jogged along, neither one realizing that they were unhappy. Clare was not breaking up anything."

At this time, Clare was also having legal problems. George Brokaw had never stopped drinking and finally drowned in the swimming pool of a nursing home where he had been confined with a nervous breakdown. The legal question was whether the income tax on Clare's alimony should be deducted from her former husband's estate.

Harry, too, was now embroiled with lawyers. He told Clare that his divorce would only take three months. While Harry waited for the divorce, Clare went to Europe. She felt that this would give them both more time to be certain of what they were doing. An observer commented, "When the going got tough and Lila's lawyers wouldn't agree to anything—just when it seemed to me Harry most needed the woman he loved—Clare packed her bags and sailed for Europe."

Harry's friend Ralph Ingersoll heard Clare tell her fiancé: "Harry, Lila and your damn family and your directors are your problems, not mine. So you settle them. When you have, I'll be back."

Such calculated coldness might have given Harry pause, but it didn't. He thought of his new passion as the great love of all time. Yet he still was imbued with Presbyterian guilt. To break up the family almost broke him.

Ingersoll remembered Luce calling him around midnight one night, "frightened and stammering that he was alone in a hotel room and afraid that he might jump out of the window."

Ingersoll was terribly concerned and persuaded Luce to put himself in the hands of his old friend Louis Bishop, a heart specialist, not a psychiatrist. "I trusted his medical judgment and common sense as no other man's," said Ingersoll. "So that night when Harry called me, I called Bish and it was together that we walked the floor with him." Ingersoll recalled thinking, "Where the hell was that dame that Harry was putting himself through all this for? Why wasn't it she who was walking at his side?"

"He was quite happy to talk to me anytime about Clare, Lila, Lila's goddamn lawyers, and the institution of divorce in general," Ingersoll noted, "but his eyes went blank whenever I mentioned anything to do with such trivia as the production of a magazine called *Fortune.*"

Clare, meanwhile, sailed for Europe with Buffy Cobb. She also took her daughter, Ann, and promptly left her with a governess while she toured the Continent. Clare and Harry exchanged a flurry of cables and she used the code name "Mike," which she always used thereafter. One of Harry's cables expressed his mortification at having forgotten Ann's birthday. He also kept telling Clare of his love and his irrepressible joy. Her joy was perhaps more repressible, but it was there.

In their time together, she had had a taste of the man, and she was happy about the prospects. Moreover, she was delighted with the idea of being the wife of a celebrated publisher. Her imagination worked overtime on the potential of her role.

Clare recalled that shortly before her ship sailed, Harry had told her that he didn't want any more babies, and that if she married him, he would start her magazine, and she could be co-editor.

Meanwhile, Clare did a lot of shopping. A bill from Jean Lanvin in Cannes itemized some twenty pieces of clothing and perfume. Clare also ordered a silver pattern engraved with the Yin/Yang symbol. She collected more china, artwork, and books. She thoroughly enjoyed herself. Besides shopping, Clare flirted. A columnist even reported that she was seen so often with the divorced publisher of *Film Daily* that "they may tell it to a foreign preacher."

While in Austria, Clare received a visitor. Luce had sent his friend Daniel Longwell, then in Europe on business for *The March of Time,* to give Clare his greeting and see if she wanted anything. A man of great enthusiasm who bubbled with ideas, Longwell had edited picture books for Doubleday and had tried to persuade Luce to start a picture magazine. Longwell and Clare toured Salzburg and got friendly enough for Longwell to advise her: "Don't get involved with the magazines; stay home and have lots of babies." Clare then burst into tears, saying she couldn't have any more babies. Nor was Longwell's advice what she wanted to hear.

As the weeks progressed, Clare grew restless. The divorce was taking longer than expected. She let Harry know how unhappy she was. He was similarly restless and impulsively joined her in Paris in June 1935. It was a reunion of lovers, but Clare soon pressed her point: Why was it taking so long? When would the divorce finally happen? How much money did Lila want? Who would get custody of the children? Harry blamed Lila's lawyers for creating difficulties and told Clare that Lila had promised to go to Reno in September. He would request that it happen earlier so that the divorce would be final before his sons started their new school term. If she delayed going, he would consider either a Mexican divorce or going to Reno himself. Then, immediately afterward, he and Clare would marry and honeymoon in Hawaii.

Clare tried to persuade him to go home and stay home, that they should not again see each other until the divorce was granted. Luce then discovered that Lila and their sons had also come to Paris, where Lila planned to stay for six weeks while the lawyers fashioned a new agreement.

"He was *furious.* That's one of the few times that I ever actually witnessed how he looked when he was angry," said Lila. "He came over to the Vendome Hotel, where I was staying with the kids. He was outraged because he thought I'd done something really immoral—to witness his love affair with Clare! He had every right to be there, but I didn't . . ."

So Lila and the boys took off for Badgastein, Austria. She always had been a loyal, obedient wife, doing what he wanted, and she still loved him. Clare promptly headed for Africa, leaving Harry behind in Paris because she hoped it would hasten the divorce.

The disconsolate Harry returned home to hear about a two-month delay caused by Lila's lawyers. Finally, they agreed upon a settlement of almost $2 million for Lila, who also got the country house. Luce told Billings that this left him with about $5 million on paper—but practically no cash. He couldn't even raise $60,000 to buy his mother and father a home.

Harry also set up trust funds for the children, but he did not give away any Time stock, nor did he sell a single share of his own. Time stock was his power.

Lila returned from Austria and went to Reno. "I took my mother and my two sons and the French nurse and lived in a cottage out there for six weeks. After that, we went for a month to Lake Tahoe. Harry was so gracious. He wrote me lovely letters, which absolutely made me burst into tears."

When Clare returned, she took the advice of her friend Maggie Chase, who told her to stay with Baruch at Hobcaw "and make Harry even more jealous and more anxious to get married." Her room was always waiting. There was a fresh fire in the fireplace in every room, breakfast served in bed, clothes pressed, cleaned, and laid out to wear. The imported French soap in the bathroom was replaced as soon as a bar was used even once. An impressed guest observed that a servant removed exactly five sheets of toilet paper from the roll every morning, then placed them back for easy accessibility.

Baruch rushed to Clare's side at Hobcaw. He didn't want any man to have her and so his advice was predictable. He counseled against her marriage to Harry and mentioned his reputation for coldness and ruthlessness. When Baruch sensed that she had already decided on the marriage, he openly hoped that it would not end their relationship. It didn't.

Years later, Baruch reminisced about their relationship. "She is thirty-three years younger than I." He then told the story of how Clemenceau was accused by a much younger woman of not loving her. Clemenceau had said, "I love you with all the passion of my eighty-four years. Someday you will die and go to Heaven. Just beyond the gate to the left, there is a little ante-room. I shall be sitting there, waiting for you."

While at Hobcaw, Clare had invited her vivacious friend Laura Hobson to visit her. Laura was reluctant to come; she had just gone to work for *Time* writing promotion and advertising copy. Clare said she already had arranged it with Harry. "I did see Harry, each of us deadpan," said Laura, "with no mention of Clare or where I was going." She was met at the station by Baruch's car and chauffeur and driven to the dock where Baruch's yacht was waiting. Though it was early in the morning, Baruch himself came to welcome her.

"Clare was nowhere in sight," recalled Laura. "There had been a large house party in progress for several days with various senators, generals, and writers, all well known. But the guests were leaving that morning or afternoon, including Baruch himself. Clare and I were to be alone, yet I never saw Clare until we met for lunch. She was writing a play; I think the title was to be 'Napoleon Slept Here.'"

Both women rode horseback, took walks, and commiserated on Laura's divorce. Clare lectured Laura on being "a softy" because she hadn't held out for alimony. She also counseled Laura on dating after the divorce: "Everybody who sees you with a man will leap to the conclusion that you are having an affair. Just ignore them. Let them guess. Because all the time you'll be happily sleeping with the doorman . . ."

Clare confided to Laura that she and Harry had been writing to each other constantly and that she had even asked whether he wore pajamas in bed and, if so, whether he preferred the tops or just the bottoms. Laura had hurt her

nose and it was swollen. Clare suggested it was probably a good time to get
her nose reshaped surgically, as she had done. Clare's nose had been stronger
originally, indented near the brow by two short lines.

"One evening, just after dinner, we were in the living room," recalled Laura,
"and Clare was talking about Harry and their plans. Clare was telling me about
some letter she had just received from Harry; she never read any of his letters
aloud, but she would paraphrase and tell me bits that amused her, and things
she had written to him. Quite suddenly, she said, 'Do something for me, will
you?'

" 'What? If I can—?'

"She was looking at me very carefully. 'Take your dress off, Laura.'

" 'My dress off?'

"She made a sweeping gesture, indicating something tossed away. She was
smiling. Nothing about her voice or expression had the slightest hint of sexual
interest—the notion never even entered my head. 'Come on,' she urged. 'I'll
say why in a minute.'

"I shrugged and dropped my dress to the floor. I wore no bra and stood there
in my brief silk underpants, my evening dress making a silken circle around
my ankles. I was still near the fireplace. Clare gazed at me, mostly at my
breasts. She cocked her head to one side and stared for a moment. Then she
said, equally calmly, 'Would you lie down on the sofa? On your back?' She
knelt beside me, about three feet away, her eyes now on a level with my own.
It became clear she was interested not in my entire body, but only in my
breasts. 'Put your arms over your head, would you, just for one more minute?'
She continued to kneel there on the carpet motionless and gazing, as if at a
portrait in a museum. Clare then gave me a look of approval. 'Thanks a
million,' she said, and turned away. I arose, slid into my forsaken evening dress
in one swift movement, and then said, 'Okay, let's have it—what the hell is
it all about?'

"She laid her hands over her own breasts and made a slight grimace. 'After
five pregnancies,' she began slowly, 'and four miscarriages . . .' She didn't finish
the sentence.

" 'You've never gone through a lot of miscarriages and pregnancies,' she
continued, 'so I wanted to see what virgin breasts looked like. I'm going to get
myself fixed—I want to be perfect for Harry.' I was shocked speechless,
especially by the cool collectedness with which she brought it all off, *sans*
apology, *sans* explanation."

In every respect, Clare's stay at Hobcaw was a turning point. While there,
she also interested Baruch in her play *Abide With Me.* Clare was having
trouble getting a Broadway production. The fact that her former husband, the
villain in her play, had died several months before, did not stop her efforts.

As always, Baruch was eager to help. He showed the script to his nephew Donald, a theatrical producer, indicating how much he wanted the play produced. With his uncle's blessing and money, Donald persuaded an associate to join him in mounting a production. Clare was delighted. If only the divorce would come through, all would be well.

While waiting for the divorce, Clare and Harry decided to stop cloistering themselves. Back in New York, they made the round of parties, including those given by Baruch and Condé Nast. They even attended a heavyweight championship fight between Joe Louis and Max Baer and took with them the Ingersolls, Laura Hobson, the Grovers, the Longwells. Everybody remembered how Clare and Harry held hands, and how longingly they looked at each other.

In October 1935, the Luce divorce was made final. As impatient as they were for marriage, Clare wanted something more. She didn't want Harry to put her on his pedestal; rather, she wanted to stand on one of her own. Before they married, she wanted to see her play produced so that she could come to him in the flush of success.

It was a heady time for Clare. For the dinner party that preceded the opening night of her play, she collected such theatrical luminaries as drama critic George Jean Nathan, playwright Clifford Odets, columnist Walter Lippmann, and even her literary hero, Somerset Maugham. Told that the audience was calling, "Author, author," Clare "leapt like a gazelle from the wings to receive applause that was nowhere audible," said an observer. She called the experience "the worst thing that ever happened to me." She never again attended the opening night of any of her plays.

Abide With Me was beautifully mounted and acted. Everything seemed right for success, but it was not to be. The critics were devastating. Brooks Atkinson of *The New York Times* called it "a gratuitous horror play." The *Sun* said it was "too horrible to be real." The *Herald Tribune* wrote, "ridiculous action, sheer bad writing."

What would *Time* magazine say? This was Clare's first test case. Everybody at *Time* knew that their boss would soon marry the playwright. There was a great fear among members of the staff that Clare would thereafter have a strong editorial hand in running the magazines. Luce insisted on seeing all drafts of the review, then sent them back for changes. "Luce wanted to eat his cake and have it too—say the play was rotten and yet good," recalled Billings. "The final version of what he wanted printed didn't get back to me until eight-thirty PM."

The poor *Time* reviewer assigned this miserable job hesitantly suggested, "Perhaps we should let Mrs. Brokaw see this."

"Harry brought me the original copy of *Time*'s review and said, 'Darling, it was a bad play, and I think this notice is too gentle. See what you can do with it,' " Clare later recalled. In rewriting it, she used words such as "lousy" and "stinking." On reading her version, Luce said, "No play is that bad!" and modified it. The final copy praised the cast and the ambiance, and noted that the play might please those who liked melodrama. But before the review went to press, Clare changed it again and made it far tougher so that "it was the worst review I got." But, of course, it was not.

When all the reviews were in, Clare said bitterly: "The play was called *Abide With Me* and abode with no one." She further said that she felt inclined to find the critics and scratch their eyes out.

Yet Clare was still uncrushable. It said something about the quality and strength of her character that she could open a play one night, knowing it might be a dismal disaster, and marry the very next day. On November 23, 1935, Harry and Clare wed in a simple, quiet ceremony at the First Congregational Church in Old Greenwich, Connecticut. He was thirty-seven; she was thirty-two. "They were two people with stars in their eyes," recalled Allen Grover's wife, Bea. "It wasn't what you call a wedding," said Harry's sister. "My brother and her brother, I think, were the only two people there. It was a very quiet thing. But Harry was very firm that it would be in a church—not just at the mayor's office."

Luce wrote his own *Time* Milestone and sent it to Billings to be published as is. It omitted the usual mention of previous marriages.

The elder Luces didn't come to the wedding. "Harry's mother did not like Clare very much," said Grover. She and her husband had felt deeply about Lila, and Clare was both flashy and divorced. Divorce was inconceivable to the Luces. There was also the serious questions of the welfare of the two small boys. In addition, they were unhappy at the rather brutal way Harry broke his divorce news to Lila.

"They were not warm to me," declared Clare. To them, the sophisticated Clare was a cold, designing "other woman." "Eventually his family came to like me," said Clare, "particularly Harry's sons."

But Harry saw this new marriage as the gratification of his life. He thought he had made a big catch and had won the most attractive woman of his time. His devotion to Clare was touching. He would sparkle when she'd walk into a room, his face filled with tremendous pride. What may have endeared her to him was that she was more quick-witted than he. He would often say, "Clare told me this." She, in turn, seldom quoted him. To the outside world, it was a sort of royal marriage. Clare and Henry were two international celebrities who had joined forces to enrich each other. So they did, for a certain time in a certain way. That, too, would change.

Soon after the wedding, Clare and Harry lunched with John Shaw Billings at the Ritz. Billings was then managing editor of *Time*. The *Time* staff already knew him as an able editor, a conservative southerner. It was Billings's first meeting with Clare. He described her as having "yellow hair, slim, milky hands, no jewelry, and a too cultivated voice. Harry was the jealously attentive bridegroom. He gave me an uneasy feeling that Mrs. Luce was about to stick her delicate nose into *Time*'s affairs."

Later, Billings would single out Clare as the reason Harry was becoming colder and more aloof. "Luce is really a dog to work for—utterly cold and impersonal. Really, I like him less and less," Billings wrote, "and blame his second wife for his attitudes. She's just a yellow-headed bitch who is spending his money like water."

Clare and Harry hurried off on their honeymoon on a chartered yacht to Cuba. They took his chauffeur, Alonzo, who claimed to be a good cook and a good sailor. On their first day out, they ran into a serious storm. Clare had no wish for food. But Harry demanded that his slightly seasick chauffeur-cook prepare a three-course meal, starting with soup. Despite the skidding and the swaying, Harry ate everything. Recalling it afterward, Harry said, "It was a terrible dinner, but I certainly called that fellow's bluff."

For six weeks, they stayed in a cool, tiled palace on the outskirts of Havana, loaned to them by a Pan American Airways executive. As the new general manager of Time Inc., Ingersoll paid them a visit to clear up some year-end problems. "The hours that I remember best we spent together—the three of us—on the sand, in bathing gear, I at a table under a beach umbrella with sheets of figures from a briefcase and Harry joining me to go over them while Clare made travel poster pictures running along the water's edge, playing with a huge inflated rubber ball, leaping, splashing. She was a pretty sight, and so was Harry, happy at long last, as nearly relaxed as his grim nature could manage. I only had his full attention to Time Inc.'s affairs in spurts. At Clare's insistence, he did calisthenics under her direction. She would say, 'I'm going to keep him trim—one, two, up, down—he'd been getting flabby—stomach in, head back, up, down, up . . .' "

Then came a brisk discussion about the new picture magazine, Luce saying, "Okay, Mac, so maybe if you just took the hundred best pictures you'd have something worth looking through in a dentist's office, but you can't make them tell stories." And Ingersoll countered, "But damn it, we've been doing just that on *Fortune* for years."

"And Clare? She wasn't taking Harry on in an argument right at that moment, and she wasn't quite sure she wanted to back me. But I do credit her with an assist that was vital. After a few days, I got my cue, that if it turned out to be the right kind of a picture magazine, and there was a star part in it for her, I might still have her as an ally. She finally chimed in, 'Harry I *like* pictures—and if they are handled right . . .' "

"Okay, Mac, go ahead and see if you can work it out," Luce replied. "You are crazy about there being a million circulation in it; it's a hundred and fifty thousand slick paper carriage trade idea. But," and here came Harry's clincher, "Time Inc.'s rich enough now to afford a failure *d'estime*. It could be fun. Go ahead with it. Hell, Mac, we don't really have to burn any bridges; we can always call it off if the figures don't check out."

Though Harry may have been feeling flush, Clare's notions of wealth were quite different. "The first quarrel we ever had was when I unintentionally hurt him on our honeymoon," remembered Clare. "We'd been sitting talking one evening. After that he was in a black mood, sulking. We'd been talking about this picture magazine and he said in passing that *Time* had made a million dollars last year, before taxes. I let it pass. I'd lived among people who made much more than that. I was used to people making big money. It never occurred to me that he wouldn't make a million a year. Well—it hurt him that I didn't exclaim over that."

She later said that she had felt very sorry for him "because he was sort of vulnerable."

The honeymooners returned to their new homes in February 1936, both tanned and happy, with forty-eight bottles of perfume for female staff members. They had taken a country house in Stamford, Connecticut, and leased a fifteen-room duplex apartment with five bathrooms at the posh River House at 432 East 52nd Street, fronting the river. It was filled with valuable French, English, and Italian antiques, although Clare preferred more modern art and furniture. Luce indicated that his own preference was for "things convenient and sensible. Whatever furniture or houses we buy in the future will be my wife's buying, not mine."

Soon after their return, they gave a big cocktail party at the Waldorf to introduce Clare to Time Inc. executives and editors. She wore a simple black cocktail dress, but her charm didn't completely enchant the editors. They had a persistent worry that Clare was moving in on the magazines. The fear was real and almost accurate.

"At various times, she'd stand up and talk about her doing something or other on the magazines and all of us began to shake," said Andrew Heiskell, who would become chairman of the board of Time Inc. The real fear was that Clare would want to run the new picture magazine.

But for the moment, Harry seemed to be the creative force behind the new venture. In his prospectus, which he wrote himself, the magazine "would eyewitness great events . . . watch the faces of the poor and the gestures of the proud . . . see strange things—machines, armies, multitudes, shadows in the jungle and on the moon . . . see man's work—his paintings, towers and discoveries . . . see things thousands of miles away, things hidden behind walls and within rooms . . . see and take pleasure in seeing . . . see and be amazed . . . see and be instructed." The will of mankind, he wrote, was "to see and be shown." As he saw the draft of the prospectus, he pranced into Billings's office and cried, "I'm pregnant." Later, he amplified. "We are in labor. We are giving birth to a new child."

Clare's comment was telling: "We went off on our honeymoon and a child was conceived—a child later called *Life* magazine."

13

❧

THE birth of *Life* came at such a perfect time. Harry's wife was everything he wanted her to be: beautiful, scintillating, romantic. He envisioned a life with her of constant adventure and enrichment. No matter how big he became, she would grow with him, as Lila had not. Perhaps Clare could become a vital part of this magazine, just as she was now a vital part of him. He wanted to share everything with her now.

Luce plunged himself into the new magazine, still nameless. (They would not buy the *Life* title until a month before publication.) One story circulated that a cleaning woman came in and Luce asked her if she would pay a dime to look at the magazine every week. That's when he decided to call the magazine "Dime." Staffers started calling it "Uncle Harry's Show-Book." In a subscription letter, Luce called it "The Show Book of the World," and promised that readers would see "the faces of the poor and the gestures of the proud; the women that men love . . ."

When Luce was later sued by a color engraving expert for stealing his idea proposed in 1932, Clare rummaged through her papers and produced her own dummy for the *Life*-type magazine she had prepared for Condé Nast in 1931. She even found a memo suggesting he buy the title *Life* from the fifty-three-year-old humor magazine. The case was dismissed, but Harry told his wife, "I never want you to mention this again." Luce later told a writer, "Of course our experience with *Time* made *Life* possible, but it was Clare's idea originally."

Picture magazines had existed in Germany and England—but none of them let the pictures tell the story. "We are all amateurs in this picture business," Luce admitted later. But Harry really felt like an explorer.

His excitement for the new magazine was becoming almost feverish. Luce and Daniel Longwell, who became picture editor of *Life*, worked on two experimental versions and decided that the cover should be a photograph.

Luce once told art editor M. F. Agha that what finally firmed his decision to go ahead with the magazine was the day he spent going through some thousands of pictures and finding a photograph of twenty roasted elephants at a circus fire.

Luce and Longwell often worked in Harry's private office, down on their knees on the plush carpeting, sorting out sample spreads. Luce was the sparkplug of the whole operation. "He gets all the ideas, makes all the decisions. . . . Everything had to go to him for a final yes or no," said Billings. "When he wasn't squinting critically at the layouts or editing captions, he was filling me full of *Life*'s principles and purposes." Luce invented the picture essay—one big feature. He also believed: "A word's a word, in small type or in big, just so long as it's readable. But a picture is not."

A picture of a Chinese man being beheaded, with the blood spurting from his neck, printed one-inch square would offend no one. Blow it up, Luce said, and it becomes a shocker. Luce believed in big pictures, standing on their own.

With *Life*, photographers became the unsung heroes. Luce once jestingly remarked that Hitler was his greatest ally in starting *Life* because some of the best photographers were Jews who fled to America as refugees. Two of the best were Alfred Eisenstaedt, whose early pictures of Mississippi sharecroppers were considered the first true examples of American photojournalism, and Robert Capa, whose pictures of the coming war became classics.

Ingersoll knew that Clare was being considered for the job of managing editor of *Life*. "For my money, she has always been a fascinating textbook case of arrested development," Ingersoll said, "the arrested emotional development of a precociously bright female child at or about early puberty. After her emotional nature developed to that point, her body continued to store the purely factual content of life. She had registered life only as does a child who observes everything, but is unchanged by it because she is unaffected emotionally. It is my position that one cannot truly engage emotionally with such a phenomenon and I never tried."

To complicate matters for Ingersoll, he now got the word from Harry: Why not name Clare as the new magazine's managing editor? ("I think I could persuade her to take the job.")

"I knew I wasn't about to second Clare's nomination because a revived *Vanity Fair* wasn't my idea of what my picture magazine was all about. So I thought and I thought and finally I came up with the right way to put it to Harry, and it was the right way because it involved telling him only the truth. The truth—in correctly measured doses—is always the best medicine."

Ingersoll and Dan Longwell then invited Harry and Clare to dinner at a posh restaurant. Clare insisted afterward that Harry had hinted that the purpose of the dinner was to offer Clare the job on *Life*. He remembered her reaction as, "Oh, that's wonderful!"

Over dessert, Ingersoll was blunt: "Harry, you have got to make up your mind whether you are going to be a great editor or whether you are going to be on a perpetual honeymoon. You just can't make a success of *Life* with one hand tied behind Clare's back."

Clare broke in quickly. "Harry Luce can publish a better magazine with one hand tied behind his back than you can publish with both of yours free."

Ingersoll then took a brilliant gamble in his argument with Luce: "Look! Clare's a very, very talented woman—but she's your wife. There are only two ways you can use her to forward the success of a magazine that belongs to you; as your full partner—co-boss—or as its star contributor. You can't make her managing editor because a managing editor is only a hired hand, halfway up the executive ladder. It wouldn't be fair to her; she's too important for that job and people would wonder why she isn't in your office, in charge with you."

Clare's version, as Ingersoll recalled it, was that Harry told her before the dinner, "that I would name her as *Life*'s editor, and then she was so disappointed that she went home and 'cried all night.' Well, what I recall is her getting whiter and tighter-lipped as the evening wore on and, finally, when she could stand it no longer, demanding a silence into which she spoke these memorable words: 'I have been listening very carefully to these men. Harry, has it ever occurred to you that you have surrounded yourself with incompetents?' She then stood up from the table and left the restaurant, leaving a highly embarrassed husband."

The story quickly circulated at *Time* and the consensus was this: Harry didn't defend his wife at the dinner with Ingersoll because, deep down, he didn't really want his wife on the new magazine. If he put Clare in as the top *Life* editor, he could see the future as a series of emotional confrontations—the thing he most hated. Clare had respected and admired Condé Nast, yet had no hesitation competing with him and confronting him. Why couldn't it happen to him? "Harry Luce was a very proud man. He wasn't going to be used by her," said Wilfrid Sheed. Luce, finally, was pleased to accept Ingersoll's position.

"You know, Ingersoll is essentially crazy, but he sure has some good ideas!" Luce later said.

Clare hit back, telling Harry, "There's something very wrong with a guy [Ingersoll] who would do that to a man who has just been married and with no proof of any kind that I have been a drag on you . . ."

She later revealed her "fiercest anger" in the bedtime talk she had that night with her husband, asking for his thoughts. "Well," he replied, "you know it would be an impossible situation considering the way they feel." It was then that she vowed "never again to put foot in your office or ever intervene in any way whatsoever in your magazines."

Years later, her bitterness gone, Clare commented, "When I found that my husband's staff did not view kindly the boss's wife being an editor—and they were probably right, too—I said, 'Okay, I'll do my own thing.' "

When Clare met Gloria Steinem many years later, Steinem told her how she was turned down for a job at *Life* because "We don't want a pretty girl."

"That's how *I* lost my job at *Life,*" said Clare.

What *was* true was that the senior staff generally maintained an unwritten rule to "stay out of her way." "Don't ever invite her in, or even ask her opinion," was the word. Nobody wanted Clare having any say about the company. They even agreed never to mention her in *Time* except on the People page.

In many ways, Clare had lost the battle without even a fight. Several editors didn't like her long before they met her. They regarded her as phony, and Clare pretended indifference. She relegated the *Time* staff and most of its editors to a level of disdain. Even when they entertained her at an official lunch, she gave them minimum courtesy. More than a bit aloof, Clare wanted to let them know that she was their superior and considered them as very inferior indeed. Should Clare pass by an editor in a café or on the street, she looked right through him. If Harry's staff didn't like her, she didn't like them, she would say in her mocking style. But she resented it all her life.

As for Harry, he quickly figured out how difficult the situation was and struggled to keep Clare at bay. "He really kept her away from Time-Life. He'd have had a revolt of the editors if he hadn't. There would have been a real palace-coup revolt," said *Time* correspondent Lael Wertenbaker.

If Clare was a problem for Harry at Time-Life, she was also a source of inspiration. "I can remember no year when he bubbled with so many ideas, when his enthusiasm for well-done stories elicited so much praise, and his impatience with the inept was so brisk," wrote Eric Hodgins, who became managing editor of *Fortune.* "You could occasionally tell when Harry spoke to you about something," said Andrew Heiskell, "that he was really repeating something Clare had said, because it didn't sound like Harry and I had to say to myself, 'That was Clare.' "

Even Ingersoll had no hesitation in asking Clare to use her influence with some of her important friends. He asked her to intercede to "try to lay to rest the ghost" of a long-standing feud between Hearst and Luce.

Many felt that Clare's indirect influence on Harry was considerable, that she was always suggesting story ideas. "Clare was a very knowledgeable lady," said Oliver Jensen, who became *Life* text editor. "Where did she fit in on *Life?* She fitted into the same bed with Harry Luce, so to speak. She was keenly aware of the world of arts and theater about which Harry knew little. She knew all the notable photographers. They worked together, talked together, and she could explain the meaning and importance of all this to him. She knew what should be covered by *Life* or *Time.* And what she didn't know, she soon found out. She was a quick study."

"She changed his life as a persona," said Andrew Heiskell. "Before that, he had not been very social; he had not been an important personality in his own right. He and Clare became social lions, political personalities, They were out every night, or entertaining every night. They lived the full life together. And of course, she was a very attractive woman, and she was very bright. She was very entertaining when she wanted to be; and she had a lot to do with making him what he became."

Clare herself tried to be modest about her influence. In describing "the almost English reserve of Harry's family," Clare noted, "They didn't reveal themselves and neither did he. I was the only person who would dig under the surface for him. Harry would know what people said. I could sometimes tell him what it meant, what was behind it."

She also tried to present herself as a moderately subservient wife: "He changed me enormously simply by marrying me. Women marry their husbands' lives, not vice versa. Whenever there was a conflict of interests, his prevailed," she said.

Still, the focus was more often on her. When Luce took Clare to the Republican National Convention in 1936, *Time* correspondent Robert Sherrod remembered that Clare stole all the attention. "Oh, she was gorgeous . . . a stunning looking woman!" he recalled.

Clare soon turned her attentions away from Time Inc. She persuaded Harry to buy Mepkin, a huge estate in Moncks Corner, South Carolina. Some eyebrows were raised because the new Luce home was only a short drive away from Bernard Baruch's Hobcaw. "She had loved going down to be with Baruch," said Harry's sister Beth, "and that's where she'd gotten this bug of having a big place with lots of guests coming. She loved that part of the country and that way of life, with the birds, the grouse, the duck-hunting . . ."

Mepkin was situated on 7,200 acres, forty miles north of Charleston. The main house was on a bluff overlooking the Cooper River, surrounded by majestic oaks. It had once belonged to a Revolutionary war hero. Clare was entranced by its haunting beauty and aura of melancholy. "Nobody could not fall in love with that place, especially at certain times of the year such as when the azaleas were blooming and with that Spanish moss on the live oaks in the sun . . . beautiful!" she said.

Clare's parents, Anna Clara Boothe and William Franklin Boothe, were both strong-willed and intelligent, but ultimately mismatched.

From childhood on, Clare worried about her sensitive and manipulative older brother, David.

State Historical Society of Wisconsin, The Nettie McCormick Collection

A close-knit family group, the Luces posed for a portrait: Emmavail, Henry, and their father stand behind Elisabeth and mother Elizabeth Root Luce.

Courtesy of Elisabeth Moore

"Harry" grew up to be a serious, deeply inquisitive adolescent.

As a young woman, Clare (above) went to Europe with her mother and stepfather, Dr. Albert Austin; Clare (below: far right) dressed up for a costume party at the Castle School.

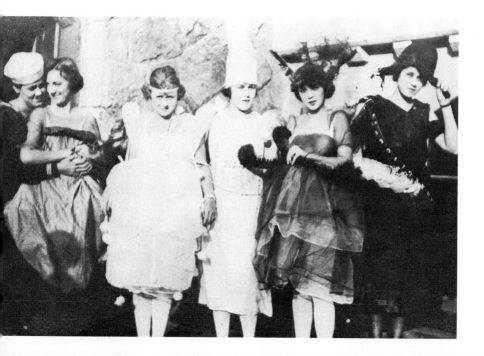

Two of the most outstanding staff members of the Yale Daily News *were Henry Luce and Briton Hadden (front row: second and third from left), who later co-founded* Time.

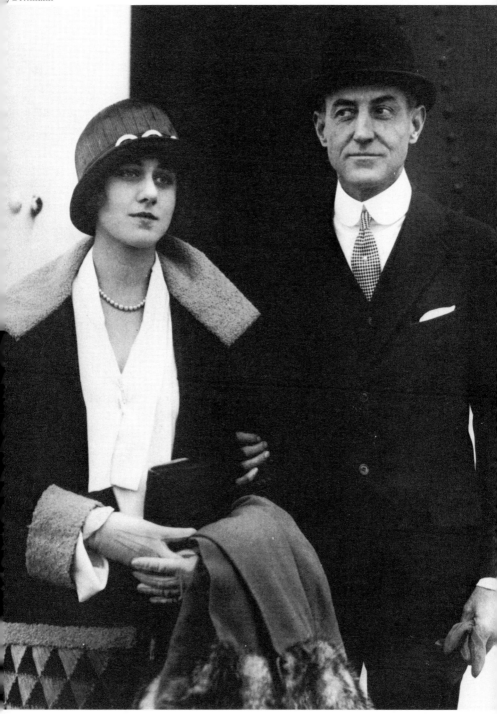

With her first husband, George Tuttle Brokaw, Clare struggled to be a good society wife, but she soon tired of the role.

Luce's first wife, Lila Ross Hotz, was devoted to their sons, Peter Paul and Henry III.

As a young divorcée, Clare took her daughter, Ann, to the beach; later, she would shunt Ann off to boarding schools.

In the early days of Time, *Harry's right-hand man was a courtly Southern gentleman, John Shaw Billings, who privately disparaged his boss.*

Before—and after—her marriage to Luce, Clare was linked romantically with Sir Winston Churchill's son, Randolph (left), and with Bernard Baruch (below), the powerful presidential advisor.

As the managing editor of Vanity Fair *in the thirties (above), Clare owed her job to her intimate friend Condé Nast (left).*

Honeymooning in Cuba in 1935, Mr. and Mrs. Luce claimed they had never been happier.

On their elaborate Greenwich, Connecticut, estate, the Luces played country squires.

Heading off on one of their first trips to the Orient in 1940 (right), the Luces visited China, where Clare and Harry were escorted by Madame Chiang Kai-Shek (below).

Two views of the freshman Congresswoman Luce: addressing the House Foreign Affairs Committee in 1943 (above) and taking time out in her library (below).

During World War II, Clare enjoyed herself with soldiers at a USO dance (left), but the British General Harold Alexander (below) was rumored to be Clare's special favorite.

With an $86,000 loan, Luce built a publishing empire that by the 1940s included Time, Life, *and* Fortune.

The main house had five double master bedrooms. There were stables for the horses, kennels and quarters for tenants. Landscaped walkways led to the boat house and bridle paths threaded through the woods. Harry complained to Billings about the huge costs for extra lights and equipment to water all the plants. "Clare did not like to walk in her gardens and see silty water," said a friend, who observed that servants floated thousands of freshly cut azaleas on the muddy river that fed the rice paddies on the estate. The thirty black servants lived in brand new cabins.

Clare was delighted with Mepkin and so was Harry. They loved it so much they didn't mind the long train ride from New York to Charleston, then the journey by boat to their property.

"I wasn't going to build a vast plantation house, because that would have been fraudulent. After all, I was a newcomer," Clare wrote in *Vogue*. She described herself as an enthusiastic convert to the South, but later explained that she and Harry had bought Mepkin from a northerner who had bought it from another northerner, and not very cheaply.

Clare hired architect Edward Durrell Stone to design four guest houses, "functional structures of chromium and glass that glitter incongruously among ancient trees." She named them Strawberry, Tartleberry, Claremont, and Washington.

Ann came to Mepkin during school vacations and loved it. She was twelve now and had Clare's curiosity but not her looks. Tall, bright, and rather opinionated, Ann adored her mother, but her mother had not yet bridged the emotional gap.

Harry did. He always had wanted a daughter, and he and Ann formed a tight bond of real affection with frequent letters between "Annie and Dad." He took her with him on vacations to Virginia and Southern California. Whatever attention Ann lacked from her mother, she got from her stepfather.

In some measure, Harry had an easier relationship with Ann than he did with his own two sons. Lila had full custody of Henry and Peter and was leery of subjecting them to Clare's presence and influence. At best, she assumed Clare would neglect them. When Harry asked that the boys accompany him and Clare on a cruise for a week, Lila agreed: "Fine. But take the French nurse with you. Then at least she'll see that they wash their hands before dinner."

Lila's negative feelings about Clare lasted a long time. But it was something far deeper than divorce and remarriage that affected Harry's relationship with his boys. "I am unaware of the boys playing any part in his life, really," said Allen Grover. "Harry was never a loving father."

Unknowingly, perhaps, he was following in his own father's footsteps. The elder Henry Luce had stimulated his son's mind and his soul; he had reasoned with him rather than disciplined him. He had trouble expressing affection. Harry, in turn, gave what he got and it was never enough for his sons.

Just as Harry found it easier to reach out to Ann, Clare was often more comfortable with her stepsons than with her own daughter. She invited them to Mepkin and put on her best camp counselor behavior. "She was awfully good at teaching the kids," recalled Harry's sister. "She taught them how to ride, how to shoot, how to play croquet and then, at night, checkers. She would play complicated word games and charades for hours at night with her stepsons."

Those who knew Clare well felt that she could do almost anything she set her mind to. Her friend Dorothy Thompson admired Clare's talents. "Her interest gives her vitality. She never stops," Thompson observed. "All the time she did her beautiful intricate needlework, she was talking or planning or giving orders about running the house. When she wanted to learn Italian, she played records while dressing."

Thompson also took note of Clare's beauty. "At Mepkin, where the plate glass windows came down to the floor, all the women would make up for breakfast, but in the blinding morning light they would look terrible," she said. "Clare, with no more than a smidgen of lipstick, looked wonderful."

Yet, there was a dark side of Clare that was beginning to emerge in the days at Mepkin. Sometimes she would get into an inexplicable black mood and disappear into her bedroom for days. Later in life, as Harry was to discover, Clare's moods would threaten to overwhelm both of them and lead to some very sorrowful times.

14

CLARE was now in her early thirties, and the world was still very much at her bidding. She had a rich, powerful husband, and was at the center of an entourage of witty, fawning friends. But something had been missing for Clare ever since Harry's editors destroyed her dream of being editor of *Life*. Once again, she decided to turn to playwriting.

"I found myself with absolutely nothing to occupy my mind, and decided, with what I sometimes tell myself now was almost a flash of genius, that writing plays was a heavenly way to fill in intellectual gaps," said Clare. A friend described her sitting in her bed in the morning with a bow in her hair, wearing a frilly bed jacket, and dictating to a secretary. "She looks like a Watteau, but the bed looks like a horror, piled with newspapers, manuscripts, menus, cards, and letters. Her correspondence, much of it written in longhand, is stupendous, and her telephone conversations exhaustive. She answers invitations, sends flowers, writes little notes of introduction, and is constantly financially rescuing some of her friends in the profession."

Ralph Ingersoll noted that Clare wrote her plays in longhand so that she would not be tempted to look back and consider what she had written—as she would if it were more legible. What she preferred was to listen to Harry read aloud her dialogue in the evenings. "He reads it very slowly," she said. "If I can stand it slowed up like that, I know it must be good."

Clare freely admitted that her plays were autobiographical. "Heavens, as if any piece weren't!" she said. "How can one help portraying what one is in everything one writes, except perhaps a check. No, perhaps after all, one's checkbook is one's real autobiography."

Perched in bed, waited on by her four maids and writing with pencil on manuscript paper bound in morocco covers, Clare insisted she wrote the first draft of her play *The Women* in three days. She claimed she got the idea in the ladies' room of the night club, El Morocco. "While I was in the loo, I heard two familiar voices at the wash basin," she explained. "They were dishing the dirt about some married friends of ours. It was the most brutal gossip I had ever heard. I just sat there until they got through with that little piece of character assassination. So I said, 'Harry, I think I'll write a play about women without any men in it.'"

"Why not?" he answered.

She set a scene she knew well—a hotel in Reno filled with frustrated women waiting for their divorces. There were parts for forty-four women—and no men. Clare seemed to be almost mocking herself because the plot featured a heroine losing her husband to a designing blonde. "I not only wrote it," she later said, "I was the leading bitchy character."

The Women quickly stirred controversy in New York. Not everyone agreed with Clare's assessment of the play's origin. "She got the idea from my hairdresser at Saks Fifth Avenue," said theatrical agent Jean Dalrymple. "He had all these rich women. And he used to get so busy that he forgot to put away the checks they wrote to him. So one woman came in, and she saw a check with her husband's name on it. And she immediately began to investigate why he had paid some other woman's bill. That started the whole thing. . . . And he told this story to Clare!"

Lila Luce had another version: "Mrs. George Kaufman told a friend of mine, 'Mary, we had a great windfall this year. You know that Mr. Luce who owns *Time* magazine? Well, he got George to come to his office, and he gave him $30,000 to write a comedy because his wife had a name for a comedy, but she could not make it into a play. She's tried for ten years to write plays. She's read most of the plays that are in the classic books, like Molière and Shakespeare, but still cannot write a play. But she thinks she has a good idea for a play about how women are to each other called *The Women*. Harry gave George $30,000 not to say anything. He was sworn to silence. He [George] wrote that play. Every time Clare's name is in the press it is followed by 'Dramatist.' But she never wrote a play."

Whether or not this is true, Mrs. Kaufman had every reason to dislike and disparage Clare. During Clare's Algonquin Round Table days, she had made Kaufman one of her conquests. "Kaufman was clearly head over heels in love with Clare. He was crazy about her," said Jean Dalrymple. At the time, Kaufman had the reputation of being "a male nymphomaniac" because actress Mary Astor had testified in a divorce court that George had made love to her twenty-eight times in a single night.

Kaufman and Clare seemed to have continued at least a professional relationship once the play went into production. Bernard Baruch had interceded on Clare's behalf with producer Max Gordon, who agreed to open the show once some revisions were done.

Gordon's story was that he had shown the play to his friend George Kaufman, a recognized play-doctor often called in "to fix the unfixable."

"He is just as enthusiastic about the possibilities of the play as I am," said Gordon. "If I were in your position," Gordon told Clare, "I would do everything possible to get George interested in working with me on the play. I think his advice is most valuable." (If Kaufman had indeed written the play, Gordon didn't know it or let on to it.)

Jean Dalrymple, who knew both George and Clare well, insists that he rushed to her side. "God, George gave hours and nights and was with her all the time, just doing a job of rewriting the damn thing. You could go through her play and pick out all of George's witty one-liners."

Right before the play went into rehearsal, Clare invited the cast to her Waldorf suite on the thirty-sixth floor to hear her read the play. She wore a Bergdorf Goodman house coat and gave each of her guests a pencil and paper pad "for notes and suggestions," and the butler served sherry. "It was exactly as though we were at a house party, playing pencil-and-paper games after dinner," observed a guest.

The leading lady in *The Women,* Ilka Chase, offered yet another version of the story. She said Kaufman and his partner Moss Hart may have offered some suggestions on the rewriting and rearrangement of scenes, but that Clare did the doctoring herself. Another member of the cast, Arlene Francis, agreed that "George only added a few laughs and curtains, nothing substantial: otherwise the play was the essence of Clare."

Harry grew indignant as the rumors spread of Kaufman's involvement. Luce wrote columnist Walter Winchell insisting he had seen the first draft of the play several weeks after Clare had outlined it for him. She had been working on it every day and had talked to nobody else during that time, he told Winchell. The first two acts he had read were almost identical with the final script. His wife had rewritten the third act before Kaufman saw any of it and it remained all hers except for a couple of lines. Furthermore, Luce continued, Kaufman and Hart had watched several rehearsals and had discussed the play with Clare for several hours, pointing out some weak spots, particularly in a curtain line, but that was the sum total of their contribution. Luce asked Winchell to doublecheck all these facts and then print the truth.

Clare's own account was that producer Max Gordon had doubts about the third act after the Philadelphia opening. Since Kaufman and Hart had seen the show that night, she did ask their advice. Before she knew it, they had found a typewriter and were at work. Their working methods astonished her. Hart would write a line and read it to Kaufman, who suggested changes, after which Kaufman would write a line, read it to Hart, and so on. She knew that she could never fit into that system, so she went upstairs and rewrote the third act herself.

Kaufman, Clare added, had made the best comment on the matter when he said, *"The Women* was one of the great hits. If I wrote it, why on earth would I put her name on it?" She also said that Kaufman made more from the play than she did, since all she received were author's royalties, and he had a share in the show. Her reason for not investing was that, as a rich woman, she did not want to give the impression that she was subsidizing her own play.

Whatever help Clare received from Kaufman, she may not have been overly gracious about it. "I was assistant stage manager of *You Can't Take It with You,* and Kaufman and Hart were working on it in Philadelphia before the Broadway opening," said Franklin Heller. *"The Women* was also in Philly at the same time and we all went to see it. I do know that George went back to Philly to help Mrs. Luce. I don't know how much. But I do know that George and his wife went to the opening night of *The Women* and they saw Mrs. Luce in the lobby afterward, and she was with a lot of her society friends, and she stiffed him, just ignored George. She didn't even invite him to the opening night party."

Once the controversy of authorship was behind her, Clare faced the jabs of the critics. *The New York Times* called the play a "kettle of venom . . . alleycats scratched and spit with considerable virtuosity. This reviewer did not like it." Neither did columnist Heywood Broun who said it degraded the whole human race. However, the St. Louis *Globe-Democrat* loved it: "glorious entertainment watching the girls take down their hair . . . only women will ever know how deep the truth goes . . . we defy any woman to read the scene between Mary and her little daughter without crying . . . the one in which she tells the child she is going to Reno for a divorce." The reviewer quoted her favorite line: "The first man who can think up a good explanation as to how he can be in love with his wife and another woman is going to win that prize they're always giving out in Sweden . . ."

In summing up the play later, Clare's friend, Margaret Case Harriman, wrote, "She tied up her own sex crisply in cellophane and delivered it to the ash can."

Clare rushed to her own defense: "My play is a slice of life; I never said it was the *whole* of life. . . . The play shows what I didn't like—idle parasitical women. I didn't approve of them then and I don't now. The women who inspired this play deserved to be smacked across the head with a meat ax and that, I flatter myself, is exactly what I smacked them with."

At *Time,* critic Louis Kronenberger had not liked the play and his *Time* review was rewritten four times. A memo was attached to it. "H. R. L. has not read this."

"Harry sent for the copy of the *Time* review and changed a few lines himself. This was the only time I can ever remember his actually changing a review," recalled Allen Grover. "He softened it quite a lot. The final review talked of 'sharp theatrical impact . . . so clever that few women would willingly miss it . . . packed with cracks which will doubtless be batted back and forth across Manhattan dinner tables the rest of the season . . .' "

The Women was an enormous commercial success and played to packed houses. It was produced all over the world, twice made into movies, and earned millions. It played in eighteen countries in ten languages. In China, Madame Chiang Kai-shek read the beauty parlor scene aloud to her husband, and he replied, "Do you mean to tell me that the women of the great, civilized Christian ally put mud on their faces and wires in their hair?" Clare was no longer simply The Great Man's Wife.

The Great Man himself was now ready to put his wife's concerns aside. It was time, at last, to launch *Life*.

Volume I, Number 1 published on November 19, 1936, sold out the entire press run of 200,000 copies. *"Life* was his wedding present to me," claimed Clare, when it appeared on their first wedding anniversary. The opening photograph was a moving photo of an obstetrician holding a newborn baby by its heels. The headline read, "Life Begins." Inside were pictures of workers at Fort Peck on a Saturday night jamboree, as well as pictures of the shanty towns where they lived. The issue also contained the first aerial pictures of Fort Knox, where the country kept its gold, and of Fort Belevedere, where King Edward VIII entertained Mrs. Wallis Warfield Simpson. There were production shots taken of the current hit play *Victoria Regina* starring Helen Hayes and the current hit film *Camille* with Greta Garbo. In addition, *Life* featured a color portfolio of John Steuart Curry's paintings and the picture story of a hunting party in honor of the British Ambassador to France—complete with a row of dead hares.

As subsequent issues of *Life* rolled off the presses, new paper and inks had to be invented, new presses had to be designed, to keep up with the demand. Sales soon reached a million a week. Pollster George Gallup had been proven right: people preferred looking at pictures to reading type.

"Bubbling with delight," as he put it, Luce lunched with the staff of *Life* at the Cloud Club on top of the Chrysler building. Ralph Ingersoll, who had been prominently involved in planning and shaping *Life,* described how he had come to Luce's office to share "one moment of happy hysteria . . . alone with Harry."

"Harry's eyes were shining. What he was saying was for and to me, but it was coming out of somewhere so deep in him: 'Mac, this is very big! I know and you know that *Life* is your baby. But it's mine too. It's actually mine. There comes a time in every man's life when he has to decide whether to take what is his, and I've made my decision, Mac. *Life* belongs to me, and I'm going to take it from you. I'm taking it over completely, and I'm going to draw on every department, for every talent I can use, and that's only part of what I've decided. You and I know that this is so big that it's going to take money, money, and more money and men, men, men. So, I'm going to take whomever I need for *Life*—from the whole organization. And about the money, you are going to have to make that, to see that it keeps coming from *Time*. So, that's what I am asking of you: that you take over *Time* and see that it goes on making the money I'll need to spend on *Life*. I am counting on you to understand. This is so big!"

Ingersoll heard himself answering, "Okay, Harry, of course I will."

"I'm not sure, in a funny way, that Luce ever understood why *Life* was a success," reminisced Oliver Jensen, "even though he had the main role."

Life was so successful the first year that it threatened to bankrupt the company. An editor described it as "dying of success." The initial advertising rates they had contracted for were so ridiculously low that the more copies they printed, the more money they lost. "We are losing money hand over fist," Billings noted.

Critics called the magazine a nine-day freak and predicted, "Luce has shot his bolt. It will bankrupt the company," wrote one. "A short *Life*, but a merry one."

The crucial decision was whether to strictly limit circulation to ensure a profit or to triple production costs and print as many copies as the public wanted. The Luce decision: Print more copies. This meant going back to the banks for more money until they could renegotiate advertising contracts at increased rates. It was a tense time.

"I once lost a trifling $5 million on a wild steer ride with a hot baby called *Life*," Luce later said, "and, believe me, that was an awful lot more excitement than I ever got out of *making* money. Of course I didn't really intend to lose all that money, but then on the other hand I had to sort of pretend I had intended to, otherwise all my friends would have thought I was a dope. It got so that every night when I came home, my wife would tell me how another one of her dear friends had consoled her about my forthcoming bankruptcy. President Roosevelt even asked me about it once. He said was it true that I was making such a hell of a success I was going bust. And in my innocent eagerness to reassure him, I said, "Well, Mr. President, I've got my next year's budget balanced." And then did I blush! But he just laughed a good-natured laugh, and I immediately began thinking up schemes to unbalance my budget and get in step again."

Life was as brassy as it was unpredictable, and everybody wanted part of the action. Movie studios delayed their film release on the promise of a *Life* spread. A Gallup poll discovered that movie studios regarded a two-page layout in *Life* as more important than a one-page news break in any U.S. newspaper. Broadway musicals happily assembled casts in full costume in the hope of a possible *Life* picture. *Life* photographers reported that starlets, even celebrated actresses, were ready to do anything, absolutely anything, to get on the cover of *Life*.

The aim of his magazine, Luce said, was to present "the good life." Though he did run pictures of chain gangs and lynchings, he killed a picture story about a riot in upstate New York at a Paul Robeson concert where state troopers overturned cars and beat up concert-goers.

Luce's hands-on approach at *Life* was a source of chagrin at times to his staff. Oliver Jensen recalls filling in once on the editorial page. "In one editorial I wrote, I made a joke about sin. 'Living in sin; sin is relative.' It was a social editorial, and Luce called me up to his office when he'd read it and said, 'Goddamn it, Jensen, don't you know what sin is?' I said, 'I'm an Episcopalian!' (Of course, he was a Presbyterian; they're a lot harder on sin.) Sin is not terribly important to Episcopalians. Anyway, he gave me a little lecture on sin—and he was deadly serious. I said, 'I was only joking! I thought it was obvious that it was just jesting.' Then he said, 'I don't joke about sin.' "

On another occasion, Luce weighed in on a delicate personnel matter. As author Peter Drucker recalled the story: a few months after *Life* started publication, Marion MacPhail, the chief researcher for *Life*, came to Luce in great agitation.

"Harry, you have to do something about that writer; you cannot imagine what he does."

It took some coaxing before she was even willing to tell Luce that the writer did his work stark naked lying on a rug in his office.

"What about his copy?" asked Luce.

"Oh, it's fine, no problem . . ."

"Does he chase your girls?" Luce asked (with a twinkle in his eyes since the writer was a well-known homosexual).

"Of course not," she said. "The very idea; I wouldn't tolerate that for one moment."

"I don't understand. I thought all your researchers were well-educated, college-bred young women."

"So they are," she said.

"Then, they surely have been taught to shut a door," said Luce, dismissing the matter.

* * *

Luce might unexpectedly wander into the managing editor's office, sit in his chair, think out loud, talk philosophy, and wonder why the staff didn't produce more ideas. Or he would discuss the advertising crisis at *Life,* or perhaps grab a layout and start critically tearing it apart.

"He tosses everything up in the air like a juggler, fussing with pictures, and then ducks out and leaves it to us to catch the pieces as they come down," said Billings. "He's got to learn that you can't put the front pages of the *Times* all into pictures. I'm so worn down by his talk that I don't even bother to answer him back. And the funny part is that he has no idea at all how I feel about him personally or professionally. Success has changed him subtly—he is no longer the shy, simple fellow I first knew."

Grover recounted a similar session with Luce and some of his senior staff: "It was really a good session with the boss in fine form and making about eighty percent sense (twenty percent was blah-blah). I think Bill Furth (who later became Luce's executive assistant) and I were the only people who didn't agree with him almost entirely, and I think he knew this and was pleased. At one point in a rather sharp passage, Harry turned to me and said, 'Well, Al, you have plenty of doubts about free enterprise—though you believe in it enough to suit me—but I'll tell you what the weakness of your position is.' Whereupon he lectured me with considerable brevity and point of view. And I then told him what I thought was the weakness of his position, which is that he is so goddam set on preserving the ultimate, final quintessence of free enterprise capitalism that he has no time for the workaday chores so necessary to make the system work better—if it's to work at all. He's like Galahad chasing after the Grail when what we need right now is a Pepsi-Cola machine on every floor. . . . Anyway, we had fun and nobody got mad."

In the midst of this ebullience, Luce received a hard slap on the face. On Thanksgiving Day 1936, *The New Yorker* magazine published a profile of Luce, by Wolcott Gibbs, "which everyone in the shop devoured," wrote Billings. An earlier *Fortune* portrait had called *The New Yorker* editor Harold Ross "a madman . . . with a face of rubber . . . a huge Hapsburg lip to which cigarettes stick." What angered Ross most were *Time*'s inverted sentences and cryptic captions—they "had the same effect on him as a dentist's drill."

"You will go through a hell of a lot of copies of *Time* without finding anybody described in a way that would please his mother," Ross later wrote Luce, signing it, "Harold Wallace Ross . . . small man . . . furious . . . mad . . . no taste."

When Harry read *The New Yorker* profile of him, he protested, "But goddam it, Ross, this whole goddam piece is ma-ma-malicious!"

"You've put your finger on it, Luce. I believe in malice."

Luce considered the printed profile a crushing disaster mainly because it was in a magazine of imagination and distinction. "And do you know what the worst of it is?" he asked. "All my friends think it's funny."

Much of it *was* funny. The most quoted line was, "Backward ran sentences until reeled the mind." Ross described Luce as an "ambitious, gimlet-eyed, Baby Tycoon," then told of his early years in China spent "under brows too beetling for a baby." The article recorded the persistent rumor that Luce had "a wistful eye on the White House . . . where it will end, knows God."

For Luce, the peaks had come quicker than the valleys. Sixteen years out of Yale, he received a reported income of $963,400 from his editorial ventures. The new offices at the Chrysler Building spread out over 150 rooms on six floors. *The March of Time* radio program reached eight million people and *The March of Time* movie appeared thirteen times a year in over 6,000 theaters. Luce was on the board of directors of many corporations, including Paramount Pictures.

"Where will he fly?" asked journalist Harford Powel. "Well, why should a man, less than forty, whose magazines are making millions, be contented until he has a newspaper or a string of them?" Another observer reported, "Henry Robinson Luce comes as close to being a Lord of the Press as America can now produce." In his new, exalted position, Harry was invited by President Roosevelt to bring Clare to lunch at Hyde Park. During the meal, F.D.R. told them that he enjoyed Clare's play but that Eleanor was simply infuriated by it. She saw it as a slander on American womanhood. This may have been the source of Clare's frequent imitations mocking Mrs. Roosevelt.

Harry and Clare were the new show pair in society, with Clare invariably at center stage. They were people whose presence made a party, but they were not necessarily charming guests. Both were slightly stand-offish, and Clare was particularly so, because she had played the society circuit many years before and had not been impressed by it. She made it clear that she thought Washington society was inferior to English. "In England," Clare said, "a group of intelligent, well-dressed, well-heeled, well-born people get together and talk about the events of the day in one-line phrases. And, if possible, you make a joke. Do you think that sounds like Washington?"

"Everything with her was on high, high voltage," said Harry's close associate Andrew Heiskell. "I think it would be exhausting." Heiskell, who remarked that Harry never relaxed, remembered once barging into his office "and there he was lying sound asleep on his couch. I almost couldn't believe it." But if Harry slept more, he stuttered less. "When I first knew him, he still stuttered," said Heiskell. "Sometimes when he made speeches it was agony when he got stuck on something. But then the stuttering practically disappeared. The self-confidence was there."

Harry's self-confidence then seemed almost supreme. Luce was filmed making a charity appeal for a newsreel at a film studio at Astoria, Long Island. The man who organized the filming was Ben Hecht, for whom Luce once had worked in Chicago as a young reporter. Hecht had since become a prominent Hollywood producer and director. Ian McLellan Hunter, who was on the set at the time, reported that after Luce had finished his speech, "twelve nude girls ran out and surrounded him. After an appalled moment, Luce recovered quite well."

The old, shy, awkward publisher had disappeared. In his place was a Harry Luce who finally had everything he wanted in life. Almost.

What Harry Luce yearned for at this point in his life was to have a moral impact on the world. The glittering prize of the White House was beyond his reach because he was not a glittering man. Recognizing this, Luce insisted that he would rather run his magazines than occupy the White House. Yet, if he could have been appointed to the presidency, he would have grabbed it.

Luce didn't want to write the country's laws, or even its policies, but he did want to shape the vision of his country. He believed in causes, and he firmly believed that there was only a right side and a wrong side. Unlike his father, who embraced a religious cause, Harry's own cause had grown in scope to embrace the whole world. Through his magazines, he would achieve his goals. He articulated this one night in 1937 as seven of his senior editors dined with him at his sumptuous apartment on the thirty-sixth floor of the Waldorf Astoria. They drank champagne and spent three hours discussing *Time* policy. Luce posed the questions: "What is the purpose of *Time* besides making money?" and "How well are we using our influence?"

One editor's answer: to amuse, instruct, and inform. Then Luce gave his own credo: "There is such a thing as right and wrong . . . liberty and human freedom are to be desired. There is such a thing as progress . . ." Luce later said, "I regard America as a special dispensation under Providence. My spiritual pastors shake their heads about this view of mine. They say it tends to idolatry—to idolatry of a nation."

Behind the philosophical rhetoric was Luce's basic belief that as head of Time Inc. he was Public Defender of the nation. *Time* took a stand on virtually everything. The magazine was an early, fervent supporter of civil rights. *Time* bitterly attacked the Ku Klux Klan long before this became a popular stance. Time Inc. magazines were once banned from the Parish County school libraries of Shreveport, Louisiana, because of their articles on segregation. A Luce rule was that no one would ever be lynched in America without *Time* running a story on it. Discrimination because of color simply went against the grain of Luce's Presbyterianism.

Nor did *Time* hesitate to interfere in business. Luce ran a series in *Fortune* that was highly critical of U.S. Steel. The piece was written by avowed radical Dwight MacDonald. Luce reluctantly had approved publication of the first two parts but drew the line at the last article, which was headed with a quote from Lenin saying that monopoly was the last stage of capitalism which inevitably leads to socialism.

The underlying factor in all of *Time*'s crusades was a deep vein of conservative moral values. The reason the average American responded to these values was that they were coupled with an emotionalism. There was something simplistic and comforting about these values. *Time* challenged its audience just enough to make its stories interesting but not frustrating.

Luce tried to infuse his staff with his sense of mission. "You would get memos from him saying, 'Please see me about war' or 'Please see me about peace,' " recalled Richard Clurman, who later became *Time*'s chief of correspondents. "He would be bothered by the thought 'What to do about corruption?' He was appalled by the idea of worldwide corruption and was constantly trying to get a handle on it for a *Time* story." Clurman once sent a cable to thirty-five correspondents around the world saying, "H.R.L. once again interested in world ethical law and worldwide corruption."

"We went in every week to remake the world," said one of the editors. Researcher Dorothy Sterling told of the *Life* photographer who quit after nine years saying, "Luce's trouble is that he tries to run the world instead of covering the news as it happens."

A journalist's job, as Luce saw it, was to find out the right side, and say so, emphatically. Once a reporter found the greater truth, Luce thought, he should not distract the reader from what he ought to know by facts that might be in his way. Accused then of being biased, he might reply, "We never said we weren't."

Something else lingered on Harry's mind. When he was a young cub reporter in Chicago headed for a date with his girl, and dressed in an elegant suit, he shared an elevator with his editor. When he first applied for the job, he had told the editor that he wanted to be a journalist. The editor had mocked Harry in his fashionable suit, "Ah, Mr. Luce, a journalist, I see . . ."

"I have sometimes said to myself that the one thing I was determined to do was to make 'journalist' a good word."

Luce had done that. He had, in fact, become the growing giant of journalism, a press lord of enormous, towering stature on the level of Hearst, McCormick, Pulitzer, and Beaverbrook. Andrew Heiskell pinpointed what set Luce apart from his peers. "Perhaps the biggest difference between Luce and other press lords was that he wanted to have it his way as the result of winning the argument, not as the result of giving the orders. He loved anybody who would argue with him. And it would get hot and heavy. It wasn't a nice social argument. It was real hand-wrestling, at the minimum. Most people dreaded arguing with him. Among other things, he usually had given himself a head start. And when he knew what he was going to argue about, he had prepared himself.

"Harry wouldn't have a confrontation showdown. I don't think it was in his nature to do it," Heiskell continued. "He wouldn't get satisfaction out of having people just obey his orders. It was: 'I made that man change his mind, you know, by sheer logic!' He was fair in an argument. He'd use the argument to the nth degree; but it was not an order. A lot of his arguments sought for the truth. When he invited you over to dinner, you'd say, 'Oh, God, now what's gonna be the subject?' You'd sort of prepare yourself. But if you weren't prepared for fair combat, 'To hell with you!' If he lost an argument, he was a reasonably good sport about it too."

Luce was merciless as a cross-examiner. Asking the right questions was his great gift. Even greater was his willingness to listen. After talking for fifteen minutes about Bulgaria to a returning correspondent, he suddenly stopped in mid-sentence. "Why am I telling you about Bulgaria? I haven't been there in fifteen years; you just came from there. I should be listening to you, rather than you listening to me. Tell me about Bulgaria."

He did listen, and would listen to anyone, no matter how young or green, but their facts had to make sense. He might even overrule someone and later admit, "You were right."

On the other hand, said Heiskell, "If he discovered you to be ignorant on some point he considered essential to your argument . . . if he had a lock on you, and had to keep that lock for another three seconds to win the point, well, he did."

Hedley Donovan, who years later would become Luce's handpicked successor, noted, "He welcomed argument so ardently that it took a certain amount of intellectual courage to agree with him when he was right, as is bound to happen from time to time." Those writers who hedged their opinions to keep them on the *Time* line were seldom successful. Luce was bored by those whose opinions suspiciously echoed his. "I like to see independent thinking," he said. "If it's going the wrong way, I'll straighten them out fast enough."

Even if he didn't bully his people, Luce still controlled what appeared in his magazines. He repeatedly trashed William Fulbright in his magazines, because the senator did not share Luce's view that worldwide communism was the enemy of the United States. For long periods, he could never be "sweetly reasonable," as he put it, about Roosevelt.

Constantly prodded about his lack of objectivity, he replied, "When Columbus discovered America, a few people thought the earth was round. Most people thought it was flat. Round or flat? The truth did not lie in the middle. Why should *anybody* be so objective? I am not objective. I don't believe that Joseph Stalin or Adolf Hitler had good ideas."

It went against Luce's grain to praise people. Archibald MacLeish once protested to him: "They work for you—or for your magazine—harder than any comparable group in the country. And they value your praise more than you could believe. If you don't [praise your staff], the last element of personal humanity will drain out of that organization and you will be left with nothing on your hands but a business which earns money."

MacLeish had his own poet's insight:

> *I wish something had gone differently with you. . . . Maybe what I mean is that I wish you hadn't been so successful. Because it's very hard to be as successful as you have been and still keep your belief in the desperate necessity for fundamental change. . . . It would have been very easy to forget everything you believed true when you were twenty. . . . That you haven't done that is admirable. I admire you for it. . . . You were meant to make common cause with the people—all the people . . . I think you hate being rich. I think you hate being a pal of the people who want you to be their pal. I think you would have liked to write "The People Yes."*

That Luce hated being rich is a very doubtful question. He had told a group of Ohio bankers, "Make as much money as you can. . . . The more money you make, the more efficient your business will probably be . . ." But there is no question that Luce would have loved to have written Sandburg's poetry. As for making common cause with the people, he always felt he was doing that.

MacLeish, together with Eric Hodgins, Dwight MacDonald, and Laura Hobson, sent Luce a more detailed list of specific stories they felt reflected *Time* bias, and even the "smell of fascism." Luce thanked them for their "steering" criticism, which he found "most valuable" and promised to investigate.

Despite MacLeish's charge that *Time* was partial to rightist views, he happily admitted that Luce never "toned down" the liberalism in his own copy. *Life* editor A. B. C. Whipple echoed that, saying that he was a Democrat and a member of the Newspaper Guild "and I was never forced to write anything I didn't believe." Ed Thompson, another *Life* editor, put it even more directly. "I realized very early on that Luce didn't care how you voted, as long as you didn't vote Communist."

One of Harry's best writers, Emmet John Hughes, sharply made the point that Luce was not only remarkable in his receptivity to new ideas but even to ideas that were contradictory. He added his judgment that Luce had much more range, much more curiosity, and much less ideology than his magazines. Hughes thought that Luce wavered back and forth between the two sides which were always fighting for his soul.

Part of Luce's problem in the mid-thirties was his persistent support of Laird S. Goldsborough, who came to *Time* as a young Yale man and almost single-handedly wrote all the foreign news for the next thirteen years. Luce relied on his technical expertise and judged Goldsborough as an eighteenth-century gentleman. Indeed, Goldsborough liked to travel abroad in royal style, complete with a chauffeured Rolls-Royce. A heavy-set, pasty-faced man, who walked with a cane, Goldsborough was also hard of hearing. All this made him a loner, easily irritated, in a world of his own. He wrote all his copy in precise script. He could talk interminably in connected sentences, often without coming to the point. And he was very difficult to interrupt. One of his associates summed up Goldsborough as simply "a horse's ass."

Goldsborough's ancestral tree was rooted in Goldsborough, Yorkshire, but he was so self-conscious about having a Jewish-sounding name that he often injected snide, anti-Semitic references into *Time*. When Leon Blum became premier of France, Goldsborough referred to him in print as "Jew Blum."

Goldsborough had interviewed Hitler and Mussolini, liked them both, and said so. Luce and Goldsborough believed early on that the moral force of fascism "may be the inspiration for the next general march of mankind." Luce changed his mind more quickly than Goldsborough. Many of the staff felt that Goldsborough remained an out-and-out fascist and that Luce preserved, protected, and defended him for too long. But Luce was nobody's dupe. Eric Hodgins, who became editor of *Fortune*, told of an editorial meeting with Luce during which Goldsborough expounded on his travels. Goldsborough described an Italian government official who was, "in purest essence, the very embodiment of the democratic ideal." Luce, who had been leaning back in his chair, suddenly snapped upright. "All right, Goldie, it's horseshit!"

"I'd never heard Harry use such a word before," said Allen Grover. "And in the course of the next twenty-five years, I never heard Harry use such a word again. He could be and was, appropriately, and sometimes volubly, profane, but this remained forever his only venture into scatology within my hearing."

At *Time* the Spanish Civil War was another source of deep controversy. The conflict soon became a small preview of the coming world war when Hitler and

Mussolini sent troops and planes to support Franco, and the Soviets bolstered the Loyalist government. The United States passed a Neutrality Act forbidding any shipment of arms to the area.

Goldsborough promptly sided with Franco, saying the Loyalists were "Red militia . . . Socialists, Communists and rattle-brained Liberals . . ." Archibald MacLeish protested both to Goldsborough and to Luce that *Time* had presented no factual proof of this charge, and that Franco's revolt, in fact, was "an inexcusable and unjustifiable act of aggression by reactionary forces against a popular government."

What made the confrontation more interesting was that Luce permitted both Goldsborough in *Time* and MacLeish in *Fortune* to write their contradictory views. Part of this stance was his delight in keeping his staff slightly "offstride." He not only welcomed opposing points of view, but encouraged his editors to differ.

Otto Fuerbringer, later a *Time* managing editor, told of attending an editorial dinner presided over by Luce. "There's a big round table and there's very animated conversation; suddenly, it's really hot and animated and very argumentative and the faces are really grim. It ends very grim. Luce looks up at me and says: 'Come on, Otto! You know I always get people against each other.' " At other times, Luce publicly admitted that fostering competition and controversy among his editors made for a livelier magazine.

Not only did Harry like to stir things up by pitting editors against each other, often leaving lines of authority unclear, he might suddenly assign new tasks to people, often seeming to support a theory of dislocation. "Uncomfortable himself," said one of his editors, "he seemed to like to make others uncomfortable."

"Harry was a great fellow for rearranging his hand under the table," said one of his best editors, T. S. Matthews. "When he wanted to make radical changes, he wouldn't tell anybody about it except the people involved. Then he'd put his cards down."

Describing the Luce mind as a blend of high-mindedness and cunning leadership, a disgruntled *Time* editor complained, "I know how to deal with Boy Scouts and I know how to deal with gangsters, but I'm damned if I know how to deal with people who are both at the same time!"

Another analysis came from Peter Drucker, who said Luce's techniques were more Chinese than Machiavellian. "Mao Tse-tung ran his government and party exactly the way Henry Luce ran his magazines: by creating factions; by working around people who had the title, office, and responsibility; by encouraging juniors to come to him but enjoining them not to tell their bosses; and by keeping alive feuds, mutual distrusts, and opposing cliques. His system of control was that of the Chinese ruler who remains far from the scene of action and takes no direct part, but who makes sure that no one else can become a threat by organizing countervailing officials, bureaucratic factions, and competing personal networks. Every American and European I have known who grew up in rural China the way Henry Luce did has acted much the same way."

At *Life,* managing editor John Shaw Billings shouldered the brunt of Luce's antics. Luce would hold long sessions with *Life* staff on how to improve the magazine. "When I started to speak," said Billings, "he said 'I don't want to hear from you.' So the junior editors had the floor. They wanted more 'Socko' and 'Wow' in *Life.* The implication of the three-hour discussion was that I was a bum editor and that any of my juniors could do a better job . . ."

On the other hand, Luce would take Billings to lunch at the Biltmore and have a long philosophical talk about his search for what he believed in. Then, he would ask: "What are you for? What are you against?" Even the critical Billings admitted it was "interesting."

Luce was always stressing the sense of the "family" of Time Inc., insisting that all the magazines must sink or swim together. He did not understand anybody on his staff feeling "alienated." He was an organization man long before the term was coined and believed in absolute loyalty. He couldn't understand why someone would not willingly want to work eighteen hours a day and survive with a sandwich, as he once did.

Luce was also kindly and paternal. He wrote personal notes when a staff member took ill and sent a solid silver porringer from Tiffany to any Time Inc. employee who became the parent of a new child. The porringer was inscribed with the name of the baby "From his father's friend, Henry R. Luce."

Most of Luce's top editors shared an ambivalence about their boss. They felt respectful, admiring, often awkward in his presence. His relations with them could be both intense and impersonal. He was not a man for back-slapping warmth, but he was still perceptive about their needs and their talents, always open to their questions and arguments. He dazzled and baffled them, and hence they were drawn tightly to him.

Periodically, Luce would get the editing itch and want to take over a whole issue. He'd prepare himself by looking at the photograph and name of everyone on the staff so that he could identify them when he saw them.

When Luce edited *Time* for a week, said Billings, "it was somewhat like working directly behind a buzz saw, chewing metal faster than the eye can follow and throwing off an unremitting shower of sharp and shining filings." Another editor described it "just like a gale-force wind, blowing through the office . . . everyone rushing around, trying to rescue bits of paper and everything. He'd send people off on terrific wild-goose chases. But they all got very much excited. Then, about midnight on Saturday, when things were really tough, Luce would just put on his hat and say, 'I'm going home,' and leave somebody else to pick up the pieces. Everybody would breathe a sigh of relief when he was finished. Yet they all had to admit it'd been an invigorating and exhausting week."

When Luce edited, his staff knew that his instincts for a story were often excellent. "If Harry didn't like something," said T. S. Matthews, "he'd call in the writer and explain to him what he thought the story ought to be. If the writer didn't do it, Luce would can the story. I remember pieces of copy when Luce would circle a sentence here and move it up to another place, and it was just absolutely right."

"I remember Louis Kronenberger once telling me that he got a good piece of advice from Harry," said *Time* editor Tom Griffith. "He was writing a piece for *Fortune,* and received it back from Harry, saying, 'This is too well-written.' Louis always wrote this balanced, eighteenth-century prose. What Luce had done was, in almost every paragraph, to take out the first sentence. 'I got very offended at first,' Louis said, 'then I got reading it and it was a lot livelier!' "

"Totally specious," was one of Luce's favorite phrases. His great aim was to reduce redundancy. Instead of tearing out everything and starting fresh, "Harry would just take the banalities out of things with one clean little phrase. He'd just lift the whole damn piece," said Griffith. One of his memorable editorial written comments was, "Make your emphasis come from STRUCTURE not STATEMENT."

Smooth transitions didn't necessarily interest Luce. "Some *Time* editors, such as Otto Fuerbringer, put out issues that were seamless. Every paragraph flowed into the next. Fuerbringer's issue was a beautiful performance, beautifully orchestrated," noted Griffith. "When Luce edited, there might be a little repetition and it was often jumpy, but oh boy was it good!"

Harry also edited *Fortune* on occasion and won praise for his efforts, particularly from John Kenneth Galbraith, who later became ambassador to India. Galbraith had done some writing for *Fortune* and Henry edited one of his pieces. "Nothing so troubled him as wasted words. It was a marvel to see how much more Harry, with a few sweeps of a soft, black pencil, could remove, and how little in consequence would be lost," said Galbraith. "Not since working for Harry Luce have I gone over a manuscript without the feeling that he was looking over my shoulder, that his pencil would presently pass through my paragraphs as he said, 'This can go.' " When Galbraith later joined John Kennedy's staff, Luce told the president, "I taught Galbraith to write. And I tell you, I've certainly regretted it."

Editing *Life* was a real challenge for Luce. "I think Luce came down from the mountain top to edit once every six months, for a week, but it took us weeks to get over it," said Billings, then managing editor of *Life*.

"Luce was very impatient with pictures. He'd look at them and say, 'If this picture and that picture were together, I could see it working.' Now, you could put two paragraphs into one, but you couldn't put two photographs into one. He'd suddenly walk off and go upstairs or something, really depressed. He didn't have the patience for them, and you have to have enormous patience. 'Patience' was not a Luce word. 'Persistence,' that's more accurate."

What Luce was best at was brewing ideas for fundamental changes in *Life*. He wanted more narrative pictures, more solid information. He had his own concept of picture essays: "It's like being a Southern preacher. First I tell them what I'm going to tell them; then I tell them; then I tell them what I told them."

Harry often shared some of his ideas with Clare. She had a sharp editorial mind and made all kinds of suggestions about story ideas, people, pictures. She even urged him to hire some writers she knew. Yet Clare still felt only at the edge of things and was frustrated and envious. This probably explained some of her need to constantly travel. Harry, after all, had his family at Time, Inc. She no longer had any sense of family.

Clare did have a set of friends, including theater people, whom Harry did not like, and literary people, whom he tolerated. Clare occasionally invited some of these friends to be weekend guests at Greenwich. This was mostly for Clare's entertainment. Harry was more interested in playing tennis, taking brisk walks, swimming some, and reading. He tolerated the company but only until ten PM. Then, no matter who the guests were, Harry would pick up his briefcase and say, "See you at seven in the morning."

Harry generally slept well, ate anything, chain-smoked, and was always punctual. During the work week, he arrived at his office at nine-fifteen. He was a very busy man, and time was a precious word at Time Inc. Luce expected visitors to state their business quickly and then he let them know when the time was up. Luce claimed his hobby was "conversing with somebody who knows something. I would rather talk to a man from Texas than to a roomful of the brightest people in New York. I believe in human beings, but I do not idealize them," he once said. People who impressed him most were people with style and grace, because he didn't have any of his own, noted friends. And yet his very strength was his lack of grace, his audacity, his brusqueness. He never had the instinct to be one of the boys, to fit in, to get along.

Everything about Luce was intense. Evenings meant little to him because he usually left the office with a load of work. He resented hearing that he had a golden touch, or that he was lucky. Luck had as much to do with the shaping of his career "as it has to do with directing the course of an army tank," he liked to say. The proper word was "ambition," he carefully pointed out.

Luce's focus was so intense that the mundane parts of life escaped him. "I was taking care of the Letters Department," remembered Marion MacPhail. "That office was on the same floor as his, and we were both going down on the same elevator. Just to make conversation, I told him how it was pouring outside. He looked at me, terribly surprised. He didn't know it had been raining outside. I mean, he had these big windows, and didn't even look. . . . So he stopped the elevator, and went back upstairs, to get an umbrella."

Coupled with his single-mindedness was his absentmindedness. "Everything had to be in its place," said his secretary. "For example, his briefcase opened at the top. On the right-hand side, you'd put his passport and tickets. If they fell out of that place, he was totally lost. He'd say, 'The tickets aren't there.' Also, when he was going out we'd give him bios on the people he was to meet as well as little cards with detailed instructions on how to get to the Waldorf, etc."

What Luce did *not* go out with was much money. And what he had, he spent very carefully. Correspondents traveling with Luce knew to check his dinner tips so that they, and the magazine, would not be embarrassed. Left to his own devices, Harry might well leave a $1 tip for an $80 dinner.

Marion MacPhail discovered this for herself: "Toward the end of a party, he said, 'Marion, I'm hungry. Why don't we go out for a bite?' So I went with him. He loved scrambled eggs. We were supposed to eat at the hotel restaurant. We went out. I think he paid the cab; but I know I tipped the doorman. But then I thought about Reuben's; so we went there. He did not have an account at Reuben's, so he couldn't sign the check. He said, 'But I'm Harry Luce!' It's lucky I had money, as he did not; and so I paid the check. About a month later, I got a note from him, thanking me for the meal, and sending me a check for fifty dollars. I told this whole story to his sister Beth, who said, 'I believe the whole story, except the part where he sent you a check.' "

Harry was so absentminded that he often left his coat somewhere. His secretary had a standing order at Saks Fifth Avenue to replace Luce's coats.

"It was impossible for me to do anything about his clothes," said Clare. "He'd go to the office with one black shoe and one brown shoe. He wore a sort of drab gray kind of clothing. He simply could not match colors. He was indifferent, not color blind. He didn't spend money on himself. His dress shirts were all frayed. His handkerchiefs were a horror. When I'd protest, he'd get cranky and call it nagging."

"Clare would just yell at him because his dinner shirts were turning yellow with age, and say, 'Harry, buy some new ones,' " noted Allen Grover. "He would just say: 'They haven't worn out, they haven't worn out yet.' "

Still, Clare tried. She took him to the best tailors, and bought the most expensive clothes, but he couldn't care less, and it showed. He wore a gray felt Borsalino hat but he wore it always and refused to part with it, no matter how battered it became. He was more concerned about having his pants pressed. "I've been in more darn hotels while Harry was in his undershorts waiting for his pants to come back," said *Time* correspondent Frank White. When White planned a white-tie formal party for Luce and invited top diplomats, "Harry came in his gray suit." One of the great laughs at Time Inc. was Harry's nomination by the Merchants Tailor and Designers Association as one of the nation's twenty-two best-dressed men, "because he clings to many of the archaic elegancies of the nineteenth century."

Harry *did* receive an award that meant a great deal to him: an honorary degree from Rollins College in Florida. What made it important was that his parents were in Florida at the time and came to hear him, the first time they had heard their son make a live speech since he was a boy. They had heard him speak the previous summer on the radio. Harry's father wrote about it to Clare and was ecstatic; he called it a red letter day and quoted an elderly friend saying it was the finest speech he had heard in a decade.

Whatever hurt his parents had over his divorce from Lila was now pushed deeply within themselves. In writing to Clare, her mother-in-law expressed warmth and affection and signed her letters, "Mother." When Ann was ill, Mother Luce offered to come and help. The Luces invited Clare and Harry to Thanksgiving dinner, and to a family weekend in Pennsylvania at Christmas. In return, the elder Luces occasionally came to Mepkin. Harry also made certain his parents had every luxurious comfort when they planned a visit to Washington. Clare kept a flow of birthday presents arriving on time. On the surface, everything was going extremely well for Harry, personally and professionally.

Luce was now thirty-eight years old. Through his magazines, he had carved a place in American life and entered its "golden age." *Time*'s readers relied on the magazine and awaited it expectantly. For Luce, the satisfactions were enormous. He saw *Time* in good hands, *Life* safely launched, and *Fortune* progressing nicely. The goals and challenges were met; the patterns set. It was time now to focus more on his personal life.

15

A thousand days after he wrote his first letter of passionate love to Clare from the Racquet and Tennis Club, in New York, Luce wrote another letter from the same club to his beloved darling. It was a remarkable piece of correspondence from a man sometimes described by his colleagues as "a Frigidaire." He talked about how he longed for her lovely body, how much he mentally kept squeezing her and crushing her, about his burning memory of their blissful nights, and how much he loved her, loved her, loved her.

Harry had married her because he had admired all of her, not just her body. He didn't marry her simply to sleep with her. He desperately needed the constant play of the breadth of her mind, the glamour and possession of her presence. But the physical was a strong part of his attraction.

Yet Harry wanted more than Clare was ready to give. An early feminist, she believed that a liberated woman must renounce being a sex object and must admit that the Prince Charming story is a fairy tale. Marriage, she said, "ain't no perpetual honeymoon."

Clare's feelings for Harry were those of admiration and deep affection. She believed that he still had a pinnacle to reach. She appreciated his voracious intellect and vice versa. But the primal bond seemed to be their shared common dream of power.

She idealized his power, just as he idealized her glamour. Both were disappointed; neither got everything they wanted. He wanted warmth from her, and never totally received it. She wanted to *share* his power, pull the strings, and he wouldn't let her. The honeymoon was over.

In 1938, the Luces bought a Georgian style estate in Greenwich on fifty-nine acres overlooking Long Island Sound, bounded by King Street and the Byram River. The property included a main house with twenty-one rooms and eleven baths, a greenhouse, and several farm buildings. Harry and Clare called it "The House," and even put that on their stationery.

In the reception rotunda, the Luces displayed their collection of Chinese art objects, icons, chests, and paintings. A glass circular staircase led to the second floor. In the living room to the right of the staircase, great mirrored panels could be adjusted to catch or deflect the light. Countless photographs of the famous people who had touched their lives were arranged on tables. The chairs and sofas in the large living room were all big and squashy "because the Luces just like to lie around and read most of the time," explained their decorator Gladys Freeman, Donald Freeman's sister.

To the left of the staircase was a large library filled with bookshelves that reached to the ceiling on all sides. Over the fireplace was a Matisse. In the adjoining music room was a grand piano and an antique backgammon table. Flowers and family photographs were everywhere. Ten live-in servants made sure that everything was dusted and cared for to the lady of the house's satisfaction.

To summon her staff, Clare used one of the first push-button telephones. The first three priority buttons read: "Office, Kitchen, and Pantry." The button after "Pantry," fourth on the list of Clare's priorities, read "Luce."

The view from the huge picture windows looked out over a rolling valley, white-fenced horse meadows, a tennis court, a lily pond, and a sparkling swimming pool.

The House was a showcase to which Clare soon invited a parade of prominent people. The guests were mostly Clare's friends, who were primarily there for her entertainment, though she did allot her guests time for bridge, backgammon, and sometimes tennis.

The same year that the Luces bought their Connecticut home, they moved from their fifteen-room duplex in the River House on 52nd Street to another posh suite on the forty-first floor of the Waldorf Towers. There were three bedrooms, one for Harry, one for Clare, and a small one for the maid.

The separate bedrooms were symptomatic of the state of the Luce marriage. Though both were aware of the growing distance between them, Harry still professed deep love, especially in his letters to his beautiful, beloved darling, saying how much he adored her, how grateful he was for their years together and for being everything she was. He was always able to say in letters what he could not verbalize. He knew how difficult it was for her to be the wife of a publisher whose magazines sometimes made fun of her friends. (Elsa Maxwell was so incensed at a *Time* item that she didn't invite them to one of her big parties.) He did mention a frustrating phone call with Clare and observed that sometimes Clare could be cruel.

In so many ways, they did not mesh. Harry was so much more ascetic than Clare in his manners and habits. The one vice they shared was heavy smoking. She was a highly sophisticated woman with the wit and gift for making people open up to her. She might have done so much more for this rigid man because she knew the fervent passion within him. Before their wedding and in the early months of the marriage, she had succeeded in unleashing Harry's passion. But once he was caught and he was hers, Clare's restlessness urged her on to other places, to other men. Her private papers include folders of love letters from a variety of men. In one, the sender called Clare "the simple girl, more tender and true and much more rare than any spirit I've ever touched or known . . ." In another, written at four-thirty AM, the smitten lover proclaimed: "After four scotches on the train, I've decided I adore you when I'm both drunk and sober . . ."

Yet another admirer referred to Clare's "remarkable chassis—a tenderness and a hardness I adore . . . a slender thing of steel and Dresden . . ."

At first, Harry suspected little. He thought that men gravitated toward Clare in social situations only because she was so glamorously beautiful. He would eventually learn otherwise.

In the early years after their marriage, Clare was often away. She traveled restlessly to Europe to see friends here and there. Harry was a lonely man. When he was at Time Inc., he was home, he was busy, and he was happy. But when the day was done, he would often return to an empty apartment or an empty house. Harry found it difficult to lift a phone and invite somebody to share his time. When he did, he summoned people from Time Inc.

John Hersey, a Time writer, was a favorite dinner guest. He was an uncanny copy of Luce. He, too, had grown up in China, a mishkid—son of a missionary—and gone to Hotchkiss and Yale. A sensitive human being and a talented writer, Hersey soon found himself absorbed into a kind of father-son relationship.

"We had lunches and dinner together about once a month," remembered Hersey. "He became more paternal and fraternal. And he would take me to the opera. He loved the opera and Clare didn't.

"I remember during intermission, going into the sort of restaurant they had at the old Metropolitan Opera House and having a drink between the acts. The thing that was touching to me, and hit me very hard, was his pointing out to me all the important people in that place: 'There's a Rockefeller over there.' He was still impressed. And it was not name-dropping in the sense of being proud about having these connections. It was sort of, 'I hope you'll share my excitement about . . .' Yes, that these are important people.

"I was invited to dinner parties at his apartment. He was fun to listen to.

He wasn't a barrel of laughs but he had such a lively turn of mind." Hersey saw Luce as a warm, compassionate man, a kind man, "a walking wonder of possibilities to a mishkid like me. He was so astonished and delighted by whatever he had not previously known." Hersey said that Harry never verbalized about their relationship, but the warmth of feeling was obvious. "And I really reciprocated in those early years—he was one of the most important men in my life."

Yet, Harry's loneliness increased. He was often withdrawn and taut. Even an old Yale friend like Archibald MacLeish, who admired Luce so much, later admitted that when he was in New York, "the last person I'd think of to call was Harry. He was so awkward to be with, so heavy-handed, so lacking in a sense of humor . . ."

In his frequent letters to Clare, Harry poured out his loneliness. Always skilled at manipulating men, she filled her letters with a lot of affection she may not have felt. If she had felt it, she would have tried to spend more time with Harry instead of constantly roaming the world.

Harry occasionally turned to his first wife for companionship. Lila confided that Harry told her, years later, that he had wanted a divorce from Clare before he had been married one year, and that he wanted one every year after that.

"It's crazy, when you think about it," she said. "One saw pictures in the paper of Clare and Harry holding hands. They were always in the news, lovely pictures, all the time. How could I know they weren't happily married? If I had suspected that he was unhappily married, I could have said, 'Let's have dinner together. Let's go to the opera. Let's *do* something.' But I kept hands off because I thought he was happily married. And he never implied that he wasn't."

"He later told me that Clare had a love affair with an aviator before they had been married six months," continued Lila. "And Harry told me, 'You know, I didn't have any trouble getting her to get rid of that guy, because I pointed out what a moron he was. He wasn't educated . . .' He was able to exert some control and get rid of her lovers. But, then, I think he couldn't do it enough because he didn't even know whom she was running around with. So he came to see me; and he gave me a beautiful gold bracelet with a great big aquamarine in the middle and diamonds and rubies on each side. He bought it in Tiffany. And he'd send me flowers once in awhile."

Another confidant was Allen Grover. One evening when the marriage was still young, Grover received a call from Luce at home.

"Are you doing anything?" Harry asked.

"No, I'm just talking to [his wife] Bea."

"Well, could you come over?"

"Sure."

When Grover walked into the Waldorf suite, Harry had his head in his hands, and there were tears in his eyes. "Al, what would you think, if you came into this room and found out that I had jumped out of the window?"

"What are you talking about?"

"Well," he said, "I just discovered that Clare doesn't love me, as much as I love her."

It was Harry's second suicide threat, again triggered by Clare.

What prompted Harry's misery was a broken engagement. They had had an important dinner-date that night to celebrate an anniversary. Harry had been looking forward to it. Then, he received a message that Clare's secretary had called to cancel the evening because of a business appointment. It was a deep hurt, not only because she canceled the date, but because she'd had her secretary call his secretary, rather than tell him directly. This, coupled with all his knowledge of her other men, triggered his deep despair.

"What do you know about women?" Luce asked Grover. And then Luce added unhappily, "I don't know anything about them."

"I spent the rest of the time just talking to him, trying to calm him down," said Grover, "trying to invent situations in my own marriage where that kind of thing happened, and told him it happened all the time. But I understood that what Harry was feeling was just a repeat of what had happened before."

Grover kept talking for the next hour or two. Harry just sat there and listened to him; he would say "Yes" or "No," or shake his head. After it was all over, he said, "Thank you, Al, for coming. I'll see you tomorrow."

The crisis was over, but not the problems. Harry confided to a friend that Clare no longer wanted to sleep with him. Yet, in a reflection later in life, Clare implied that the curtailment of their sex life was more to do with her work habits: "Harry often came home and after we'd had dinner, I'd 'go to bed' and start to write a play. Obviously I didn't know what a *bed* was *for,*" she said.

Her recommendation to other women was that they should never let their husbands see them in bed until they are ready to make love.

Clare added a telling footnote that a woman should never marry somebody who has walked out on a good wife because he is as cheerful as someone who has killed his mother.

Harry seemed to blame the failure of his marriage on himself, not Clare. His friend Allen Grover confirmed this. "It was a terrible shock to him. It took him quite a while, many months, to adjust to the fact that their marriage was going to be a much more regular, ordinary marriage than he had thought of it as being. When he was under the spell of Clare's infatuation for him, and his for her, he had a very different attitude toward her. It had been worshipful. And that came to an end. They had to readjust to a more normal American marriage and to the notion, 'You do this for me; I'll do that for you.' He found that this woman that he'd idolized was very human."

As the marriage worsened, Harry sought friendship from Clare's old confidante Laura Hobson, who was working in the promotion department of *Life*.

Laura was a dynamo, hard-driving and ambitious, and had no hesitation telling Harry exactly what she thought about anything. She spoke loudly and distinctly, so that he had no trouble hearing her. She would throw up her hands and say, "Oh Harry, you don't understand!" He would almost look sheepish! Laura could do that to Harry; not many people could. When he handed her the proof of an ad, and asked what she thought of it, she replied, "Pretty pompous and pretty dull."

"Fine. I wrote it myself." His big eyebrows shot up, and he said briskly with his usual abrupt style, more interested than annoyed, "Do you think you can do better?"

Yes, she thought so, and she did.

Harry liked Laura. He liked the dynamo and the excitement and the talent and the woman. She was extremely attractive. Shortly after he hired her, she became the highest paid woman on staff and, later, the only woman to have Time stock. Luce and Laura spent lunches, dinners, and entire evenings discussing promotion ideas. Harry's highly efficient and protective secretary, Corinne Thrasher, suggested to Laura that Luce was "so tired of restaurants" and would much rather dine at Laura's apartment. "I don't have a cook," Laura said. "He never thinks about food," answered Corinne.

The set-up was perfect for an affair, as Luce's *Time* associate Andrew Heiskell noted. "I don't know whether they ever had one or not," he said. "I suspect, but I don't know. But she had considerable influence on him. She was a very, very smart copywriter." Ralph Ingersoll, who later had a prolonged affair with Hobson, openly speculated that Harry had always seen much more in Laura than her considerable promotional talents, and that the two of them had "pursued a cautious fling . . ."

While Harry spent more time with Laura in the late thirties, Clare restlessly sought out a new cause and a new hero. Soon she found both.

Clare met the magnetic Harry Bridges at the home of her friend Helen Brown. In 1937 Helen had married Jack Lawrenson, a founder of the new militant National Maritime Union. Harry Bridges was a friend of the Lawrensons. Clare was immediately mesmerized. Bridges was a long, lean, hawk-faced labor organizer with the speaking style of a rabid preacher. Brilliant, shrewd, and cocky, Alfred Renton Bridges had the fire and force to move people. Within four years after he arrived in the United States, he encouraged long-shoremen to strike in all West Coast Pacific ports. When 2,000 National Guard soldiers crushed a strike on July 5, 1934, "Bloody Thursday," wounding hundreds and killing two, Bridges organized a protest parade of 40,000 men, women, and children marching eight abreast through San Francisco to the music of Beethoven's Funeral March. The result was the first coast-wide contract in the industry. Three years later, Bridges set up the International Longshoremen's and Warehousemen's Union, and was elected president. For seventeen years afterward, the United States tried to deport him without success.

Bridges was a staunch Communist sympathizer, though he did not join the party. "The Communist Party did not permit anyone to join who was not a U.S. citizen," said Helen Lawrenson. "I doubt if Bridges ever was technically a member, even after he became a citizen, although there is no question where his sympathies lay . . ."

Bridges had the kind of power and magnetism Clare loved. "He almost talked me into communism," she said. "I suspect now that the appeal of communism, for me, lay in its religious aspect. It provided a complete, authoritarian religious structure. In my teens, I read Karl Marx's *Das Kapital,* and was very much inclined to believe that he had found the perfect blueprint for the happy society," she continued. "My favorite memories of Marx's thesis gave me an increasingly uneasy feeling about the wealthy society in which I was moving. No Communist front organizations solicited my name in those days, for it was not well-known enough. But it might have been had a hundred times over, for the asking. It was the emotional content that made communism appealing to me for a long time. It is really no accident at all that the intellectuals of my own circle who most strongly deny any need of a personal faith are the ones most drawn, even today, to the Communist religion."

Clare had been a taster and a wanderer all her life, and suddenly the taste of communism seemed tempting. She tried "society" and found it empty. She had enjoyed the literary life, without finding it fulfilling. She had lived in a dozen places without having a home at all. Her first marriage had been to a drunk and this second marriage had grown dry and dull. Clare found much lacking in being the frustrated consort to a king. What she wanted was an overwhelming sense of purpose.

Bridges seemed to offer more than that, much more. He gave her what she no longer received from her husband, the stirring of a physical passion. With their own busy travel schedules, their relationship was difficult. Still, when Bridges was hospitalized in New York, Clare was at his bedside. She tried hard to find ways to rendezvous, despite their schedules. What finally turned Clare away was when a Communist recruiter arrived to persuade her to be an active agent for the Communist Party in America. She strongly suspected Bridges had sent him. Clare was too individualistic to be an agent for *any* group. The offer shocked her into weighing what she wanted and where she was going. The Communist credo was too hard, and its purpose too cold. It was not the religion she was seeking.

About this time, Clare was rocked out of her political crisis by a personal one: Her mother and her friend Joe "Riggie" Jacobs were killed in a car collision with a Florida East Coast passenger train at a crossing. Ann Clare was fifty-two.

Clare and her mother had been very much intertwined. Ann Clare had been her model, and she had been her mother's clay. Her mother had shaped her and pushed her. She had absorbed her mother's attitudes toward men and life. She had envied her mother's beauty long before she had developed her own. As a young girl and as an adult, she had frequent nightmares watching her mother's teeth fall out. (Ann Clare had perfect teeth, and Clare did not.)

Ann Clare's final days had been deeply unhappy. Just as Billy Boothe once left her for another woman, Dr. Austin found his nurse more attractive. Ann Clare had suffered a mental breakdown, and extended hospitalizations. Then came the terrible accident.

Her mother had seen Clare as the justification for her own life. Clare was devastated by her mother's death. Her friends felt that perhaps she would now turn to her own daughter for love and solace, but no. Ann was a timid girl and not a very pretty one. Clare simply could not reach out to her. She had frequent surges of great guilt because they had spent so little time together. Ann had been in boarding school for five years and wrote again and again how much she missed her mother, adored her mother, how she was almost dying of homesickness. When Clare called her occasionally, Ann wrote to thank her a billion times, apologized for disappointing her by not getting better grades, and asked if Mummie would please not forget to send the biscuits and cod liver oil for her dog.

Ann also wrote that her friends were only concerned about their coming-out parties. She said college was a waste of time but that she wanted to go to college, that she loved her mother very, very much, and would do anything she wanted. When was she going to hear from her? When was she going to see her?

As always, Harry tried to fill the gap. He was not a man who hugged many people, but he hugged Ann. They had a loving relationship. To Ann, Harry was now "Pop."

But Clare could not seem to find time for Ann, and when she did plan a visit, she often canceled it. In 1938, however, both Harry and Clare felt it was time to attempt to knit a close family group. Clare was still in the aftershock of her ending with Bridges. Harry wanted his wife back. Both seemed to be trying harder. After a small party, Fred and Adele Astaire wrote Clare to say how much they had enjoyed it, and added that they were glad to see her so happy and they would "never forget that little 'Sappho' kiss your darling hubby gave you . . ."

Clare and Harry decided to go to Hawaii for six weeks on a "second honeymoon." They would take his two sons, aged thirteen and nine, as well as Ann, who was fourteen. Harry also invited his brother Sheldon and Sheldon's wife to join them.

The night before Harry was to fly to Hawaii with Clare, Time Inc. employees gave him a farewell black-tie stag dinner in a private dining room at the old Blackstone Hotel in Chicago. Afterward, Harry cornered Ingersoll, who had been his frequent confidant at Time Inc. "Come with me," said Harry, who led Ralph to his cluttered hotel bedroom. The luggage was lying about only half-packed. Ingersoll described Luce as "very tense, tight-lipped, hard-eyed."

"Mac, what I am going to say to you, no one else knows, not even Clare. There is a time in a man's life when he has to make a decision by himself and I have made mine. I brought you here to tell you that when I go away tomorrow, I may never be back!"

Luce paced the room and stood towering over Ingersoll. "I am telling you," Luce continued, "because if I do not come back, you're the one who will have to explain it, as best you can, to the directors first, I guess, however you like. This is my decision, Mac: That my love for Clare means more to me than this company, even though I've built it myself, and it's mine. So if I have to choose between them, I will choose Clare."

It was a monologue not meant for rebuttal or response. "He was making a confessional in that room, and I was the invisible confessor behind an invisible screen," Ingersoll said. He was astounded and speechless. Nor could he believe Harry really meant it.

Harry's marriage had been imperfect, unfulfilled, and perhaps he felt that if it were not purified and made right, then all his life had been for nothing. He was therefore willing to give it his total dedication and prepared to forsake all else, past and present. In a sense, Harry was reaching back to his youth, to his fervent belief in absolutes.

It was a happy time, and the children made it happier. When Harry practiced riding a surfboard, his children would yell at him, "Stick with it, Pop." Ann wore her hair in a long bob, and she and Clare rode their surfboards tandem with Hawaiian beach boys. Ann wanted so desperately to show her mother that *she* could do things too. But she sadly told her Aunt Kit, "I can't even beat Mother at tennis . . ."

On their return from Hawaii, an expectant Ingersoll anxiously searched Harry's face and words for some sort of sign on what he wanted to do with Time Inc. and with his life.

"But there was no communication with me in Harry's eyes," recalled Ingersoll. "There was not a vibration in the air; Harry and Clare were just two married people, almost middle-aged, and the night in the Blackstone Hotel had never happened."

Of course, Clare did not want Harry to give up his empire any more than Wallis Warfield Simpson wanted the king to give up his throne. If there was no empire, there would be no power. If there was no empire, she could no longer play the part of empress. Nor did Luce really want to surrender that power. Not yet forty, he was too young and restless to retire.

Harry returned recharged and ready to be boss again. In a memo to his staff, Luce announced his new title: editorial director of *Time, Life,* and *Fortune.* He wanted to signify loud and clear that he was boss, and he was back in charge, available for consultation on any editorial matter, day or night.

In a telling exchange, Clare had criticized the fact that Harry had all his money tied up in Time Inc. stock. "You know, Harry, that's a terrible mistake, having all your eggs in one basket."

"No," he said, "not as long as it's my basket."

16

In 1938, *Time* was fifteen years old. To commemorate the anniversary issue, Luce requested a letter from Franklin Roosevelt, then in the middle of his second term. When F.D.R. complied, Luce offered effusive thanks. But privately, Luce was extremely ambivalent about Roosevelt. *Time* writer Tom Griffith noted that "it bugged Luce" that F.D.R. photographed so well and "made a terrific *Life* cover" while most Republican candidates "looked like accountants." But more significantly, Harry took it personally when Roosevelt granted recognition to the Soviet Union. Basically a conservative Republican, Luce retained an independent mind on many issues. He saw much worth in the structure of the early New Deal. He felt sympathetic to many of its issues. He certainly believed in many of Roosevelt's international views—except on Russia.

The White House was *not* amused when *Life* described F.D.R. as "this shrewd, bold, lusty, self-willed man who now truly bestrides the world like a Colossus. His ambition and power are cut to fit . . . President Roosevelt has never shared the majority opinion."

"Roosevelt hated him [Luce]," explained *Time* editor T. S. Matthews. "He thought he had an unfavorable, unfair press from Luce. He was right, too, because Luce's theoretical idea was to have *Time* fifty-one percent against the government—no matter who they were. With Roosevelt, instead of fifty-one percent, it was about eighty-nine percent."

Harry was not a man who showed his hate, yet John Shaw Billings once wrote, "God, how he hates Roosevelt, as I do too." Yet, when Billings wanted to run a picture in *Life* of the crippled president in a wheel chair, Luce flatly refused. A year later, in a speech at the Ohio Bankers Association in 1939, Luce also gave a speech lauding F.D.R.

Luce praised the president for making "the first concerted attempt to adjust the inequalities and to attack the accumulated evils of a system that business-men were either too afraid or too lazy to change."

Again and again, Luce would change his opinion about the president. The relationship was a love-hate one that would last for years. Clare, however, had none of her husband's ambivalence about F.D.R. She described Roosevelt and his circle as "ramsquaddled, do-gooding New Deal bureaucrats." Clare never forgot or forgave overhearing the voice of President Franklin D. Roosevelt, after a White House meeting with her, saying to an aide, "Get that woman out of here!"

In May 1938, Clare and Harry departed on an inspection tour of Europe to assess the growing Nazi threat. The Luces were delighted to be in the thick of things. Though the Nazis had already marched into Austria, London society geared up to give the Luces a reception that was almost royal. They were "feted, dined, wined, complimented, and plastered with praise," observed British columnist "Cassandra." London newspapers mentioned Luce as a presidential possibility.

Great Britain was always a favorite place for Harry and Clare. While there they renewed their acquaintance with U.S. Ambassador Joseph Patrick Kennedy. The year before, there had been friction when *Fortune* was doing a story on Kennedy. Presumably, *Fortune* planned to deal with Kennedy's longtime affair with actress Gloria Swanson whom he had squired on his yacht and even taken home to Hyannisport, Massachusetts, to meet his wife. "The story I heard," said *Life* photographer Dmitri Kessel, "was that Joe said, 'Look, Harry, we don't need a conference. Meet me for lunch.' So Luce met him for lunch, and Joe said, 'You publish that story and you're going to lose your *Time* magazine.' The way it was put, I don't know, but Joe was going to buy him out. Whatever happened at that lunch, the Kennedy story was published in *Fortune*, 'but with changes.'"

The two men remained friends. Nevertheless Luce's view of Joe Kennedy remained ambivalent. He had a lingering envy for Kennedy's life-style as a rogue and a pleasure-seeker. What disturbed him about Kennedy was his cynicism and pessimism.

"Kennedy was sure the British would be defeated," Luce reported back to Billings. "I told him I could not match him argument for argument. I could only tell him I did not believe they would be, and so I prayed."

In London, Harry and Clare also touched base with another rogue, William Maxwell Aitken Beaverbrook. The son of a Scottish Presbyterian clergyman, "the Beaver" was a self-made millionaire, who owned the *Daily* and Sunday *Express* and the *Evening Standard*. The author of a book on success and another on power, Beaverbrook usually epitomized both. Yet, he occasionally championed causes he regarded as grand and romantic. Those who didn't like Beaverbrook called him "Wrong Horse Max" and a pompous martinet. His granddaughter would play a pivotal part in Luce's later life.

Clare also had a fond reunion with her adoring Randolph Churchill, who still called her "honey child" and vowed to follow her to Paris. Luce still knew nothing of this, but he instinctively never liked Randolph.

In Paris, the Luces dined with the duke and duchess of Windsor. How Clare must have smiled at the memory of her mother hurrying down to Greenbrier because this prince of Wales would surely fall in love with her when he saw her. How proud her mother would have been to see her now.

Clare's bemused impression of the duke was that he was so short and slight. Yet, she found him sparkling and well informed. He told the Luces that money could buy your way out of anything in France

In Berlin, the Luces hoped for an audience with Hitler. When they did not meet with the Fuehrer and moved on to Czechoslovakia.

Faced with a Nazi invasion, Czechoslovakia's president, Dr. Eduard Benes, told Luce that totalitarian systems would collapse and democratic systems triumph within ten years because the dictatorships would go broke. *Time* had scheduled a cover story on Benes that month, and Luce cabled to make certain the story did full justice to the great leader of a brave people who were determined to fight and die for country and for liberty.

Finally, the Luces headed home to New York. Luce took no notice of the time change after the long overseas flight; he went directly to work. "He sat on my big picture table," said Billings, "and swung his legs and talked about all the bigwigs he met."

Several months after the Luces' return, in September 1938, they and the world learned that the Czechs were not going to fight Hitler after all. British Prime Minister Chamberlain had negotiated a four-power pact at Munich with Hitler, forcing Czechoslovakia to surrender its Sudetenland to Nazi Germany. Chamberlain returned to Britain, waving his umbrella, declaring that the pact would now bring "peace in our time."

The whole tone of *Time*'s Foreign News department changed when the talented, liberal Robert Neville replaced Goldsborough. Neville was an intense man, but with a warmth and a twinkle, an observer who believed in respecting facts as facts and not twisting them. Goldsborough even went to Mrs. Luce to use her influence with her husband to get him reinstated, but Billings had put out the word that "Goldy has cracked up and doesn't even know it." Some years later, wearing a topcoat, his homburg, carrying his briefcase under one arm and a heavy cane in the other, Goldsborough jumped out of a window. When the body crashed to its death onto the pavement, the cane was still clutched in his fist, the homburg still on his head.

Clare reacted to the world crisis by writing another play, *Kiss the Boys Goodbye*, which she insisted was an allegory about the rise of fascism in America. Critics saw it as a satirical play about Hollywood and southern womanhood. It was listed as one of the ten best plays of the year. Columnist Heywood Broun panned it, but Clare still asked him to write the introduction to the printed version of the play. He panned it again.

At the start of 1939, Luce and Ingersoll had a strained confrontation but agreed with the selection of Adolf Hitler as Man of the Year. The quarrel came about the art work that would go on the cover. The art department offered Ingersoll a glamorized portrait of Hitler in a dignified uniform. "Where the hell did they get such a portrait?" asked Ingersoll. "From Goebbels?" Instead, Ingersoll commissioned a black-and-white lithograph of a tiny, evil-looking Hitler playing a giant organ surmounted by a wheel cover with naked bodies of his victims. The caption read: "From an unholy organist, a hymn of hate." The text of the cover was something that would never ever have appeared during the Goldsborough tenure.

Luce approved the text, with some qualifications, but didn't see the cover until it was already printed. Ingersoll described their subsequent meeting at his office. "Luce's face was white; the blood seemed to have drained even from his lips."

"Who did this?" he thundered.

"I did."

"You did? Have you any idea what you've done? A basic tradition destroyed—everything I've built, in one gesture . . ."

He and Luce sat there, in utter silence for a full minute, staring intently at each other. Then Luce said simply, "Split milk."

"What deep waters had I stirred?" Ingersoll reflected later. "Had it been like that between Harry and Brit when they differed? A periodical is a living thing, the product of thousands upon thousands of decisions, made by the men who create it, down to and including the placing of commas. Harry was right to have been so shaken when I changed the course by taking an open editorial position on the very cover of *Time*. The sacred essence of *Time*'s plausibility was its pose of impartiality in public matters and I had, as the cloak-and-dagger boys put it, blown the cover (no pun intended). But Harry never intended not to take sides in handling news.

"In his first writings about what he proposed to do," continued Billings, "Harry laid that on the line: '*Time* gives both sides but clearly indicates which side it believes to have the stronger position.' So from the beginning he must have been in torture. If *Time* revealed his prejudices, it would lose its plausibility. Yet his basic convictions were very strong, and to be objective in areas they touched upon seemed a betrayal to him."

At one of his many soul sessions with his editors, one of them asked Luce what would motivate him to use *Time* as a political instrument. Luce replied: "If I thought the republic was in danger."

By early 1940, Harry increasingly felt the war in Europe was a U.S. war, and the sooner we got into it the better. Clare said no, we weren't ready for it yet. "Go see for yourself," Harry told her. After that, it was easier for her to persuade him to let her be a *Life* correspondent. Billings was then managing editor of *Life*. "Of course," he noted, "I had to say yes."

Clare sailed for Naples in February. A reporter asked if she thought there would be a war crisis the next month. "Oh yes," Clare replied.

Aboard ship, the guilty Clare wrote a long letter to her daughter. In it, she said how she hated to leave without her, how much she missed her, how she kept looking at a picture of Ann doing the hula—which she kept on the table near her bed. She sent her a million kisses. At the bottom, she drew a cartoon of a lady weeping out of a porthole.

Shortly after Clare arrived in Europe, the signs of war grew more ominous.

She had an audience with Pope Pius XII and claimed she was timid about going. She felt he was the one man in the world who might perform the miracle to stop this war.

There was no miracle. The pope told her that he loved America, then made the sign of the cross and said, "God bless America!" She left unhappy that "so good and wise a man seemed to have so little power to avert the catastrophe that threatened the world."

In France, Clare was angered by what she heard. The French did not want to attack Germany, they told her, because that was what Germany wanted them to do. Besides, if they bombed Berlin, then the Germans would bomb Paris, and Paris was more beautiful than Berlin. Besides, they were much too busy having fun. What about her, they asked. Was she afraid being in the war zone?

"No. I've noticed that bombs never make hits—on people who live in the Claridge or Ritz."

In war, Frenchmen said, "Never buy anything you can't hop over the back fence in an emergency." Drinking at the Ritz, Clare wondered what would happen if the Germans arrived at the hotel. She felt the hotel manager would probably bow and greet them in polite, correct German.

Clare's suite at the Ritz was filled with "soldiers, generals, newspaper men and women, all getting information for her, drinking her whiskey, phoning the mistresses of deputies for their influence."

Clare tried to persuade the French Army to permit a *Life* photographer to go to the front. "Why should France make propaganda?" was the reply. The people in France, Clare decided, despised America, loved Roosevelt, and firmly believed that F.D.R. felt that this war was America's war, and would come to France's aid when a crisis came.

Clare was determined to visit the supposedly impregnable French Maginot Line, the massive concrete and steel fortification near the German border. Women were forbidden there. But Clare finally met and charmed the reportedly inflexible General Gamelin, and soon found herself on a rainy hillside in a muddy village in Lorraine called Metzevisse. She had come to visit the men of the 11th Regiment of the Foreign Legion. The legionnaires, representing thirty-three nations, stared at this attractive woman as she walked by in a smart blue tailored dress which might have been a perfect model uniform for women driving army ambulances. She ate with them under an old oak tree in the school yard and listened to the men sing. The colonel gave her a flag of the regiment and kissed her on both cheeks. Then Clare descended into their deep fortification several hundred feet underground. She entered a steel room where two guns rotated on a 200-tun turret and began to fire. Their guns could have demolished the largest tanks, if there were any. In a dramatic ceremony, the men of Maginot for *Le Mont des Welsches* made Clare their *marraine,* their godmother, and presented her with roses. Clare reciprocated by supplying the 600 men with cigarettes, champagne, and a gold-embroidered flag inscribed with *"Ils ne passeront pas"* ("They shall not pass"). The band played "The Star-Spangled Banner," and Clare said, "I cried a little because I am at heart idealistic, evangelical, and easily stirred by crusader emotions. She felt, too, that she was performing some morale service because "all the officers were quite pleased just to sit and look at me, just because I was a woman, and most of them hadn't seen a woman in months. An occasional feminine chortle or gurgle from me was quite enough to evoke a whole train of nostalgic memories."

The scene was interrupted by a pale-faced radio operator with a message: Germany had occupied Denmark and was invading Norway. Clare felt she was watching the making of history. "No gambling table was ever more thrilling and no spin of the wheel more precarious than the roulette of political events," she said.

Clare then hurried back to Paris and cabled her husband: "Come, the curtain is going up."

Luce swiftly decided to join Clare in Europe. He assured his senior editors that he wasn't going "for love." He had been "highly pressured" by Ambassador William Bullitt, the U.S. ambassador to France, that his trip was necessary.

Harry joined Clare in London. The couple found the city gayer than Paris with, as Clare noted, "very good Hungarian music at Claridge's for women in low dresses and men in dinner coats; fine Italian food at Quaglino's where young frilly girls danced with young sleek officers . . . cocktail bars and night clubs everywhere . . . dozens of theaters open, a rash of strip-tease burlesque shows. So much frivolity—so much 'splurge of wealth.' " There were also jokes about everything from gas masks to barrage balloons. The Luces sensed a smugness and complacency in France and Britain. Clare observed, "A nation which is overripe with tradition is overripe for ruin."

Clare and Harry spent some time with Churchill, who would soon replace Chamberlain as prime minister. Beaverbrook had been wrong about Germany, wrong about Hitler, wrong about the threat of war, but Churchill had converted him, then created a Ministry of Aircraft Production, and put Beaverbrook in charge.

In the rising sense of crisis, Harry and Clare went to Holland on May 7, for an interview with Queen Wilhelmina. With reported German troop movements on the border, the queen was too busy to see them. A Dutch diplomat told them he had excellent sources in Germany and knew about the invasion of Norway five days before it happened. Did he tell the French and English about it, the Luces asked. "Certainly not," he said indignantly. "Why should we? They're not our allies . . ." Amid rumors that the Dutch would open the dikes to flood the countryside before the Nazis attacked, Harry and Clare went to Belgium for a hurriedly arranged interview with King Leopold.

The exhausted Luces went to bed at midnight. At five-twenty-five on the morning of May 10, Harry recalled, "a maid rushed in and shook me by the shoulder: 'Les Allemands revienment!' "

"The show's begun," Harry told Clare, waking her.

"We just had time to go to the window, which overlooked a lovely square."

It was a beautiful summer dawn, overlooking a quiet lovely square with the early sunshine steaming in. Then—BANG! "The blast knocked me half across the room. I like to say it was the first bomb of the blitz," said Harry. Everybody rushed downstairs in confusion. The square was now filled with dust from the blast. Clare decided to make some coffee and scrambled eggs. She then filled her purse with an extra supply of powder, lipstick, and cold-cream and put only flat-heeled shoes in her suitcase.

Harry, meanwhile, walked to the main square to see the damage. When he returned, the ambassador told him, "I've got a car you can have. You had better leave at once."

"But you are giving a dinner for us tonight," Harry reminded him.

"Dinner or not. You'd better go. If you stay, I take no responsibility."

"We'll stay."

"The dinner came off—very gloomy," Harry remembered. "The next day, I wangled a car from American Express. When I picked up Clare at a hotel, I was startled to see she had two British airmen with her with enormous duffel bags. They had been interned and now released. That afternoon we started for Paris. We saw the last of the British Army going up to the front."

The Nazi tanks were close and coming closer. Clare recorded the sighting of the British Queen's Own Westminsters going to the front and the terror of the refugees streaming the other way, including "half-mad mothers, starving children, the young, the old, the crippled . . ." One woman, discovering her baby was dead, handed it to a Red Cross worker, saying, "Here, he is yours now."

Crisis and conflict always united the Luces, and the war brought out the best in them. An American woman, who was with the Luces for an hour in the middle of another air raid, later reported, "In such moments one gets to know people far better in a few minutes than one normally can in many months, and it was clear to me from a score of little signs that the Luces are a most united couple and that Clare is an adoring and happy wife."

Clare was eager to write about the war, and Luce duly sent a cable urging *Life* to use Clare's piece as part of its lead story. He added that he wished a pious pacifists could see what he saw.

Clare then sent in a piece on the first day of the war in Brussels. In her piece, she had written: "Do you know what big guns and incendiary bombs and machine guns are? Do you know what they can do to people and houses and roads? Imagine the worst things you can. They have all happened."

"It was good and I was glad to use it as spot news in the lead," Billings recorded. "Later Norris [Frank Norris, an editor of *Time*] came up with 'condolences' at my having to run it. I took him down sharply, saying I was glad to run it, and the trouble with *Time* was that it was too sophisticated for such simple emotional writing."

The Luces got to Paris in time for lunch at the Ritz the next day, and they could feel the wave of fear sweeping through the crowd. Clare and Harry were disgusted at the abject fear of the rich, so severe that they were willing to agree to any German terms to stop the war. Clare was similarly revolted by those who were still talking about money and possessions.

In another cable home, Luce reported that he had talked to half of all the people in the most responsible positions in France and the most intelligent conversations he heard concentrated on airplanes. He warned that America must go into high gear and build every military plane it could in the next six months. He saw it as absolutely essential. No country, he said, must be too fat to fight. Statements by the pope and President Roosevelt, which generally echoed his own feelings, sounded so wonderful to Luce that he said he was always ready to become both a Catholic and a Third Termer unless the Republicans changed their isolationist tune.

Billings recorded in his diary, "Luce is about ready to declare war! What a guy!"

In the middle of the war, Harry and Clare found time for a literary interval. The most famous American expatriates in Paris were Gertrude Stein and Alice B. Toklas, who had been at the literary center of Paris during the Picasso-Hemingway period. Stein was a solid and powerful woman with a loud, hearty laugh. The more feminine Toklas had a musical voice and she gave Clare some hints on needlepoint. Toklas referred to Stein by the nickname, "Lovely," and remarked often how Lovely always exaggerated things. Stein dated the decline of America to the coming of the Roosevelts. She hated both Teddy and Franklin. Luce asked her why so many intellectuals favored F.D.R., and Stein replied that since intellectuals could not be revolutionary in their private work, they were revolutionary in their public posture. Her final dictum: A country should be peaceful and exciting as France was and America wasn't.

Toklas recalled that Clare "was embroidering in petit-point a map of the United States. Mrs. Luce was convinced her husband would become president."

After their interval with Stein and Toklas, the Luces went to Aix-les-Bains. The war seemed far away, and Clare and Harry played bezique and tennis. They got massages and took the thermal baths to relax. Clare complained that her belt was too tight and that she hated getting fat because she preferred being called slim. They read aloud to each other from a book called *Union Now,* and, said Clare, "talked and talked and talked . . ."

Was the war inevitable, and what could they do about it? Harry felt that a full war might still be avoided, and he wrote that to Lila. When they came home, he noted, he might have *Fortune* sponsor a roundtable discussion on democracy to arouse Americans about the war. Both Harry and Clare were stirred about that for a while, and then agreed it wouldn't do much good. Clare persuaded the orchestra in the dining room to play "Over There," which they didn't know very well. Clare described an image of Harry sitting in the Cure-House at Aix drinking his morning glass of lukewarm mineral water and relaxing. The Cure-House rules forbade the reading of newspapers, but Clare explained in a letter to Billings that Harry was busy with a French newspaper, which he didn't understand anyway.

Harry and Clare's time together in Europe that May of 1940 was a heady time in a heady place. They were sharing a great adventure, fraught with danger. Both were part of the making of history; both were part of a great cause in which they intensely believed. If their marriage bond had loosened, here it tightened. In a sense, this was why he had married her, and, in a larger sense, this was why she had married him. Someone once said their union represented an American variation of a marriage between Henry VIII and Catherine of Aragon. Henry Luce would never be Henry VIII, but Clare was straining hard to be a Catherine.

Clare wanted Harry to stay abroad, but he felt his place was with his magazines. So Harry headed home, and Clare stayed on. She had planned to write a report for *Fortune,* but it began growing into a book. Back in London, she again saw all the British statesmen. She was presented to the king and queen at a small tea and made blunt comments during dinner parties. She seemed to love great arguments lasting into the night. An observer wrote that her effect at a party "lies in the ridiculous disproportion of her frail face and her detached bitter wit. The effect is like being dynamited by angelcake."

Within days of his return to New York, Luce was on the radio on behalf of the Committee to Defend America by Aiding the Allies, telling the American people, "We can strip off our false cloak of neutrality and announce to the world that we refuse to recognize the Nazi domination of free peoples." The staff joke afterward was that Luce's speech "broke off Time Inc.'s diplomatic relations with Germany." Luce was so incensed that he even wrote an editorial telling Germany to quit fighting within ninety-six hours or we would go to war. His editors combined forces to persuade him not to run it. He also got involved in a secret meeting with the German chargé d'affaires to discuss whether Luce and American public opinion would accept an armed truce if Hitler agreed to stop fighting and withdraw from western Europe. The meeting adjourned at midnight with no results.

Clare, meanwhile, had witnessed the surrender of Belgium, and the dramatic evacuation of 200,000 British troops from Dunkirk. She afterward heard Churchill growl, "Evacuations do not win wars."

On her return to New York in late June 1940, she lunched with *Life* editors and she was on the platform all the time while the six editors said little. She and Harry were then invited to stay overnight at the White House; the occasion was a screening of *The March of Time*'s first full-length feature, *The Ramparts We Watch,* a propaganda film designed, said Luce, to "make viewers go out and kill Nazis." They slept in the bedroom where Queen Elizabeth had slept, and Clare later remarked that it was an unattractive room that looked as if it came from a summer stock set.

At dinner, Clare sat next to the president. He told her he had worried about her when she was in Europe. Clare described him as a good conversationalist with a hearty and friendly voice, but she felt that every time she was outspoken and political, Roosevelt seemed to put her down. She felt that F.D.R. didn't think that women should talk politics "unless they were very ugly or agreed with him." There was no question that the president and the Luces were on the same side in regard to aiding the Allies and destroying Hitler, but Roosevelt still expressed his feelings that Time Inc. had a deliberate policy of either exaggeration or distortion. He told an aide, "Pay no attention to them—I don't."

Clare then retired to their house in Greenwich to write her book on the war. She worked at an enormous table in a pale blue bedroom splattered with enormous pale pink roses. She had almost completed the manuscript when Harry called inviting her to dinner with Wendell Willkie.

Wendell Lewis Willkie was a big bear of a man from Indiana. A Democrat who had voted for Roosevelt, he was now a confirmed Republican opposed to the New Deal. Only forty-eight, he was called "The Barefoot Boy of Wall Street," because he was once a poor boy who had become president of a giant utility company, Commonwealth and Southern. At dinner, Willkie suggested that the Republican presidential candidate that year should be a new face, a prominent businessman, "Like you, Harry."

Clare quickly protested that it was not politically possible to elect a business-man in this age. Harry reportedly kicked her under the table, and when she persisted, he kicked her again. On the way home, "it was one of the few times in our life together when Harry was truly furious with me. He said that until that moment, he cherished a foolish notion that I was an intelligent woman." Harry then explained that Willkie didn't want Luce to be president—Willkie wanted Willkie.

So did Harry. He fully agreed with the president on the war, but felt that an unprecedented Roosevelt third term spelled danger to the country. He wrote a strong pro-Willkie editorial for *Life,* and *Life*'s lead story reported Willkie's growing bandwagon momentum. Russell "Mitch" Davenport was given leave of absence as managing editor of *Fortune* to become Willkie's chief strategist. Harry called Mitch "The Zealot . . . a force of spirit." Mitch sometimes rushed from the printer to the opera in his black cape and full dress. Harry also became a key advisor. Willkie would barge into his office about six-thirty PM. Nobody else ever barged into Luce's office. Willkie would put his feet up on one side of the desk and Harry would put his feet up on the other and they would talk for hours. With Willkie as president, Luce had high hopes of being secretary of state.

At the Republican National Convention in 1940, Willkie won on the sixth ballot. As the months progressed, the Willkie campaign was not going well. Ambassador Joseph Kennedy had promised the Luces that he would endorse Willkie and "put 25 million Catholic votes . . . to throw Roosevelt out." The British had been tapping Kennedy's wires, learned about the plot and tipped off the White House. When Kennedy arrived at the airport, Rose Kennedy and a White House representative were waiting to take him to Washington in a private plane. Two days later, Kennedy endorsed Roosevelt on national radio. He told Clare that he did this because Roosevelt had promised to support his oldest son for governor of Massachusetts.

Another surprise Roosevelt supporter was a lifelong Republican, columnist Dorothy Thompson. Clare, her longtime friend, promptly wrote a letter to the editor accusing her of sacrificing principles for expediency. Harry showed the letter to Willkie, who then urged Clare to make a public speech about it at Carnegie Hall that night, replacing a speaker who couldn't come.

Clare had never made a speech before, said she was terrified, a "nervous wreck," but the speech went well. She had compared Thompson's political flip-flop to a girl in an apache dance team who willingly surrenders to her partner's brutal treatment. Thompson retaliated by saying, "Miss Boothe is the 'body by Fisher' in this campaign. She's torn herself loose from the Stork Club to serve her country . . ."

"Two men disagree, and it's a disagreement," Clare said later. "Two women disagree, and right away they're all shouting 'cat fight . . . hair pulling contest!' " She vowed never again to get into another political argument with a woman in public.

Politics gave Clare and Harry a fresh shot of adrenaline. Clare made forty speeches for Willkie, and she loved it. They were both energetically promoting a political dark horse. They had earlier shared the full adventure and excitement of being center stage at the start of a war. Once again, they were exhilarated by a cause, exultant over the use of their power. Their marriage looked good again.

One night in the middle of the campaign, the Luces were dining with Allen and Bea Grover. "Harry said to me, 'Well, Al, who are you gonna vote for?' " recalled Grover, "And I said, 'I'm going to vote for Mr. R.' And he really was dejected; he fell silent for a few minutes. Then he looked up and said, 'You're not gonna change your mind?' I said 'No, I'm not, Harry; I'm going to vote for Mr. Roosevelt.' There was silence at the table; he was really put out, and Clare finally spoke up and said, 'Harry, if you can't convince Al Grover to vote for Willkie, how do you expect to win the election?' "

Luce sent a stream of memos, suggestions, and advice, almost on a daily basis to the *Willkie Special;* he even wrote drafts of speeches. In addition, he was also on a small key committee to pick Willkie's running mate. Harry sometimes called his secretary in the middle of the night to meet him at his office to type a speech and forward it to Willkie on his private wire.

When Willkie lost by a huge margin in November 1940, Luce seemed dazed and dismayed. He felt that the country was going to hell. Clare was so distressed that she told former presidential candidate Al Smith that this was positively the end of politics for her. Smith gave her a wry smile and said that in politics, "You just say *au revoir . . .* you never say good-bye."

Mulling over the defeat, Luce wrote a five-page *Life* editorial called "The American Century." The essence was much the same he had said as a Yale student in a prize-winning speech: that it was America's God-given mission to save the world, keep the seas free, feed the hungry, and live heroically.

The war and politics had once again pushed Clare's daughter onto the back burner of her life. Ann was now a senior at Foxcroft Academy in Virginia, and was an excellent student. Clare's secretary, Isabel Hill, whom Ann called "Hill Billy," served as her surrogate mother, by correspondence only. Ann asked Hill Billy to tell her mother that she had heard her on "Information Please" and thought she was wonderful and to pass along her thanks for the basket of fruit her parents sent her for Thanksgiving. She requested a schedule of all of her mother's speeches and radio appearances in case she could hear them. She also wanted a copy of her mother's book about the war, for her school library.

Ann was consistently upbeat and cheerful, but then came a bitter letter in which she said she knew her mother was a busy genius and all that, but nevertheless, all the other mothers had arranged the senior parties and dances for their daughters. Why couldn't her mother? But nothing Ann said changed Clare's ways. When the Luces were in Europe, Clare left it to Hill Billy to arrange for the removal of Ann's wisdom tooth, shopping for clothes, as well as admission interviews for college.

Ann finally decided to go to Stanford and largely made the decision alone.

For Ann's seventeenth birthday, Baruch sent her a jeweled compact. Ann wanted a ring instead and asked permission to exchange it at Tiffany. Ann had never been to Tiffany's before, and Clare went with her. Though Ann happily tried on diamonds worth $25,000, Clare insisted she buy a tiny pearl ring. Clare tried hard to keep her daughter from knowing much about the family money. In fact, Ann later claimed that she didn't know she was an heiress until she read about it in Cholly Knickerbocker's column, and she hoped she wouldn't arouse jealousy in people the way her mother did.

When it was time for Ann to enter Stanford, Clare and Harry were not there. They had decided on a trip to China. China was never far from Harry's mind; China had helped shape his soul. Both Luces had devoted considerable time to the cause of United China Relief. Harry called the trip "a busman's holiday," and Clare told an interviewer, it was "an escape to reality."

Waiting for them in Chungking was *Time* correspondent Theodore H. ("Teddy") White, who had come there fresh from graduating summa cum laude from Harvard. John Hersey, Luce's favorite protégé at the time, had hired White in 1939.

The forty-three-year-old publisher and the young correspondent struck up an immediate rapport. White was awed by the reception Luce received. "No visitor I had seen previously in China was greeted with the deference given to Luce and his wife. He was China's single most powerful friend in America," said White.

Luce, in turn, was thrilled to be back. He got very excited, because his boyhood Chinese began coming back. When he would say something in Chinese he would add, "Correct me . . . correct me."

"Suddenly he began to jabber like a kid," said White, "and he wanted to talk to everybody in Chinese."

"The Japanese were bombing the hell out of Chungking. Everything seemed larger than life. He loved every minute of it—the noise, the passion, the danger," said White. "Every time a Japanese bomb sent him to a shelter, you had a feeling of his excitement and the fact that he almost wanted to take a rifle and shoot down the Japanese plane."

The Luces then met the generalissimo and Madame Chiang Kai-shek. The generalissimo greeted them with "a few distinct grunts of encouragement. "How . . . How." "Good . . . Good." Madame Chiang was interpreter and hostess. The Luces gave her a bountiful supply of her favorite cigarettes and gave the generalissimo a portfolio of photographs of the Chiangs. Luce recorded that the slim, wraithlike Chiang grinned from ear to ear. Later, Luce would describe the "gissimo" as "the greatest ruler Asia has seen since Emperor Kang Hsi 250 years ago."

The Luces had only one request of Chiang, and it was quickly granted: They wanted to visit the Japanese front on the Yellow River.

They flew in a single engine Beechcraft, then traveled by train, and, finally, by car and Mongolian pony over the Tsinling Mountains. They could see the Chinese shelling the Japanese positions on the cliffs across the river. Though the Japanese already had captured much of the South China coast, Luce was much impressed with the quality of the Chinese soldiers he saw.

Safely back in Chungking, Luce told White to get him away from the "smothering government escort" and they sneaked off in rickshaws. "It turned out he only wanted to practice his Chinese," said White. "With glee, he commanded the rickshaw man this way and that, poked in and out of shops, examined prices, bargained in Chinese with ever-growing gusto. Another evening, he canceled a banquet of state and ordered me to assemble whatever graduates of Yenching University I could find; he wanted to dine with them. His father had helped found that university as a Christian enterprise and Luce wanted to find out what had happened since the Japanese occupation."

In Madame Chiang, better known as "May-ling" or "the Madame," Clare met her match. Educated at Wellesley, more American than Chinese, Madame Chiang had converted her husband to Methodism in a public baptism which gave Luce his great hope of a Christian China. Madame Chiang was a stunning woman in tight-fitting silk gowns. She could change quickly from a coy kitten to a queen. Dark and petite, her smooth black hair coiled simply at the nape of her neck, the Madame could dress down a general with a few well-chosen words, call a quick conference of military leaders, and also give a detailed laundry list of equipment needed for the war. She gave semi-official interviews, wrote articles for publication in the United States, and gave the impression of being a brainy American college girl who had taken over China.

With her usual intentness, Clare focused on the Madame. "It was as if she had studied her to see how it was done; and no doubt the Madame was studying her right back. It was one of the great match-ups of the century," said Wilfrid Sheed, who became Clare's confidant in later years. He added that Clare told "more stories about her than the rest of China put together." The Madame gave Clare a pair of silk pajamas and Harry a Jade T'ang horse. Harry gave her the full editorial support of *Time, Life,* and *Fortune.*

One day, Clare and Madame Chiang went shopping in Taipei. As they returned to their car, each urged the other to get in first. After three turns of "No, after you," Clare gave up and climbed in first. Madame Chiang then got in beside her and sulked all the way back to her residence in the northern outskirt. After the Madame had stalked off to her rooms, Mrs. Luce asked a secretary what she had done wrong. "I offered her three times," she said. "You should have offered four," the secretary answered. Many years later, long after they became intimate friends, called each other by their first names, and had exchanged many gifts and letters, they met at a dinner party for Richard Nixon. Instead of shaking hands with Madame Chiang, Clare leaned over and kissed her on the cheek. Despite their close relationship, the Madame considered this a breach of good manners, a gross familiarity. "I could see Madame Chiang stiffen," recalled an onlooker.

At the time of the Luces' visit, Chiang's nationalist army was more concerned with fighting the Chinese Communists than the Japanese. Moreover, corruption in Chiang's Kuomintang party was blatant and considerable. Nothing, however, could sway Luce from his support of Chiang.

When Harry was busy elsewhere, Teddy asked Clare, "Would you like to meet Chou En-lai?" Chou was second only to Mao Tse-tung in the Communist Army. "Teddy and I drove out to what my memory reconstructs as a cave, though it may have been a shack built against the mountainside, and we dined on bare boards by candlelight with Chou En-lai," said Clare. "I found him a fascinating little man. We had a long talk which I'm afraid I can't recall." She did remember asking whether he was ever concerned that Chiang might kill him. "You just don't understand the Chinese," he told her, saying that he had been a student under Chiang at the Whampo military academy, China's West Point. "He said that in China the relationship between professor and pupil is as close as the father-son relationship, and it was unthinkable that Chiang Kai-shek would shoot him."

When the Luces readied to leave after a hectic ten days, Luce decided to take Teddy, then twenty-six, back with them and make him Far Eastern editor of *Time*. Something about the young Teddy had touched a sympathetic nerve in Luce. Perhaps it hit Luce, too, that he and Teddy had both been scholarship boys at Ivy League schools and had made it the hard way. Outsiders saw it as a father-son relationship, much the same as Luce's feelings for Hersey. "He took White with him to adopt him, to take possession of him," said John Hersey, "as he had done over the years with me."

Flying home in the Pan American clipper took six days. White described stopping at all the island stepping stones that were to become famous in military history: Guam, Wake, Midway, and Hawaii. At each stop, Luce would send White by car to check how well prepared were the island's defenses for the war they were both certain was coming. They also stopped at the Philippines, where they met General Douglas MacArthur. MacArthur had been a star student at West Point, an aide to President Theodore Roosevelt, a hero in World War I, and was now the commanding general of the American Armed Forces in the Far East. An imperious man with a giant ego, he told the Luces that he was the one man who could stop Asian world dominance. After meeting him, Harry declared, "He's either a great fraud or a genius. Probably both."

In the Philippines, they dined with the high commissioner and the commissioner's teenage stepson, who was aghast at the way Luce peppered his stepfather with questions. The teenager, Ralph Graves, later became the publisher of *Life.*

As White and the Luces were flying over San Francisco, recalled Teddy, "Harry harumphed, stammered again, and said, 'Teddy, you've read all this stuff in business magazines about how the boss' door is always open to everyone? Well, that's not the way I run my magazines. Everybody's door is open to me. But my door is open to people only when I want to see them. We're friends, Teddy, but at the office, my door is closed.' "

Two months after their return, "word came down from Luce, who was sitting on his throne on the thirty-third floor, that Clare should go to Manila to do text pieces for *Life,*" reported Billings. "We all think it is a waste of money, but if Luce says so, then she goes and to hell with the budget. Luce is hollering for big names, and Clare Boothe is such a name."

Clare went back to the Philippines to write a profile of General Douglas MacArthur. Despite some nagging neuralgia, Clare kept up an exhausting pace. She credited her husband with her ease of access to anyone. "Not that I didn't fight and write as hard as anyone else," she noted. "But the introduction as Mrs. Luce was an advantage."

Clare soon made another intimate conquest of the man closest to MacArthur, General Charles Willoughby. He was an impressively huge man, covered with war ribbons. He talked to Clare about coming home one day with MacArthur to lead an American movement to prepare for the inevitable war with Soviet Russia. He also gave her a book about war military strategy.

Clare found MacArthur a difficult man to interview. What was incredible to her was the fact that MacArthur spoke the same pearl-shaped purple prose both in public and private. She later reminisced that MacArthur's temperament was flawed by an egotism that demanded obedience not only to his orders, but to his ideas and his person as well. His condition for the interview had been that he could read the article before it went to press. "One remark concerned how he folded his sparse locks from left to right, 'like a raven's wing, over his bald head.' He told me quite a lot in exchange for blue-penciling that," said Clare. "He plainly relished idolatry."

Clare admitted to *Life* editors later that she could have said many unpleasant things about MacArthur in her article, but that American prestige in the Far East was tied up with MacArthur. If she had weakened him, she would have hurt America's prestige. He was an ambitious swashbuckler, she felt, but not a phony.

"Clare Luce's piece on MacArthur arrived—seventy-three pages," Billings recorded. "I took forty-five minutes out to read it—and it stunk! It gushed about MacArthur. It told *nothing* about him in the Philippines, just a jumble of words. What a mess! Luce came down, said his wife's piece was "good stuff" or something, and then began to figure how soon we could get it into print. It shocked me to see Luce standing up for his wife's tripe when in his heart as an editor he must know it was awful. Busch [a *Life* writer] and I hedged and fenced around, and finally won a great victory over Luce: postponement of Clare's piece until it could be 'fixed up.' "

"Mr. Luce used to call me up when I was playing tennis over at the River Club," said Dan Longwell, then managing editor at *Life,* "and about every week he would call me and say, 'Don't you think you ought to run Clare's piece on MacArthur, put MacArthur on the cover?'" Longwell hedged, said he wanted to wait until the war seemed closer.

Back in New York in November, Clare saw a small article in *The New York Times* in which Philippine President Manuel Quezon personally threatened to hang the U.S. high commissioner if the Japanese bombed the Philippines because he had prevented the construction of air raid shelters. Clare linked that hysterical announcement with her memory of Quezon's supposed pipeline to Japan and wondered if Quezon was trying to exonerate himself because he knew an attack was coming. Clare discussed it with her husband that night and Luce agreed with her. He made an appointment to see President Roosevelt, but Roosevelt canceled that appointment without explanation. Harry always felt that if he could have met with Roosevelt, he might have made an impact. The next day, Luce met with an army general in charge of intelligence. "That general made me feel very insignificant," Luce said later. "I almost asked him to excuse my impertinence and went home with my tail between my legs." The general felt that his own intelligence sources were perhaps better than Mrs. Luce's intuition.

Years later, when Quezon was dying, Clare asked him if her intuition was correct, that he had known of the coming Japanese attack from his Japanese pipeline. He said yes and that he had passed on his information to Washington. Their reply was that they knew the Japanese fleet was on maneuvers, but they were then talking peace with Japanese envoys in Washington and that the Philippines would not be attacked.

On December 7, 1941, the Luces were giving a dinner party for the Chinese ambassador, when the butler interrupted, something he was ordered never to do during a meal. He handed Luce a note from the *Time* office. The note read: "C. D. Jackson on phone. Pearl Harbor bombed."

Harry jumped up knocking his chair over and saying, "It's come. It's come. Pearl Harbor has been bombed."

Clare said, "We've expected it." Then she grabbed a spoon and clinked it on a water glass to get attention: "Listen to this, please. Japan has just bombed the Philippines, Pearl Harbor, and San Francisco."

Her guests laughed, but Luce said loudly and sternly. "She means it. Please read it again, Clare."

"She did, and this time the guests left their desserts and scattered. Cars rushed out of the garage. Harry received a call from *Time,* jumped up, and rushed away. Clare was to give a radio speech and started dictating to her secretary from the bathtub. Suddenly, she said: "Oh my God, Ann, she's out there! Bernie," she told her secretary, "keep trying—get Ann!" There were no lines available to the coast. Clare soon discovered there had been no bombing of San Francisco, but the fleet at Pearl Harbor had been devastated.

Clare Luce's profile of MacArthur had finally gone to press the night before Pearl Harbor, with her own photograph of the general on *Life*'s cover. The article discussed the American showdown with Japan and observed, "The stage was set for war, a distant, dangerous, hard amphibious war for which the American nation was not yet fully prepared . . ."

In his own two-page editorial in *Life* Luce wrote:

"This is the day of wrath. It is also the day of hope. We accept only two alternatives—either to die in the smoking ruins of a totally destroyed America or else to justify forever the faith of our fathers and the hopes of mankind."

On the day Pearl Harbor was bombed, Luce had called his father at his sister Emmavail's house in Haverford, Pennsylvania, to share the latest news. "I'm so glad Harry called," Dr. Luce told his wife. "His faith reassures me."

After the call, Luce said, "Well, Father will get a good night's sleep."

That same night, the man who jokingly referred to himself as "Father Time" died in his sleep. The *Time* obituary noted that he was seventy-three and "largely responsible for the establishment of Shantung's first Christian University and Peking's Yenching University. He was a dynamic worker for the political, cultural, and religious education of the Chinese." His best known scholarly publication in Chinese was, *A Harmony of the Gospels.*

The *Christian Century* editorialized, "Within the seven seas, all men are brothers. There was no 'impossible' in his vocabulary. Perhaps some of this same spirit passed on to his son."

The death of Luce's father was the end of an era for Harry, just as Pearl Harbor represented the onset of a new and dark horizon. Both were cataclysmic events for Luce, events symbolizing a bleak and uncontrollable future he was not certain he wanted to face.

17

CLARE'S approach to war was simple: She wanted to be there. It was an excitement that heightened all her senses, put her on a par with any man. She knew she was a good observer, knew how to wheedle an interview out of anyone and to report sensitively on anything she saw and heard. She wanted to return to the Far East because that's where the action was, and she knew the principal players.

Because General MacArthur would go to Australia after the fall of the Philippines, Clare wanted to follow him. She mapped a route from Bermuda to Brazil then across Africa, Egypt, India, Sumatra, and Java, a trip of 75,000 miles. Her trip would include stops in the Caribbean, Liberia, Palestine, Trans-Jordan, Syria, Iraq, and Iran. Clare arranged with the American Red Cross to report for them as a roving observer, checking on their programs.

Clare saw her upcoming three-months' tour of the war as a time of freedom and adventure. She did have a lingering worry about her husband, sensing the danger of leaving him alone for such an extended period of time. She knew that his power, particularly during a war, would be an aphrodisiac for other women, just as it was to her.

She felt it necessary to put her concern in a thirty-page memo to Harry summarizing the bitter, fruitless arguments that had strained their marriage during the past three years. She promised from then on to agree with him as much as she could, and when she didn't, to try to keep her mouth shut. She reminded Harry that the Chinese word for love was made of the characters for heart and gift, and that love, therefore, was the gift of one's heart.

Keeping her mouth shut was an impossible promise, as impossible as giving him the gift of her heart. One of the wistful things Clare once said was, "Women do generally manage to love the guys they marry more than they manage to marry the guys they love." This was certainly not true of Clare.

It was now a war of the world. The Japanese were moving quickly through Malaya, the China coast, and the Philippines.

Time Inc. correspondent Annalee Jacoby, returning after the fall of the Philippines, was invited to the Luce home in Greenwich to report to some senior editors. Jacoby remembered that Luce was stammering that night, his words jamming up and coming out in bursts. Clare would coolly interrupt, "What Harry is trying to say is . . ." Jacoby recalled that Clare did it at least twenty times. Harry was humiliated.

Clare's journey was at last under way, with many stops eliminated because of the war. En route to India, her fellow passenger on a Pan Am clipper was brusque-talking Major General Joseph ("Vinegar Joe") Stilwell, who was being sent to command the Chinese armies. Clare would soon need his help.

Clare found India complacent, but fascinating. She saw too many people at military headquarters still dressing for dinner, giving large cocktail parties, and living the peace-time Colonial life. In a way, it was so similar to what she had seen in Paris during the phony war. When she discovered that the air route to Australia was now closed, she settled for Burma, where the war was still fierce. This meant hitching a ride on a twin-engine army transport loaded with bales of American and Chinese money and six Chinese soldiers. It was a long trip through very rough weather and the Chinese soldiers were soon sick. Clare helped them unbuckle their seat belts while they covered themselves with a greasy ointment called Tiger Balm, which some claimed would cure anything. The combined smell of the ointment and the vomit forced Clare to plead with the pilots to let her sit up front.

In Burma, Clare again ran into Stilwell. "Burma is no place for a woman," he told her. But, then Stilwell added with a half-snort, "Tomorrow at dawn, I'm driving to Maymo. If you get up that early, you can join me on the road to Mandalay." She went to Mandalay, where the smell reminded her of a dog that had been dead for days under her veranda porch one hot summer. "The stink permeated every cell of my mind."

Clare eventually won herself the chance to profile Stilwell for *Life*. She highly admired this "lean, little, grizzle-haired general who marches with his men, eats with his men, sleeps with his men, speaks fluent Chinese, and understands the Chinese soldiers better than any other living American . . ."

While writing about Stilwell, his camp was bombed and Clare shared a slit trench with the others. She wrote about her shaking fear when the shells seemed too close, and she became suddenly more sharply aware of her mortality.

* * *

Some seven thousand troops had been fighting the oncoming Japanese without relief of air cover or supplies. General Harold Rupert L. G. Alexander, British commander of the forces in Burma, admitted to Clare that their campaign was hopeless but they would hold Burma as long as they could. "We have more than a sporting chance," he told her. "Guts and determination will decided the issue in Burma, and we have both."

Alexander had supervised the successful evacuation of British troops at Dunkirk, and was the last man to leave. In the course of the war, he would be known for his shrewd tactical judgment. Restrained and self-effacing, Alexander became the British general that Eisenhower most admired.

When Clare was invited to join the blue-eyed general for lunch, she was still wearing her muddy slacks. He served her a gin drink with real ice and they spent a long afternoon together. It was said of Clare that she never met a general she didn't like. She seemed to have a weakness for generals who controlled the lives of so many and lived with death and danger. This one was particularly handsome. Clare was not a woman of conscience or guilt when it came to romantic affairs. She was a woman of impulse as well as design. The design might have been subconscious, or an extra dividend. He was a source of strategic news and she was a correspondent. The impulse was easy to understand. She had shivered in a slit trench when falling bombs could have ended her life. The danger of war reminded her again to grab what she could get. She was good at that.

General Alexander dropped her a note after their lunch saying he was off to the front and almost asked her to come with him—but hoped she would still be there when he returned.

She would meet Alexander many times during the war, and their names were so often romantically linked that Churchill's wife, Clementine, later refused to sit at a table with Clare because of an alleged affair she had "with one of our best generals." Long afterward, *Life* correspondent Robert Coughlan saw Clare and Alexander in an elegant restaurant having a candle-lit dinner, "and the way that they would look at each other, it really looked like what they call an '*intime*' relationship." Even Harry later learned of it and referred to him as "Clare's general."

The war made Clare's earlier memo to her husband full of regret and guilt and promises seem part of another life on another planet.

Clare later tried to get on a plane, already loaded, that was headed for Chungking. If she didn't get on that plane, she would have to make the long haul overland. Her only chance was to charm the pilot, a living prototype of a character in the cartoon "Terry and the Pirates."

"Hello, Dude, my name is Burma Boothe and I am a lady in distress which I gather is your specialty."

"Well, beautiful, if you are in distress it's probably your own damn fault for being in China. What am I supposed to do?"

"Take me to Chungking. It's the only way I can get out of here and then from Chungking to Calcutta."

"Have you got a ticket on the plane?"

"Obviously not or I wouldn't be in distress, would I?"

Instead of going to Chungking, she stopped off at Kunming, the base of the Flying Tigers under the command of General Claire Lee Chennault. In her *Life* story, Clare told the dramatic story of how these hundred pilots fought with fifty-four obsolescent P-40 fighter planes and destroyed 500 Japanese planes. She called these pilots "valiant, drunken, disorderly, chivalrous" and gave them full credit for denying the Japanese an easy victory. Afterward one of the pilots said he thought the Flying Tigers name was first used by Clare Luce.

A Chennault staff officer recalled how he was awakened by the noise at the pilot's bar late at night when pilots were supposed to be asleep getting rested for the dawn mission. He saw this "attractive blonde in a well-tailored version of Churchill's air raid suit. She was charming everyone, and it was a great party." He announced that the lady must leave.

"But don't you see who she is?"

"I don't care if she's the queen of England—it's time to go."

That same staff officer went to breakfast with General Chennault the next morning and saw him with Clare Luce. When the general introduced her, she replied coldly, "We've met."

The general gave her a farewell present—an automatic pistol with seven shots. If she stayed near the Japanese front, he warned her to save the last shot for herself. If she was caught by the Japanese, he said, she would be good for only one thing when they got through with her "and that's the taxidermist."

Three months was a long time, and Harry was a lonely man who did not like being lonely. He was always welcome at his sister Beth's home and could always invite any of his staff for dinner or drink, but that was not enough.

Harry then found his own romantic diversion. She was a talented author, a friend of Clare's. A highly attractive woman, she had been a free-lance journalist all over Europe and had written several books. She was also married. Harry's relationship with this woman started slowly, almost casually, but she intrigued him. Their affair was sporadic and stretched out over some months. For both, the relationship was one of excitement, not depth. She was too similar to Clare in too many ways to reach anything deep within him. She also misjudged her man. With the idea of titillating him, she arranged for him to be at the corner of her street at a certain hour of night when the street was deserted. She knew he could see her bedroom window from there. Her shade was down but her light was on and she proceeded to undress completely in front of the shade. Instead of turning him on, it turned him off completely. He considered it cheap and shocking. Their relationship abruptly ended.

Clare, meanwhile, continued her travels. *Life* gave great play to her pieces, including her photographs, but *Time* still kept clear of Clare. She kept trying. John Hersey recalled walking into managing editor Gottfried's office where Luce and editor Tom Matthews were discussing a story Clare had sent.

The discussion between Luce and his editors was whether *Time* should print Clare's story and give her a byline, something rare at *Time*. "Matthews had decided that Clare's piece wasn't good enough for *Time,* and Luce was begging him to run it," said Hersey. "And Matthews, in his forthright way, was telling Luce just what was wrong with the piece; that it could not run in the magazine. Gottfried stood silent behind Matthews while this was happening. And there came a moment when you saw that Luce knew he was licked, and that it was not going to run. At that very moment, as he was leaning against the door, Roy Alexander opened the door and the steel handle hit Luce right in the kidney, just at the moment when he knew that he was down. He was double-wounded, said Hersey.

En route home, stuck in Lagos, Nigeria, for a week waiting for a plane home, Clare broke open the seal of the British censors on her notes and started writing a detailed private report of her trip for her husband. The report contained considerable information that would have been valuable to the enemy. In her report, Clare noted General Stilwell wanted to form a fighting force of thirty Chinese divisions, but that Chiang was more concerned with appeasing the many Chinese warlords who had helped put him in power. Clare sided with Stilwell on this, but disagreed with him on reopening the Burma front. Clare recorded Stilwell's reference to Chiang as "the peanut" and "that bastard." She also gave a detailed description of the Libyan campaign where British officers in Cairo regarded the whole war as a highly social affair. She discussed the exclusive floating night clubs down the Nile and how the officers had more concern for getting starch in their shirts than putting starch in their soldiers.

Clare finally got a seat going home on a plane that stopped in Trinidad, where the British customs officers examined her papers, including her long report, and promptly put her under house arrest. She was detained in custody for a week and then finally sent home, accompanied by a courier who took her papers to the British ambassador in Washington. Harry offered to accompany her to see the ambassador, but Clare insisted it was her mess and she would face it alone.

Clare entered the British ambassador's office, carefully attempting to hide her nervousness. Lord Halifax looked at her sternly over his glasses, hesitated before speaking, making Clare increasingly anxious, then said, "Good, accurate report, Mrs. Luce. I have forwarded it directly to Prime Minister Churchill."

Shortly afterward, Churchill visited the Libyan front, replaced some generals, and put Lieutenant General Bernard Montgomery in command. The headquarters was soon moved out of Cairo.

Clare was scheduled to write a Burma story for *Life,* using her own photographs. Billings recorded how she dawdled over photographic identifications, telling minor stories as she went along. "What an actress! Every move a gesture," sighed Billings. "But we don't like each other perhaps because I won't bow and scrape around her. With the pictures out of the way, we discussed what she could write and she proved difficult and headstrong. She said she couldn't finish her Burma piece till Monday, and we go to press Saturday. Upshot was that she finally agreed to write all she could before press time. 'I'll work all night and take Benzedrine,' she said, asking for pity. Really a horrid woman and not professional." Billings admitted, however, that Clare was a professional photographer, and he defended her when someone accused her of passing off other photographers' pictures as her own.

Eventually, Billings decided to postpone Clare's piece and give her more time. "I took my decision to Luce who approved it." Some days later, Billings got a call from Harry. "Clare has finished her piece on Burma. What was I going to do with it? I'd tell him after I'd read it." Billings later noted: "Clare Luce's Burma piece—118 pages—good narrative and observations. Can edit it down and make a notable two-page piece out of it." Billings also cut Clare's article on the war in Egypt almost in half. "I'm good at that!" he said. "But even then it wasn't as good as it should have been." Billings called Clare's story on North Africa "real sob stuff."

"On all sides I hear we are running too much 'Clare Boothe' and her pieces are becoming a general joke," complained Billings, who observed that one of *The New Yorker*'s fourteen war points was: "Bring Clare Boothe back from the war front and keep her at home."

The ongoing conflicts with her husband's magazines deeply troubled Clare. She was still trying to reinvent herself. She constantly questioned her future and her limited role as a power behind the throne. Increasingly, she wanted her *own* power. As *Vanity Fair* friend William Harlan Hale told author Dorothy Sterling, about Clare's yearnings: "Nothing less than the power to direct the destinies of nations will be enough."

For Clare, power was in politics. She had seen the excitement of politics during the start of the Roosevelt era, and she got a small whiff of it again when she visited her stepfather. In 1938, Dr. Albert Elmer Austin had been elected a representative from the fourth congressional district. Austin served only one term and was defeated for reelection. He died a few months later.

Albert P. Morano, a young politician who once worked as a gardener for Clare's stepfather, and then had served on his congressional campaign, saw Clare as a successor to her stepfather. Morano tried to arrange a meeting with Clare, but she was en route to China or else too busy after her return. For somebody supposedly hungry for power, she was indeed playing coy. When Morano finally set a date on a Sunday morning at her home in Greenwich, she kept him waiting more than an hour, but kept him supplied with coffee and cognac. When Clare finally admitted him, she was "in a great wide bed looking like a doll you'd put in a bed after it was made up," he reported. "After I had given her all the reasons why I thought she could win, she called for Mr. Luce. It was the first time I had ever met him." She said, 'Harry, Mr. Morano wants me to run for Congress. I want your advice.' " In retrospect, many years later, Clare insisted, "I never wanted, really, to run for Congress."

Luce and Morano walked for an hour in the garden, and Morano later said that Luce obviously didn't know anything about a congressional race, but was interested and full of questions. Luce told him that he and his wife agreed not to interfere with each other or give advice to each other. This, however, was exactly what he was being asked to do. What Luce indicated most strongly was that he didn't want her to run unless she could win. Success was very important. Failure would stamp a stigma on the Luce name.

Luce had two critical questions: Would the campaign embarrass him or Time Inc. in any way, and how much would it cost?

When they returned from the walk, Clare was dressed and gave Morano the strong feeling that she would be a candidate. Later Clare said, "Harry was very eager that I should do it. It was Harry who urged me. Our life together was altogether more agreeable when we did things that interested Harry. Therefore, I chose politics over playwrighting."

Morano leaked Clare's interest to his friends in the local press. He got statements of support from the Republican state chairman and the national committeeman.

Luce brought in some high-powered experts to face the final question of Clare's candidacy: Bernard Baruch, former New York *World* editor Herbert Bayard Swope, and *Time*'s Washington correspondent Felix Belair, among others. Everyone favored it but Belair. His blunt argument was that it was a mistake to mix politics with the running of a magazine. Even if Harry distanced himself from the campaign, people would assume his magazines were partisan. Clare listened thoughtfully, then called up her manager and dictated a statement, declining to run. The next morning, Harry Luce told Belair at breakfast how very much he had wanted his wife to run and almost growled, "You certainly messed things up."

In bowing out of the race, Clare told the state Republican chairman that while she was a Fairfield resident since childhood, she had spent most of her adult life in New York or traveling and knew too little of the Fairfield people or problems to represent them in Congress. Morano persuaded her to drop the word "irrevocable" from her decision not to run. "You said the Republican Party did not want you. Let's see if they do or not." She agreed.

Clare's potential rival for the Republican nomination was a vitriolic Westport manufacturer, Vivian Kellems; she hinted openly that Clare was simply afraid to run against her.

That was all Clare needed to change her mind, and she decided to run. Harry suddenly seemed to matter more to Clare. She needed advice, help, a private cheering section. As much as she argued with him, she respected Harry's pragmatism and his insight.

Clare's initial hurdle was the Connecticut Republican Convention, where she would be the keynote speaker. Harry asked one of his best editors, Mitch Davenport, to write a speech for Clare, and she delivered it brilliantly. Suddenly, Clare was the center of the biggest stage she had ever imagined. Every flick of her finger seemed to be news. Every word was an item, every quote a story. She was the most colorful candidate Connecticut had seen in years.

The delegate vote wasn't even close: eighty-four for Clare, only two for Kellems. In accepting the nomination, Clare said, "I want you to know that I accept this nomination as eagerly as I sought it."

Now came the much tougher general election. Clare's Democratic opponent was the incumbent, Congressman Le Roy Downs, publisher of the daily newspaper, the Norwalk *Sentinel,* who felt he didn't even have to campaign. Downs encouraged many Broadway and New York personalties to speak on his behalf, but this became more of a negative than a positive. None of them lived in Connecticut, and they couldn't vote.

She wanted a bright young man named Eddie Fay to be her press secretary, but he said he couldn't because Downs was his best friend, and he was voting for him. It was to Clare's credit that she and Fay still became good friends. When Fay mentioned a city in Connecticut and asked her what Clare would say to the people there, she ad-libbed something acceptable and he said, "Great, but it isn't in your district." Fay's message was to learn fundamentals, a basic lesson she never forgot.

As the campaign heated up, *Time* staffers worried that it would be very difficult for them to be nonpartisan. "It will be interesting to see if you fellows can be as objective as I can be about this matter," Luce told his editors. Many wondered why Luce wanted her to run. Clare had her own wry explanation for that: "To get me out of the house." Others felt that Luce was simply curious to see what would happen.

"He was *very* interested in her going into politics," said his sister. "He worked very hard at getting her elected. He'd have loved to have been a politician, to have been a senator. So, failing that, he poured a lot of energy into getting her elected, and advising her and helping her afterward."

"I was the chin that Harry led with," Clare concurred. The idea was that, if elected, she would be the national voice for so many ideas that they both believed in. She had no complaints about this. On large principles and issues, they were of one mind, with very few exceptions.

Clare had another reason: "There could be no legal discrimination against women in Congress because the law would not permit it," she observed. "If you are a congressman, you're going to be paid what any other congressman is going to be paid. You're going to have just as much chance to talk on the floor of the House. You are in every sense the equal of a man in the eyes of the law. The discrimination that exists against a woman in politics is of a very subtle and complicated kind. But, at least, she has access to the same amount of power as a man has."

What made her bitter was that, for a publisher's wife, "I got less support from the publisher than any character in history." *Time* did print a three-column story, largely biographical, not mentioning the other candidate but noting that she was married to the *Time* editor in chief, and referring to her as Miss Boothe. Luce also told Billings he wanted a close-up profile of Clare in *Life,* and even took the writer to lunch to tell him how he wanted it written.

"I don't know what goes on in the public mind, but there's always been an assumption that the *Time* Inc-ers write my books and plays, and that I write their editorials. I'd like to point out that as a rule we each do our own work."

Luce did assign *Time* reporter Wesley Bailey to supervise all of Clare's campaign advertising and printing and give strategic advice. Said Bailey: "We conspired to keep Luce out of the campaign because it was hard to give Clare orders, and with Luce it would have been worse. Luce couldn't talk the language of people or politicians." Bailey spent six months on her campaign, and also sent in stories about what she was doing. Despite his professed editorial neutrality, Luce did run some of them. Luce also asked some other people to help her with some speeches and even wrote a few himself.

During the campaign, some of Clare's old salvos came back to hurt her. She had blasted Roosevelt in the previous presidential campaign and F.D.R. neither forgot nor forgave, despite Baruch's intercession. The president said to his vice president, Henry Wallace, that he had to hope that there were still enough good solid people in Connecticut who would not elect, "a Luce woman." The president added, "You know she was Barney Baruch's girl . . ."

The great unknown plus and minus of Clare's campaign was the women's issue. Would women vote for a woman? Clare felt that they would if they were convinced she was competent enough. Baruch suggested she give a big dinner for working women in Bridgeport, and Clare afterward wrote him what a huge success it was.

But the women's issue wouldn't go away. Male reporters often confined their comments to her clothes. "For example, if I wear a dress that is all frilly, they are likely to say: 'Looking far too feminine to be in politics.' On the other hand, if I wear strictly tailored suits: 'Wearing a mannish suit, which ill-disguised her femininity.' In either case the implication is that, regardless of how a woman dresses, her place is not in politics, but in the home."

She deeply resented the fact that every political interview always geared back to the issue of women in politics. "When being interviewed, I sometimes feel like a black supreme court justice who would like to talk about the Constitution but is always being asked how the Negroes are faring."

A big surprise announcement came from Clare's one-time critic, Dorothy Thompson, who now said that she was voting for Clare Boothe Luce because "she knows more about world affairs than any other candidate—what she has is brains, freedom, a considerable knowledge of the world. Mrs. Luce is a liberal Republican."

One of Clare's great assets turned out to be her insomnia. She needed little sleep, she said, and proved it often by finishing a day's campaigning at two in the morning and getting up the next day at seven-thirty. "She claimed to fall asleep listening to linguaphone records in any one of five languages."

Harry was seldom far from her side. Her political fever was infectious. Moreover, he liked her dependence on him, and this time it was real because she was in strange territory.

Clare's margin of victory was only 7,000 votes out of 120,000 cast. It was the first time in the state's history that a woman had been elected to Congress. In conceding, Clare's opponent said, "I guess I just haven't got glamour."

Harry was exultant. Her success was his. He made arrangements to come to Washington almost every weekend. During the week, they would keep the phone lines busy. Whatever help she wanted, he was ready to give. She had made the Luce star a little brighter.

Clare had been so skeptical of victory that she had signed a contract with Warner Bros. to write a movie about China which would deal partly with

Madame Chiang. So, Clare headed off for a short interval in Hollywood before taking office in Washington. Harry and Ann joined Clare for Christmas. Clare mentioned how sad she was that Ann was growing up so fast, but thought she had enormous possibilities.

After Harry returned home, Clare still managed to play the part of the concerned wife from afar. She asked Luce's secretary, Miss Thrasher, to be sure to give her husband a vitamin B tablet every day after lunch so that he would be less tired. Miss Thrasher briskly replied that she would not give Luce any vitamin pills without orders from a doctor. Clare intervened directly to Harry, assuring him that he needed no prescription for such a vitamin. Clare also interfered with Thrasher's purview by suggesting what Christmas presents Harry should give to his staff. She advised him to send a card with an artificial rose to some of his senior executives, indicating that they would get real rose plants in the spring in time for planting. (Harry's Christmas present to Clare that year was 150 shares of Time Inc. stock.)

The friction between Clare and Thrasher sometimes exploded. Clare never forgot the time when she wanted use of their only car one day in New York. Thrasher icily informed her that Mr. Luce needed the car for an afternoon appointment.

"Well, he can just bloody well take a cab!"

While Clare was still in Hollywood, a Gallup poll mentioned her as a potential candidate for president. The Washington *Post Parade* supplement observed that it was the first time a woman president was being seriously discussed. It also reflected that in the 1942 congressional elections, more votes were cast by women than men. Two weeks earlier, Washington commentator Paul Mallon put Henry Luce among possible presidential candidates. Neither Luce made any comment.

Hollywood columnists constantly wrote items about Clare. One suggested that the young writer with whom Clare was working on the script was so enamored of her that he was ready to chase her all the way back to Washington. Clare, however, seemed more interested in a navy man she had met. She classified him along with Orson Welles and writer Michael Arlen as the only people she had found in Hollywood who really mattered. Reminiscing later of her Hollywood stay, Clare admitted that she was neither overpaid nor overworked.

On the train to Washington, she wrote lengthy love letters to her navy conquest, saying how much she missed him and loved being with him. She vividly recalled the wave on his forelock, his eyes that seemed to change colors, his blistered hands, large pink ears, and wide V-shaped mouth. Most of all, she missed his infectious laugh. She asked for a photograph of him.

As she headed East, her mood seemed to sober. She spent much of her train trip to Washington reading a thick book on congressional procedure. If she had read that book earlier, she noted, she might not have run for office. She also fretted that her life would be like a frenzied goldfish bowl.

For all her known poise, Clare must have experienced strong emotions on arriving in Washington. What a strange, long road from a New York tenement to Newport society to this. She had once recalled Congress as "the biggest tent show on earth." And yet the show was real compared to the tinsel of Hollywood. It could be just as callous, but a Hollywood film studio street scene was all front and no structure; in Washington, the structure was solid, and a little forbidding.

Clare checked into the Wardman Park Hotel and soon had two parakeets named Frankie and Winnie and a cocker spaniel puppy named The Speaker. On the wall, she hung two photographs of General MacArthur. On her desk, she placed pictures of her mother, her husband, his sons, and her daughter. Her personal library included Toynbee's *Study of History,* Fulton Sheen's *The Mystical Body of Christ,* Mackinder's *Democratic Ideals and Reality,* as well as *How to Reach the Top in the Business World* and *How Never to be Tired.*

"Work hard and keep your mouth shut." That was the advice of one of her more ardent admirers, Representative Joseph Martin, who would soon become speaker of the House of Representatives. An older congresswoman disagreed, "Nothing to it . . . I have been quiet in the House all these years, but what has it got me? Not even a decent committee assignment."

On the opening day of the congressional session, Clare gave doorkeeper William "Fishbait" Miller a freezing look when he told her that her slip was showing. Fishbait later had a confession: "She was beautiful. I think most of the congressmen were half in love with her and I'm afraid I was no different."

Clare swiftly let it be known that she had not come to Washington to merge with the woodwork and become one of the "boys." She came here to make things happen, especially to make things happen for Clare Boothe Luce. The world was changing and she would help it change. And, surely, it would change her.

In her maiden speech, Clare decided to be provocative. Vice President Wallace had appealed to the world for a good neighbor policy for freedom of the skies. Clare now called that policy "globaloney." Republican newspapers gleefully headlined her phrase. Baruch sent a long telegram to Ann saying how proud she must be to have such a wonderful mother with so much brains and sweetness and gentleness.

But there was no sweetness or gentleness in that Globaloney speech, and the astute Mrs. Roosevelt quickly jumped on Clare. She pointed out to the vice president that Clare's speech was probably a political payoff. Pan American Vice President Juan Trippe had provided planes for Harry when he was courting Clare in Cuba, and many times since then. He had been a strong supporter during Clare's election. Because open skies meant more competition for Pan Am, Trippe clearly welcomed Clare's stance.

Congressman William Fulbright (Democrat-Arkansas), one of the top debaters on the Hill, was chosen by the leadership to refute Clare. It was a dangerous assignment. He proclaimed that the congresswoman had "inferred that Wallace's plan for free skies would endanger the security of the United States." Jauntily, Clare Luce corrected him, "I inferred nothing," she snapped. "I implied and the gentleman from Arkansas did the inferring."

The face of Rhodes scholar Fulbright went red. Clare soon got her comeuppance. The National Press Club held a congressional spelling bee with Speaker Sam Rayburn as schoolmaster. Clare was on stage. Rayburn asked for the spelling of "feline." An Atlanta reporter jumped up and spelled it: "L U C E."

The hundred or more guests laughed hilariously, but Clare was furious. Her face turned white and she unsmilingly faced the audience. She deliberately misspelled the next three words to put her out of the game, and rushed off the stage. For the next couple of weeks, members of the club took turns seeking Clare out to apologize and butter her up.

Clearly, no one wanted to offend Clare for long. Something about her signified power. Reporters observed that she always drew a full house when she spoke. At first, they thought it was curiosity, but then they saw she held her audience. She was definitely a phrase-maker and quick with rejoinders. Representative Knutsen of Minnesota said on the floor of the House that she had a "masculine mind," hoping to give her a compliment.

Clare's response was swift. "I thank the gentleman from Minnesota, but I must refuse the compliment which he has so graciously paid me by saying that I think like a man. Thought has no sex. One either thinks, or one does not think."

Invited to the traditional president's reception for freshmen members of Congress, she responded by sending a letter to President Roosevelt—simultaneously released to all newspapers—criticizing his administration in great detail. Asked why she had done it, she calmly replied, "It was my first chance to reach the president's ear directly. Wouldn't I have been a fool to ignore it?"

When she did arrive at the White House reception, the president greeted her curtly, "How's Harry?" and passed on to the next congressman.

Congresswoman Luce found herself creating the impression that she was tackling too many problems at once. She ruefully agreed that in Congress it is optimum to be a piccolo player, stick to one note, and hit it all the time—but she never did it. It just wasn't in her nature.

Clare confounded Republicans by her "soak-the-rich" tax program and her pro-labor votes on various bills. She even voted against the appropriation for the Dies Committee on Un-American Activities (the House of Representatives' precursor to McCarthy's Senate committee). *Progressive* magazine called her a "C. B. L." (certified public liberal).

Clare's congressional office seemed to resemble a Wall Street brokerage house on a big day. While the average congressman then had a single secretary, Clare had five, and her incoming mail was enormous and national.

Clare and Harry talked about everything she was doing, especially on weekends when he came to visit. But Harry did not try to impose his own views, if they differed from hers. He was simply doing what he did with his own editors at Time Inc.: He tried to influence her, but let her run her own shop. He had little alternative because Clare liked being a force of her own. In fact, the longer she stayed on the job, the more she learned, the more independent she became. Harry felt a danger in her growing independence. Once again it weakened the tie between them. He wanted her to need him, and the less she needed him, the less he liked it.

He persisted in trying to get stories about her into *Time*. "If Clare was anybody else's wife, *Time* would just *love* to write about her," he complained to his editors. A more specific complaint to the managing editor was Harry's reminder that Clare had been the first person in elective office to propose an alliance with Great Britain, that this was a newsworthy fact that should be mentioned in *Time*. Finally, it was.

"It's not that I care what *Time* says about me," Clare remarked, "but it's embarrassing in Washington."

Clare finally felt compelled to issue a press release that she had nothing whatever to do with the management or editorial policies of Time Inc.

For Clare, life in Washington was a cocoon. Once again, she pushed everything aside to achieve her goals, and once again, she seemed to forget she had a daughter. Her secretary Isabel Hill kept apologizing to Ann, explaining that Clare simply had no time to write. "Your mother just keeps on writing and writing and broadcasting and 'speaking' and then writing and broadcasting and 'speaking' and then writing and broadcasting and 'speaking' and then writing . . ." A friend of Ann's shocked Clare by writing to suggest that she take time out from her busy life to write her daughter who adored her. The friend insisted that Ann knew nothing of the letter. Clare guiltily wrote to Ann thanking her for some anniversary gift, describing a party, gushing how much she missed her. Ann was in her sophomore year at Stanford. Clare also wrote her stepson Hank, then entering Yale. She predicted he would be the president of Time at thirty and of the United States at forty, and she hoped he would want to interview her someday.

If Clare had little time for her family, she did not neglect her romantic life. She was a woman alone in Washington, but seldom lonely. The press noted that her favorite escorts included handsome army colonel Matthew G. Jones, stationed at the Pentagon, and former movie czar Eric Johnston. Harry was usually there on weekends, and Baruch was a frequent visitor. When Baruch appeared before the Congressional Committee on Military Affairs, Clare came from her seat on the dais to greet him with a full kiss and a tight hug. She referred to herself as the pumpkin seed with the watermelon heart so far as Baruch was concerned.

He wired her once that he had been getting newspaper queries about her rumored nomination for vice president. He hoped it would not swell her "pumpkin seed noodle."

Clare was not simply a congressional freshman—she was a national exhibit. It was all going the way she had hoped: The excitement, the brouhaha, the frantic fun. There was no shortage of pending projects, and it was almost as if there was a national searchlight zooming in directly on her. Everybody seemed to want to know everything about her.

Clare was such a focus of publicity that when her maid quit and complained to the press, it made headlines. Clare made her usual saucy comment, "We have lost an old family retainer who has been with us for almost two weeks." When a columnist questioned the dignity of a national poll selecting Clare's legs among the most beautiful in America, she replied, "Don't you realize that you are falling for the same subtle New Deal propaganda designed to distract attention from the end of me that's really functioning—it's the other end of me, I hope, that's important."

MGM had produced a new movie called *Woman of the Year,* starring Katharine Hepburn. Clare received a letter from a *Life* movie reviewer saying that the film was obviously patterned after her, Dorothy Thompson, and five other women. *Life* wanted to photograph all of them attending a preview together, but Clare declined. She disliked being only one-seventh of a woman.

What she did do was to accept an invitation from her old Connecticut friend Eddie Fay who was then in an army training camp south of Washington. Fay had been one of the few to predict her congressional victory, even coming close to the actual vote margin. When she was in Hollywood after the election, she had sent him a big brown envelope full of photographs of Hollywood glamour stars, and forged intimate messages inscribed to Eddie Fay, some even smeared with lipstick kisses. "It didn't hurt me in the company at all," said Fay. He now invited her to visit him in the camp some evening. She came incognito so as not to cause a stir, ate in the mess with the men, and spent the evening drinking beer and telling stories about Hollywood. Fay found her warm and wonderful.

Clare was on a high. She would later tell an interviewer: "As a girl, I used to keep a diary and confide to it all my hopes and aspirations. Last year I came upon my diary and re-read it. On my sixteenth birthday, I said that I hoped to write books, be married to a publisher, live in a house in the country, and have three children. The last was a bad break, but I have everything else. And that is the kind of a future I would want for talented girls today who are wondering about choosing a career."

18

ANN had grown up almost without a mother. Clare later admitted that she had shamefully neglected her daughter over the years. She had lived in consuming worlds, sometimes several at a time. She had been an editor and an author and a playwright, a war correspondent traveling the world, juggling her time between articles and affairs. Now she was a member of Congress and a national celebrity with huge piles of mail, an unending flow of work, constantly in demand for speeches and appearances. Hers was a life of many men, little sleep, and five secretaries. What growing child wants a secretary as a surrogate mother?

Clare's shy little girl became a tall, shy young woman. In 1943, Ann was nineteen, and a senior at Stanford, scheduled to graduate magna cum laude the following June. She was a warm, lively, friendly girl. Her laugh and voice were like Clare's, and so was the contour of her face, but her nose was a little thicker at the end. Her hair was brown, her complexion light, her eyes dark, a cross between blue and hazel. Unlike her tone-deaf mother, Ann sang sweetly and played the piano well. There was also a grace about her as well as an obvious interest in people. Friends described her as unspoiled and very simpatico.

Clare had insisted that she had kept Ann out of her public life because she hated "people who exploit their children." But her detractors felt otherwise: "Clare didn't like Ann because she was a reflection of her own passing years, so she made her go as far away as possible," said Tom Matthews.

More than anything, Ann wanted to be part of her mother's public life. She shared all of her mother's opinions, studied hard about politics, and claimed that she hadn't liked F.D.R. even before he had a feud with their family. She was disturbed when press critics called Clare "a beautiful liar," and "the congressional snake charmer." Clare finally told her secretary to send Ann only the favorable newspaper clippings. Even the flow of clippings seemed to stop for a while until Ann pleaded for more. "She was such a sad little girl," said Grover. "She got the material things but not the love."

Ann told her mother that she wanted to take the State Department's examinations for diplomatic service, and that her ambition was to be "a magazine editor or a diplomat."

Clare replied how proud she was. But the pride was distant and dim.

It was so distant that one of the young men who had been courting Ann took it upon himself to write Clare, explaining how disturbed he was that Ann, or "Ace" as he called her, was talking of leaving Stanford to live in Washington, closer to her mother. The young man discussed in detail Ann's problems in living in the lonely, enormous shadow of her celebrated mother. In a long letter, filled with guilt, Clare told the young man how much she wanted Ann to develop her own personality, how she only wanted Ann to be happy.

"People often blamed Clare for setting too high a standard for Ann," said Bea Grover. The gist of their criticism was that Clare was making a nervous wreck out of her child. "She kept trying to live up to you," people told Clare, who passed this on to her daughter.

Ann was furious and replied in a letter that if she wanted to make a nervous wreck of herself trying to be like her mother, that was her business. Ann added that there were so many things she needed to learn from her mother, especially since she planned to spend a weekend with her boyfriend in San Francisco. In a sad afterthought, Ann worried that she just couldn't seem to get excited about anyone anymore. In her growing independence, she seemed to become more resentful.

Her resentment became bitter, even sarcastic. She would write more often, Ann said, if she had any hope of ever getting a reply. When Clare *did* write, Ann expressed surprise that her busy mother had time to write to anybody outside of her constituents. When Clare did make an occasional call, Ann announced her pleasure but tinged it with anger saying she hoped her mother would call again, if her budget permitted. Ann also notified her mother's secretary that she was not going to send any flowers for Mother's Day because her mother was probably tired of receiving flowers. In the course of time, Ann's letters to "Mummie darling" became "Mother dear."

Ann still kept trying to reach her mother, to intrigue her. She sent an essay she had written about her room. It was a sensitive essay about the way the light was thrown up through the glass shelves repeating the color of the flowers in the mirror, the glow of sunlight on the canary when it sang. When Clare received the essay, she corrected one of the words.

Ann's despairing letters finally touched Clare deeply enough to cause a sea change. Perhaps Clare now saw more and more of her young self in her daughter. Clare's trickle of letters became a small stream, caring letters full of genuine concern and affection. Earlier, she had been motivated by guilt, but no longer. She seemed to be falling in love with her daughter. With her letters came a steady flow of gifts: Valentines, stockings, candy, dresses, jade pins. In return, Ann sent her mother a coffee ration coupon that she wasn't using because she knew how much her mother liked coffee. When Ann mentioned some problems with her teeth, Clare promptly contacted her daughter's dentist for a full report. It brought back all her own problems with her own teeth.

Clare now even involved herself with her daughter's love life. A young man wrote despairingly to Clare. He claimed he loved Ann and wanted to marry her but that she said that she didn't love him. What should he do?

Clare replied with a single-spaced, three-page letter, saying that Ann was still unsure of herself, searching for a life similar to what she thought her parents had, that she wanted a husband like Harry Luce. Clare added that Ann didn't know how much of the Luce life was shallow, sterile, and very boring. Nor did Ann know, Clare said, that Harry Luce, as a young man, was very opinionated, stuttered, was balding, and covered with cigarette ashes—and that then he would not have impressed Ann. Clare's advice to the young man: Ignore Ann for six months or a year so that she wouldn't take him for granted. Clare added that it was nonsense to think that she controlled her daughter's life with a silver cord, but she did recognize her influence and Harry's.

"Harry really was close to Clare's daughter," said Jean Dalrymple, the theatrical agent who knew Clare in the days of *The Women* and soon would have a far greater role in the Luces' lives. "Oh, he felt so sorry for that girl. He used to talk to me about how Clare ignored her. How unhappy the child was. Clare used to say that Ann was unattractive, and she didn't know how to dress, how to put herself together. And Harry was always hugging Ann and telling her that she was a lovely girl."

When Harry met Ann's suitor, Norman Ross, Ann briefed Ross, "Be sure to look my father straight in the eye when you talk to him. He hates people who don't do that."

Ann wrote of seeing her mother in the newsreels, and how proud she was. Her mother could be anything from ambassador to China to president of the United States, and was certainly one of the great women of the century, said Ann. She now only hoped people wouldn't expect her to be like her mother because that was impossible. Ann would write to her mother about how she loved her, adored her, absolutely worshiped her, and missed her terribly. They were letters so sad, so lonely, and so hungry for a mother's love. Clare replied with real regret that they could not celebrate Christmas together but promised her daughter that this would be their last Christmas apart, and that they would celebrate together every Christmas after that to the end of the world.

The end of their world soon came. Ann had come after Christmas for a short holiday. Clare recalled it as one of their warmest times together. Mother and daughter then traveled on the Sante Fe Chief to Los Angeles. "Ann took the upper berth and I took the lower berth, and I can still see her funny little face sticking out:

" 'Mother, I know the strangest thing. I know, all of a sudden, that I will never be married.'

" 'What a funny idea! You're beautiful—of course you'll be married. Don't you want to be?'

" 'Yes, I do. Of course. But I never will be.' "

They were really mother and daughter again, really sharing. Clare showed Ann a speech she was scheduled to give in Los Angeles, promising unity in support of the war effort. Ann liked it very much and liked even more the standing ovation of the audience at the Biltmore Hotel. Harry had joined them for a few days in Palm Springs, a quiet family interval, and had returned to New York. Clare and Ann went to San Francisco, where Clare had scheduled another speech. The two had five days in the area together before Ann had to return to Stanford. On one of their city walks, they passed a small Roman Catholic church and Ann suggested they go in. They stayed there through Mass, then back to their hotel for breakfast. That night, they both went to a small dinner party given by one of Clare's old classmates at the Castle School.

Ann was heading back to Stanford early the next morning and Clare planned to drive her there. It was only twenty miles away. The night before, Ann came into her room at the Mark Hopkins and said that her mother didn't have to drive her to school the next morning because she was getting a ride with a friend. Her mother could join her later for lunch. The two then talked until midnight.

Clare now felt that she could talk to her daughter about almost anything. She saw in her the same sensitivity and understanding she liked to think that she had at that age. Beyond all that, this was somebody who loved her more than herself, more than anything. The clear adoration was always in Ann's eyes. Nobody ever had loved her like that; nobody else ever would.

Clare was still asleep early the next morning when she was awakened by her hysterical secretary shaking her and saying, "Wake up! You wake up! Your daughter is dead!"

The two girls had been driving in an open convertible. They were only two blocks from campus when a car came down a side road trying to beat the light and sideswiped the convertible. Their car spun around, the front door flew open and Ann was hurled out into a tree. She was crushed between the car and tree and died immediately. The other car was driven by a German assistant instructor in an army specialist training unit at Stanford. The girl who had been driving was only slightly injured.

Clare felt shattered, in complete shock.

"I don't know what I want to do," she told her secretary, "but whatever it is, I want to do it alone. Please get out of here."

When she called Harry with the news, "I remember the first words he said: "Not that beautiful girl. Not that beautiful girl. I'll be right out to take care of everything." Clare then dressed slowly and walked down the hill to the small Catholic church she and Ann had visited the day before. The only prayer she knew was the Lord's Prayer. Her grief became bitter against a God who had let her daughter be killed.

She didn't want to be with her secretary, and she didn't want to be alone. She remembered a man she had seen again at a party that week, a Colonel Townsend who had shared a slit trench with her during a bombing in Burma in 1942. She called him. "I am in more trouble now, much more than we were in Burma. Will you come and help?"

He came and they walked in silence for hours. Clare later called them the darkest hours of her life.

Sitting stunned in her room, Clare told her secretary to ask the priest of the small Roman Catholic church to please come to her. He was a young man and Clare asked for the meaning of life and death and the answer to her angry question, "What kind of God would take my child?" His answers, she later said, were too pat and shallow.

"When Ann died," Harry said later, "I thought Clare was going out of her mind."

Clare herself admitted, "I had a nervous breakdown."

It was as if her breakdown had created a private space in her life where no one could enter.

Clare's maid phoned Irene Selznick, a close friend and confidante, from her early *Vanity Fair* days. "I don't know what to do. You must help us. Mrs. Luce is sitting in a little straight chair, tearless and glassy-eyed. She keeps talking about plans for the evening. She keeps saying: 'Don't tell me my daughter is dead. That's nonsense.' Oh, Mrs. Selznick, send us a doctor."

"Irene routed out one of the great psychiatrists of San Francisco," recalled Buffy Cobb. "He was with Clare for hours. She talked brightly about everything. Each time he said gently, 'Now we must talk about your daughter's death, Mrs. Luce,' Clare would say, 'Absurd! My daughter's not dead,' or else, 'Yes, but first I want to know how you feel about the Pavlov theory.' Finally after four hours, Clare broke down in screaming hysterics. Then the doctor gave her a sedative." Buffy felt that the doctor saved Clare's reason.

Clare had once talked to Buffy about her life and her future. "If everything were lost, I'd still have you and Margaret Harriman and Dorothy Thompson and Bernie—but he's so old." She had made no mention then of Harry Luce. But now she would need him more than ever.

"Clare was beautiful, brilliant, kind, but not endearing. You cannot imagine cuddling her," remarked Buffy. "But once she got crying so for her lost daughter that day, I thought she would die."

Condolence letters came from all over the world, including one from a young John Kennedy, who had lost his brother in the war. He wrote that he thought he had become so hardened to losing people, but that Ann was such a wonderful girl, "so completely unspoiled and thoughtful and so very fond of you. I couldn't have been sadder." In another note, his mother, Rose, added her prayers.

When Laura Hobson sent her condolence note, "I got her reply on plain black-bordered notepaper that made me weep for her." Replying to condolences from war correspondent Robert Sherrod, Clare wrote how she worried about him covering the war and couldn't he stay home a while and be with the ones who loved him? She added that the only security and certainty in her life was in the exchange of love.

Driving to the funeral with Harry and his sister, Clare asked them to stop the car because she was going to be a little sick. They gave her some gum to chew. Clare later recalled a vignette. "Harry had my arm. A photographer came up and wanted to get our picture. Harry said, 'Get the hell out of here.' The man said, 'Well, a camera isn't permitted by the editor of *Life?*' Harry later said to me, 'I must never forget—every other journalist has the same right I have.'"

On the night of Ann's funeral, her old suitor Norman Ross and a friend overheard a distraught Harry Luce emotionally wondering aloud whether he should have become a missionary like his father.

"Clare's daughter was buried in a little small burying ground near a little old church just at the edge of Mepkin. The funeral was held on one of those beautiful days that touch the South in January. In the one-room church, all the flowers were gay and brilliant in color. All through the service, the sun was streaming through the windows. It was a short walk to the cemetery. A cow with its head over the fence mooed. Birds were singing. If it had to be, there was consolation in the beauty of the day," said Clare's friend, Dorothy Burns Hallorand.

The only note of color was one large pink camelia near the head of Ann's grave. The huge live oaks on either side of the plot formed a magnificent cathedral as the sun shone through the Spanish moss.

Clare could not stay at Mepkin after Ann's death, so she and Harry moved into Baruch's Hobcaw for the next two months. Harry read aloud a great deal to Clare. They took furious walks, consumed by a terrible restless energy. She and Harry remembered vividly how much fun Ann had had at Mepkin with the two Luce boys, and how Ann had laughed when Harry had phoned from Mepkin, after his first visit, that there "were snakes in the bathtub."

Clare hardly ate, even when they tempted her with her favorite food—fried egg sandwiches, Campbell's tomato soup, fancy cookies, chocolate cake. All her animation seemed gone. She would mostly sit and stare at nothing. It was as if all the past had descended on her, all the guilt of her neglect of Ann. Her health was very poor and many wondered whether she would survive. Those who came with comfort told her that even if she could no longer live in her daughter, her daughter was now living in her.

Time reported "the accidental death of Ann Brokaw, daughter of Mr. and Mrs. Henry Robinson Luce." Felix Belair had been called in to write the item, which Luce dictated. He corrected Luce to say, "Harry, it's not your daughter."

"Don't quibble. Put it down as I say."

"Harry, if that's what you want, that's the way it is."

Billings was shocked by the way Luce looked and sounded. "He was in the depths." When Billings asked what they should do about the coming campaign, Luce bitterly replied, "Laugh it off. It's nothing important. The country has gone to hell anyway."

Months afterward, Luce went to Stanford's graduation ceremony to pay tribute to "his daughter."

Clare later said, "I didn't realize until my daughter died how many plans I had made for my grandchildren, without even knowing I had." Later she added bitterly, "You're always sorry for the things you didn't do."

Clare somehow discovered that Ann had bought a bottle of Joy perfume as a gift to be sent to her at the Waldorf—her last gift—and it had never arrived. Clare wrote the store, insisting on having it. She received a long letter from a young man describing his trip with Ann to Yosemite, how she had told him that she had resolved her differences with her mother, how much fun she had had with Father in christening a ship and going with him to important dinners, how she had switched from agnosticism to a belief in God. Clare sent him a flower from Ann's grave.

The Trappist monks took care of the graves. Clare returned on every anniversary of Ann's death. One of the young Trappist monks once said to Clare, pointing to one of the empty grave sites, "Lady Foundress, that is where you will be."

"It gave Clare a chilly tingle up her spine."

Soon afterward, Clare requested that the urn with her mother's remains be transferred to South Carolina for burial alongside her daughter. And she told her husband, "Dear, I'm going to be buried next to my mother and daughter." And Harry said, "I will, too, if a Presbyterian minister will read over my grave."

Some months after Ann's death, a *Time* researcher, in charge of Back of the Book department was summoned to see Luce.

"He said that he would appreciate if I would interview a certain young woman. If she was qualified, and *only* if she was qualified, I might hire her as a researcher. I did. This young woman was the driver of the car in which Clare Boothe Luce's daughter was killed. Then I got a call some time later from Clare Boothe Luce. Her voice was very frosty, almost angry: 'I understand you hired So-and-So as a researcher.' From her voice, I could tell that she was saying, 'I understand you hired the girl who drove the car that killed my daughter.' But all I said was, 'Yes.' Then the frost and the cold sort of disappeared from Clare's voice, there wasn't much more to be said."

Once in a while after that, Clare walked to the Brokaw house. "I wasn't interested in anything about the house. There was only one room I cared about," she said. "That was the room where my Annie was born. I just liked to walk by the house and look up at that room."

Clare still kept her own baby pillow on her bed, and now she used Ann's baby pillow, too.

19

CLARE grew bitter and sour and angry. She was angry at God for taking away her daughter, bitter at herself for giving Ann so little of her time and love, and sour at the world for suddenly seeming so empty.

Never more lonely, never more vulnerable, she remained a recluse at Hobcaw, searching for something stronger than herself, something she could grasp. She even deeply involved herself in a mystical study of reincarnation. Politics finally pulled her back into reality. It was 1944, time for Clare to run for re-election. "I'm sure Ann would want me to continue," she told a friend.

Clare returned to Greenwich to face physical memories of a home where her daughter had lived. Everything reminded her of Ann and once again she fell into a depression. Harry, too, was distraught. A weekend guest, Alexander King, told of finding Harry wandering around the house after midnight because he couldn't sleep. Clare relied more and more on pills.

In Washington, it was easier for Clare to recover emotionally. She immersed herself in her work.

A reporter described a typical day:

She had two Washington and three New York newspapers brought to her with her breakfast in bed at seven o'clock. Sitting up in bed, she flipped through the twenty-four most important letters of the 112 she received in the first mail of the day. (Her normal mail runs to 1000 letters a week.)

After breakfast, dressed in one of the tailored suits she usually wears, and with her daily rose in her lapel, Clare received a correspondent from a French magazine and posed for his photographer. She took three long distance and eight local telephone calls and arrived at the meeting of one of her committees at ten. When this broke up an hour later, she returned to her hotel suite and received one group of high school admirers, then five constituents of other Republican congressmen friends who wished to give their home-folks a treat.

In the same period, she received two batches of mail from her office, lunched with Anne O'Hare McCormick, a columnist for The New York Times, *and stole away for fifty minutes, to the amputee ward at Fort Belvoir to visit a group of Fifth Army veterans. At six o'clock, Mrs. Luce drank a cup of tea while she signed eighteen letters, glanced at her press clippings and talked to her husband by long distance. She then bathed, changed into a pair of Chinese pajamas (the gift of Madame Chiang Kai-shek), dined with a book on religious philosophy propped on the tray, and was ready at nine-thirty to greet three Republican Party leaders to talk over a thorny problem in foreign affairs. At midnight she settled down at her typewriter and began a 2,000 word article for a magazine. And when she went to bed at two, she left a call for seven-thirty.*

"No woman I know would willingly change places with Miss Boothe today," wrote Margaret Case Harriman. "The girls feel uncomfortably that something peculiar has happened to Miss Boothe. Like Superman, she has grown an extra set of practically everything and the effect is unsettling to plain people. We used to say 'Isn't it marvelous, all the things Clare has done?' And now we just say, 'For godsakes, why does she do those things?' "

Although a member of the minority party, she took a leading part in initiating and influencing the passage through committee and the House of considerable constructive legislation, particularly to aid the rights and health of children. She also introduced a draft bill for the military ineligibles to work in war-related industries. She even challenged the president's wife on her advocacy of a large post-war army.

The war was going well on all fronts. U.S. planes were battering Tokyo as well as Berlin. Japan was slowly surrendering the islands it had so bloodily won. A Russian advance had captured 100,000 Germans at Minsk. The Allies were preparing for D-Day landings in France.

Clare petitioned the president to disclose his peace plans but he simply ignored her. Clare countered by saying that every great leader had his typical gesture—Churchill the V sign for Victory, Hitler the upraised stiff arm. Roosevelt? Clare wet her finger and held it up. This was her designation of F.D.R. as a man of cautious timidity, waiting for public opinion polls to show him the direction of the political wind. She never could forgive him saying, "Get that woman out of here!"

Since his election loss in 1940, Wendell Willkie had emerged as a strong liberal, but with a weak political organization. Determined to run again for president, Willkie asked Clare's advice. She told him sharply, "Stop drinking, lose forty pounds, and adopt a more realistic understanding of the Communists' announced plan to conquer the world." She had called communism "the opiate of the intellectuals" and "no cure except as a guillotine might be called a cure for a case of dandruff."

But publicly, Clare called Willkie "a global American Lincoln." Harry, too, did everything he could to help Willkie. The day Willkie lost the critical Wisconsin primary, the word around Time Inc. was: "Don't go near the thirty-third floor today [where Luce's office was] . . . don't go near him." Earlier, Harry had told his staff, "If the Republicans don't nominate Willkie, I'll vote for Roosevelt." Now Luce was in a rage. He felt Willkie had let down the American dream. Billings privately confided to his diary that he was secretly happy about Willkie's defeat. "I disliked him only because Luce, Larsen, [Roy Larsen, then publisher of *Life*], and Davenport [Russell Davenport, *Fortune* managing editor] have been ramming him down our throats for four years. It's a relief to vomit right in Luce's face." As working editor that week, Luce edited the lead *Time* story, which reported that the people had voted "against a crusade which had never been clearly defined." Willkie was plainly unhappy with *Time* coverage. Luce described their dinner afterward: "His face became a bowl of fury. He half-rose and I really thought this giant of a man was going to reach across my sister and sock me."

"I'm really a dirty politician," Luce later confided to Billings. "Willkie made the mistake of accepting me as an intellectual adviser instead of as a back-scenes wangler." Mutual friends felt that Harry and particularly Clare "treated Willkie very badly, even cruelly, after he was defeated."

A month later, Luce walked into Billings's office, closed the door, pushed his hat on the back of his head, and confided that the company was too big for him to keep track of editorially. He wanted Billings to be editorial director to ride herd on all three magazines. When the change was announced, Billings recorded, "I see where I must spend much time listening to his roaming rambling ideas and try to make sense out of them, to myself, and to the rest of Time Inc. He's rushed and distracted."

The marvel was that Harry Luce never really knew what Billings was truly thinking and feeling about him—but then neither did anyone else at Time Inc.

For a time, Luce focused his attention on his wife's re-election. Clare was to be a speaker at the Republican National Convention, and Harry was at her side in a white suit, with a rosebud in his buttonhole. All through Herbert Hoover's speech, Luce sat with his feet on the gallery rail reading a newspaper. When Clare came to the speakers' stand, however, Luce dropped his newspaper and listened, rapt.

She spoke about G. I. Jim, the brother of G. I. Joe. G. I. Joe, she said, was the returning war hero, but Jim was the one killed and buried in an unmarked grave. She mainly blamed G. I. Jim's death on President Roosevelt who "lied us into war."

Many felt her speech boomeranged. Many called it "cheap demagoguery" and *The New Yorker* commented that her speech "made it difficult to keep anything in our stomach for twenty-four hours." Most Americans didn't want to feel that Roosevelt, who had done so much for the country, was responsible for the death of their sons. A reporter overheard Clare say, "I'll dance on Franklin Delano Roosevelt's grave." A decade later, Clare admitted that she wished she could apologize to Roosevelt for that statement, "because lying was clearly the only way to get us there."

Luce, for his part, was indignant that *Time* had failed to report the convention's reaction to his wife's speech, which he described as extremely moving. He soon sent a memo to senior editors of all his magazines:

> *The matter of Clare Boothe Luce seems to be recognized as a definite Time Inc. problem. Anyone who goes into politics must expect to take plenty of attacks and even smears. At the same time, practically all politicians can expect to get a lot of puffing and praising from their own side. And Clare has had more than her full share of attacks. But she has so far got relatively little puffing and praising . . . from her own side. One of the reasons is that other publications—both newspapers and magazines—are not overeager to give strong favorable publicity to the wife of Publisher Luce. Meanwhile for many years, one of the main smears against her has been the thousand-time repeated allegation that she owes practically everything to the enormous press buildup she has received in the enormously powerful Luce press. It is, I think you will agree, a bit tough on her.*

Years later, seeing this memo for the first time, Clare said: "I was greatly touched by the memorandum Harry sent his editors on the score of *Time*'s handling of his wife. What a rough thing it all was on him, too. Vis-à-vis me, he always defended the editors. When I wasn't around, he defended me to his editors. You know, I never knew this before."

One charge against Clare backfired. Critics pointed out that she missed twenty-one of the seventy-one recent roll calls on legislation. The bulk of her absences occurred after her daughter's death and during her trips to the war front.

To run against Clare, Democrats picked Margaret Connors, who was a former deputy secretary of state, a dozen years younger, and also attractive. President Roosevelt congratulated Connors on "your determination to continue the fight until the Congress is rid of the untamed shrew . . ."

With Roosevelt as her enemy and with a penchant for angering even her supporters with her tart, often ill-conceived barbs, Clare fought a heated battle. She had serious doubt about winning. She later described those final days before the election as sheer misery and torture. She had taken a number of bets that Roosevelt would lose the election, but she gradually changed her mind. Clare wrote her husband a letter eight days before the election in which she predicted a Republican defeat, particularly a Dewey defeat. Her main reason: lack of warmth. She viewed the Republican campaign without anger and without promise. She claimed Republicans had failed to prove that they liked people as much as they like power.

Expecting Clare to lose, her Time aide, Wes Bailey, wrote an explanatory memo in advance blaming her G.I. Jim speech and her frequent attacks on Roosevelt, that grew so heated that she often seemed to be running against Roosevelt rather than Connors. Bailey also decried her acid quips, including, "Back on relief with the commander in chief."

A Winchell column also reported that a Republican leader had told Dewey that Clare Luce's speeches were doing him more harm than good. "My wife told me the same thing," Dewey replied.

Speaking in Hyde Park on election eve, F.D.R. observed that Clare Luce seemed to be trailing badly and volunteered that he thought her defeat "would be a good thing for this country, and it's a rough thing to say about a lady."

Until eleven-fifteen P.M., that night, Connors was leading Clare by 200 votes. But in the final tally, Clare squeaked in 2,013 votes, carrying nineteen out of twenty-three towns in Fairfield County. In view of Roosevelt's sweep that night, it was considered a political miracle.

The winning margin came from the industrial areas of Bridgeport, Hartford, and Stamford—the working women she had courted rather than "the station-wagon set." There were rumors that the fine hand and checkbook of Bernard Baruch again had made itself felt. Helen Brown Lawrenson, a confidante of both Clare and Baruch, confirmed this. And Patricia Coughlan, a *Fortune* researcher, quoted her former boss, publisher Eric Hodgins, "The election was sewed-up, paid for."

The political campaign had provided both Harry and Clare with a kind of therapy for their deep depression over Ann's death. With the campaign now over, Clare needed something new to distract her. When the Congressional Military Affairs Committee proposed that she visit the Fifth Army in Italy, Clare knew she had found her next diversion. Though she protested, she couldn't say no. The soldiers were the same age as Ann. Also, the commanding general of Allied Forces in Italy happened to be the handsome General Alexander.

En route to Italy, the committee stopped in London, where Clare caused her usual flap. Congresswoman Luce was firmly informed by the military that she was not permitted to talk to the press. Clare quickly fought back by repeating this gag order to reporters, who soon made headlines out of it. She then appealed to Americans to send more aid to Britons suffering from the effects of missile bombing.

From there, they went to France, where Clare again raised hackles. She described the French in Cherbourg as "having no food, no homes, no clothes, nothing." The press clustered close to her as she toured the Third Army front in France with General Patton. The driving, determined Patton was her kind of general, and the press dutifully reported that "she wore an officer's pants and blouse, topped off with a brown, spotted handkerchief tied over her curls and a matching scarf." Reporters did not describe what the other congressmen wore.

Clare found Commanding General Dwight D. Eisenhower a personal challenge. When he offered her a cigarette, she took a firm hold on the package. The general had a reputation for not being generous with his cigarettes and Clare had made a bet she could scrounge the pack. "The minute he felt the pressure of my fingers on the cigarettes, he withdrew the package, extracted one, and handed it to me. And all the officers laughed, and I said at once, 'General, I've just lost a bet.' Of course, when I got back to my quarters that night, I found six cartons of cigarettes from the general. At any rate, I felt that I had made a warm human contact with him at that point."

Commanding General Mark W. Clark was particularly attentive to Clare. *Stars and Stripes* combat correspondent Jack Foisie, reporting on Clare's tour for the army newspaper, later privately noted that it was the only time he had ever seen General Clark surrender his seat in his Jeep to anyone.

At Christmastime, the rest of the congressional committee returned home, joking that Mrs. Luce had been "lost in a fog over Italy." The truth was that she wanted to spend her holiday with Fifth Army soldiers instead of a Christmas at home without Ann. She traveled by Jeep through a blizzard to sing carols with patients and nurses at the 94th Evacuation hospital. While she was there, an Associated Press poll of American newspaper editors selected her as "woman of the year."

The war seemed to have given Clare a concentrated purpose. When she returned from Italy, she had a ready quip. "Well, who does the press say I'm in love with now? I'll tell you who I'm in love with—I'm love with the whole Fifth Army!"

She was indeed. She had made the Fifth Army her urgent cause. "The press has failed in one place: Italy. It is the forgotten front. It was the forgotten front because the D-Day invasion of France was more dramatic, the push to Germany more historic."

She spoke everywhere about these American soldiers fighting a terrible war with heavy casualties and insufficient supplies. At a meeting of the New York State Publishers Association, her voice was loud and clear, angry at the American people who had forgotten their fighting sons. Fred Archibald, who presided, remembered, "She was radiant, beautiful . . . completely dominated the scene. She spoke of her husband in a rather condescending way . . ."

When Luce was finally introduced to speak, he said a few rather unimpressive words and added, "My wife does the talking for this family. She does it much better than I can," and sat down.

"I felt almost sorry for him," said Archibald. "He seemed so modest, so retiring, so humble, so completely in the shadow of this beautiful, brilliant, and glamorous woman."

In contrast to Clare, Harry was indeed a far more sober, almost gray presence. The two seemed totally opposite. She liked glamorous people and glittery parties. He gravitated toward what he called "typical" types, such as a professor from a midwestern college or a small town manufacturer. Generally, he regarded New Yorkers as "smart alecks" and "insular" and preferred the company of those he met on his fact-finding trips around America.

Harry also distrusted many of the trends and movements that swept people's imagination in New York. When modern art became all the rage in the forties, Luce was enraged. He put it in the "smart-aleck" category and was particularly revolted with abstract expressionism. Nelson Rockefeller was privy to Luce's feelings about art. Said Rockefeller, "He was beginning to feel that maybe modern art was one of the most dangerous factors threatening the strength of democracy, and that he and his editors were considering whether they should expose and denounce it as a destructive force in America. I was then president of the Museum of Modern Art. I said, 'Harry, we all better sit down and talk this over before you take a stand.' First, we had dinner, and then we went to the museum to talk some more, a sort of illustrated convention. The fascinating thing about this experience is that we ended that evening with Harry being convinced that modern forms of art were the only area left in democracy where there was true freedom, where you had absolute freedom and there were no holds barred. He went from a deep concern that modern art was a destructive force, to the conclusion it was one of the great areas of freedom, one of the bastions of freedom and strength in our lives."

Such a willingness to shift positions was part of Luce's willingness to listen and be convinced. Researcher Rosalind Constable was hired to sit in a mysterious back office and do nothing but report regularly to him on what was going on in the avant-garde. "Harry *loved* new ideas, loved honing them out, loved arguing about them. To say nothing about *fighting* over them!" said his sister Beth. "Clare was a lot of fun to argue with and, boy, they had *violent* arguments, which he loved, sharpening his mind. Clare was a key part of his art enrichment because she was so interested in a lot of areas that he didn't know much of anything about. She was always interested in something new; and that fitted in exactly with the way he liked to think. They did contribute a lot to each other but he enriched Clare more than she enriched him! No *question* about it! A lot of people think otherwise; but they don't know. And she knew that, too."

Their intellectual exchange would always be of great value to both Luces. But the rest of their marriage had shifted in the ten years since their wedding. They had become two powerful forces moving in separate orbits. Luce was now an eminence, on a level with presidents and kings. His magazines, radio shows, and newsreels reached millions. His orbit was an expanding world of foreign correspondents, almost a private State Department, which sometimes seemed to have equal influence. Politicians and leaders in every segment of society yearned to be on the cover of *Time* as a peak fulfillment, on the cover of *Life* as a celebration, and on the cover of *Fortune* as a special distinction. Luce had many critics, but most of them were discreet.

Clare was in her own orbit, spinning even faster. "Something was *driving* her all the time," remembered Beth. More and more polls ranked Clare next to Mrs. Roosevelt as the most important woman in America, and one of the most important in the world. Women marveled at her energy, her brains, her ability to fight her way into the man's world and push to the top.

She seemed to put herself on a different level from most women. The wife of a *Time* publisher, noting how Clare wore her emeralds to one party and her sapphires to another, said: "She tried to look regal, as if she was doing you a favor shaking your hand."

Many Republican leaders now talked of Clare as a candidate for the U.S. Senate, or for vice president.

Despite their power and status, the Luces were privately frustrated, rootless, lonely people. They lacked any central core of love in their lives. Clare had repeatedly said, "I think love is still the name of the game for all human beings." Ann had been a major part of that love, and now she was gone. Her death and their mutual mourning had bonded Clare and Harry for a while, but no longer.

The marriage was at a crossroad. Clare, always searching for an escape, jumped at the chance to return to Italy, only two months since her previous visit. Anna Boettiger, the president's daughter, asked Press Secretary Jonathan

Daniels to check into the reason for Clare Luce's trip. Daniels soon reported that the British War Office spokesman had told him that she "was on her way to Italy to visit the Italian front at the personal invitation of Field Marshal Alexander, Allied Commander in the Mediterranean." The spokesman said he did not know the purpose of her visit.

Daniels added his own comment: "I cannot dismiss lightly the fact that Clare as long ago as 1942, and in an unhappy Burma, was writing about Alexander: 'his keen honest blue eyes blazing faintly.' There may be a gleam in 'em still in Caserta." [Alexander's headquarters were in the royal palace in Caserta.]

Field Marshal Sir Harold R. L. G. Alexander was still impressively handsome—and still married. The ostensible reason for his invitation to Clare was that he wanted her to promote Anglo-American cooperation in Italy. Clare's friends quickly noted that there was little question who was the Anglo and who was the American. But Alexander, like many other men, would only be an interval in her life. She left in March for a planned trip of two months.

While Clare was away, Harry moved out of Greenwich and into their small apartment at the Waldorf Towers. It was a bare place described as entirely cold with no homey touches. But there was a portrait of Clare on the wall "looking like an angel," as one observer archly noted.

Once again, Luce had to ferret out dinner partners. "I felt sorry for Harry because he had so few friends," noted Allen Grover. "Partly, I suppose, this was because so many people were so opportunistic and he knew it. Everybody wanted something from him. In a strange way, I think one of the people most intimate with Harry, on whom he depended a lot, was his valet." John Hersey added a footnote: "I don't think Harry was a person who dealt in friendship. He couldn't give of himself. I think that's probably it."

As a substitute for friends he had his employees, some of whom he preferred to call his "colleagues." It was not a bad substitute, for Luce's conversation was always shoptalk and his employee-friends were eager to join in.

Luce's standoffishness was even apparent to the vice president, Henry Wallace. "I would judge that he is rather lonely, self-torturing, and uneasy in his success," noted Wallace. "He rather wants to do good for the world, but doesn't know just how to do it. He rather acts to me like a man who's done wrong in some respect, but doesn't know just how or just what to do about it."

Still, Harry Luce developed a more confident presence than in the early years. His shyness never left him, but it was mostly evident now to people who knew him well. He was still a trim, handsome man, though his hair was thinning. He was a man women would look at quickly when he came into a room. "I found him very very attractive physically," said the wife of an associate. "A marvelous specimen of a man—tall, slender, and very handsome. He would talk to a woman as he would talk to any man. When he had something to say, sex didn't make any difference."

No man was more hungry for affection, for a sympathetic ear. No man was more ripe for a love affair.

20

❧

ONE evening in 1943 while Clare was out of town, Luce accepted an invitation to a party Elsa Maxwell was giving at the Waldorf. One of the guests was Jean Dalrymple, an attractive woman with striking eyes, a sensitive face, and a good figure. She had long been an acquaintance of Clare's, but had never met Harry. Jean had been one of the prime movers for Mayor Fiorello La Guardia in organizing the Center for Performing Arts and also had helped assemble the New York City Opera Company. Besides, she was known as one of the most aggressive theatrical agents in town. Still, there was a feminine softness about her, a certain air of quiet mystery. Jean could not compete with Clare in the same room, but she was a far merrier, warmer woman. Unlike Clare, she did not need to be center stage all the time. She had the greater gift of knowing when to listen and, therefore, was on everybody's select party list.

"Elsa was a very close friend of mine," recalled Dalrymple. "Harry was alone at the party, and Elsa introduced me to him. We talked awhile, but I had an appointment, and I had to run. I told him, 'I'm terribly sorry, I have to go.' He was taken aback. I said, 'Grace Moore, a well-known opera singer, is one of my important clients. I have to take her to "21" to meet a man who's doing a story about her, which I arranged."

" 'And then you'll come back?'

" 'Well, I told Elsa that I'd try.'

" 'Well, please do.' "

As Dalrymple remembered, "He looked so unhappy, as if he needed somebody to talk to. So, I said to myself, 'Gee, I really ought to go back.' I will!' "

When Dalrymple returned, much later than she had anticipated, she feared he would be gone. But Harry was still there.

" 'Oh, you did come back! I was just going to leave; I'd given you up!' Then he said, 'Oh, you don't want to go back in there to the party. You came back to meet me! Let's go and have a drink, together.' And I said, 'Fine!' And, much to my astonishment, he took me up to his apartment. 'Now that you're here and we're going to order a drink, let's order some dinner. How would that be?' he asked.

"I had a date elsewhere, but decided that my date wasn't as important as this, so I told him, 'I have to make a phone call, and get out of another date.'

"He replied, 'Yes, you do that.' Then, he ordered up dinner. The waiter came and gave us menus. And he began, right then and there, asking me questions. He was *delighted* to find out that I was a Presbyterian," she recalled.

Jean left him later that night when she thought he was tired. The next morning, the phone rang when she was half asleep.

"Well, I didn't finish my conversation with you last night," he told her. "And I woke up this morning determined to talk to you again—so have dinner again with me tonight."

Dalrymple was busy, but Luce persisted.

"He began to call me quite frequently and asked me always to dinner and to the movies. He treated me like any man would who wanted to know me."

But more than wanting to know *her,* Harry wanted her to know *him.* He *needed* somebody to know him.

Luce could always order an audience from among his associates, but that was an audience bought and paid for. What he wanted and needed was a woman who regarded him not as an icon or as a power, but as a man.

While Luce was courting Dalrymple, Clare was busy with yet another lover. While she was flying over Germany, the pilot turned to her with the information that his instruments had malfunctioned and they might have to make a crash landing through a bad fog. "Are you ready for it?" he asked. "No, not quite," she said. The plane flew on for almost an hour, eventually finding a break in the fog. During this tense period, as the gas was running low, Clare was busy finishing some sonnets she had been writing about the Anzio beachhead. She had been taken there by General Lucian Truscott, another one of the generals in the ardent Clare corps. Truscott commanded the Third Infantry Division, which had swept through Sicily. Before that, he had organized the Rangers, the tough American version of the British Commandos. He was one of the generals Eisenhower relied on most. A strong, dynamic, attractive man, it was Truscott who showed Clare the misery of the war in Italy.

Clare had first met Truscott at a dinner at 10 Downing Street in London, attended by Prime Minister Churchill and Field Marshal Montgomery. Near the end of the meal, Clare did what she often did at a dinner table, and what her husband often did. She tapped her glass with a knife to get everybody's attention, then posed a question for discussion: What did the gentlemen think was the most perfect thing in the world?

Truscott took a drag on his cigarette, looked her in the eye, and answered promptly: an infantry battalion.

"Why?" she asked with a thin smile.

"Because an infantry battalion will do any goddamned thing you tell it to do," said the general.

The military men at the table all applauded.

Clare announced her surprise that the general did not champion a woman as the most perfect thing in the world.

"What for?" asked the general. "I never met a woman who would do anything you told her to do."

Everybody laughed. Clare only smiled, but she was intrigued.

They soon embarked upon an affair and continued it whenever they could throughout the war. In a book he later wrote, the general's grandson Lucian Truscott IV discussed the affair, including the fact that "Clare Boothe Luce spent the rest of her life bragging to anyone who would listen about her wartime affair with the general." As for Truscott, he "relished the rumors," and "did nothing either to shut her up or dispel them."

The Truscott affair was more serious than most. It was so intense, Clare later confided, that she really thought he wanted to go home, divorce his wife, and marry her. Clare said she almost believed it, but it never happened. He went back to his family.

So many other men almost fell in love with her. International News Service correspondent Frank Gervasi recalled a brief encounter when Clare stopped off in Paris. "I know she could be cold and businesslike, but I only saw the warm, charming part of her. I almost fell in love with her. I thought she might have even liked me a little bit because it was only our second meeting, but she looked me in the eyes and kissed me full on the lips. It was enough to capture me for good. She is the kind of woman whom most men adore and most women definitely don't. Women say and write things about Clare which should neither be said nor printed, but invariably are."

Luce, for once, was enjoying himself while his wife was off with other men. He confided to Jean Dalrymple how very unhappy he was with Clare.

"The marriage was terrible for him," she said. "I don't think it was so bad for her. She just seemed to carry on her own life, and not pay much attention. I said to him once, 'You ought to take a stand with her!' You have to say to her, 'Do you want to live with me, or don't you? You have to live where I want to live for once!' But he never did; he never could. He somehow could never face up to her.

"With us, it was never any flaming, passionate love affair. He's not that type and I'm not that type. Every once in a while, he would say that he wanted to marry me. I would say I was terribly sorry, but I would never marry him.

" 'Why not?' he would ask me.

" 'You feel guilty now about having left Lila for Clare. Eventually, you would feel the same way about leaving Clare for me. I don't care to have that on my conscience. I have a Presbyterian conscience, too.' "

One day, Dalrymple received a call from another woman whom she knew well. The woman, a well-known writer, had been an intermittent part of Luce's life. She said, "I understand you've taken Harry away from me."

"And I said, 'Well, I never knew that he looked at anybody but Clare!' She then said, 'Oh, I'm just one of quite a few.' She didn't say who the others were. Harry was no womanizer, but he did like women. He found them easier to talk to than men."

On her return, Clare quickly learned about Dalrymple. They had many friends in common and Dalrymple was not pledged to secrecy. She and Harry had dined in restaurants and were the subject of talk.

Clare swiftly called Billings at home and demanded to know everything he knew about Dalrymple. She thought Billings was one of the few to whom Luce confided. But Billings, who *did* know, denied the whole thing.

Clare wanted their open marriage open only for her. She had underestimated Harry. She had considered him a shy, safe man too much in love with his magazines to think much about women. In some measure, Clare was right. Harry had his tough side. He was still in his forties, and the women he knew were on the fringe of his life. In the early days with Clare, and in his relationship with Jean Dalrymple, they were a compelling attraction, often pulling him from his work, but the work had such a gravitational force that it always pulled him back. It was the center of his being. Women could complete his life, but almost never command it.

Dalrymple was right about their relationship. It was deep and important to him, but it was not an overwhelming passion.

Clare now made a concerted campaign to regain her husband. From Washington, or anywhere else, she sent a stream of messages, telegrams, and letters full of loving words, telling again and again how much she missed him, how grim it was without him, how badly she wanted him to come to her, wherever she was.

But Luce was preoccupied with Dalrymple. Increasingly, he found himself seeking her company instead of going into the office. For a brief time, he let Billings have control.

One of his senior editors, Eric Hodgins, soon ventured some criticism: "You are facing the major problem that every head man of every successful enterprise always faces as he and his organization grow and mature. You are growing remote . . ."

But Luce was unconcerned. Dalrymple had given him a new contentment.

He felt so much at ease with her. There was no edge in her speech, no bite in her look, no scorn in her spirit as there was with Clare. He continually raised the question of marriage. But Dalrymple regarded this as an exciting interval with a fascinating man, and that was enough for her, at least for then.

Thanks to Luce's new contentment with Dalrymple, those at Time Inc. now found him much more approachable, much less tense. "I really love the boss," Grover told Billings, but expressed the hope that he "doesn't break some vast new concept upon an unsuspecting world without having it thoroughly thought out. You know our sainted boss is not the greatest organization man."

Luce's greatness as an editor, said his associates, was in his intuition, his sense of timing, his keen ear and quick eye. His senior staff felt that the secret of Luce's editorial success, "was not his intellectual profundity but his intellectual naiveté, that he was unashamed on strange territory, honest with himself." Coupled with that was a passion for history and the spreading of ideas. "An idea does not exist outside the human skull," he once said. "Therefore, you tell your story in terms of a person's emotions."

Occasionally, Luce reigned from an office on the thirty-third floor of the Time-Life headquarters in Rockefeller Center. Harry referred to his office as a box, but others called it "the cathedral." Billings joked that the office was fit for Il Duce and called it "Il Luce." Certainly, it was an impressive expanse, that opened onto a sun deck. Wide windows a story and a half high faced across the East River. On one side of the inner office was a gallery of one hundred candid photos of key staff members at Time Inc., mostly taken by *Life* photographer Alfred Eisenstaedt. At the end of the table, all alone, was a framed photograph of Ann. On Harry's desk was a small, framed photograph of his father. At the window shelf to the right of his desk were four more photos: a glamorous one of Clare; one of his brother Sheldon, stationed with the Air Force in Ohio; one of his son Hank, a twenty-year-old graduate of the Navy-V-12 program at Yale; one of Peter Paul, then sixteen and a student at Brooks School in Massachusetts.

Occasionally Luce still went down to the twenty-ninth floor to put out an issue of *Time*. He felt that the red-bordered weekly needed most of his day-to-day attention. *Life* was on a different wavelength and took more advance planning. He was more unhappy with *Fortune*. "*Fortune*, though doing fine statistically, is reported dead on its feet, with nobody around to bury it," Billings reported. "Nobody bothers to read it; it's that dull."

Fortune's losses coupled with other problems had caused Time Inc.'s income to drop appreciably, but not enough to stop the company from buying two transport planes. For a time, there was some budget-conscious talk about cutting out drinks charged to *Time*. (The company's liquor bill for the previous year was reportedly $10,000.) But gradually, the financial picture improved.

On a more global scale, Luce was pleased with events. The war was going well, and so was his relationship with the White House. The president still periodically asked Luce to come down and talk, and Harry sometimes even invited himself to Washington. F.D.R. floated occasional ideas to Luce, one of which was for a *March of Time* film about the development of rural areas after the war was over.

While the relationship between F.D.R. and Luce was now comfortable, it was not cozy. Luce was irate when he felt F.D.R. had ceded too much to Stalin at Yalta "and didn't leave a limb to climb back on."

On April 12, 1945, President Roosevelt died. For millions, F.D.R. had been the only president they had ever known, their commander in chief, the man who had shaped their time and their history.

Luce told his editorial voice, Jack Jessup, that he was afraid Roosevelt "would escape history and be credited with being more interventionist than he really was." He felt that Roosevelt had done too little too slowly in preparing the country psychologically to take sides in the war, forcing it to make up its mind, and that he shirked the mission for which God had ordained him. Luce disagreed with the draft of a *Life* editorial crediting Roosevelt for preparing the country for taking sides "sooner and more effectively than we had any right to expect."

"I sometimes pray," Luce told author John Kobler, "forgive me my sins as I forgive that sonofabitch his."

Roosevelt's primary sin, according to Luce, was his final softening toward Soviet Russia. "Luce had a phobia about freedom," commented Berlin bureau chief John Scott. "His kind of freedom, American freedom. And everything else seems to be dangerous. That's the main policy of his magazine . . ."

That phobia about freedom was at the heart of Luce's violent anti-Soviet feelings. He truly believed that Soviet Russia was an evil empire determined to spread communism all over the world. A Communist world to him was a world of slaves—without religion. This, of course, was a key factor in his mind. A godless world was an empty world. A world without freedom and religion was no world at all.

Luce's anxiety about communism intensified to the point that he notified his editors that he no longer wanted any Communist sympathizers working for Time Inc. He ordered them to start a dossier.

Communism was one issue on which he and Clare were in complete, enthusiastic agreement. They were almost equally intense about it, although Clare was much more outspoken than Harry. She could say publicly what he could not. John Kenneth Galbraith had a vivid memory of Clare, glittering in a rhinestone evening gown, delivering a radio broadcast about the American surrender to Bolshevism "in taut, high-pitched, frantic tones . . . so awful was the effect that there was a full minute of silence at the end of the broadcast."

At *Time,* the foreign news editor Whittaker Chambers, a former Communist, was even more obsessed with the threat of Soviet Russia than the Luces. Chambers was a short, stocky man who dressed like a pallbearer. He was conspiratorial and secretive by nature and always locked his door.

Emmet John Hughes later told David Halberstam that Chambers was so intent on his anti-communism that "you could try to do a review of a French pastry, and he would put anti-communism in it." Hughes lunched with Chambers and told him he thought he was carrying his anti-communism editing too far. Chambers disagreed.

When foreign correspondents complained that Chambers was coloring all their dispatches, Luce countered, "I've read all these things, and I've been following what's going on. As far as I can see, Chambers is on the right track."

Luce would later change his mind about Chambers, but for the time being he was willing to maintain *Time*'s editorial stance and focus his own energies on forging a relationship with F.D.R.'s successor, Harry Truman. Both Truman and his wife, Bess, had been victims of Clare's tart tongue in years past. Luce was nervous.

She had called them "Kickback Harry" and "Overtime Bess." (Truman's wife was on his payroll in the Senate when he was still paying off debts for a failed haberdashery business.) Truman might forgive what you said about him, but not about his wife or daughter. During Truman's presidency, Clare was never admitted to the White House.

Truman did not transfer his ill will to Harry. Luce was nervous. After the Germans surrendered on May 19, 1945, Truman made Luce a very happy man by giving him clearance to tour the Pacific combat zone. Luce took off with senior editor Roy Alexander. Liberals on *Time* categorized Alexander as "one of the hard-eyed boys." Alexander had been a star reporter on the St. Louis *Post-Dispatch,* a Marine in the first World War, then a military expert on *Time.* The story circulating around *Time* was that if you had been a marine and applied to Alexander for a job, you usually got it. Alexander had an easy warmth and a ready remark to break any tension and was the perfect companion for Luce. In thirty days, Luce and Alexander traveled 30,000 miles. They stopped in Guam, the Philippines, Iwo Jima, Saipan, Kwajalein, and Hawaii. Luce even visited the destroyer escort *McGinty* to see his ensign son, Hank. For the five-minute chat the navy allowed Luce with his son, he had to travel by mail plane, destroyer, and packet boat.

On his return to New York, Luce was "bursting with ideas about Pacific coverage," including a special issue of *Life*. He had spent four hours with an angry General MacArthur. The general resented some remarks against him in *Time* and *Life* which, he claimed, threatened his whole strategy. Luce, in turn, blasted his editors, reaffirming a policy, not subject to rebuttal, that Time Inc. was not against MacArthur.

"We sat on the terrace sipping tea," said Billings, "as Harry began his saga. He was quite interesting—but refused to stop for questions. We moved to the supper table and it was dark and the moon was coming up before the meal was over. All we had to do was to sit still and listen to his monologue. He is a good reporter: He thinks the war could be won in three or four months if we combined our political and psychological warfare with the military forces."

Luce took his ideas to Washington and dined with thirty-three senators. He detailed his recommendations that the government modify its demand for unconditional surrender and permit a peace that would allow Japan to keep its emperor on the throne. Otherwise, he warned, it would take a year of bloody fighting and heavy casualties to invade Japan and defeat it. He did not believe Japan would be a menace to the United States in the foreseeable future. Luce even scheduled an interview with President Truman to present his argument, but the interview was cut short before Luce could make his case. When the atomic bomb was dropped on Hiroshima on August 6, Harry felt he had another mission. He and his friend Joseph P. Kennedy went to Francis Cardinal Spellman, requesting the cardinal to ask President Truman for five or six days' truce to give Japan a chance to surrender. The next day, the second atomic bomb fell on Nagasaki, and, within a week, the Japanese unconditionally surrendered.

"In America, the celebration outdid anything within the living memory of man," wrote Sergeant Hilary H. Lyons in *Yank, The Army Weekly*. "It made V-E Day seem silent. A chapter, perhaps a whole book of history had ended, and a word that had figured much in American thoughts for three years, eight months, and seven days—a word often spoken, but always in terms of the past or of an unsure future—could be spoken now in terms of the living present. The word was peace."

Japan's defeat still left China facing civil war. From his post in China, correspondent Teddy White reported the impending strife and urged *Time* to take a neutral stance for a democratic solution instead of unconditional backing of Chiang Kai-shek. Luce did not question the quality of White's reporting. What Luce soon did question was his partisanship. He felt White sympathized too much with the Chinese Communists and ascribed too many virtues to the peasants and too few to the leadership of Chiang Kai-shek. White believed that Chiang's Kuomintang Party was corrupt and could save his government from the Communists only by giving the people more liberty and more land. He repeatedly tried to express his opinions to Luce, to no avail.

White finally put up a sign in his office in China which said, "Any relationship between this correspondent's dispatches and what appears in *Time* magazine is purely coincidental."

It was no surprise when Harry announced plans for another trip to China, this one at Chiang's personal invitation. Luce hitched a ride from the U.S. to China in a general's private plane, outfitted with five beds and a lounge and a bar. "Harry thinks he's going out to help the generalissimo and general marshall bring peace to China," observed Billings in his diary.

At a party for 300 in honor of Mao Tse-tung, Luce, the only foreigner, came to hear Mao shouting that China must find unity under Chiang Kai-shek. At that time they wanted a unity government.

A major objective for Luce in China was to meet more of his enemy, more Communist leaders. A meeting was arranged with Chou En-lai, the Communist next in command to Mao, and the one much respected by many Western intellectuals. From the moment they sat down, recalled Luce, their conversation was completely frank. Chou promised to put Luce in touch with Communists in Shantung, but complained that *Time* had not been very nice to them recently. Luce blamed this on world-wide, left-wing propaganda, which had turned increasingly nasty. It was a meeting of tough minds. Harry left much impressed, but unconvinced.

During Luce's visit to Tientsin, a U.S. marine who felt that Luce was responsible for keeping marines in North China, decided to shoot him. Just as he was taking aim at Luce's back, some buddies forcefully took away his M-I rifle.

Luce left China optimistic about its potential for rapid recovery. But Billings, after debriefing Harry, said, "I suspect he is less pro-Chiang than he was but he didn't say so." Nor was Luce any more willing to listen to Teddy White. He soon replaced him with another correspondent, who regarded Chiang as "a truly great man."

He also sent highly respected Robert Sherrod to write about Chiang's "wonderful army," but Sherrod decided they were not so wonderful. His article was not printed. Luce did, however, print another story later on corruption in China.

At a dinner in November 1945 with the Luces, former Vice President Henry Wallace felt that Clare was more realistic about the Chinese than Harry was, that Harry was continually modifying his sentences, trying to twist the truth in order to come out with the answer he wanted. "Mrs. Luce was enjoying the luxury of saying what popped into her mind first," observed Wallace.

* * *

The dinner with Wallace was a symbolic occasion for Clare. It was rare those days that Harry included her in his life. During his tours of the Far East and China, Luce had sent cables to Clare, but they lacked his old intimacy and affection. The marriage was on a totally new footing. Jean Dalrymple was now the woman Harry cared deeply about, and Clare knew that. Yet, things were at a standoff. Harry hated confrontations and was not ready to ask Clare for a divorce. Clare, for her part, had no reason to change the status quo. Publicly, they were still the powerful Mr. and Mrs. Luce. Privately, Clare probably assumed that she could yet win Harry back.

Still, there was a growing malaise about Clare. Distressed about the state of her marriage, she was also increasingly unhappy in Congress. More and more, she felt overworked, trying to perform "the menial and the miraculous," as she called it. The phones were always ringing, the buzzers always buzzing for upcoming votes. There were constant committee meetings to deal with and an unending stream of visitors with requests and demands and advice, as well as mountains of mail, some filled with love, some with hate. One was even addressed simply to " 'That Woman,' Washington D.C."

Washington reporters floated a rumor that Clare was being considered as editor in chief of a new Luce magazine for women. At Time Inc., the notion was "viewed with alarm." There was an idea for a woman's magazine, but Clare was never considered as editor.

In her search for something diverting, Clare accepted the title role of George Bernard Shaw's *Candida* at a summer playhouse in Stamford, Connecticut. One of her few unfulfilled ambitions was to be a successful stage actress. Her previous attempts were almost disastrous, but she was determined to try again. She had told Harry about her childhood role in *The Dummy,* where she played her only scene bound and gagged by kidnappers to a chair. "Harry said he would be willing to have me return to the theater if I could find a similar part."

Clare spent a week rehearsing on the porch of her Greenwich home. "It took me a little while to get over the first stage fright. But I had a lot of fun." So did the critics. "No warmth . . . ham hands . . . school girl diction," carped one.

Luce claimed he couldn't understand why reviewers didn't give her a break: "What do they think she is—an actress?" he asked. Going backstage after the final curtain, Luce's only comment was one of relief: "It's over."

During the rehearsals, Clare had left most of her congressional duties to her assistant, Albert Morano. A Connecticut paper soon ran a headline calling him: OUR REAL CONGRESSMAN.

Faced with all this unpleasant publicity, Clare was increasingly bitter about her "worthless and unhappy self." She needed a rest. Harry suggested they take a two-week vacation in the White Mountains, but Clare canceled because "she didn't think two hotel rooms were good enough for her." Baruch then chartered a plane to take Clare and Harry to Hobcaw. They shot quail, rode horses, and retired at ten o'clock. For a time, the marriage seemed back on track. Harry had always been willing to help Clare through rough spots, and this was no exception.

As the second anniversary of Ann's death approached, Clare succumbed to an attack of hysterics; she even talked about suicide.

Clare and Nehru had met during her travels to India and had become correspondents. Her last letter to him was in June 1942, delivered by Wendell Willkie. In that letter she had urged Nehru to come to the United States to meet President Roosevelt and resolve the fate of India. When Clare heard that Nehru had been imprisoned by the British, she berated the president for his silence in the matter. Nehru wrote to Clare from the Liddar Valley in Kashmir:

> *You are not a person one can easily forget, and though I seem to have given you the impression that I was not sufficiently impressed by your beauty and your intelligence, you are clever enough to know that this impression was wrong. It may be that I am rather afraid of Woman, especially when she has the quality of moving and disturbing the mind. . . . I have come to realize more than ever that in the pain and torment that are the inevitable accompaniments of life, a certain detachment is the best armor. Not that I have succeeded in attaining it, but even an attempt in that direction has helped me. For you that may not be necessary, and yet I doubt if anyone can dispense with it easily without having to face the consequences of too much entanglement in life's maze. . . .*

From his distance of space and time, Nehru had touched some tremulous chord in Clare. She, too, had tried using a certain detachment as a kind of armor, but without success. The pain and torment of life Nehru had talked about were deep within her. The pressures on her had become cumulative and overbearing. On top of it all was the blow to her ego—her husband's love affair with another woman.

Clare was clearly suffering. Behind her sharp tongue and willingness to conquer the world was a curious fragility. Moreover, she felt doubts sweeping over her. She told friends that there were even nights when she couldn't write three lines at the typewriter that made sense. The idea that she might have petered out as a writer made Clare panicky. Too many people expected too much of her, and now she seemed to be unable to do anything at all. She felt herself a failure. Elsa Maxwell described Clare's condition as "complete collapse verging on melancholia."

Out of such melancholia, came despair. Out of despair, came a wish to die. Clare had felt this death-wish before but had been able to blot it out through work; now she couldn't. It seemed as if everything in her life had come to a full stop. Clare had told her friend Ruth Burns, "I envy people who can believe. But I can't understand about you Catholics. You always get up for church. Do you feel you have to?"

"No," said Burns. "We want to."

"It must be a wonderful religion," Clare replied. "Someday I'm going to study it."

Clare sat in a darkened room, day after day. She later confided to a friend that Harry didn't know how to help her. "He'd come in, sort of pat my hand, and walk out." What she wanted, she said, was for him to put his arms around her and hold her. "But he didn't put his arms around anybody."

She was wrong about that. Harry was putting his arms around a woman who gave him the quiet, loving attention he had never seemed to get from Clare. He had found what she had not.

21

As her despair increased, Clare found herself crying and reciting the only prayer she had ever memorized, the Lord's Prayer. Wandering aimlessly around her room, seriously contemplating suicide, she noticed an unopened letter on her desk from a Jesuit priest, Father Edward Wiatrak, who taught in a parochial school for boys in Cincinnati. He had once written her a fan letter about an article of hers. When she replied, he wrote to her regularly over a period of years. His constant theme: God and love are the part of the soul. Never once had he asked for a favor or a contribution.

Clare was restlessly picking up things, putting them down again. She started seeing faces: Her mother looking at a water lily, saying, "My religion is flowers." She saw the glowing face of her daughter with her red brown hair, her eyes closed. Then she saw a parade of faces of people she had known. Clare thought she was going crazy.

Unable to find a Bible, Clare instead found a telephone book and called Father Wiatrak.

"Father," she said, "I am not in trouble but my mind is in trouble."

"We know," Wiatrak replied. "This is the call we have been praying for."

Wiatrak, however, said he was too simple a priest to counsel her and referred her to Father Fulton J. Sheen in Washington.

Walking past St. Patrick's Cathedral early in her marriage, she and Harry had gone inside and Harry had told her, "Darling, if you ever become religious, you'll become a Catholic."

A dinner was arranged, and Father Sheen set the ground rules:

"First, we will consider the existence of God. I will talk for fifteen minutes without interruption and at the end of that time you can talk as you like—two, three, or four hours and ask any questions you please."

Sheen later recalled that it was silly to think that anybody could talk to Clare for fifteen minutes without interruption. "Actually I talked for about five minutes. Then Clare jumped up and shook her finger under my nose and said, " 'If God is good, why did he take my daughter?' "

Sheen replied, "Perhaps it was in order that you might become a believer. In order that you might be here tonight and to start on the road to wisdom and peace. In order that you might discover God's truth. Maybe your daughter is buying your faith with her life. . . . Ann's death was the purchase price for your soul."

After that, they met frequently for sessions that lasted up to four hours. Sheen later said although he had devoted his life to instruction in the church, Clare raised difficulties "the likes of which I never heard before." He described it as a battle of wits.

Clare insisted that Ann's death was not responsible for her conversion, but many thought otherwise. And Father Sheen said that Clare's eventual conversion came as a result of intellectual conviction. "We do not allow a leap of faith."

"You cannot realize the depth of her," Sheen said of Clare. "Her mind works like a rapier. There is no bludgeon about her mind. It has the quality of a rapier and cuts like a sword to the truth, almost intuitive flash of truth. Like a sword it cuts away all the merely incidental things that are not to the point."

Most of his courses of instruction averaged fifty hours, Sheen added, but Clare took hundreds of hours, "longer than anyone else I had ever known." Clare often sat on the floor while he sat on the chair and systematically tried to prove the existence of God. One night they discussed Hell, which Clare refused to accept. He told her he would give her as much time as she wanted to argue against it, and she argued for more than an hour. "I never heard such arguments against Hell in my life." Sheen then had his hour of counterargument. Clare then jumped to her feet, looked up, and cried, "Oh God, what a protagonist you have in this man!"

Clare's friends credited Father John Courtney Murray, an attractive and powerful Jesuit theologian, chief architect of the Declaration of Religious Freedom, as being the final force in shepherding her to conversion. He was a big, tall, attractive, whiskey-drinking priest who wore his habit all the time.

Father Murray would become a key person in Clare's life, and in Harry's. At the end, he became closer to Harry than to Clare. It was said of Father Murray that he seemed more at home in the Luce home than they were. *Time* would later do a cover story on him.

That Christmas Day of 1945, the Luces had been invited to a family dinner in Haverford, Pennsylvania. Clare, by then, seemed quite different. She had been hard like crystal but now the brashness had dissipated, and there was an obvious quiet about her.

If Clare's soul was now full and warm, her mind was still cold and clear. Her political instincts also stayed intact. She was scheduled to attack the administration in the Republican Lincoln Day dinner in Johnston City, Tennessee. She called Walter Winchell to ask him "as a personal favor" that he delete his story about her coming conversion from his nation-wide broadcast over the ABC network. He did. Clare felt her speech would be better received in the South if it were not known that she was becoming a Roman Catholic.

When Clare was received into the church at St. Patrick's Cathedral on February 16, 1946, only a half dozen people were present. Clare explained that she had become a Catholic "to get rid of my sins and start living again . . . and the need to find meaning in all this torment.

"I became a Catholic—one of the better decisions of my life. It permitted me to love and be loved. Never having had a father, it was a great joy to discover I had the greatest of them all." She also added that women "must be prepared to leave the home awhile in order to save the home," that they must obey the Pope's injunction to participate fully in the political life of the nation and "we should soon see the end to communism in Europe and here at home . . ." Her postscript was that the most important domestic issue was to ensure that working men are paid enough so that they could marry and raise families.

Clare later revealed that she had been "seeking God in my analyst's office, and it is quite clear to me that this experience was also one of the real reasons I became a Roman Catholic." Analysis could not answer her persistent question: What was the point of striving or keeping alive or fighting, "if only an ominous silence reigned throughout all creation when Death came?"

"I think she liked the idea of the confessional," said Wilfrid Sheed. "To confess whatever all those dreadful sins were . . . apparently, she felt guilty about Ann. I think that would be one reason why she'd want something like a confession."

When Fulton Sheen asked Clare to whom she wanted to confess, she replied, "Bring me someone who has seen the rise and fall of empires." She later said she had been joking. But she told Edward L. Bernays that she preferred confession to a priest than confession to a psychoanalyst, recognizing that both were methods of ridding oneself of a sense of guilt. "She told me about it," said Bernays, "because she knew I was a nephew of Freud and would understand." Bea Grover felt that Clare had an ambition to be bigger than anybody, and "I think her happiness in the Roman Catholic Church is partly that it is bigger than even she could hope to be."

There were those who believed Clare's conversion was for a different reason entirely. The rumors of an impending Luce divorce had become persistent. "Clare, being the political operator that she was," said Robert Coughlan, "figured out how to stop the rumors. And that was to become a Catholic convert. You can't divorce a Catholic. A marriage could be annulled, but not after ten or fifteen years. And not just because this guy has got a lech for somebody else . . ."

Harry was exultant about Clare's conversion. He felt that Clare had found a home for herself, and now she no longer needed him. Now, she might let him go.

"Harry was in San Francisco," said Jean Dalrymple. "I was in my house in Beverly Hills. The phone rang very early one morning. And it was Harry. 'Did you read the morning paper? Look down at the bottom of the page.' So I turned, and it said, CLARE LUCE BECOMES CATHOLIC.

" 'I suppose that means that now you're stuck for life.'

" 'Not at all! She has just divorced herself from me.'

" 'Not in her mind, she hasn't.'

"Harry was insistent. 'In her religion, we are no longer married, because in her religion I'm still married to Lila. She cannot live with me as my wife. I'm going to fly down and have lunch with you. I want to talk.'

"So I cooked lunch for him and he said, 'I want to marry you.'

" 'You're childish! She'll never give you up! I don't know how she'll arrange it, but she'll never, never give you up.' "

C. D. Jackson, a Time vice president, then told Billings that he, Luce, and Luce's attorney had dropped in on Clare at the hospital, where she had recently undergone a hysterectomy, and pressured her for a divorce. Jackson said that he'd bet 50-50 that there would be a divorce with Clare getting a big cash settlement.

Clare went directly to Baruch for advice. He told her to ask for fifty-one percent of Time Inc. stock and four million dollars.

Billings soon reported further developments: "Clare and Church investigated Harry-Lila marriage to see if it could be annulled. Luce to Clare in anger at being 'closed in on' like this: Clare on knees, holding Harry's legs, big melodramatic tears and crying, 'It's all because I couldn't give you a baby that you don't love me anymore.' Harry ordered her to get up and stop that nonsense."

Clare then told Harry her terms for divorce. Harry refused. He would give her money, yes, but Time stock, no. He would never ever sell control of Time. It was his life.

Harry then presented Clare with some lawyers, who threatened to annul the marriage on the ground that she was frigid.

"Oh, so far am I from being frigid. Let's go upstairs, Harry, and show these guys!"

Luce quickly backed off.

Clare now made a threat of her own: If Harry didn't give her the stock and the money, and if he tried to divorce her in a foreign country, she would give him the most terrible publicity—call him "an old lecher" and tell about all the different women that he'd gone out with.

"I think he was scared of her turning on him—you know, blowing the whole thing—or else afraid that she'd kill herself," said Dalrymple, who then revealed some astonishing statements Harry had made to her about Clare. "That worried him more than anything else, because she tried, twice [to kill herself]. She drew a knife across her wrists. Hardly enough to kill you, but enough to scare you to death. He even told me that she had threatened to kill him."

As the divorce battles continued, Luce's secretary Corinne Thrasher reported regularly, mainly to Billings, that Luce was "in a perfect rotten mood." Billings would find Luce "holding his head in his hands, looking sour and miserable." To some, he seemed suddenly disagreeable, talking in "evil grunts" and snarling. Once he went into "a quivering rage" saying that *Life* was going "degenerate" because of a scheduled article on a psychotic boy. Or else he would shut himself in his office all day. "And I have no idea what he is doing. He looked like a gray death's head, with an off-stage sense of doom," said Billings.

"Poor lonely soul," Billings wrote of Harry in his diary, "unable to get any normal wholesome fun out of life—and when he does try, it all goes rotten. . . . Sex makes more damn fools out of more people than liquor. . . ."

Grover, who had been privy to Luce's previous suicide threat, was particularly concerned because Luce seemed "erratic and contradictory, in fact crazy at times. He's trying to escape by overwork. He drives himself unmercifully, and doesn't know how to let go and take it easy . . ."

A long scheduled profile of Clare for *Life* was then canceled. "Thank God . . . what a relief," Billings recorded. Luce also turned down an offer from a close friend of Clare's to write an article about her. *Time* treated Clare's conversion with a simple item in its People column.

All was now in a kind of legal limbo. Clare refused to budge. Harry would not surrender his stock, worried about her threats of publicity and suicide. He told Jean the divorce looked dim. Dalrymple was not surprised. Ostensibly, it did not change their relationship, but it did give Jean more to think about.

However shaky the marriage, this didn't manifest itself to their friends. Harry and Clare were still seen together at public functions and parties. When someone snidely mentioned Dalrymple to Clare, she airily dismissed the comment, saying that Harry was simply "straying from the ranch." Later, she would even say, "Harry liked me much better as a Catholic than as the secular character he'd married."

"In every marriage, there are two marriages," Clare once told an interviewer. "His and hers. His is better."

22

⚜

I N the midst of his struggles with Clare, and with his heart and mind filled with Jean Dalrymple, Luce headed off for Zurich en route to Germany. He had been invited by the War Department to view postwar conditions in Germany with a group of VIP journalists. The American consulate in Zurich was responsible for the care and comfort of the group, but somehow no one had been told in advance that they were coming. Most of the staff was away, and a young vice consul was faced with the job of entertaining the illustrious visitors.

He quickly summoned Mary Bancroft, a vivacious American woman living in Switzerland. A former wartime spy, Bancroft, then forty-two, was witty, outspoken, and fiercely intelligent, and he felt sure the journalists would like her. Would she come for drinks? At first, Bancroft said no. But when she heard that Henry Luce was part of the group, she swiftly changed her mind. She had angry questions for Luce on many inaccuracies in *Time*'s Foreign Affairs articles. Furthermore, Bancroft had recently given a talk to a group of French children who had been evacuated to Switzerland.

"All the questions without exception were based on something the children had read," Bancroft explained, "either in Teem (as they called *Time*) or in Leef (as they called *Life*). I was appalled by the influence of these publications. I'd heard, of course, about Harry Luce being a missionary's son, with a great desire to do good, plus all this high-blown talk about this being the American Century, so I was just lying in wait for him, like a cobra about to strike.

"Finally, he came hurrying in the Bauer Au Lac. He walked in a rather peculiar way, a little bit like Donald Duck. And as he came over to where I was standing, I said, 'So there you are, Public Enemy Number One.' And he, startled, said, 'Public Enemy Number One? Me, you mean me?' And I said, 'Yes, you!'"

She had quickly caught his attention and held it for the next twenty years.

Over drinks, Bancroft began telling Luce in sharp language all the things she didn't like about his magazines, from the style to the slant. He protested that this was not the way to talk to "the man who invented the American Century," but he listened, intently, and was alternately angered and intrigued.

Mary was quickly captured by this man, whom she saw then as basically shy and unsure, more compassionate than kind, but sensitive to what she was saying. "I felt that here was someone I could say anything to—absolutely anything that came into my head and I wouldn't be hurt in any way as a result.

"At the dinner table, I had Mr. Adler [Julius Ochs Adler, the publisher of *The New York Times*] on my right side and Harry on my left. At one point, Harry said, 'Does she remind you of anyone, Julie?' And Mr. Adler said, 'Sure, Dorothy.' That infuriated me, because I loathed Dorothy Thompson, and I certainly didn't think I was like her. You know, women think I am masculine. Men don't, but *women* do. I think that has something to do with my talking so much and not really giving a damn what people thought. What really intrigued Harry was that I just simply wasn't impressed by him, or by Cowles [Gardner Cowles, publisher of *Look*] or by Mr. Adler. After all, I didn't consider their publications as good as *The Wall Street Journal!*"

Bancroft's memory of Harry Luce that evening was that he seemed "like some kind of factory that was making steel, with the blast furnaces going full force."

"The next day, I received an envelope from the Hotel Bauer Au Lac, containing a little note that said, 'Thought you might be able to use these.' And enclosed were some rationing coupons and meal tickets that Harry, as a foreigner just arriving in the country, had been given at the frontier.' "

Luce decided to leave his group in Zurich and make his own tour of Germany and Austria. Joining him was Raimund Von Hofmannsthal who had worked for *Time* in New York and London, and would now serve as Luce's companion and guide.

For most of the tour, Von Hofmannsthal felt that Luce was distracted. He escorted Luce through a Nazi prison camp still filled with Jewish survivors. He also took him to official receptions in several cities, and on a trip to Vienna. Driving back to Switzerland, Luce's mood suddenly changed. He asked Von Hofmannsthal to arrange a huge champagne party, complete with music and dancing, actresses as well as celebrities. This was so unlike him, but perhaps Mary Bancroft had sparked his spirit.

Von Hofmannsthal sensed Harry's impatience to return to Zurich. When a customs man delayed them at the Swiss border because of a passport irregularity, Von Hofmannsthal described Luce as "white with rage." "He leaned over and was almost about to grab the border man's stamp and stamp the papers himself," recalled Von Hofmannsthal. Back in Zurich, Harry again seemed to relax but only after he had called Mary.

"Hello, I'm back again. Can you have lunch with me?"

"First we had lunch," said Mary, "then we had dinner, then we walked around the city, and he cross-examined me until I was so tired I thought I was going to faint. I thought I knew everything about Switzerland, and I did know an awful lot. But he got to the bottom of that in no time."

Luce and Bancroft shared an insatiable curiosity about everything. Mary was primarily interested in people; Harry was also, but he was primarily obsessed with facts. Many of their arguments concerned what he considered "facts."

A typical altercation occurred when they went to buy a watch.

"Do you want the most expensive," Mary asked, "or do you want the best?"

"Then there was this dialogue about whether the best is the most expensive, and if it is not, why not? Of course, the point was that the most expensive might not be the best, but just might have a diamond wrist-band or something like that. And Harry acted as if this was all a revelation to him. I have never known anybody who could ask as many questions about any given subject as he."

"No, the best is the least expensive in the long run," she told him.

"In watches?" he queried.

"No, stupid, in everything," she replied.

Nobody, but nobody, *ever* called Luce "stupid" to his face. But he would take it from Mary.

"When he left, he said that when I came to New York, I must look him up." And so she did.

Mary Bancroft was simply like no woman Luce had ever met.

Bancroft was the child of a Boston Brahmin and an Irish chambermaid. Her mother had died after childbirth and Mary was raised by her grandparents. Her grandfather had been Cambridge mayor four times and then president of the Boston Elevated Railway.

She was a wildly imaginative child. "God offers every mind its choice between truth and repose," Mary said, quoting Emerson. "Granted my curiosity, the choice was simple. I could do nothing with repose."

Her stepmother's stepfather was C. W. Barron who took over *The Wall Street Journal* and founded *Barron's Weekly.* She said she learned more from Barron than she ever learned from school. He was the one who said to her what she often repeated to Luce: "Facts are not the truth. They only indicate where the truth may lie."

"I never learned anything at school," said Mary. "It's always been men I've learned things from."

Mary quit Smith College after three months to marry the coxwain of the Harvard crew. They had two children, divorced, and Mary moved to Switzerland in 1935 where she married a businessman of Turkish ancestry. She wrote articles, was analyzed by the famous C. G. Jung, and—when Americans entered the war—she became a spy.

When the U.S. entered World War II, it formed its own spy service, the Office of Strategic Services (OSS) with Allen Dulles in charge. Upon meeting Dulles, Mary decided almost immediately that she would work for him as a spy and became his lover.

"I have a very peculiar reaction to danger," said Mary. "It's just simply stupid. Most people, when anything gets dangerous, or they hear shooting, want to run and hide. Well, I want to run and see what's going on."

Mary was then forty and Dulles fifty. "I can't marry you and I'm not sure I would if I could," Dulles told her. "But I want you and need you now." Mary liked that.

"We can let the work cover for the romance and the romance cover the work," Dulles told her.

Both her husband and his wife were aware of the romance and didn't seem to mind. Mary said Dulles's wife told her: "I can see how much you and Allen care for each other—and I approve."

One of Bancroft's OSS tasks, she said, was to be a contact in the crowd that was trying to kill Hitler at Berchesgaden on July 20, 1944. "Allen told me that if I opened my mouth 5,000 people would be dead. The thing I did best was talk, because you just push a button and I could go on forever—I never think anything is real until I've shared it."

Bancroft talked to her analyst Jung about it. "Jung threw back his head and howled with laughter," she recalled. He said, "Well, I think Dulles is right. I think you can keep your mouth shut, but I think only the idea that if you open it, 5,000 people would be dead is the one thing that would make you keep quiet."

"Your friend Dulles is quite a tough nut, isn't he? I'm glad you've got his ear," Jung told Bancroft. When she asked what he meant, he said that men like Dulles, men of power, needed to listen to what women were saying in order to exercise their best judgment. "To get such a man's ear," Jung added, "was not easy."

By the time Mary met Luce, she knew all about men of power and was very skilled as a questioner—and a listener. Luce found himself telling Mary things he had told absolutely no one else. There were few people in the world to whom Luce poured out his heart and soul, and Bancroft was one of them.

He told her he had thought he and Lila were happily married, that they had a good life together. They had two children, and he believed everything was fine. Then, after they'd been to Europe on a vacation and were heading home by ship, she had asked him one day, "Why don't you love me anymore?"

"If she'd never said it, if she'd never brought it up," Harry told Mary, "I don't think it would ever have occurred to me."

Harry told Mary that after he began to make money, "I realized I was a tycoon. I felt I must get a mistress. The very first thing that I did when I realized that I was rich was to get a car and a chauffeur. That was something I'd always wanted. That was the most important thing." Harry also told her that after he got the car and chauffeur, he went looking for a mistress, and he picked Clare.

After Harry returned to New York, he and Mary began a correspondence. Her letters, noted Allen Grover, were long and intense.

"Mary's correspondence with Harry was on a very high level, philosophical, not loving, and sometimes violent. They began arguing with each other about the belief in God! They were into everything—not only about God, but the 'meaning of meanings,' things like that. It was a marvelous exchange of minds. I don't think he ever had an outlet anywhere else in his life like Mary Bancroft," reflected Grover, who compared the intensity of Harry's relationship with Mary Bancroft to that of his original infatuation with Clare.

Harry kept his new private life a very private secret. Neither Jean nor Clare presumably knew about Mary. Even if Clare had known, it was hardly a matter she could complain about. Clare had been writing intimate letters to men all her life. If she had known about Harry and Mary, it might have raised her estimate of her husband. This was a dimension of Harry she did not know. A romance with Jean Dalrymple she could understand, but an intellectual affair was something else entirely.

But was it *only* of the mind? Occasionally, Mary visited New York and they had long evenings alone.

Physically, Mary was not a beauty, but she was striking and vivacious. "Her skin was blotched, her hair stringy, her figure nondescript, but she had a good smile and a jolly laugh and fine mind! She was alive, she exuded energy, and she was a beautiful conversationalist," said Grover. "She talked to Harry as he had never been talked to before."

Both insisted strongly that their relationship was strictly platonic.

"Look, the only reason that I'm making such a hullabaloo about the fact I never slept with Harry Luce is that I think this is very important to an understanding of his character," Mary insisted. "That he had a close and enduring relationship with a woman for twenty years, that was merely platonic."

Still, Mary once told Harry, "I wish you'd get rid of Clare and come live with me!"

"For Harry, the intellectual thing could be just as important as sex, probably more so," said Grover. "I think Harry could have strong emotional feelings about a woman who could cope with him, maybe even lead him. In many ways Mary was rather a simple woman but in many others she was a mystery."

Bancroft once wrote to Luce: "I don't love you for your mind, Harry, really I don't, much as this thought insults you. 'Tis your soul I love. And I bet you don't even know what it looks like. It is blue, Harry. Quite light blue and there is a lot of white fog in the valleys of it . . ."

Luce's deep friendship with Mary only heightened his desire for a divorce from Clare. Both Mary and Jean had taught him that a woman could be caring and kind, qualities he no longer saw in Clare. Furthermore, he sensed that Jean Dalrymple would not be there for him forever. Dalrymple was a celebrated woman of the theater, and her efforts to help organize City Center and the New York City Opera were widely noted. She enjoyed her life, but she also relished her relationship with Harry. She knew how happy Harry was with her and how unhappy he was with Clare, and now she finally encouraged his idea of a divorce.

But first came a fresh crisis. Before Dalrymple, Harry had conducted a brief affair with a member of his and Clare's circle. Now, she was threatening blackmail. "The little bitch really has Harry by the short hairs and every time she pulls 'em, it costs Harry another $100,000," explained C. D. Jackson, a Time vice president, to John Billings. "He feels not only like a fool to have gotten into this mess, but also like a heel. That's why Luce is having constant sessions with his lawyer, Bromley, who's trying to save him from public embarrassment. Now Clare has just gotten word of it. Luce has been most shut-mouthed."

As the threat continued, Luce was incommunicado at the Waldorf. When he did show up at his office, Billings found him sitting "for fifteen minutes, holding his head, almost paralyzed . . . a strange performance which suggested acute mental fatigue." Billings heard that Luce's doctor had diagnosed his condition as "chronic exhaustion."

"Grover and I suspected something like this but we couldn't believe it," noted Billings. "I wasn't really sorry for him because he is so cross and bad-mannered and inconsiderate that I like to see him suffer. Yet, I hope his private dirt doesn't splatter on the company and therefore on me."

Once the blackmail threat was finally resolved, Luce again raised the question of divorce. Clare had impressed upon Harry the fact that divorce was rampant in her family and that she considered it a defeat.

Harry was torn. Divorce was a defeat for him, too. The guilt and stigma of his first divorce had never left him. His contentment with Jean Dalrymple had been enormously important to him, but divorce would tumble his life upside down once again. Besides, Clare showed no sign of retreating from her impossible demand for Time stock. Nor did Luce dismiss her threat of a public scandal. He knew her too well for that.

Harry broached the subject with Billings. "Luce said he was at a crisis with Clare and didn't know how much I knew or wanted to know ('Nothing,' I said). He looked unhappy and never mentioned the other woman. He asked me what my 'hunch' was about his making up with Clare. I said he'd try to make a go of their marriage but I doubted if Clare would. 'That's just what she says about me,' he said bitterly."

Privately, Harry and Clare hashed out their differences, confiding in almost no one. Whatever their rationale, they finally decided to reconcile. "Grover came in with news," reported Billings. "Luce told him that there would be no divorce, that he and Clare had decided to make things up and try their marriage again. Clare was going to Hollywood to write a movie script for Darryl F. Zanuck, and Luce might even go with her."

Harry then told Dalrymple that he could not divorce Clare because she needed him. They would have to break off their relationship.

Awkward and tactless in such circumstances, Luce handled it badly, just as he had once done with Lila. Jean understood Harry's abruptness but did not totally want to give him up. She tried to maintain at least a friendship. When Luce was hospitalized later with a gallbladder attack, she even tried to see him. But Harry did not change his mind—the affair was over.

After breaking with Jean, Luce deepened his hurt by breaking with his two protégé sons, John Hersey and Teddy White. Hersey had gone to Japan for *The New Yorker* to do a story on Hiroshima. His article filled the whole issue, and received sensational publicity. Luce was shocked that Hersey would write for another magazine. He regarded it as disloyalty, especially since he now hated *The New Yorker*. (Later, Time Inc. writers had strict guidelines about "outside" writing.) Harry and Hersey fought, and Hersey left Time Inc. Luce afterward referred to Hersey as "an unfaithful man."

"There was pain on both sides in this parting," said Hersey. "I know I felt pain."

"Luce and John were not on speaking terms for a long time," said *Life* photographer Dmitri Kessel. "I remember when they were both invited to the same wedding. John went over and said 'Hi, Harry.' And Luce looked at him, turned around, and walked away. John was so hurt."

"Sometime later, I saw Luce walking toward me on a sidewalk in New York," said Hersey, "and he saw me, and it was clear that he intended to cut me dead. I blocked his way and spoke to him." Luce looked at him, then said "in a kind of mean way, 'I was in Japan recently and flew over *your* city.'" He was still bitter about Hiroshima. When *Life* later wanted to republish "Hiroshima," Luce vetoed the plan. Despite his many negative articles and comments about Time Inc., Hersey maintained his basic affection for Luce. Years later, the two reconciled.

"Harry was bitter about my leaving," said John Hersey, "but he was much more bitter about Teddy. To him, I was just somebody who had defected, who had betrayed his personal trust. With Teddy, it was more."

Theodore White had left China and had written a highly successful book about it. Still employed as a writer for Time Inc. in New York, "Teddy would find out where Harry was going to speak about Chiang Kai-shek, and then turn up at the gathering," recalled Hersey. "He would ask questions from the back of the hall. I was there, at one of these meetings. He'd deliberately bait Luce with loaded questions. Or, he'd say 'No, that's not so!' Things like that."

White got increasing pressure from his China-expert friends to cut loose from Time Inc. and get out from under the stigma of being paid by somebody they felt was on the wrong side.

White finally asked to become a correspondent in Russia. Luce was negative. "The basic question is whether, despite our acknowledged difference of political opinion, you feel that my reporting is no longer reporting," said White.

After a seventy-five-minute talk, Luce asked White: "Are you willing to take any job I assign you, from copy boy to managing editor?"

"No."

"Will you take any point in the foreign field that I assign to you?"

"No."

Teddy shared an office with photographer Carl Mydans. Mydans recalled Teddy returning from that meeting: "He came in the room, opened the middle drawer, took out a few things, a few pencils—those were the days when you had pencils with 'Time Inc.' on them—handed them over, and said, 'These are all yours, Carl. I'm through here.' In a minute or two he was gone."

Luce's explanation to his editors was that while he respected White's rugged individuality, Time Inc. was not a plum pudding from which writers extracted plums of choice. He wanted a happy staff but a disciplined one, and White wasn't able to submit to that discipline.

T. S. Matthews remembered a dinner with Luce some time afterward. "I told him I felt Teddy was right, and he was wrong. He admitted it, but blurted out, 'What can I do? I can't admit to Teddy I was wrong. So what can I do, but just stick with it?' " White afterward listed Luce as one of the most brilliant men he ever knew. He included Chou En-lai on that list.

While Harry was sorting out his staff problems and trying to put his life in better order, Clare, now forty-two, was facing some decisions of her own. Once again, it was time to run for re-election and she had grave misgivings.

As one of the eleven women among 424 men in Congress, Clare had made her mark. Most recently she had worked closely with Baruch proposing international control of atomic energy. She had also proposed a detailed plan for massive aid to postwar Europe, which was a precursor of the Marshall Plan made effective the following year.

What distressed Clare was the bureaucracy and slow action.

To her friends, she claimed that Congress had brutalized and toughened her spirit. To an interviewer, she later insisted, "I always regretted that I shifted to politics. You can do nothing truly creative in politics by yourself. You're working with a team all the time. At least when you write a play, it's your own, and you've done your thing."

The real reason Clare wanted out of politics was something else entirely. With Dalrymple out of the picture, she had a fresh chance to renew her marriage. She wanted Harry back, because she knew no man who matched him in power and prestige. Baruch still wrote that he laid the passion of his years at her feet, but he was now sadly too old.

Of course, Clare was still fiercely ambitious. She did know that politics drew her closer to Harry. Republicans still saw her as a political prize, and prominently mentioned her as a candidate for the Senate. "It certainly is no insult to be discussed as a candidate for the U.S. Senate," Clare told reporters. "But it is a bore to have to keep saying 'No, no, no, no, no' so many different ways and at so many different times."

But she said it softly. Being senator was a cherished dream, a national prize, a chance to sit on an equal platform of power with Harry—or without him. Clare seemed to be putting herself in a position for a draft and even hired public relations guru Edward L. Bernays. Harry Luce hurried to Connecticut's Governor Baldwin to talk about it. But Baldwin had his own ideas for the Senate and Clare was not part of his plans.

When she realized the Senate was impossible, Clare put up her best front, saying that she had refused to run because "I wanted to be with my husband more. At that particular moment in my life, I had to choose whether I could keep my marriage together or whether I wanted to be a senator. I just wanted to be home. You see, I haven't really been home in six years. I wanted to see something of my husband again, to be able to plan holidays with him, to spend more time with our family and friends. It is my firm conviction that a woman's first duty is to her husband and home. In America, a full-time federal office is no job for a woman with family obligations." She then added a sharp thrust: "My husband would *never* have had to make such a choice. So the price is still high for a woman."

Harry personally wrote Clare's farewell-to-politics story—to spare the staff embarrassment. In it, he said *Time* had fumbled the story of his wife, "because they were too fearful of being damned if they told it or damned if they didn't." The story was printed.

Harry and Clare decided to start their renewed life together in a new home. In 1947, they bought a red brick Georgian mansion complete with swimming pool and tennis court in Ridgefield, Connecticut. Once again, they decorated their home with the Far Eastern furnishings Harry loved. Their decorator was still Donald Freeman's sister Gladys.

While the mansion was being readied, they rented a country farm house from singer Grace Moore. Ironically, Moore was a longtime client of Jean Dalrymple.

Harry and Clare seemed to be at an impasse. Tom Matthews described their show of public affection at a restaurant "like two Hollywood stars—everybody watching. And damn bad actors!" Clare had made divorce impossible, and they were too much in the limelight to live their private lives outrageously, so they had to survive together. He had his morality, his reputation, and his conscience to consider, and she had lingering political ambitions. So, they maintained a serene public posture.

Clare often seemed to be trying hard to be a good corporate wife. Coughlan told of a dinner where she was the only woman among a group of Time Inc. editors discussing world matters. After dinner, she sat there on the sofa, listening to the men resolving international problems, quietly working on her needlepoint. But she couldn't totally restrain herself. "Every now and then, she'd come in with some zinger," said Coughlan, "and then go back to her needlepoint."

No matter how much they both tried, the competition between them remained fierce. The Luces were held together by the pull of power. No longer happy, they were always lively. There were indeed cordial, supportive moments, and they stimulated each other. But they would often compete at the dinner table for control of the conversation. Clare could not become a kinder, gentler person, no matter how she tried.

Clare now constantly invited a steady stream of celebrities to their new

Connecticut home. Visitors could be expected to earn their weekend lodgings by filling Clare's evening with intelligent conversation. Harry, too, constantly prodded his guests for opinions and information. A weekend at the Luces could be hard work.

Andrew Heiskell remembered a dinner in the Luce's austere dining room. Clare soon made it clear why she had invited them: She wanted Heiskell's actress-wife Madeleine Carroll to read a play she had started writing. Carroll tried to be polite. "Well, Clare, you know the theater well enough to know it's very difficult to read material when you have no idea what the content is."

Clare was insistent, and Madeleine had no choice.

The play was about a saint who'd been raped and survived the raping.

Reading the rape scene, Carroll struggled, then said, "I can't go on."

Heiskell recalled with grim satisfaction the way he took his revenge on Clare for submitting his wife to this sorry scene. He and Clare were on the same side in a tennis doubles match, "and I took careful aim and deliberately hit her in the ass three times in a row. I still can't believe I did it."

Harry seemed to be seeking escape anywhere. T. S. Matthews was amused when Harry joined the local Silver Spring Country Club to play golf, usually alone. "He took it up the way a patient would take up a doctor's prescription," said Matthews. "The doctor said golf would be good for him; he went out and played golf. He hated it, and was no damn good at it."

Visitors saw Harry still playing the role of the solid, middle-aged husband. His friend attributed this in some measure to his Presbyterian conscience and his guilt.

Mary Bancroft would say of Harry, "I've never known anyone who wasn't Jewish who felt as guilty as Harry did. He felt terribly guilty because he divorced his first wife. And I think he felt guilty because he loved his mother more than he loved his father. I think he felt guilty because he got an 'A' once at Yale. I think he felt guilty that he was rich. In fact, guilty about just about everything. He stuttered and felt guilty about that."

When he felt too guilty about being rich, Luce badgered Clare about household extravagances. She promptly suggested a long list of cuts: fire the chauffeur and take taxis to the train; restrict gardening to keeping the lawn green and the pool clear; stop maintaining the tennis court because he didn't play anymore; rent or sell the Ridgefield house and she would go abroad for a while and he could live at the Waldorf. And, finally, she told her multimillionaire husband, she could cancel all their magazine subscriptions, and he should bring home his office copies.

After weekends arguing over such matters with Clare, Luce would arrive at the office depressed and cross. His secretary Miss Thrasher became verbally bitter about Clare. Thrasher, "whose enthusiasm for Harry was almost obscene," said Billings, told him about Clare "acting insanely" and even said she had been a secret drinker, though this does not seem to have been one of Clare's vices.

"I wish she had croaked," Thrasher told Billings when Clare had a serious virus.

He usually made his points by striking the blue-stone ring on his left little finger hard upon the table. Now he seemed to strike more often with it, and harder. Friends observed new furrows in Harry's skull and noted how he nervously stroked an invisible beard. He seemed much more snarling and destructive and often bemoaned the sea of troubles around him. He also talked of retiring. Billings got word one day that Harry and Clare had had another big row and the whole problem of separation was again up for debate. "God, but what a miserable life they must lead," he said.

Billings noted in his diary: "What's wrong with Luce? He's lost all his human sparkle. He holds me at arm's length. . . . Miss Thrasher also worried about his depressed conduct and reports his sister Beth Moore is too. . . ."

Harry later confided to a woman who would become his lover and intimate confidante that Clare was truly a manic depressive, living a life of highs and lows. When she was manic, she was in high gear, touring the country to talk to Roman Catholic groups, writing about her conversion, being the first woman to address the Chamber of Commerce in New York.

When she was low, she wanted to kill herself. Her conversion had helped minimize Clare's suicidal tendencies, but could not wipe them out entirely. Throughout her private memos and personal papers, her constant question was: What did God want her to be?

Clare's old friend Laura Hobson recalled hunting for some aspirin in Clare's bathroom one night in a hotel room. While looking in the cabinet, Hobson wondered whether Clare used any "white night" sleeping pills. "I yielded to my curiosity and performed my shameful little act. One by one, I took up each bottle or box, read the prescription label, and when that was ambiguous, even looked inside. There wasn't a sign of a sleeping pill in any of them. I felt that it must be that Clare had indeed found peace and inner quiet from her new religion. Confirmed agnostic that I was, I was impressed.

"As I went out through her bedroom, I stopped. At either side of her bed was something too valuable to be part of any hotel's furnishing, something that must have traveled along with Clare in her luggage. It was a pair of small crystal bottles, each encased in a delicate filigree of silver. On one side of the bed, the crystal bottle was filled with bright blue capsules, at least thirty or forty of them, and on the far side of the bed, the bottle was filled with an equal number of red ones. I knew the blue were sodium Amytal. The red were

Seconal. How often, in those periods of anguish in my own life, had I taken one or the other to get me through some endless night? And then I thought: Well, so much for one's new religion and peace of mind. I stood still for a moment, just looking at those lovely crystal containers. Briefly, I found myself wishing that those two lamps had not been lighted, so that the shining crystal beneath them would never have caught my eye."

Clare's private demons often consumed her. She had little room in her emotional life for Harry, and he badly needed a friend. He asked Mary Bancroft to come to New York, and she came quickly. "I think part of our friendship, Harry's and mine, was based on the fact that after he became a tycoon, nobody would tell him the truth anymore. They were just telling him what they thought he wanted to know. And the poor thing used to read bestsellers to try and find out what life was really like. Harry had a wicked, razor-blade shrewdness when power was involved, and actually a kind of 'street-smarts' in such situations. But otherwise, he was a babe in the woods. I think that the real reason he liked me was that I wasn't the least bit afraid of him. Most people were. But I wasn't working for him. I didn't want anything from him.

"Once, when I said I didn't want anything from him, he looked a little hurt, and he asked, 'Don't you like my money? Wouldn't you like some of my money?' And I said, 'Wouldn't I like your money? Sure! I adore your money.' He opened his wallet and took out some money, actually a thousand dollars, and put it right over there, on that table. I said, 'Oh, thank you! That's nice. You can give me money anytime you want. I like your money, and I like the fact that you made it. But I don't want anything from you, not even your money!'

"Then I said, 'By the way, if you ever have any trouble and lose all your money, you can come and live with me, and I'll take care of you. And if you have any trouble with God, I'll intervene.' I think Harry honestly thought there was a chance he'd fry in Hell."

Bancroft took special note of the fact that Luce had a private elevator in the new Time headquarters, and that he would ride alone from the ground to his office on the thirty-third floor. "I asked him, 'Harry, what the hell do you do in the elevator, all alone in the morning?'" recalled Bancroft, "And he said, absolutely sincerely, 'I pray.' And I said, 'Whatever for?' And he said, 'For forgiveness.'"

Luce squired Bancroft all over the city during her visits, almost as if he were courting her. Before Mary returned to Zurich at the end of that summer in 1947, Luce asked her, "Would you leave me something in your will? Would you mention me in your will? I sometimes think—I bet—nobody is ever going to remember me in their will."

On a ship heading back to Europe, Mary met the talented and handsome Charles Wertenbaker, who had left his job as head of *Time*'s Paris bureau, to write novels. He tried to persuade Bancroft to involve Luce in a passionate love affair. Wertenbaker felt that if Luce had a romance with such a liberal lady, it might change his conservative Republican viewpoints. The truth was, Bancroft now needed no persuasion. But Harry still mainly wanted her mind, and her friendship.

What he wanted from Clare became even more questionable. Despite her protests that she had given up politics to be with him, they were often apart. She went to Hollywood to work on a movie script about two nuns and he went to Europe. Still, they wrote to each other often and with concern. He still sent her roses and even rubies. Frank White, *Time*'s Paris correspondent, told of a memorable Luce visit: "Luce stayed, as always, at the Ritz, which is in the Place Vendôme. We arrived through the back and he said, 'That's Van Cleef & Arpels, over there, right? Let's go there. You look for some rubies.' Then a guy came out in a square-cut, black business suit, and black tie. He said, 'Can I do anything for you?' I said, 'I would like to look at some rubies.' So he said, 'Suivez-moi.' We went into an antechamber, and Harry was right behind me. He showed me some cut rubies; and I got sort of a knee in the back and a word in the ear, which was 'a necklace of rubies, please.' Well, now I got some kind of sign from Harry that I'm on the right track. A new guy came out. This guy was in a swallow-tail coat. He ushered us into a place where the buyers go. After a wait, he came out with black-velvet trays. The guy was bumbling on about Burma and Rangoon, and holding two big necklaces. Both were very similar, but exquisite and extraordinary. Finally, there was dead silence. I hadn't received any more instructions. So I turned, like this, as if I were thinking; and I heard a word in my ear. 'Both of 'em!' I turned to this guy and said: 'We'll take 'em both; wrap 'em up.' There was no mention of price at all, though I found out later that the first one, the smaller one, was $250,000. I never did find out about the other one. But it was bigger and better."

Who got the bigger necklace? Harry's sense of guilt may have prompted him to give it to Clare. But she was again making him feel tense and bitter. It is quite conceivable that Luce gave Mary the bigger necklace. At this point in his life, she was a far better friend to him than his own wife.

23

I N 1948, *Time* celebrated its twenty-fifth anniversary and Luce turned fifty. Several editors wanted to put his picture on *Time*'s cover, but he refused. Luce settled for a birthday cake with five candles on it and a floodgate of reminiscences about the early days when it was "one hell of a fight." Harry's staff gave him a French silver box inscribed with a quote in Latin from the first *Time* circular: "All things knowable and various other things." Few quotes fit Luce better. At the time, an interviewer observed something else about Harry: "His inner loneliness is surrounded by a mass of people and faces."

Still, the anniversary had lifted Harry's mood. He seemed more cheerful and optimistic, particularly because his empire was flourishing financially. Time Inc. assets were at their peak, with revenues over $120 million. *Time* and *Life* were thriving, as were *Time*'s four international editions. Only *Fortune* was losing money.

Politically, Luce was also feeling optimistic. The mood of the country was more upbeat. People were generally prosperous. Europe with all its problems seemed faraway, and nobody was interested in any more war. The men were back home, back at their jobs, and women wanted babies. Harry Truman had turned out to be a surprisingly good president. Congress passed the Marshall Plan for Europe's economic recovery. An American plane was the first to fly at supersonic speed. Clare's old friend, Cole Porter, wrote "Kiss Me Kate," and her new friend, Irwin Shaw, wrote *The Young Lions.* Harry Luce's old Chefoo schoolmate, Thornton Wilder, wrote *The Ides of March.* And Hollywood gave an Academy Award to a movie called *Hamlet.*

This was also a presidential election year and there was again some occasional comment about Clare as a possible vice presidential nominee. Again, there were rumors of Harry as a dark horse candidate for president. Luce was even chided for presidential aspirations at the annual Time Inc. stockholders meeting. Hearing this, Clare pointed mockingly to a passing servant, "You might just as well say *he's* going to be president of the U.S. Our being in the White House is ten million times as fantastic as that!"

"Well, there's no point in exaggerating," Luce interrupted. "You might just say it's twice as fantastic."

As the election neared, the Republicans were getting ready to choose Thomas Dewey, who had lost to Roosevelt in the previous election, or Senator Robert Taft of Ohio, or Senator Arthur Vandenberg of Michigan to battle Truman. Clare and Harry preferred Vandenberg, primarily because his internationalist view on foreign policy was closely akin to theirs. Vandenberg, however, had been a pre-war isolationist and a *Life* story highlighted this in interviews with thirty-three senators. When Luce saw the manuscript, he slashed lines through the unflattering comments about Vandenberg with his red pencil and wrote in the margin, "Change from stem to stern—H.R.L."

At the Republican National Convention, Clare was picked as one of the speakers. She tossed gay kisses to the crowd while the orchestra played "O Beautiful Lady," and then started her speech "with a smile of childlike innocence." Some felt she was not as good as she had been four years before in Chicago, that her speech was not as well-rehearsed. Critics called her strident and ill-at-ease. They also admitted she held her audience in the palm of her hand. She dramatically held up a carton of milk and a steak when she blasted Democrats for inflation.

Before the final vote, Harry and Clare tried desperately to make a full effort for Vandenberg's nomination. *Life* had called him "the brightest dark horse," but Vandenberg had taken the position that if he was wanted, he would accept, but he wasn't making any effort to get the nomination. Clare had furiously solicited delegates for her candidate.

When Dewey failed to win the nomination on the first two ballots, Harry Luce made a final effort. "Roy, you've got to swing Kansas and Missouri behind Arthur on the next ballot," he told his friend Roy Roberts, owner of the *Kansas City Star.*

"Harry, I couldn't do it if I wanted to and anyway it wouldn't do any good. Arthur doesn't have a prayer." Harry stomped angrily away. Part of Luce's reasons for supporting the dark horse were very personal. There were rumors that if Vandenberg were elected, he might make Luce his secretary of state. But Dewey won again.

Vandenberg died three years later. Shortly before his death, he explained to Clare that he didn't fight for the nomination because he knew he had cancer and was dying. He had left it up to God, he said, to decide if He wanted a sick man for president who would die in office. But, just in case, he showed Clare a copy of the acceptance speech he had written.

A feisty Truman whistle-stopped across the country, and made seventy-one extemporaneous speeches in two weeks, "giving them hell." It was Dewey who seemed the man of phlegm, staying largely in New York and confidently picking his cabinet. Most Republicans were equally confident. *Life* captioned a picture of Dewey in their pre-election issue: The Next President. *Time* described Dewey as acting like a winner.

Luce even held a luncheon meeting for eight of his editors at his Waldorf apartment to meet Foster Dulles, often mentioned as Dewey's secretary of state. Billings and the others wondered whether Dulles would appoint Luce to some big job as ambassador when Dewey was elected.

"His magazines never did tell the truth about me," Truman told Merle Miller, who would later write an oral biography of the thirty-third president. "During the campaign, they took all those pictures at places I spoke trying to prove there weren't any crowds turning out for my speeches, which was a damn lie, of course. They say pictures don't lie, but they do. Pictures can lie just as much as words if that's what the big editors and publishers set out to do."

When *Time* received a report that Dewey was slipping and prepared to publish it, Luce commented that *Time* didn't have to tell everything it knew. Matthews replied that he knew that recording a falling political barometer caused inevitable storm warnings, but he felt that the news should be told.

After Truman's election, *Life* described the media as "eating crow, wearing sackcloth and ashes." Managing editor Joe Thorndike added that "we were misled by our bias." Luce called the coverage of Truman a spectacular blunder and accepted prime responsibility.

Once again, politics had given the Luces a renewed sense of mission and togetherness. But once the election was over, Clare again grew despondent. And she had good reason. The campaign loss had hurt, but now that it was behind her, the trauma of shock returned. A few months before, in September, her brother David had hired a plane and flown out over the Pacific until the gas ran out. The plane crashed two miles offshore, and his body was never recovered. Although there was no suicide note found, Clare always assumed the plane crash was no accident.

David's life had been a frustrated shambles, except for his war years when, as a pilot in seven campaigns, he earned six air medals, a Purple Heart, and two presidential unit citations. But after the war, David seemed deeply troubled. In a sudden, uncontrollable rage, he once almost killed a servant. Then David wanted to open a gambling casino in Las Vegas and Clare refused to finance him. After that, she had to hire private detectives to find David because he had threatened suicide.

Clare arranged for a thirty-day vigil light to be placed on the altar at St. Jean Baptiste in New York in his memory. David was the only one who had truly loved her. It was as if a part of her heart had died.

In the midst of this sorrow, Harry's mother died, at age seventy-seven, a few days after the election. She had lived the last years with her daughter Emmavail and Emmy's husband Leslie Severinghaus, headmaster of Haverford School in Pennsylvania. Her stream of letters were always adoring, "You know how much I love you and thank you." The prayer book he had sent her for her last birthday was her prize present, the red roses he had sent her for Easter filled her with overflowing joy, and she said, repeatedly, how happy she was in her old age. She applauded his indomitable courage in the holy combat he was waging to improve the world, and she prayed for him every day.

She left behind for him a verse in Galatians 5:1, which began, "Stand fast therefore in the liberty . . ."

Harry never saw her in her final days. He had planned to visit her three different times and canceled each time. There was the press of the presidential election, but was it more than that? Was there, possibly, some lingering guilt over his divorce that had ruptured something in his relationship with his religious parents?

On his return to the office after the funeral, Billings remembered him as looking gray, haggard, abstracted, and in a remote daze.

His mother had been the central force of the family, and Harry's sister Beth wrote that he was now the family's heart and fountainhead.

For a man who was the family fountainhead, for a man who could penetrate anybody with his constant flow of quick questions, Harry found it remarkably difficult to reach his sons. His losses did not bring him closer to his sons. Harry scribbled occasional notes, mostly apologizing for not writing more often and not coming to visit. To his former wife Lila, he wrote a worried note about Pete, simply observing that young people face a lot of uncertainties in life. To Pete, who was to appear in a school play, Luce asked a curious question: Did he want Dad to come and see the play? When Luce *did* schedule a visit in a private Time plane, his secretary notified Pete that Luce's stay would be only for the night, as he was en route somewhere else. Pete soon made it even more clear that he was not interested in being part of the Luce heritage at Time Inc. He was more interested in planes, and later he bought his own rickety Piper Cub.

Distanced from Harry's children and filled with sadness, Clare and Harry decided to take a holiday in Jamaica; this was private time on a private beach. They were now a middle-aged couple wanting to get their marriage back on track. She was still attractive enough for men, and there would be more men.

He was still open to the magnetism of women, and there would be more women. But at this point, Clare was tired and drained and ready for peace. And so was Harry.

Upon their return, to please her, Harry bought Condé Nast's triplex apartment opposite the River Club with a view of the East River. To please her even more, he bought a Picasso and a Manet. The Luces had become public citizens, sponsoring the arts. They contributed heavily to the New York Philharmonic and Clare was elected a trustee. Harry became a board member of the Metropolitan Museum of Art. Clare now ranked in a Gallup poll as one of the most admired women in the world—after Mrs. Roosevelt and Madame Chiang. Madame Chiang was reportedly shopping for a house in Connecticut near the Luces in case she and her husband had to make a hurried exit from China.

To please Harry, Clare gave big dinner parties for visiting celebrities, including the Windsors, President Gabriel Gonzalez Videla of Chile, and Queen Frederika of Greece. In a different life in a different world, he would have liked to have married a woman like Queen Frederika.

In April 1949, Harry left for his annual trip to Europe, this time accompanied by Allen Grover. The trip buoyed him. The Marshall Plan had worked. Most of western Europe had rejected socialism. Time-Life, he now decided, would not have to tilt to the left to reach the readers of Europe.

Luce specifically had requested that he not be given the red-carpet treatment on his trip, but it was a treatment he could not avoid. World leaders were waiting to see him, from the Pope to Charles de Gaulle. Many of them had been on *Time* covers, or soon would be. Beaverbrook's London *Daily Express* treated him to some "Timese" enthusiasm, calling him, "Vigorous nonstop magnate Luce."

In Zurich, Luce visited Mary Bancroft. She introduced him to her friend, Prince Constantine of Lichtenstein. She remembered her surprise that Harry was ill at ease and even intimidated by this man who ruled over a country of only 12,000 people. Unsure why, she could only imagine that the boy from China was still awed by the ancient heritage of Hapsburg blue blood.

Charles Wertenbaker, still believing that Harry needed a tempestuous love affair with Mary to recharge, sent her a one-word telegram: ATTACK. But Luce and Bancroft, at least publicly, maintained their platonic relationship.

Besides, not even Bancroft could keep Luce in one place for long. "In Switzerland, the plane was delayed," said Dmitri Kessel. "Luce was just too restless to wait for a plane, or wait for anything. So he said, 'What do you have next, going anywhere?' They told him about a plane to Amsterdam in twenty minutes. 'Let's take it!' Well, there was a panic in trying to rearrange all kinds of schedules. But that was typical Luce. He wouldn't wait for the planes; he wanted a plane waiting for him."

After a packed day of interviews at the Hotel Excelsior in Rome, Luce said to an exhausted Grover, "Al, we have two hours until dinner. How shall we make use of the time?"

"At the end of the trip," said the harried Grover, "Harry had gained six pounds and I had lost ten."

Grover later made a private report to Billings: "Luce is a good man on the great issues. He wants to do right, to think right. But on the small issues, the personal relationships, he is a very bad man, thoughtless and arbitrary, and he leaves hurt feelings strewn in his wake."

That summer of 1949, Clare had a guest, eighteen-year-old Wilfrid Sheed. Invited for the weekend to the Luces' Ridgefield home, he stayed for the summer. Young Sheed's father, Frank, was a prominent Roman Catholic, who ran a publishing house and was a friend of Clare's. Wilfrid had been a polio victim, and he and Clare spent hours at the pool, where Sheed tried to strengthen his muscles. "She was a marvelous swimmer, but she raced me one time and barely let me beat her. At that age, you're vain enough to think you did it."

For young Sheed, Clare was a warm, shining light, neither an angel nor a dragon lady; for Clare, Wilfrid was a son to replace her daughter. The two became lifelong friends, and he even wrote a book about her in 1982. His father suggested the opener: "She was the best of dames, she was the worst of dames."

Though Clare, then forty-six, seemed content to maintain her maternal role with Sheed, he noted how casually she wandered in and out of his room at any time. "One evening, she reclined on my bed in a way which was over too fast to be called an invitation by anyone short of Harpo Marx, but which suggested a possibility—in a different time and circumstance, perhaps."

The observant Sheed noticed that the walls of her study were covered with pictures of herself in her many roles "and in so many of them there was no other woman in sight." He watched the parade of people passing through the house that summer, people she called "stuffed shirts," and he wondered whether she wanted "slightly dumb company in order to shine more." He watched her being slightly coquettish, "even a touch giggly with a handsome dinner escort." For most guests, she put on a public performance—clever, with some self-mockery, ardently trying to be taken seriously. But, when an old school friend like Buffy Cobb visited, Clare was equally funny and girlish.

"Watch out for envy," Clare once told him.

"I don't see why anyone would envy a guy with polio," Sheed said.

"Yes," she said, "I guess that might slow them down some. But they'll find a way."

At summer's end, Clare gave Sheed a gift of a new Oldsmobile. The two conditions of the gift were that he mention it to no one, and that it must not contain a radio. The car radio was on when her daughter was killed in that accident. She made one other request of the shy Sheed: "You can thank me by kissing me in a crowded place."

That fall, Clare decided to go to Rome, and persuaded her friend Buffy to go with her. Buffy had also converted to Roman Catholicism under the guidance of Father Fulton Sheen.

Clare listed her required items for the trip: "Aspirin, Alpine stock, sleeping pills, cold-cream, Energine, Benzedrine, and missals, reading specs, seasick-specifics, soporifics, liver-pills, dollar-bills, walking shoes . . . Long black gloves, i.e. the Pope, diamond rings, aspirin, and soap."

"I was sick with fatigue," said Buffy. "Usually I cannot sleep in a plane, but I could have slept on anything. Just as I was conking off, Clare poked me: 'Wake up! Wake up. I have just met the most fascinating man, a wonderful old monsignor. He knows everything and is very wise.' The monsignor was brilliant but I was too shot to enjoy him. Just as I was conking off again, Clare jabbed me: 'Wake up! Wake up! I want you to talk with the pilot. He has a matrimonial problem, and we need your advice. Besides, he's going to let us sit in the control cabin when we land in Rome.' We advised the pilot, and he circled St. Peter's three times. It's a wonder he wasn't pinched. At four o'clock she was shaking me again, 'Wake up! Wake up! We're going to a most interesting dinner.' She had a list of engagements made beforehand by telephone and cable. Everywhere we went, the first appointment had been made with a hairdresser.

"On our last day in Rome, we were invited to the wonderful Colona Castle out in the country," continued Buffy. "I was dying to go. Clare was irritatingly vague. 'I don't think so. Something I must do,' she said. We got in a car and drove into the humble suburban section of Rome to a school for boys. A beautiful blond boy came running out to the car and kissed Clare's hand. She hugged him hard. Then she began to question him about his studies: What was he doing? What did he want? He wanted a watch and a bicycle." (They were sent next day.)

Later, Clare talked with the people in the school and spent most of the afternoon with the boy. When they were alone Buffy asked Clare: "How did you get that child?"

"When I was in Rome during the war," Clare told her, "I found some nuns taking care of a group of lost babies in an old abandoned warehouse. There I saw this baby who was so beautiful and so sick. I took him back to my hotel and got an Army doctor who shot him full of penicillin. I got a nurse for him, and we managed to pull him through."

Rome was so crowded that Clare could not get a room for the child, so he and the nurse slept on her bed while she rested on a couch. Then she got the child into this school, a sort of Boys Town. Ever since then, she had taken care of him. "My beautiful American mother," he called her.

Buffy later learned that the nine-year-old boy was named Augusto and that he had been a mass of sores when Clare had found him as a baby, and that she had washed him and fed him until she could get a doctor.

This was a side of Clare few people knew. Somewhere beneath the cool, often brittle exterior was a warm, loving woman. It was rare, however, that these qualities emerged.

Most of the time, Clare was her usual driven, self-absorbed self, moving through Europe like a steam roller.

"Clare is a real adventurer," said Buffy. "She speaks to everyone; is afraid of nothing."

Clare even said to the pope, "What do you do for fun?"

"I have my canary," said the pope. "He always sits on my shoulder when I am shaving." Clare later sent him some English records.

In Florence, they visited the Uffizi Gallery.

" 'There's a lot of junk here and we haven't much time,' I said. 'We'll head straight for the gallery with the primitives.' The pictures were superb. Clare was thrilled, but I was worried. There was a small dark man with corduroy pants following us. Clare looked awfully expensive with lots of diamonds and a light mink coat.

"The man finally spoke to her. 'Have you seen the Botticelli Room?' Clare had not and he guided us there. He talked brilliantly about the pictures and finally Clare told him who she was and where we were staying.

"When we left, I said, Clare, I could slap you. That was a stupid thing to do. How do you know he won't follow us and rob us or break into our rooms later?'

" 'Oh, anybody who loves beautiful pictures as much as he does can't be bad,' said Clare."

Buffy snorted that it had nothing to do with the case and pointed out a few historical villains who loved beautiful pictures. About six months later, Clare and Harry were going to Mexico City. Harry called Nelson Rockefeller and asked him to give him some introductions and pave the way. At the airport in Mexico City, they were met by a special car belonging to the president of Mexico. Out of it stepped the president himself, who happened to be the small dark man from the Uffizi.

In Paris, they visited with the duke of Windsor ("the little man," as the duchess called him) who was working on his story for *Life* with Charles Murphy. Murphy later commented to Luce that getting the Windsor story "cost twice as much and took three times as long as was required for Stanley to produce Dr. Livingston from the heart of darkest Africa."

Clare afterward described the Windsor dinner as wonderful, the duchess' clothes perfect, the duke chatty and affable. But she categorized the Windsors as a frail, lost, and unhappy little pair of might-have-beens with nothing left but golden memories. Her remarks about the duchess were tinged with an almost tangible contempt.

At Versailles, Clare wanted to see the closets. "She says Versailles is one of those impossible houses that husbands are always finding, with no place for the vacuum cleaner."

And then, in Paris, recorded Buffy, there was a mysterious visitor "The Grand Duke Otto came to call on Clare, and thrust this note in her hand: 'I want to tell you something extremely important concerning our last conversation. There is almost certainly a microphone in this room. So please mention nothing. In two or three minutes I'll suggest we go, and if you don't mind, we will continue our conversation just walking out in the Jardin du Louvre, because that is entirely safe.' " And she added, "Clare disappeared in a cloud of perfume and blue-chiffon scarfs. Grand dukes and mystery!"

Reminiscing about Clare, Buffy said, "You could push her out of a window and she'd find a bagful of diamonds falling beside her." Of a gourmet dinner they both attended, Buffy added that she would still prefer being alone with Clare "with a drugstore sandwich and a bottle of lemon pop."

While Clare was off in Europe, Harry was forging a deep new bond in New York. This time, it was merely friendship with yet another of his younger, liberal protégés. As a successor to White and Hersey, he chose Emmet John Hughes.

"Emmet Hughes was a precocious young man," said *Time* correspondent Dave Richardson. "His senior thesis at Princeton was literally on the Roman Catholic Church. He took the liberal point of view that the Church had to change. On this basis, Luce hired this brilliant young guy and sent him to Rome. He was in his mid-twenties and still wet behind the ears. He got to Rome when the Christian Democrats were coming up. I always said he had imaginary sources. He was a romantic from the word 'go.' Women melted at the sight of him."

Luce liked this sly approach, this sweeping sense of history he felt Hughes had. And he was willing to forgive Hughes's lack of detail, his lack of hard-nosed reporting.

"Emmet had this real dramatic way of writing," Richardson continued. "He could write like a dream but it was not news writing. It lacked the discipline and was full of emotion, full of flavor, and mood. And then, when the Soviets blockaded Berlin and the Allies ordered the airlift, oh my God, this made Emmet. Berlin was also his territory and he gave readers the emotion, the tension, the dramatic story. And mind you, he didn't do reporting. He had a bevy of brilliant young German researchers. He'd then come out with a story which was half-true, maybe, but boy, it was full of oomph! You'd cry when you read it. Well, Luce loved this."

In his two years overseas in the forties Hughes had more bylined stories in *Time* than almost any other correspondent before or since. Moreover, because Luce had issued orders that Hughes be left alone, he had no experience with *Time* twisting or manipulating any of his copy.

Once Hughes returned to New York, he lived in the Hotel des Artistes in an apartment decorated with purple velvet walls, religious art, and a huge candelabra. He seemed to be always broke, but he still bought a house on Long Island in Locust Valley. Hughes reputedly drank a quart of scotch a day but seldom seemed drunk. Friends described him as profoundly lazy, but with the brilliance of a fellow who always got an A on exams without cracking a book. Though a devout Roman Catholic, he had married three times. Hughes was an outrageous talker, a very odd fellow with a kind of mysterious standoffishness.

"I don't think he liked Clare," said the Luces' friend, Richard Clurman, "but he and Clare and Harry became kind of a ménage à trois. Emmet knew every ounce of Harry's personal life. Harry was ready to turn over the keys of the kingdom to him. He liked brilliance. He liked his mind. He liked his theology."

Hughes's Catholicism was a major influence on Luce. He was impressed by Clare's newfound devoutness, but Hughes somehow made a deeper impression. *Time* devoted so much space to Roman Catholic news in 1949 that Billings wondered in his diary, "Is Luce flirting with Catholicism?" He observed that Harry had gone to a three-hour service with Clare at St. Patrick's Cathedral. Grover also reported to him that Clare was "putting steady pressure on Harry to become a Catholic." Even Thrasher was "in a tizzy."

"There's something terribly wrong with Mr. Luce," she told Billings. "I don't know what it is, but I'm afraid he's going to turn Catholic." The word also circulated through *Time* that Father Fulton Sheen had Luce's private phone number.

Emmet Hughes felt that at one point Harry was quite close to becoming a Roman Catholic, "when you could sense his proximity to the Catholic

Church." There were some around *Time* who felt that "If Emmet had ever suggested to Harry that he become a Catholic, he probably would have!"

The one factor that kept Luce from joining the Church was China. The Protestant missionary background was just too deep in him. In fact, when a midwestern Presbyterian minister expressed to Luce his concern that Clare might convert him, Harry wrote that he was happy that Clare had found her faith, but that he was happy with his own faith, which had been his salvation since childhood.

Religion became another form of competition for the Luces. Clare much admired her Roman Catholicism and rather wore it as a badge of pride. Harry felt equally strong and dedicated about his Presbyterianism. The conflict had a way of sharpening, in a competitive way, their relationship.

"Harry almost always went to church with Clare," remarked Buffy Cobb. "He always took a Presbyterian Bible along and read it through Mass. Luce was also conscious that all eyes were upon him when he did attend Mass with Clare."

"He also told me," said Thomas Griffith, "that as he walked up the aisle, he had developed a little stumble as he entered the pew, which could be interpreted as a genuflection toward the altar."

"Of course her great interest is that I should follow her," said Luce. "But that won't happen. I have what has been called, 'The Presbyterians' invincible ignorance.' "

One day in the middle of a blizzard, Buffy was accompanying Clare to a church on the West Side, where Monsignor Sheen was going to preach. When she got to the Luce's apartment, Clare was ready. Buffy asked, "Where is Harry?" because he always went, too. Clare explained that Harry had said grumpily, "I suppose even with this weather, that man will pack the church."

"I suppose so," Clare had answered.

"Well, I'm going to the Presbyterian church. And I'm going to walk. You can have the car."

"Why are you going there?"

"Because there'll be nobody there."

Nor was Luce's interest in religion only a Sunday matter. Gloria Mariano, Luce's secretary who succeeded Corinne Thrasher, reported that Luce never traveled anywhere without his Bible in his briefcase, and seldom made a speech without mentioning God. His adherence to Presbyterianism was profound. He fully accepted its tenet that man is a lowly sinner to whom worldly success must mean nothing. This gave him his outward serenity. Theologian Reinhold Niebuhr, whom Luce much admired, told a reporter, "I once got a note from a *Time* editor, saying, 'Could you please do something to keep our boss from getting more pious and more conservative?' "

* * *

The strong, but unsuccessful appeal of Catholicism for Harry was matched by the equally forceful pull of politics. In 1950, one of Connecticut's senators had resigned. Governor John Lodge owed much to Clare and could have appointed her to the unfulfilled term. The other candidate was Prescott Bush, father of a future president. Harry felt it was important for Clare to be senator, that it might pull her out of her emotional funk. Luce pressured Lodge, but Lodge refused to commit himself.

Once again, Clare announced that she preferred to be "companion in life" to her husband, and publicly praised him, saying, "It takes a big man to let his wife grow, and he did." She tried again to return the favor, prodding Harry to run for the other Senate seat. She saw this as a bulwark for their shaky marriage because then he would need her more.

The Fort Lauderdale *Daily News* soon headlined a story: A LUCE FOR SENATE; WILL IT BE HE OR SHE?

Luce admitted that he had been approached by several Republican leaders. They, in turn, reported that he showed "a keen interest" and planned to tour the state and determine his prospects.

Harry then asked everybody's views. Billings told Luce that he had no talent for electioneering and would get beaten, and even if he did win, he would be bored and frustrated as a freshman senator. Harry's brother-in-law and lawyer, Tex Moore, felt that Luce's genius in breaking tradition would make him a force in the Senate. Matthews warned Harry that his departure from *Time* would throw the whole editorial structure in question, and this could be ruinous.

At a lunch for managing editors, Luce raised the issue of his Senate candidacy, saying the odds were five to one that he'd say "no" at the end, but the way he talked, he was concentrating on the "yes." He explained that he felt like a Pentagon general in charge of propaganda, who had a chance to face the fire of the front lines and couldn't say "no."

When Harry talked to Republicans in Washington, they called his patriotic issues "baloney" and they said the big question was whether or not he really wanted the job. Billings was with Luce when he said, half to himself, "I feel miserable, perfectly miserable." Billings saw Harry as somebody cold and frozen, sunk deep in indecision. "I shouldn't have gotten into this," Luce said, "and it's going to take a lot of coping for me to get out."

"Maybe you ought to run and get it out of your system," Billings told him.

"Hell, it's not *in* my system," Luce insisted.

"Then get it out of your friends' system."

Harry decided to confer with his son Hank, then a reporter on the Cleveland *Press.* Hank was against the campaign and felt that his father would be making a big sacrifice and would waste a lot of time talking to stupid people with little chance of making a real impact on Congress. His son did note that a Senate seat might make sense if his father had future political ambitions for a Cabinet job.

Mary Bancroft even weighed in from Switzerland on the subject. She told Harry that she found it hard to imagine him on the campaign trail, kissing babies.

Finally, Luce scheduled another lunch with his managing editors and told them he was not running for the Senate. "They almost cheered," he noted. His major concern, he said, was how to tell Clare his decision because she was his prime sponsor.

In the end, Luce's decision was not so much intellectual as from the heart. As he told one of his correspondents, "The way I feel today after a bad night on the train, it would be plain silly to take up a new career."

But Harry needed something new and exciting. The old career had lost its glow. Luce felt so depressed and frustrated that he sent his staff a memo saying he no longer wanted to see any *Time* copy, that he was going away for a while, that he never got any credit for the good things about the magazines—but got all the blame. Harry added that he wasn't worried about *Time*. Though he felt it lacked an editorial vibrancy now, he thought it would snap out of its slump. Moreover, he promised he wouldn't leave his magazine out on a limb. "I won't be irresponsible in my decision," Luce told his staff, but added that he had to work out a formula as to what he was going to do.

He soon found it. It wasn't a formula; it was a cause.

24

HARRY fell in love with Eisenhower as people fall in love with beautiful girls," said Allen Grover. "Here was this marvelous man who came from the heartland of America, the fair-haired boy, the leader of the great armada of World War II, a crusader, honest and straight. And Harry really fell for him. He idolized Eisenhower as he did almost no one else."

Eisenhower was a man that others intuitively liked. He made men smile and had an open warmth, easy charm, and relaxed presence—all the things Harry did not have and desperately wanted. There was a whole generation of Americans who worshiped Eisenhower. He had been the commanding general for more than 14 million men and women. His name was a household word. MacArthur had been a hero, too, but somewhat more aloof and godlike. The public couldn't call him "Mac" but they always called Eisenhower "Ike." With his flashing smile and midwestern manners, Ike was accessible. The American people were ripe for Ike, and he became their hero.

One of Luce's deep wishes was to be a public hero. It was one thing to be a giant in communications, a great national power and a man who saw himself as a moral force, but it seemed an insurmountable step to emerge as a hero. He had finally satisfied himself that he could never run for political office. His only hope now was a political appointment—the possibility of being secretary of state. He had the mind for it and the background. If Luce could make his mark in the cabinet, he might earn a national respect and international reputation and come as close as he ever could to being a hero.

Clare visited Ike at Columbia University and urged him to run, but he was evasive. "Just as I was leaving," recalled Clare, "I asked, 'How many politicians give you advice?'

" 'Nobody can go through that door without giving me advice,' he replied.

" 'I'm no exception. If you take my advice you will be president. This is my advice, *Don't take any advice.* Just pursue what you are doing until your own instincts tell you where else and what else you should do.' He looked very much relieved and gave me one of his great grins and said, 'Now, I will take you into my confidence—that is the only piece of advice that I have received since I've been here that I intend to take. I tell you if I do get to be president, you're going to be one of the people I want on my team.' "

Clare and Harry both went into high gear. At a *Time* managing editors' lunch, Harry expressed his feeling that Ike was someone who was all things to all men. Billings disagreed and felt as if Ike had "too big a grin and no principles behind it."

Soon after that, Ike told *Time*'s Charles Wertenbaker, "I will only run for president—if I'm nominated by both parties."

"Now, wait a minute! You can't do that!" Wertenbaker told him and tried to give him the full picture. "But Eisenhower literally said that," he noted. "He was a political innocent."

In 1951, a *Life* article appeared comparing the presidential potential of General Dwight David Eisenhower, then supreme commander of NATO forces in Europe, and Senator Robert A. Taft, the Ohio senator who was known as "Mr. Republican" because he seemed supreme in the party. Taft and Luce were in full accord on most issues, including the danger of communism. Taft's brother and campaign manager were both personal friends of Luce. Moreover, Luce and Taft were also bonded by Yale's Skull & Bones.

For Luce, the Taft issue was a real dilemma. "Harry felt that from all kinds of points of view, the man best qualified to become the Republican candidate that year was Senator Bob Taft," noted Clare. Yet, Harry also felt that "Taft simply had no style."

Harry believed that if the Republican Party lost the election, it would cease to be a national party. Making his painful choice, Luce said, "I was sure Eisenhower could win. I was not sure that Taft could." He had admitted to his wife that he had never voted for a winning presidential candidate.

Like Harry, Clare, too, was in a quandary. "To be elected president, I think a man has to be the type that could pass as any woman's husband, brother, sweetheart, or uncle," Clare said. "He needs to be the kind of man that appeals to a woman."

She said she personally preferred Eisenhower, but that if Eisenhower and MacArthur should both run for president, "it would tear out my heart. I love them both." MacArthur was then commanding an international United Nations force against North Koreans who had broken through the thirty-eighth parallel to Seoul.

When Harry finally wrote to Eisenhower, urging his candidacy, Ike wrote back to "Dear Henry." Luce was miffed. "If he doesn't pick up that it's 'Harry' very quickly, then we can't have him," Luce told a meeting of his managing editors. It was difficult to tell if he was kidding.

Harry soon decided upon a trip to Paris to persuade Eisenhower to resign from NATO and come home and campaign. "He'd asked me to meet him in Paris," said Mary Bancroft. "He'd come over to inspect Eisenhower, to see if he would 'do' for president. This was when I thought he should back Bob Taft. I was so annoyed with his whole procedure, about how he said he wanted to evaluate Mamie's drinking for himself. He seemed to think he was God, being able to sit in judgment over everyone and everything. I was so furious with him that I actually wanted to just leave him and take the train back to Zurich," she recalled. "But he wanted to talk it over afterward, so I had lunch with him and we fought some more. He said he was going to do something 'nice' for Stevenson, and then he was going to do something 'nice' for the Taft family, and then he was going to endorse Ike and go all-out for him.

"I think," she continued, "that he felt that with Ike he'd have a finger in the pie. He'd have the run of the White House; maybe he'd even be able to manipulate Ike, who did like rich men. With Bob Taft, he felt he'd be helpless."

Taft was far colder than Ike, a matter-of-fact, highly organized man. His door would be open for Harry, but not wide open.

Luce's conversation with Ike helped to clinch his decision that the political time had come for him to resign and return to the U.S. Earlier, he had announced that he would run for president if the Republicans nominated him, but he would not quit his NATO job to campaign.

"Oh, so coy and self-righteous!" commented Billings. "I hope he doesn't get it, to spite Luce who is deeply in love with his candidacy."

Frank White, *Time*'s Paris bureau chief, recalled, "Harry was all charged up. And he wanted a full-blown staff meeting. Luce said, 'Pick a restaurant. I have something to disclose to you all.' So we went to a famous one called The Barclay, off the Champs-Elysées. There might have been twenty-five around a big table. Harry said dramatically, 'I've been here on a mission to talk to Eisenhower, the commander in chief of NATO.' He evolved this drama of how the purpose of his mission was to see if Ike had agreed to run for president. At this dramatic moment, he sat down and speared the soufflé. And by the time he'd reviewed Ike's answer, the soufflé was running water. He had actually put the fork into it! And the headwaiter was going bananas!"

Luce's dramatic success with Ike was enough to make his trip a triumph. But Frank White felt there was something more Luce should do before returning home: reconcile with Teddy White. "Why don't you guys knock off this sort of dumb thing, and have lunch together, or drinks together, and see each other, in any case?" Frank asked Luce. "And they did. They both told me to bug off. I wasn't even invited to the lunch. Teddy said, 'We don't need any more Jewish mothers.' Even though there was no kiss-and-make-up, they agreed to disagree. They both liked each other. They had *always* liked each other. I don't think Harry liked more than four or five guys."

Upon his return to New York, Luce had the usual Time Inc. lunch with his editors to report on his trip. This time, the concentration was on Eisenhower and why he could and *should* be elected. Luce simply assumed all his editors were for Eisenhower, and most of them were.

In the midst of his political discussions, Luce did allow himself a few diversions. One of them was a lunch with the duke of Windsor. The former king was then in New York, completing his memoirs for *Life.* At lunch, noted Oliver Jensen, then text editor of *Life,* "The duke made a comment on the fish, and how he liked the kind we were having. Luce kept going on about fish, and fishing, and eating fish, until everybody was dying of boredom. He had been told that you allow the prince, or the king, or the queen, to set the topic. Finally, I think it dimly occurred to the duke to change the subject. He sort of leaned over, and asked in a low voice, 'Where's the men's room?' So Luce, stuttering, said, 'Oliver, will you show-show-show the duke the men's room? You know where it is.' I said, 'Yes.' "

Luce invited other visiting celebrities to a Time Inc. lunch as well. Leonard Lyons reported that Luce once met King Peter of Yugoslavia in an elevator at the Waldorf-Astoria. "We're expecting you for lunch at our office," Luce told him.

"Of course, of course," said King Peter.

The next day, the king's equerry called to inquire about the date of the Luce luncheon. Luce's secretary checked and discovered that the scheduled lunch was with Prince Peter of Greece. A new lunch for King Peter of Yugoslavia was hurriedly arranged.

As the 1952 election grew closer, Mary Bancroft returned to the States for her daughter's wedding to Senator Taft's son. "I was infuriated at Harry for coming out for Eisenhower, when I knew he admired, almost worshiped Bob Taft," said Bancroft. "I knew how dreadfully Taft felt about the whole thing from my son-in-law. I was at dinner at Allen Grover's, and I was lashing out at Harry. He had a dreadful temper—the temper of a redhead. His eyes began to flash. Grover was kicking me under the table, to make me stop, but I was going to make Harry blow up. Harry got so mad he actually began to tremble.

"When it was time to leave, he said, 'Where are you going?'

" 'I'm going home.'

" 'Well, I'll take you.' He had brought me, but I thought he was so mad he wouldn't take me home. But I was wrong, and he never mentioned losing his temper.

"The next day, Al Grover called me up and said I shouldn't do such things, and I said, 'Why in the world shouldn't I? It was a dreadful thing to do, endorsing Eisenhower when he thinks Taft should be president. He is impossible, but I'm sorry I did it in front of some of his employees.' "

But Luce did have a long-standing problem with Taft, who had supported the charges of Wisconsin Senator Joseph R. McCarthy. McCarthy had come to Washington as a freshman senator in 1946 and received little notice until he defended the Nazis who were blamed by the U.S. Army for the Malmedy massacre of American troops in the Battle of the Bulge in World War II. McCarthy then hit his real stride in attacking what he called, "the Communist infiltration of the U.S. government." In one speech, McCarthy claimed he had the names of eighty-one Communists and party-liners in government, but refused to name any of them. His charges increased in number and volume, but always without evidence. He aimed his charges at the State Department, saying that Communists known to the secretary of state were still shaping American policy.

In a matter of months, McCarthy created a national hysteria and managed to destroy many lives and reputations, wreaking particular havoc among creative-minded liberals. *Time* called him "loud mouthed . . . irresponsible . . . wretched . . . a fool or a knave . . ."

In *Life,* an editorial deplored Taft's support of McCarthy, and noted, "It is right to fight communism; it is wrong, wicked, to smear people indiscriminately, most of whom are good Americans. What you can best do for America and for American principles is not to join the McCarthy lynching bee." In this, Time Inc. was far ahead of the American press, ahead of a fearful American people, and even in advance of the historic TV treatment of McCarthy by Edward R. Murrow. *Life* called on Taft to repudiate McCarthyism "because truth and decency are at stake."

Luce was personally contemptuous of McCarthy and regarded him as a bungler and a liar. He saw him as a menace "because he distracts Americans from serious consideration of the really great things they should be doing for peace and liberty throughout the world."

While Harry's antipathy toward international communism never changed, he now told his *Life* editorial writer, Jack Jessup, "Communism has become too much the scapegoat of everything that's wrong with us. The fact is that communism is no longer a real issue, even indirectly in America." For Harry, this was a sea change.

Eisenhower had refused to confront McCarthy during the campaign, even though McCarthy had denounced his hero and friend, General George Marshall, as a traitor. McCarthy's prime supporter, Senator William Jenner, who had called Marshall "a living lie," appeared with Eisenhower on an Indianapolis platform. Eisenhower had asked Emmet Hughes to write a paragraph for his speech praising Marshall, but was persuaded not to use it. Instead, he allowed Jenner, as well as McCarthy, to embrace him. Yet, Luce was so enamored of Eisenhower that he did not denounce him for this.

On April 11, 1951, General MacArthur was fired by President Truman for disobeying orders in trying to widen the war in South Korea. MacArthur, *Time* Man of the Year, felt he could return as a public hero and sweep the presidency. When he was defeated badly in the Wisconsin primary, Taft became the party favorite. But Luce still felt that only Eisenhower could win.

He then played a crucial role at a critical moment in the convention balloting. At national conventions there are often conflicts between competing sets of delegates claiming voting recognition. The Taft-dominated convention committee approved the slate of Texas delegates favoring Taft, instead of the ones for Eisenhower. This was typical and unsurprising. *Time* however dramatized the story under the headline, "THE TEXAS STEAL."

Luce then did something unprecedented by printing *Time* one day early "because if that story hit the delegates before the crucial ballot at the convention, it would make a great difference." *Time* men were seen carefully placing that particular issue of the magazine on the chairs of delegates. Harry admitted to Clare that it was all his idea and acknowledged that it was a really dirty trick, "the only thing that weighed heavily on his conscience." Clare claimed: "He suffered greatly."

Given all their back-room dealings, both Luces had a right to consider Eisenhower's nomination a personal victory, and so they did.

President Truman had decided not to run again, and he privately solicited Illinois Governor Adlai E. Stevenson to be the Democratic nominee. *Time,* meanwhile, ran an enthusiastic cover story on the Illinois governor, edited by Matthews who was Stevenson's close friend and classmate at Princeton.

When Stevenson was drafted as the nominee at the 1952 Democratic National Convention, he made a memorable acceptance speech with the theme, "Let's talk sense to the American people." It caught fire all over the country. *Life* called him "the Democrat's best foot."

Luce had met Stevenson and liked him. Stevenson was going up in the elevator in the Waldorf Towers one night and saw this man slouched under a hat in an untidy coat in the back. After a while the man said, "Hello, Adlai." Stevenson was startled to find it was Harry Luce. They laughed and chatted. Stevenson afterward went with the Luces to the theater. Their mutual friend,

Bill Benton, owner and chairman of the Encyclopedia Britannica Company, even arranged for Adlai Stevenson to join him and Luce on Benton's yacht.

No matter how much he personally liked Stevenson, however, Luce was adamant about the need to elect Eisenhower. Luce asked Time Inc. vice president, C. D. Jackson to head up Eisenhower's speech-writing staff. Ike wrote Luce that Jackson "saved my sanity." Luce also sent Emmet John Hughes to act as an Eisenhower speech-writer. Clare predicted a disaster because Emmet's style was so ornate, involved, and intellectual. Still, it was Hughes who wrote Eisenhower's most sensational speech in which he proclaimed, "I shall go to Korea!" This became a slogan that helped win the election.

Luce could not control all his staff. Jackson tried to recruit Eric Hodgins at Time Inc. to work for Ike, but Hodgins had said, "Piss on you, C. D. I'm going to work for the right man." Another Time Inc. editor who volunteered for the Stevenson staff was Robert Manning. Luce, who admired both men, was pleased to tell outsiders that Time had editors on both sides of the campaign, to show how the coverage was even-handed.

But *Time* was not very even-handed. Luce told his editors: "Eisenhower is right for the country and therefore it was *Time*'s job to explain why. Any form of objectivity is therefore unfair and uninvolved."

During the campaign, *Time* printed twenty-one photographs of Eisenhower, all highly attractive, smiling, and warm. In that same period, there were only thirteen pictures of Stevenson, two of them thirty years old and the rest mostly unflattering and frowning. There was the often-repeated story at *Time* that photographers going out on assignment asked only one question of their editors, "Good guy or bad guy?"

In the midst of the political heat, Luce often sought the companionship of Mary Bancroft. Now divorced, she had moved to a New York apartment on 86th Street, near the mayor's mansion, facing the East River. She lived simply, much as Harry would. For Harry, it was a needed retreat, and he came often.

"He'd phone, but wouldn't identify himself, just say, 'Hello, Five o'clock.' I'd say, 'Yes.' And plunk down would go the receivers on both ends.

"As the clock struck five, the doorbell would ring, and in he'd stroll. My daughter Mary Jean claims that when Harry and I were together, we both talked incessantly all the time. 'Both of you are talking,' she insisted. 'Neither of you listens to the other. I wonder why in the world you bother to meet.' Well, I think that a slight exaggeration, but I do think we did an awful lot of overlapping in our talking! And then, at exactly six o'clock, he'd get up, nod, and out he'd go."

Much of that time, the talk was politics. Mary attacked Harry for his adoration of Eisenhower. Harry, who almost never lost control, once shouted at her, Mary shouted at him, and then both apologized.

One day, Mary came to Harry's office and met Corinne Thrasher, who had transcribed so many of their letters. The two later had lunch and Thrasher talked about Clare and Harry: "You know, it used to bother me, the way they treated each other. But now I think they deserve each other. Better that they torture each other now than that each of them should be torturing somebody else."

Mary once said to Harry: "You tell me that when you hear her voice on the telephone, your mouth gets dry. What are you afraid of?"

"I am not afraid of her."

"You tell me she's got a sharp tongue, and you don't want me to meet her. I've got a sharp tongue, too. I am taller than she is. She doesn't impress me. I don't even think she's very bright. I hear that she is a good military strategist—so what?"

And he said, "What you don't understand is the importance of a pretty face."

"Are you telling me that I haven't got one?"

"No, you are not pretty!"

"Well, there are some people who think that I am more interesting-looking than Clare!"

Mary realized that Harry really minded having her meet Clare. "I told him several times, 'Harry, I'm not afraid of her tongue, I've just as rotten a tongue. If she hits me, I'm bigger than she is. I can knock her out, and I'd really like to have a go with her.'

"Then he'd say, 'Please, don't, please.'

"He once told me that she said that she would kill herself if he ever left her, that he was the only friend she had. I asked him if he believed that, and he said, very seriously, that he did. I doubt if she'd have killed herself, except out of spite!"

In a note of triumph, Harry added, "I've been married to her now for fourteen years. It's been fourteen years of sheer hell." Then he grinned and said, "But by God, I've fought her to a standstill."

If Mary could not understand the almost Darwinian battles in the Luce household, she knew that nothing would change. Besides, Harry once again needed Clare's help in his crusade to elect Eisenhower. A far better speaker than Harry, Clare had made dozens of speeches for Ike.

By October 1952, it was time to push even harder. *Time* scheduled cover stories on the two presidential candidates.

The Stevenson cover story carried the blurb, "Does he make sense to the American people?" *Time*'s answer was "No." But the Eisenhower cover story was a glowing tribute.

Matthews, who had fought furiously to soften the Stevenson story, now bitterly asked Luce whether it might be better for *Time* to openly declare itself as a Republican magazine.

When Ike won a sweeping victory, Luce went from desk to desk, shaking hands with his editors, glowing happily.

"I was one of perhaps fifty people invited into the private rooms of the elected president of the United States on election night," Clare told an interviewer. "I remember, we were in a suite in the Commodore Hotel. The president-elect showed all the evidence of utter campaign exhaustion. His eyes were glazed, his voice cracked, his shoulders drooped. He threw himself down in a chair, spread his legs out, and his arms fell on either side of the chair, and he said, 'That is the last thing anybody's going to get me to do for the next twenty-four hours.' I went over to him and I said, 'No, Mr. President, there's one more thing.' He said, 'My God, what's that? And the answer is no.'

"There's an old gentleman sitting over in the Waldorf who is the last Republican president of the United States, called Herbert Hoover, and I think it would be really awfully kind of you just to give him a ring on the telephone." He pulled himself out of the chair, and he and I went into the bedroom of the suite, closed the door, and he lay down on that bed, hardly able to lift his head. I called up the Waldorf, and I said, "President-elect Eisenhower would like to speak with former President Hoover."

Hoover had just gone to bed, thinking that Eisenhower wasn't going to telephone. "Then Hoover came on, and there were only a few words exchanged," remembered Clare. " 'You're the first person I would like to see, whose advice I would like to get,' Eisenhower told him. Hoover said, 'Congratulations.' Afterward, Hoover told many people how grateful he was for the sensitivity that Eisenhower had displayed that particular night."

Soon afterward Harry asked Clare, "Well, what are you going to ask Ike for?"

"What do you mean?"

"Well, he's certain to offer you something. He *has* to. I mean, he's got to have a woman on his team somewhere."

Only a few months before, Clare had once again put herself in the running for a Senate seat that had become available in Connecticut. She tried desperately to get the nomination and failed, and now professed no interest in public office.

"Well, you know, Harry, I've decided to leave politics and try to stay at home as much as possible, and I certainly don't want another round of Washington."

"Now, come on, you must think of something."

"I might ask him if he would make me a representative to the UN, because it's right across the street and I can always get home for lunch and dinner."

"Oh, I feel sure that he would do that."

Luce later confided to Hedley Donovan that Eisenhower once had asked him during the campaign what job he wanted. "He said the only thing I really want, you'd be crazy to give, and that was the secretary of state."

Luce knew it wouldn't happen, but he *wanted* it to happen. It wasn't just that he wanted the power of the position, but he saw it as a bigger stage to put all his ideas into action in a way that he never could at Time Inc.

"Luce never talked to me about wanting to be secretary of state," said Hugh Sidey, a key member of *Time*'s Washington's bureau. "But when he'd be around the president, he'd get that wonderful sparkle in his eye, that kind of kiddish delight. I always felt he would've loved something like that. Basically, he was beyond ambition. He was a realist about it."

But Sidey was not entirely right. Luce was not beyond ambition. "He had to be talked out of it," said T. S. Matthews, "I was one of those against it. I said, 'You've effectively disenfranchised yourself, by the job you've done in publishing and the way you do it.' " Despite their many disagreements, Matthews served not only as a kind of liberal conscience for Luce, but occasionally his voice. In discussions with top editors, when Luce failed to make himself clear, he would turn to Matthews and say, "You know what I mean, Tom. Why don't you explain?"

Any hope of being selected secretary of state disappeared when Eisenhower picked John Foster Dulles. Harry and Dulles agreed on almost all international issues, but Luce did have some serious questions as to whether Dulles could shake up the diplomatic establishment.

Sensing Luce's disappointment, Frank White asked him, "Why don't you become ambassador someplace?"

"And he gave me some sort of funny answer, like, 'Why doesn't somebody ask me?' "

Washington insiders had speculated that Luce might well be the next ambassador to the Court of St. James. Eisenhower later said he never offered Luce any spot in his administration because he never thought Luce was interested.

But Emmet Hughes, like Frank White, knew the depth of Luce's unhappiness when Ike didn't offer him something important. He felt a big government job would have "conferred upon him a kind of legitimacy that he has always felt escaped him."

Clare, too, was waiting: "I rather expected to be offered some job if we won. I never said anything about it. But I asked myself, Should I do something? I really did not want to. I had written a play, *Child of the Morning,* which I closed on the road campaign for Ike. There was a Hollywood movie that looked good. I wanted to go on writing, and do those things. After we won, I talked it over with Harry. He said, 'Don't go near him. If he wants you, he'll offer you something and you can decide whether to take it. If not . . .' He shrugged. Everybody else had been called. I did not want a job, but I wanted to be asked. Harry said, 'You are being absurd. You will hear from the president.'

"Then Harry decided to go out to the Orient," said Clare. "I never heard a word from Ike. I began to feel hurt. One appointment after another would be announced. I thought, well, he's just forgotten."

Finally word came, "The Boss wants to see you."

As Clare recalled the meeting, "I went in and Ike was very businesslike, very glad to see me. He thanked me for the part I'd played in the campaign, and then he twirled his pencil between his fingers and looked at me and said, 'Now, we've done a great deal of thinking about all these posts and positions, and I would like to ask you what you would think about becoming secretary of labor?' "

Clare felt she wasn't qualified, that Ike needed someone with a far greater knowledge of labor. She said, without a smile, "I am not your man."

"All right, now, what would interest you?" countered Eisenhower.

"Well, now, Mr. President, I was thinking you might put me over there on the UN." She already had asked Ed Thompson of *Life* to look into the details of the job's hours, pay, and rank.

"Nonsense, I'm not going to waste one of my stars on a small job in the UN. What about an embassy?"

London and Paris were no longer available, he told her. She then eliminated Germany, Mexico, and Spain for her own reasons. Eisenhower mentioned Italy.

In 1940, when Clare was in Europe researching her first book, she had visited the American embassy in Rome and called it, "The most beautiful in Europe. How I'd love to be ambassador here."

Clare's account of how Eisenhower offered her the ambassadorship has been disputed. A Luce intimate insisted that Harry had told her that he himself was offered the ambassadorship to Italy, but had suggested that Eisenhower appoint Clare instead. Harry even mentioned that Ike later told him that he had also offered the job to Bill Benton.

Whatever preceded Ike's offer, Clare insisted that she was reluctant to accept it. She told the president that the Rome ambassadorship would be most difficult. "You know there will be sharp criticism. People will object to me for four reasons. First: I am a woman and the Italians will not like dealing with a woman. Second: I am a Catholic. The Bible belt will think I am giving our top secrets to the Vatican. Third: Since my husband is a great publisher, they will say that my being in Italy will prevent his reporting the news from there objectively. Fourth: I am known to be so anti-Communist that the very large number of Italian Communists and leftists will be infuriated."

After further discussion with Eisenhower, Clare agreed to consult with Harry, who was in Indonesia. She wouldn't go to Rome without Harry.

Clare knew what she was saying. If she went without him, seeing her husband only on intermittent trips, then the marriage was finished. The Dalrymple affair was still bright in her mind. Harry would find somebody else, because she knew now, better than ever, that Harry always needed *somebody*. She knew this because she was the same way. They had traveled apart, grown apart, but the marriage was no longer strong enough for them to live apart, and survive. If she still wanted him and the marriage, she would have to bring Harry with her to Rome, at least half the time.

Clare wrote Harry a long letter saying that she didn't know whether it was a good thing to do for him and for her and for their marriage, and it would altogether depend on how he felt about it. She said that she had no intention of taking the job if it kept them an ocean apart.

He cabled back: LETTER FOLLOWING. ACCEPT AT ONCE.

Then he sent what she called an extraordinary letter. "He wrote that it would be an injustice in history if I were not to take the job," said Clare, "and that he felt that I really should do it, and that I owed it to my sex because he knew how I felt about discrimination against career women." He suggested that he could arrange to spend alternate periods of six weeks in Italy and asked whether six months of the year there would be enough. Finally, Luce added, that she "must keep her personal rendezvous with history."

The gossip in Washington was that Clare was Eisenhower's discarded mistress and therefore he had sent her to Rome to get rid of her. But the Luces refused to let anything put a damper on their enthusiasm.

When Clare's appointment was formally announced, Harry's editors noticed that he "even sported a carnation." It was his victory, too. As much as anyone, he had helped pick and create a president. The ambassadorship for Clare was part of the prize.

An even more remarkable testament to Luce's delight was his decision to leave Time Inc. for six months a year to be with his wife in Rome. This was an extraordinary act for Luce. It seemed completely out of character. Time Inc. was not only his love, it was his life.

The political dream of being secretary of state had proved to be a fantasy. The satisfaction of finding and promoting a president had been an enormous satisfaction, but that was done. Beyond that, he now felt a deep bitterness toward him at Time Inc.

Luce's pro-Eisenhower stance had deeply angered the supporters of Stevenson on the staff, including T. S. Matthews, who wanted to resign. Luce sent him to London to explore the possibility of a new magazine there. Matthews finally got the message that it was simply a ploy to get rid of him and he sent a memorable cable: WHY DID YOU KEEP ME STANDING ON TIP-TOE SO LONG IF YOU WEREN'T GOING TO KISS ME? AH WELL.

As managing editor of *Time,* Matthews had done more to change *Time* style than anyone. When Luce gave him that job, Matthews told him: "I am married, *Time* is not the name of my wife. I hate the Republican Party. As a reader and as a writer, I consider *Time* badly written."

Harry respected Matthews, leaned on him, used him often as his voice and conscience, but finally, didn't want to fight him anymore and let him go.

He was less lenient with the rest of the pro-Stevenson staff. He grouped them together in a postmortem to tell them that if they didn't like it, they could leave. He reminded them that he was their boss and could fire any of them, and said, almost wistfully, "but I don't know anyone who can fire me. Sometimes I wish there were."

Besides his malaise at *Time,* Luce had another reason for wanting to go to Rome. He had suffered through a serious gallbladder attack and surgery, which gave him the sense that he was "an old crock." He had an increased sense of mortality, a stronger desire to adventure into new things.

In his persistent Presbyterian way, Luce was still the optimistic romantic hoping again to make his marriage work. He and Clare had never spent any concentrated time together. Going to Rome might give their marriage the lift it needed.

This would be another chance, another challenge. Clare now had climbed another pedestal. If he had reached the top of the mountain, she once again seemed to be getting closer. It was Clare who had said often, "Love is possible only among equals."

25

CLARE was not fifty years old and had reached a political pinnacle: She was the first woman the United States had ever appointed as an ambassador to a major country. When a reporter asked Clare what she thought of the possibility of a woman becoming president, she answered, "It makes so much sense that they'll never allow it. That is, in our time." When another reporter suggested that certain international inconveniences might result if a woman were president and became pregnant, Clare answered, "I don't see why. Pregnancy is not an illness." Pressed further on the awkwardness of a woman president giving birth during a world crisis, she said, "Would that really be any more awkward than if a male president were taken to the hospital with a heart attack?" She then added a postscript, "If there were a woman extraordinary enough to be president and also be pregnant, then that would definitely be an extraordinary woman I'd like to see elected."

She was undoubtedly one of the most celebrated, most controversial women of her era, and still quite beautiful. But Clare had a gnawing sense of uneasiness as she sailed on the *Andrea Doria* for Naples on a cold April day in 1953. The situation was complex. Jean Dalrymple had caused a very deep hurt. Clare had underestimated her husband. There were obviously facets of him she had not known, depths she had not plumbed. She thought she held Harry safely in tow, quietly corralled; suddenly he had strayed and now was back. She sensed a fresh restlessness in him; it could happen again. She would have to keep him close to her, watch him more carefully, cater to him a bit more. Clare had invested a large part of her life in him now, and he was too good to lose.

For both of them, this ambassadorship gave everything a new dimension and a sudden spirit of adventure. She had achieved a greater importance now. He respected that. In Italy, she would sit at the head of the table and he at the far end. Yet, she knew this was no time for her to preen. She could not overstep. He was a proud, sensitive man. Clare must always keep reminding herself, and him, that she was still basically his wife. She must ask his advice, respect his judgment, request his help. And, he must always feel himself a full part of this adventure. He must always believe that she needed him. If she could maintain that impression, then he would stay; if not, there would be another Dalrymple, and maybe then the bond might really break.

As the American ambassador to Italy, she faced her greatest challenge. In an article for an encyclopedia on being an ambassador, she wrote, "An ambassador is an honest man sent to lie abroad for his country, a glorified messenger boy." She was much more than that. She soon described it as very hard work.

"To govern Italy is not only impossible, it is useless," Mussolini once said. Italy was in serious trouble. Poor in natural resources, plagued by unemployment, Italy faced bleak economic prospects. With the fall of Mussolini's fascism, the 47 million Italians had renounced the royal rule of the House of Savoy and proclaimed a republic. The Americans had supported the new premier, Alcide de Gasperi, leader of the Christian Democratic Party. As Clare arrived, the political situation was highly unstable.

Gasperi's government had been distressed by Clare's appointment. A female ambassador was an affront to Italy's male-oriented society. Also, Italy was a Roman Catholic country, and both Luces had previously been divorced. *Candido,* a satirical weekly, highlighted both issues by calling Clare "Mr. Boothe Luce" and running a cartoon showing the American embassy flying a flag of laced-edged panties.

There was, in fact, some confusion about what to call Clare. State Department policy decreed that she should be called Signore Luce—ambasciatore not ambassatrice. ("Ambasciatore" is masculine, whereas "ambassatrice" means the wife of an ambassador.) At a banquet of the Chamber of Commerce at Turin, Clare asked, "Please call me ambassatrice." However, the main speaker stuck to his protocol. "He kept talking about, the male ambassador, she does this," remembered Clare. "A waiter standing behind me got the giggles. Soon everybody was smiling." Gradually, Clare was known in Italy as "La Signora."

To make matters worse, there was even confusion about what Clare looked like. There was another Clare Luce, an actress of some repute, who was known in Italy. The Luces had once offered her money to please change her name, but she refused. Then, one of the leading Italian photo magazines published a picture of the actress Clare Luce in an embrace in *Antony and Cleopatra.* The caption read, THE NEW AMERICAN AMBASSADOR.

As if all this weren't enough, Clare replaced a beloved icon. The departing ambassador, Ellsworth Bunker, an able career diplomat, had been so popular that Italians cried when he left. Italian officials bitterly questioned why Bunker was followed by, as one of them put it, a woman who, "became a career diplomat five minutes after she was appointed." Moreover, Italian matrons were reportedly appalled that any woman so wealthy and good-looking should be interested "in such an unpleasant job."

But Clare was undaunted and looked for reasons why she would succeed. Being a playwright, she said, "is really excellent preparation for diplomacy. I watch a man's inflections, his gestures, his manner of speaking and try to determine what his inner convictions really are, very much in the way that a playwright casts the characters for one of his plays." Public life, she said, had no horrors for someone "who had once been raked over the live coals by a group of professional theater critics. It is the quickest way I know to acquire a spiritual elephant hide."

In addition, Clare said, "a celebrity ambassador can draw more attention than a diplomat should, but she can also publicize certain national interests better than a faceless functionary." And she promised to make noise only about the few things that mattered.

She had to do all this, and more. "Because I am a woman, I must make unusual efforts to succeed. If I fail, no one will say, 'She doesn't have what it takes.' They will say, '*Women* don't have what it takes.' "

Clare also liked to point out that women throughout the ages have excelled in the art of diplomacy. "Women take naturally to it," she noted. "The great trick in diplomacy is to make some unwitting man think your idea is his idea, and women have been doing that all their lives."

The man who would help pave Clare's way agreed with her. "Actually a woman has advantages," said Elbridge Durbrow, minister counsellor of the embassy. "She can often put over a story, make them take a bitter pill better than a man can. If a man talks straight, he is apt to get thrown out before he can finish. But a woman will be listened to out of politeness. When they explode and protest, her needling can be subtle and she can say gravely, 'That's very interesting—are you sure you really feel that way?' "

Nevertheless, before Clare's arrival, a nervous Durbrow had written to his friends who had served under women, asking, "How do you handle these ladies?"

Both Luces found it strange that the flag was not flown at the embassy on their arrival, as was traditional. Clare, Harry, and Harry's sister Beth were in the limousine, Harry sitting on the edge of his seat. The streets were lined with people cheering "La Luce! La Luce!" Beth gave Harry a poke. "Your wife's had a tough day, she looks like a dream. Why not tell her so?"

Harry said, "She looks all right." Then, he turned to her and said, "Now, Clare, about this flag business. You have that flag hoisted tomorrow!"

Harry's sister had accompanied them at his specific request. "I went over with them, because Harry was worried that everybody here was saying, 'Oh she's just going over there to give parties in that beautiful house and she's not interested in the politics of it.' He wanted to make absolutely clear that she wasn't having anything to do with the household arrangements. So he asked me if I would go, and see how the house was really running."

It was said of Clare that she could rise to any challenge except housekeeping. "She was allergic to servants and convinced they were enemies. She needed a wife more than any other career lady I know," said Beth.

The U.S. ambassador lived in the Villa Taverna, a large, sixteenth-century Italian-style country house built by Cardinal Taverna and bought by the U.S. in 1948. "The Villa Taverna was beautiful, but terribly run down. It had been terribly neglected, but Harry supplied money to put it in good condition," noted Beth. "He wanted to be sure there was marvelous food at the dinners, and he didn't want her to have anything to do with it."

In the heart of Rome's residential section, only one block from the zoo, Taverna seemed a world removed. Set in a park-like seven acres, it was a serene enclave filled with sweet-smelling cypress trees, statues, and fountains. Taverna was important enough to have its own private catacombs with underground passageways that once reportedly connected to St. Peter's Cathedral. On his first inspection tour, the ever-curious Luce was accidently locked in the catacombs for several hours by a gardener.

Visitors were immediately struck by the lovely winding staircase, and the succession of small, elegant rooms. A landscaped terrace led to an expansive, justly famous, classical garden. An unusual feature of the villa was the way the floors were suspended on heavy chains, presumably to make the building less vulnerable to earthquakes.

In describing the villa, Clare's assistant Tish Baldrige wrote: "You find yourself in a large front hall of cream-colored stone, with ceilings so lofty you feel you are entering the foyer of a cathedral. Medallions of carved white marble decorate each of the four large columns, and attached to each post there is also a tall mirror over an antique Venetian marble and gold-wood table. Large Chinese jardinieres containing green plants stand guard at the entrance of the *piccolo salone* [a small living room], and azalea plants the size of small trees cover the whole lower part of the big glass doors opening onto a tiled terrace."

Most of the floors were covered in a fancy mosaic pattern of ceramic tiles; the chandeliers were of delicate Venetian glass. The pale blue and gold brocaded chairs in the dining room matched the gold and blue tiled floors. The ceilings were made of wooden beams, and the walls were covered with rich satin damask.

"A guest could sit on the rose-satin bench in front of the fireplace and look out of the windows onto acres of mysterious lights and shadows flickering through the foliage, an effect created by lights placed strategically all over the garden in wax-filled bronze pots that could burn for three days continuously," noted a member of Clare's staff.

The Luces had shipped over some of their personal belongings to feel more at home. They hung art by Matisse, Gauguin, Dufy, Delacroix, Utrillo, and Chagall, as well as a study of a North African native by Sir Winston Churchill, and an artistic effort by Clare's friend Noël Coward. They also displayed sculptured heads of both Henry and Clare by American sculptor Jo Davidson. As if all this weren't enough, they decorated the villa with their Chinese porcelain horses, their beautiful jade collection in white, pink, and green, and a painting of the Madonna of the Roses by Francesco Ferrentina—a gift to Clare from her husband.

Among the personal photographs the Luces also sent was a framed, autographed portrait of Winston Churchill and another of Bernard Baruch. Under the Baruch portrait was a verse inscribed to Clare:

> *The World was sad, the garden was a wild,*
> *And man, the hermit, sigh'd—till woman smiled.*

When Harry and Clare finally arrived at the Villa Taverna, somebody released white doves. They were the last symbols of peace she would see for a while.

Edward C. "Kip" Finch, Luce's sophisticated new assistant, and researcher Margaret Quimby, had preceded Harry to Rome to set up his Rome office: six rooms in an apartment building with a view of the pine trees of Villa Borghese, only five minutes from the *Time* headquarters. Finch felt that Luce would need guidance in Roman society as well as in business and politics. He thought that many people would try to get to the ambassador through Luce. His guest list had to be properly screened. For this, he got Duchessa Elena Lante della Rovere, also known as "Nellie," who knew society. Luce, meanwhile, busied himself with an Italian instructor and tape recordings to learn the language. "I think he was slightly homesick," recalled Quimby.

Finch also made himself personally responsible to see that Luce was properly dressed. About a half hour before they were due to leave Taverna for the Presidential Palace for the ambassador's presentation to President Luigi Einaudi, "I went into Harry's room and here was Harry struggling with a soft-collar shirt. He'd brought his Prince Albert with him for the occasion, but he didn't have a stiff shirt or collar. I said 'Harry, my God, you can't go to this thing in a soft-collar shirt.' He said, 'Oh really? Really? Why not? Why not?' I said, 'It just doesn't go.' I took off with Mario, the embassy's driver, to the haberdashery nearby. They didn't have anything. So then we drove to my digs at the Excelsior Hotel. I brought back my own stiff shirt and collar and studs. Precisely on the stroke of the hour of departure, Luce came out properly dressed. He afterward said to me: 'Well, Kip, you were right, they all had these damn shirts on.' This was typical of H.L.'s naiveté."

There was nothing naive about Clare or how she dressed. As her husband watched her descend the marble stairway for her presentation to the president, he was visibly impressed and remarked, "How beautiful!"

When Clare heard her name called out, "Ambassador Plenipotentiary and Extraordinary," she whispered to an aide, "Extraordinary, yes; plenipotentiary, no." With her usual sharp tongue, Clare described the president "looking like a farmer at his daughter's wedding in rimless specs, white thinning hair, leaning heavily on a cane."

It took time to win the approval of the Italian people. Beth said that one of the first things that swayed the hostile staff was the party Clare gave for three hundred of them at their villa. They all knew she'd been working until six-thirty and figured a beautiful woman needs an hour, at least, to get beautiful. They did not expect to see her until seven-thirty. Instead she was down in ten minutes, looking perfectly exquisite. "This really gave them a thrill," said Bea Grover, who later replaced Beth Moore as Clare and Harry's "wife."

The embassy economics minister, Joe Jacobs, afterward admitted that he planned "to scoff" when he met the ambassador. "But I stayed to praise," he said. Durbrow also admitted to a bias: He thought Mrs. Luce would spend much of her time getting inside information for her husband for a series of articles for *Time.* He would later learn that this was not the case.

Clare quickly got down to business. Each morning she dressed in her "favorite uniform," a simple linen dress. "I have it in several colors. Raglan sleeves and the pleated front give it softness and grace. But here's the secret," noted Clare. "See these pockets? They're full and lined, just like a man's suit. They hold everything I need: pencils, keys, lipstick, purse, powder. I dislike carrying a handbag during office hours." She also put on low-heeled shoes, "because high heels hurt my feet when I have to stand at official receptions for hours." Clare always wore her trademark—a red rose in a tiny water-filled vase clipped to the left side of her dress.

Each morning, she was driven to the American embassy, the Palazzo Margherita, once the home of Italy's queen mother. A massive place, guarded by marine sentries in dress blue, the embassy had thirty-foot ceilings. The doors and windows were twelve feet high. The central staircase, noted an author doing a profile of Clare, "would have fit nicely into one of the sets of *Quo Vadis.*" The anteroom which overlooked the Via Veneto, was one about the size of center field in Yankee Stadium.

The ambassador's office had been the dining room of the queen mother. From the ornately carved ceiling hung a spectacular chandelier of exquisite Venetian glass. Decorative maps in pale blue adorned the cream and gold walls. At the far end, there was a big staff table with seats for fourteen. But the Luces soon discovered that this impressive embassy had no linens, no pictures, and no silver.

A reporter described the setting: "The ambassador's desk, hardly noticeable in the huge room, is uncluttered. There is a gold clock, a cup of paper clips and pencils, including a gadget that clamps onto papers, given to her by Sir Winston Churchill. There are photographs of President Eisenhower and John Foster Dulles, inscribed 'with high regard.' "

Behind Clare's mahogany desk were two flags: The American on her right and beside it the ambassador's flag—forty-eight white stars on blue edged with a heavy gold fringe. On Clare's desk was a framed motto:

> *Lord Thou knowest I shall be verie busie this day.*
> *I may forget Thee, Do not Thou forget me!*
> *—Lord Astley before the Battle of Edgehill*

Near it, was a quotation on a card, "Above all, not too much zeal."

The British ambassador had advised her to go to the office only in the morning, see as few people as possible, leave everything to her staff, read no official reports or memoranda, take long siestas, and enjoy herself in the afternoon.

That surely was a joke. "It is really a grind," said Clare. "I'm up at the crack of dawn and keep going until one or two o'clock. What keeps me going? I have the constitution of an ox. Also, there is the excitement and exhilaration of doing this job."

"Clare's physical stamina was amazing," said Beth Moore. "Few people could keep up with her. At nine o'clock every morning, she was at her desk in the embassy, which surprised a lot of people (including some of her staff, who weren't used to getting in that early)! And, boy did she work them!"

"A dynamo in a Wedgwood china house," wrote *Newsweek* about Clare. "Up every morning at seven-thirty at the Villa Taverna (she rarely sleeps more than five hours a night), she goes through half a dozen Rome papers, including the Communist daily *L'Unita,* orders her calendar, plans dinner menus—the things an ambassador's wife normally does, and looks through her private mail. Then, she is rolling along to the embassy in her gray Cadillac. She receives callers, diplomats, Italian politicians, visiting Americans until one-fifteen, when she goes, generally, to an official lunch or takes time out for the hairdresser. She has a standing line for the hairdresser, 'You have exactly fifty-five minutes. Make me beautiful.' Between three and four, she returns and works until six or seven. Then she prepares for dinner or a diplomatic reception."

Her days were crammed and unending, so much so that her husband substituted for her on a variety of occasions, including some lunches. She always managed to be there if there were visiting American generals or key American politicians such as Adlai Stevenson. And it was a plus to have her husband with her when she dined with the president of Italy.

Her presence gave protocol specialists the worst headache they'd had in years. They had to decide who sits where. Mrs. Luce's invitation cards did not help. They read: "The American Ambassador and Mr. Luce." Paul Ghali, the Rome correspondent for the Chicago *Daily News,* reported his view that Mrs. Luce's "greatest handicap in her functions as U.S. ambassador is Mr. Luce." Ghali admitted that Mr. Luce was "scrupulously discreet" and would not discuss embassy matters "under any circumstance." But he observed that Italians were unable to distinguish between Luce, the publisher, and Luce, the husband of the American ambassador. "His magazines, therefore, are of peculiar interest to Italians who search them for views they associate with the embassy."

To help her, Clare had a detailed list of the most important people in the country, with personal descriptions. About one monsignor, she was told, "You should try to see him. They say he's the next Holy Father." Another member of the Rome hierarchy was described as "The Frank Crowninshield of Italy—gay, chic, charming, and *social*—a good one to lunch and dine with." Clare was also advised to establish a personal friendship with the Pope's two nephews.

Then, there was this added piece of advice: "Unhappily, everyone in Rome is poor as a church mouse. So don't be surprised if no one asks you to lunch or dinner—but all will accept with alacrity if you ask them! And they'll be delighted."

No sooner had she settled in when the storm broke. Clare arrived only a few weeks before the national election. As Clare said, "It was a bad break."

Clare saw the masses of underemployed people in Italy—many of them worried about earning their daily bread. She viewed them as a kind of sponge that absorbed Communist propaganda and Communist ideological promises. Clare felt the need to issue a warning and make a point.

"Diplomatic procedure was for the embassy staff to write your public speeches for you," she noted, "so I was handed this little speech for Milan (she was scheduled to speak before the American Chamber of Commerce), and I took it home and showed it to Harry. 'Look, you know all the briefing I got in the State Department about the sensitivity of these people. There's a phrase in this speech that might make a little trouble.' It was rather delicately expressed, but the effect was that if the Communists took over Italy, we might possibly, perhaps, who can tell, you never can say with any certainty, but *might* withdraw our aid programs and our financial help. I said, 'I don't think the speech would lose anything if we left that out.' So I blue-penciled it. And in comes Durbrow." Durbrow persuaded her that this tough phrase was important.

"I said, 'Well, you fellows know Italy better than I do so, OK, back it goes.' "

The actual phrase read: "If the Italian people should fall unhappy victims to the wiles of totalitarianism of the right or of the left, there would logically follow grave consequences." American aid to Italy then totaled some $650 million in addition to $300 million more for a NATO procurement program.

"We stuck her out there in front," said Durbrow. "What she said had to be said, but nobody could say it as well as she could. It wasn't her decision alone, though. It was the decision of the entire embassy, and it was a calculated and necessary risk."

De Gasperi lost the election and an American columnist blamed the defeat on Clare's speech. Italian newspapers resented an American telling them how to vote and threatening them if they voted wrong. Clare saw it as her low point in Italy. "I'd arrived, I'd not been well received, I was a woman, didn't know my potatoes . . ."

Besides being attacked in the Italian press for intervening in Italy's internal affairs, Clare took the heat at home. At a Democratic dinner, Democratic Party leader Averell Harriman called it a "blunder." Senator Wayne Morse, then a member of the Senate Foreign Relations Committee, also denounced Clare's speech.

As she was feeling so unsure of herself, Clare achieved a striking public relations success. A terrible flood engulfed Salerno, and the ambassador rushed to the scene to judge how much food, medicine, and other help might be needed. One newspaper described her as "a porcelain figure of a fairy godmother."

Whenever disaster struck, Clare had an innate sense of public relations. She was in the States when news came of the crash of an Italian plane. Clare immediately changed her return reservation from an American airline to the line that had experienced the crash. Her move was much heralded all over Italy.

* * *

Ambassador Luce soon became one of the sights of Rome. "The Coliseum comes first, of course, and a few other things, but I am generally on the list for tourists," she said. At an embassy reception, a flustered American girl actually told the ambassador, "It's so wonderful to be over here in Rome seeing all these old, romantic ruins and you, too."

Clare usually received as many as eighty or ninety tourists in the great hall of the embassy, on a fairly regular basis. "How would you like to meet and be sweet and gracious to some four hundred strangers every seven days?" she asked an astonished journalist assigned to write about Clare. He added that "Clare had at least fifty ways of telling a bore to shut his trap without insulting him."

When Mrs. Eleanor Roosevelt stopped off in Rome, Harry was her escort and guide. As Clare noted, "He was the big shot in the family." Despite her pretense of pride, Clare clearly did not like having anyone upstage her when she gave a party for Mrs. Roosevelt. A reporter observed Clare's nervous and wistful look when the former First Lady became the center of attention and nobody wanted to leave.

At another reception, the wife of a *Time* correspondent was so beautiful that all the Italian men at the party surrounded her. "Clare had stationed herself in the center of the room," noted *Time* correspondent Dave Richardson, "and you could see her eyes darting toward the crowd of men around that woman. 'Who is she?' Clare finally asked, and then added, 'Bring her over here, please.' Her idea was, I'm sure, that if this woman was to be the center of attention, she wanted that center to include *her.*"

When Italy's American hero, baseball star Joe DiMaggio, arrived for a visit, Clare clung to his arm and steered him to a café on Via Veneto to ensure maximum public exposure.

Wherever she went, people gathered to see Clare. Few heads had ever turned for any previous ambassador, but for her, everybody gaped.

Another Italian paper, *Il Giorno,* pointed out that the Italians "applauded her and hissed her, raised her up for worship and threw her down in the dust; above all, they chose her as the favorite target for slander: And this, in Italy, is the most certain indication of popularity."

In America, however, Clare was often attacked in the press. "Henry is sticking by his ambitious wife's side," wrote one journalist. "Perhaps he feels that if she were tempted in Washington, it would be dangerous to turn her loose with Latin lovers with an ocean between the two of them. Of course, Clare continues to act like a goody-goody girl headed for sainthood. But if she makes it, you can take odds she'll be the first Patron Saint of Gold Diggers."

Slowly, however, Clare won applause on both sides of the Atlantic. The

Italians realized that Mrs. Luce was a real diplomat and very powerful because she had the ear of both the president and her husband. It was then that they began to appreciate her, not as a woman, but as an ambassador.

Her first task was to master Italian. The moment she had been appointed, Clare busied herself studying Italian with a dictaphone and a verb wheel. "I try to learn a new verb every day," she said, adding, "I could hold a pretty good conversation at a political level, but I couldn't possibly order a dress."

Then she began mastering all the intricacies of protocol. But Clare still had a lot to learn. "At my first official dinner [at the Spanish embassy] we did not dine until ten o'clock," Clare said. "The State Department had told me that the protocol was simple. Everyone had to wait until the ranking guest left. At this dinner, I thought British Ambassador Sir Ashley Clarke was the ranking guest. Dinner ended at eleven-thirty. I was dying to go home and kept watching Sir Ashley. We sat and talked. Nobody moved—twelve o'clock, twelve-thirty. Finally I said to the Spanish ambassadress, 'When does Sir Ashley usually go home?'

" 'When the ranking guest leaves.'

" 'But who is the ranking guest?' I asked.

"The Spanish ambassadress' eyes were slits of black fire. 'You are,' she hissed.

"I went out of that house like a fireman to a three alarm."

Virtually every day, Clare faced a social hurdle. "In Rome," she told an interviewer, "there are sixty-nine officials from other countries upon whom I must call. Heads of missions must call me. That makes 138 calls at our offices or theirs. Then I must call—with Henry when he is available—upon each foreign official and his wife, if he has one, at his residence. And he must call on us. That makes 276 more calls. We also give two or three dinners a week and are invited to an average of fourteen social functions a week—dinners, luncheons, and cocktail parties." Yet, Clare claimed to enjoy all this in a certain way: "I've never met a representative of another country who hasn't told me something interesting I didn't know. And information never bores me."

Clare soon had her own D.D.I.—Diplomatic Digestive Intelligence. She knew an astonishing amount about the eating habits of local and visiting V.I.P's: senators on diets, Americans who prefer scotch to wine, committee women who are reducing or can't eat garlic.

Because the protocol was so important, Letitia Baldrige arrived to help. "Tish," as everybody called her, was so capable that she would later serve as Jacqueline Kennedy's social secretary and write books on etiquette. Tish not only knew social protocol, but had a great instinct for weeding out phonies.

Baldrige, who was six feet tall without heels, and Clare quickly became close friends. The ambassador felt free to ask Tish about her love life. Tall Tish had a favorite story about two Italian men who told her, "Signorina, you obviously need two men, both working hard at once, to make love to all of you properly, and here we are, both of us, at your service."

But Clare gave Tish little time to enjoy herself. Tish handled the daily mountain of mail, which included many requests for jobs or handouts. Italians even sent Clare plays to translate. "One young man wrote enclosing his picture and saying that if Mr. Luce died, he would like to marry her," recalled Baldrige. "Then we had one man who wrote really lovely verse in stilted Italian, like a voice from the seventeenth century. He wrote at least one poem a week."

Baldrige also handled the inquisitive press. In response to a question, she told reporters that the ambassador had a hairdresser once a week to style her hair, that she never wore a mud mask, that she had never had a face lift, that she never wandered around the house in a hostess gown or told the cook how to cook something. She also tried to keep Clare informed of her public image. "I brought her a Communist poster I had ripped off a wall near my apartment that called her an Evil Witch," recalled Baldrige. "The poster had a huge photo of her, all distorted to make her look like Madame Frankenstein. Clare burst out laughing at my indignation. 'Tish, you have a lesson to learn that I learned long ago,' she told me. 'Never take yourself seriously—or anybody else, for that matter. Why, I think this poster's a charmer.' "

Both Baldrige and her boss were continually astonished by the pressures of Clare's social life. "I don't think I've been to more than two private dinners in the three months I've been in Rome," remarked Clare. "Everything that I've attended has been in the nature of a diplomatic or a political or a business occasion. Yesterday, we had a buffet lunch for thirty or forty people for Mr. Hugh Baillie, head of United Press, to which we invited a number of Italian journalists. I've had a dinner party for the American Ballet Company, a very large party, probably one hundred and fifty. And I had a Fourth of July party, to which we invited about 3,000 people. I have a guest book at the Villa, and I think at this point there are over 6,000 people who have come in the last three months I've been here. I haven't gone to bed before one o'clock practically any day since I've been here. And I've had one weekend during which I've had personal control of my time."

Clare tried to approach her social life with pragmatism. "She liked the businessman's lunch way of doing business, to call informally some minister and say, 'How about lunch tomorrow and talking things over.' That is characteristically American but it isn't done that way here," said R. D. Grillo, head of the American section of the foreign office. "People were offended, though she meant no offense."

Nor could Clare put aside her outspokenness, which was part of her American upbringing and part of her nature.

The New York Times correspondent Cyrus Sulzberger dined with her one night and recalled: "I spend the entire evening until after midnight talking to her, that is to say, listening to her. I was appalled. I am rather fascinated at the way in which she acquires knowledge here. I presume it must be by osmosis because surely she does not listen to what anybody has to say. She is not interested in listening because she is talking all the time herself. She is an exceptionally beautiful woman—quite astonishingly so when one considers her age. She has an excellent figure. But this exterior conceals the most arrogant conceit and the most ruthlessly hard-boiled self-assurance it has ever been my privilege to come up against."

Sulzberger also observed that at a typical dinner party, Harry played the part of consort. He would sit with the women at one side of the room, while Clare sat in a small room having brandy with some correspondents and Durbrow. "As she explained the intricacies of the situation and her own brilliance in handling it, she would occasionally turn to Durbrow and say, 'Durby, isn't that so?' Whereupon Durbrow would nod sagely and add a platitude like, 'Yes, the ambassador really handled that one well.' With a claque like that it is easy to see why her self-esteem floats blandly along," commented Sulzberger.

Sulzberger refused to accept Clare's concept that Italy was going Communist unless the U.S. intervened. "I think she's nuts and merely wants to make a big name for herself as an activist in her first diplomatic job. I mistrust her judgment and think she bullies the regular career men on her staff who have been rendered gutless by McCarthyism. I have a dreary suspicion she is trying to cook up some kind of violent action to ensure that the Communists are not going to gain power in Italy. And if she has a hand in it, I gravely fear it is going to be a fiasco."

The Communist papers referred to her as "The old lady with the evil eye." In posters, pamphlets, and in speeches by Italian Communists, Clare was called all kinds of Kremlin-inspired epithets. Palmiro Togliatti, Italy's leading Communist, made her the target of a major address on the floor of the Italian Parliament.

Politically, Clare's task seemed practically impossible. She had so far confronted the Italian elections, the weak new government of Giuseppe Pelle and the attacks of the Communists. Whatever she said seemed wrong in some circles. But she persisted.

In her first sixteen months, Ambassador Luce visited every important region of the country and traveled more than 35,000 miles on official business. During her first year in office, she made eighteen speeches on topics such as peaceful applications of atomic energy, the unity of Western nations, the evolution of relations between Europe and America, U.S. overseas private investment, and international cooperation in education.

Even if the Italians didn't always agree with her, they got to know her. A newspaper poll reported that almost half of the Italian people knew Clare's name, compared with only two percent for the previous ambassador, Ellsworth Bunker.

At the U.S. Embassy, there was an enormous lift in staff morale. Elbridge Durbrow summed up the feelings for Clare, saying: "As an old careerist, I could ask for no better boss, for three reasons. One: She is intelligent. Two: She seeks advice and takes it with an open mind. You can say what you think, but she makes up her own mind. Three: She has a wonderful sense of humor.

"You could not ask for more. She has won over the staff one hundred percent, and it didn't take her long, either. She played it very well." He then added, "One gets so used to laughing and smiling when one works for her."

Clare was in her element, at top form. It was going exactly the way she had hoped. When she talked, everybody listened. When she went anywhere, everybody watched. When she did anything at all, everybody buzzed about it and tried to interpret her intent. Clare was a daily headline. It seemed almost too good to be true.

26

ONE of the most remarkable things about Ambassador Luce was her husband. This was a man whose whole life was rooted in his magazines and in his work. Luce did not have social lunches. He seldom even had social dinners. Whatever he did, wherever he went, whatever he thought was almost always tied up somehow with his magazines. He was constantly thinking of ideas for his magazines, stories for them, changes in them. Time Inc. was his world and his life.

And, now, suddenly, for six months a year he jokingly called himself "the ambassador's wife." Frank White said he was the perfect ambassador's wife, because he would do whatever she said. In Rome, at least, Clare appeared to have more impact on him than he had on her.

Or did she?

A favorite question at dinner parties in Rome and New York was whether Luce was a prince consort or a behind-the-scenes king.

A few friends felt that Harry was constantly telling Clare exactly what to say and what to do on most key decisions. Clare herself described his importance as "enormous." He generally made an effort to stay out of the limelight, but he could talk to political leaders, newspaper editors, and other influential people as they could never talk to his wife. Clare constantly sought his counsel. She was no puppet, but there were discussions, advice, and strong suggestions. And both knew when to hold fast, not only against each other, but together against everybody else.

Both Luces strongly resisted the pressure of Senator McCarthy's traveling team of witch-hunters, who arrived in Rome to tell the ambassador to fire one of her staff. It seemed that this young man had served in China with the American embassy at the time when some in the State Department regarded the Communists as agrarian reformers. In this case, neither Luce confused personal convictions with party loyalty. They knew that this staff member was on too low a level to have been involved in any policy-making. Yet, McCarthy painted all old China hands with the same red brush. Clare knew her man well, fought for him, and won.

Harry sent his own reports to President Eisenhower. The president replied: "Of course, I never had any doubt that our new Italian ambassador would get started on her work with the good will of everyone who knows her, on both sides of the water. Likewise, I have no doubt as to the effectiveness of the official performance *you* will turn in."

His unofficial role seemed to give Luce some of the excitement and power he had hoped to have as secretary of state. Harry was happy, and this affected his relationship with Clare. They shared a closeness they had seldom felt before. The Luces took more trips together, too. Greek shipbuilding tycoon Stavros Niarchos made his spectacular yacht, *Creole,* available to them for a Mediterranean cruise. They joined the yacht at Lisbon and planned to stop at Nice for a visit with Joe Kennedy at nearby Eze. The trip also included stops at Venice, Trieste, Brioni, Ismir, and Istanbul.

Some said Harry's job was more trying than his wife's. "He has to go everywhere with her, yet he goes in a secondary role and with a feeling among the Italian people that he and his publications are not friends of Italy," said an American journalist.

"I really have two professions," Luce told a foreign reporter. "On the one hand, I am the big editor, of whom you have undoubtedly heard, and on the other hand, I am the assistant to the U.S. ambassador in Rome." And then he smiled. "It is difficult for me to say which of the two jobs is the harder."

Clare was admittedly startled at the pleasure with which Harry embraced Roman society. "I took these occasions for granted, but he found them glamorous. He could be both thoughtless and generous. Harry's thoughtlessness was really bad manners. But when he wanted to have good manners, he had them. When he was in Rome, his manners were perfect."

But not always. As he was jabbering away with the ladies at a reception one day, Luce looked at his watch, and suddenly said: "It is twelve o'clock. The embassy car is here waiting for you, Mrs. Cannon." Lily Cannon, wife of the U.S. ambassador to Greece, was apparently in the middle of a story. There was a dead, embarrassed silence all around. Then everybody got up and Luce practically pushed them out the door.

On the other hand, one visitor told her friends in Washington, D.C., what a big hit Luce made with the ladies in her touring group. Acting as the embassy guide, she said, "He seemed to know exactly what the women wanted to know. He told them about the intricacies of embassy housekeeping and told them that the fine paintings on the walls, the china in the dining room, and the Oriental rugs on the drawing floors had all been brought by the Luces from America. And lastly he showed them a portrait, a very fine portrait, of Clare Luce, of which her husband was obviously proud."

Sometimes, Clare and Harry presided over two or three cocktail parties held concurrently in different sectors of the Villa Taverna gardens. On Sunday nights, they showed movies. "Feed them and sit in front of a screen. You don't have to waste energy talking," said Clare.

At one of the more elegant parties, the guest list included eight ambassadors, eleven foreign ministers, a large sprinkling of Italian industrialists, assorted patrician members of Roman society and café society, and Elsa Maxwell who was visiting. For this party, the Luces brought out the gilded silver, white and gold embassy china, the gold-plated candelabra as well as the Belgian damask tablecloths. A delighted Maxwell tried to organize a conga line, but only two of the ninety guests joined her.

"Harry loved the elegant parties," said Clare. "He loved the people, and everyone in Rome seemed attracted by him. One of his favorite cracks was, 'I only help Mrs. Luce at social gatherings. I pour tea.'"

Luce said it without resentment. This was a new role, and he was still exploring it. He had never been a man of much vanity. When he had questions, he asked them. When he was bored, he walked away. He thought Italian women were especially attractive and he loved to look at them, lunch with them, and listen to the musical lilt of their language. Though the ambassador was considered too high a prize for most Italian men, the Italian contessas saw Harry Luce as a more accessible challenge. Yet, there is no indication of any conquest.

"Harry did have a wonderful time!" said his sister Beth. "It was a vacation for him. He'd done everything at *Time*. Of course, he was still editor in chief, but he had put good people in charge and he wasn't running things anymore. He felt he hadn't any free time like this in all those years. He had always been under such pressure. So, he was really glad to come here, because he felt it was time that he should study the trends in Europe. And that's exactly what he did. It was a sabbatical, and he knew he needed it."

Beth was absolutely right. Harry was living the life he had wanted to live for years. He had long ago said, "Someday I will go to Europe, to Asia, anywhere, and study one country, not just move from place to place. Learn the language, get to know the people, their philosophy of life, and their hopes, past and present."

"Luce unconsciously fell into the role of a Henry James character," said Beth. "He was an honest, straightforward American, defending and promoting the simple ideas Americans abroad believe to be theirs above all."

ublicly, the Luces appeared a happy and adoring couple on their Connecticut estate;
rivately, their marriage would soon turn sour.

Shortly before Ann's death in 1944, Clare and her daughter posed for a portrait.

Two of Clare's favorite generals were Major General Charles Willoughby (left), an aide to MacArthur, and General George S. Patton (below).

Acting in Candida *(above) was a pleasant diversion. Much more important to
Clare was her role as a devout Catholic.*

As America's most powerful publisher, Luce befriended many world leaders, including Winston Churchill.

Clare always kept in contact with her old friend Bernard Baruch.

As the U.S. ambassador to Italy in 1953, Clare was a constant source of curiosity.

Consort and advisor to Clare during her years as ambassador, Luce accompanied his wife to Capri.

Obsessed with Roman history, Luce was an enthusiastic tour guide for President Harry Truman.

Joseph P. Kennedy entertained the Luces at his villa on the Riviera.

Theatrical agent Jean Dalrymple (left) was the first woman who nearly broke up the Luces' marriage; later, Lady Jean Campbell (below), Lord Beaverbrook's granddaughter, became the love of Harry's life.

As one of the most powerful women in Republican politics, Clare gave advice to President Eisenhower (above) and Vice President Nixon (below).

John F. Kennedy invited the Luces to his inaugural and paid them special attention.

President Johnson demanded advance copies of Time *each week and often conferred with its editor in chief.*

Attempting a semi-retirement in Phoenix in the 1960s, Luce kept his lifeline to New York.

Near the end of their lives, the Luces reached an accord with one another.

UPI/Bettmann

At Luce's funeral, his older son, Henry, escorted his stepmother Clare.

As a widow, Clare struggled to stay active politically and socially, but discovered that life with Harry had been far better than life without him.

Luce soon became obsessed with Rome. He knew equally well the decayed as well as the energetic and beautiful parts of the city. He knew all the obscure churches as well as the animals in the zoo. No tourist ever studied more art and travel books with such fervor. His chauffeur had to follow him in case he got lost, as he sometimes did.

He took a special pleasure in taking Harry and Bess Truman on a tour of his city. He even corrected the guide: "No, that building has three columns, not two." The former president felt so at home with Harry that he played the piano at Taverna.

Frank White remembered Luce saying that all experiences should go "by fours—this was to be his four-year sabbatical." *Life* editor Ed Thompson agreed that the Rome experience wasn't out of character for Harry. "You have to realize, it goes back to his curiosity. He was curious about a hell of a lot of things besides journalism."

Still, it was somehow difficult to imagine Luce sitting at the lower end of a table making small talk, dinner after dinner, party after party. And Harry finally did tire of the entertaining. "I'm so damn sick of this," he told a friend after some months had passed. "We have these diplomatic state dinners. I always sit next to this same bloody woman. If I have to sit next to her again, I don't know what I'll do!"

Yet, he did not forget about his magazines. He was eager to know what the Rome bureau of *Time* was saying about Clare. Nevertheless, if he constantly visited the *Time* bureau, other news organizations would feel he was funneling news about Italy from the ambassador directly to Time-Life. Harry, therefore, seldom came anywhere near the bureau. He did, however, ask the Rome correspondents to file their stories before noon so that he could read them during lunch. That was his freest hour.

"When he was over there in Italy," recalled *Time* editor Robert Manning, "we covered Italian politics in *Time* as thoroughly as any two or three Italian newspapers. Harry was always sending in long reports on everything. We had stories on Italy almost every week."

Harry even tried to persuade Emmet Hughes to spend two months researching flying saucers because the Roman Catholic Church had a committee studying the duties of the Church toward creatures from outer space.

Even if Harry bent over backward to keep a distance between Time Inc. and the embassy, Clare did not. Bob Neville, the Rome bureau chief for *Time*, told correspondent Ed Clark that Clare wanted to see all his copy on Italy before he sent it to New York. "She periodically would try to throw her weight around, and get the bureau to report things that she wanted us to report, or do stories that she wanted done; that was a kind of pain in the neck," said Clark. "But Harry was a tower of strength in that situation; he just basically said, 'Don't pay any attention to her,' which was a great reassurance."

At the same time, Luce watched "like a hawk" to make certain Clare got all the prerogatives and deference her position deserved. "He told me off because I seated Mrs. Luce on my left in the rear seat of the car, saying that her rank entitled her to the right side of the car," said William Morrow Fechteler, a member of the embassy staff. Clare herself was equally aware of her status and bristled at any slight.

Ambassador Luce made a sharp point of reminding her husband that *she* was the ambassador. Her political sections Councillor Francis Williamson remembered driving from Naples, with Harry sitting in the front seat and she and Durbrow in the back. Durbrow was briefing her on some classified material and Clare pushed a button raising the glass separating the front, cutting out Harry.

Still, noted Clare, "Harry really enjoyed it more than I did, because I had the rough end of it and he had the fun end of it. He often spoke of 'my time in Rome' as one of the happiest of his and my life together."

The Luces often took side trips to other parts of Europe. *Time*'s Paris bureau chief Frank White hosted the Luces in the fifties. "The French franc was in dire trouble, as it usually was in those days. We gave this dinner for the minister of finance and his wife, Ambassador Douglas Dillon and his wife, and the Luces. I was at the opposite end of the table from Clare. But she absolutely interrupted conversations everywhere. To the finance minister's wife, Clare said, 'Chère Madame, I understand that your husband has some interesting theories about finance.'

"The finance minister was sitting there, too, and there was a deathly hush all over the room.

" 'What is that you hear about my husband?'

" 'I understand that your husband's currency is such that people would rather have diamonds, instead.' She looked pointedly at the wife of the finance minister, who was dripping with diamonds.

"My wife, Drew, hurriedly suggested, 'Clare, will you and the rest of the ladies join me in the other room?' Clare looked Drew right in the eye and said, 'No! The most interesting people here are the men; and I'm going to talk to the men! You can go your way.' "

*   *   *

Clare occasionally came to Paris and London on her own, primarily to do some shopping, but also to relax out of sight of the watching press.

"John Phillips [a *Life* photographer] and I took Clare dancing one night," said White. "She danced like a dream. We had such a grand night and about two o'clock in the morning, she said, 'Let's go to the Montmartre!' "

Those were the days of troubles with the Algerians in Paris. Montmartre, heavily populated with Algerians, was regarded as dangerous late at night. The driver flatly refused to go. But Clare was determined, so White hired a taxi and Phillips went home.

"She was wearing a necklace with round blue beads. I said, 'A good job. Those things look like sapphires!' " recalled White.

"Yes, but they are," she told him with a mixture of humor and defiance. Clare was *not* the kind of woman to be fearful about anything.

White recalled the evening as such casual, delightful fun. "You could yak and argue with Clare like she was a college girl. She could talk about everything and switch around. She loved conversation. Late in the evening, she'd tell you how it was to be a kind of motherless, fatherless foundling. I tell you, she was special. She was marvelous."

On another of her trips without Harry, Clare attended a meeting of European ambassadors in Luxemburg. There, she horrified the guests at a dinner party attended by many dignitaries. She told the guests that she had been asked by an American magazine to write a review of the Kinsey report on women. After serious consideration, she decided she couldn't do it in her present position. Then in a loud voice she added that it wouldn't have taken her any 480 pages to prove, as she felt that Kinsey had tried to say, that all men are dopes. All conversation ceased; her male colleagues perked up their ears. "After all," she said, "women are not interested in sex. All they want is babies and security from men. Men are just too stupid to know it."

Harry, too, made his solo trips when Clare was busy. Frank White accompanied him to Hamburg on a tour of the bordello area. "Harry was interested in Hamburg whores as people; he wanted to know how they lived. When we went into one of those houses, God, they descended on Harry like you wouldn't believe. I was at least fifteen or twenty years younger than Harry, but they weren't coming on to me. If I had one girl on my knee, he had seven. I couldn't help mentioning to him that he was getting a lot of attention. The women must have smelled power. And he said something to me like, 'It wasn't always this way.' "

Harry also made a trip to Cairo during a rebellion. He immediately became a reporter, doing interviews and returning with piles of notes for the *Time* correspondent who was writing the story. The correspondent wrote the story with Harry's quotes and put Harry's name in it. Harry crossed out his name. When the story appeared without Harry's quotes, he was indignant: "They were good quotes," he protested. The reporter reminded him, "You should have let me use your name."

"That's all right," said Harry. "It's just poor journalism. They should have used those quotes. They were good."

When Harry was not in residence, Clare did not stay monastic. One of her favorites was Michael Burke, a very attractive sports executive who later bought the New York Yankees. He came to Rome often and always called Clare. "They were great buddies," said a mutual friend, "but I don't think there was anything beyond that, although they were both handsome, intelligent, accessible, and available. Yet, there's no question there might well have been."

Other names were frequently linked with Clare's, including that of noted novelist Luigi Barzini, and Eric Sevareid, the handsome celebrated CBS-TV correspondent.

Stan Swinton, the Associated Press bureau chief in Rome, a dashing, unusually talented reporter, had been a special friend of Clare's until his fiancée, Helen, came to Rome to marry him. "Clare came to our wedding," said Helen, "but she looked through me with the coldest blue eyes you can imagine. I mean, I didn't exist! She still came to all our parties, but she looked right through me. And then, I got pregnant. We were going through the receiving line, when she said, 'Helen, dear!' Embraces, kisses, hugs, you name it! It really was funny. Yes, it took a child to make her a human being. Or, maybe in her mind, it meant that the marriage was permanent."

Clare was both discreet and careful about her liaisons in Rome. The whole world was watching. It was easier for her to see men in London, where a *Time* editor arranged a couple of evenings for her. "She got a little sloshed on martinis. I got her a date with a Conservative M.P., known as a great womanizer, a big tall guy; I thought there might be something there! Also I fixed her up with a young, up-and-coming Tory, named Ted Heath, and a couple of others, all Tories," he recalled. "She really looked down on all these people I'd assembled for her. She treated them as little kids. She wasn't rude, but arrogant, yes."

When Harry returned to New York, as he did every few months, Clare had more time for romance. But Harry was basically lonely without her. He felt comfortable at the home of his sister Beth and her family, and he went there often for dinner parties. Jean Dalrymple was married now, but Harry and her husband liked each other. Luce sometimes dropped in to talk and listen.

Dalrymple had no problem in their new platonic friendship. He still fascinated her.

Laura Hobson felt the same way. Now divorced from Thayer, she was Harry's frequent dinner guest. Their earlier encounters gave them a full freedom with each other. Laura was always chic, an attractive woman with luminous dark eyes and a mind that earned her a nickname, "The Big Smart." She recalled dining with Luce alone in his huge triplex apartment on the East River, "at a table that could have seated twenty." She dropped him a note the next day thanking him for their "stimulating and provocative hours." If they did have an affair, it was not a deep one.

His primary companion was Mary Bancroft, now permanently living in New York. She remembered a particular conversation about Harry's theory that great men shaped the dynamics of history. Bancroft quoted Churchill that the most important ingredient of greatness was luck. Harry told her the story of Churchill saying we were all worms "but I have always thought I was a glowworm." Mary reminded him that only a glowworm can produce light without warmth.

In a way, Harry felt like a glowworm in those days. He didn't want to be. He was still searching for something beyond himself. The experience with his wife in Rome was partly what he had hoped for. Their time together had improved their marriage and enriched them both. But the great problem was that Clare was also a glowworm, light without warmth.

Yet, he tried. His letters to Clare were loving and full of news. The greenhouse was almost built. There was a new path around the pond in their home in Ridgefield. The Rockefellers had come to visit, and so had Wendell Willkie's wife, Edith. He had lunched with John Foster Dulles, dined with Chiang's son, spent an evening with Richard Nixon, to whom he had sold the importance of Italy. He had also softened a rough *Time* review of Elsa Maxwell's new book, played golf with his brother Sheldon, took his grandchildren to the rodeo, and read them *The Wizard of Oz*.

Harry told his wife how much of the stamp of her spirit and imagination still filled the house and reminded him of her and her beauty. He hoped he was being helpful to her in Rome, and he was anxious to be back with her again. He thanked her for bringing joy to his life, and he created an ungrammatical corny Valentine telling her again that he was always the man who loved her.

There was almost a wistfulness in his letters and a sadness.

27

ROME had recharged Harry and given him a sense of pleasure he had seldom felt in his lifetime. A staff consensus was that Harry seemed less combative in his fifties, less rude, and more open-minded. Hedley Donovan, who would later become his successor as editor in chief, said of Harry, "He had achieved what he had wanted in life; he'd made a president and had been very powerful for twenty years. He was on a plateau."

Now Harry had something up his sleeve. "Anybody can make money with money," Luce told his staff at a luncheon in 1953. "But we are supposed to be magazine publishers. Wouldn't it be a good test if we found out we could bring out another successful magazine?"

He then told them he was considering a sports magazine. "Too much of the world news is dull news," Luce said and added, almost apologetically, "Well, sports is a big thing in the United States."

"But you're not interested in sports," someone said.

"It doesn't matter what I'm interested in," Luce answered.

Indeed, Harry didn't have any knowledge of most sports. He had to work at school jobs while other boys played baseball or football. He had been a poor boy and poor boys didn't play tennis and golf, and they don't ride. He learned those later, mostly out of embarrassment and as an act of defiance to be a regular guy. He approached sports the way he did anything he was interested in—questions, questions, questions.

At Time Inc., many people thought Luce was crazy and they mockingly referred to the magazine as "Muscles" or "Jockstrap." Finally, it was named *Sports Illustrated.*

At a staff lunch, Luce tried to get his editors to come up with a concept for *Sports Illustrated,* without success. "Everybody broke off and went back to their offices," said *Time's* A. B. C. Whipple, "and finally, two hours later, Luce had an answer: "I give you a quotation from the Bible: 'Be not afraid to teach.' "

He told the same thing to 175 newsmen at a conference in Oregon. He decried the idea that the press must publish in order to amuse the reader or give them a variety of viewpoints. He called that "cynicism at the heart of American life." *S.I.,* as it was called, would teach people about sports.

Luce launched his new magazine on August 9, 1954, with an initial circulation of 450,000. He needed a strong managing editor, and Mary Bancroft recommended André LaGuerre, who had been head of the Paris bureau and also had been Charles DeGaulle's public relations man during the war. "André loved sports and understood power," said Bancroft. "Harry could see both things were relevant, although he never thought of André till I suggested him. The reason I suggested André was that I knew that in order to get the job done, it would have to be someone able to stand up to Harry. If anyone could deal with Charles DeGaulle, well, they could deal with Harry."

LaGuerre had many of the qualities that somehow attracted Luce. "He was grumpy and never went out of his way to kiss Harry's ass or be in any way congenial," said Frank White. "He was a medium-sized guy, not particularly handsome—kind of flabby. He drank whiskey all the time. But he was so smart. If you were working in Europe and wanted to find out what was going on, he was *terrific.*

"André admired Luce enormously," White continued. "I can't tell you how much, or why Luce was such a fantastic figure in André's life. André was a very cynical guy. He was another sort of alter-ego type for Harry, but Harry never understood LaGuerre. Not many of us did."

When Luce offered André the top job at *Sports Illustrated,* he didn't really want it, but said yes. What he really wanted to do was be managing editor of *Time* and this seemed a foot in the door.

While Harry met LaGuerre in New York, he saw that André had somehow lost a front tooth. "How can a really big editor of mine go on and on without a front tooth?" Luce grumbled.

"André took offense at this, and till the day he died, he never had that front tooth fixed," noted White. "But I don't know anybody that Luce paid more attention to than LaGuerre. He was kind of a dissenter. It was under LaGuerre that the magazine made money."

However, it would take years and losses of $33 million to turn *Sports Illustrated* into a profitable magazine.

Clare had her own comment on the magazine: "Ah, yes, the only good things in it are Charles Goren on bridge, which I suggested, and my articles on skin diving." Goren was known as "Mr. Bridge."

* * *

While Harry absorbed himself in sports, Clare was continuing her endless round of duties in Rome. On the 700th anniversary of the death of St. Clare at Assisi, she knelt to kiss the ring of Cardinal Micara. "Best wishes on your name day, Clara," the crowd yelled in Italian.

"Clara" came from the Italian word *chiara* which meant "clear." Italians coupled that word with Luce, which meant "light" in Latin. Clare then became "clear light."

But "clear light" was not how she felt. Clare had begun to despair about her lack of real accomplishments in Italy. While she was there, the government had lost a new election and Italy was in a turmoil of internal political friction. Ambassador Luce stirred up some friction in the international press when she attended the opening of a housing development in impoverished southern Italy and handed the tenant a key to the house and a crucifix. Critics claimed she had usurped a privilege usually reserved for the clergy.

As Clare's mood darkened, Luce took Emmet Hughes aside and said, "I'm worried about Clare."

"Why?"

"Well, she has to be persuaded that she's not carrying the entire world on her shoulders."

Emmet looked at Luce, the man who always carried the world on his shoulders, and began to laugh. "Harry, you're just the man to do it," he said.

Harry returned to Rome for his usual visit, and Clare tried to put her troubles aside. She even set up an audience with Pope Pius XII for her husband to present an album of pictures that had appeared in *Life*. The photos, taken in the Vatican garden, showed the pope and a crowd of visiting children.

Luce brought his Rome employees and the Time-Life bureau staff to the presentation. The Luce contingent included secretaries and even some of their mothers—a total of twenty-two. When the pope was ten minutes late, the punctual, restless Luce asked his assistant, Walter Guzzardi, "Damn it, Walter, where the hell's the pope?"

Nan Orshefsky, the wife of Rome correspondent Milt Orshefsky, recorded the scene:

"We arrived at the inner sanctum of St. Peter's and boarded an elevator up to the pope's audience chambers. The elevator was the last semblance of the twentieth century we would see. An attendant dressed in scarlet brocade ushered us through about ten audience chambers, each more magnificent than the last, with great painted ceilings and scarlet-damask walls and golden thrones. The pope came in from a door on the left, frail and gentle, and looking very well for his eighty-one years. He wore red-silk slippers with gold embroidery, rather in the Chinese style. All the Catholics knelt and kissed his ring. He spoke to each in excellent English and gave us each a medal. He stood in the center of the room with his arms outstretched and explained that the blessing he was going to give us extended to all of our families. Then he went into Latin. Most of the people kneeled. I kept my eye on Mr. Luce, for a cue. He stood for most of it. I think the pope was speaking toward Mr. Luce's deaf ear, so it was a rather strange presentation!"

When Luce finally presented the pope with the large, leather-bound album of photographs, Guzzardi silently moaned as Harry interrupted the pope to point out some of the children's faces which had particularly appealed to him. Nobody, but nobody, ever interrupted a pope.

Clare herself finally managed a private audience with the pope. As a Roman Catholic, Clare had always tried to distance herself from the Vatican so that no one could argue that she was betraying the United States "into the arms of the Vatican." The stress was on secrecy. She was driven to the Apostolic Palace in a Vatican limousine and took a private elevator directly to the papal library. Not even the top official in the Vatican knew that the meeting was taking place. When the interview ended, she returned home in the same anonymous limousine. The papal secretary breathed a sigh of relief that the whole thing had been brought off without publicity. But when Mrs. Luce saw an Italian journalist, she exclaimed jubilantly, 'Guess where I have been! I have just had a private audience with the pope!' "

After the war, the Allies had divided Trieste and the Istrian peninsula into two zones, one Italian and one Yugoslavian.

When Clare had first arrived in Rome, Yugoslavia's Marshal Tito threatened war if Italians moved into the Yugoslavian zone. Secretary of State John Foster Dulles called a conference of European ambassadors in Luxemburg to discuss the situation. Clare told them: "I think this thing can be settled, for one very good reason. It's a pain in the neck to both countries, and there is nothing to be gained by their going to war. If we can find what each of them really wants, besides territory, we can settle it."

During this period, Clare was once called to the phone in the midst of a dinner party and was gone a long time. When she returned, Harry asked, "What's the matter, dear? I thought you had settled that Trieste affair." And then he laughed, and so did everybody else—except Clare.

Clare pressed the urgency of having President Eisenhower put the Trieste problem before the National Security Council, something the State Department had so far not been able to do.

How could she get the issue to the president of the United States? "If only

I can get the president to focus on this matter for one minute, to say, yes, go ahead and try to work it out, we may get it settled," she said.

Knowing that Eisenhower liked one-page reports, Clare sat down at her typewriter and began to try to explain the problem of Trieste on one page. "I'd get four pages, three pages, then four pages, then five pages—and I'd tear all these things up," she said. Then came an inspiration and she capsulized it all in a poem:

> For want of a Two-Penny Town [called Trieste]
> A Prime Minister was lost [de Gasperi]
> For the want of a Prime Minister . . .
> Italy was lost . . .
> For the want of Italy, NATO was lost . . .
> For the want of Europe, America was lost . . .
> All for the want of a Two-Penny Town [called Trieste].

"I sent it to Ike through the *Time* correspondent, because I knew he would drop it on his desk," Clare said. "I did not dare send anything so unorthodox through the State Department. And Ike read it aloud to a State Department meeting. They said, 'What does she want?' 'Permission to try to save the two-penny town,' said Ike. And they all said, 'Well, sure.' Boom, we were off. We got the White House's approval to try to settle it."

Under American pressure, Italy and Yugoslavia both agreed to secret negotiations in London. A CIA operative told Ambassador Luce privately that Marshal Tito's problem was the failure of the country's wheat crop. Without wheat, there would be famine in Yugoslavia. If he got wheat, he might soften on Trieste. Clare hurried to Washington and met with President Eisenhower. Twelve hours later, Tito received a personal letter from Eisenhower offering wheat.

Finally, one and a half years after the partition of Trieste, the issue was settled. Italy got the city of Trieste, and Yugoslavia the surrounding territory. Within three weeks, Yugoslavia received 400,000 tons of wheat from the United States. None of these secret negotiations were made public.

C. D. Jackson, who didn't like Clare, was proud enough to send a message saying, "I told you that you would be Miss Trieste, 1954."

Luce sent Clare an exultant letter offering her a 101 gun salute. He was filled with pride about her accomplishments during her Roman years. He was like a proud parent. Harry added how much he loved her.

A negative opinion came from a highly respected Italian expert, foreign correspondent Graham Hovey: "If she had not felt compelled to talk about the pact before it was signed and sealed, it could have happened much sooner."

Furthermore, once it *did* happen, not everybody was happy with the settle-ment. There were street riots in various parts of Italy. "Clare had been to Trieste to see the British ambassador," said Elbridge Durbrow. "She was alone in the car with Gino, our old chauffeur, when the car got blocked on a side street. Clare said 'I'll walk.'

"I went and begged her to come inside," said Durbrow. "Clare said, 'I'm an old fire horse, I'm going to stay here and watch.' All hell was bursting loose right across the street—tear gas bombs, fire engines pouring colored water through high pressure hoses, people yelling, jeep sirens going—all not twenty feet away." Nothing daunted Clare.

After a celebratory lunch with the Italian foreign minister, Clare returned to the embassy in a great excitement. Her friend Bea Grover was there to greet her.

"Clare came running upstairs, 'Look what they gave me!' It was her vanity case which was covered with pictures representing every stage of her career: *Vanity Fair, The Women,* Congress, etc. There were two blank spaces. The Italian foreign office got her maid to swipe the case for them. At the luncheon, the foreign minister said: 'Mrs. Luce, you left something very personal at the foreign office.' He then handed her the vanity case. In one blank space, they had put the crest of Trieste set in rubies and diamonds. Clare was almost in tears. The foreign minister then said, 'The emblem of the grand duenna of the Diplomatic Corps.' This meant that he hoped Clare would be in Italy for an extended numbers of years and that he would make her dean of the Diplomatic Corps."

Soon after the Trieste triumph, Clare developed a severe viral infection in her mouth that affected her teeth. When her maid informed her she had lipstick on her teeth, she replied, "Great! The important factor nowadays is not whether I've got lipstick on my teeth, but whether I have teeth!" she said.

Besides losing her teeth, she began losing her hair. Her alabaster skin complexion suddenly turned sallow, and she no longer had the energy for her occasional swim. She also claimed a slight motor loss in her right leg. Tish said Clare looked like a "picked chick."

Clare later claimed that her Italian doctor did a urinalysis and said she was being poisoned. A checkup at the American Naval Hospital reportedly re-vealed arsenic in her urine. Clare further reported that CIA investigators moved in and informed her that she had been absorbing small amounts of arsenic for a long time. They suspected, she said, that somebody might be trying to kill her. Then came the delicate, probing question: What about her husband? Were they having problems?

Clare's version of the story had the CIA men checking for Communists in the kitchen. Then they noticed thick gray dust on the phonograph record in Clare's bedroom. Further investigation revealed that every morning, when the washing machine upstairs was being used, the vibrations shook the ceiling. A fine dusting of paint filled with lead arsenate was falling from the stucco roses that decorated the room. The conclusion, as Clare told the story: Her physical condition was the result of a daily diet of inhaling arsenic dust.

This, at least, was the account that leaked to the press. No one came forward to refute it, and Clare emerged as a tragic heroine. However, Richard Clurman, then chief of correspondents for *Time,* has set the story straight: "The whole arsenic story was a fake. She was never poisoned. She had to have massive dental work, and she didn't want to say that."

Frank White has also confirmed this and amplified the details: "Clare had to be in the States for six months. So the Luces called in Charles Murphy, [a *Fortune* editor] and Charlie concocted this story. Clare *did* have some serious viral infection at that same time which presumably caused her visible signs of illness. Nobody bought Charlie's story but it showed up in *Time*'s poop sheet for internal use about stories not for publication, and the thing leaked out. Of course, Clare was delighted because it was the perfect excuse to get away. But the whole thing was ridiculous."

It gave Clare the perfect cover to return to the United States for her dental work, and her resignation. She wanted to quit Rome while she was at the peak. It had been a great experience, but she now wanted something else. She had the same restlessness about jobs that she had about homes. She always wanted a new one. She now felt that the ambassadorship gave her a stronger springboard for the Senate.

Eisenhower asked why she wanted to resign. She detailed the story about the arsenic poison—not about her teeth.

Clare indicated that she wanted a piece done in *Time* on her so-called poisoning. "So we did it," reported a *Time* editor. "Intrigue, cloak and dagger and all. It should never have been printed."

In Italy, the rumor was that Clare took arsenic to clear the skin and create an alabaster look. But what most intrigued the Italians was the unexpected knowledge that the Luces had not slept in the same bedroom, since Harry was not affected.

After seeing her dentist, Clare spent some time at a luxurious health spa. When she emerged, she had a long talk with Eisenhower, who persuaded her to stay on until the next year. Publicly, she announced, "I want to be where he wants me to be." But, privately, she told him that she wanted to campaign for him again in 1956, and she would not be able to do it unless she surrendered her diplomatic status.

Aside from poor health, Clare confided to friends that another reason for quitting was that Harry wanted to go home. He had told a *Time* editor, "Three years of this is too goddamn much." He then added: "We have better things to do."

Clare, too, was thinking of "better things to do." She wrote Eisenhower asking for his help in getting her consideration for a new Senate seat in Connecticut. Congressman Albert Morano talked to some of the Connecticut party leaders and told her: "Don't do it. You can't make it."

Suddenly, Clare saw an opportunity that excited her greatly. All over the country, there was increased talk of "dumping Nixon," as vice president. Eisenhower himself was quoted as saying Nixon was "acceptable" to him, but so were others. Clare badly wanted to be one of the "others."

She approached Meade Alcorn, then in charge of the Committee on Arrangements, at the Republican National Convention, and asked him to intervene for her with President Eisenhower. "She wanted that nomination so badly, she could taste it," said Alcorn.

But in the end, Republican leaders strongly opposed the "dump Nixon" movement because they feared it would damage the Republican Party.

So Clare returned to Rome, as Eisenhower had requested, to complete her duties. Then, when Italy's European ally Hungary revolted against Soviet Russia, fully expecting American support, it received none. Clare pleaded with Dulles and Eisenhower to intervene, but to no avail. "An ambassador is just a messenger boy," she complained. "He can influence policy, but only if he goes home and argues it out, and then waits for a cable to come back, giving him the directive."

Harry had his own bone of contention with the man he had helped promote for the presidency. "This was the time for American leadership," he declared. "It was no time for a trumpet with an uncertain sound."

At a farewell dinner for the Luces, a *Time* staffer, Dora Jane Hamblin, felt brave enough to announce loudly, "I miss Harry Truman. Truman would have done something . . ."

In the sudden silence, Luce said to her, "Do you know what I hope happens to you?"

"No sir," replied the young woman, now almost paralyzed.

"I hope that when you grow up [long pause] you will get to be editor of a great big magazine . . . and that everybody who works for you is a Republican. . . ."

Everybody burst into laughter.

Richard Clurman was at a Time Inc. lunch when Luce asked his senior editors, " 'Have we gone too far, in praising Eisenhower?' Everyone said, 'Oh, no, no!' But the next week," noted Clurman, "we absolutely trashed Eisenhower in *Time.*"

As Clare's departure neared, one of the fresh rumors was that she might succeed Oveta Culp Hobby as secretary of health, education and welfare. Clare denied this. Another rumor speculated that Harry would become the U.S. ambassador to the Court of St. James.

The Luces were people about whom there would *always* be all kinds of rumors, most of them untrue. This never bothered them, and they seldom responded. But both of them were probably secretly pleased.

Before coming home, the Luces went on a holiday to Spain. Clare was in a mood of nostalgia and longing. She told Harry she wanted a castle in Spain on fifty acres on the Costa Brava with a good beach for rock bathing. She wanted it all ready for her to move in. She reminisced about how the smell of mimosa aroused powerful emotions in her and brought back memories of southern France when she was sixteen and romantic. The dreams she had dreamed then, she said, had never come true.

They never would. Clare had always wanted too much. She was, however, more pragmatic now about her concept of her ideal man. She defined him as "that particular man with whom a woman happens to be in love at that particular time."

Harry never had verbalized what he wanted in an ideal woman, but it was no longer Clare.

28

HARRY Luce finally found the woman he loved more than he had once loved Clare, the woman he wanted, the woman who changed his life and almost changed Clare's.

When they fell in love, she was twenty-seven and he was fifty-eight and that seemed to mean nothing to either one. It was the kind of love he had never had, a sweeping, passionate, overpowering love that made his initial love for Clare seem more like an infatuation. With this young woman, he felt absolutely fulfilled. She was a fantasy come to life.

Harry first met her in a villa in southern France. She was the granddaughter of a man he considered his friend, and one of the few peers he admired and envied, Lord William Maxwell Aitken Beaverbrook.

Jean Campbell was tall, about 5'10", with a full, sensuous figure. Her penetrating brown eyes were serious under a shock of dark wavy hair. Then a lilting, sometimes riotous laugh, would reveal her great sense of humor. Jean's regal air was inborn, born to the manor, but nobody could have been less pretentious. She laughed when she said she was "born in a drafty castle." Jean often acted as hostess for her grandfather, and she was perfect at it because she had the marvelous gift of welcoming people with such natural ease that it made even the most stuffy, unsure people suddenly relax, and feel wonderful about themselves.

Beaverbrook, the Canadian-born tycoon of British journalism, had written books on success and power, and epitomized both. Son of a Scottish Presbyterian clergyman, a self-made millionaire, Beaverbrook owned *The London Daily* and Sunday *Express* and the *Evening Standard,* and was a fighting force in the British Conservative Party. He had earned his peerage as a member of Parliament and had helped engineer the election of David Lloyd George as prime minister. When another friend, Winston Churchill, later became prime minister, Beaverbrook energetically served as minister of aircraft production.

"What a man!" Harry exulted about his friend. "Power, power, power!"

More than his power, Harry envied his reputation as an international rascal. Something in Harry—the good, proper little boy—always envied the rascal and the pirate, because he knew he could never be like that himself. They got along marvelously well.

Beaverbrook was seventy-seven, almost twenty years older than Harry, but, in many ways, much younger. A man of medium height, he seemed smaller because he moved so quickly. He had a powerful physique, favored a black trilby hat, and like Harry, was unconcerned about the frayed collars on his white shirts. He had an enormous mouth with an urchin's grin. Beaverbrook had a reputation for boldness. He would try anything, including lost causes. His worst defeat was his inability to form a King's Party to keep Edward VIII on the throne after he married Wallis Warfield Simpson, an American divorcée.

Beaverbrook, or "the Beaver" as he was often called, was a wicked old man. Any attractive woman within his physical reach was considered fair game. Women seldom forgot the mischievous wink in his puckish face. Most found him difficult to resist. Even his granddaughter regarded it as likely that Clare Boothe Luce was one of his early conquests. Clare always made it a point of coming to see Beaverbrook whenever she was in Britain.

Lady Jean Campbell, the daughter of Beaverbrook's daughter and the Duke of Argyll, had been born in a castle in Scotland. Her parents were divorced when she was three, and each remarried, so Jean moved in with her grandfather. "He was my 'parents' in many ways," she always said.

It was a strange, weird world in which to grow up, a world mostly of men. During the war, her grandfather was in government and their home was a buzzing hub of politicians and journalists. Jean may well have met Harry Luce on one of his frequent visits to Beaverbrook in those years, but she was too little to remember.

Jean was educated at an English boarding school, and then decided to study Shakespearean acting at the Old Vic. In 1949, she moved back in with her grandfather and worked as his assistant. Jean was totally caught up in his frenetic world. They migrated between houses in Surrey and London, and she was with him for almost five years. "I learned so much from my grandfather," she said. The Beaver didn't like to pin himself down with unnecessary engagements. "He wanted to always be able to say, 'Well, I'm leaving tomorrow,' " reflected his granddaughter.

"We'd go to America in October," remembered Jean, "and stay at the Waldorf Towers, then go to Canada, back to New York. Then off to Nassau, then to Jamaica, back to Nassau, back to England, then to the south of France. This was the round. He had houses in all of those places, except New York.

"The difficulty for a young woman," Jean added, "is that you can't form any relationships with men when you travel that much and that fast."

Feeling she must experience life on her own, Jean came to New York in 1956 and got a job filing photographs at *Time*. She was in southern France on a two-week holiday with her grandfather when she met Harry Luce. "I remember that he was very surprised that I worked at *Time,*" said Jean.

She considered him handsome, but "very, very shy and remote." Harry, however, thought Jean was fantastic.

Back in New York, Harry told Mary Bancroft about his first meeting with Jean and confessed that he would like to make love to her. Only Harry didn't use the word "love." He used a word almost nobody had ever heard him use before.

Mary simply said, "Well, why don't you?"

His reply was, "I'm afraid that if I tried, I couldn't. I'd be too nervous."

But Luce couldn't get Jean out of his mind. One day in 1956, he simply walked into the *Time* photo department and said to her: "Would you like to come and have dinner tonight?"

"Yes, I'd love to."

"Well, I'll send my car for you."

"At half-past six, the car came," Jean recalled. "I arrived at the Luce triplex, facing the River House. I expected it to be a big dinner party, but no one was there, so I went out on the balcony. Then Harry came. There were no other guests! We went into dinner and talked for a long time.

"The next morning, he called to ask if I would have dinner with him that night. I said yes, even though I didn't then find him attractive. But that evening at his apartment, we sat on the balcony and talked about everything in the world. And I saw this man, who had been very cold, very hard, in the morning, suddenly unfold with a flowering of enthusiasm into somebody wonderfully warm and human, with such depth and humanity. And laughter. He loved to laugh. The transformation was so unexpected, so complete, so absolutely fascinating. And he became very handsome to me," she reflected.

"By the end of the evening I was in love. And I knew, right away, that this was going to be a tremendous love affair. I knew everything about it, everything that was going to happen. Yet, there had been no romantic conversation at all. I was terribly frightened—frightened because I knew, and yet I didn't know. Nothing had been said; nothing had been done. We talked until twelve o'clock, then he took me home in the car. When we said goodnight, Harry said, 'Oh yes, be sure to ask your grandfather to spend election night with me.'"

The next day, Campbell was scheduled to move out of her hotel to her cousin's apartment. "When you fall in love," Campbell continued, "your life is so completely overturned and I realized that I wasn't even collecting my mail for two months. He'd left two books for me at the hotel. One by Santayana, *Letters From England,* and the other was O'Connor's *The Last Hurrah.* He also left a letter, written that night. But you see, I didn't go back there to pick it up. I think we met on the ninth of September; and I didn't pick it up until about the twenty-sixth of October. So all during that time, we didn't meet."

Jean admitted that she was quite unnerved by her feelings for Luce and therefore did not respond to his letter. Nor did she pass on Luce's message to her grandfather. When she did check her grandfather's diary, she discovered that he was scheduled to dine that night with the owners of *Newsweek.*

Six weeks later, when she finally told her grandfather about Harry's invitation, as casually as she could, he replied, "If he damn well wants me to spend election night with him, he can ask me himself."

This forced her, finally, to write Luce a note. She sent him a book on Middle Eastern archeology and suggested that he ring up her grandfather.

"So I arrived in the office. I remember I had on my overalls for filing. Harry walked in and said, 'Well, all right, I'm going to call up your grandfather. By the way (he was very sharp), do you think your grandfather would like to go to a musical or a play or something?' I said 'Yes, I'm sure he'd love to go to a play.' "

Luce made it clear that Jean was to join them. "I remember I wore a simple black dress. It was a dreadful night. It was sort of a party evening, lots of people at small tables. I was so nervous that I kept putting my finger around the rim of the glass, and my grandfather glared at me and said, 'Stop doing that. Behave yourself.'

"Grandfather and Harry were discussing the Suez crisis and they did not agree. We left very early, almost immediately after dinner. Harry took us back to the Waldorf Towers and told grandfather 'Max, don't worry, I'll take Jeannie home.'

'No, you won't! She's got to come upstairs and talk to me.'

"He must have sensed something," said Jean. "He just didn't want me to go home with Harry."

Jean later spent that Christmas with her grandfather in Nassau. When she returned to New York, there was a call from Harry: "I want to have dinner with you."

Jean was then living on the eleventh floor of a small apartment house with a sitting room and two bedrooms. She invited Harry to dinner there, not quite knowing what would happen. So far, there had still not been a single romantic word between them. Then after dinner, Harry told her, "Of course, you know I've fallen very much in love with you."

"And I said, 'And of course, I've fallen very much in love with *you!*' " And so it began.

An hour after he left her that evening, Harry called to ask what was the color of the blouse she was wearing that night. It was pink. The next morning, he sent her fifteen dozen pink roses.

"Then we saw each other as often as we could," she said. "It got more intense, more intense, more intense."

For Harry, it was easy to understand Jean's appeal. She was a free spirit with her own natural style, the complete opposite of Clare. Jean wasn't trying to impress anyone, had no desire to be center stage, and felt no need to make herself heard. Still, she was never at a loss for words or opinions. Jean not only listened, but listened intelligently. She had a broad knowledge of all kinds of things. She found it exciting to keep pace with Harry's mind, and she could.

Friends say that Jean never took herself too seriously, but was always alive, vital, ready. She had no interest in designer clothes, and her style was most natural. One of the most admirable qualities about her, according to others, was that there was no spite in her, never a mean thought in her head; nobody ever heard her say anything bad about anybody.

Jean's interest in Harry was more difficult to grasp. Though she had never really had a father, Luce was not a father substitute for her. Jean laughed at that suggestion. "There was not an inch of father-figure in him. That would be the very last thing in the world I would ever think of in terms of Harry. Never, never!"

What first intrigued Jean was Harry's looks. Yet, he seemed so cold. Then, on their first date she saw him emerge into this "very, very tender man, like a big bear, clumsily tender. He was so masculine, but there was something inside him that wasn't developed. I'd never met a man who was so totally male, who knew nothing about females. He was very boyish in that way, very innocent in certain matters of life. I'm not talking about sex. I mean all kinds of things. He had no street smarts. He had a great appetite for life, but there were all kinds of things he had never really explored."

As their affair progressed, Harry transferred Jean to *Life* magazine as a researcher, a better, more interesting job.

"I had a very peculiar time at *Life,*" she said. "I hardly had any friends there. It was so weird. I felt very odd. I wasn't talking much, really not at all. I remember the head of research sent for me and said, 'Jeannie, is anything wrong with you? I mean your love life or your sex life? Is anything wrong?'

"I said 'No, no, no. Everything's lovely, thank you.' And I thought, 'Oh, baby, if you only knew! Was anything wrong!'

"But it was such a weird feeling, being there as an employee. I was totally cut off from all the others, because I never wanted to go to the parties or anything like that. So I kept very much to myself. And being very gregarious by nature, that was a rather odd situation to be in."

Even though she distanced herself, Jean was liked and admired. *Life* writer Joseph Kastner remembered her vividly: "She wore a sheath dress, and came out of it in front and behind. It would knock your eyes out. She was gay, effervescent, and bright, and she was so *nice.* She did a certain amount of checking and researching. But she wasn't very good. She could never get to work on time in the morning, so she arranged with another researcher, who would go to the drawer, take out a pocketbook that Jeannie had left there, and put it on the desk. She also put a lighted cigarette in the ashtray. Nobody was fooled."

"I caught her at that trick twice," said Marion MacPhail McDermott, then head of *Life* researchers. She recalled that Jean was beautiful, bright, eager, and energetic, "but she just didn't want to work."

Jean's mind was obviously on Harry and little else during her *Life* period. Needing advice, she told her grandfather about the affair. "I was estranged from my father and didn't have much other guidance. My grandfather and I had had our tiffs but we were very, very close," she said.

Jean was excited about telling him because he always had told her that men were only after her money. "So now I had somebody all to myself who wasn't after me for my money," she explained. "At first he was enthusiastic about us. He thought it was a marvelous match, despite the age difference, and he thought it would be absolutely wonderful for the both of us. Then, later, he came to my bedroom and said, 'I am an old man. I am the son of a Presbyterian minister, and I can do nothing to help you. I am going to die soon.' So on one hand," said Jean, "he wanted it very much and at the same time he wouldn't lift a finger."

Beaverbrook had sensed the romance from the time they all went to the theater. He knew all the symptoms because he had suffered them so often himself. He truly loved his granddaughter and was happy for her, although he might have selected a younger man for her, someone who might marry her and give her children. He knew Harry Luce was seeing something in Jean that he himself had seen so often in so many younger women. He could not fault Harry for wanting what he himself had always wanted. Beaverbrook knew Harry as a good human being. He did not truly understand him, but he liked him. Besides, it was all out of his hands. Beaverbrook could only give them his good wishes. They had his blessing, but it could not be a public blessing. There were too many people in too many positions of power who would not understand.

Jean also said that her grandfather had described Harry's Presbyterianism as "God-ridden" while his own was only inherited. Jean felt, though, that her grandfather was Prometheus-ridden, wanting to be a huge figure of power. But, then, so did Harry. Which is why, perhaps, Jean understood him so well, and so quickly.

At first, Harry and Jean always met at her apartment. Soon they were seeing each other constantly. Harry sent her roses almost every day. "He'd never send a bunch of roses. He'd send something like fifteen dozen roses at a time," she recalled. "They were always pink, because he knew I liked pink, but I mean it was absolutely absurd! All those roses! And I didn't have enough vases for all those roses, so I had a terrible time. That kind of thing Harry didn't understand—he didn't understand numbers. To tell you the truth, I wasn't too appreciative, because it made my apartment seem like a funeral home, and it was very difficult to explain my roses to anybody who came to visit."

For months, the couple never went to any public place. "My apartment was our private place." She explained, "In retrospect, what young girl could have put up with that? Maybe it was because I had lived a public life for so long and so it was now wonderful to have a private one. Otherwise, it wouldn't make sense. But then, I adored him so much."

Harry, she said, was completely relaxed and happy. "He talked and talked and told me the whole story of his life. He was the biggest talker I ever met in my life. He was just busting with talk. I never got a word in edgeways hardly." Jean also noted that Harry, who most people felt was dour and humorless, loved to laugh. "Clare later told Randolph Churchill that the reason Harry loved me was that I made him laugh. It was not a loud laugh, not an outburst, but it was a real laugh. And he would even tell funny stories," said Jean. "You should have heard him tell about the time in Portugal when he thought he was being followed. He had read in some spy novel about how to use discreetly placed cotton to test whether spies had entered a room and opened cabinets and cases. And he tried it, but there were no spies. The way he told it, was just so funny."

Harry also shared his fondest memories with Jean. "He told me how he adored his mother. He once sent me a letter about his grandson, whose mother would put him on her lap and calm him down when he got upset. And Harry said to me, 'I want you to read this letter very carefully because he's very much like me,'" she recalled.

Harry told her other things as well—that his favorite reading material as a little boy was train schedules, that he had been a virgin until he was twenty-three. He also discussed his marriages. "I know he was faithful to Lila for a long time. He felt Lila was a fine woman with good taste, and all that, a sweet person, but conventional," she continued. "He told me about this society woman he was involved with in the fashion industry. She had a crush on him, but it was no big affair. And then there was this writer with whom he *did* have a romance. But she did something that shocked him. It was something she considered a turn-on, but she turned him off, completely. He wouldn't talk about it. [This is the same woman who undressed while Harry stood outside her window years ago.]

"And then there was Clare.

"He told me that he and Clare stopped sleeping together after six months, that it was his decision; she had persuaded him that she wasn't interested in sex. When it came to women he was *so* naive; he was an innocent. Because of what Clare told him, I don't think it entered his head for one moment that she was having all those other affairs. He thought that all these men were simply filled with admiration for her. Nothing else would occur to him. I admit it sounds crazy, but I know he just thought that way."

However, Harry did talk about a general in Clare's life. "I don't know which general that was," said Jean. "There were rumors about her and our General Alexander, but this one, I think, was an American general."

Harry also complained to Jean of a seemingly trivial thing that had embittered him about Clare early in their marriage. He had shown her a speech he had written and she made fun of it. He neither forgot that nor forgave it.

Jean listened to Harry's confession, without adding her own knowledge about Clare. How shocked Harry would have been, she felt, if she had told him that his old acquaintance, Joe Kennedy, had had an affair with Clare. "Oh, no question, they did," she said. "He grabbed everybody attractive. He was nonstop!" (Clare confided to Shirley and Paul Green that John Kennedy had told her of his father's advice that a day without a lay was a day wasted.)

Jean told about how Joe Kennedy came often to visit her grandfather. "He would go to bed with one of grandfather's researchers, give her presents, and then she would mail Joe a weekly report on everything happening in our household. But grandfather's secretary would steam open the letters before she could post them, copy the contents, and give them to grandfather." This was during the war, she noted.

But Jean did not tell Harry any of this at the time. Nor did she talk about her old friend Randolph Churchill. Randolph had told Jean all about his love affair with Clare. Jean also knew of Clare's friendship with a prominent British politician and barrister—"a great ladies' man and the odds are good that she had an affair with him." Jean also knew of "a very attractive man who became an ambassador, and made a pass at Clare. He got an unusual response: 'Oh, I'm sorry, but I'm not very good at this sort of thing.' " Jean, however, did not consider Clare promiscuous.

Harry and Jean did talk a little about Jean Dalrymple. He showed Jean a letter from Clare, in which she wrote that she thought Dalrymple was probably in love with Harry. "I know Clare was obsessed with Jean, hated her, loathed her," said Campbell. "She was desperately jealous of Jean." Later, Campbell noted, Clare would find out about *their* affair and become irate. "In a letter to Harry, she referred to us as 'those big-busted women' and indicated that she had a mind and we didn't. I don't think Jean Dalrymple ever knew how near Harry came to marrying her. When I asked Harry to tell me more about Jean, he just bowed his head and said that it was a very sad story. He added 'I don't want to talk about it. Don't make me talk about it.' "

Harry told Jean about Mary, too, but insisted that she had never been his mistress. Harry even showed Jean some of Mary's letters. "Harry had talked so much about Mary that I always longed to meet her," said Jean. "Years later, we did meet, and I said 'Why on earth didn't Harry introduce us? We could have been friends all those years.' "

"I think Harry needed a female bond desperately," reflected Jean, "whether it was his mother, Mrs. McCormick, Jean, Mary, me . . ."

The marvel of all this, and perhaps a commentary on Harry Luce, was that the two Jeans and Mary really liked each other and became close friends. They were three women sharing someone very special, so special that somehow it did not stir any major jealousy in them. The only woman they resented was Clare, not simply because she was the one married to him, but because, as they saw it, she was the one hurting him.

Before long, Harry was talking about marrying Jean. He first did so in a discussion about money. "Harry had no concept of money. He had all the money in the world, but he really didn't know how much he had. He once said, 'You know, when you marry me, your standard of living is not going to be the same as it was. I'm not as rich a man as your grandfather. You can't expect to live *that* way!' And when I told Grandfather that Harry says you're three times richer than he is, Grandfather just said, 'Yeah. Quite true.' But it really wasn't."

Clare was then winding up her affairs in Rome, and Harry joined her for the farewell parties. Jean continued her work at *Life*, still keeping her secret.

George Harris, a *Life* editor, was fascinated with Jean. He found it difficult to believe that she didn't have a long line of admirers.

"Jeannie was this absolutely charming, full-bodied woman, a vivid, full-of-laughter lady. The only woman who tempted me, just being around her," he said. "She was *powerful,* one of the most powerful presences I've ever seen. She was close to a true Rubens lady. She was somewhere in between one of the Demons and Little Orphan Annie. Yet, there was this quality of innocence about her, mixed up with something else."

While Harry was in Rome, Harris took Jean home to meet his wife. Harris and his wife soon plotted to find somebody who deserved her. The man they thought of was young Hank Luce, who was in town from Washington.

The Harrises could not understand why Jean was reluctant to meet him, and when she did, why she seemed so nervous. "We couldn't figure out what's going on. I just decided that Hank's not interesting enough for her," said Harris, "but I wasn't giving up."

Several months later, when Harry was still away, Harris again invited Jean. He told her, "Jeannie, dammit, it's time you came to dinner again. And Hank's gonna be in town.' " And she laughed and said, "George, for reasons I can't tell you, this is not going to work." Soon enough the Harrises would understand what she meant.

While Harry was in New York with Jean, Clare was concluding her tenure in Rome. In December 1956, she threw her silver half-dollar into the green pool of Rome's Trevi Fountain to ensure her safe return and came home to the United States. Eisenhower and Nixon had been re-elected. There was speculation in the press that Clare might want to be ambassador to the Soviet Union, and a state department official verified her desire for the post. But her health was bad, her ambition low. She no longer felt like "the pale goddess." She went to Phoenix, Arizona, for several weeks to Elizabeth Arden's exclusive Main Chance Spa where she could be coddled, massaged, and comforted. But she was soon bored by the small talk of moneyed women. Clare wired Harry to come and keep her company at a nearby hotel, and he went. Perhaps he felt that her suspicions might be aroused if he insisted on staying in New York. And, in any divorce agreement, he would need her good will.

Clare knew nothing then of Jean Campbell. But she knew her man well enough to sense his restlessness. She also felt the need to put down new roots. Rome had been a success for both of them and she felt that it had strengthened her hold on him. In a way, it had, until he met Jean Campbell. Now, he was again torn, as he had been with Jean Dalrymple. Clare had made divorce impossible once before, and he knew she would now make it even more impossible. It was difficult to see the future clearly.

After Clare felt rested and rejuvenated, she and Harry took long walks. The winter air in Phoenix was dry, pleasant, and warm. One of the houses that caught their fancy in Phoenix was a tile-roofed Mediterranean villa with a giant olive tree out front. The house had a tremendous living room, a glassed-in porch, and ample servants quarters. It also faced the fifteenth green of a golf course.

Luce impulsively suggested they buy the house. He felt inspired and excited by this idea. Perhaps, if Clare could be happy in Phoenix, and stay there, he could more easily have an alternative life in New York with Jean. Perhaps, too, it would make a future divorce easier.

Clare's explanation for Harry's sudden decision was, "Harry's in the midst of male menopause. He likes houses." Clare enjoyed moving into different houses. She had lived in twenty-eight different places in her lifetime and seemed to regard each new one as a fresh chance at happiness. And this was a lovely house, light and airy. Clare felt at peace there. The distant mountains looked bronze. The desert, she said, "looked like Egypt without the Arabs." After a rain, "the blossoms had all the smells of Paradise." Pink and white cyclamens grew in her bedroom window; bougainvillea vines covered the terrace. She swam every day in her heated pool, drove a car for the first time in fifteen years, had her Rolleiflex and Leica cameras always available for the quick picture. To make her pleasure complete, her black poodle, Cosi Fan Tutti (named after her favorite opera), had just given birth.

Harry, naturally, found it necessary to be needed in New York and flew back frequently to continue his romance.

The happiness Jean Campbell gave him was not only the full passion of love, but of an undemanding love. She wanted nothing from him but himself, and he gave it totally. He cleared his mind of all the guilt he had ever felt, confided dreams he had never confided to anyone, and revealed a side of himself nobody had ever known.

Harry told Jean that he was going to a psychiatrist, a very famous one. He confessed that he had discussed their relationship, but had not mentioned her real name to the analyst. "What name did you use?" Jean asked.

"Kate," he told her.

"Why Kate?" she wondered.

Harry told her it came from a character in a Hemingway novel.

By this time, Jean had moved to an apartment on 94th Street, near Fifth Avenue. It was a pretty place with a bow window in the living room, and Harry came often. He surprised her by not only talking garrulously, but drinking. "I know Harry almost never drank during the day or at Time-Life dinners or parties, but he really drank a lot with me," she said. "He never drank liquor straight. He loved those Old Fashioneds and Manhattans. Drinking made him more enthusiastic and made him talk even more nonstop."

When Jean and Harry eventually started to go out occasionally for a beer, Luce lost his calm. "Who's going to see us?" he constantly asked in a state of nervous guilt.

Even though Jean never talked about her relationship with Harry at *Life,* news of their affair got around. "People began to catch on," said Robert Coughlan. In the beginning, Luce's secretary, Corinne Thrasher, let a few people know that Jean had called to ask for Harry's address. Soon, the affair became a flagrant topic of discussion among the staff.

"Harry finally made me quit *Life,* and he was right about that," said Jean. "It became too difficult."

While Harry was off with Jean, Clare was slowly recuperating after her years in Rome. She busied herself with paintings and mosaics. She planned to make a big golden tiger mosaic and even taught mosaics to the children of her servants. Through research into mosaics, she discovered the California artist, Louisa Jenkins. They met in Monterey, and Clare quickly commissioned Jenkins to design a mosaic for the chapel at Stanford as a memorial to Ann. When Jenkins mentioned her interest in scuba diving, Clare proposed they go to Florida where they would exchange lessons: mosaics for scuba diving. Clare even wrote a three-part series on scuba diving for *Sports Illustrated* and supplied her own photographs.

Scuba diving became a mystic challenge for Clare. Several times a year, she had the same nightmare of a gigantic wall of green water advancing on her and then beginning to crash over her from a hundred feet up. This dream was always deep in her soul whenever she went scuba diving.

Luce found it easier to commute from Phoenix to New York than from Mepkin to Connecticut. For a diversion in Phoenix, he and Clare frequently invited friends from New York for short stays.

One visitor was Laura Hobson, who flew in the same plane as Luce. Hobson once again worked for Luce at Time Inc., writing promotion for *Sports Illus-trated.* "Harry's relationship with Laura was now on a plateau of easy friend-ship. She was then involved in an intense affair with Ralph Ingersoll, Harry's close friend, who had left Time Inc. years ago and was now president of an investment company."

Laura sat separately en route to Phoenix because she knew he had a fetish about not sitting next to anybody he knew on a plane. In those days, it was necessary to change planes in Chicago with a half hour wait.

"Of course, I seated myself at the other end of the waiting room," said Hobson.

Luce was reading a current best-seller, *Rally Round the Flag, Boys,* and called Laura over because he couldn't understand much of the slang, "although I hear so much of it from my two boys. Should I read it and see if I can come up with some sort of glossary?" he asked her.

On the plane again, Laura passed Luce's seat en route to the lavatory and tried not to look at him. Still, she did see him out of the sides of her eyes, and what she saw startled her. "He seemed slumped sideways in his seat. He was pale and waxy-looking," she remarked. I knew something was very wrong; I knelt beside him, right there in the aisle. 'Harry, are you all right?' A stewardess came rushing over. I reached for his wrist to try for his pulse, but he yanked his hand back. 'It's nothing,' he said. 'I'm all right.' But I stayed there, kneeling beside him; his color began to return. He sat back, straightening himself up. He did look more like himself, but I was glad we were approaching the airport. Harry's chauffeur met us. During the drive to their house, Harry remained silent and so did I. Clare noticed nothing unusual when we arrived, and he told her nothing of what had happened in the plane, at least not then."

Five days later, Harry had a chest cold and Clare called the doctor. As usual, Harry minimized everything. But, afterward, when Clare brought him some soup, he sat, staring, and said, "I'm dying."

A doctor and ambulance soon arrived. "I can still vividly remember being outside in the garden when the stretcher came out carrying Harry, looking so ill, so unlike the powerful Henry Robinson Luce the whole world knew," Hobson remembered. "Clare went with him in the ambulance to St. Joseph's Hospital, and I followed. When I saw Clare at the hospital, she was talking to a nun. She then came over to me weeping. 'If anything happened to Harry, my whole life would be over,' she told me."

But Harry soon perked up considerably and told Clare: "This is not *it*. Don't pay any attention to what I said."

He was hospitalized for three weeks, and his son Hank and Tex Moore flew out to see him. When Laura went to visit him, "I myself was oddly ill at ease to see him there in bed in his pajamas, so shorn of his usual Harryness."

For Luce, the visit seemed a strain also. "I think he was unwilling to have anybody see him so ill and not in command," explained Laura.

Harry was told he had suffered a pulmonary embolism followed by a coronary occlusion. For the rest of his life, he would be on anticoagulant drugs. "The decision had been made there in the hospital, surely by Clare herself, that the full truth must be kept from the press, from the stockholders, from the stock market, where Time stock might plummet," said Hobson. "As far as the world knew, he had been ill with pneumonia. Clare told everyone that Harry simply had pneumonia."

While Harry was recovering, he and Clare played bezique and Scrabble. She had artfully learned the subtler way of losing to him in Scrabble. The ferocity of their competitiveness had lessened.

They also played bridge. Harry grew fascinated, and invited *Sports Illustrated* expert Charles Goren, who soon became a fixture in Phoenix. Goren gave them both lessons and also played with them in New York. It was best to play with Harry while you were "dead tired," said Goren, "because you can always take a nap while Harry counts his points." Goren observed that Harry might be a better player if he wasn't so afraid of making a mistake: "He's too proud." Luce put Goren on a *Time* cover.

Clare invited Father Murray to stay with them for a while, because Harry liked him. Perhaps, also, Harry now had a greater sense of his mortality and therefore a fresh interest in conversion. But Harry's religious sense remained fixed. Nor had his illness precipitated any soul-searching. "Looking into himself was no habit of his," said Father Murray. "He said his prayers on his knees every night. He said he'd try to do better. After that, he'd sleep soundly, leaving things up to God."

Jean was worried. When Harry was in Phoenix, or anywhere, he wrote or called her regularly. Suddenly, there was this long stretch of silence. Then came word from friends that Harry was ill. "I rang up his secretary right away, and said, 'Is it true that Mr. Luce is ill?' And she said, 'Yes, he's ill.' The word she used was 'pneumonia.' I got a letter two days afterward. He wrote to me from the hospital, saying that he'd had a heart attack and that it was all hushed up."

After some months, Harry was back at work in New York. But he now seemed changed. He told Corinne Thrasher: "I'll never retire. I'll die at my desk."

"Harry talked about death and age," said Jean. "He felt he was very old.' This was just two months before his sixtieth birthday. He said that, even at *Time* magazine, he was feeling like an 'old chicken.' He certainly didn't look old. He was still a vital man. But he couldn't put death out of his mind."

"Every time I pass a graveyard," he told Jean, "I think I'm going to be a much longer time in that graveyard than I've been on earth here. This sense comes to one as one grows older. Death: You think about it every day, in some way or another."

" 'When you are old and gray and full of sleep . . .' That's the poem he told me to remember always," said Jean.

HARRY'S illness had diverted Clare for a time, but now he was better, and so now she began to grow restless. With restlessness, came a revival of her fierce ambitions. Scrabble and bridge were not enough for Clare at any age. She told her friend Elsa Maxwell that she might write a new play, and that she had definitely had had enough of public life.

President Eisenhower's chief of staff, Sherman Adams, knew otherwise. "After she got through being the ambassador to Italy, she made a probe of the possibilities of becoming, if not a roving ambassador, a personal presidential emissary around the world," he reported. "We had an interesting debate and discussion at the White House as to just what we were going to suggest that Mrs. Luce might usefully do and nobody could think of anything."

That October, President Eisenhower sent Clare as his personal representative to attend the funeral of Pope Pius XII. She went in the same plane with Secretary of State John Foster Dulles and returned five days later as Eisenhower's emissary to the coronation of Pope John XXIII.

When reporters asked if she would take another ambassadorial job, Clare replied, "Irvin Cobb was once asked if he planned to attend a big society party. He said, 'No, I'm not, for three reasons. Number one is that I haven't been invited. Which makes the other two academic.' "

Ellis Briggs, the U.S. ambassador to Brazil, repeated a story, most probably apocryphal, that Dulles had queried Mrs. Luce about a return to diplomacy, and she reportedly proposed that since Great Britain had a queen, the United States ought to have an ambassadress in London. Dulles pointed out that the U.S. embassy in London "had been rented to a solvent young American called Jock Whitney for the duration of the Eisenhower Administration." But, if Mrs. Luce would be good enough to put a globe in front of her and spin it, and then spear the globe with her forefinger, any place her finger touched would be hers for the asking.

"And Clare is supposed to have said, 'Thank you very much, Mr. Secretary.' Zip! And she poked Rio de Janiero, which was the end of my assignment there," said Briggs.

Three months later, John Foster Dulles asked Harry Luce about his wife's health. The White House then leaked the news that Clare Boothe Luce was slated to be the new ambassador to Brazil.

Clare's version of this varies. She claimed it was Dulles's idea and she was "absolutely flabbergasted." She had discussed it with Harry who had said, "It's a great country. You haven't been able to get back on track [with writing] and you enjoyed being an ambassador, and you did well—so sure."

"Same conditions?" asked Clare, thinking that he would spend six months a year with her.

"Well, I don't know Latin America, and I think I ought to. So the same conditions would interest me."

Harry was even more interested in the way her appointment would reframe his life. Once again, he could commute between two separate lives. It would be difficult to spend too much time away from Jean, but he might always manage to come back a little more frequently and a little more often. Time Inc. had its demands, too.

Clare had recently undergone two minor operations on her foot and refused to come to Washington for briefings until she didn't have to arrive in a wheelchair. "I'm going to walk in there on my two feet," she insisted.

Meanwhile, she started studying Portuguese and scoured her files for South American contacts. Clare also ordered 10,000 new calling cards as the ambassador to Brazil.

As it turned out, all this was slightly premature.

Clare's first problem arose when Time quoted an unidentified American embassy official, saying that American aid to Bolivia had been wasted and that the only solution was to "abolish Bolivia—let her neighbors divide up the country and its problems." Bolivians promptly stoned the American embassy and burned the American flag, as well as copies of Time. Columnist Drew Pearson quickly questioned the advisability of sending Mrs. Luce to Brazil, since Bolivia had a long border with Brazil.

The Senate usually waived hearings for anyone who had previously been confirmed as an ambassador, but Senator Wayne Morse of Oregon had some scores to settle. Time had hit him hard when he switched from the Republican Party to become a Democrat. As a member of the Foreign Relations Committee, his voice had some clout. He couldn't stop her nomination in the committee but he did make a three-hour speech against Clare, using the theme, "Is she honest? Is she reliable?" He quoted her many diatribes against President

Roosevelt. Republican Senator Dirksen protested these earlier references, saying: "Why beat on an old bag of bones?"

Quick with a quip, Democratic Senator Hubert Humphrey stood up with a smile, "I must rise to the defense of the lady . . ."

An embarrassed Dirksen rose to explain that the "old bones" referred to the old references, not to the lady.

Discussing these distressful events with her husband, Clare said: "Harry, it's not too late for me to go to Ike and say, 'I think perhaps this is something you should give to a career man, not only for my sake. I mean, I was perfectly willing to ride out the storm for the sake of Nixon and the upcoming American elections [Clare supported Nixon in the upcoming election and did not want to be a liability for him].' "

"At this point, I think, Foster [Dulles] died," Clare explained. "Right before, he called me from the hospital, and it just really broke my heart, because he said, 'Well, Clare, you're one of the few people that I'm telephoning, and I'm calling you because I know you will go down there and straighten that thing out. I have every confidence in you. God bless you.' "

The Senate agreed with Dulles, not Morse, and voted 79–11 to confirm Clare.

Brazil was attempting to industrialize, but agriculturally, it was still a one-crop country, which was crucifying the Brazilians economically. The Eisenhower-Dulles plan was to send Clare Luce down with the message that Brazil wasn't going to get any more American money. "I knew my mission was going to be a hideous failure, sheer disaster," said Clare.

Failure was something Clare never wanted to face. Furthermore, she began to feel that Brazil would be a bureaucratic nightmare, and to make matters worse, she had heard that the mosquitoes were formidable.

Meanwhile, Harry had already arranged for an office and a manager in Rio, similar to his setup in Rome. His secretary was soliciting Clare's help in getting Luce some lightweight clothes for the hot weather. She attached a copy of his clothing needs.

But Clare was clearly unhappy. "The more I found out about Brazil, the more certain I was that it was the worst can of worms that could possibly have been handed to anyone. Furthermore, I wouldn't have time to make a record, because if Nixon didn't make it, I was out with the bad end of the stick in Brazil," she said.

"I knew Clare didn't want to go to Brazil," said her friend Shirley Clurman. "She'd say, 'Well, Beth tells me so-and-so about Brazil.' She didn't want to *say* she didn't want to go. She'd prefer to do something complicated than do something simple."

Clare's solution was to issue a statement via her old friend Stan Swinton, then a top executive at the Associated Press. "Just say this, Stan," Clare told him. " 'I am grateful for the overwhelming vote of confirmation in the Senate. We must now wait until the dust settles. My difficulties of course go some years back and began when Senator Wayne Morse was kicked in the head by a horse.' "

It was vintage Clare, acid and witty. But Swinton quickly warned her, "Clare, you don't want to say that. You won. This will just start things all over again. You know how clannish the U.S. Senate is. Morse can make lots of trouble."

Clare insisted, and Swinton released the statement. The country laughed and the Senate bristled. Clare next heard from her friend Senator Lyndon Johnson. "Now Clare, honey, you know how fond I am of you, but you have insulted the dignity of the Senate."

Dignity, she replied, was a two-way street, and Morse had not been very dignified about her and she reserved the right to reply.

Johnson warned her that if she didn't apologize, the hearings might be reopened. "Good, that's exactly what I want them to do."

President Eisenhower publicly defended Clare, saying her remark was "ill-advised" but "perfectly human."

"I knew Clare well," Swinton later told a friend, "and I think it was her way of saying she really didn't want the job."

Clare then told her husband: "You got me into this, now help me get out of it."

Luce issued a statement, saying that he had asked his wife to resign the appointment because the attacks on her had been too bitter and because they had been aimed at him.

In her letter of resignation, Clare talked of the climate of good will being poisoned by "extraordinarily ugly charges," and the threat of "a continuing harassment of my mission." The underlying message was that many men hate women who fight back.

Eisenhower was not happy when she told him.

Senator John F. Kennedy was one of those who voted for Clare Luce, saying, "I've known Mrs. Luce all my life. I think she did a fine job in Italy." Years later, Kennedy told her, "You know, Clare, I think you made a terrible mistake in resigning from Brazil."

"Well, could be, but history runs on one track only, and you never can tell how things would have turned out had I gone."

"I can tell you how they would have turned out. I would have kept you there."

"You would have, Mr. President?"

"Certainly."

Clare reminded him that John Cabot had replaced her and was himself replaced within six months. "The only difference between me and Mr. Cabot is that he was kicked out on page twenty-two of *The New York Times,* and I would have been kicked out on page one."

For Clare it was a bitter pill—the first time she had ever really quit without fighting.

Harry kept Jean updated on the running fight. Jean was not happy that Harry contemplated the six months' arrangement, because he was the love of her life and she wanted him close. Harry had mixed feelings, uncertain now of the immediate future. Clare was too restless to spend most of her time in Phoenix and she would be in New York longer, and more often. Things would again get more complicated. He liked neither complications nor confrontations, but he did know one thing for certain—he truly loved Lady Jean Campbell.

Clare accepted an offer from *McCall's* for a monthly column, and decided to spend more time in Ridgefield. She also spent a great deal of time with her dearest friend Buffy Cobb, who was dying. Buffy had been the little girl who shared her apple tree, and later shared all her dreams and frustrations and some of her travels. She even converted to Roman Catholicism, with Clare as her godmother. Buffy had made some small marks of her own: She had written a play, a biography of her father, and a novel which was made into a movie. Buffy's final days were filled with intense suffering, and Clare was there with her, at all hours of the day and night. Those who long ago had classified Clare as cold would have marveled at the compassionate woman at her dying friend's bedside in the hospital. Clare could not afford to lose a friend; she had too few.

Harry's time with Jean Campbell was gloriously happy for him. He laughed more with her, drank more with her, and made love more with her. He also shared poetry with her.

Few at Time Inc. would have recognized this man they thought they knew so well. None of the other women in his life would have believed it. The caterpillar had become a butterfly.

He kept revealing himself to Jean in a way that would have made his analyst envious. One of Luce's big regrets, he told her, was that he never had fought in a war. It was the main way, he felt, that a man might prove himself. He also regretted that he had never belonged to a small American community, and thus established roots.

Luce also revealed that he cared much more about the niceties of life than he had ever let on. "I know people have said that he didn't notice good food, but that was absolute nonsense," said Jean. "He always noticed *everything* about the food we ate when he was with me, everything! He *did* care about it. I had a French cook and she was extremely good. Then I started doing it myself and took great care with it. I'm afraid he liked all the wicked things best—pies of all sorts. He loved sweets, absolutely adored them. When we were both making plans for our future, we were going to have an apartment in New York and I said, 'Great! Then we'll have a cook.' And he said, 'Cook? No way—you're doing the cooking.' And if I felt angry about something and didn't bother much about the meal, just threw things together, he noticed it immediately, and said that the food was not so good."

As their relationship entered its second year, she observed more and more things about him: How proud he always was of the high polish on his shoes, but otherwise how dowdy he was about his clothes. He had a funny old gray hat he refused to part with. She bought clothes for him, especially shirts. She thought he looked marvelous in a blue shirt with a blue tie. The only jewelry he wore was a silver ring with a blue stone "a very male ring, and he would lend it to me sometimes. He had the most beautiful hands of any human being I've ever seen, long, not thin, but with thin masculine fingers. They were so sensitive, they looked exquisite," she recalled.

Luce was with her almost every night when he was in New York—if Clare was in Phoenix or Ridgefield. Music had long been part of his life, but it was not with Jean. With her, it was books and poetry. When they were not making love, they were reading aloud to each other. He loved anything by Willa Cather, preferred Roman history to Greek, and appreciated anything theological, particularly the Bible. Marcus Aurelius was another favorite.

"He loved Yeats," said Jean. "He once gave me a copy of Yeats's poetry and showed me that lovely one about 'The Pilgrim Soul.' "

"I loved the one about 'A Pity Beyond All Telling,' and a day or two later, I read it aloud to him."

Two of the lines read:

A pity beyond all telling
Is hid in the heart of love.

"I hate that poem," he said. "I hate it. There is no pity in love. It has nothing to do with pity. Nothing."

"I think love has *everything* to do with pity," Jean told him. "It may be that Clare played on his pity too long," she reflected. "She gave him the feeling that she needed desperately to be looked after. The hold she had on him was completely a hold of tremendous compassion."

And Harry was still very much in Clare's grasp. When he was with her, he quietly settled into a routine of walks, bridge, golf, and a small circuit of social dinners. If Clare had any inkling of Harry's double life, she did not show it.

It was not difficult for Jean to get a job with one of her grandfather's London newspapers, the *Evening Standard.* "Harry helped me write my first political article, and it was about Nixon, who was then vice president. Harry gave me some great ideas, terrific ideas. He was a superb editor, and he could see what was wrong with a story. But that was the only time I asked him to help me on a story. I never asked again.

"I did go to the Soviet Union for the *Standard.* He hated the idea of my going there and didn't want to hear anything about the plans for the trip. When I came back, my apartment was filled with 15,000 pink you-know-whats."

It was almost three years before Jean and Harry left their cocoon for more than a quick beer in the neighborhood. "It was very strange. I would say, 'Let's go out to the Bronx and have dinner tonight.' He always found it very difficult to talk to waiters; I had to do it. Or, I used to insist sometimes that we meet in funny parts of New York. Once I asked him to meet me in Union Square to show me where *Time* first started. But outside our cocoon, he was always very nervous. And when he was very nervous, he still sometimes stuttered."

But in the offices of Time Inc., Harry did not stutter.

He was also a commanding, assured presence in his role as behind-the-scenes statesman. Luce was often invited to Washington to meet with the man he had helped make president. Though he quickly grew disillusioned with Ike and felt that he was not dynamic or assertive enough, he never gave up his dream of serving him in an official capacity.

When John Foster Dulles died in 1959, Luce really wanted to succeed him as secretary of state. "He talked to Emmet John Hughes about it, and he talked to me about it," said Grover, "and he hired Raymond Lesley Buell, former editor of *Foreign Affairs,* as a full-time employee to draft position papers. It was almost a joke among us that Harry was practicing to be secretary of state." Eisenhower, however, had other plans, and named Christian Herter to the post.

Once again, Harry turned back to a world he could still control: Time Inc. By 1960, the total assets of Time Inc. were $230,585,000. Luce decided it was time for a "reorganization of expectations." His heart attack, still stark in his mind, prompted him to focus on a successor. He picked forty-five-year-old Hedley Donovan, a handsome, serious man with a decisive mind and quick smile who, as managing editor of *Fortune* for six years, had transformed it into the magazine Luce always wanted.

When Luce began inviting him to dinner at his apartment, Donovan, a former Rhodes scholar "was shocked the first time I noticed in the beautifully paneled library that the book spines were fake."

In a succession of one-on-one dinners, recalled Donovan, Luce talked about "the bad state of the modern novel, the politics of America, Asia, and Europe, a couple of good movies he had seen lately, and the theories of a certain theologian I hadn't heard of."

These dinners usually ended around ten P.M. "He would stop talking, slap his hands down on his knees, peer at me pleasantly from under the massive eyebrow-thatch, and if necessary haul out his vest-pocket watch," recalled Donovan. "If you still didn't get the idea, he might say, 'Well, I mustn't keep you.' "

One evening, as Donovan recalled, Luce said "in a somewhat apologetic way, that he had a personal matter to discuss. He wondered if Donovan would be interested "not right away, in a few years or so," in having his job as editor in chief of *Time.* He added that he had considered "just leaving it up for grabs, you know, blood running in the streets." However, he preferred to have it settled.

Donovan said he would not be interested in the job unless Luce understood how he felt about certain past unfairnesses in *Time.*

"I felt *Time* had been quite unfair in several instances to Harry Truman. Harry agreed that this was so. I also felt *Time* had been somewhat unfair in the first Eisenhower-Stevenson campaign." Luce agreed the magazine had been rough on Stevenson, but felt it important that the Democrats not become the permanent governing party.

When Hedley came home, his wife Dorothy asked, "Did you get fired?"

"No, he wants me to be *him,*" said Donovan.

A friend who heard the news later said: "It must be like being elected Moses."

Two other men might have had Donovan's job. John Shaw Billings, Luce's deputy, had been a clear favorite. Before becoming editorial director, he had been managing editor of *Time* and the first managing editor of *Life.* Billings was held in high regard by much of the senior staff as a true professional. But Billings, who had detested Luce's liberal stance on civil rights, had moved back to South Carolina after a black couple moved into his New York apartment house.

After Billings's death, his diaries revealed his love-hate relationship with Luce. Incredibly Harry had never suspected any bad feelings from Billings.

The other possible candidate for Luce's mantle was Emmet John Hughes. His peers felt he was more of a staff officer than a commanding officer, and

Clare said, "Emmet wasn't really that ambitious to run the empire, he only wanted to be secretary of state."

Emmet was the last in Luce's line of surrogate sons. Harry seemed to need such sons. Shy with his own boys, he searched for substitutes who could argue with him without qualm, probe him sharply, give him respect and deep affection. He wanted young men to remind him of what he was and what he might have been.

Like John Hersey and Teddy White, Emmet was a liberal. His thesis at Princeton was "The Church and the Liberal Society." In his days as a Time-Life correspondent in postwar Europe, Hughes's code name was "the Florentine." He was a suave courtier, handsome, brilliant, smooth, and very sharp but ephemeral.

With the death of Stalin, Hughes (and Eisenhower) saw a chance to thaw the cold war. But Luce did not. He and Hughes disagreed on many issues, often strongly, but their relationship remained warm and deep. Luce confided his personal problems to Emmet as he did to few others, and Hughes reciprocated. "When Emmet had problems with his marriage, he came to Luce. And Emmet was one of the few who knew all about Harry and me," said Campbell.

When Hughes returned from his tour of duty in Rome, Luce asked Donovan to put Hughes on *Fortune.* Donovan thought his articles were excellent after they had been "duly de-purpled." Hughes then became head of all *Time* foreign correspondents. "At one time," said Hughes, "Harry made a pitch to make me ambassador-at-large for *Time* and travel all over the world. But I didn't want any part of it." Hughes finally left to work as senior advisor to Nelson Rockefeller.

Still, he and Luce remained friends. The break ultimately came when he wrote *Ordeal of Power,* a book detailing his disillusionment with Eisenhower and bitterly attacking him.

Emmet sent Harry a note saying that *Time* could review his book in whatever way it wanted. But he did not want to have the experience of Luce saying he hadn't read the review. He wanted to make sure that, like so many stories in *Time,* it had Luce's imprimatur. Luce read the book. "I remember Harry turning to me and saying, 'How could Emmet *lie* that way?' recalled Shirley Clurman. "I got him that job! He doesn't say that in the book. I *hate* that book!"

The *Time* review that finally appeared, with Luce's approval, referred to Hughes as "a disgruntled ex-employee of the Eisenhower administration," and a Democratic agent who somehow infiltrated the Republican establishment. According to one editor, Luce personally made the original review "even more savage" but had been persuaded to tone it down.

Hughes then fired off a letter to Luce. The tone and language was so unforgivable to Harry that it ended their relationship for good. In fact, when Luce and Hughes ran into each other at a party given by Dick and Shirley Clurman, Luce refused to shake his hand. "Luce just walked away," recalled Dick Clurman. "They never spoke again, never made up. And Luce had *loved* Emmet Hughes."

In 1960, Time Inc. had a new home in Rockefeller Center. The new forty-seven-story Time-Life building had a spectacular view of the city, the river, and the gardens. Presiding over the new headquarters was a new chairman of the board, Andrew Heiskell, the former publisher of *Life,* who had replaced Luce's brother-in-law, Maurice "Tex" Moore. Moore stayed on as chief counsel and director.

In the new hierarchy, James Linen became president of Time Inc. Linen was the grandson of the old family friend on whose Pennsylvania farm Luce had once worked. Luce had regarded Linen's family almost as warmly as his own. Roy Larsen, formerly Time Inc. president, became chairman of the board of directors executive committee. C. D. Jackson was made publisher of *Life.*

Bernard Yudain, a Time Inc. executive, finally asked Luce what everyone in the company wanted to know.

"I have one question about Heiskell and Linen," he said.

'What's that?"

"Who's the boss?"

Yudain recalled that Luce "actually had sort of a Machiavellian grin on his face. He raised those big eyebrows and said, 'That's what we're gonna find out!' "

"That, to me, was one of the most revealing sides of Harry I've ever heard," Yudain said. "He did that once before with two men vying to be managing editor of *Time.* He just wanted to throw them in the pit and see what happens."

Having settled the top management of Time Inc., Luce again turned himself to national affairs. It was 1960, and John F. Kennedy was running for president.

Harry had a complicated concern about the campaign. Part of it was expressed in his reply to his friend Bill Benton, who had asked why he had written an introduction to young John Kennedy's first book, *Why England Slept,* in 1940. Luce simply snapped, "Joe."

Joseph Kennedy, then ambassador to the Court of St. James, had called Luce from London asking him to write a foreword for his son's book. Luce read the manuscript, liked it, and agreed to do it. He did not remember meeting the young Kennedy before publication.

Luce would not have been flattered to know that he was the second choice. The first was Professor Harold Laski, who had taught Kennedy at the London School of Economics. Laski had refused on grounds that it was "the book of an immature mind; that if it hadn't been written by the son of a very rich man, he wouldn't have found a publisher."

On another occasion, Luce had yielded to the senior Kennedy's persuasive power. In 1956, when J.F.K. had made a run for the Democratic vice presidential nomination, the Luces were Joe Kennedy's guests on the French Riviera. Luce cabled his editors that they might well devote more space to John Kennedy because he had emerged as a considerable national figure.

The political problem for the Luces was not only the father, but the son. As they got to know Jack, they both liked him. Clare liked him very much indeed. Ted Sorensen, Kennedy's longtime aide and friend, recalled that during the campaign in the southwest, John Kennedy stopped off in Phoenix for a long private visit with Clare Luce. Later, Sorensen perceptively said, "They liked each other in the way that two tigers like each other."

Kennedy told Sorensen: "She's bitter because her power and influences are derived from her association with men."

Clare was still a highly attractive woman. Was she attractive enough to intrigue John Kennedy? It would not have been the first time that the son followed the father in a romantic encounter with the same woman. There was also a political prize in the package. Clare had been a devastating hatchet man for Republicans during previous elections. Whatever was said or done that afternoon with Kennedy, the result was that Clare Luce sat quietly on the sidelines during the election She did not allow the Republicans to use her against Jack. Nor did she give him any strong voice of support.

Harry still had mixed feelings about Kennedy. When J.F.K. won the Oregon primary, *Time* correspondent Stanley Karnow recalled Luce saying, "Well, it looks like we'll have to stop Jack." However, when Kennedy became the front runner for the Democratic presidential nomination, *Time* did its first cover story for him, which even the highly critical Joe Kennedy considered "a great job."

During the Democratic National Convention in Los Angles, Luce received a call from Joe Kennedy saying he was en route to Europe and was stopping off in New York. Could he see Luce that Friday? They made an appointment for five PM at Luce's Waldorf apartment.

Luce then made plans to have dinner with his son Hank at seven, assuming that his talk with Joe Kennedy would be done by then. The elder Kennedy had given Hank a job as his special assistant on the Hoover Commission, the young Luce's first job after college.

Kennedy's plane was late and he joined them for dinner, ruddily hale, hearty, and happy. He consumed a couple of lobsters, and then discussed his son's future policies. Luce said that it naturally must be assumed that young Kennedy would have to be "left of center" on domestic affairs.

"Old Joe broke in with blazing blue eyes, 'Harry, you know goddamn well no son of mine could be a goddamn liberal,' " Luce recalled.

Luce insisted Kennedy had to take a liberal position to win as a Democrat, but then added, "If Jack shows any sign of going soft on communism [in foreign policy], then we would clobber him."

During the evening, Joe Kennedy discussed Luce's son Hank. "Why don't you buy him a safe congressional seat?"

"What do you mean by that?"

"Come on, Harry, you and I both know how to do that. Of course it can be done."

Joe Kennedy and Harry watched the Democratic National Convention together on TV. As Adlai Stevenson and Hubert Humphrey preceded Jack to the rostrum, Joe made derogatory remarks. "There was no respect for *any* of these liberals," said Harry's son Hank. "He just thought they were all fools on whom he had played this giant trick."

Luce was not overly impressed with Kennedy's acceptance speech but did not puncture his guest's glory.

"I want to thank you for all that you've done, Harry," declared Joe Kennedy as he said good-bye to his host. Then he effusively repeated his thanks.

Luce later recalled being "a little taken aback by it. I began to wonder—did we do too much?"

Time soon did much more. Managing editor Otto Fuerbringer became ill and was replaced for the duration of the campaign by Tom Griffith. The more liberal Griffith quickly announced a policy of absolute fairness, saying the best that could be said of each candidate each week, "and the worst." A disgruntled Republican leader was quoted: "This is a heck of a year for *Time* to turn objective!"

Griffith recalled that Luce never asked to see a story in advance, although he did discuss what stories were being planned. Noted historian Arthur M. Schlesinger, Jr., a friend and aide to the Kennedys, then commented, "This is the best *Time* political coverage since 1936, the best and the fairest."

Luce's curious new stance of fairness attracted much attention in the press. *The New York Times* quoted Harry as saying, "Mr. Luce has in no sense of the word come out for Richard M. Nixon and neither have any of the Time Inc. publications." *The Wall Street Journal* reported: "*Time* toys with the surprising notion of backing Kennedy." Kennedy himself asked Bill Benton if there was any chance of Luce ever becoming a Democrat. Benton's answer was a quick and curt "no." In his thank-you note to Harry for an editorial lunch, Kennedy added that he had "a faint feeling that your 1960 endorsement of the book may be the last one I shall get."

During the campaign, Luce gave a dinner at the Waldorf for Vice President Nixon and invited eight of the top Time Inc. editors. "Nixon was his usual stilted self, and he talked in his almost speechlike manner. At one point he said, 'If I weren't a Quaker, I think that I'd rather be a Presbyterian more than anything else because it's so easy,' " recalled Otto Fuerbringer. There followed a terrible moment, absolute silence. "Everybody looked at Luce and you could see him looking at Nixon and wondering whether to argue with him, whether to pick him up on it, whether to explode. There was about a thirty-second silence. Finally, Luce let it pass."

"I think Harry thought Nixon was not classy enough to be president," said *Time*'s Washington correspondent, Hugh Sidey.

"I don't know, I just don't like Nixon. I guess we have to support him, but I don't like him," Luce said. "I don't agree with Kennedy on most things. But I like him." Later Luce expanded on that: "Dammit, why am I so attracted to Jack Kennedy? I've always been attracted to radicals and Communists and people like that, but why am I so attracted to Jack Kennedy?" Later he concluded, "He seduces me!"

Yet, Hedley Donovan insists that Luce was never seriously tempted by the notion of endorsing Kennedy. The decision was made by a small group whom Luce called The College of Cardinals, "leaving it clear who was pope," noted Donovan. They included the editorial director, the managing editors, and John Jessup, the chief editorial writer of *Life*. They were all for Nixon, whom they felt had the edge of experience. They also felt that Kennedy's attacks on Eisenhower policy "were generally unconvincing." Tom Griffith argued for Kennedy, but the *Life* editorial finally came out for Nixon, saying that he had "done more for the nation and the world."

But Luce was still vulnerable to the persuasiveness of the Kennedys, as Jean Campbell recounted. "Harry told me that *Life* was going to run a story saying that Billy Graham was going to come out for Nixon. And then Jack Kennedy found out about it and rang Harry up and said, 'It's just not fair, you know,' and persuaded Harry not to run the story. I thought it was a strange thing for Harry to do, especially since he had supported Nixon. Maybe Joe Kennedy called Harry and put the pressure on too. The double-whammy. But he only told me about the Jack-whammy, not the Joe-whammy. Maybe because he knew how I felt about old slimy Joe.

"Anyway, if Jack had been running against Eisenhower, and had called Harry to stop the article, Harry would have told him to 'forget it.' But with Nixon, it was different because he didn't really like Nixon. I was infinitely more liberal than he was, and we never talked politics, but I just thought it was an unfair thing for him to do."

Luce himself privately anticipated the Nixon defeat, but saw a Democratic victory as something journalistically exciting, something which would shake up the country. Moreover, a Democratic president might even sock the idle rich with a tough program of tax reform, which he thought Eisenhower should have done.

After Kennedy's victory, Bill Benton reminded the president-elect that Luce treated him very well in his magazines during the campaign and that this may have accounted for the one tenth of one percent that was his margin of victory. Kennedy agreed.

Luce himself wrote Kennedy a note, pointing out that the *Life* editorial had said respectful and complimentary things, comparing Kennedy to Theodore Roosevelt. This, Luce noted, was as praiseworthy as he could get. Donovan then wrote Luce a note saying he felt Time Inc. might have more influence on Kennedy than they had on Ike since Kennedy was "a reader." Eisenhower, basically, was not.

Once again, the issue of secretary of state loomed large in Luce's mind. He knew he had no chance this time, but he still was concerned that Kennedy was considering Senator William Fulbright for the post. He asked his *Time* Washington bureau chief, John Steele, to pass on his concern to Kennedy. The president then called Luce for his recommendation.

Luce's choice was Dean Rusk, who had made a deep impression on him at a dinner of the China Institute with an all-out attack on Chinese Communists. Others gave similar support to Rusk, and Kennedy finally gave him the position.

"I like Luce," Kennedy once said. "He reminds me of my father. He's entitled to have his magazine say what he wants because he made it. He's like a cricket chirping away. After all, he made a lot of money through his own individual enterprise, so he naturally thinks that individual enterprise can do anything. I don't mind people like that. They have earned the right to talk that way."

At the Inaugural Ball, the Luces were guests of the Kennedys. On the bus to the gala, Lyndon Johnson sat next to Clare. She could not pass up the chance to ask him about something he had told her shortly before the Democratic National Convention, where it seemed certain that he would be the presidential nominee. Clare had asked him then, "Lyndon, what are you going to do if you don't get it? Will you agree to go on Kennedy's ticket?"

"Well, you should have heard him," Clare said later. "He had a terrible foul mouth, you know. He and I knew each other well. He said, 'Clare honey, no *way* will I ever join that sonofabitch.'

"So now here I am on the bus, and here is the vice president and I said, 'Lyndon, come clean. Come clean.' And he said, 'Clare honey, Bird's been wanting me something fierce to slow down, and my health ain't been good lately, and, well, I thought this job might suit me a spell.'

"I leaned forward and repeated, 'Come clean, Lyndon.'

"And he leaned close and said, 'Clare, I looked it up; one out of every four presidents has died in office. I'm a gamblin' man, darlin', and this is the only chance I got.' "

30

✥

THE 1960 election had absorbed much of Luce's attention, and Jean Campbell wisely stayed in the background. She was there when he needed her, but did not pressure him for time or attention. But now, things were different. With an exciting young president, the world was at a crossroads; and so was Lady Jean. She had come to a turning point in her relationship with Luce. She loved Harry more than anyone and always would. She knew how completely content and happy he was with her. If Harry could have frozen this moment in time, he would have. But Jean increasingly felt herself living at the end of a long string. Harry could only see her when Clare was in Phoenix or Ridgefield, or off scuba diving. This made their life together unpredictable. She now wanted predictability. She wanted Harry always. She wanted a home. She wanted children.

Earlier, she had confided to an old friend, Nicholas Phipps, and he had advised her that her situation was intolerable, that she should confront Harry and insist that he divorce Clare and marry her.

"I remember the date. It was March 15, the Ides of March," said Jean. "Harry was coming over for tea that day. And I said, 'Harry, there's something I want to discuss with you.'

"His reaction was that I should give him time, until the fifteenth of July. I asked him what he had to do and he said he had to talk to his lawyers. And that's when he told me again about Clare being a manic-depressive and suicidal. He feared what she would do if he again raised the issue of divorce."

Jean then told Harry, "Well, before you even *approach* thinking about it, I want you to go and have a checkup to make sure you can have children. I don't want to marry you if you can't have children."

The doctor discovered Harry had a prostate condition that required surgery, but that the surgery could be done in such a way that he could still have children. He proceeded with the operation.

"I think he loved the idea of our having children. Had he married me first, Harry would've been a different human being. Oh, we'd have had an incredible life," Jean said.

The marriage idea increasingly excited Luce. Knowing that Jean had always wanted to be a Catholic, he urged her to pursue it. "You don't want to get into it after we've married," he told her. But after making some inquiries, Jean learned that her marriage to a divorced Presbyterian would present problems. "But at that point, I was willing to give up being a Catholic so I could marry Harry," she said.

Then Luce began happily redesigning the house in Ridgefield. "He even drew diagrams," said Jean. "There would be a bedroom for both of us, for one thing. It had grated upon him, living with Clare, sleeping in two bedrooms."

For the rest of her life, Jean wondered: "What would have happened if I had never proposed to Harry? Our relationship would have gone on forever and ever, amen. But my great urge was to have children."

During this period, Clare felt that her life with Harry was pleasant, but dull. He seemed much more distant and was less frequently in residence. His power no longer spelled anything important in her future because politics was dead for her. She could not expect any prize political plum from a Democratic president, no matter what their relationship. Perhaps this was now the time to leave Harry.

Harry had agreed months before to let her build an idyllic house in Hawaii. With that house, and all the money she could ever spend, she could explore her writing talent, enjoy her many friends, travel the world. She could also pick and choose among the many men still willing to court her and do it without fear of publicity or guilt.

She confided all this to Shirley Clurman, who had become a kind of substitute daughter. An attractive, bright young woman. Shirley now handled Time Inc. promotion and publicity. Clurman would later be one of the few beneficiaries named in Clare's will.

Talking about Harry with Shirley, Clare remarked sadly, without bitterness: "We never see each other. You know, when I'm here, he's away; and when I'm away, he's here. There's really no sense going on."

Harry carefully made his move. As his personal advisor, he chose Roswell Gilpatric, a young partner in his brother-in-law Tex Moore's law firm, Cravath, Swaine, and Moore. Gilpatric's name frequently appeared in the social columns, coupled with some of the most celebrated beauties of his time. Gilpatric was not only handsome, but had a reputation for brains and great sophistication. He had been one of Kennedy's ardent supporters and would later serve in his administration as assistant secretary of defense. Like Luce, Gilpatric was a Presbyterian with a Hotchkiss-Yale background.

"Luce had decided to get a divorce, and for some reason had insisted that I be his lawyer," recalled Gilpatric. "I told him, 'I'm not a divorce lawyer; I'm a corporate lawyer.'" But Luce insisted on Gilpatric.

When Harry initially approached Clare for a divorce, this time things went smoothly. She got a tough divorce lawyer. Luce's attorney intimated that there really wasn't any dispute about money. Clare was to get some $200,000 a year plus the new Hawaiian house and the house in Ridgefield.

Harry then told Jean that Clare was not only very amenable, but had even suggested to him, "It would be much easier for me to get a divorce if I knew you had somebody else."

Of course, she didn't mean it. When she read an item in Cholly Knicker-bocker's column in the New York *Journal American* that suggested an impending Luce divorce and mentioned Lady Jean Campbell, Clare was enraged.

"I got a telephone call in the office," said Shirley Clurman. "Clare screamed at me, 'How could you not tell me? I thought you were my friend. All you care about is your loyalty to Harry!' I was so shocked. I hadn't even seen the story yet! I told her, 'I swear to you. I knew absolutely nothing.' Then Harry called up. If any press calls come through, he told me, I was to issue a denial. For some reason, the national press did not pick up on the story. At the end of the day, I told him, 'Mr. Luce, there haven't been any calls.' And that was that."

Clare, however, was calling everybody who might have information for her. One of them was Frank White.

"Do you know anything about the Jean Campbell thing?"

"I don't know nothin' about nothin'," White replied, and Clare told him: "I've got to buy a lot of clothes. If there's any truth in this, it's gonna cost Harry a lot of money!" She later told White, "Do you know what it's like to have your husband carrying on with another woman?"

Though Clare certainly knew all about infidelity, she had completely obliterated her long string of so many affairs with so many men, throughout her marriage. She had also completely forgotten her own liberal philosophy of open marriage, which she had so often preached. All that mattered to her now was "saving face." It hurt her ego to discover once again that Harry preferred another woman, a younger woman. She became furious.

She once berated Harry when they were together and he wasn't talking to her: "Why don't you speak to me?" "I'm reading," he replied. "I bet you would talk to Jeannie."

Meanwhile, Harry warned Jean to expect calls from the press. He also told her of Clare's rage. Jean found it amazing and unbelievable that Clare truly didn't know about the affair until she read it in the column.

It took some time before Clare cooled off. "At one point Harry called me," said Jean, "and then put Clare on the phone, saying, 'Have a chat with each other.'

"It was a lovely conversation, as you might imagine," she recalled. "Clare told me how old Harry was and how I would hate to be married to him, and things like that. And then Harry got on the phone again and he said to me, 'You've won this round.' "

Harry told Clare that he was going to move to his club.

"Clare was my enemy, and I wanted to know all about her," said Jean. "I know she wanted to know all about me. But she once told Randolph Churchill that *she* was not my enemy. *Beth Moore* was my enemy. Harry loved his sister. They were *so* close. He had been dying to tell her everything about us. He was really so excited about it. But I knew there was a danger. I didn't know how much until I met her.

"We met at her place on Park Avenue. Beth shared Harry's deep-seated faith in their religion, and she told me her concern about another divorce for Harry."

About that time, there was a massive scandal in England about Jean's father, the duke of Argyll, and his third wife. "It was absolute dynamite, one of worst divorce cases in the history of British law," said Jean. "The headlines in all the tabloids were a horror story beyond horror. The timing for me was hardly perfect."

Beth Moore then told Jean she thought it would be wiser if she went back to Scotland for a while until everything calmed down.

So Jean returned to Scotland. She then stayed with her grandfather in London. "It was a very difficult time," Jean said sadly. "Harry was just a cold mystery to my old British friends." They would ask her, "How's that fascist friend of yours?"

But Luce wrote to her every day, sometimes twice a day. "And he telephoned every night," she recalled. "And he'd talk for an hour or two. I had a special phone installed in the library downstairs for Harry's calls."

While Jean was in Britain, Luce took a five-week world tour, accompanied by *Time*'s new editor Roy Alexander, who soon knew of Harry's heart condition because he had noticed his pills. The trip was a whirlwind. Bureau chiefs awaited every plane at every stop. Luce had a tightly packed schedule and met everybody who was anybody. Harry would not have it any other way. But knowing his limitations, Luce did check into a doctor's office every two weeks.

He wrote Clare that the briefcase of work he carried was as heavy as a trunk, that he thought of her often with prayers for them both and for understanding and strength.

Hong Kong correspondent Stanley Karnow accompanied Luce and Alexander to attend Generalissimo Chiang Kai-shek's third inaugural ceremony as president of the Kuomintang, the National People's Party, now restricted to the island of Formosa. As their plane landed, Luce asked Karnow about their luggage, "You don't think they lost our luggage, do you?"

"You never know," said Karnow, "they lost the mainland."

"Madame Chiang and the general were constantly playing to him," said Karnow. "They flattered him. They told how much they needed him and how right he was. They gave him what he did not get in his own country, a feeling of how important he was, how dependent they were on him. On that tour, we'd see Chiang three times a day: morning, noon, and night. It was exhausting." Chiang was seventy-three, frail, and no longer sharp. When Luce pressed him on his plans to invade the mainland, he could only reply, repeatedly, 'I see big dangers ahead . . .' "

Clare, meanwhile, was writing letters to Jean that she never mailed. "I saw copies of them, years later," Jean said. "She called me 'baby doll.' She even sent me a telegram I never received." Jean later saw a copy of that telegram dated June 1, 1960, addressed to her at Inverary Castle, Argyll, Scotland. It mentioned that Harry wanted to marry Jean and would soon be in a position to do so. She included her congratulations.

"What I did get then was a telegram from Harry saying that I should disregard the telegram I got from Clare, a telegram I never got."

On June 4, 1960, Jean received a letter from Harry, which in essence said: Good-bye forever.

Clare wrote a long letter to Harry on May 16, 1960. She was trying to put him more at ease with his decision to break with Jean. Clare noted that Jean had prepared herself psychologically for the end of the affair when she insisted on a marriage she knew could not happen. It could not happen because, as Jean knew, Clare had refused to agree to a divorce. Clare pointed out the frustrating problem of any affair between an unmarried woman and a married man. This, of course, was something about which Clare knew much. Clare made a great point in saying that Jean was young and that the young always adjust and survive. The most important thing of all, Clare asserted, was that now they could both wipe the affair out of their minds and concentrate on the survival of their own marriage. What was extraordinary about the letter was how objective Clare appeared, as if she were watching the whole scene from a distance, without bitterness.

The reason Luce was so harsh to a woman whom he called the love of his life was Clare. She had made a serious suicide attempt in Phoenix by taking an overdose of pills. Luce could not bear the thought that he was the cause of a possible loss of life. Furthermore, Clare's suicide attempt may have reminded Harry of his own dark thoughts of ending his life years ago when he felt Clare didn't love him.

"I think it was a perfectly genuine attempt at suicide, a profoundly serious attempt," said Jean. "I think Father Murray saved her. There was another 'un-serious' suicide attempt later, climbing over the ledge to jump out of the window. But there were people in the room to stop her."

Once again, Harry told Jean that Clare was manic-depressive. "She's always on the verge," he said.

Harry had stopped going to his psychiatrist, but he was so overwrought that he sought his pastor, Dr. David Read, head of the Madison Avenue Presbyterian Church. Dr. Read, pledged to confidentiality, would only say, with considerable pity, how terribly troubled Mr. Luce was.

Luce also shared his grief with Jean Dalrymple, who remembered vividly how tormented he was, and how passionate he was about wanting Jean Campbell.

He had so few people he could turn to. Luce had spent his life trying desperately to avoid hurting others and had tried even more desperately to avoid confronting them. One evening, Harry visited his former wife, Lila, who was staying at her mother's apartment on Park Avenue. He was careful in what he told her—he did not discuss Jean Campbell. Nevertheless, he still told her much. It was almost as if he were himself in a kind of suspended time: Their early intimacy seemed intact. Lila still loved him.

"He came over for lunch, and we talked all through lunch and kept on talking all afternoon. Finally, at about six o'clock, he said, 'Can I stay for dinner?' And I said, 'Perfectly wonderful! I've no date, so why not stay?' We went downstairs to the restaurant called 'La Rue.' We had dinner and he came up afterward."

Lila reminded him that years ago he had told her that he had wanted to divorce Clare the year after he married her, "and then every year after that."

"My great regret," reminisced Lila, "is that I didn't ask him, 'Why don't you get the divorce you say you wanted every single year? Why don't you get it?' "

Harry implied to Lila that he didn't think he could face the kind of hatred Clare would spread about him. He also confided to Lila that he had been told by their doctors that Clare suffered from paranoid depressions. When she was in the limelight, she'd go into one of her depressions, then behave badly.

"Many a time, she hurled accusations at me—bad names, names you don't know the meaning of, Lila, because she came from the gutter," said Harry, "and she acted as if she came from the gutter. She knew that language."

Harry stayed late that night, and the next morning Lila called to invite him to join her at the opera. But he had already left for Arizona.

Harry could not let Jean go. He had so few things he truly wanted in life, and he wanted Jean. He impulsively wrote that he was coming to see her in Europe, completely ignoring the good-bye letter he had written. Jean had reconciled with her father and was staying with him.

"We met at Oxford, and it was nerve-racking," she said. "He was meeting my father, and it was one of the few times I had ever been with Harry and somebody else. Daddy was so nervous and Harry was so nervous. But my father thought Harry was absolutely charming, and they seemed to like each other very much. And the last thing Daddy said was not, 'When is something going to happen?' or anything like that. He simply said, 'When will you be coming up?' And Harry, said, 'Well, I hope very soon.' "

Harry was desperately trying to restructure his life, to combine reality with fantasy. If he couldn't divorce Clare, why not let her stay in Hawaii while he once again commuted on their six months' plan. He asked Jean to buy a house in Jamaica for the two of them. He also proposed that they might divide their time between Jamaica and Lake Louise in Canada.

Harry insisted to Jean that he and Clare had discussed all this in a preliminary way. As seeming proof that there had been such discussion, Jean later saw a letter from Clare, written in Hawaii, thanking Jean and Harry for giving her a happy respite. Clare called them blessed people and sent them thanks from the bottom of her heart. It was a strange, weird letter. Once again, Clare expressed her feelings in a letter she did not mail.

The world still knew nothing about Jean and Harry. Then *Time*'s Paris bureau chief Frank White got a call from Sam White, a Paris correspondent for the London *Express*.

" 'What are we gonna do about Topic A?' asked White and then explained, 'Your boss and my boss' granddaughter, you numbskull!' I asked him to tell me more. He said, 'Well, Harry is squiring Lady Jean Campbell around to all the socially elite nightclubs in our town! We're walking on thin ice all the time. It's not gonna be in *Time,* or the *Express* but god damn, it's gonna be some-where!' " But somehow, Harry and Jean again escaped detection in the press.

When Harry was ready to leave for home, Jean sensed how worried he was about all their tentative plans, which could so easily collapse. The more he talked, the more she understood that the six months' plan didn't really suit him in any way.

"He seemed to feel more and more that we must get married, or else nothing," she said.

When Luce returned to New York, he urged his lawyers to get busy again about the divorce. In Clare's papers there is a record of a call Clare made to Margaret Case Harriman, asking, "Please come to my apartment. Harry is crying because he wants a divorce to marry Lady Jean Campbell."

Jean got two letters from Harry saying that the situation looked bright and asked her to return to New York, which she did.

Harry told his lawyer to check into getting a "fugitive divorce," in Tijuana or the Dominican Republic. He said he didn't care whether she attacked the decree.

"Now Randolph Churchill got into the act," said Jean. "Just the person! Like putting an elephant into a bird cage. Harry loathed Randolph because he felt Randolph was forever trying to make trouble. He felt Randolph was far too irreverent and dangerous."

"Anyway," Randolph said, "I have the solution to the whole thing. I'll marry Clare and that will make everything all right. It will be wonderful for her. She'd love to be called 'Churchill' and I've got a great house and she'll enjoy the garden and all that."

Indeed, Clare loved to tell about how Randolph Churchill used to say, "And how's old Henry! Stuffy old bastard! Why don't you dump that old goat and marry me?" He thought he had reason to be hopeful. Her most recent letter to him had suggested they both take a Baltic cruise on a four-masted sailing ship.

"Eventually, Randolph wrote Clare a very serious letter of proposal," said Jean, "and she wrote back a very nice letter of refusal. And that put us all back to square one."

Clare seemed to be seesawing in the divorce discussions, as if she herself was no longer certain what she wanted. Jean's impatience with matters increased, and she and Harry had some stormy scenes. It was after one such scene that Harry left quickly for Greece. This time, Jean felt that this was the end of it. "I thought I would never see him again and it was *ghastly.*" But then came a love letter from Harry, tender, romantic, passionate. She was his beloved and he missed her desperately.

"The day he got back, round he came as if nothing had ever happened. I'd see him pretty well every night, for supper, then all evening. I was getting fed up by then. I was young, and I wanted children. We had been together four years. It was very hard to listen to someone saying how much he loved you, loved you more than anything else in the world, and still be in the same situation. It was very hard and I was getting angry." She remembered it as a tough and terrible time.

Feeling depressed, Jean left for Jamaica to be with her grandfather.

"And Harry would still ring me up every single morning at half past eight," she said.

In one of his calls, Harry was excited about the fact that Governor Nelson Rockefeller was getting a divorce. If a public man like Rockefeller could get away with a divorce, why not Luce?

Harry kept pleading with Jean to come back, and so she did. "By this time we were having a lot of rows, and I was being very difficult," she admitted. "I do know I was being harsh; I was the stormy one. I just knew I was getting fed up, really fed up. And acting beastly, horrible, angry, grumpy, cruel, dreadful—dreadful! I mean, I was a monster!"

And then, the world crashed in on them. Leonard Lyons, in his national column, "The Lyons Den," printed the item that Luce would marry Lady Jean Campbell.

Now it was a national story with headlines everywhere. When the columnist Cholly Knickerbocker, who had been the one to first print the rumor months before, reached Luce on the phone at his Ridgefield home, Harry would only say, "Clare and I are here together. It is all very premature to say the least." The key word was "premature."

Once again, Harry urged Jean to say as little as possible. Her response to reporters, was "I am reminded of the inscription over the gate of the beautiful flower garden of St. Andrew's University in Scotland. It's by an anonymous sage, circa 1720, and carved in stone. It reads: 'They have said; they will say; let them be saying!' "

Clare, too, denied any separation rumors. She had been hospitalized in Phoenix with pneumonia when the news broke and said, "So help me heaven, there's nothing to it." She then added, "I've already denied it. Harry has denied it. It's just too bad we have to keep on saying so." She later quipped: "If I divorced Harry, and married The Beaver, I would become Harry's grandmother . . ."

Privately, she was more venomous. "Clare again let it be known that she would not go quietly. She would raise a national scandal and keep it blowing hot," said George Harris, a *Life* editor. She reportedly told Harry, "I will sue you in every court in America. I'm not going to have this little British trollop make a fool of me."

As the scandal worsened, Gilpatric struggled to come up with a solution. He reported to Harry on alternative divorce in Mexico, where they wouldn't need Clare's agreement, but Harry never said more on this.

And, Clare, he added, was hitting where she knew it would hurt Harry most. "She didn't care about the money," said Gilpatric. "She wanted control of Time Inc.—*active* control. She wanted a say in the editorial policy, too. She must have realized that Luce would never leave her editorial control of *Time,* even when he died, and that's why she took such a strong position, wanting control now, when they were talking about a divorce. Harry wouldn't give it up."

Clare had asked for the impossible. If he gave it to her, it would open a new world of power for her. If he didn't give it to her, she would still have him. The trigger was the national publicity on the story. If there had been no publicity, the divorce might still have happened quietly. She might have settled for her original plan to get the houses and the money and roam the world with her attentive men. But the publicity was a hard slap in the face, and nobody did that to Clare Boothe Luce.

Why didn't Harry proceed with an alternative divorce in Mexico, or some other place? For the same reason he didn't do it when he wanted to marry Dalrymple. The surrender of editorial control of Time Inc. was unthinkable. National scandal was degrading. His love for Jean was overwhelming, but Time Inc. was his whole life. In the final analysis, he chose propriety over love. His Presbyterian upbringing was back in control.

Harry was so distraught that he failed to call Jean one day. "I remember it was a Tuesday, March 15, the Ides of March," she recalled. "It was very strange."

Sensing the affair was over, she accepted an invitation to a party at Gore Vidal's house. There, she met author Norman Mailer. "I threw myself at Norman," she admitted. "It was a very wrong thing to do. I was on the rebound. I did it for survival. I had to make a break, and I had to go on with somebody else. I was beginning to get really broken by Harry, in every way. I wanted children desperately. And Norman was terribly attractive and very interesting. I've always had great guilt about what I did because it wasn't fair to him."

Jean told Norman a little bit about Harry, but not much. "Norman hated Harry. Norman was very, very immature really. Compared to Norman, Harry was unbelievably complicated with depths and banked fires of passion. Compared to Harry, Norman was like Little Lord Fauntleroy. Literally! But the truth is that you cannot end a long, long, long love affair and go into another."

Had she not met Mailer, Jean reflected, "I don't know what would have happened with Harry. We might just have drifted on for years because Harry didn't have any real motivation to change things. He was absolutely blissfully happy the way it was, the best of all worlds. Or maybe he might have pushed again for a divorce. I don't know. I know he wanted us to have children so much. If I had gotten pregnant then, that would have made it urgent to push for a divorce again. I wish I had, but I didn't."

But Jean did get pregnant right away with Mailer. "Norman and I went to see grandfather, who said to me, 'Don't marry him. Have the baby but don't marry him.' "

"Oh, come on, grandfather, I can't do that!"

"Of course you can!"

Harry, meanwhile, had reacted swiftly to Jean's affair. Jean claimed that during her time with Norman, she noticed that they were being followed by two detectives. "Clare must have told Harry about it right away. It was too peculiar," she said. "The day after I met Norman, Harry changed his private phone number which I still have in my old passport. Anyway, he never called me again."

But Harry was still obsessed with Jean. Campbell and Mailer soon married in a quiet, unpublicized ceremony.

"Mary (Bancroft) later told me that the day I was having my baby, Harry kept ringing her up from Canada," Jean explained. "She said he was drunk. He kept calling Mary up to find out how the childbirth was coming. At that point, I hadn't even met Mary yet. We became good friends later. When my daughter was born, Mary told Harry and he said, 'Oh well, now I suppose she'll wait and have a boy . . .' "

Campbell's marriage to Mailer would be short and fiery, and Harry was always in her mind. "You know, I've loved Harry more than I've loved anybody except my children," she said years later. "I loved him as he was. I loved the man in our cocoon, and it had nothing to do with the image. I hated all that.

"When he came through my door, he was part of my world. I wouldn't have minded being part of his world and I might have brought him into another dimension. We *did* have fun. And we *did* have laughter. With me, he might have flowered into a different kind of a giant human being. And I think we would have been able to do more wonderful things, good things. And I know," she added after a long, reflective pause, "that he would have lived longer."

31

FOR their twenty-fifth wedding anniversary, Harry bought Clare a silver gilt cactus plant from Tiffany. In many ways, it was symbolic of their marriage. The cactus is a prickly plant that survives with minimal nourishment. Some cacti even have succulent fruit and a lovely flower. Once, Harry might have likened Clare to that species of cactus. But now, the lovely flower was fading, the fruit was no longer sweet. Only the prickly needles remained.

Tiffany owner Walter Hoving wondered about the cactus. "I couldn't figure out whether it was because it was Arizona or because it was Clare," he said.

Whatever Harry intended with the gift, he was miserable. He and Clare were tied together by circumstance, pretension, and power. Their lost loves were sharp aches, and their future resembled a cold fog.

Harry again retreated to his inner self. His break with Jean Campbell had been swift surgery, and he still felt the pain of it. He had been so abrupt, because that was his way of decision-making. He could do it no other way. When he broke with Lila to marry Clare, he had been equally brutal, though he did write subsequent letters to her, thick with guilt and uncertainty.

After leaving Lila, Harry was so torn that he had even considered suicide. Once again, he was tormented. His guilt was lessened because Jean had rushed off to marry Norman Mailer. Still, he knew what he had done, and where the fault lay.

Clare knew, too. She would live all her life filled with guilt about her daughter, but she felt no such guilt about holding Harry from his true love. For one thing, she knew he had a certain salvation in his work. Time Inc. gave him a peace with himself and with the world; a wider horizon, a soul-healing.

Clare had no such form of therapy. Her conversion had given her critical help at a critical time, but it could not wipe out her lifelong restlessness and dissatisfaction. These were things deep within her. Her playwriting was of little interest now. Needlepoint was merely a diversion. Scuba diving was no longer exciting.

"I was constantly bumping into fish that look vaguely familiar to me, like old friends. There was one barracuda with a hideous, toothy grin who reminded me of somebody, though I can't say who, because it wouldn't be charitable," she said. "My last dive was in Bermuda, and my diving buddy was Sir Julian Gascoigne, the governor of the Bahamas. He and I dove on a wrecked French frigate lying at about thirty feet off the reef. We shook hands over a submerged cannon. Sir Julian, most gentlemanly, removed his glove before taking my hand.'

"I'd done it," she continued. "I had reached my depth. If I went deeper, I felt I would perish, and there was no point in doing the same thing over again."

This quote said a great deal about Clare. She cared more for the challenge of scuba diving than the fascination of the ever-changing sea life.

Whenever Clare was bored, she sought a new home. This time she persuaded Harry to sell their triplex apartment and move to a smaller, but still elegant apartment at 927 Fifth Avenue, near 74th Street facing Central Park. It had several bedrooms and a large living room decorated in the French-Provincial style. Clare needlepointed the rug years ago; her first piece of needlepoint had been for Harry, and it read, "Love Will Conquer All." It had been wishful thinking.

For at least half the year, they lived in Phoenix. Though they had been competing with each other all their lives, there now seemed nothing more to compete about. There were no more grand prizes. She seemed to have surrendered the idea of ultimately converting him to Roman Catholicism, even though he still escorted her to Mass every Sunday (some said it was part of a deal they had made when they decided to stay together). But he also attended his own Presbyterian church services, although not every Sunday. "He was ecumenical," said Clare. "He stayed with the faith of his fathers, but he was never unhappy with mine." But then she added, "He had a deep sense that he was a sinner."

She might have added, "a lonely sinner." One of the beliefs of Luce's life was that he could make religion and success come together—that if you were good, then you were successful.

For Clare and Harry, it was their longest stretch of time together in many years. They had reached a silent accord: They would live their lives together with as little rancor as possible.

Every morning, the maid set up a folding table in Clare's bedroom and Luce would trundle in barefoot, usually wearing his crimson dressing gown to join her for breakfast. She would talk and he would read his paper. Their pet cockatoo would sing "Stars and Stripes Forever."

They regularly watched *Perry Mason* on TV, each trying to guess who committed the crime. They both read voraciously. And every night, he would read to her, "sometimes detective stories, sometimes more serious stuff," she told friends. "There's nothing I enjoyed more, and he never got tired of it. Sometimes he would read for a couple hours at a time. It became a precious ritual."

While Harry read, Clare made Christmas tree ornaments. "I get restless if I'm not doing something." She bought synthetic foam balls in all sizes and decorated them with jewels and velvet. Harry called them "imperial baubles," even though Clare sold them for charity. Clare also made a seven-foot long mosaic of a medieval Madonna, which she donated to her parish church.

Harry's hobby was golf, which he did not play particularly well. He had a favorite caddy who would pick him up in a cart and friends observed that he seemed in a hurry all of the time and would roar around the golf course. He didn't seem to enjoy himself. In fact, a friend said he played as if he was fulfilling a doctor's prescription.

When Harry returned to New York, he would visit Jean Dalrymple and her husband. To his old love, Harry confided his inner despair. "He was never content in Phoenix; he hated to go there! And he had a big fight with her, every time they went," she said. "At first, he fought about her wanting to live in Phoenix. He said, 'Why? We have a beautiful home in Connecticut.' But he said she was never satisfied with any place they lived. She always wanted to go somewhere else. She moved from place to place, but she never made a home, never."

Still, something bound him to Clare. His dislike of her was mingled with his admiration.

They discussed anything and everything, including whether or not Mao Tse-tung was America's greatest ally because he was the prime force in preventing the Soviet takeover of Asia. "We both had strong views," said Clare. "Usually we'd agree. Rarely we'd disagree. Then we might argue the question intellectually for days. Sometimes I'd win the argument. More often he did. He'd bring in a battery of proof that bore out his points. On those rare occasions when he lost, there was never any masculine sulk. On to the next case!"

Clare liked Harry's response when she broke in on his argument, "For God's sake, dear, will you stop talking when I'm interrupting . . ."

She once complained to Harry, "You have time for everything but me."

Very seriously, he quietly replied, "Do you realize that I have given you more time and thought and concern than all the other people of my life put together?"

Harry often used Clare as a sounding board for some program *Time* was considering. "He would outline it to me and say, 'What do you think?' So I'd give him my views carefully—not all pro. Then he'd say they were going ahead with it."

"If you had your mind made up, why did you ask my opinion?" she'd ask.

"I'll have to defend my decision," he told her, "and I knew you'd give me the best argument."

The Campbell affair was never far from Clare's mind, and she wrote Father Murray in January 1962, disagreeing with him that Harry had left her because she had hurt his masculine pride, that he would never have strayed if she had been more of a submissive wife. She refused to accept any principle that man was superior to woman. She had fought her battles of the sexes, she said, and, admittedly, had lost most of the battles, but she did not plan to stop fighting.

Clare had embarked upon a campaign to assure that she wasn't left alone in her old age.

In a moment of despondency, Clare once said to her husband, "Harry, you're married to an old woman."

"She had a Prince Valiant haircut, wore no makeup, and some drab-colored clothes and was covered with paint," said Shirley Clurman. "She was really looking bad."

It was one of the few times Harry was ever graceful. He said: "Yes, but such a beautiful old woman."

He was graceful again when Clare teased him, "What happens with all those attractive women you go out with to dinner?"

"They all copy you," he told her. "I want the genuine article."

Harry might even have meant it at that moment. At times, Clare was unique. She had many facets and many virtues and she could be very helpful to Harry. When he expressed curiosity about some UFO sightings over Mexico City she had mentioned, she promptly researched the matter and sent him a long letter. She also protected his privacy at home. "His orders are firm: He wants to talk to no one, except from the office, until one o'clock." Even if he was doing no writing, "no one will knock on his door," she told potential intruders.

Harry helped her, too. She was often called upon to make speeches. When she was asked on short notice to give a talk at the Waldorf about great writers who became politically involved, she needed emergency research. Harry asked a *Time* writer to do it for him. "I did absolutely nothing that day but keep feeding him that stuff," said Max Gissen. Only later did Luce admit to Gissen that the material was for his wife.

* * *

Throughout this latest period of reconciliation with Clare, Harry exhibited a more subdued, conservative presence at Time Inc. There was a collective feeling that Harry suddenly seemed closer to all those boring people who would have bored him in earlier years. He now seemed to want the respectability that came with awards and titles and positions. His editors felt he really didn't know how powerful he had become and didn't realize that most people needed him more than he needed them.

The proof of his power was always in evidence when Luce was called upon to speak at a Senate committee hearing. The senators listened with obvious deference. Most were prepared to hear the unexpected. He seldom disappointed them. Testifying against communism, he had made clear his agreement with Robert Kennedy that communism was only a minimal problem within America. "I yield to no man in my distrust and hatred of communism, but I'm not going to give all my time to it." International communism was something else. He said he did not consider peaceful co-existence possible with Russia and Red China. He paraphrased Lincoln on slavery, saying, "Communism must be stopped from spreading that men can confidently foresee its withering away."

The shy young man in his badly shaped Chinese-made suit who had stammered when he waited on tables was the honored guest at the forty-fifth reunion of his class at Hotchkiss. He now had a pre-tax income of one million dollars and occasionally lunched with the president of the United States.

When Kennedy assumed the presidency, Luce wrote him a poignant note saying that would be the last time he would address him as "Dear Jack," that it would now have to be, "Mr. President."

But Harry was really more concerned with what the president was calling *him*.

"Well, his father was one of my best friends. I've known him since he was a little boy. Yet every time I see him, he calls me 'Mr. Luce.' He insists on this; I don't know what he's trying to do to me!" grumbled Harry to *Time* executive Bernard Yudain.

Luce seemed absolutely stunned when *Time*'s Washington bureau chief John Steele assured him that Kennedy was simply being very correct and well-bred because Harry was his father's contemporary and knew Jack when he was a boy. Kennedy queried *Time*'s Hugh Sidey on the same issue: "What do I call him? I can't call him 'Harry.' It was always 'Mr. Luce.' "

Kennedy had no hesitation about "Mr. Luce's" magazine. Few presidents took *Time* as seriously as J.F.K. "I go overseas and the only way those people there overseas, the ambassadors and people like that, get their news is *Time,*" Kennedy said. "People who made opinions in Europe were deeply influenced by *Time* and read *Time* perhaps more than any other American publication. They really read that goddamn magazine."

Kennedy got early copies of *Time* and *Life* hand-delivered to his office a day ahead of publication. They were airlifted from the Chicago printer to the White House. When someone borrowed his copy, Kennedy was furious. Luce once complained that Kennedy saw a copy of *Time* before he did.

Kennedy's interest in *Time* was almost fanatic. "He wanted to know the deadlines," said Hugh Sidey. "He wanted to know how they did a cover story, how the selection of cover art was made, how they chose the people to go on the cover. He wanted to know how much employees were paid. Was it really true that we paid more than other magazines? He wanted to know about the writers and researchers. He wanted the biography of everybody even at lower echelons. It was incredible."

"Well, what happened to your magazine last week?" the president asked Luce on one of Harry's visits to Washington. "Did Otto Fuerbringer go on vacation last week?" Luce was shocked that Kennedy could detect a tonal change in the magazine and admitted that Fuerbringer had been sick.

Because *Time* went to press by Saturday afternoon, if Kennedy was making an important speech on a Monday, he'd make sure that *Time* saw an advance copy to get it into that issue. After reading his early copy of *Time,* Kennedy would call Sidey on a Sunday evening and "would complain, in cheerfully profane style, about some choice of phrase or photo." He was especially annoyed about a *Time* story on how his brother-in-law Prince Radziwill got an annulment so that he and Jackie's sister Lee could be married in the Church.

Kennedy didn't measure his support by degree—he wanted one hundred percent. No matter how approving, or even flattering, an article was, if it contained anything critical, Kennedy automatically accentuated the negative. Luce and Kennedy largely agreed on foreign policy, but differed on domestic issues. The core of their difference was that Kennedy was a Democrat and Luce was a Republican. Also, *Time,* inevitably and invariably, felt it necessary to be critical of every president—even Luce's icon, Eisenhower.

Kennedy found such criticism deeply annoying. Hugh Sidey vividly recalled one particular blast from Kennedy when *Time* reported that the president had posed for the cover of *Gentlemen's Quarterly.*

Speechwriter Ted Sorensen and Press Secretary Pierre Salinger were standing in the room, while Kennedy was at his desk reading the magazine. "Where did you get this story?" he asked me. He threw the magazine on the desk, and he said, 'Now, I'm not kidding. I'm getting goddam sick and tired of it.'

"Suddenly I realized how really sore he was. He came out from around the desk, and he walked up and down in front of me. 'This is all a lie. This isn't true. I never posed for any magazine, never posed for a picture.'

"Just at that moment, I remember Tazewell Shepard, his military aide, came dashing into the room and said, 'Mr. President, Mr. President, Colonel Glenn is on the line.' Colonel Glenn had just returned from space and gotten on the destroyer. And I remember the president turned to me and said, 'All right,' whereupon he got on the phone and immediately changed his mood. With a happy, boisterous voice he said, 'Hello, Colonel Glenn, we're glad to talk to you.' Then, immediately after he hung up, he came around the desk, stood in front of me, and went into this thing again and talked quite awhile about it."

It was the day John Glenn had orbited the earth.

J.F.K. was so obsessed with *Time* that he even enlisted the help of Clare's old friend, Tish Baldrige, who worked as a White House aide. Tish called Clare to say the president was unhappy about some of the things about his family in *Time* and wanted to see her. It was a time of national tension. The Eisenhower administration had trained an exile force of Cubans for possible use against Communist dictator Fidel Castro, and the Kennedy administration further organized this exile brigade to invade Cuba. Rumors of this invasion filled the press.

It seemed unlikely that the president could be concerned at this time with *Time*'s treatment of a family incident. He wasn't. He felt Clare was privy to her husband's views—views that Luce as head of Time Inc. could not express but that Clare could. Furthermore, he respected the quality of her mind. Clare and J.F.K. had once written a "thought-provoking" series of long letters to each other on the need for international control of nuclear weapons.

Clare agreed to meet Kennedy at the White House. Baldrige remembered her former boss's delicate stomach and ordered a lunch for Clare of thin consommé, scrambled eggs, and custard.

There was no small talk that day. Clare told Kennedy one of her favorite phrases, that "a great man is one sentence, with an active verb in it, describing a unique action, and you don't have to know the man's name." She then illustrated her point. "He died on the cross to save us" or "He sought a new way to the old world and discovered a new world."

She wondered aloud what sentences would be written about Kennedy after he left office.

"You're talking about Cuba," Kennedy replied.

"No, I wasn't, but I can imagine such a sentence. 'He broke the power of the Soviet Union in the Western world' or 'He failed to break the power of the Soviet Union in the Western world.' One of these two sentences will be written after your name. Maybe you'll write a greater one."

"Well, what you're talking about is my using force in Cuba."

Clare said she didn't think he could resolve the crisis without using force.

They walked to the balcony, with its lovely view. "Well," he said, "I'll have to go to work on that last sentence."

Clare later quoted the president as saying that he did not think Cuba was as big a threat to American security as she did. She asked why he thought the presence of Communist power in Vietnam, 9,000 miles away, was more of a threat. He mentioned the U.S. commitment to Vietnam and added that *Time* had urged the government to take action there, but not in Cuba. She said *Time* may have been wrong, and she didn't speak for the magazine or edit it.

"You surely have some influence," he said.

"Such as I have—very little—I am urging them to keep their eye on Cuba now. Why wait until a war will be more costly in American lives?"

"Then you are for a war in Cuba?" he asked.

"Not unless you know of some peaceful way we can break out of the double bind."

Clare was referring to the possibility of the Russians moving into Berlin if the U.S. invaded Cuba. She also knew how much Kennedy worried about the threat of nuclear war. "I do not wish to be the president who goes down in history as having unleashed nuclear war," he told her. Then he added, ruefully, "It looks easier when you are on the outside."

Kennedy walked Clare to the door and she kept talking, so he walked with her to Pennsylvania Avenue to her car. Shortly afterward, Kennedy saw Sidey, "She was too much for me, Hugh; I'm going to turn her over to you."

The Cuban invasion of April 1961 was a fiasco. It took Castro only three days to crush the rebels and capture them. The president accepted full responsibility. Khrushchev promptly reassessed his strategies, and considered Kennedy an easier target.

Shortly after the disastrous invasion, Luce lunched with the president. "He came down the elevator and he pulled two or three memorandums out of his pocket. One of these was from the chairman of the Joint Chiefs, and I think he had one or two others, military reports. He displayed a good deal of disgust with these reports and asked me what he should do now," recalled Luce, "and I said, 'Well, in my mind the answer is very simple, namely that a strong application of the Monroe Doctrine should be reapplied, reasserted.'"

Kennedy then asked Luce to undertake a special mission of advice and counsel to the president—the only time Luce was ever asked to do this. The president wanted him to review the question of the admission of Communist

China into the United Nations. Ten days later, Luce returned his verdict, "No."

Kennedy's overture to Luce didn't deter the preparation of a *Fortune* article blaming Kennedy for the Bay of Pigs defeat in Cuba because he had refused to provide critical air power. Kennedy had found out about the major points in the article in advance. Were the piece to be published, he felt, it would damage national security because it gave away secrets, and it also totally distorted the situation.

In an unprecedented action, hoping to stop the article from being printed, Kennedy sent General Maxwell Taylor, head of the Joint Chiefs of Staff, on a personal mission to complain to Luce about errors in the piece. Taylor started his point-by-point critique, then quit in the middle because it was evident that the critique was not substantiated. General Taylor later let it be known that he found this assignment demeaning. The article was printed.

Kenny O'Donnell, the president's close friend and appointments secretary, told *Time* editor Robert Manning about J.F.K. summoning Luce to the White House to complain about a *Time* story. O'Donnell claimed he had seldom seen the president so angry. Luce tried to present his argument but Kennedy only got more furious.

"It was a hell of a scene," said O'Donnell, who was the only other person in the room. And, suddenly, Kennedy yelled, "You sonofabitch, you get out of my office."

O'Donnell remembered that Harry Luce left the room, dejected, with his head bowed.

It did not end that way. Kennedy was too keenly aware of Luce's power. J.F.K. had been a longtime admirer of Franklin Delano Roosevelt's use of the stick and carrot. During the campaign, Luce had admitted that he was a victim of the Kennedy charm. Kennedy knew when to use it with Luce. Discovering that Luce had made a quiet visit to Washington, he promptly sent him a message, "Harry, how can you be in town without coming to see me?"

Only a president could do this to Luce. Only for a president would Harry return—but he would neither forgive nor forget.

32

THE women in his life saw Harry more clearly than anyone. Jean Dalrymple sensed a change of mood. Mary Bancroft, who saw Luce whenever he came to New York, felt an inner struggle.

Harry was almost sixty-five, and he was depressed. He seemed to be spending an inordinate amount of time reading his Bible, even before cocktails, as if he were somehow trying to find his answers there.

One day, while crossing a street with a *Time* associate, waiting for the traffic to stop, he suddenly turned and said, "You know, I dread old age. In old age, I'm gonna be so damn bored."

Fear of boredom was now his driving fear.

Harry talked to Mary much more about death. With Jean Campbell out of his life, it was as if his last hope of real living was also gone. Mary emphasized all the awesome power he held, and how much good he could do with it.

In October 1962, Luce finally understood his power when Kennedy summoned him to discuss a crisis that could have meant the end of the world.

Kennedy asked Luce and Fuerbringer, then *Time*'s managing editor, to the White House for a conference. "What's he going to do? What's he want to say? What's he want?" Luce asked.

"I think he wants to explain to us what he's doing," said Fuerbringer.

"That's pretty good, isn't it? Calling us down," said Luce, obviously pleased.

Kennedy's practice was to probe the best brains in the nation for their judgments on crucial situations before making his own decisions. Luce recalled how tired the president looked, how deep was his emotion. Harry expressed his thanks for being consulted, and Kennedy said with a smile, "Well, you've been very interested in Cuba for a long time." Harry replied, "Not just Cuba, the global situation."

The Russians had put nuclear missiles in Cuba, within easy range of the southern United States. Kennedy was again concerned that the Russians might take advantage of the missile crisis to overrun Berlin. He feared a nuclear war. He kept asking Luce, "Are you for or against invasion?"

Luce said he was not for an immediate invasion, but he did endorse a naval blockade, searching incoming Soviet ships for more missiles.

"Then we went over to the Pentagon and were shown this extraordinary display of reconnaissance photographs," Luce recalled. Some of these photographs were then made exclusively available to Time Inc.

Time Inc. supported the president in his final showdown until the Russians took out their missiles and the crisis was over.

If Luce's involvement in the Cuba crisis were not enough to convince him of his power, the fortieth anniversary of *Time* in May 1963 did the trick. This was a jolt of jubilation for Luce at a time when he needed it most.

"People don't celebrate anniversaries except the twenty-fifth or fiftieth— why the fortieth, Harry?" Clare asked him.

"Because I won't be here for the fiftieth."

So, he invited 650 people who had been on the covers of *Time* and almost half of them accepted—and paid their own way to New York.

"He wouldn't let me approach Eisenhower," said John Steele. "This was so important to him that he approached Ike himself. And Ike opted not to come because he had a standing date to play at the Masters golf tournament in Augusta, Georgia. He could've played golf a day later. We could have sent a plane to fly him up, and fly him back that night, if necessary. But Ike just wouldn't put himself out." After all Luce and *Time* had done for Eisenhower, he was deeply disappointed.

Luce also extended a personal invitation to President Kennedy during a meeting in the Oval Office that was supposed to be short but went on for more than an hour. Kennedy wanted to discuss the state of the world and got Luce to agree that it was pretty good. "But in your magazine you just say it's lousy," said J.F.K. He then turned to Hugh Sidey, asking, "[Does] the average man on the street in the city, Washington, think that *Time* magazine has been fair to me?" Sidey felt forced to say no, but reminded the president that Washington was a Democratic city, and would probably be prejudiced. Luce immediately brightened and said, "Ah, yes, in Phoenix, where I go, they think we've been very kind to you."

Harry felt shaken when he left, and told a sympathetic Sidey, "I've got to have a drink, I've got to have a drink." He said he didn't like having the president of the United States feel that way about him and the magazine. "I don't like it at all."

Luce then said that perhaps *Time* had been unfair, dwelling too much on the small things, the swimming pool parties and that sort of thing, giving a negative impression. The fact was, he said, that after the Cuban blockade, the state of the world was pretty good.

Luce had yet to persuade Kennedy to come to the anniversary party. "Kennedy called me over and asked me what he should do," said Sidey, "and he said that the people would say he was a sap if he went, that he was trying to curry favor from *Time,* and he didn't want to be put in that position. So he sat down and wrote Luce a letter in longhand in which he expressed his regrets."

Steele concentrated on getting Vice President Lyndon Johnson as a substitute. "My wife and I were dressing at the Dorset Hotel in formal clothes for the party," recalled Steele. "And Lyndon was still on the phone, saying, 'John, I've got to go to Lucy's girl-scout meeting tonight. I haven't been there in two years!'

"And he called back saying how much this hurt him, and to 'please apologize to Luce for me.' And I said, 'Oh, Lyndon, fuck yourself!' " Steele hung up the phone. A minute later, Steele recalled, Johnson called back and said, "John, I can't do this to you. I'm gonna fly up."

It was an evening of glitter and elegance, a champagne reception in the Waldorf-Astoria ballroom for everybody to meet Luce and his editors. Among the 284 cover subjects who had accepted was a range of celebrities from baseball manager Casey Stengel to General Douglas MacArthur. A succession of toastmasters included Bob Hope. "This is what the UN would look like if it had Mr. Luce's circulation," quipped Hope.

The guests filled 144 tables on the main floor and up into the two balconies. Celebrities were almost outnumbered by the photographers snapping pictures on the flower-bedecked three-tiered dais.

Even though Kennedy was not there, he sent a message praising Luce as "one of the creative editors of our age." He said of *Time* that it "had instructed, entertained, confused, and infuriated its readers for nearly half a century. Like most Americans, I do not always agree with *Time,* but I nearly always read it." Then he added: "I hope I am not wrong in occasionally detecting these days in *Time* those more mature qualities appropriate to an institution entering its forties—a certain mellowing of tone, a greater tolerance of human frailty, and most astonishing of all, an occasional hint of fallibility."

In his reply that night, Luce said, "I hope that *Time*'s number one subscriber will always be the president of the United States." He also hoped that his degree of personal dialogue with the president would always continue. Then he quoted his old friend, Roy Roberts of the Kansas City *Star:* "Don't get too mellow with age!"

One of the most poignant moments of the evening was when Luce introduced his wife, who was decked with emeralds and diamonds. Clare, he said, was "One who has never been on the cover of *Time* for a very poor reason—she married the editor in chief."

Clare later told an interviewer that she had a *Time* portrait of her done by Boris Chaliapin. "Three times it was supposed to go on the cover but Harry decided at the last minute to yank it off. He thought it would look like he was using the magazine to build me up."

This was Luce's night, and he picked as the principal speaker, a man of God. Dr. Paul J. Tillich, a white-haired seventy-six-year-old-theologian from the University of Chicago School of Divinity, who had escaped from the Nazis, talked of "the negative forces of our one-dimensional culture." It was characteristic of Luce to select a speaker who would prod *Time* rather than pat it on its back. Tillich attacked the concept that everything American was always right and those who criticized it were always wrong.

All in all, it was a celebration of success. "Never in our experience have so many titans and titanesses of industry, sports, music, theater, philanthropy, politics, publishing, finance, science, medicine, government, advertising, and religion taken spotlighted bows in one place," said Geoffrey Hellman, a writer for *The New Yorker.*

Lyndon Johnson looked around the room and said: "I have realized that many of us owe Harry Luce a very great debt for being the first publisher to select magazine cover models on a basis other than beauty. We have here in this room tonight the conglomeration of viewpoints that could only be assembled in a free land."

Luce had a new hearing aid and may have missed many of the anniversary speeches. But his pleasure was evident. After all the sorrows of recent years, Luce delightedly basked in a moment of pure glory.

At five o'clock in the morning, Hubert Humphrey was still dancing with Gina Lollabrigida. It was the party Luce had yearned for.

But the glow was short-lived. Soon Luce—and the nation—was embroiled in another controversy. The voice of *Time* was not speaking softly on the emerging war in Vietnam.

With Chiang's China overrun by communism, the Luces were loud and fearful that it must not happen in Southeast Asia. Clare wrote just such an article for the *National Review.* In a speech afterward, she decried the false American morality about force saying that the American people wanted to stop communism but didn't want to get hurt in doing it.

Luce's successor, Hedley Donovan, felt that Luce was not that concerned with the early stages of Vietnam because he regarded it "as somewhat messy." Through his editorial voice, Jack Jessup, he questioned whether the U.S. had a responsibility in Asia. Luce told Jessup: "Some liberals who would not want to see Europe overcome by communism may actually think communism is a good thing for China—and perhaps for the rest of Asia. The same liberals who want to be color-blinded in the U.S. seem to be quite color-conscious when it comes to world affairs."

Clare and Harry both felt that the inevitable outcome of Vietnam would be a negotiated peace, and that the area then would be controlled by Chinese Communists. Donovan felt that Luce was more open-minded and less militant about Vietnam than people thought he was.

Charles Mohr, *Time* correspondent in Saigon, wanted tougher coverage of the growing war, and complained that his reports were being softened and sweetened at *Time.* He threatened to quit. Luce sent his trusted chief of correspondents, Dick Clurman, to check the facts. Meanwhile a *Time* story accused the American press corps of favoring the Communists. Clurman returned, agreeing with Mohr that the war was being lost, and *Time* was not printing Mohr's dispatches.

At Clurman's urging, *Time* prepared an article that began: "*Time* was wrong." This was calculated to soothe Mohr's righteous anger. Luce read it and approved. But just before the plate was printed, managing editor Otto Fuerbringer eliminated the first sentence. He could not admit to himself or anyone else that *Time* was wrong. Mohr resigned.

The conflict continued in the White House. Kennedy had sent Secretary of Defense McNamara to survey the situation. McNamara later revealed that "We were all in the Cabinet Room a month before Kennedy died. We were discussing his authorized withdrawal of a thousand troops from Vietnam by December. There was a lot of pro and con at the meeting, but the final decision was Kennedy's. His reason there was that our role in Vietnam should be limited to training and assisting Vietnam to carry on their war, but it was their country and their responsibility and their war. All we could do, and should do, he said, was to provide the hardware and a certain degree of training."

All the controversy suddenly stilled with the news that an assassin had shot and killed the president.

At Time Inc. on November 23, 1963, there was chaos. Harry Luce was too busy to grieve and Clare Luce grieved too much to be busy. The next issue of *Life* had already closed and 300,000 copies were in railroad cars at printing plants in Chicago. A crew flew out to Chicago to do new layouts and replace the cover. With the slaying of Oswald, the issue had to be changed again.

Normally *Life* reached the newsstands on Monday. However, because of the extraordinary events sixty percent of the copies appeared on newsstands on Tuesday, the rest the next day.

The new president was now that "gamblin' man," Lyndon Baines Johnson. L.B.J. started touching important bases and quickly called Luce in Phoenix. As Luce's son Hank remembered, "He just wanted to say hello and tell Henry Robinson Luce he was president." During the call, Clare whispered, "Tell Lyndon hello for me." Johnson replied, "She's the sweetest little woman I ever served with in Congress."

Clare and Harry had the highest regard for the power and presence of Lyndon Johnson. Harry liked him partly because he felt they both believed in the American Century, that here was a patriot as well as a pirate.

Clare remembered Johnson's force in Congress, his skill at manipulation and the impact of his poor childhood, with which she freely empathized. This was a man of strength and determination.

Eliot Janeway, who had introduced Clare to Johnson when she first came to Congress, said afterward, "I'm sure she had an affair with him, although I wasn't there."

The attraction seemed obvious, and with Johnson such attractions were almost always physical. It is surely not inconceivable. Johnson was a raunchy man with the reputation for reaching quickly for any pretty woman. In his oral biography of Johnson, Merle Miller told the story of Lyndon waking in the bed of a strange woman whose name he did not know, and saying to her, "Thank you for your contribution to my campaign."

Clare was often sexually attracted to a man of power. The awesome power of the leader of the Senate might have been irresistible.

But now Johnson was president, and Harry was the one impressed by Johnson's power. "Harry never lost his sense of awe of the presidency," said Clare, "be it F.D.R., Ike, or L.B.J. Soon after Johnson became president, Harry spent much, much longer than the usual twenty minutes with Johnson. Harry came home, his nose twitching with pleasure, and told me about it. Well, L.B.J. had been showing off before him. While Harry sat there, Johnson spent most of his time on the telephone with Lady Bird and others, tossing questions like Vietnam back and forth. I said to Harry, 'I don't think the president should have kept you like that.' Harry beamed. He said, 'I was watching the president of the United States transacting the business of the United States."

Luce respected Johnson's strength of purpose. Once, ordering a drink, he asked for Cutty Sark. "That's what the president drinks," he explained with a twinkle. "I figure if it's good enough for Johnson, it's good enough for me."

Like Kennedy, Johnson was an avid reader of *Time*, perhaps even more so.

When Johnson had been Senate majority leader, he would set aside Thursday night for *Time* magazine. "At six o'clock every Thursday he'd call me up," said Hugh Sidey. "He knew my deadlines and he'd brief me. He'd call up and say: 'All right, it's *Time* magazine time.' We'd drink scotch. He would say that he'd rather have one story in *Time* magazine or *The New York Times* than three or four everywhere else."

As president, Johnson enjoyed certain perks. John Steele remembered the White House car and driver pulling up to the Merkle printing plant in the Northeast section of Washington about ten o'clock every Sunday evening. The driver would enter a certain door and be handed a copy of *Time* still damp from the ink of the presses. This would be rushed to President Johnson. If he was at his Pedernalles River ranch in Texas, the copy of *Time* would be flown by courier plane early the next morning.

Like Kennedy, Johnson was not always happy with *Time*. An article entitled, "Mr. President, You're Fun," told of him racing up a Texas hill at eighty-five MPH, passing two cars, and almost colliding with a third, "his paper cup of Pearl beer within easy sipping distance." As *Time* reported, "Speaker of the House John McCormack was next in line for the presidency, and a passenger groaned aloud, 'That's the closest John McCormack has come to the White House yet.' "

To *Time,* Johnson was "a cross between a teen-age Grand Prix driver and back to nature Thoreau in cowboy boots." In the course of the ride, *Time* told how Johnson gave a newswoman, "a very graphic description of the sex life of a bull."

Johnson and his staff were not happy with the story. "He had a hawk-like memory," said Steele. "He even remembered a single, unfavorable line."

Time later wanted to do a cover story on Johnson but, in a blistering memo, Johnson accused *Time* of being liars and cheats, destroyers of government, etc., etc. And he pledged that he would never talk to *Time* reporters or sit for their photographers. After reflection, he changed his mind. Arrangements were made for a long interview, which lasted five hours. Johnson even sat for an artist's sketch. "He was an entirely different Johnson," said the reporter. "It was just night and day."

At this time of recognition, Harry was preparing formally to step down into a valley of greater personal peace. He would no longer be "Owner/Editor, Big Boy of the Works," as he once put it. No more would he be the ringmaster crusading for a new American century, building a world that God wanted. No more would he call for filling his magazines with both "titillating trivialities" as well as "the epic touch." No more would he invite a writer to join him for coffee and doughnuts at his favorite drugstore in Rockefeller Center.

The time had come for Luce to leave his magazines—and the world—alone and to turn inward to his own soul and his own private life, remembering the line from a Latin poet saying, "Death plucks my ear and says, 'Live—I am coming.' "

33

WHEN Luce turned sixty-six, he decided the time had come to pass the scepter to forty-nine-year-old Hedley Donovan. Observing this extraordinary change of command, Teddy White issued a ripe remark: "When the tree begins to fall, for the first time you see how tall it is. Harry's the biggest timber in American journalism. It was exciting to be around him. He's prayerful, rough, and great."

Everybody agreed that it was not in Luce's character to step down. Observers quickly pointed out that Luce was not stepping down, but sideways. In his new post as editorial chairman, he announced, "It is my intention to work for Time Inc. approximately full time."

Still, the succession had begun. Luce talked about traveling and writing memoirs. He also said he would do a little backward looking and "perhaps get to a college campus once in a while to see what the rising generation is thinking." Then he made a very telling point: "I will contribute, criticize, and suggest, but my advice does not have to be taken."

It seemed as if he had finally come to terms with himself and decided on a more peaceful approach to his life and work. Ambition was no longer a big word. Though Luce received various offers of ambassadorships, he said: "The only ambassadorship I would take is to a restored democracy in China."

In officially taking over as editor in chief in April 1964, Hedley Donovan told the assembled Time Inc. staff, "We do not claim to be neutral; we do claim to be fair. But our occasional lapses hurt us among some of the very people our magazines are meant for. We do indeed have some enemies to be proud of, and we want to keep them. We also have some unnecessary enemies whom we acquired rather carelessly." And then came Donovan's declaration of independence: "The vote of Time Inc. should never be considered in the pocket of any particular political leader or party. The vote of Time Inc. is an independent vote . . ."

* * *

In the 1964 presidential campaign, Donovan's candidate was a progressive Republican, Governor William Scranton of Pennsylvania. Scranton was also Luce's candidate. James Linen, who was Scranton's brother-in-law, was a big supporter. But Scranton's chances became slimmer when he delayed too long in declaring himself. Even so, *Life* editorialized, "We would far rather see Scranton than Goldwater as president of the United States."

Senator Barry Goldwater was a Phoenix neighbor of the Luces and an occasional bridge partner. As she got to know Goldwater, Clare gradually decided that he best represented her own views on the extreme right. Goldwater asked Clare to make a seconding speech for him at the convention, and she agreed. Luce edited Clare's speech, but otherwise stayed politically aloof.

In her speech, Clare called Goldwater "a prophet of a free and fearless America." Her stepson Hank sent her a telegram congratulating her on her eloquence, even though he disagreed with her choice of candidate. At sixty-one, her hair now white-gold, Clare looked deceptively fragile until she started speaking. Her name was again mentioned as a possible vice presidential running mate for Goldwater, but most political observers regarded Clare's prospects as dim.

For Harry, the convention was momentous for a very personal reason. "The last time I saw Harry was at the Republican convention," said Jean Campbell. She was there covering it for the London *Evening Standard*. "Marion Javits invited me to lunch. Her husband came up from the convention floor, and who do you think he had with him—Harry! And, of course, Harry was so nervous; he didn't know what to do. So, I went over and sat next to him on this tiny bench and just made light conversation. Poor darling! He had a coffee cup in his hand, and it was trembling. When he left, he didn't go out the door—he walked into the cupboard. And Marion yelled after him, 'You're in the cupboard!' He practically ran out.

"Then afterward, he rang me up straightaway," Campbell continued. "He started ringing me up again, every day, twice a day, until he left for Japan. He called me up from the airport, but then I never saw him again. And he never wrote again."

Whatever Harry's feelings about this encounter with his lost love, he revealed nothing to friends, and certainly not to Clare. In fact, once again he involved himself deeply with Clare's career.

There was some serious talk that she might run as a Conservative Party candidate for the U.S. Senate in New York. It became more than talk when Harry, somewhat apologetically, called New York's Republican incumbent Senator Kenneth B. Keating to tell him that his wife had made up her mind to run against him. Harry then put Clare on the phone to talk to the senator. Keating felt that Mrs. Luce was not serious but was playing a cat-and-mouse game to pressure him to endorse the Goldwater ticket. Clare then announced publicly her intention to run on the Conservative Party ticket.

Republican leaders roared in protest. Clare finally bowed out on the eve of the Conservative Party convention and announced, "Oh, no, of course I couldn't win. If I were to win, it would be one of the great flukes of political history."

As the election neared, the Time Inc. magazines were not by any stretch in Goldwater's camp. "How can we expect to win when even your magazines say such things about Senator Goldwater?" one of the senator's aides asked Clare. Her reply: "Well, in the first place, they're not my magazines . . ."

At a managing editors' lunch at Time Inc., Luce said, "Well, you know Clare. She's after me to vote for Goldwater, but I don't think I will."

"So help me, I do not know *how* Harry himself voted," Clare later told author W. A. Swanberg. "He never told me. I never asked him." She knew he didn't like Goldwater.

One of Harry's peers, Herbert R. Mayes of *McCall's,* asked him what would happen if he preferred candidate B and his editors wanted candidate A: Who would his magazines support?

"They will support candidate B," said Luce.

Life magazine finally endorsed Lyndon Johnson. Commenting on it, Clare said, "I don't disagree with them. They disagree with me. I endorsed Goldwater before they endorsed Johnson."

Clare's feelings for Johnson were more emotional than political. Goldwater had promised to give her what L.B.J. wouldn't—a position in his Cabinet. Goldwater had publicly named his choices for the Cabinet if he won. Clare Boothe Luce would be his secretary of health, education and welfare.

Luce avoided the political flak of the *Life* endorsement by going to the Far East and staying away for five weeks. "We met him in Bangkok," said *Time* correspondent Frank McCullough. "We cleared him through all the customs and immigrations. But he did have to fill out a financial form. I said: 'Harry, how much money do you have?' He said: 'What? What?' I said, 'How much money?' He said, '$700 in cash and $2000 in traveler's checks.' Five weeks later, after thirty-five lunches and thirty-five dinners with Harry Luce, most of them enormous state affairs, and after buying all kinds of gifts, it's time to go home. At the airport in Japan, I say to him: 'Harry, how much money do you have?' He says, 'You know damn *well* how much I have.' And it was $2000 in traveler's checks and $700 in cash. It must have cost $50,000 to arrange whatever we were arranging—and he never personally spent a nickel."

Luce still traveled like a king whenever he went anywhere, a badly dressed and rumpled king but still a king. Dick Clurman, *Time*'s chief of correspondents, accompanied Harry to Chicago for a black-tie dinner. They shared a living room, two bedrooms, and two baths. Clurman recalled, "He comes out in a towel, his chin covered with shaving cream, and says, 'How much does this suite cost?' I said, 'I don't know, Harry. I suppose $150.' He said, '$150! We can change in the men's room. Let's leave here!' And I said, 'Harry, you don't understand. When I come here without you, I stay in this suite!'"

Yet, despite his penny-pinching, Harry was indignant when Clare suggested that he might take a tax deduction for a forthcoming trip. If he wasn't successful enough to pay his taxes, he noted, then things were pretty bad.

In fact, Luce had a typical, poor boy's attitude about money. He guarded it carefully and wanted to be richer than anyone else. He also coveted the social acceptance that comes with money. One of his seldom-expressed regrets was that he had never been fully socially accepted, that the Rockefellers never had invited him to their homes.

If the Rockefellers were negligent, the president was not. After the election, Luce visited Johnson often. He was particularly pleased with L.B.J.'s inaugural speech on "The Great Society," which Luce called "the best speech of the decade." The fact was that Luce earlier had used the phrase "The Great Society" in one of his own speeches. In April 1939, he had said, "The business of business is to take part in the creation of The Great Society."

He was similarly pleased when Johnson got his Civil Rights Bill passed within the first hundred days. "Well, thank God, *that* problem is solved," said Luce. "Now we can go on to something else."

Harry seemed to mellow. He had found another woman to listen to him. She was the gentle, adoring princess of Lichtenstein who operated a store in Phoenix called the Princess' Pantry. She was an American from the Midwest, an attractive woman much younger than Harry, and her first name was Jean. Phoenix friends gossiped about how often Harry and the princess were seen together, but there were no details or evidence of any romance.

The princess and her husband and the Luces even played bridge together. The prince of Lichtenstein was a wiry man with a goatee, some twenty years older than his wife, and generally impoverished. Columnist William Buckley knew them both and recalled the prince had a pleasant smile, a good sense of humor. Presumably, while the prince was away, Harry became more intimate with the adoring princess. Buckley considers a romantic liaison between Harry and the princess unlikely because, while she had an attractive personality, "she was not at all seductive." Harry, however, was appreciative enough to send her and her husband on a world tour.

Harry's attentiveness to the princess may well have been what triggered a hot argument with Clare. She hurried to New York, and sought refuge with Irene Selznick.

"Clare was not fond of women," said Irene, "but she said I was one of the three women she loved. (As I didn't much admire the other two, may they rest in peace, I was unmoved.) From time to time, she would declare her devotion to me, sending me any number of affectionately inscribed photographs of herself in silver frames. She would occasionally even present me as 'the woman I love,' but the next time I saw her, she could give me a very cool, 'How do you do?' "

To Irene, who had cared for her after Ann's death, Clare poured out the full story about Luce and Lady Jean Campbell. She also told Irene that she was now "ready for a divorce."

When Clare left several days later, Irene called Jean Campbell in Jamaica and told her, "You must come back here now!", but gave no details.

Jean quickly returned. "I had told Irene all about Harry and she hadn't believed me; she thought it was my invention," said Jean. "Then Clare came and told all about it and she finally believed it."

For Jean it ended on a flat note. Once again, Clare had changed her mind. There was no further mention of divorce.

Clare had once said: "Life is not a series of bridge hands that you can keep dealing yourself until you get a grand slam." Now, she may well have thought that her grand slam days were over, and she had better hold the hand she had.

Most of the other men in Clare's life were gone, most notably Bernard Baruch. He had died in June 1965 at the age of ninety-four. For his birthday, Clare had sent him a telegram with the word "LOVE" repeated 94 times. Shortly before his death, he had phoned to say how ecstatic he had been over their recent evening together, that she looked more beautiful than ever, and reminded him of when she was a very young girl. Clare had replied that she could not imagine her world without him. Baruch had helped shape the young Clare, helped her emerge into politics, helped get her first plays produced, helped elect her to Congress, was always there with love, advice, and friendship. Bernie had been one of the rocks of strength in her life. Whenever she was hospitalized, he called her constantly. She kept pictures of him in her rooms, happily served as his hostess in Washington, kissed him effusively without shame in public whenever they met, sent him a steady stream of notes from wherever she was. In the last years, he had complained of some neglect from her, but never for long. His death was a hole in her heart.

As for Harry, he still mourned the emotional loss of Jean Campbell. Her marriage to Norman Mailer had been filled with strange parties, and Mailer wrote a novel based on it all. Their marriage ended in December 1963 with a Mexican divorce. Jean married soon afterward to a gentleman farmer from Maryland, the grandson of a Drexel and a descendent of the founder of Cooper Union. This, too, was not a marriage that would last long. The love of her life would always be Harry.

After his meeting with Campbell at the Republican convention, Harry let matters rest. He was not a man to reminisce. He did not like to look back, possibly because this would remind him of his advancing age. Coming back from a school reunion, he said, "I must look in the mirror—the old classmates are all looking older."

Jean Dalrymple also noticed Luce's fear of aging. "I gave him something to read," she recalled. "He had glasses on, and he couldn't read with them, so he took them off. He fooled around, and finally said, 'God damn this old age!' I know just how he felt."

Although Harry had formally surrendered his editorial title to Hedley Donovan, founding father Luce still sat at the head of the table during any editorial meeting he attended. Time Inc. was still his store. When a British author blamed Time Inc. for failing to give Americans the facts on China, Luce bristled, flushed, almost trembling with indignation and exclaimed, "I am responsible for my magazines in a great measure and any attack on them is an attack on me."

Yet, he tried at other times to move offstage gracefully. Harry now would go to Donovan's office rather than calling him to come to *his*. "I have to watch out that I don't get into Donovan's hair," he said.

His old secretary Miss Thrasher, as he always called her, had retired after twenty-eight years. She had protected him against everybody and everything, including Christmas parties. His new secretary, Gloria Mariano, (he called her "Gloria" from the first day) scheduled Luce for a dozen different Time Inc. parties, including one for the telephone operators. "He went to all of them and had the most marvelous times!" she said.

Luce had told Donovan that he no longer wanted his name on the *Time* masthead, but the new editor in chief insisted it remain. Luce still wrote comments on the margins of every issue of TIME for the staff to read, but he knew they paid less attention to them.

Some months after turning the top job over to Donovan, Luce made one of his frequent trips to Washington. He was escorted to his hotel by John Steele. At the door, Luce stopped for a moment and asked, "Do you think I made a mistake in naming Hedley to the job?"

"I was flabbergasted," said Steele, "and remained silent for a moment."

"Oh, that's an unfair question," Luce snapped. "Don't answer it." Then he turned on his heels and went into his room.

Steele had known Harry long enough to know what was going on. Luce was suffering temporary withdrawal symptoms. Harry had no doubt about Hedley; he simply missed what he had surrendered. He had given up a part of his life.

When an associate asked him how he liked retirement, Luce's reply was curt: "It ain't good."

But he refused to let retirement slow him down. Luce still dropped in at *Time* bureaus, still made speeches all over the country on his favorite subjects of American morality, justice, the responsibility of journalism, and the future of the Far East. He still wrote most of his own speeches. The wish of Luce's life was to be a great orator.

Luce also involved himself in an international convocation of statesmen and scholars to discuss world peace; he toured U.S. Air Force bases as chairman of the Air University's board of visitors, and attended a world law conference in Washington.

If that weren't enough, he spent time as a Chubb fellow at Yale. In seminars there with students, Luce spent most of his time defending or explaining *Time*. Answering the charge that *Time* was not objective enough, Luce said, "If you read a column by Reston in *The New York Times,* you know you're reading Reston. If you read *Time,* you know you're reading *Time.*"

On another occasion, he lectured at Brandeis. Students asked Luce how he could call *Time* a news magazine "when you're so unfair." He thought about that a moment, then replied, "Well, since I invented the term news magazine, I can make it mean anything I want it to mean."

In Paris, he once wistfully asked a *Time* correspondent, "Are the French happy?"

The correspondent replied that it was impossible to tell.

"Why?" asked Luce.

"You can't even tell if a single person is happy."

Luce just stared at him, "We sent you here to find this out."

Harry had not changed much physically. His red-gray brows were as imposing as always. There was perhaps more gray in his thinning hair, more of a stoop in his shoulders. He still punctuated his staccato-like conversations by pausing with his finger pressed against a front tooth.

Luce seemed more aware now of people's feelings. When Gloria Mariano came in with laryngitis, he would say, "Go home and take care of that, Gloria." Years earlier, such concern would have been beyond Harry's capabilities.

Family relationships, however, would never be easy for him. He saw his brother Sheldon several times a year, and they played golf. He also enjoyed being with his grandchildren, nieces, and nephews. With smaller children,

Harry was at his best, his most relaxed, his warmest. When Hank's son was nine, Harry Luce took him to Europe and was most proud when the boy corrected the guide at St. Peter's, just as his grandfather would have done.

With his sons, the relationship was more strained. Perhaps he expected too much from them. His younger son, Peter Paul, was a very outgoing young man—tall and good looking. He attended M.I.T. for three years and then worked at Grumman Aircraft on Long Island for a while. He liked to collect old cars and airplanes and wanted nothing to do with Time Inc. Peter would take his father for a flight in a small plane or pick him up for lunch in his antique Rolls-Royce.

Harry was amused and baffled by Peter, who eventually went to live in Denver with his wife. There, they raised four daughters, and Peter worked as a consultant.

Henry or "Hank," as everybody but his father called him, stayed with *Time*. Luce had a father's pride whenever Hank did well in any of his Time Inc. jobs. But he wanted to learn and do on his own.

Early in his career, Hank had talked to Frank White about being in Paris, and White thought it would be fine. He then mentioned it to Luce, whose cautious reaction was "Are you sure you need him?"

"Of course," said White. "And then he said something odd," White remembered. He said, "I'll talk about it with Clare." "I had never before heard this kind of family thing in any conversation I had with him," White declared. "And then he said, 'I want to thank you for your interest in my son.' "

Instead of allowing his son to go to Paris, Luce put Hank in charge of the construction of the new Time-Life building.

Then when Richard Clurman was chief of correspondents, Hank applied for a job in the London bureau, and Clurman suggested he first talk to his father.

"Twenty minutes later," Clurman recalled, "Harry called me, and said, 'Can you come up?' He was sitting there, with his feet on the desk, in a reflective mood, and asked. 'What do you think?'

"It's a gamble," I told him.

"He said, 'I'm gonna let you make that decision.' Then, he added, rather reflectively, 'You know, I haven't always been a good father . . .' "

In December 1966, Clurman dropped in on Luce, and said, "Harry, I've just come from London, and I'm pleased to tell you that Hank is doing very well there."

"Harry was *visibly* moved," Clurman recalled.

In his new, more mellow retirement mood, Harry liked parties. "Clare really wouldn't entertain for Harry," said Shirley Clurman, who knew her friend well. "It was part of her subconscious hostility, although a lot of it was conscious. She didn't want attention taken away from herself. If he was there, she was afraid people would want to talk mostly to him. It was sad."

Even more sad was Clare's behavior when she and Harry went out to other people's parties. "She would get looped on one martini, smashed on two," confided an intimate. More often now, she had two.

One night, the Clurmans invited Harry to a party in New York with a lot of literary and theatrical celebrities. Harry made a point of asking playwright Edward Albee why he wrote such sad plays when he might have written happy ones. He liked probing, provoking. Luce asked Shirley, "How do you give a party like this? How do you get these people to come?"

"And then I said the most graceful thing in my life—which wasn't true. I said, 'Because I tell them you're going to be here.' And I think he liked that. I got flowers afterward."

In her job handling public relations for Time Inc., Shirley arranged for Harry and Clare to make their first joint television appearance on a Martin Agronsky show. Clare refused because she claimed her life was empty of any plans or ambitions. This was unlike Clare, who was always ready to get into the pit, into the action, ready to fight back at any interviewer. Now she felt she had nothing to fight about.

Clare was still planning her million-dollar home in Hawaii, and spent much of her time there at a rented house nearby. She wrote Harry that she found life without him like being in an Italian palazzo in the winter without heat. Clare was a good letter-writer, and she knew what to say. At this point in her life, Clare was savvy enough to see an emptiness without Harry. Also, very simply she again needed him at her side.

"He felt she kind of planned it that way so that she could have him out there, captive," said Jean Dalrymple.

Harry felt very isolated in Hawaii. Luce would pad around barefooted in shorts, looking ill-at-ease. Clare spent her time in a billowing mu-mu, painting at an easel beside the swimming pool. An interviewer suggested he couldn't imagine her "undertaking anything at which you expected to be a failure."

"I'm already better than Churchill was," Clare said. In fact, Churchill himself had given her a painting set in 1955. She had cabled him then that she had everything a painter needed except a little touch of genius.

In Hawaii more than in Phoenix, Clare seemed willing to entertain. Perhaps it was a way of holding Harry. The Honolulu *Advertiser* society columnist reported "a swing supper party" at the Luces and described Clare wearing "an emerald green brocade gown slit to the knee on one side to balance the intricately cut side drape on the other." Another columnist observed Clare doing a hula interpretation of swaying palms and reported that she would soon be making a serious study of the hula, as well as of porpoises in Hawaiian waters. "Porpoises," she said, "are the most intelligent animals I have ever encountered."

When he could escape from Hawaii, Luce tried to continually broaden his experience. He eagerly accepted an invitation to speak to students at Yale, even though the overture came from John Hersey. After their break in 1945, the two had lost contact. But Hersey was then master of Pierson College at Yale.

"I wrote him a friendly letter, said that I wanted to see him again," Hersey explained. "Why did I want to be friends with him again? Well, I *liked* him. There was a warmth in his enthusiasm that was very exciting. And I know Luce wanted his old friendships restored."

When Luce arrived, said Hersey, eighteen students came to meet him. Luce recommended to them the experience of being a cub reporter "whether or not you're going to be a poet or a banker. Being a cub-reporter," he said, "enables you see life in the raw, perhaps more raw than life."

Luce felt too many of the students had lost their faith in God and country. Some Yale students afterward admitted being impressed by his dynamism, his confidence, and his candidness, even though they could not share his faith.

"At about eleven or eleven-thirty, they all went home," said Hersey. "These sixties kids were a little bit hostile in the way they dealt with him. After they'd left, he had a scotch, and said, 'Oh, John, I've been experimenting with LSD, and it's the most wonderful thing! You look at that glass on the table, and see shimmering colors on either side of it.'

"This was at a time when LSD was ruining lives at Yale," recalled Hersey. "I thanked my stars that he didn't say that when the kids were there!"

Harry was not so reticent at the Hunt Ball, a traditional, formal annual dinner for the staff of *Life,* at the Waldorf. In a brief speech, he told about how he and Clare had experimented, under controlled conditions, with LSD.

"I remember there was absolute silence," recalled Andrew Heiskell. "Not a person could think of a proper response to this declaration! You don't applaud. You don't hiss. And then you say, 'Well, why did he tell?' I guess he had to prove that at past sixty-five, he was still young, still one of the boys."

Later, it came out that LSD experiments had begun with one of the Luces' house guests, a doctor, who had been researching the effects of LSD on creative people. Under his supervised guidance, the Luces "took a trip." Clare reported a heightened appreciation of color, and Harry heard magnificent music, so much so that he walked toward their cactus he had never liked, a squat one with long hair, and came back saying, "Did you ever see anything more beautiful?" Father Murray, observing this, laughed out loud.

Luce's public admission about LSD did not affect his status as journalism's elder statesman. Yale gave Luce an honorary doctorate of law and so did Williams. Syracuse University School of Journalism also gave him its Distinguished Service Medal. *Der Spiegel,* the German magazine, summed up Luce's status by saying, "Luce printed products are the intellectual supplement of Coca-Cola, Marilyn Monroe, and dollar diplomacy."

Pleased with his grand stature, Luce was still plagued by the advanced age that went with it.

On a short trip to New York, he invited Tom Griffith and his wife to dinner at his apartment, then to the theater by limousine. Griffith mentioned a friend who had a pacemaker installed in his heart, and Luce soon exhausted Griffith's knowledge of the subject. At the theater, the curtain was delayed because a man in the balcony suffered a seizure. As they heard the ambulance arrive, Luce suggested they go to the foyer to see the man being carried out. Griffith's wife refused, feeling the man was entitled to some privacy. Luce rushed out alone. Later, they realized that it wasn't simply his insatiable curiosity about everything. He had suffered a heart attack himself and wanted to see what he knew might happen to him again.

Perhaps sensing his mortality, Luce once again wanted to see Jean Campbell. He missed her deeply. He asked Jean Dalrymple to try to find her and set up a lunch. "I was in Washington, when she called and gave me Harry's message," said Campbell. "I got back to New York and was so excited. I thought, 'Oh, how lovely!' And then she called again, and said, 'No, he just can't do it.' " Harry simply could not summon the courage for an emotional confrontation. It could cause an explosion within him, and he feared he could not cope with it.

It was far easier for him to simply do Clare's bidding and not risk any unwanted inner turmoil. So, when the Commonwealth Club in San Francisco asked Clare to speak about the United Nations, Harry went with her and even helped write the speech.

The next day, before Clare's talk, Harry wanted to see Haight-Ashbury, the gathering place for California's counter-culture. His guide was *Time* reporter Justin Gooding, who faced the usual barrage of Luce's questions about the hippies: Where did they come from, what did they want? Harry asked to see the Chinese art at the museum in Golden Gate park. The curator opened the storeroom to show him a four-foot-high clay camel, not yet on display. "How much do you want to see?" asked the curator.

"I want to see all I can," said Luce, as if he knew that he would not have many more chances.

That Saturday, after their return to Phoenix, Harry played nine holes of golf, had drinks and lunch with friends, and joined a dinner party at the Arizona Biltmore. He also wrote a note to Griffith complaining that there had been no recent strong editorial in *Life* or any deep analysis in *Time* about the American attitude on sanctions against Rhodesia.

On Sunday morning, Luce was uncharacteristically still in bed when the cook brought him his breakfast. He couldn't eat it, and later he vomited. He was too restless to stay in bed, so he wandered over to Clare's studio to watch her paint. She took his temperature, which was 102. Clare then called Dr. Hayes Caldwell. By the time he arrived, Harry had a nosebleed and was coughing up bloody sputum. His blood pressure and pulse were both normal, and the doctor decided to let him rest. Harry stayed with Clare in her room, tried eating some soup and again vomited. His blood pressure and pulse were still normal when the doctor came that night, but the doctor ordered a nurse to stay with Luce. The next morning, Harry wandered into the kitchen asking for cornflakes. Again, he vomited and the doctor ordered an ambulance.

Luce walked to the ambulance, refusing assistance from Clare. She had packed some books he had been reading: a paperback Perry Mason mystery, a theological work, and a Bible. Clare followed in a car behind the ambulance, and Luce playfully waved at her through the ambulance window. But when he settled in at the hospital, he admitted to the doctor, "I seem to be unusually sleepy."

For the rest of the day, he underwent medical tests. Luce persuaded Clare to keep a dinner date with the in-laws of California Governor Ronald Reagan. When she phoned him that night, he told her he planned to watch *Perry Mason* on television. "Should I come over and we'll watch it together?" Clare asked. He said no.

That night, he slept poorly, and kept getting out of bed, and pacing the floor despite the nurse's protests. About three AM, he went to the bathroom, and the nurse heard him yell, "Oh, Jesus!" Hearing him fall, she rushed to find Luce on the floor, already unconscious from a coronary occlusion. A hospital emergency team applied shock treatment and heart massage. The Mother Superior of St. Joseph's Hospital told Clare to hurry over. But by the time she arrived, Harry was dead, five weeks short of his sixty-ninth birthday. The date was February 28, 1967. On this day, exactly forty-four years before, the first printed copy of *Time* had been delivered to his door.

Luce was fortunate in that he had suffered no disabling stroke that would have robbed him of his mind or his voice. Nor had he suffered any prolonged pain. It seemed somehow right that he had died with "Jesus" on his lips.

Yet, this was not the way Luce would have wanted to go. He had once said that he wanted to die in the *Time* offices. After all, his magazine empire was his child. It was his love, and it was his life. He had given more of himself to Time Inc. than he had to any human being—to any woman, child, or friend.

The week Luce died, Jean Campbell was on a Greek ship going around the world with her husband and daughter. "I said to my husband, who knew all about Harry: 'I have the most extraordinary feeling. I know Harry is somewhere around here. I know I will see him when we land in Australia. I just *see* him here. I'm sure he's here.'

"We went to Perth, and then to Sydney, and I checked for him in all the hotels. I could feel something weird. Then we got to Fiji. I went into a pharmacy shop and suddenly I saw a copy of *Time* with Harry's picture on the cover. It was as if he was saying to me, Do you want to see my picture? He had died some ten days before, while I felt him on that boat."

The memorial service for Luce at the Madison Avenue Presbyterian Church on March 3, 1967, was packed with some 800 prominent people. A private hookup transmitted the service to the auditorium and reception lounge of the Time-Life building for some 1200 employees, who sang the hymns in unison with those in church. Dr. H. C. Read, Luce's friend and pastor, called him "a man of unlimited imagination who reveled in hard facts, an idealist who made his judgments with utter realism, one of the decision-makers of our time. To talk with him was a signal to shift the mind into high gear, for his was never in neutral," said Dr. Read.

He stressed Luce's belief that behind the chaos of men and nations, "in the journey of man from the slime to the stars," there was a divine purpose. He was a pilgrim, who had set forth on a pilgrimage.

Luce's burying ground had been a subject of intense family discussion. His sister felt he might want to be buried near his parents, at his mother's family plot in Utica, New York. Clare had recalled that she had told him she planned to be buried at Mepkin. "I'd be happy to be buried there, too," he had said, "providing a Presbyterian reads the service." Hank Luce, flying in from London where he was then *Time* bureau chief, confirmed that his father wanted to be buried at Mepkin. He had loved the peace of the place and went back there even after they had sold it to the Trappist monks. He would be buried near his stepdaughter Ann, whom he truly loved.

Those close to Luce knew of another fitting reason for his being buried in South Carolina: It was on a moonlit night in Camp Jackson that young Luce and Briton Hadden had made their final decision about starting *Time*.

On the day of Luce's burial, the sun came out and the service was ecumenical, a touch his family felt Harry would have loved. "The monks sang ancient

Gregorian chants and the service was read from my mother's Presbyterian Book of Common Worship," recalled Harry's sister Beth. "Father John Murray pronounced a eulogy. The monks, led by Father Moses, a convert from Judaism, held a High Mass. The casket was opened to reveal the body—his face beautiful and serene."

Harry's grave, marked by a simple, four-foot marble stone carved with the abstract motif of an old live oak tree, was on a hilltop. The Mepkin monks would care for the grave site.

After Luce had been laid to rest, Father Anthony, one of the Trappist monks, said to Clare, "There's a little marble left over from his headstone. Shall we run one off for you?"

She gave a little start, then answered, "That'd be very nice!"

Father Anthony also asked Dick Clurman whether he thought it was possible for Time-Life to "provide some liquid refreshments for lunch?" "So I sent the limousine to the nearest town, and the driver came back with three cases of booze and a case of wine for the Brothership. They lived it up," Clurman reported.

It is most likely that Harry would have been pleased.

The company Luce had started with a loan of $86,000 in 1923, now had a market value of $690 million. His personal holdings in Time stock totaled 1,012,575 shares worth about $109 million. Most of it was set aside for the Henry Luce Foundation, created in honor of his father to promote Christian education and intellectual exchange between the United States and Far Eastern countries. The Foundation became the largest single stockholder in Time Inc., and Henry Luce III was made president. Clare received various properties plus stock shares worth $19 million. She was not included on the board of the Foundation. Even in his death, Harry would not leave her any editorial control over Time Inc.

All his life, Luce had been an outsider craving to become an insider. Yet the profession he chose made it impossible for him to become an insider. Perhaps being an outsider gave him a special brilliant vision, an unclouded vision—even if it was sometimes wrong-headed. It enabled him to bring to *Time* a simplicity and idealism that attracted the general public. His magazines, especially *Life,* gave people the image of an America they *wished* they knew.

When people picked up Luce's magazines, they felt his influence. He was always searching for simple answers, and he was vain enough to feel he could find them. And, sometimes, he did. A great part of his strength was his naiveté, "so innocent that he didn't know there were things he couldn't do, so he went ahead and actually did some of them," as T. S. Matthews said. At the core was Luce's insatiable curiosity. If Harry found himself in the presence of God, said his pastor, the first thing he would want to do would be ask some questions.

But, sometimes, he wanted too much. If somebody pleasantly said to him, "It's a nice sunset," he might quickly ask, "Why?"

One of Luce's critics insisted that all his energy and religious zeal "confused more issues than it clarified, harmed more people than he helped, and contributed more to the Gross National Product than to American culture." The question raised, said this critic, was not how much but "how little he used his strength." Was he more obsessed with the idea of power than with the power of an idea?

Others disagree. "It didn't seem to me that he ever did editing for profit's sake. He never did stories, or chose them, because they'd make money for the magazines," said John Hersey. "I think he always cared about the subject itself. In that way, he was a true journalist."

The sorrow of Luce's life was that he never got what he truly wanted—the lifetime love and laughter of a tender woman. For that, he deserved compassion. He remained a man of frustrated hopes, banked fires, and deep passions. Yet his soul was always his own and he was never truly defeated. More than anything, he wanted to be a great patriot and a true Christian who believed, "There is no such thing as right, left, and center. There is freedom and lack of freedom. We are for freedom."

Though Luce had his enemies, they objected mostly to his beliefs. "I have never heard anyone, in all the time I've been there, say anything shabby about him personally," said a *Time* editor. "I have never heard anything said about Luce, really, that couldn't be repeated to his face."

Luce was a man who lived with God, but wistfully envied the pirates. He was a man of words, who personally could not communicate, a man who wanted a love he did not know how to keep. He was a man untarnished by money, a man for whom faith was a shining light. He was a man who made his own world, but was still lost, a man who could build an empire, but not a home. Yet Luce had discovered the great gift of life: to wake in the morning filled with the excitement of what he would do that day. It is a gift given to few. It was a gift he had earned.

34

NOBODY saw Clare cry when Harry died. There was grief, but no tears. Those who knew her well wondered if the grief was for Harry or for herself. Clare was alone now with all the houses and all the money she would ever need. But she was sixty-four years old, and she felt empty and confused.

"She was devastated," said Shirley Clurman, who went to Arizona to stay with Clare. "She was very angry. One night, I had gone to bed and I heard this scream coming from her room. I quickly ran in. She was in the bathroom on the verge of hysteria, and said, 'That sonofa*bitch!* How could he do this to me? Why didn't he wait for ten years, or why didn't he go ten years ago?' "

"It's funny; I learned so much when I went out there," Clurman continued. "She said, 'You'll stay in Harry's bedroom.' She had the single most beautiful suite of rooms that any woman would ever dream of. Just for her luggage, she had a room with high ceilings and racks going up, filled with all that old Vuitton luggage. She had clothes racks like cleaners' racks; you'd just push a button and they'd go around. The bathroom was a thing of glory. She had equipment for her own hairdresser and makeup person there. I stayed in Harry's room, which was small, with twin beds. It really was nothing, you know. That was representative of their marriage, in a large sense."

Clare had lost her throne but not her royalty. She was still on the lists as one of the most outstanding, most important, most admired, best dressed women in the world. She still received invitations, requests for articles, and solicitations for political support. The telephone was always ringing. Her name on a committee board was considered a coup; her presence at any party was regarded as a special event. Her tongue was as tart as ever. She had earned her own way and had sampled enough careers to satisfy a dozen women, but she was still restless for more.

To outsiders, Clare was the model for the self-made woman, but she did not fit easily into that or any category. For some, she was too elegant to be intelligent, too sharp-witted to be ladylike. Many of the stories about her were myths of her own making. She was clever enough to realize that people would make up stories to explain a phenomenon they couldn't understand, but she had been inventing the stories long before they did.

In some of her more depressed moments, Clare would freely disparage the phenomenon she had created. "I've never thought of myself as successful," she said. "One achieves so much less than one's expectations. I was thinking at one time of writing my memoirs and calling it, 'Confessions of an Unsuccessful Woman.' I've done too many things and it all doesn't stack up. The truth is, my private life has been sad, unhappy, and sometimes tragic."

For Clare, the truth about Harry and his women reflected her own failings as a wife. How could she, as beautiful and gifted as she was, desired by men everywhere, lose her husband to other women?

One interviewer observed that "a couple of times when Clare mentioned some intimate recollection of Harry, tears would fill her eyes and she'd make herself another drink." However, others felt that her tears seemed staged. Yet she insisted to interviewers that she had loved Harry deeply, that her personal loss was terrible. She described him "as a man who was sometimes difficult but always interesting, always stimulating, always provocative." And there was often genuine affection in her voice when she referred to him, as "that old sonofabitch."

Clare soon started to sort out her life. She gradually felt a sense of freedom and space. She no longer had to cater to Harry's schedule or his eccentricities. It became a liberating time for her. She hurried to complete her house in Hawaii.

"At my age, the big problem is not accumulating property but getting rid of it," said Clare, who soon sold the house in Phoenix and the apartment in New York. Ever since she was nineteen, she said, she always had lived in three homes. "I had one great desire, which was to have just one house. I had two conditions. It should be under the American flag, and it should be as livable in winter as summer. I'm too old to shovel snow off my doorstep in Connecticut."

The house in Hawaii, fanned by the trade winds, sat on a beautiful beach with a sweeping view of the sea from every room. Elegant, airy, and expansive, it had an Oriental feel but was utterly modern with twenty-foot ceilings. Clare could press a button and electronically seal herself off from the world behind shatterproof windows.

She settled easily into the soft, slow pace of Hawaii. The oils she painted hung from her walls and so did her colorful mosaics. The sofas were covered with her needlepoint pillows. Dominating the drawing room was a portrait of Clare in her full ambassadorial regalia. Underneath the portrait were shelves filled with her jade collection. Scattered through the house were tiny Chinese vases, each holding a single orchid.

In her "glory hole," her indoor-outdoor office, were hundreds of tropical plants; tiny white temple birds, freed from their cages, flew overhead. The furniture was white and the rugs brilliant blue; books were everywhere.

But Clare had moments of deep discontent.

Clare confided to Father Murray that she was quietly drifting away from the Church because she resented its concept that Man represented the active brain and Woman the passive heart. Furthermore, she began questioning the value of her pampered life and her possessions.

"Yes, I have all of this, living in Hawaii, and I have a Chinese couple to take care of me, and I have a hundred million dollars. But why am I so upset? Because I am wondering if I will wake up tomorrow and it will all be gone." What one of her friends felt she meant was that "when she doesn't wake up in the morning, it will all be gone.' "

When guests arrived at Clare's house, which was called Halenai'a, the "House of the Golden Dolphin," she kissed them on both cheeks and draped each guest with a lai of ginger, tuberoses, and pikake blossoms.

In a typical week, Clare's guests included hydrogen bomb scientist Edward Teller, her old arch antagonist Senator Fulbright, and Mortimer Adler, originator of the Great Books of the Western World series. She was not intellectually lonely.

"I'm home and mother to people traveling across the Pacific. I enjoy the role, but I keep the number of guests under control by having only one guest room. The room is small so they won't be tempted to stay too long."

The prince and princess of Lichtenstein had moved in on Clare. She earlier had hired the prince to supervise construction. She had told him then, "Alex, just tell the architect this: If when the sun comes down, I can't sit in my lanai, with my dry martini, and watch the sun come down over the ocean, there's going to be one less architect in Honolulu!"

Oceanography became a fresh excitement for her. Walter Cunningham, an expert on the subject, came to discuss it with her: "From time to time, we would take a dip in the bay but never let it interfere with the conversation," he said. "On one occasion, we were idly swimming toward the mouth of the bay, chatting as usual, and forgot the time. She swam along very slowly in an easy little breast stroke, while I did a backstroke beside her. When we finally stopped to take our bearings, we were at the mouth of the bay and the open sea."

They had been swimming with the tide, and the way back was now another hour's swim, against the tide.

"I was sticking close and trying not to show my concern for her, but she just kept chugging along. After another fifteen minutes, we noticed an outrigger canoe coming toward us from the beach. It was apparent that the lifeguard on board was concerned for our safety. Explaining they had lost many swimmers in just this fashion, he began to escort us back to the beach. I expected Mrs. Luce to get into the canoe, but that just wasn't her nature and she insisted on swimming all the way back to the beach. With all her other accomplishments, Clare Boothe Luce is one hell of a swimmer."

Guests understood that Clare worked in the morning, dictating in bed to her two secretaries. She swam in the afternoon, and talked in the evening. Punctuality was almost religious—lunch at twelve, supper at seven. Promptly. "My cook gets noivous," she explained, with a staged Brooklyn accent.

Clare was the queen of Honolulu, the focal point for every visiting celebrity. She had a rapid succession of big dinner parties. Everybody loved her, wanted her. She had little interest in going to Washington, where, she said, "the average age was *death.* "

"When I was in my twenties," Clare said wistfully, "I'd get up in the morning, and I used to think there was time to swim and have lunch and go to an art gallery and have a drink and go to dinner and then on to a club. Now I can do two things a day, and that's all."

Visiting Clare in Hawaii, Shirley Clurman found that her mood was now upbeat. "I had the best time with her. We'd stay up and watch those late movies until four in the morning; she said to me one day, 'Isn't this wonderful! If Harry and Dick were here, wouldn't it be boring? We couldn't *possibly* watch a movie like this.' "

And she kept her sense of humor.

When *Harper's* magazine headlined an article, "Clare Boothe Luce, from Courtesan to Career Woman," Clare commented: "If only it had read, 'Clare Boothe Luce, from Career Woman to Courtesan.' At my age, *that* would have made me sound more interesting."

Clare played more bridge and painted more. Her paintings now reflected her early life. One was a picture of a little girl with long blond hair, sitting on a stoop. A small portrait of her father showed him with a violin under his chin, but there were no strings in the violin. When somebody saw that as symbolic, she said, no, she simply didn't remember how many strings there were. It was the only painting she kept on the wall alongside a Monet, a Pisarro, and the oil by Winston Churchill.

Though Clare had plenty of money, she worried about it anyway. Her childhood poverty always haunted her. With Harry alive, her wealth was limitless, and she felt completely protected. Now that he was gone, she feared that the money she did have might slip through her fingers. She complained that Harry had never trusted her with money and so she had never really learned about it.

On visits to New York, she moved into a hotel room at the Sherry Netherlands, the same place she had lived when Harry Luce came to propose. Clare invited her friend Wilfrid Sheed to come and visit. "I was relieved to find her more or less the way I'd left her, sunny and gentle and life-size," he said. "The media monster was nowhere in sight. She was beautiful as ever, though she didn't think so herself."

"Fame? I always knew that *that* wouldn't last forever," she told him. "The night *The Women* opened, I went to the top of the Empire State building and realized that none of the ants on the street had ever heard of me. So much for being famous. You do miss being recognized at airports and being sent to the head of the line, but that's about all. What I miss are my looks."

With time, Clare felt more keenly the problems of a single woman. "I would enjoy a good friend and companion I could go to the movies with, sit and yap with, count on as an escort," she said. "But most of the intelligent men who would interest me are married to other women. I do miss very much some one person I can really be close with. We still don't live in the kind of world where women can travel alone. And when they travel in pairs, it complicates the lives of their friends, because they have to find two pairs of trousers to put under the dinner table. But men friends—I have none that I can count on, none that I can travel with."

Still, Clare confessed to a friend that she had dated a man younger than she was. He was "awfully cute, and I had such a nice time. I found myself batting my eyelashes at him, and asked him if he'd like to come up and I heard myself saying, 'Why don't you mix us a drink while I get into something more comfortable.'" Then she admitted, "I began to feel very foolish and it was making me nervous, so, finally, I asked him to go home."

Another time, Clare had a date with "a terribly handsome" *Life* foreign correspondent, who was married. "She was so excited," said her friend. "She was just ready to have an affair. The next day, I called her: 'Well, did you have fun?' Her voice was absolutely dead. She said to me, 'You know what he wanted? He wanted to know if I'd talk to Stavros Niarchos [the Greek shipping tycoon] about him.' She did, and he got his job."

Occasionally, Teddy White and Dick Clurman and their wives would ask Roswell Gilpatric, the handsome attorney who had been Harry's lawyer during the attempted divorce, to come along for an evening and be Clare's date. Clare didn't seem to fault Gilpatric for his role as Luce's divorce lawyer.

"They would arrange it," said Gilpatric. "I didn't do it on my own. They just thought that I'd be somebody good for Clare to play with. We didn't hit it off," he continued. "It was later that I began going out with Jackie [Onassis] and I found her more interesting than Clare! Clare worked a room, or worked a table, according to how she ranked in importance the people who were there. One felt in her company that she wanted to extract as much out of you as was there. I just had the feeling that, whatever the situation she was in, she was going to see what there was in it for her. After she extracted from you what there was, she might just tune out and never pay any more attention to you. She called the shots. She was a *very tough* lady."

Gilpatric remembered playing tennis with Clare at her sister-in-law's place in Weston. "Clare would never change courts," he said. "She wanted to keep her back against the sun. She had very diaphanous clothes, and she figured that, instead of watching the ball, you'd be watching between her legs. That's true!"

Observing the Clare that emerged after Harry's death, Gilpatric said, "I don't think she was capable of a deep emotional sense of attachment. I don't think she missed Luce very much. It was more of a social relationship."

That was the evolving pattern of Clare's life. She kept close to the few friends she trusted, enjoyed herself with sophisticated people who could stir a conversation, selected handsome men who could also be entertaining. There was not a lot of depth in this new emerging life-style—no serious writing, no dipping into politics. Clare was now another rich, relaxed woman of many moods.

"One thing you have to say about Clare," said Bill Benton, "you never mention her name without starting a conversation."

Critics called her brittle and harsh, and felt she knew nothing of values and principles. Clare had long had a reputation for being particularly insensitive to people.

Yet, Lyndon Johnson told *Time*'s John Steele that Clare had written him "every day after I had my heart attack."

Clare still made her trips abroad, mostly to see friends. In London, Mary Lee and Douglas Fairbanks gave a posh party for Clare. Her old friend Irene Selznick was one of the guests. When Clare was in a room, Selznick noted, "the talk would sparkle." But Selznick, too, sensed the brittleness in Clare. "Her ambition was so great that she never stood a chance of happiness," reflected Selznick.

During her stay in England, Clare visited her stepson Hank, at *Time*'s

London bureau. Over the years, he and Clare had formed a close relationship. Their correspondence reflected a warmth and mutual concern.

When Clare went on to Paris, she expected *Time* bureau chief Curtis Prendergast and his wife to arrange a dinner and supplied a list of important people who were supposed to come without their wives. "She didn't want competition," said Prendergast, who noted that he and his wife were not invited.

The years passed in a smooth, uneventful flow, without many bumps. Clare's health was "exceptionally good," because she was not driving herself hard. She even stopped smoking. One night, Clare bet a friend that whoever smoked first would give the other ten thousand dollars. When she woke the next morning and reached for her usual cigarette, she thought, "Well, I can afford the ten thousand dollars, but I don't want to give it to *her!*" The other woman felt the same way, and they both stopped.

But once again, she became restless. Playing the role of a pampered rich woman was not for Clare. Life's stage was too big, and Clare was an actress in need of a big part. Politics had always been an integral part of the pattern of her life, and as the 1968 presidential campaign neared, Clare found a new calling.

She now positioned herself as "the Conservative," and took a pro-war stance on Vietnam. Clare sided with those who espoused the domino theory—that Vietnam's fall would mean the fall of many nearby nations. Vietnam had become to Clare what China had been for Harry. If she stopped short of being a true hawk, she still did not believe in "being chicken." We were in this war and we must win it. "Clare loves the military for its latent power," said a friend.

"A lot of young Americans feel it is patriotic to try to criticize your country when you think it is doing wrong," she said, "but they have very few constructive ideas."

Considering the tortured political road Clare had traveled, the short flirt with Italian fascism, the strong involvement with Roosevelt's New Deal, the quick temptation of communism, and finally the complete acceptance of the Republican Party, she had come full circle to strong conservatism.

Feeling that Henry Kissinger would in some measure share her views, she introduced presidential candidate Richard Nixon to Henry Kissinger, three week before the election. The two men had met casually before, but Clare felt they belonged together. "I knew that Henry was not a Nixon man, that he didn't like him or trust him. But I thought they would hit it off. I told Nixon, 'I think you'll admire Henry.' I knew that if Henry spent an hour talking to Nixon, the two men would get along famously."

Several weeks after the election, Nixon gave Kissinger the second most powerful job (presidential assistant for National Security Affairs) in foreign policy in the world. Clare once again delighted in her role as political manipulator.

Nixon soon made Clare an offer: the job of U.S. ambassador to UNESCO in Paris. At first, she was intrigued because she felt she would only have to spend a couple months a year in Paris, and the rest in Hawaii. However, upon reflection, she notified Nixon that she now considered "9,000 miles of commuting too much." The job went to Shirley Temple Black.

As a staunch conservative and as a longtime friend of Chiang's China, Clare now felt it possible to applaud Nixon's visit to Red China. "America gained the credibility and prestige that always flows to a nation whenever a long-standing enemy decided that it is, after all, better to be a friend. It's better, as Churchill once put it, to jaw than to war," she said.

Harry would have detested Clare's comments, but she was proving again that her quixotic mind was her own political instrument. Furthermore, by supporting Nixon, she would soon earn a payoff.

Invigorated by her taste of politics, Clare even went back to playwriting, but her one-act play, *Slam the Door Softly,* opened in Los Angeles without much fanfare. The play was a companion piece to Ibsen's *A Doll's House* and was filled with Clare's usual sharp lines.

Besides her renewed interest in playwriting, Clare again tried to cultivate a television persona. She appeared several times on Bill Buckley's TV program, *Firing Line.* She invariably took charge of the interview, which seldom ever happened on any Buckley show, and she discussed, among many other things, the original male chauvinism in the Old Testament when God created Adam in the Garden of Eden.

One of her biggest admirers during this period was Richard Nixon.

"I only wish that the Clare Luce I knew in the fifties was around today!" Nixon told her. "You would have been a lead-pipe cinch to become the first woman president."

In 1973, Clare finally received a bone from President Nixon. He appointed her to the PFIAB, the President's Foreign Intelligence Advisory Board, designed to assess American foreign intelligence efforts. The board consisted of a small group of similarly bright people with inquisitive minds. For Clare, the appointment was a pure treat. She saw it as being in a highly charged environment— just what she loved. Most of the members were not national names, but they were known to her.

Her PFIAB job meant reading and discussing a lot of secret documents that might influence national policy, a task that greatly suited her. She had once given her definition of greatness to Churchill: "to see, to say, to serve." Once again, after a long hiatus, she was doing just that. PFIAB meetings meant prolonged visits to Washington, D.C., where she got her "intellectual fix" and also basked in her status as an anti-Communist icon, charming a new generation of conservatives.

Because she anticipated more time in Washington, she took an apartment at the Shoreham West. "I've been coming to Washington since the days of Harding; that's almost sixty years. I don't remember ever getting here and not being told everything is a mess, that the president is not doing as well as he should, and he's got all the wrong advisers around him. That's part of the Washington game," she observed.

She would later say that her life spanned twenty administrations of fifteen chief executives, eight of whom she had known personally, and some of them, much more intimately. When her latest presidential friend faced impeachment, Clare wrote him a long letter of advice and encouragement. She told him that history would always regard him as a great president—no matter what had happened.

Nixon received a note from Clare, right after Watergate first broke: "This was Sir Barton's Ode: 'I am hurt, but I am not slain! I will lie me down and bleed awhile—then I'll rise and fight again.' "

Clare tried to help Nixon. When she learned that her stepson Hank was writing the *Time* editorial urging Nixon to resign, she tried to stop it. Obsessed with a cause, there were no strings she would not pull, no people she would not call. Such a kind of frenzy made her feel more vividly alive, more purposeful. She regarded Watergate as a political Alamo, and she and a small determined group were defending the president of the United States against the rebels. Hank rebuffed Clare's efforts to intercede at *Time*.

She then sent Hedley Donovan an impassioned letter, arguing that it would be unconstitutional for a president to resign. She wanted her message published in *Time*. Donovan sent back word that they would be glad to print her letter, but would follow it with an Editor's Note: "Let Reader Luce reread her U.S. Constitution, Article II, Section 1, Paragraph 6, and the twenty-fifth Amendment." Clare then withdrew her letter.

Later, she wrote a letter to *Time,* attacked the magazine "for its editorial over-investment in the destruction of the president." Clare blamed the press for savaging Nixon and applauded him as a gutsy fighter. If Nixon lost, she said, the country would lose.

Harry would probably have disagreed. He had never liked Nixon. Furthermore, Luce was a stickler for what was right, and this was a clear break with the law.

Harry might have smiled at the fact that the only way Clare could get into *Time* was by writing a letter to the editor. If he had won no other battle with her, he had managed to stop her from having any editorial control.

After Nixon resigned, Clare once again retired to her Hawaiian home. Now, almost ten years after Harry's death, the sun seemed dreary, the beach forlorn. Life had lost its tang. Clare's guests became more occasional. People now dropped in on her only if they happened to be in Hawaii with nothing else to do. She told her sister-in-law Kit, "All my friends have either died or moved back to the Mainland."

Finally, Clare sold her Honolulu house, for about seven million dollars. "I think her life came to an end when she sold that house," said Shirley Clurman. "She should never have sold it. She had a good life there."

At first, Clare rented a small, dreary apartment in Washington. Eventually, she bought an elegant five-room apartment in the Watergate complex. She looked out through a glass wall onto the Potomac River, Key Bridge, and the spires of Georgetown University. She used a catalog to select the same kind of furniture that Ari Onassis had bought for his boat and the Nixons for San Clemente. Her sofas were in a sea-green that matched the carpets. She selected overstuffed chairs that pivoted to face a TV chest made from a beautiful old Chinese screen. The handpainted wallpaper was Chinese. Clare filled the apartment with her own needlepoint pillows and assorted Chinese works of art. Her immediate neighbor, directly across the hall, was Attorney General Griffin Bell. Later, Clare bought another Watergate apartment to use as a separate office.

Clare now described Washington as "a city of human proportions." Here, her friends always eagerly awaited her. In 1980, one of her friends, Ronald Reagan, became president of the United States. Reagan reappointed Clare to the reconstituted PFIAB, which had been disbanded by President Carter.

Clare also belonged to the Committee on the Present Danger, whose particular concern was Soviet Russia. She believed firmly in maintaining a first strike nuclear capability. Without it, she argued, the U.S. conceded to any enemy the choice of time and place of attack.

"It's such a different America than it was eight or nine years ago," she said. "I think my husband would be very distressed by much that has happened in the country—Vietnam, Watergate, the general collapse of morals, the growing isolationism . . ."

As awards and medals streamed in, including an honorary degree from Mt. Holyoke and the Distinguished Service Award from Congress, the one that pleased Clare the most was the highest honor bestowed by West Point. When Clare received it in 1977, she was the first woman to be so honored. She also enjoyed her annual reunion with the Fifth Army and applauded a new fellow-ship at Yale established in her husband's name "for the purpose of promoting Chinese-American understanding."

By this point, one of Clare's admirers had even called her "a national resource." If she was, she was more often a sad and lonely one. She had proposed marriage to Stan Swinton, a vice president and international editor of Associated Press, whom she had known so well in Rome. Swinton had been her bachelor escort before he married. And he was a talented, handsome man with a wonderful mind and an easy manner. But it was an offer Swinton could refuse. He had no intention of giving up his lovely wife and family. Stan's refusal did not stop Clare from calling up the Swintons to ask if she could join them if they were going to the same party. "And she'd take Stan's arm," said Helen, "and stay with Stan the entire evening. They'd go around together, meeting and greeting."

When Sandra Day O'Connor was named to the Supreme Court in 1981, Clare admitted that she was envious. "I would just like to have had that kind of chance," she said. What she really wanted, said a critic, was the life of an actress without going to the trouble of acting.

As always, Clare still had some admirers. A prominent four-star air force general who held the Distinguished Flying Cross wrote her lovingly and regularly, inviting her to share his hot tub. "Since I cannot be with you to help keep you warm on your cruise, I am sending you something as a substitute," he wrote to Clare, enclosing a warm jacket.

But Clare showed little interest in romance at this point in her life. She was more concerned with solidifying relationships with family and the few old friends she had left.

At the National Press Club in 1979, she remarked, "I see a lot of friends and at least one warm personal enemy. There are all too few of my enemies left. I've outlived all the SOB's." Gleefully, she told a friend that since she had joined the Roman Catholic Church, she had made up with all of her enemies, from William Fulbright to Henry Wallace.

"A funny thing has happened to me. I tend to like people I used to despise. One man I disliked intensely for years, Hubert Humphrey, is a man I'm very fond of now. Hubert is a cute, dear, cozy old character to me now. We don't agree, but so what?" she said.

Some of this newfound spirit of compromise came with age. Clare was now seventy-seven. Seventy was the springtime of senility, she declared, and eighty was the summer. Old age, she said, meant a crown of thorns and the trick was to wear it jauntily. She told a friend that life was two locked boxes, each containing the other's key.

As Clare approached eighty, she grew more and more autocratic. Wilfrid Sheed, who took her to a party at Bill Buckley's house, marveled at how she became another Clare, "the autocrat of the dinner table." He added, "She would have shone at a pit auction. Her style was the rather old fashioned one of setting up a topic and inviting everyone to speak to it." Harry Luce had been particularly good at that same technique.

Clare often talked throughout an entire meal. Shirley Clurman once told her, gently, " 'The dinner party I can't stand is when some bore starts talking at the beginning and doesn't stop till the end!' That did it. It sunk in, and she didn't do that again."

In the end, too, Clare dramatized the many men in her life, claiming some affairs that never happened. Shirley Clurman was convinced, for example, that Clare never had an affair with CBS boss Bill Paley.

She invented more and more stories, and was upset when she was caught in a flat lie. A friend told her, "Oh, Clare, why don't you take some of your jewelry out of the vault?" And she said, "This is all real; it just looks fake!" "But nothing about Clare looked or sounded right, at that point . . . she was so frail."

She confided to a reporter that if she didn't fill her remaining years with intellectual relationships and work, she knew she would wither away. "I don't feel older than I did when I was young," she said. "The really sad part is the recognition that your only future is your past. People think I'm tough and that I've always known what I've wanted," Clare continued. "I wish that were true. I would have done much better in my life."

The reporter then asked whether she still believed in love.

"It has always appeared to me that love makes the world go round, but money greases the axle. Life without love is satisfactory to no one. I'm not just talking about a physical relation, like dogs can have on the street or people in the privacy of 'your place or mine.' But love, children, family—I think you simply cannot live without them and remain, or become, a whole person," she reflected.

In interviews and with friends, Clare didn't talk much about her marriage to Harry. "She reproached herself for not having played more golf with Harry during those last days," said Bill Buckley. "She always spoke of him admiringly, and a little bit distantly. But Clare was that way about everybody. One of her strengths, in a sense (and I suppose in some ways one of her weaknesses), was when she was talking about somebody, it was as if that person had no relation to her. It's as if she was in a portrait. Even if she was saying intimate things about that person."

Buckley had his own highly perceptive analysis of the Luce marriage: "She was a Catherine Wheel of curiosity and insights—so was he. So, in that sense it was a mismatch. 'All the world's composed of helpers and helpees; and it's disaster when a helper marries a helper.' They were both helpers."

At Clare's eighty-third birthday party, when asked what a woman should do to be successful, she answered with a straight face: "Get herself elected to Congress, become an ambassador, and marry a rich man—all of this." Then as an aside, she added: "It would have been awful if I had fallen in love with a man who had no money."

At another time, Clare was asked if she had any regrets. "Yes, I should have been a better person, kinder, more tolerant," she said. "Sometimes I wake up in the middle of the night and I remember there was a girlhood friend of mine who had a brain tumor and called me three times to come and see her. I was always too busy, and when she died, I was profoundly ashamed. I remember that after fifty-six years."

What *did* please Clare was that she had lived to see women's role change so that she was no longer "ahead of her time." She had always predicted change and was delighted when her visions came true.

As she moved through her eighties, there were larger intervals of loneliness for Clare and fewer friends to call. She drank more whiskey.

"I don't go to beauty parlors anymore," she complained. "My hair's so thin and my nails won't grow." Her voice became tremulous.

Then, doctors discovered that Clare had a brain tumor, and started her on radiation. She treated her illness with her customary courage. Clare was not one to whimper. "Perhaps I'll make it to December," she said.

When Clare realized that the end was near, she refused to stay in a hospital saying, "A hospital is no place to be sick." Instead, in typical fashion, she took center stage and orchestrated a series of gatherings to say good-bye to her friends. At a party for twenty-two people, reported Sylvia Morris in *The New York Times,* "she made a painful slow entrance, supported by two attendants. We were shocked at her skeletal appearance, made more macabre by a silver wig. Clare held court on a low couch, munching popcorn and drinking Perrier. Dinner was served almost at once. It consisted of borscht and sour cream, pasta with shrimp, and goulash. Dessert [her final mischievous joke?] was a DoveBar, complete with stick, laid across fine china."

That morning, Clare had received word that there was no further point to treatment, that nothing could be done. Still, she tried hard to keep the talk away from her condition. She even directed a conversation about the Iran-Contra hearings. The evening was a living wake. Everybody at the party knew they would never again see her alive. But she was going out in style, grace, and dignity.

That evening was her final performance. Clare died a week later on October 9, 1987, at six in the morning. She was eighty-four.

At Mepkin, she would rest close to her husband, closer than they had been in their lifetime. Nearby was her mother, whom she had loved early, but not late, and her daughter Ann, whom she had loved too late.

As Clare was lowered and placed into the ground in a gleaming pine coffin next to her husband, one of the Mepkin monks said softly, "There is no distance between them now: it's vault to vault."

Clare's farewell advice to her friends had been: "Do not defend me!" She had also quoted Mencken, saying: "He told me once that he answered all his mail, pleasant and unpleasant, with just one line: 'You may be right.' That's the way I feel now. It is the realm of possibility, just barely, that I could be the one who's wrong."

In those last years after Harry died, what Clare missed so much in her path of glory was that she was no longer the eye of the storm. With Harry, she had been part of the hub that moved the wheel. Without him, she was simply a lesser part of the wheel. She had experienced a life full of excitement with Harry, and she didn't have much of a life after he died. Perhaps that's why she probably loved him more after he was gone.

When Henry Robinson Luce married Clare Boothe, some called it a mating of eagles, and perhaps it was. He surely was an eagle, soaring high above his peers. But she was more of a peregrine falcon, who could soar as high as he—only if she followed in his current.

He did not put her on a pedestal: She built her own. She had made herself into an international celebrity, carved out her own careers in theater, magazines, and politics, and she raised herself up to be one of the most admired women in the world. Her life was a glittering Christmas tree, but in her own final summation, she admitted that she never fulfilled the dream of her life; she was never *really* a writer. The power was his, and she knew it, and he would not let it go.

Their relationship was fascinating to watch, sad to see. He found a field, exploited it to the hilt, and built an empire. He had a clear vision, a strong faith, and a great mind. To the watching world, the Luces represented the peak of power, the ultimate American dream. Their words could reach millions of people, shape ideas, and help elect presidents. Popes, kings, and prime ministers were always eager to see them and listen to their views. Celebrities of every kind groveled before them. Their names opened every door.

But without Harry, Clare was tolerated and smiled at but rarely listened to.

She wanted people to pay attention to her, as they did to him. Her final frustration was that she wanted all the perks, kudos, and trappings to continue. She was more emotionally bound to him and his position than she knew. At her death, she must have known that he had given her more than she had given him.

CHAPTER NOTES
AND CRITICAL BIBLIOGRAPHY

1

Interviews with Richard Clurman, William F. Buckley, Jr., were most important here. Laura Hobson's memoir, *Laura Z* (New York: Arbor House, 1983) had some key material. Also important were Hobson's private papers at the Manuscript Room of Butler Library at Columbia University. Luce's private secretary, Gloria Mariano, provided the passport story. Mrs. Henrietta Rogers was also most helpful.

2

The most important core in this chapter comes from interviews with the person closest to Henry Luce, his sister Mrs. Elisabeth Moore. Her memories of Luce family life in China are truly sharp and remarkable. Another valuable research resource are the papers of Mrs. Nettie Fowler McCormick at the State Historical Society in Madison, Wisconsin. As the close friend and financial patron of the Luces, Mrs. McCormick had a large file of correspondence and photographs with the Luce family, particularly with the young Henry Luce.

Also valuable was B. A. Garside's biography of Henry Luce's father, Henry Winters Luce, *One Increasing Purpose* (New York: Fleming H. Revell, 1948). The best genealogical source was the Genealogical and Family History of Southern New York (New York: Lewis Historical, Volume III, 1914, pp. 1425–26).

John Hersey, who was also born in China, the son of missionaries, had very relevant memories of missionary life in China at that time. Henry Luce also had revealed pieces of his China memories to various friends such as Ed

Thompson, Allen Grover, Mary Bancroft, Jean Dalrymple, and Lady Jean Campbell, among others. He also reminisced about it in several interviews and speeches, particularly in a speech at the Waldorf-Astoria on May 4, 1950. He confided about it also to his pastor, the Reverend David Read at the Madison Avenue Presbyterian Church.

An especially good interview on his life in China is by Alden Hatch in the Rare Books/Manuscript Division of the University of Florida in Gainesville Florida (Box 5, File 37). Another useful interview was by Betty Jo McLeod in the Lakeville, Florida, *Ledger,* November 7, 1948. For background, there is a valuable interview of Mrs. Leslie Severinghaus, Harry Luce's sister, in the Swanberg Collection at Columbia University. W. A. Swanberg also had an excellent interview with Clare Boothe Luce on February 21, 1969 (Box 17-F). The Columbia University Oral History Library has other interviews with Luce friends and associates that touch on this time.

Some books that offer additional interesting background on China at that time include, *The Siege of Peking* by Peter Fleming (New York: Harper, 1959), especially on the Boxer Rebellion. Also, *Manifest Destiny* by Albert K. Weinberg (Baltimore: Johns Hopkins, 1935); *China Images* by Patricia Neils (Savage, MD: Rowman & Littlefield, 1990); *Missionaries: Chinese and Diplomats* by Paul A. Varg, (Princeton, NJ: Princeton University Press, 1958). Of the several biographies of Henry Luce, the best on this period is *Luce and His Empire* by W. A. Swanberg (New York: Scribner's, 1972). *Luce: His Time, Life and Fortune* by John Kobler (New York: Doubleday, 1963) had some interesting material. *Life Sketches* by John Hersey (New York: Knopf, 1989) is also excellent. The New York Public Library also had other helpful historic pamphlets and reports detailing missionary life.

Henry Luce III provided some important insight in a speech he made about his father, "The Faith of Henry Luce," on October 9, 1984.

For background, there is also an interesting letter to Henry Winters Luce from John L. Thurston, February 19, 1904, in the Thurston papers at the Yale University Library, Manuscript and Archives (Box 1, Folder 27).

3

The most important source of material on the early life of Clare Boothe Luce is in the vast collection of her personal papers at the Manuscript Division of the Library of Congress in Washington, D.C. The Boothe genealogy in Box 859 indicates that the name "Boothe" was spelled without an "e" throughout the early family Bible record but was changed in 1840.

The C.B.L. papers include a copy of the *Musical Courier,* January 1929, which has some of the best background about Clare's father. There is also an interesting article in the White Plains *Daily Argus,* May 20, 1910. For background, there is also an interesting letter from Mrs. Ruth G. Raley of Mechanicsville, Maryland, dated August 12, 1981, an undated letter from Edward Boothe of Portchester, New York, and another undated letter to C.B.L. from Cary Reeder, all dwelling on their heritage. A more important one, dated June 18, 1949, is from "Uncle Charles" in Los Angeles.

Her various school records, diaries, and letters are also among these early papers.

Clare Luce gave a great many interviews in a variety of newspapers and magazines, many of them contradictory, all of them available in her papers. Among the best is by Alden Hatch at the Rare Books and Manuscript Division in the University of Florida. Hatch also did an important interview with Clare Luce's best friend, Buffy Cobb, who dates back from her early school days.

Wilfrid Sheed was a most valuable interview for me because C.B.L. had reminisced so much with him about her life, and his book about her, *Clare Boothe Luce* (New York: Dutton, 1982), is the best and most intimate portrait. Stephen Shadegg's book *Clare Boothe Luce* (New York: Simon & Schuster, 1970) also has some pertinent material.

4

Again, the prime source on H.R.L.'s school days in China, as well as Hotchkiss, comes from his sister Mrs. Elisabeth Moore. Also, again, the McCormick Papers in Wisconsin. And, again, the Garside biography of H.R.L.'s father. An interview with John Hersey revealed an interesting anecdote about H.R.L. at Chefoo. The Swanberg research on this period is particularly good. Luce's schoolmate Thornton Wilder was excellent on the subject on Chefoo as revealed in his personal papers at Yale. Also check for background Gilbert A. Harrison's biography of Wilder, *The Enthusiast* (New Haven and New York: Ticknor and Fields, 1983) and *Thornton Wilder: An Intimate Portrait* by Richard H. Goldstone (New York: Saturday Review Press/Dutton, 1975).

Dr. Martin F. Schwartz, director of the National Center for Stuttering at New York University Medical School, was most revealing on the subject in *The New York Times,* May 14, 1989, in an article by Michael Ross.

George Harris, in Tarrytown, New York, a former *Life* editor, had his own memories of Hotchkiss, and stories H.R.L. told him. Ralph Ingersoll's private papers in Cornwall, Connecticut, made available by his widow, also had interesting sidelights. The records and periodicals of the Hotchkiss School were most valuable, particularly the *Hotchkiss Literary Monthly* of June 1916.

Noel Busch's biography of his cousin Briton Hadden (New York: Farrar, Straus, 1949) is brightly written. A more objective one, though, is in the superb intimate history of Time Inc. (New York: Atheneum, 1958) by Robert T. Elson (1923–1941). The Elson book is the best written and best researched on the whole early period of *Time*, including preliminary background of Luce and Hadden. James L. Baughman's book *Henry R. Luce* (Boston: Twayne, 1987) also has several interesting anecdotes and letters on this period. One can find scattered material of interest in the John Shaw Billings papers, The South Caroliniana Library, University of South Carolina, particularly in Volumes 18 and 20. Also of some interest is John Jessup's *The Ideas of Henry Luce* (New York: Atheneum, 1969).

5

The C.B.L. papers in the Library of Congress supply the best background material for this chapter, much of it in letters, papers, diaries, and many published interviews. There were also her school yearbooks supplied by the Historical Society of Tarrytown. Most interesting was an undated article, "Echoes from Miss Mason's Chapel Talks." In Box 506 F, there was an interesting article by Frederick Van Ryn, called "Dream Jobs."

Best of all, for me, were her personal reminiscences as told to me by Wilfrid Sheed, especially on Sheed's own observations on C.B.L.'s meeting with her father. There were also some important school materials of C.B.L. among the Hatch papers at the Library of Congress, Manuscript Division, and a C.B.L. interview with Hatch (Box 5, File 36).

Some sidelight material was available in both the Shadegg book and a biography by Faye Henle *Au Clare de Luce* (New York: Stephen Gaye, 1943).

6

Interviews with Allen Grover, who also went to Yale when Luce was there, were most important.

The Busch book on Hadden is good here, and so is the Harrison biography of Thornton Wilder, who also went to Yale with H.R.L. Another biography on Wilder is by Linda Simon, *Thornton Wilder and His World,* (Garden City,

NY: Doubleday, 1979). The Thornton Wilder Papers were also useful for this chapter.

The Yale University Library, of course, has all the files of the Yale *Daily News* and the Yale *Literary Magazine* of this period, 1917–20. The Yale Alumni Records had a variety of interesting material, including a revealing H.R.L. speech given there on July 6, 1958, "Conscience of Yale Men." Another pertinent speech was at the Missouri Bar Association in St. Louis on September 26, 1958. Worth examination was a book by Morehead Patterson, *History of the Class of 1920* (New Haven: Tuttle, Morehouse and Taylor), and another edited by C. Stuart Heminway, *Twenty Years with Nineteen Twenty* (Pasadena, CA: San Pasquel Press, 1940). Elson, again, is excellent on this period.

A speech by John S. Martin at the dedication service of the Hadden Memorial Building at Yale, April 27, 1932 had worthwhile observations on both Hadden and Luce.

T. S. Matthews had some interesting observations on this time of Luce's life. H.R.L. wrote revealing letters to Mrs. McCormick during this period in which he confided in her many of his plans and dreams.

An excellent book on the Chicago *Daily News,* where H.R.L. worked briefly, is *Deadlines* by Henry Justin Smith (Chicago: Covici McGee, 1923). Hyman Benjamin Turner, also made available his unpublished master's thesis on Henry Justin Smith, written in 1940 at the University of Missouri School of Journalism. Turner also related some specific stories told by one of the reporters at the time who knew Luce.

Luce himself reminisced about his time working on the newspaper, in an interview with *Berlingske Aftenavis* (Denmark) on January 12, 1963.

Some Baltimore atmosphere of the time comes from *The Amiable Baltimoreans* by Francis F. Beirne (New York: Dutton, 1951). Andrew Turnbull's *Letters of F. Scott Fitzgerald* (New York: Scribner's, 1963) also enrich the picture of the time.

The first Mrs. Henry Luce, now Mrs. Lila Tyng, was remarkably forthright in her own memories of the courtship and their relationship.

7

For the beginning of the chapter, most useful were the Matilda Young papers on Alva Smith in the Manuscript Department of the William F. Perkins Library in Duke University, Chapel Hill, North Carolina. Young worked as Mrs. Belmont's nurse and was her confidante in her latter years. Most useful too was Elsa Maxwell's book, *R.S.V.P.* (Boston: Little, Brown, 1954). Martha Weinman Lear had an excellent interview with C.B.L. in *The New York Times Magazine* and so did Digby Diehl in *Supertalk* (Garden City, NY: Doubleday, 1974).

C.B.L.'s own scrapbooks in the C.B.L. papers in the Library of Congress likewise detail the subject. Sheed also had perceptive comment on this period. Buffy Cobb dealt with it in her interview with Alden Hatch, now at the University of Florida library.

A good survey of the social scene at that time can be found in Walter Lord's *The Good Years* (New York: Harper & Brothers, 1960). But, best of it all, C.B.L. thinly veneers her own life in high society in *Stuffed Shirts* (Freeport, NY: Books for Libraries Press, 1931). Society gossip was even more realistically detailed in the weekly, *Town Topics,* and the daily Cholly Knickerbocker columns in the New York *Daily American.* C.B.L. also wrote about it herself in the New York *Evening Telegram,* "A Day in the Society World," November 18, 1931.

Genealogical sources on the Brokaw family can be found in *Huguenot Immigration to America,* Volume 1, p. 188; *Genealogies of Southern New York Families* by Reynolds, Volume 1, p.463; *St. Nicholas Social Register,* 1916, pp. 11 and 79. C.B.L. also hired genealogists to trace her family lines so she could become a member of the Daughters of the American Revolution and Ark and Dove. The results of this research are in the C.B.L. Papers at the Library of Congress. In C.B.L.'s papers there is also an undated article called "The Wreck of the Brokaw Mansions."

A good reference of C.B.L. relations with Somerset Maugham can be found in a published seminar on the author with C.B.L. participating, published by Friends of the Libraries, University of Southern California, 1966. There is also Ted Morgan's excellent biography *Maugham* (New York: Simon & Schuster, 1980). A first-rate profile of C.B.L. is "The Candor Kid" by Margaret Case Harriman, in *The New Yorker,* January 4, 1940.

The obit of Billy Boothe appeared in the *Musical Courier,* January 3, 1929.

8

Mrs. Elisabeth Moore had vivid memories of the early days of *Time,* of which she was a part. Mrs. Lila Tyng, H.R.L.'s first wife, similarly had specific memories of those early days of their marriage. Her recall was phenomenal. Mrs. Sheldon Luce, widow of H.R.L.'s brother, was also most helpful.

The Elson book, again, is the best description of early *Time* history. Otis

Chatfield-Taylor has produced a most interesting "The Timeditors" (*Ringmaster,* November 1936). Very important is the material in the Swanberg collection at Columbia University, especially interviews with *Time* associates who have since died.

Among those I had interviewed, those most fruitful for this period were John Steele, Joseph Kastner, Thomas Griffith, T. S. Matthews, James Bell, Curt Prendergast, Richard Clurman, Andrew Heiskell, Wilfrid Sheed, Dmitri Kessel, Allen Grover, Frank White, Gloria Mariano, John Hersey, Dave Richardson, A. B. C. Whipple, Lael Wertenbaker, and Otto Fuerbringer. Most valuable were interviews by David Halberstam, again with Time Inc. people who have since died, for his superb book *The Powers That Be* (New York: Knopf, 1979). Halberstam's papers are in the Special Collections at Mugar Memorial Library at Boston University. Especially important was his interview with Emmet John Hughes.

Wolcott Gibbs's profile of Henry Luce in *The New Yorker* had much rich material. Also very important was *Laura Z,* by Laura Z. Hobson (New York: Arbor House, 1983) for a great deal of background for this chapter. Hobson not only had a sense of fact but a sense of drama. Her relationship with Ingersoll heightens the importance of what she writes. Ingersoll's private papers are once again of great importance here as were his papers at Boston University.

On the use of *Time* language, two articles of interest were in *American Speech* of February 1932, by Robert Withington, and in October 1940, by Joseph J. Firebaugh.

Worth consulting were articles by Roger Butterfield in *The Saturday Review,* May 28, 1949; R. H. S. Crossman in *The New Statesman and Nation,* September 3, 1949; Carol Bjorkman, *The News American,* Baltimore, Maryland, March 28, 1967; Garland Smith, "The Young Man Behind TIME," *The Brooklyn Eagle,* October 6, 1929; and "Sharpshooter of American Periodicals," by George Payne, January 1927.

9

The prime source of material comes from the C.B.L. papers in the Library of Congress, and her own book *Stuffed Shirts.* The files of *Vogue* and *Vanity Fair* are especially rewarding. Most useful were *Vogue's First Reader,* edited by Frank Crowninshield (New York: Julian Messner, 1942) and *Vanity Fair,* edited by Cleveland Amory and Frederic Bradlee (New York: Viking Press, 1960). Also, *Always in Vogue* by Edna Woolman Chase and Ilka Chase,

(Garden City, NY: Doubleday, 1954) and *The World of Carmel Snow* by Carmel Snow and Mary Louise Aswell (New York: McGraw, Hill, 1962). Also check *Au Clare de Luce: Portrait of a Luminous Lady* by Faye Henle (New York: Stephen Daye, 1943).

Most helpful was a very revealing article by C.B.L.'s former friend, Helen Lawrenson, in *Esquire,* August 1974. Very worthwhile was an interview with C.B.L. by Lillian G. Genn in *The Seattle Times,* January 24, 1932. Another good interview with C.B.L. was in an undated clipping in the New York *Graphic* by Margaret Sandy. There is also a very good article by Marie Brenner on C.B.L. in *Vanity Fair,* March 1988.

Alden Hatch's interview with C.B.L. was useful here, and so was an unsourced radio interview with C.B.L. in the C.B.L. papers. Most valuable were the Donald Freeman letters in the C.B.L. papers.

An interview with Howard Byrne revealed some interesting C.B.L. stories on *Vanity Fair.* Wilfrid Sheed also contributed some interesting sidelights. So did Mrs. Elisabeth Moore.

Some good background on the period can be found in "A Memorable Guest List of Great Dinner Parties" by Helen Lawrenson, *The New York Times,* October 10, 1979, and *A Fashion of Life,* by H. W. Yoxall, (London: Heinemann) and an article in the Baltimore *Post,* "No Humor in Society," by Evelyn Seeley, December 4, 1931. Laura Hobson's book, *Laura Z,* should also be read. Another interesting book, helpful in this chapter, was *Libido in the Female Child* by Ada Adler, edited by H. L. Mencken (New York: Liveright, 1930). Also *In My Fashion,* by Bettina Ballard (New York: David McKay, 1960) and *Run-Through: A Memoir* by John Houseman (New York: Simon & Schuster, 1972)

10

Vital to this chapter were my interviews with Mrs. Lila Tyng.

The story of *Fortune* comes from a variety of interviews, particularly with Allen Grover, Andrew Heiskell, Joseph Kastner, Mrs. Elisabeth Moore, Frank White, Mrs. Henrietta Rogers, Oliver Jensen, John Hersey, and T. S. Matthews. Most helpful were the recollections of Mrs. Ralph Ingersoll and the private papers of her husband.

Also very worthwhile is Margaret Bourke-White's autobiography, *Portrait of Myself* (Boston: Hall, 1985). Miss White's material is of special importance for the *Fortune* story. Interesting, too, by Dwight Macdonald was *Discrimination: Essays and Afterthoughts* (New York: Grossman, 1974); *James Agee, A Life* by Lawrence Bergreen, (New York: Dutton, 1940) and Agee's introduction to his own book, *Let Us Now Praise Famous Men* (Boston: Houghton Mifflin, 1989); *The Collected Short Prose of James Agee,* edited by Robert Fitzgerald (Boston: Houghton Mifflin, 1968); *The Span of TIME* by Eric Hodgins (New York, Time Inc. 1946); *Writing for FORTUNE* by Nineteen Authors, (New York: Time Inc., 1980); and the biography *Ralph Ingersoll* by Roy Hoopes (New York: Atheneum, 1985); Charles Fountain, *Another Man's Poison* (Chester, CT: Globe Pequot Press, 1984). The Elson book, as always, is invaluable. Another excellent book is *How True* by Thomas Griffith (Boston: Little Brown, 1974). So is *A Life in Our Times,* by John Kenneth Galbraith (Boston: Houghton Mifflin, 1981)

A rich resource of interviews and background can be found in the Dorothy Sterling papers, Special Collections, University of Oregon. This was research done for her unpublished manuscript, "The Luce Empire."

The John Shaw Billings papers at the Library of Congress (Box 1, Folder 14) and the Billings papers at the University of South Carolina also have interesting memoranda of this time, as well as an interesting speech on Luce by Billings in Des Moines, Iowa, before Delta Sigma Chi. Among the Swanberg papers at Columbia University, the recollections of Leslie Severinghaus and Archibald MacLeish were similarly especially useful. A good source on Archibald MacLeish is a book by Bernard A. Drabeck and Helen E. Ellis, *Archibald MacLeish Reflections* (Amherst: University of Massachusetts Press, 1986) and *Letters of Archibald MacLeish, 1907–1982,* edited by R. H. Winnick (Boston: Houghton Mifflin, 1983).

The Anson B. Stokes papers at Yale University Library are worth checking. So is another excellent book by Thomas Griffith, *The Waist-High Culture,* (Westport, CT: Greenwood Press, 1959) and *Adventures of a Bystander,* by Peter F. Drucker (New York: Harper & Row, 1978).

Other pertinent articles: "The Education of Henry Luce" by Kenneth Stewart, *PM,* September 3, 1944; *The Saturday Evening Post* article by John Kobler, January 16, 1967; *The New York Times Book Review,* September 5, 1969, interview by Francis Brown; and "Romantic Business," by William Lydgate, *Scribner's,* September 1938.

The New Haven *Journal Courier,* April 20, 1930, has a good report of H.R.L.'s Bromley lecture at Yale.

11

My interview with Robert Coughlan, who wrote extensively about Baruch, and knew him well, was particularly important in this chapter. So was my interview with John Hersey. *LIFE Sketches* by Hersey supplemented much of this. His papers at Yale University provided a good supplement. Again, the C.B.L. papers were vital, especially the many Baruch letters to C.B.L. My interview with Sheed about Baruch was most enlightening. My interview with Shirley Clurman and Mrs. Patricia Coughlan was even more so.

Alden Hatch's interview with Baruch was interesting, but circumspect. So was his interview with Buckminster Fuller. His interview with Helen Lawrenson was important. The biographies of Baruch have little to offer on the Luces, but are worth examining for Baruch background, particularly *Mr. Baruch,* by Margaret Coit (Boston: Houghton Mifflin, 1957).

Digby Diehl did an excellent interview with C.B.L. for *West* magazine *(Los Angeles Times),* May 14, 1972, and Martha Weinman Lear did a very good interview with C.B.L. for *The New York Times,* both of which also deal with this period. Good general background on this time can be found in *George Kaufman and His Friends,* by Scott Meredith (Garden City, NY: Doubleday, 1974) and *The Enemy Grows Older,* by Alexander King (New York: Simon & Schuster, 1958) and Elsa Maxwell's autobiography *R.S.V.P.*

More pertinent was Wilfrid Sheed's book. My interviews with Jean Dalrymple, who knew Clare then, were of great importance in this chapter.

The Oral History Library interviews at Columbia University with C.B.L., Mary Bancroft, and Charles Poletti were all most valuable.

Some books of background helpful here include: *Special Relationships,* by Henry Brandon (New York: Atheneum, 1988); *Walter Lippmann and the American Century,* by Ronald Steel, (Boston: Atlantic/Little, Brown, 1980).

12

The private papers of Ralph Ingersoll represent the most important research for this chapter, along with Laura Hobson's autobiography and the C.B.L. papers. Laura Hobson's papers at Columbia University provided good additional material. Also *Point of Departure: An Adventure in Autobiography* by Ralph Ingersoll (New York: Harcourt, Brace & World, 1961). The John Shaw Billings papers at the University of South Carolina add vital information, and so did my interviews with Sheed, Bell, Jensen, White, Heiskell, Matthews, Bernard Yudain, Shirley Clurman, Jean Dalrymple, Bea Grover, Mrs. Moore, John Steele, Otto Fuerbringer, John Dullaghan, Mrs. Pierrepont Isham Prentice, Ed Thompson, and Lael Wertenbaker.

Dr. Murray Krim, former president of the William Alanson White Institute, and nationally known psychologist, gave me some important insights on the relationship of C.B.L. and H.R.L.

Interviews with Mrs. Lila Tyng were again pivotal here.

Elsa Maxwell's *The Celebrity Circus* (London: Allen, 1964) had some key personal material about the courtship. Equally important was Helen Lawrenson's memoir *Stranger at a Party* (New York: Random House, 1972).

C.B.L. also made reference to this part of her life in an interview with Christopher P. Anderson in *People,* July 25, 1977.

Countess Rose Waldeck, at whose party C.B.L. and H.R.L. met the second time, was formerly Rosie Goldschmidt Graefenburg, also known as "R.G.," a former journalist, banker, spy, celebrated in Paris for her sparkling literary salon.

Margaret Case Harriman's profile of C.B.L. in *Ladies' Home Journal,* November 1938 had useful material. So did "As Manhattan Goes," *Mademoiselle,* 1935.

13

The key material on the birth of *Life* comes from interviews with its former editor Ed Thompson, former text editor Oliver Jensen, its publisher Andrew Heiskell, as well as some of its writers and editors, Bill Brinkley, Joseph Kastner, John Hersey, Lady Jean Campbell, and again, Allen Grover was indispensable.

The best research sources are in Ralph Ingersoll's personal papers in Connecticut and the Billings papers in South Carolina. Both have an extraordinary wealth of detail about the magazine's beginnings. Daniel Longwell also has recorded a history of *Life* at the Rare Books and Manuscripts Room at Columbia University Library. His personal papers at Columbia were also quite helpful as was his correspondence on the subject with John Billings which are at the University of South Carolina Library in Columbia.

An interview with Robert Sherrod put many things in perspective. Allen Grover's views on the changes in the marriage are also vital. Jean Dalrymple's views are more partisan, but also significant.

The New Yorker story is best found in the Ingersoll private papers, the Hoopes biography of Ingersoll, and Ingersoll's own autobiography, *Point of Departure* (New York: Harcourt, Brace, 1961). One should also read Dale Kramer's very good *Ross and the New Yorker* (Garden City, NY: Doubleday, 1951), James Thurber's excellent book, *The Years With Ross* (Boston: Little Brown, 1957), and Brendan Gill's *Here at The New Yorker* (New York: Random House, 1975).

For other background in the chapter, there was Guy J. Forgue's *Letters of*

H. L. Mencken (New York: Knopf, 1961) and *Ben Hecht* by William Macadams (New York: Scribner's, 1990).

14

Mrs. Lila Tyng's reflections on her divorce, and on Clare's playwriting, are most revealing. The Kaufman biography does not amplify C.B.L.'s collaboration with Kaufman and neither does *Act One, An Autobiography* by Moss Hart, Kaufman's partner (New York: Random House, 1959).

Most important were interviews with Jean Dalrymple, Allen Grover, Franklin Heller, and playwright Max Wilk. The C.B.L. papers was a good source for all the reviews and interviews.

The development of the *Life* story is best told in *The Great American Magazine,* by Loudon Wainwright (New York: Knopf, 1986). The Elson book, as usual, is excellent. The Ingersoll papers were a prime source. My interviews with Oliver Jensen, Marion MacPhail McDermott, and Ed Thompson were invaluable. Peter Drucker's book had some excellent background stories.,

Most important is Wilson Hicks's book *Words and Pictures* (New York: Harper & Brothers, 1952). The Roy Hoopes biography of Luce and the Bourke-White autobiography are both important here, as well as *Trolley to the Moon* by Eric Hodgins (New York: Simon & Schuster, 1973). *The Fun House,* by talented William Brinkley, is a revealing novel about working on *Life.* David Halberstam's book *The Powers That Be* (New York: Knopf, 1979) is also excellent.

A footnote of interest was the Harry Hansen column in the New York *World Telegram* of December 4, 1936, referring to a study that year of Yale alumni in Who's Who, noting that children of missionaries succeeded in greater proportion than any other profession—and only one out of ten became ministers.

15

My interviews with Mrs. Lila Tyng, John Hersey, Allen Grover, and George Harris were basic to this chapter. Also most helpful were Mrs. Elisabeth Moore, Andrew Heiskell, Dmitri Kessel, Robert Manning, Lael Wertenbaker, T. S. Matthews, Thomas Griffith, Richard Clurman, Ed Thompson, Connie Clark, Bernard Yudain, A. B. C. Whipple, Joseph Kastner, Otto Fuerbringer, Arthur Hadley, and John Steele.

The Billings papers were again invaluable and so were the C.B.L. papers, the David Halberstam papers at Boston University, and the Hersey papers at Yale. So were the Dorothy Sterling papers at the University of Oregon.

The interview by the Oral Research Library at Columbia of Max Gissen was most worthwhile.

Two novels worth reading with a Time Inc. background, both excellent, were *The Death of Kings*, by Charles Wertenbaker (New York: Random House, 1954) and *The Big Wheel* by John Brooks (New York: Harper & Brothers, 1949). Again, the Griffith book *The Waist-High Culture* was most pertinent here. The Drucker book was also very useful. So were the Hobson memoirs.

David Garroway did an excellent interview with H.R.L. on March 3, 1961. And Joseph Epstein wrote a penetrating article in *Commentary*, November 1987. A similarly important article of great use was Lester Bernstein's "TIME Inc. Means Business," in *The New York Times Magazine*, February 26, 1989.

Wilfrid Sheed had some key remarks on C.B.L.'s relationship with Harry Bridges, but Clare's own writings on this supply the detailed material. Her private papers are also the best single source on her relationship with her daughter. Their correspondence was enriching. All of Ann's school records are also there.

16

Interviews with Tom Griffith and T. S. Matthews were important here. So was Dimitri Kessel. The Billings papers were again valuable as were the C.B.L. papers—which also had her letters from Randolph Churchill.

The Beaverbrook material comes largely from interviews with his granddaughter, Lady Jean Campbell. The biography *Beaverbrook* by A. J. P. Taylor (New York: Simon & Schuster, 1972) tells much about him but almost nothing of his relationship with the Luces.

The Ingersoll private papers background much of this material. So do the Dorothy Sterling papers and the MacLeish letters and his biography.

The best published source is C.B.L.'s own book *Europe in the Spring* (New York: Knopf, 1940). She also referred to portions of the trip in various interviews, articles in *Life*, conversations with friends. Billings reports on her detailing the trip for him and others at *Life* lunches. HRL also discussed the trip with Billings and others, and in an interview with Alden Hatch, as well as in occasional speeches at the time. Check a radio address by H.R.L. on June 1, 1930, at six-thirty PM over WABC. Elson also had dealt with it in detail.

Check *The American Century with Commentary by Dorothy Thompson* by Henry Robinson Luce (New York: Farrar and Rinehart, 1941).

The single best overall book on the war is *The Second World War* by Martin Gilbert (New York: Henry Holt, 1989). An interesting book of the time was *Why England Slept,* by John F. Kennedy (New York: Wilfrid Funk, 1940) with an introduction by Henry Luce.

The Gertrude Stein story comes partly from *What Is Remembered* by Alice B. Toklas (New York: Holt, Rinehart and Winston, 1963).

The Franklin D. Roosevelt archives at Hyde Park, New York, is the source of much of the comment and letters by the former president and his aides concerning the Luces. The letter from June Hamilton Rhodes to the president's secretary, Margaret LeHand was dated April 20, 1939 and can be found in PPF 3338. Some of the other Roosevelt-Luce material is in Box 2442. Other material is in Boxes 3297–3343. The memo from F.D.R. to Lowell Mellett of December 31, 1940, comes from PPF 3338. An excellent reference book on this part of the Roosevelt era is *The Age of Roosevelt: The Coming of the New Deal,* by Arthur Schlesinger, Jr. (Boston: Houghton Mifflin, 1959).

Allen Grover detailed the stories of H.R.L. and Wendell Willkie, and so did T. S. Matthews and Ed Thompson. A good biography of Willkie was *Dark Horse* by Steve Neal (Garden City, NY: Doubleday, 1984). Another good reference book was *Land of the Giants* by C. L. Sulzberger (New York: Macmillan, 1970).

Material on Ann comes largely from C.B.L. papers.

A great part of this China material comes from the private papers of Theodore White at Harvard University Library, as well as White's superb autobiography, *In Search of History* (New York: Harper & Row, 1978). Also see *The China Hands: America's Foreign Service Officers and What Befell Them* by E. J. Kahn (New York: Viking Press, 1972). Halberstam's interviews with White in his private papers were also excellent. Much of this was elaborated in Halberstam's book, *The Powers That Be.* Dave Richardson provided a most illuminating interview for me on Teddy White and China, as well as the Pacific War Theater which he covered so notably. Richardson also discussed MacArthur at great length. So did Robert Sherrod. A good book on MacArthur was William Manchester's *American Caesar* (Boston: Little, Brown, 1978). There was also the C.B.L. profile of MacArthur in *Life.*

17

Yank Magazine war correspondent Ed Cunningham wrote extensively and wonderfully well about Stillwell and India during the war and had given me much background about it. So did Dave Richardson. C.B.L. also wrote about Stillwell for *Life* and in her C.B.L. papers. Robert Sherrod told me what C.B.L. told him about MacArthur. An excellent book is *Stillwell* by Barbara Tuchman (New York: Macmillan, 1970). Halberstam's interview with Annalee Jacoby was penetrating.

The General Alexander material comes from a variety of sources, ranging from Robert Coughlan of *Life* to C.B.L.'s own words in her private papers and in her *Life* articles.

John Hersey told me of the incident in Gottfried's office when Luce asked them to publish a C.B.L. story in *Time* with a byline and was refused. Matthews gave me his similar version of that same story.

The most important sources on C.B.L.'s entry into congressional politics came from Eddie Fay, Ed Plaut, and Bernard Yudain. The Hatch interview with Al Morano was very good. So were his interviews with Dorothy Farmer and Dorothy Burns. Bea Grover was helpful as well as Hatch. The Henry Wallace stories about C.B.L. and H.R.L. come from his Oral History at Columbia University as well as interviews elsewhere.

Aside from C.B.L., the other women in Congress included Winifred Stanley (NY), Mary Norton (NJ), Jesse Sumner (IL), Margaret Smith (ME), Edith Rogers (MA), and Mrs. Chester Bolton (OH).

C.B.L. has written and spoken extensively about this herself, and there is some good material in the Shadegg biography as well as the Henle book. C.B.L. deals with this in her oral history interview at Columbia University by John Luther. The Fishbait story comes from *Fishbait* by William Fishbait Miller (Englewood Cliffs, NJ: Prentice-Hall, 1977). Some newspaper articles to check: The Bridgeport *Sunday Post,* July 18, 1943 and the *Capital Journal,* in Salem, Oregon (undated clipping, but in this time period). Some useful magazine articles include Gretta Palmer's in *Look* magazine, April 15, 1947, and Maxine Davis's also in *Look,* January 25, 1944.

Sheed's observations were especially valuable. Allen Grover's insights were particularly important, as well as Ed Thompson's and Andrew Heiskell.

The C.B.L. papers are rich in this period, particularly with her scrapbook of clippings, interviews, and letters. The Ann material, again, comes from the C.B.L. files.

18

The life and death of Ann is documented in great detail in the C.B.L. papers. C.B.L. also has written about it in her various articles and spoken about it extensively in interviews. Important observers were Allen and Bea Grover.

Clare confided much about this to Shirley Clurman. Richard Clurman had a fascinating sidelight about C.B.L. at the gravesite. The Hatch interview with Buffy Cobb was important. So was his interview with Dorothy Burns Hallorand, Isabel Hill, and Baruch. Eddie Fay had some comments for me on Ann's relationship with her mother. The Hobson autobiography had material on this, too.

C.B.L.'s exchange of letters with Ann's boyfriend after her death was most revealing, as was her other correspondence with friends and family.

19

The mystical study C.B.L. involved herself with was soul transmigration advocated by Peter Demianovich Uspenskii in his book *A New Model of the Universe.*

The daily congressional routine was reported in an article by A. E. Burton Stickels in *Look,* then reprinted in *Everybody's,* November 12, 1949.

The Roosevelt Library at Hyde Park has a relevant letter from Mrs. Roosevelt to C.B.L. dated April 28, 1944.

See the Neal book on Willkie for background on this period. The Margaret Case Harriman quote comes from her article in *Reader's Scope,* November 1945. The Billings papers are of paramount interest here, especially his H.R.L. quotes on Willkie. Elson is again valuable here, this time in the second volume of the *Time* history.

The C.B.L. radio interview was with Mrs. Clapper, June 21, 1944, over the Mutual Radio network. The Morano account of the G. I. Jim speech comes partly from an interview with Hatch. The convention description was reported by Kenneth Stewart in *PM,* September 3, 1944. India Edwards reaction to the C.B.L. speech was in an interview with Jerry Ness, filed in the Oral History Collection at the Harry S Truman Library.

Important here were interviews with Isabel Hill by Hatch, and Chester Bowles by Neil Gold at Columbia University Oral History Library.

C.B.L.'s comment on lying was in her article for *Vanity Fair,* October 1930, "Ananias Preferred."

Sheed's comments to me about C.B.L. at this time were most valuable.

The Wes Bailey comments on H.R.L. come from his interview with Dorothy Sterling in the Sterling papers at the University of Oregon Library (AX 539, Box 14). The various F.D.R. comments on C.B.L. can be found at the F.D.R. Hyde Park Library. The Henry Wallace lunch with F.D.R. on the subject of C.B.L. was February 19, 1944. For other background on F.D.R., check *Frank-*

lin D. Roosevelt: A Rendezvous With Destiny (Boston: Little, Brown, 1990) by Frank Burt Freidel. Another interesting source is *Architects of Illusion: Men and Ideas in American Foreign Policy 1941–1949* by Lloyd C. Gardner (Chicago: Quadrangle Books, 1970).

Ed Thompson gave me much relevant background on the *Life* role in the election. *Life* reporter Jeanne Perkins Harmon reported some stories on it in *Such Is Life* (New York: Crowell, 1956). Swanberg and Elson were both good on this. The files of the Bridgeport *Post* for the election provide excellent background. So does the C.B.L. interview at Columbia Oral History, which also deals with her trip to Italy and contact with Eisenhower.

Jack Foisie gave me some of the background of C.B.L.'s trip to the Italian front.

Margaret Case Harriman's article in the *Ladies' Home Journal,* November 1938, had some interesting Luce quotes that fit here. The Rockefeller story comes from an article in *The New York Times,* April 9, 1967.

Luce's sister Mrs. Moore had pertinent comments about the H.R.L.-C.B.L. relationship at this time. Henry Wallace discussions in his Columbia University oral history interview were also of value.

20

Jean Dalrymple was the prime source on Jean Dalrymple. Her memory for detail was truly remarkable and she was most forthcoming.

The background on General Truscott comes partly from John Chamberlain material at the South Caroliniana Library, University of South Carolina (Folder 30 TLF B-1, September 22, 1943), material from some Eisenhower biographies, particularly the one by Merle Miller, and most of all from *Army Blue,* by Lucian K. Truscott IV (New York: Crown, 1989).

The Frank Gervasi story comes from my interview with Gervasi. The Hodgins material comes from Elson. The Matthews quote from a Matthews interview. The Billings papers were again important. So were the C.B.L. papers. The Kobler book was the source of the Roosevelt quote. A book of excellence was *The Ideas of Henry Luce,* with an introduction by John K. Jessup (New York: Atheneum, 1969).

Mrs. Sheldon Luce was most helpful here. The Dorothy Sterling papers were again valuable. John Kenneth Galbraith's memoir recorded the vivid memory of the C.B.L. speech. The Halberstam interview with Hughes on Chambers was in his papers at Boston College. Other Chambers background comes from his book *Witness* (New York: Random House, 1952). The Truman background comes from Merle Miller's biography of him, and my own biography *Harry S Truman,* (New York: Messner, 1964).

The White papers at Harvard were most valuable for the China trip. *Thunder Out of China* by Theodore White and Annalee Jacoby (New York: Sloane, 1946) was most useful. Robert Sherrod's interview also was most pertinent. So were interviews with Dave Richardson, John Hersey, and Chet Hansen.

21

C.B.L. has written extensively about her conversion to Catholicism in books, magazine articles, newspaper columns. Most important was her column in *McCall's,* "The Real Reason." Her C.B.L. papers are rich in clippings and interviews and personal observations. The Hatch interview with Bishop Sheen is most valuable and the Sheen book *Guide to Contentment* (New York: Simon & Schuster, 1967) has much to offer. So does Martha Weinman Lear's interview in *The New York Times,* April 22, 1973.

The Billings observations in his papers are most revealing. So were the memories of Allen Grover and his wife, Bea. Particularly perceptive were the observations of Wilfrid Sheed and William Buckley, Jr., on this. Robert and Patricia Coughlan were also most important. The Hatch interview with Buffy Cobb and the Halberstam interview with Emmet Hughes were very good. Frank White also gave some perceptive observations, and so did Jean Dalrymple, Shirley Clurman, T. S. Matthews, and Lael Wertenbaker.

Cobey Black's article in *Parade,* April 21, 1974, was worth reading and so was the Harriman story in the *Ladies' Home Journal,* November 1938. Also worth noting is *An Open Letter to the Right Reverend Fulton Sheen . . . Regarding the Activities of Mr. and Mrs. Henry Luce and of Time Magazine* by Randolph Churchill (Suffolk: Stour, East Bergholt, 1962).

Also worth reading was *A Private View* by Irene Mayer Selznick (New York: Knopf, 1983). Selznick was an intimate of both Luces.

The Billings papers record the dramatic stories from C. D. Jackson as well as the Corinne Thrasher comments.

22

The Mary Bancroft material comes from an oral history interview by Peter Jessup at Columbia University, her own *Autobiography of a Spy* (New York: Morrow, 1983), my interviews with her close friend Lael Wertenbaker, and with Allen Grover who knew her well. Lady Jean Campbell was also most helpful. Bancroft's letters are in assorted places, the Swanberg Collection at Columbia, also at the Arthur Schlesinger Library at Radcliffe. Jean Dalrymple also knew her well. But the best words on Bancroft are her own.

Billings again records all the C. D. Jackson stories, particularly on the divorce negotiations.

Hersey detailed for me his break with Luce over the Hiroshima story. Dimitri Kessel amplified it. Hersey also provided more insight into Luce's break with Teddy White. White's own letters to Luce in his papers at Harvard Library amplify this in greater detail. A letter from John Fairbank to White (February 3, 1946) is especially illuminating. Halberstam's interviews with Carl Mydans and Hersey added still more background. My own interviews with Richard Clurman, a close friend of White's, and my own memories of conversations with White, as well as talks with Dave Richardson, T. S. Matthews, Robert Coughlan, and Robert Manning, all helped complete the picture. The Elson book was also excellent on this.

Much of the Baruch material is in the C.B.L. papers.

A good article on CBL politics is by Doris Fleeson, "They Wear No Man's Collars," *Nation's Business,* September 1946.

Andrew Heiskell's reminiscences to me about the Luces' life in Ridgefield were most revealing.

The Laura Hobson autobiography has some dramatic stories about C.B.L. at this time. The jewelry anecdote came from my interview with Frank White, who had wonderful stories about both Luces.

23

There was an excellent interview and profile of Luce by a Swiss correspondent in *Die Weltwoche* in Zurich, March 2, 1951. My interviews with Frank White were enormously helpful for this period. The Billings papers were again a rich source. So was Elson's *The World of TIME Inc., Volume II: 1941–1960,* edited by Duncan Norton-Taylor (New York: Atheneum, 1973). Andrew Hopkind had a most useful article in *New York Review of Books,* September 12, 1968. Equally useful was an interview with Luce in *Berlingske Aftenavis* (Danish), January 12, 1963.

To be read is *A Free and Responsible Press* by the Commission on Freedom of the Press (Chicago: University of Chicago Press, 1947).

Useful, too, are the Dwight D. Macdonald papers at Yale University.

Shirley Clurman was most important, and so were the Swanberg papers at

Columbia, as well as the C.B.L. interview at Columbia Oral History, and the C.B.L. interview with Alden Hatch. The Hatch interviews with Baruch, Anne C. Fuller, and Buffy Cobb were likewise valuable. The Shadegg book had some good convention material. Two books of value were Robert H. Ferrell's *The Eisenhower Dairies* (New York: Norton, 1981) and Merle Miller's *Plain Speaking* (New York: Putnam, 1974).

My interviews with Matthews and John Hersey were pertinent here. The comments on her brother come from Matthews. Much about her brother, including complete correspondence, is in the C.B.L. papers. A provocative interview with Luce is in the Miami *News,* January 13, 1949.

Good background on Madame Chiang can be found in *The Soong Dynasty* (New York: Harper & Row, 1985). Also check *No Feast Lasts Forever* by Madame Wellington Koo with Isabella Taves (New York: Quadrangle/The New York Times Book Co., 1975). Good material on the Luce tour came from an interview with Dmitri Kessel, the Mary Bancroft interview with Columbia Oral History, and most important of all, from interviews with Allen Grover, who went with Luce.

Wilfrid Sheed, of course, was the prime source on his summer with the Luces, both in our interview and amplified in his book.

The Buffy Cobb interview by Hatch is the best source on her European trip with C.B.L. The C.B.L. papers are full of material on this, too, including a delightful scrapbook Cobb assembled for C.B.L. as a gift. So are some of C.B.L. interviews after the trip.

The Emmet John Hughes background comes from assorted sources. Interviews with Richard Clurman and Dave Richardson were revealing. So was the Hughes interview by Halberstam in the Halberstam papers. Material in the Billings papers is penetrating.

Luce's secretary Gloria Mariano filled in with some intimate anecdotes. So did Mrs. Elisabeth Moore.

On the campaign section, the Morano interview by Hatch was again of value. An interview with C.B.L. by Digby Diehl in *Supertalk* was excellent. Inez Robb did a very good reporting job on this in the Washington *Times-Herald,* June 22, 1950. The Dorothy Sterling papers had some good material. A letter from Grover in the Billings papers had pertinent observations.

24

Allen Grover was excellent on the H.R.L. relationship with Eisenhower. The Mary Bancroft interview at Columbia Oral History was similarly vital. Frank White was most knowledgeable here. The Billings papers were very good. Worth reading was Dora Jean Hamblin's *That Was the Life* (New York: Norton, 1977). Oliver Jensen had some good stories.

Some articles to read: *The* (Cleveland) *Plain Dealer,* September 30, 1951; *San Antonio News,* October 8, 1952; *Commentary,* by Joseph Epstein, November 1967. The *News* had a good quote on the McCarthy issue. The John K. Jessup Papers at the University of Wyoming Archive on Contemporary History has some relevant material.

An interesting anecdote on Eisenhower-Stevenson comes from Mrs. Ernest Ives, Stevenson's sister, in an oral history interview at Columbia. Some background also comes from *Stevenson Speeches,* by Ralph G. Martin and Debs Myers (New York: Random House, 1952).

My interview with Tom Griffith was most illuminating as was his book, *How True* (Boston: Little, Brown, 1974). Interviews with Matthews, Lael Wertenbaker, Richard and Shirley Clurman, Otto Fuerbringer, Frank White, and A. B. C. Whipple were all of great benefit. Robert Manning was also excellent.

Hugh Sidey also gave me most valuable insight into this whole political scene, and the Luce ambitions. Hedley Donovan's book *Right Places. Right Times* (New York: Henry Holt, 1989) is must reading for this period, as is *Mandate For Change 1953–56: The White House Years* by Dwight D. Eisenhower (Garden City, NY: Doubleday, 1963). Lady Jean Campbell had some reminiscences on this, too. The Hatch interviews with C.B.L. and Al Morano were most pertinent. So was the William Benton interview by Newton Minow at the Kennedy Library in Boston.

25

The remark about the woman president was made in an interview with Alan Brien, on March 25, 1957, in the London *Daily Express.*

My most important interviews for this chapter were with Mrs. Elisabeth Moore, Bea and Allen Grover, Milt and Ann Orshefsky (who were with Time Inc. in Rome then), Frank White and Ed Thompson, Ed Clark, Robert Manning, Dave Richardson, James Bell, Jean Dalrymple, T. S. Matthews, William Buckley, Jr., Mrs. Pierrepont Isham Prentice, Shirley Clurman, Mrs. Robert Neville, Stan and Helen Swinton, and Graham Hovey.

The best source books are *Roman Candle* by Letitia Baldrige (Boston: Houghton Mifflin, 1956) and *A Long Row of Candles* by C. L. Sulzberger (New York: Macmillan, 1969).

The C.B.L. papers, of course, are highly detailed on all this. Hatch's interviews with both C.B.L. and H.R.L., as well as with Eugene Durbrow, R. D. Grillo and Senator Stuart Symington are very good, and Eric Sevareid's interview with C.B.L. in 1954 was excellent. Interviews in the Swanberg collection with Kip Finch and Dorothy Farmer were most useful. There is also a most interesting interview with C.B.L. in *Il Popolo Nuovo,* November 26, 1953 and by columnist Bob Considine of International News Service, June 17, 1953. Other valuable ones are in *Welt am Sonntag,* December 19, 1954, and *Il Borghese,* August 6, 1954. Other newspaper articles of value: *The Washington Post,* October 4, 1953; *The New York Times,* February 7, 1982 and October 10, 1987; the Rosevilla (California) *Press Tribune,* October 2, 1953 and an editorial in the Davenport (Iowa) *Times,* July 1, 1953.

The Halberstam interview with Emmet Hughes is again valuable here. So were his interviews with James Shepley and Hedley Donovan. The Columbia Oral History interviews of most value here were with Robert C. Christopher, Prescott Bush, and C.B.L.

Other books of benefit were: *A Private View* by Irene Mayer Selznick (New York: Knopf, 1983); *R.S.V.P.* by Elsa Maxwell (Boston: Little, Brown, 1954); Peter Drucker's *Adventures of a Bystander* (New York: Harper & Row, 1978); and, again, the Griffith book *How True* and *Joseph P. Kennedy: A Life and Times,* by David E. Koskoff (Englewood Cliffs, NJ: Prentice-Hall, 1944).

Other profitable magazine sources: *Time,* February 22, 1982; *Newsweek,* January 24, 1955; *Behind the Scene,* May 1956; and an unsourced clipping in the Hatch papers, dated February 1954 by G. Harry Evans, "No Roman Holiday for Clare Boothe Luce."

26

Chapter 25 sources apply here, too. Add Mary Bancroft interview Columbia Oral History.

27

Chapter 25 sources also apply here. Add my interviews with A. B. C. Whipple, the C. D. Jackson papers at the Eisenhower Library, and the memoir by Meade Alcorn,

28

Lady Jean Campbell was the basic source of material here. She was forthright and compelling. Jean Dalrymple, Kelly Brook, Marion MacPhail McDermott, Ed Thompson, Richard and Shirley Clurman, George Harris, and Joseph Kastner amplified many of the details. My good friend Martin Gilbert was most helpful in filling out some background on Randolph Churchill. Wilfrid Sheed had his own comments of great interest. The C.B.L. papers had a fascinating supply of letters, sent and unsent, as well as other material. Robert and Patricia Coughlan offered valuable background. Laura Hobson's memoirs *Laura Z* had descriptive memories of Luce's first heart attack.

The *Beaverbrook* biography by A. J. P. Taylor (New York: Simon & Schuster, 1972) has good background on Beaverbrook but almost nothing on the Luces.

29

Helen Swinton was an invaluable source on her husband Stan's involvement in C.B.L.'s Brazil appointment. Shirley Clurman was also excellent on this and so was Bill Brinkley, a close friend of Swinton's and mine. The Eisenhower papers at the Eisenhower Library in Abilene, Kansas, shed some documentary light on this and so did his diaries. The C.B.L. papers were most useful. The Elson book has some good material. Worth reading by the Committee on Foreign Relations is "Nomination of Clare Boothe Luce," hearing 86th Congress, 1st session, on the nomination of C.B.L. to Ambassador to Brazil, 15 April, 1965.

Lady Jean Campbell continues as the richest resource on her relationship with H.R.L.

Allen Grover provided excellent insights into the Eisenhower story. Hedley Donovan's memoir adds needed detail, particularly on his succession to Luce's job. The Billings papers, as always, are vital. Emmet Hughes's book *Ordeal of Power* makes interesting reading. Richard Clurman had much to contribute here. So did Andrew Heiskell and Bernard Yudain.

Some of the Kennedy background comes from some of my own books, *Ballots and Bandwagons* (Chicago: Rand McNally, 1956); *Front Runner, Dark Horse* (New York: Doubleday, 1960) written with Ed Plaut; and *A Hero for Our Time* (New York: Macmillan, 1983).

My interview with Ted Sorensen was most helpful. Also interviews with Tom Griffith, Otto Fuerbringer, and Hugh Sidey.

30

Lady Jean Campbell supplied the heart of this chapter in her interviews. Shirley Clurman was most important in the C.B.L. reaction to the Campbell-

Luce relationship. H.R.L.'s lawyer on the divorce, Roswell Gilpatric, could not have been more cooperative, in detailing the negotiations. Frank White was excellent. The C.B.L. papers filled in many gaps, especially the letters exchanged between the Luces.

Dr. David Read, H.R.L.'s pastor at Madison Avenue Presbyterian Church, was most forthcoming in talking to me.

Mrs. Lila Tyng described her last meeting with HRL in revealing detail.

31

My own previously mentioned books on Kennedy were most useful here. So was Ted Sorensen's book *Kennedy* (New York: Harper & Row, 1965) as well as my interview with him.

Richard and Shirley Clurman were again important here. Jean Dalrymple added some needed details of their time together. The C.B.L. papers and her clippings from many interviews were most helpful. One of her best interviews was with William Buckley on his *Firing Line* television show, September 28, 1966 and later with Christopher Anderson in *People,* July 25, 1977, reminiscing about this period.

My interviews with H.R.L.'s secretary Glora Mariano, John Steele, Hugh Sidey, Bernard Yudain, Thomas Griffith, T. S. Matthews, Robert McNamara, A. B. C. Whipple, Jerry Goodman, Robert Sherrod, Mrs. Sheldon Luce, Reverend David Read, Andrew Heiskell, Milt Orshefsky, Robert Manning, and John Hersey were all important here.

The Halberstam interview with Hugh Sidey added helpful information and his interview with Pierre Salinger amplified an earlier interview of mine. His interview with Otto Fuerbringer also complements mine.

The third volume of the Time Inc. history *(The World of TIME Inc., 1960–1980)* by Curtis Prendergast with Geoffrey Colvin was equally vital for me. In his interview with me, Prendergast was enormously helpful in amplifying certain parts of the book and suggesting new sources.

Some good background books here were *Walter Lippmann and the American Century* by Ronald Steel (Boston: Little, Brown, 1980); *Special Relationships,* by Harry Brandon (New York: Atheneum, 1988); *The Enemy Grows Older* by Alexander King (New York: Simon & Schuster, 1958); *Hopes and Ashes* by Alice G. Marquis (New York: The Free Press, 1986); Jean Perkins Harmon's book *Such Is Life,* and Harrison's biography of Thornton Wilder, and Laura Hobson's memoir. Also worth noting is *The Sin of Henry Luce: An Anatomy of Journalism* (Secaucus, NJ: Lyle Stuart, 1974).

Charles Spalding's interview at Columbia Oral History by John Stewart should be read as well as the H.R.L. interview by Richard Callener for the John Foster Dulles Oral History Project, July 25, 1965. Parts of the C.B.L. interview for Columbia Oral History were pertinent here.

The John Knox Jessup papers at the University of Wyoming, Archive of Contemporary History, have proven value for this part of the book.

Some newspaper articles and interviews worth reading: New York *Herald Tribune*, February 16, 1964; article by Warren Rogers, *Times-Union*, Albany, NY, June 11, 1964; *Newsweek*, June 29, 1964; "The Gospel According to St. Luce," by Peter Matthews, *Fact*, Volume 4, 1967.

32

Many of the notes in Chapter 31 apply here, especially the Kennedy material and the interviews, particularly with John Steele and Hugh Sidey. Steele's description of the preparations for the Time Inc. fortieth anniversary party was marvelously graphic.

The Donovan memoir and the Jessup papers at the University of Wyoming were important. Richard Clurman's account of the Vietnam War coverage, particularly the Charles Mohr story, was of considerable value. An earlier interview of mine with Robert McNamara for a biography of Kennedy fit in well here. Merle Miller's biography of Johnson added much needed background, as did *A Very Personal Presidency: Lyndon Johnson in the White House* by Hugh Sidey (New York: Atheneum, 1968).

33

The Donovan book is best here in detailing the leadership transition at *Time*. Jean Campbell's description of her final meeting with H.R.L. was vivid. Buckley's view of the political situation then was most perceptive. Swanberg's papers and his biography add a different dimension and perspective. The C.B.L. papers were very helpful here. Richard Clurman was excellent on his relations then with H.R.L. Shirley Clurman filled in some of the relationship of H.R.L. with the prince and princess of Lichtenstein, and so did Buckley. The Irene Selznick memoir had some key anecdotes of this time. Jean Dalrymple had some reminiscences of this period. Gloria Mariano filled in much necessary detail about H.R.L. in his last days. John Steele had some dramatic stories about this time. So did Frank White, Shirley Clurman, and John Hersey. Hersey's account of their reconciliation at Yale was amplified in *The Pierson Sun*, February 25, 1966.

Andrew Heiskell and George Harris were both vivid in their descriptions of the Luces and LSD. Tom Griffith had a graphic account of their night with H.R.L. at the theater.

The Prendergast book was excellent about the final days of Luce. I am grateful to Dr. Read for his description of the services and to Richard Clurman for his personal account of the funeral.

34

Richard and Shirley Clurman shared with me anecdotes on C.B.L.'s final years in vivid detail, and I am most grateful to them. The C.B.L. papers on this period are packed with detailed correspondence. She gave a great many interviews during this time, some of which were contradictory.

Her friends Bill Buckley and Wilfrid Sheed had some excellent stories to tell. So did Roswell Gilpatric, who had dated her. And Curtis Prendergast who was with the Time Inc. Paris bureau when she arrived there. Hedley Donovan had some revealing remarks about C.B.L.'s involvement with the defense of Nixon during the impeachment hearings. Helen Swinton's memories are key here. The Digby Diehl interview with C.B.L. was one of the best. The Chester Bowles interview by Neil Gold in the Columbia Oral History proved interesting.

Richard Milhous Nixon by Roger Morris (New York: Holt, 1990) has useful background on Nixon but not much on the Luces. Richard Nixon himself had more in *In the Arena* (New York: Simon & Schuster, 1990). Hedley Donovan's *Roosevelt to Reagan* (New York: Harper & Row, 1985) was of great value. William Buckley's book *On the Firing Line* (New York: Random House, 1989) and Richard M. Clurman's *Beyond Malice* (New Brunswick: Transaction Publishers, 1988) both had excellent material on the Luces. Buckley's book *A Hymnal: The Controversial Arts* (New York: Putnam, 1978) also had some very good background for me.

There was a good perspective on "Spectrum," CBS radio, March 21, 1972, and several excellent articles in *The New York Times,* by Judy Klemensrud, October 18, 1971; by Clive Barnes, October 27, 1973, November 3, 1981, February 7, 1982; in the *Sunday Magazine,* September 3, 1972, and *Time* magazine of March 8, 1974. An interesting article appeared in *The San Francisco Chronicle,* April 14, 1978. Cobey Black's article on C.B.L. in *Parade, Daily News,* April 12, 1974 was very good.

Oliver Jensen offered some good comments and so did Lael Wertenbaker, Wilfrid Sheed, and Paul S. Green.

INDEX